Parley P. Pratt

Parley P. Pratt

The Apostle Paul
of Mormonism

TERRYL L. GIVENS

MATTHEW J. GROW

OXFORD
UNIVERSITY PRESS

OXFORD
UNIVERSITY PRESS

Oxford University Press, Inc., publishes works that further
Oxford University's objective of excellence
in research, scholarship, and education.

Oxford   New York
Auckland   Cape Town   Dar es Salaam   Hong Kong   Karachi
Kuala Lumpur   Madrid   Melbourne   Mexico City   Nairobi
New Delhi   Shanghai   Taipei   Toronto

With offies in
Argentina   Austria   Brazil   Chile   Czech Republic   France   Greece
Guatemala   Hungary   Italy   Japan   Poland   Portugal   Singapore
South Korea   Switzerland   Thailand   Turkey   Ukraine   Vietnam

Copyright © 2011 by Oxford University Press, Inc.

Published by Oxford University Press, Inc.
198 Madison Avenue, New York, New York 10016

www.oup.com

Oxford is a registered trademark of Oxford University Press

Library of Congress Cataloging-in-Publication Data
Givens, Terryl.
Parley P. Pratt : The Apostle Paul of Mormonism / Terryl L. Givens, Matthew J. Grow.
p.   cm.
Includes bibliographical references and index.
ISBN 978-0-19-537573-2
1. Pratt, Parley P. (Parley Parker), 1807–1857.   2. Church of Jesus Christ of Latter-day
Saints—Apostles—Biography.   3. Mormon Church—Apostles—Biography.   4. Church of Jesus Christ
of Latter-day Saints—History.   5. Mormon Church—History.   I. Grow, Matthew J. author.   II. Title.
BX8695.P7G58 2011 289.3092—dc22
[B]
2011005099

1 3 5 7 9 8 6 4 2

Printed in the United States of America
on acid-free paper

To Sylvia I. Givens—more the pillar than she ever realized,
and
Robert J. Grow—dad, champion, friend

Contents

Acknowledgments

SEVERAL SCHOLARS HAVE been generous in reading drafts, sharing research, and providing feedback and suggestions throughout the writing process. We owe a considerable debt to R. Steven Pratt, who spent years collecting and annotating Parley P. Pratt's letters and materials, greatly aiding our work by his efforts and generosity. Financial support was provided by the Charles Redd Center for Western Studies and the College of Liberal Arts of the University of Southern Indiana. Several excellent historians of Mormonism and American religion reviewed early versions of this book, including David Whittaker, Steven Harper, Patrick Mason, John Turner, and Benjamin Parks. Glenn Rowe, Christopher Blythe, Brett Dowdle, Mauri Pratt, and Rachael Givens tracked down difficult sources and provided other research assistance. Jayne Fife graciously shared her own manuscript on Mary Ann Frost Pratt and responded to ours as well. LaJean Purcell Carruth's meticulous transcriptions of Pratt sermons from nineteenth-century shorthand added greatly to our source material, as did typescripts provided by Dorsey Ford. Robert and Linda Grow read the manuscript with careful attention to detail and readability. Our wives, Fiona Givens and Alyssa Grow, gave their usual criticisms—painfully perceptive and typically invaluable. We are especially grateful to Cynthia Read at Oxford, friend and editor extraordinaire.

Parley P. Pratt

FIGURE I.I Early undated photograph of Parley P. Pratt. Courtesy Utah State Historical Society.

Introduction

Earth ought to be full of prophets and heaven and earth
full of angels.
—PARLEY P. PRATT, *sermon, 10 July 1853*

ON A SPRING day in 1853, a forty-six-year-old Mormon apostle sat in his modest home just outside Temple Square in Salt Lake City to respond to a request from a long-lost friend from his youth for a sketch of his life. Reflecting upon his experiences, Parley P. Pratt mused that "such a history would overload the mail" and would appear "far more strange to you than the thousand volumes of Modern Fiction." Against the background of their shared boyhood in the backwoods of New York, Pratt's subsequent life appeared improbable, even fantastic. Since that time, he had traveled widely throughout the United States and Canada, led Mormon pioneer companies past the "moving masses of wild Buffalo on the boundless, treeless plains" to Utah, preached in San Francisco during the Gold Rush, crossed the Atlantic Ocean six times, and eaten "figs from the tree" in Chile. His life had been one of extremes, of "poverty and riches, peace and war," sublime joys and devastating sorrows.

Controversy had perennially stalked him, Pratt continued, as he had "been received almost as an Angel by thousands and counted an Imposter by tens of thousands." Fifteen years previously in Missouri, he had "lain months in gloomy dungeons, and been loaded with chains," though he had "been visited there by visions of Angels and Spirits, and been delivered by miracles." As a defender of Mormonism, Pratt had publicly debated "priests, learned men and Infidels," "stood before senators and Governors," and had "edited periodicals and written and published books." In his private life, Pratt would marry a dozen times and father thirty children. "In short," he wrote, "I have been a farmer, a servant, a fisher, a digger, a beggar, a preacher, an author, an editor, a senator, a traveler, a merchant, an elder and an Apostle of Jesus Christ." Pratt exclaimed, "Is not truth stranger than fiction!!!"[1]

Pratt's well-honed literary instincts were correct; the narrative of his life could have formed the basis of a page-turning novel. By 1853, he had already become, after Joseph Smith and Brigham Young, the most influential figure in shaping early Mormon history, culture, and theology. Pratt exerted that influence across an astounding spectrum, excelling as a missionary, explorer, hymnist, pamphleteer, autobiographer, historian, and theologian. The final four years of his life only solidified his place as one of the most engaging, colorful, and powerful figures in early Mormonism. In 1857, to the unrestrained cheers of the national media and the laments of the Latter-day Saints, Pratt was murdered in Arkansas by the estranged husband of his twelfth wife.

Born to a hardscrabble family in New York in 1807, Pratt struck out in the late 1820s for the frontier of northern Ohio, where he converted to the religious message of the Campbellites, modeled on the primitive Christian Church of the New Testament. Inspired by his newfound faith, Pratt became a freelance minister during the chaotic years of the Second Great Awakening, but an encounter with the Book of Mormon in the fall of 1830 changed his trajectory. By converting to Mormonism, Pratt added doctrines of priesthood authority to the primitivism and millennialism of the Campbellites. The Book of Mormon fired his religious imagination, both as a harbinger of millennial events and for proclaiming American Indians to be the descendants in part of an Israelite civilization. He joined the infant Mormon movement in September 1830, six months after its formal founding. Soon after his baptism, Joseph Smith, the youthful Mormon prophet, appointed him as one of four missionaries to the "Lamanites," the Book of Mormon people whose descendants early Mormons viewed as contemporary American Indians, in Missouri. Pratt's decision to take his fellow missionaries to visit his former religious mentor, Campbellite Sidney Rigdon, in Kirtland, Ohio, altered Mormon history, as hundreds of conversions followed and shifted the Mormon center of gravity from New York to Ohio. Soon Smith announced a revelation proclaiming a gathering of his followers in that area.

Pratt spent relatively little time in Kirtland in the early 1830s, opting instead to live in Missouri, which Smith's revelations proclaimed the site of a New Jerusalem. Driven from home there, as were other Saints in late 1833 in the first of a five-year-long series of increasingly violent clashes between Missourians and Mormons, Pratt served a pivotal role in the Zion's Camp expedition, which sought to restore the expelled Mormons to their homes and lands. In 1835, Smith called twenty-seven-year-old Pratt (along with his twenty-three-year-old brother, Orson) as a member of the newly formed Quorum of the Twelve Apostles. Pratt's apostolic position vaulted him into the forefront of Mormonism for the remainder of his life.

Our subtitle dubs Pratt the Apostle Paul of Mormonism. Certainly, key differences exist between Paul and Parley—between a first-century educated scion of the Jewish diaspora and a nineteenth-century self-taught backwoodsman; between a reputed champion of celibacy and a promulgator of polygamy. Nevertheless, both men possessed a deep sense of the divine importance of their apostolic calling and a bold, blunt, outspoken style that led to frequent controversies. Just as Paul clashed with Peter, Pratt dissented at times from both Smith and Young, making clear that his commitment to Mormonism rested not on devotion to a charismatic leader but spiritual and intellectual assent to the religion's doctrines. Religiously devout even before their conversions to Christianity and Mormonism, Paul and Pratt passionately devoted their lives to advancing their new causes, driven by a belief in an oncoming millennium.[2] Pratt's millennial urgency stands out even from his peers among Latter-day Saints and other religious enthusiasts of the era; he titled his first extensive printed work, Mormonism's first book of poetry, *Millennium*.

We make the comparison between these religious figures for three key reasons that transcend the stylistic similarities between Paul and Pratt. First, in early Christianity, Paul's writings (or at least those attributed to him)—including thirteen of the twenty-seven canonical New Testament books—systematized and popularized Jesus's teachings. Pratt's extensive writings served the same function in early Mormonism. His newspaper articles, pamphlets, and books explored the implications of Smith's revelations and the Book of Mormon, clarifying and expanding Latter-day Saint doctrines, including key theological points such as the physicality of God, the domesticity of heaven, the possibilities of theosis (human divinization), and the religious rationale for plural marriage.

In his letter to his boyhood friend, Pratt emphasized the drama of his life, while only mentioning in passing his literary and intellectual contributions to the development of Mormon thought. In many respects, though, Pratt exerted his influence most powerfully through his writing. Early Mormonism achieved its reach through both ambitious evangelizing and an extensive print culture based in newspapers, pamphlets, and early theological treatises. Heavily involved in all of these media, Pratt ranged across many genres: poetry, hymns, short stories, satire, apologetics, history, and theology. He lived in an era when print culture was rapidly democratizing, and like other religious and reform leaders, Pratt took advantage of inexpensive pamphlets and the popular press to spread his message. He pioneered Mormon print culture, writing the first handbill, first book of poetry, first work of fiction, first apologetic pamphlet, and first successful missionary book. The father of Mormon pamphleteering, Pratt wrote more than two dozen tracts to spread the Latter-day Saint message, combat its detractors, and explore its theology. In 1840, he served as the founding editor for the *Latter-day Saints' Millennial Star*, the church's influential British periodical, and he later edited a New York newspaper called *The Prophet*. Two of his books—one written near the beginning of his writing career and one near the end—attained near-canonical status, remained among the most widely read Mormon works for several decades after his death, and continue to shape the contours of Mormon theology. His millennial *Voice of Warning* (1837), which clarified Latter-day Saint doctrines for both outsiders and church members, proved exceptionally effective as a missionary tool. In *Key to the Science of Theology* (1855), Pratt ambitiously reached beyond first principles to attempt a comprehensive cosmology and ontology. While still recognized for his *Voice of Warning* and *Key to the Science of Theology*, Pratt made many of his most profound theological contributions to early Mormonism in long-forgotten but once-influential short pamphlets.

Pratt's writings, which deeply influenced other Mormon authors, particularly his equally prolific younger brother, Orson, not only helped convert thousands to Mormonism but also shaped the Mormon theological system. In 1870, Mormon dissident Edward Tullidge commented on the influence of the Pratt brothers: "Ask the people what brought them into the church, and you would hear from every direction Parley Pratt's 'Voice of Warning' or 'Orson Pratt's Tracts,' until it would almost seem to you that the Pratts created the church. Indeed the best part of Mormon theology has been derived to a great extent from them, and so it may be said that they also, to a great extent, originated Mormonism."[3] While the first half of Tullidge's statement would have gratified Pratt, he likely would have objected to the claim that he had "created" or "originated" Mormonism. Though combative, Pratt consistently demonstrated his commitment to the revelations and teachings of Joseph Smith, whom he revered as a prophet and restorer of ancient truths. Only once, in a personal dispute over a failed business transaction in 1837, did he clash openly with Smith, and even then he reiterated his devotion to Mormonism's scriptural canon. Pratt saw his role not as innovator, but as systematizer and popularizer.

Nevertheless, his speculative writings also pushed Mormon thought in new directions. Many modern Mormons imagine a relatively linear process of doctrinal development in the church's early years, with Smith revealing each new doctrine to the church in orderly sequence. Smith, however, viewed himself as both revelator and inspired eclecticist, pulling truths not only from heaven, but also from his culture and his contemporaries. Pratt's writings and interactions with Smith suggest a more nuanced and messier process of doctrinal development; with some issues, he took germs of ideas from Smith's revelations and explored their implications, thereby extending the boundaries of Mormon thought and suggesting doctrines that later received Smith's imprimatur. Pratt's extensive writings, which systematized, expanded, and made accessible Smith's teachings, illustrate a crucial stage of any new religious movement: the creation, explication, and popularization of a theological system.

Second, like Paul, Pratt's extensive missionary travels helped put his movement on the path from small sect to worldwide religion. Paul primarily proselytized in Jewish quarters of cities in the northern Mediterranean. Similarly, while Pratt spent much time preaching in small towns, particularly in the early and mid 1830s, he concentrated his missionary labors in large cities, including Toronto; New York City; Manchester; Liverpool; San Francisco; and Valparaiso, Chile. His public proselytizing during the Second Great Awakening—first as an itinerant minister loosely affiliated with the Campbellites and subsequently as a Latter-day Saint missionary—demonstrates the rich public culture of religious debate and dissent. Like Paul, who "almost persuaded" Agrippa to be a Christian, Pratt was a tireless and persuasive preacher. The *Edinburgh Review* deemed him in 1854 as "chief of the Mormon missionaries."[4] His converts filled not only Mormonism's rank-and-file, but also included future leaders such as John Taylor, the church's third president.

Pratt contributed to the expansion and internationalization of early Mormonism by serving crucial missions in Canada (1836) and in England (1840–1842), when thousands joined Mormonism and immigrated to the United States. Following Joseph Smith's death in 1844, a vigorous battle occurred within Mormonism over who should succeed Smith as leader, with the claimants including Brigham Young and the Twelve Apostles, Pratt's former teacher Sidney Rigdon, and the charismatic James J. Strang. Pratt first helped Young and the apostles win over most Mormons in the Latter-day Saint headquarters of Nauvoo, Illinois. Then, during missions to the eastern states in 1844–1845 and to England in 1846–1847, Pratt's actions helped ensure that the majority of Mormons outside of Nauvoo, particularly the large numbers of British converts, remained loyal to apostolic authority. In the 1850s, Pratt's two missions to California and a mission to Chile (the first Mormon mission in Latin America) helped orient the church toward the

Pacific Rim and Latin America. Pratt's missionary work also serves as a window onto the finances and family life of early Mormon missionaries and of itinerants of the era more broadly.

Third, like Paul, Pratt reveled in opposition and persecution, and in his own eyes and the beliefs of the Latter-day Saints, met a martyr's death. Writing of the death of his five-year-old son, Nathan, in Nauvoo in 1843, Pratt stated, "He died an infant, but he can say with Paul, 'in prison oft, in stripes more abundant, in tribulations, in persecutions, in perils by the sea and land, in perils among robbers, and among false brethren, and in travels more abundant.'"[5] Pratt viewed himself in the same way. Imprisoned for eight months in 1838–1839 as a consequence of his participation in a battle between Mormons and Missourians, and held longer than Joseph Smith and any other Latter-day Saint, Pratt compared his prison experience to Paul's in a letter to his wife.[6] En route to a mission to California in 1851, reflecting on his "travels more abundant," Pratt wondered "how many of the days of our manhood, and of our strength and vigour are thrown away in apparent uselessness without enjoyment to ourselves or usefulness to our family or any boddy else. Some, on the sea, and Some on land and in the desarts or in Prisons." But, he reminded himself, "It was so with Paul, and with Peter and John, and others of old."[7]

Crucially, Pratt not only saw himself as the object of persecution; his writings shaped a Mormon memory and collective identity forged in persecution, particularly in the expulsions from Missouri. His *History of the Late Persecution* (1839) persuasively developed a narrative of persecution that shaped Mormon culture throughout the nineteenth century and, in some ways, to the present day. Pratt deeply believed that the Mormons' suffering revealed they were God's chosen people. Joseph Smith expressed this belief in 1842: "I feel, like Paul, to glory in tribulation."[8] Pratt, likewise glorying in his persecution and proclaiming himself a martyr as he died in 1857, personified the early Mormon culture of persecution.

We are not the first to tell Pratt's story. He did so in a well-regarded autobiography, posthumously published in 1874, which remains widely read and is a classic statement of the nineteenth-century Mormon experience.[9] Pratt wrote his autobiography in the mid-1850s, using a variety of already published materials and his own memory. In so doing, he established for posterity the legendary Parley P. Pratt, the trickster of bulldogs, the jailed apostle, the intrepid and indefatigable missionary, the fearless explorer. His autobiography is a crucial source for this book—particularly for information on his early years, for which other records are scarce.

Writing about a subject who is a capable autobiographer both helps and complicates the biographer's task. Autobiographies are a window into an individual's motivations, actions, and thoughts. And yet they conceal as much as they reveal. Like all autobiographers, Pratt selectively fashioned his history. The problem is not factual accuracy. Indeed, Pratt's memory of names, places, and events is remarkably (though not completely) correct; most can be confirmed in other contemporary sources. The challenge, rather, is that Pratt constructed his autobiography to reveal how he became the apostle he was in midlife. He cast events to explain his crucial role in early Mormon development and omitted or underemphasized events and issues that did not fit within this central narrative.

Pratt's autobiography is uneven, with about a quarter of the published text devoted to his eight months of imprisonment in Missouri. In addition, the quality of the autobiography drops off noticeably after 1851, as the fluent narrative is replaced by episodic journals, letters, and newspaper articles. Like other early American autobiographers, such as Benjamin Franklin, Pratt largely omitted information on his family life. His private letters, by contrast, demonstrate great concern and longing for his family when absent, suggesting the abiding tension in Pratt's life between a religion that exalted family life (and Pratt's own writings were crucial in developing Mormon theology of family life, including the concept of a domestic heaven) and yet required his continual absence from it for short preaching tours and long missionary journeys. Pratt felt genuine joy in his family circle and strongly saw himself as a celestial patriarch-in-the-making, and yet his devotion to Mormonism required a kingdom-or-nothing-attitude that led to frequent absences even with family members ill, with babies about to be born, or with his family in deep poverty. Everything had to be subordinated to the needs of the kingdom and the oncoming millennial timetable. Pratt's family life, particularly after the onset of polygamy, dramatically reveals both the struggles and the joys of the new marital system. His letters, and the statements of his wives and children, serve as a window onto the daily reality of plural marriage. Our biography aims to restore Pratt's family life—from his monogamous marriage in 1829 with Thankful Halsey to his large polygamous family of the 1840s and 1850s—as central to his story.

In addition, while Pratt's autobiography mentions his other various writings, he did not generally elaborate or summarize them. Understanding Pratt's significance requires placing him within his intellectual and theological worlds, both within early Mormonism and beyond. Finally, Pratt underplayed controversial events in his autobiography. Strong-willed, he clashed with his

religious leaders and family members, including Joseph Smith; Brigham
Young; his brother Orson; and his second wife, Mary Ann Frost. These con-
frontations reveal changing ideas of religious authority within the early
Mormon movement as well as the domestic challenges occasioned by the
transition from monogamy to polygamy.

Perhaps because of his perennially published and highly readable autobiography, Pratt has never received the scholarly biography that has long been
overdue. In recent decades, a wonderful trove of primary sources has been
amassed, primarily by descendant R. Steven Pratt, who graciously allowed us
access to the materials. Archival repositories, particularly at the Church
History Library of the Church of Jesus Christ of Latter-day Saints and at
Brigham Young University, have preserved Pratt's insightful letters and journals, as well as minutes of meetings he attended and records of some members
of his family (including several wives and his brother Orson). In addition,
many of Pratt's associates left many records detailing Pratt's life.

In his letter to his boyhood friend in 1853, Pratt stated that he had written
only the "thousandth part" of his own life. The conclusion of Pratt's letter to
his friend nevertheless captures the core of his self-identity as a single-minded
apostle preparing the world for the millennial reign of Jesus Christ. After
providing a quick overview of his life, Pratt quickly pivoted to a "testimony in
regard to our *religion*": "Angels have ministered to some of us in the present
age and have ordained a new apostleship and renewed the commission to
preach the Gospel and baptise all who turn to the Lord and believe our testimony. This new dispensation is a special message to all the world: in order to
prepare the way for the second coming of Jesus Christ." He encouraged his
friend to investigate the Latter-day Saint message, convert, move to Utah, and
"renew the covenant of Eternal frindship which so early existed between us."
Finally, he invited his friend to join in the central cause of Pratt's own life:
"Yea come and help us to build up the kingdom of God."[10]

I

The Young Seeker

We live somewhere in the latter end of the sixth
millennium.
—PARLEY PRATT, *"The Millennium," Latter-day
Saints' Millennial Star, August 1840*

PARLEY PARKER PRATT, third son of Jared and Charity Pratt, could trace
his ancestry back several generations—five on his father's side and six on
his mother's—to the first waves of Puritan settlers in America. Tracing the
family history of a biographical subject can often be a simple gesture in the
direction of genealogical background, a kind of obligatory research into earliest origins. In Pratt's case, however, his American family's beginnings were
strikingly prescient of his own life trajectory. Biology may not be destiny, but
genealogy—especially one that is internalized—can be. Pratt was a
larger-than-life figure, a colorful, passionate, and intrepid man of action and
of words, who lived with the certainty that he was an important actor in an
unfolding drama with cosmic significance. In the prime of his life, Pratt
learned the details surrounding the first Pratt, William, to come to America.[1]
He doubtless found in the patriarch of his line both a model and dramatic
validation for his own embattled life.

William Pratt was a member of the congregation of the Puritan exile
Thomas Hooker, a religious refugee who fled, like the Pilgrims before him,
from England to Holland and thence to Massachusetts Bay Colony. Serving
some time as pastor of the church at Newtowne (later Cambridge), Hooker
grew dissatisfied with community leaders and struck out for new lands with a
hundred followers, including William and his brother John, thereby becoming
dissidents from their fellow dissidents. The Pratts' father, Reverend William
Pratt, also likely sympathized with Puritanism, though he never emigrated like
his sons to New England.[2] Persecuted in their native country, self-exiled as
seekers of a purer Christianity, and refugees once again going from the frontiers of civilization to utter wilderness, Hooker and the younger Pratts reached
the Connecticut River and founded the settlement of Hartford in 1636.

Two years after Hartford's founding, an ancestor on Parley Pratt's mother's side similarly found herself a religious exile from that same Massachusetts Colony of religious exiles. Anne Marbury Hutchinson was convicted in that year of heresy for propounding the exact doctrine that Parley Pratt would one day call the centerpiece of his own religious vision: "an immediate revelation" from God, as court documents at her trial noted. So while William Pratt was making his new home in the wilds of Connecticut, a dissident twice exiled, Anne Hutchinson wended her way through heavy snow on an unseasonably wintry spring day to refuge on the island of Aquidneck—later the colony of Rhode Island. She lasted four years before wandering farther, this time to Pelham Bay, New Amsterdam, where Native Americans killed her and several of her children in 1643.[3]

John Lathrop, another Puritan ancestor, renounced his ministerial duties in 1623 in protest against the Church of England. The government banned his congregation of "Independents" the following year, though they continued to meet in secret until 1632, when Lathrop was jailed. After agreeing to leave England with his followers two years later, Lathrop was released and sailed for America with Hutchinson. His separatism and doctrinal views created tensions with Massachusetts Bay officials, leading to his congregation's decision to settle in the more distant town of Barnstable (on Cape Cod). Parley's brother Orson once told him of a vision shared by Joseph Smith "that our fathers and his all sprang from the same man a few generations ago."[4] Lathrop fit the description and was a progenitor not only of the Smiths and the Pratts, but of many early Mormons including Oliver Cowdery, Frederick G. Williams, and Wilford Woodruff (as well as nineteenth-century luminaries such as Ulysses S. Grant, Oliver Wendell Holmes, and Frederick Law Olmsted).[5]

Like William Pratt and Anne Hutchinson, John Lathrop represented a "radical fringe element" of New England Puritan society. These Puritan dissenters were disproportionately the ancestors of early Mormons and passed down within their families a unique set of beliefs—including the necessity of a restoration of New Testament Christianity, revelatory communication between individuals and God, spiritual gifts, and a more positive sense of human potential. These beliefs prepared their descendants, including Parley Pratt, to embrace the Mormon message.[6]

Intervening generations of Pratts included Joseph, a large landowner; William, an influential civic and military leader in his Connecticut community; Christopher, of whom little is known; and Obadiah, Parley's grandfather.[7] Born in 1742, Obadiah relocated from the colonial home of Connecticut to New York, where he enlisted as a private in an Albany County militia during the War for Independence.[8] He settled in Canaan in Columbia County, New York, where he farmed and worked as a tanner and currier.[9] He died before he could tell Parley of his war experiences, but the heritage of a revolutionary veteran in the family undoubtedly fed the patriotism that would burn so fiercely in his grandson and make the religious persecution he would experience that much more bitter.[10]

In what appears as an almost mythically familiar narrative of the early nineteenth century, Jared Pratt, born to Obadiah and Jemima Tolls Pratt in Canaan in 1768 as the oldest of eleven children, was an itinerant laborer, moving from place to place to place, always searching for better opportunities, respite from penury and want, hoping to find in the next verdant field the elusive grail of prosperity or at least security. Obadiah trained Jared as a weaver, a trade in which he might well have expected to find both.[11] Generations of weavers had found self-sufficiency in the centuries-old cottage industry. But when Jared was sixteen, the first power loom was built in England, launching a revolution in textile production that would soon affect thousands of craftsmen like him. The industrial revolution of the late eighteenth century would lead to the greatest leap forward in Western standards of living that history had yet known, but advances in agricultural production and technological efficiency came at great personal cost to those caught in the transition. This was particularly true in England, where the Acts of Enclosure that promoted farming innovation and economies of scale displaced thousands of peasants. The introduction of the factory system likewise turned individual craftsmen into inefficient practitioners of outmoded trades. The weaver Jared Pratt was, his son Orson remembered, simply "thrown out of employment" by the course of history, forced from the promising trade of weaving to working on others' farms and occasional school teaching.[12]

The result was catastrophic for his family. Upstate New York was rich in farmland, but Jared had neither the resources nor the experience to set himself up as a small-time farmer. He could do no more than hire himself out as an unskilled laborer at subsistence wages. Around 1792, Jared married Mary or Polly Carpenter, likely the daughter of one of Obadiah's Revolutionary War companions. The following year, she gave birth to a namesake daughter.[13] Jared's wife soon died, however, leaving him a widower in his twenties. In 1799, Jared married twenty-three-year-old Charity Dickinson, the daughter of Samuel and Hulda Griffith Dickinson and a fellow native of Canaan.

They were still living in Canaan when Charity gave birth to Anson, their eldest son, in 1801. By the time of William's birth the next year, Jared had made the first of several migrations, to Worcester, almost a hundred miles to the west. A few more years, and the family's westward migration had drawn them another thirty miles, to Burlington, an isolated town of the state's interior. Burlington was first settled in 1790 and given autonomy from neighboring Otsego in 1792, just fifteen years before Parley was born there in 1807. A land of gently rolling hills and deep valleys, the county occupies the geographical center of New York. The Pratts' relocation to Burlington was part of a larger influx to the area, which rapidly pushed the town's population from twenty-four hundred in 1800 to almost thirty-two hundred by 1810.[14] Thereafter Burlington entered a steep, consistent decline to half those numbers over ensuing decades. Jared seems to have moved out, as he had moved in, with other hopeful then disillusioned waves of itinerants pursuing elusive success. By the time Orson was born in 1811, the Pratts had crisscrossed the state back in the other direction, 120 miles northeast to Hartford.

During these years of Parley's youth, the War of 1812 ravaged areas too far removed for the family to take note of its impact—until 1814. In that year, fifteen thousand British troops crossed the Canadian border into upstate New York, striking at Plattsburgh, 120 miles to the north of Hartford. Parley proudly noted that his father "shouldered his rifle at the call of the Governor, and assisted in gaining the battle of Plattsburgh."[15] The overwhelming British defeat in this campaign meant that whatever threat England had posed to communities to the south was past and that the war was essentially over.[16] By 1820, the Pratts had circled back to the neighborhood of Canaan, in what is now called New Lebanon.

Those born to the hard toil of farming seldom romanticize their childhoods. It is mostly left to poets to laud pastoral Edens, as the distinctly non-farming Oliver Goldsmith did with "Sweet Auburn, loveliest village of the plain, Where health and plenty cheered the labouring swain."[17] When he wrote his autobiography, Parley tersely avoided the subject of his toilsome boyhood: "Of my early youth I shall say but little." Certainly he would have recollections that preceded the age of seven, but Parley drew attention only to those episodes that went furthest to explain the essential meaning of his adult life. In seeking to "examine how far Nature and Education had qualified him" for his divinely appointed vocation, the poet William Wordsworth lit upon scattered "spots of time" that shone with "distinct pre-eminence."[18] Likewise, Pratt first invoked those recollections that he thought most formative of the intrepid Mormon apostle he had become at the time he recorded his childhood memories. His earliest recollection was of his kind and pious mother teaching him scripture lessons when he was seven. He found himself immersed in biblical stories such as that of Joseph, a faithful Hebrew who served years of bondage for his love of God and truth. His next recorded memory, five years later, was of his own scripture reading, and of the religious anxiety induced in his twelve-year-old mind by learning of the impenitent throngs who would slumber for a thousand years while the righteous reigned with Christ.[19]

Pratt's imagination was fired by the dramatic and heroic, but he was also prone to bouts of melancholy and pathos. His spiritual agonies were not likely provoked by zealotry on the part of parents. Sporadic in his own church attendance and committed to no one faith in particular, Jared imbued his son with an openness to genuine religion but a suspicion of clericalism. Though Parley had good reason to emphasize the religious orientation of his youthful character, he likely presented an accurate picture of his earliest disposition. Orson, four years his junior, remembered him as sober and thoughtful.[20] Religious yearnings would become the paramount drive in Parley's life even before he attained to full manhood.

The essential rhythm of the young Pratt's life was unrelenting physical labor mitigated by the single diversion of books. This was a common motif in the early Republic. "The young men who joined the mobile bands of restless youth ferreting out opportunities placed great importance on their early love of books," notes one historian.[21] In Pratt's case, his life-long obsession with writing bore out his early fascination. "I always loved a book," he reminisced. "If I worked hard, a book was in my hand in the morning while others were sitting down to breakfast; the same at noon; if I had a few moments, *a book!* a Book! A book at evening, while others slept or sported; a book on Sundays; a book at every leisure moment of my life."[22] But there were never enough of those leisure moments. Even school was a luxury when there always seemed to be fields to plough and crops to plant and harvest. Parley attended just often enough to get familiar with "the four great branches" of learning, likely referring to history, poetry, theology, and moral philosophy.[23] Mostly, his smattering of schooling just whetted his appetite for more. But with limited success on the family farm, Parley frequently had neither leisure nor schooling. Then at fifteen he was hired out to a kindly Presbyterian family, the Herricks. That must have been a time of exceeding penury and heartbreak at home, for that same spring Orson was sent away in another direction at the age of ten. This was a pattern in the hard-pressed family: young sons sent off to work for hire, then afterward left to fend for themselves. Neither brother would reside long term at home again. Thus both were deprived of parental instruction, Orson recollected, at the very time they needed it most.[24]

With the end of the farming season, Parley did not return to his parents'
crowded home, which included not only the five hungry sons but also a boarder
at least some of the time.[25] Probably, the family's impoverishment influenced
the decision to have him board with his "kind-hearted" and more prosperous
aunt Lovina Van Cott, Jared's sister in Canaan. Food and respite may have been
more abundant at his aunt's, but the real joy for Parley was the chance it
afforded him, for the last time in his young life, for sustained formal schooling.
Orson stated that Parley had, "even in youth, an originality of mind, seldom
exhibited."[26] Parley attended the local Gilbert School, and the schoolmaster
frequently held him up to his classmates as a model they should emulate, he
recalled. No bragging here, just the truth, he insisted in his autobiography. He
had been, Parley said decades later, "a sportive, careless, innocent boy."[27] But as
the school year wound down, his life assumed a harsher regimen.

With the coming of spring, Pratt turned again to work on his aunt's farm.
Canaan was but an hour's walk from the little hamlet of New Lebanon, where
his family had established itself a few years previous, and the birthplace of
Thankful Halsey, a comely widow of twenty-six. He described her as "tall, of
a slender frame, her face of an oval form, eyes large and of a dark color, her
forehead lofty, clear complexion, hair black, smooth and glossy," with a "mild
and affectionate disposition."[28] She was ten years Pratt's senior, but the lad was
profoundly smitten. Apparently she reciprocated his love, though any mean-
ingful relationship seems to have been deferred by mutual agreement.
Meanwhile, Pratt worked side by side with his cousin William, the son of
Jared's younger brother William, planting crops and tilling the soil through
one more growing season. By then, Pratt had tired of spilling his sweat on land
not his own. He decided to work no more for family or employer, but strike
out on his own. At the age of sixteen, accompanied only by his brother
William, Pratt headed for the frontier that fall of 1823, "in search of some spot
of ground in the wilderness which we might prepare as our future home."[29]

Like Daniel Boone, who had similarly embarked on his first extended
wilderness expedition as a youth of sixteen with a single companion, Pratt
knew his destiny was westward.[30] But the wilderness Pratt referred to was
already a sparsely settled Lake Ontario community a few years old—Oswego,
New York—that would be connected to the bustling thoroughfare of the Erie
Canal before the decade was ended. His journey into the unknown culminated
in a simple real estate transaction. Pratt likely believed that a prospective canal
spur, linking Oswego with the Erie Canal, would make a land purchase there
a shrewd economic move. The Pratt brothers bought seventy acres of tim-
bered land for $280, putting $70 down and agreeing to pay the balance, with

interest, in four annual installments. They then returned eastward to earn the money due.[31]

The disparity in the Pratts' ages—William was twenty-one—would suggest that Parley was the junior partner, a kid brother along for companionship and an extra pair of hands. But events soon revealed the precocious leadership tendencies that would mark Parley's life. William failed to contribute a dime to the looming debt. Parley, on the other hand, found work with a disagreeable taskmaster, farmer Eliphet Bristol, back in the neighborhood of the Van Cotts. Long months of service, during which Bristol treated him as a "machine," secured him the money to make that year's payment, with enough left to purchase two axes. This time, his father, not his brother, accompanied him the two hundred miles back to Oswego during the fall of 1824. While working to pay for their own expenses, they managed on the side to clear, fence, and with the coming of spring, plant ten acres with wheat and Indian corn. They planned to sell the crops to meet the next payment.[32]

As father and son toiled together through that spring and into summer, Parley's thoughts turned again to religion. Though sparsely settled, the area was a microcosm of the religious marketplace of the frontier, with several competing clergy contending for converts, and Parley was caught up in the holy angst. Presbyterians had organized first in Oswego, meeting in a schoolhouse from 1816 until they completed a church building in 1835. A few Methodists were also worshipping in the area, which had seen circuit riders since the outbreak of the last war with the British. Episcopalians made their appearance in Oswego just the year before Pratt did. The Baptists came a little late to the scene, not organizing a church until 1828 and erecting a frame building in 1831.[33] In this spring of 1825, Parley found Reverend William A. Scranton, a teacher at a Baptist seminary in Hamilton, seventy-five miles to the southeast, preaching to a group of Baptists who regularly assembled for worship.[34]

Pratt sampled liberally of the religious offerings on hand, evaluating each by the light of his own study of the Bible. Methodists and Presbyterians he rejected for their baptism by sprinkling. With the Baptists, on the other hand, it was not their mode of baptism but their doctrine of baptism that troubled him. He complained to his father that the Baptists did not baptize "for *remission of sins*" and required "*an experience*" of conversion.[35] Pratt had not had any such experience, and he sought baptism rather as a means to a more spiritual life. Even so, and lacking an identifiable moment of rebirth, he petitioned for and was accepted into fellowship with the Baptist flock; Scranton baptized him that summer. Still, Pratt found that his public profession of faith did little to resolve the unease he felt over many points of salvation, personal as well as doctrinal. He singled out as especially unsatisfying Scranton's claim that spiritual gifts were intended by Jesus to accompany only the original apostles, not modern believers.

On October 25, 1825, the long-awaited opening of the Erie Canal took place. Ready transportation from western New York would greatly stimulate agricultural production in the region—but not in time to help Parley. Oswego did not yet have its canal spur, prices had not yet begun their dramatic rise, and demand for his fine crop of wheat and corn was nil. Two seasons of hard work, the clearing and planting, the labor for the payments, an investment of more than $150—all had gone for naught. An unyielding creditor retook possession of a now much improved seventy acres.[36]

Pratt appears at this point to have been too disconsolate to even settle his affairs in Oswego. He left his father to tie up the loose ends and sought escape from the disaster by fleeing to a pair of uncles in Wayne County—his father's younger brothers Ira and Allen, who lived thirty miles to the west. After a respite of some months, he struck out again during autumn 1826. This time, he did not anticipate attempting another entrepreneurial experiment from the security of a home base. Rather, he would "bid farewell to the civilized world" and head for Indian country. It was a dream-obscured effort to escape his own failure to make a living as a farmer, combined with a fear of permanent bondage to the same cycle of petty failures that dogged his father's cautious peregrinations around the state. Fear and frustration drove him west, but later he couched it as the romantic dream of being a savior to the Native Americans of the frontier: "I will win the confidence of the red man; I will learn his language; I will tell him of Jesus; I will read to him the Scriptures; I will teach him the arts of peace; to hate war, to love his neighbor, to fear and love God."[37] Naïve and romantic his notions may have been, but his dream would find expansive opportunity for fulfillment a few years later, and goes a long way to explain his enthusiastic embrace of Mormonism when it came. For his love of the Indians was rooted in his belief, confirmed in a youthful dream, that they were a remnant of Israel who would one day be restored to their place as a covenant people. "When the Book of Mormon revealed who that remnant were," he later said in a sermon, "it was no news to me but a confirmation of what I believed."[38]

Missionary work among American Indians was beginning a period of rapid growth at this time. Traveling from Oswego to Canaan and back again would have taken Pratt very near Stockbridge, New York. Elizabeth Camp, a devout Congregationalist, had visited the Stockbridge Indians in 1819 and found many Christians already among them. She returned herself the next year as a missionary.[39] Pratt had more western parts in mind, however, and after purchasing a pocket Bible and making his way to Rochester and thence to Buffalo via the Erie Canal, he took passage on a steamer bound for Detroit. He made it only as far as Erie, working for his fare, before poor weather drove him to continue his way by foot. He walked to Lorain County, west of Cleveland. By now, the rainy season made the roads increasingly impassable. Thoroughly discouraged, out of money, with no friends or family within hundreds of miles and with winter coming upon him, Pratt, not yet twenty years old, hunkered down for the season while he took stock of his situation and future. He found enough odd jobs to buy some foodstuffs and an ax, fashioned a crude hut, and settled down for the season in sparsely populated Russia Township. And so, almost twenty years before Henry David Thoreau would embark on his own, somewhat artificial experiment in woodland self-sufficiency, Pratt began such a life in earnest:

> Some leaves and straw in my cabin served for my lodging, and a good fire kept me warm. A stream near my door quenched my thirst; and fat venison, with a little bread from the settlements, sustained me for food. The storms of winter raged around me; the wind shook the forest, the wolf howled in the distance, and the owl chimed in harshly to complete the doleful music which seemed to soothe me, or bid me welcome to this holy retreat.

Pratt spent the winter immersed in reading, both the scriptures but also books about the West, including Alexander MacKenzie's *Voyages from Montreal, on the River St. Lawrence, Through the Continent of North America to the Frozen and Pacific Oceans: in the Years 1789 and 1793* (1801)—a Scottish explorer's account of his search for the Northwest Passage—and the journals of the Lewis and Clark Expedition (1814).[40]

With the coming of spring, Pratt found he had grown attached to his wilderness home and decided to sink down his roots. All that was lacking to his New World Eden was the Eve he had left behind. Knowing he could not hope to lure a bride to a squatter's hut, he bargained for a piece of land, built a house, and spent the next months clearing the land for a farm. Only then did he head back for the woman he had left almost three years earlier.[41]

Pratt started his six-hundred-mile journey back to his aunt's Canaan farm in the summer, arriving on July 4. But he passed by the house, going first to the Halsey home in nearby Ghent. There, a thirty-year-old Thankful listened as a weath-er-beaten, bearded man of twenty recounted his past years of travel, toil, and disappointments. Whatever impression he had made as a youth of sixteen and whatever love he had engendered in her heart were not diminished by his failure to secure status, prosperity, or even reasonable prospects in the interim. Neither was she dissuaded by his eccentric idealism: his inchoate plans "to try and teach the red man."⁴² A widow with delicate health and a decade older than the median age for female marriage in her era, she may have been content to over-look the age difference. Pratts had married across such disparities before, but in the other direction. (Parley's grandfather Obadiah was twenty-six when he mar-ried his fourteen- or fifteen-year-old bride Jemima.)⁴³ In any event, in early September, two months after Parley's return, he and Thankful were wed by a Baptist lay minister, Electa Palmer. He passed the subsequent months working again as a hired hand for William Herrick. A kind and appreciative employer, Herrick paid him double wages and these, together with his wife's modest dowry, enabled the couple to return to Pratt's refuge in Russia Township, Ohio, weeks after the wedding and pay off his small holding. Younger brothers Orson and Nelson (sixteen and twelve) made the journey with the newlyweds.⁴⁴

MAP 1.1 Early Life

Pratt's plot of ground was in an area of the United States with a complicated history of ownership. By royal charter in 1662, Charles II granted the colony of Connecticut lands comprising portions of present-day Pennsylvania and Ohio. Connecticut relinquished most of its holdings west of Pennsylvania to the federal government in exchange for forgiveness of war debts in 1786. The state maintained, however, its rights to the portion immediately west of Pennsylvania, the Connecticut Western Reserve, which it sold to private investors ten years later, finally giving up all control over the area in 1800. In 1803, this area that had once been the Western Reserve and had since become part of the Northwest Territory was incorporated as the northeastern portion of the new state of Ohio. Local tribes, however, still possessed the land west of the Cuyahoga River, which empties into Lake Erie at Cleveland. Two years later, the United States, by the treaty of Fort Industry, acquired title to those same lands from local Native Americans. Lorain County, where Pratt established his homestead, was in the heart of the area that had been opened to settlement only twenty years before.[45] By 1817, a village was established at the mouth of the Black River, and a few years later the legislature created the county of Lorain. When Pratt spent his first wilderness winter in that area, thirty miles west of Cleveland in 1826–1827, he said he passed months without seeing another human being, as the inhabitants of the area were widely diffused.[46] The pace of settlement had so accelerated just two years later that Thankful kept a school with twenty children, and several houses and farms had sprung up in the vicinity of the modest frame dwelling Pratt had built.[47]

As Pratt settled down to a happy if penurious domestic life, his thoughts once more turned to religion. His spiritual quest had never been satisfactorily met by his brief engagement with the Oswego Baptists, nor had they resolved his lingering doubts about the nature and purpose of baptism, a topic of fierce dispute among American Baptists at this time. In the spring of 1829, a fiery preacher would sweep into the area with a modified version of the Baptist faith that addressed Pratt's specific concerns and forever altered his spiritual trajectory. The backdrop to these events was one of the most important developments in nineteenth-century American religion. Barton Warren Stone, an ordained Presbyterian minister, had recently left that denomination and taken upon himself the designation Christian in lieu of a sectarian label. Two other ex-Presbyterians, Thomas Campbell and his son Alexander, were similarly eschewing labels and creeds, opting to self-identify as Disciples (or sometimes, "Reformers"). The senior Campbell, who had emigrated from Ireland in 1807, rejected the Calvinist teaching of salvation only for a predetermined elect, preaching instead that all were free to choose redemption. But he went much further than simple

Arminianism. Campbell published a "Declaration and Address" in 1809, laying out a manifesto of a movement soon to spread like prairie fire. He emphatically advocated a "simple original form of Christianity," stripped of any human accretions in "doctrine, worship, discipline, and government" not expressly found in the New Testament. He explicitly disavowed any intention to establish a new church, claiming rather to serve, along with his son, as "advocates for Church reformation."[48]

For many like-minded primitivists, who looked toward the "primitive" church of the New Testament as a guide, Campbell had raised a clear and appealing standard. Rejecting infant baptism as unscriptural, Campbell and his son Alexander naturally found themselves aligned with American Baptists. By 1830, just as Pratt was returning to his religious investigations, fissures between the Campbellites and the Baptists over several doctrinal issues, including baptism, had split the two groups decisively. Reformers and Baptists alike repudiated infant baptism, but differed on the importance and purpose of baptism. Campbell and Stone insisted that profession of faith in Christ qualified one for baptism, an ordinance that effected remission of sins and was essential to salvation. Other Baptists saw baptism as a sign of a remission of sins already effected.[49] Some Baptists (Landmark Baptists) would eventually affirm their difference by emphasizing the symbolic nature of baptism, officially denying its salvific efficacy.[50]

Sidney Rigdon, a Pennsylvania native, affiliated himself with a local Baptist church in St. Clair Township, near Pittsburgh, in 1817 and soon became a licensed, but not ordained, minister.[51] After a months-long apprenticeship, Rigdon headed for the Western Reserve of Ohio, settling in Warren, a bustling little town sixty miles east-southeast of Cleveland. He immediately set to baptizing converts, adding dozens to what was already becoming one of the largest denominations in America. The eighteenth-century dominance of the Presbyterians, Congregationalists, and Anglicans had been shattered by the rise of Methodists, Baptists, and, emerging at the turn of the century, the first of numerous Restorationists.[52] The summer of Rigdon's arrival in Warren, Alexander Campbell came to debate a Presbyterian minister on the question of baptism. Intrigued enough by Campbell's version of the gospel to strike up an association, Rigdon soon became an ardent disciple and mesmerizing preacher in the growing cause dedicated to restoring the ancient order of things. In January 1822, Rigdon assumed pastorship of a Baptist church in Pittsburgh and soon alienated many conservative Baptists with his reforming ideology. Two and a half years later, in a pattern typical of the age's Baptist factionalism, Rigdon and most of his congregation broke with the local church, disavowing them and being rejected in turn. They found a new home with Walter Scott, a Scottish immigrant who urged a restoration of New Testament practices and forms and rejected the authority of creeds. Scott would soon become, after Stone and the Campbells, the most influential figure in the emerging Disciples movement, best known for his "five-finger exercise," a mnemonic for teaching the essential gospel principles of faith, repentance, baptism, remission of sins, and gift of the Spirit. With Scott's impassioned preaching, the Campbellites truly began to gain traction in the Western Reserve.[53]

After imbibing Scott's influence, Rigdon moved back to Ohio to head a small congregation in Bainbridge, and he preached in a circuit to surrounding areas as well. In 1826, he answered a call to pastor the Mentor congregation of Baptists twenty-five miles east of Cleveland. He continued as an associate of Scott and the other reformers, finally shedding the last vestiges of Calvinism when he adopted in 1828 Scott's teaching that baptism, not faith, effected remission of sins.[54] That would be key to why Pratt fell under his influence when Rigdon's circuit took him west of Cleveland in 1830.

By 1828, the doctrines espoused by Stone, Campbell, and Rigdon were no longer amenable to traditional Baptists, and the Grand River Association in Ohio withdrew its fellowship that fall. But the appeal of the "gospel restored" grew only more powerful, as hundreds and then thousands flocked to the movement. Rigdon preached, baptized, and organized congregations of Reformed Baptists throughout the region that year and next. An ironic development occurred when the famous atheist communitarian Robert Owen debated Rigdon's co-religionist Alexander Campbell on the "evidences of Christianity" in Cincinnati in April 1829. The contest spanned eight two-session days, and when the dust had settled, Campbell expressed concern that the sedate audience reaction during the proceedings would be inaccurately reported as apathy. So he proposed that as a final disposition, those in support of the Christian religion and its propagation should stand. "An almost universal rising," the event's reporter duly noted. Those doubtful of Christianity and opposed to its "spread and prevalence" were likewise invited to stand. Three rose.[55]

The meeting then adjourned with mutual courtesy and decorum—at least according to the official report. British observer Fanny Trollope gave a slightly different version of what she had learned of the meeting's final moments (not deigning to attend herself, though residing in Cincinnati). Owen protested against Campbell's populist ploy, she reported, insisting that no responsible father with children to feed would "hazard the sale of his hogs, or his iron, by a declaration of opinions which might offend the majority of his customers."

In any event, she concluded, the debate failed to change a single mind in the capacity crowd of twelve hundred.[56]

The battle of the titans may not have changed Rigdon's mind, but it did alter its direction. Rigdon had been edging toward disaffection from his fellow reformers, largely over the question of how far the recuperation of New Testament practices should extend and how to interpret the prophesied millennium. Scott, Stone, and Campbell sought to restore a gospel of simplicity, purged of creedal complications. But Rigdon was increasingly looking for a broader restoration, including "supernatural gifts and miracles," and Owen had provoked Rigdon to ask why not a restoration of New Testament communalism as well.[57] Rigdon's interest in communalism was not just a return to primitive practices for their own sake. He was simply taking the audacious praxis of Owen, who had founded a short-lived communitarian experiment in New Harmony, Indiana, and merging it with the theology of Campbell. Owen's vision of social reformation had its Christian parallel in *post*millennialism, the belief common to many Baptists that Christ's kingdom would be ushered in through a human work of spiritual renewal. Campbell himself had been quick to point out such a parallel in his debate, impishly imputing to the atheist Owen a kind of crypto-Christian endeavor: "At one time, I would think he was preaching to us concerning the millennium; that he was a herald of a better day. Sceptical as my friend is, I must infer that he is a *believer* in the millennium; and, for aught I know, he may be doing as much as a thousand missionaries to induce it."[58]

However, whereas Campbell's version of millennialism implied a modest, conservative approach, Rigdon in his zeal wanted a vigorous, proactive strategy. Campbell himself explained in the inaugural issue (January 1830) of the *Millennial Harbinger*, "This work...shall have for its object the development, and introduction of that political and religious order called THE MILLENNIUM, which will be the consummation of that ultimate amelioration of society proposed in the Christian Scriptures."[59] Nevertheless, unlike Owen, Campbell did not believe that organizing into communal families would speed up the process, even if it was practical. Like many of the spiritual gifts, communalism, he believed, was never intended by Christ to be an enduring feature of church life. Rigdon grew increasingly impatient with such gradualism. As Campbell came sadly to realize, Rigdon "held to a literal fulfilment and application of the written word" and became convinced that scriptural prophecies portended dramatic events that would definitively herald Christ's coming in glory, "something extraordinary in the near future."[60]

Rigdon felt New Testament precedent and the urgency of millennial prep-aration both argued for at least experimenting with communitarian practice. Accordingly, he returned to Mentor and over the next year persuaded several of his parishioners, headed by Isaac Morley and Lyman Wight, to establish a small communitarian order; he also organized a smaller effort at Mayfield. Within months, more than one hundred of his flock had joined the "Family."[61] Rigdon's communitarian order was by no means unique. In addition to the secular versions, such as Owen's New Harmony, the Shakers were approach-ing their zenith. In 1840 they would peak at more than thirty-six hundred members spread among some twenty-two communal settlements.[62] The first of these had been formed in 1787 at New Lebanon, New York, where the Pratt family settled. Several of Pratt's relatives joined Shaker communities; in fact, his extended family was "shot through with Shakerism."[63] In addition, many smaller groups experimented with recapturing this aspect of the New Testament church. For example, during Pratt's youth, nearly a dozen Reformed Methodist farmers established a community of believers near the New York and Vermont border, at Shaftsbury, in 1815.[64]

During this very spring of the Campbell-Owen debate (1829), the spiritual journeys of Rigdon and Pratt intersected. Pratt's study of the scriptures had led him, like thousands of his countrymen, to desire a more primitive version of Christianity in accordance with New Testament principles. Rigdon's preaching confirmed his own views that baptism was both by immersion and for the remission of sins. This was indeed the "ancient gospel," he said in recounting the moment years later.[65] Nevertheless, the absence of any claim to authority in Rigdon's version of the gospel troubled Pratt. Thomas Campbell had been emphatic on this point: "As for authority," he wrote in his *Address*, "it can have no place in this business; for, surely, none can suppose themselves invested with a Divine right, as to anything peculiarly belonging to them, to call the attention of their brethren to this dutiful and important undertaking. For our part, we entertain no such arrogant presumption."[66] No man had any authority to dictate to the Body of Christ, and no divine commission to do so was looked for. The spirit of Campbell's rhetoric infused the Second Great Awakening, encouraging the rise of populist spiritual leaders, the prolifera-tion of new religious movements, and denominational democratization. This reflected changes in the broader culture, which increasingly assaulted the authority of the traditional economic, political, and religious elite.[67] Such cultural celebration of democracy justified the widespread fear and criticism of groups—such as Masons, Catholics, and, later, Mormons—perceived as authoritative, hierarchical, and secretive.[68]

This repudiation of authority, however, did not resonate with all Americans. Dismayed by the diversity and disunity of the contemporary religious scene, many like Pratt sought for the reassurance of authoritative truth claims and hierarchical religious structures.[69] Nevertheless, the Baptists had shown no more interest in priesthood authority than had the Reformed Baptists, and clearly the deficiency did not loom large enough in Pratt's mind at the time to dissuade him from switching allegiance from the former to the latter. That summer of 1829, Pratt joined Rigdon's flock.[70] As a Reformed Baptist, Pratt began—along with Rigdon—to move in the direction of expecting a more imminent millennium, one preceded rather than followed by Christ's dramatic return. "The prophecies of the holy prophets were opened to my view," Pratt wrote of this formative period. "I began to understand the things which were coming on the earth—the restoration of Israel, the coming of the Messiah, and the glory that should follow."[71]

In the midst of these personal religious developments, Pratt discovered that his brother William was living only ten miles away. William seems to have had a striking disregard for communication with family, even to the point of callousness. He had dropped out of the family's lives five years earlier, at the time of the loss of the farm he had purchased with Parley. Perhaps felt or imputed blame led him to abandon his family, who soon interpreted the ensuing silence as a tragic death. Years later, after William reconciled with his family and was laboring as a missionary under Parley's direction, the pattern continued. "Let him communicate with us from time to time," Parley wrote in a church newspaper which he hoped William would read, "and let us know that he is alive."[72]

In the present case, Parley was thrilled to learn his brother was not only alive but a near neighbor. He hurried to a joyful reunion with William, but perhaps the most salient part of his recollection was a point Parley remembered making about scriptural interpretation. He had by this time decided to strike out as an itinerant preacher to spread his millennialist fervor. To William, he expressed his willingness to rely upon the Lord for sustenance in his destitute circumstances. "Experiment shall now establish the truth of Christ's promises, or the truth of infidelity," he boldly pronounced. "For my part," William responded, "although I always believed the Bible, I would not dare believe it *literally*."[73] Following Rigdon, Pratt insisted on biblical literalism, a stance that became a touchstone of his career and that indelibly left its imprint on Mormon scriptural interpretation.

Pratt did not manage to resolve all his financial obligations, but he disposed of his assets, took his wife in tow with all of $10, and headed back east, presumably to start witnessing to his own acquaintances. Though Pratt's decision to become an itinerant evangelical preacher, without institutional affiliation or support, may seem eccentric today, it was actually quite common at the time, as many believers found themselves caught up in the religious excitement of the era, even as they struggled to articulate the precise nature of their own beliefs and find a like-minded community. In addition, the most rapidly expanding movements—Baptists and Methodists—often relied on lay ministers and teachers out of both doctrine and necessity. (By 1835, the proportion of "fairly educated" ministers was 55 percent and falling.)[74] Evangelical fervor frequently captured entire families. When Rigdon got the bug, three of his cousins also became Baptist ministers in the years following.[75] Austin Cowles was a minister before joining the Latter-day Saints in 1832, as were six of his brothers.[76] Four of Brigham Young's brothers preached at least part time, with Lorenzo Young and his brother-in-law John P. Greene serving without a home church or support.[77] At times, in the swath from the Western Reserve to the Burned-Over District of New York, it must have seemed there were more preachers than preached-to. "Every theological vagabond and peddler may drive here his bungling trade, without passport or license, and sell his false ware at pleasure," grumbled a Swiss immigrant.[78]

Ten dollars was insufficient for the long trip back to Canaan, so after walking with Thankful the thirty miles to Cleveland, Pratt hired himself out as a hand on the schooner that would take them the two hundred miles to Buffalo. To book passage from there to Albany along the canal, an additional 360 miles, he paid the rest of their money and sold some of their clothes. But Pratt went no more than a quarter of the way back to Canaan, only as far as Rochester, when he felt it "plainly manifest" by the Spirit that he should interrupt his journey in that area. Explaining to Thankful his call to disembark and await developments, he accompanied her a few miles farther to Newark, then left her to complete her voyage alone. It was approaching autumn 1830.

Pratt walked ten miles into the countryside and found a man, probably a fellow Baptist, by the name of Wells, who agreed to assist Pratt in his preparations to preach in the area. Itinerants generally looked for a local church open to visiting preachers or, lacking one, a house that could be advertised as an ad hoc venue. On one of their neighborhood visits to announce that night's event, Pratt and Wells visited a Baptist deacon named Hamlin, who told his visitors that he had recently come across what he described as a "STRANGE BOOK, a *very strange book!*" involving metal plates, a history of Israelites, visions, and angels.[79]

Newark, where Pratt had disembarked, was only eight miles from Palmyra, where the book had appeared months earlier. Though rumors of the young Joseph Smith's discovery of gold plates had floated about as early as 1827, even reaching the Western Reserve, it was not until the previous March that missionaries had fanned out to sell the leather-bound books with Bible-mimicking covers. Rigdon later recalled hearing the early rumors while in Mentor, but for Pratt, at least in his recollection, Hamlin's report was his first introduction to the Book of Mormon. Hamlin promised to lend the book on the morrow, leaving an anxious, curious Pratt to preach his millennialist message to a small audience even as he considered the unsettling message he had himself heard a few hours earlier, which aroused in his heart a "strange interest." The next morning, probably early given Pratt's impulsive and energetic nature, he returned to Hamlin and borrowed the promised volume. The book transformed his life.

In the process of reading the Book of Mormon, Pratt found the conversion experience he had long sought but never found. The concept of a personal conversion experience was at the heart of Puritanism's dissent from the establishment church. Puritans "preached for it, they sought it, they recounted it in spiritual biographies and in hagiographies, they checked its authenticity with those already converted, and they disdained those who had not experienced it."[80] This emphasis on the personal conversion experience figured prominently in the First and Second Great Awakenings. Most nineteenth-century Baptists remained committed to this core definition of the religious vocation. To join a Baptist congregation, "a believer had to make a confession of faith, relate a personal experience which gave credibility to the confession, [and] receive a favorable congregational vote."[81] This would have been the case when Pratt first requested membership in the Baptist congregation near Oswego, as a youth of eighteen. Perhaps he fudged the evidence to gain baptism, but if so it was with persistent misgivings.[82] Switching to the Reformed group the year previous would have salved his conscience some, since Campbell's group required no such membership test. Whereas the Baptists stressed experiential religion, the Reformers tended to put more emphasis on the reasonableness of revealed religion.[83]

Pratt's description of his conversion while reading the Book of Mormon is a template for a modified kind of religious experience that remains the hallmark of Mormon conversion. "[I] opened [the Book of Mormon] with eagerness, and read its title page. I then read the testimony of several witnesses in relation to the manner of its being found and translated. After this I commenced its contents by course. I read all day; eating was a burden, I had no desire for food; sleep was a burden when the night came, for I preferred reading to sleep."[84] The last year of his life, in his final testimony before a Utah audience, Pratt recounted what happened next:

> The Spirit of the Lord came upon me, while I read, and enlightened my mind, convinced my judgment, and riveted the truth upon my understanding, so that I knew that the book was true, just as well as man knows the daylight from the dark night, or any other thing that can be implanted in his understanding. I did not know it by any audible voice from heaven, by any ministration of an angel, by any open vision; but I knew it by the spirit of understanding in my heart—by the light that was in me. I knew it was true, because it was light, and had come in fulfillment of the Scriptures; and I bore testimony of its truth to the neighbors that came in during the first day that I was reading it, at the house of an old Baptist deacon, named Hamblin.[85]

Pratt's conversion involved influences from his two religious paradigms inherited from the Baptists and the Campbellites. It was marked by a dramatic encounter with spiritual powers that completely reoriented his life's meaning and purpose. But he was also seeking, and found, an appeal to his intellect, a spiritual confirmation of what he considered the restored gospel's reasonableness. He thus felt not only spiritual renewal but also a newfound conviction about particular propositions, involving a sacred text, its provenance, and the legitimate authority behind its production, claimed by a prophet named Joseph Smith. From then on, Pratt's life would be dedicated to articulating the reasonableness, even the rational inevitability, of the book's appearance and message.[86]

Independently of the spiritual power Pratt believed he had experienced as he read the book, two doctrinal seeds in the Book of Mormon struck especially fertile ground in his heart and mind. First, Pratt's millennialist expectations were nourished and heightened by the connections that the Book of Mormon explicitly made—and embodied—to latter-day events. A contemporary historian of Western Reserve religion noted that "the ardor of religions awakening . . . was very much increased about the year 1830, by the hope that the millennium had now dawned, and that the long expected day of gospel glory would soon be ushered in."[87] Pratt was caught up in those exuberant expectations, which were only heightened through his association with Rigdon, who "was prepared and preparing others for the voice of some mysterious event to come."[88] Pratt's excitement surrounding the Book of

Mormon reflected its dual relationship to the millennium. It supplemented biblical prophecies with an array of its own, expanding and enhancing Pratt's perception of cosmic forces rushing rapidly toward the final disposition of days. And the Book of Mormon was to Pratt's mind palpable proof, a concrete emblem like the budding rod of Aaron or the tablets of Moses, that God's mighty purposes were intersecting with human history. Regarding the first, Pratt later reminisced about his early conviction of the Book of Mormon's prophetic reliability.

> When I was a lad just out of my teens about 1830 I read a book that was but little known in the world. . . . It was entitled the Book of Mormon and . . . had many predictions in it that are plain and easy to be understood and the spirit and power of God bore witness to my heart of their truth. . . . Well now, these prophecies interested me I assure you. They made an impression upon my mind [which] never has been effaced. I realized the future with all of the assurances as if [I had] seen it myself. My knowledge would have been [no] stronger if I had seen Jesus Christ in his glorified body and [had] heard [the] same words from his own lips. I could rely on those predictions [and] consequently expect their fulfillment. I weighed every word and sentence over and over again carefully searching what idea was that was manifested and how and what manner [to] look for its fulfillment and soon there was not a sentence predicted in that book pertaining to our time that I hadn't gloried over perhaps one hundred time[s,] that I might perfectly and fully understand it so far as man could before it took place.[89]

Regarding the Book of Mormon's own oracular function, Pratt frequently wrote of its appearance as exhibit A in the catalog of end-time events. Ezekiel 37, with its reference to a stick of Joseph that would be joined to a stick of Judah; Psalm 85, foretelling the springing of truth "out of the earth"; Isaiah 61:9, which promises that Israel's descendants shall one day be known among the gentiles. These and other biblical prophecies were invoked by Pratt as evidence that the Book of Mormon not only *foretold* prophecy, but by its very existence *fulfilled* prophecy about end-time events.[90]

His long-nourished dreams of proselytizing the Indians also found dramatic reinforcement in a record that purported to reveal the origins and providential destiny of American aborigines. Pratt remembered how his heart resonated to the Book of Mormon's promises made to the descendants of Lehi. The Book of Mormon claims that Lehi was the founder of an Israelite colony in the New World, whose one-thousand-year history comprises the principal story line of the Book of Mormon. The same record predicts that if the gentiles (modern non-Israelites) did not repent and accept the Book of Mormon and the gospel it taught, then Lehi's descendants would be remembered by the Lord and have restored to them the blessings and promised status of their forefathers. As he read these things, Pratt said, "I felt as Moses felt when he refused to be called the son of pharaoh's daughter and chose to let his sympathies run with [the] poor trodden down and oppressed."[91]

The Book of Mormon confirmed his long-standing sense that the Indians were ripe for the gospel message. The Indians of North America, he quickly discerned (he would later include native peoples of South America in his conception), were descendants of Lehi and therefore children of the birthright by default, given the incorrigible wickedness of the gentiles and the corruption of sectarian Christianity. Other authors had long posited an Indian-Israelite connection. One popular theory connected them to the Lost Tribes of the Old Testament, the inhabitants of Israel who were carried off by the Assyrians and disappeared from history in the eighth century BCE. This theory was suggested as early as the sixteenth century by the Dominican friar Diego Duran and appeared in print in 1607 in Gregorio Garcia's *Origin of the Indians of the New World*. Thomas Thorowgood's *Jews in America, or Probabilities That the Americans are of that Race* (1650), likely the first English publication on the subject, influenced the Puritan missionary to the Indians John Eliot. By the time of the Revolution, James Adair had published his influential *History of the American Indians* (London, 1775), which argued for their Israelite ancestry. Elias Boudinot advanced the same theory in 1816 (*A Star in the West*), followed by Ethan Smith in 1823 (*A View of the Hebrews*), and Josiah Priest two years later (*The Wonders of Nature and Providence*, 1825).[92] But none of these authors affirmed the connection with the voice of scriptural authority or forecast for the Native Americans such a glorious destiny, which Pratt was anxious—and soon to be authorized—to help bring about. But first, he recorded, he was "determined to see the young man who had been the instrument of its [the Book of Mormon's] discovery and translation."[93]

Years later, Pratt reminisced how he "traveled on foot during the whole of a very hot day in August, blistering my feet, in order to go where I heard he [Joseph Smith] lived.[94] Arriving in Palmyra, he found that Smith had relocated across the Pennsylvania border to the town of Harmony a few years previous.

He encountered instead Joseph's brother Hyrum, who invited him into his
home, where they passed the entire night talking about Pratt's spiritual quest
and the history of the recently established Church of Christ (Smith's organization would not acquire its present name of the Church of Jesus Christ of
Latter-day Saints {LDS} until 1838). Hyrum likely recounted his brother's early
visions—probably not his first 1820 vision of God and Christ (which Joseph
rarely discussed in these early years), but almost certainly the visits from 1823 to
1827 of the angel Moroni who had led him to the gold plates, which Joseph
then claimed to translate from an ancient language to English. Pratt raised his
perennial preoccupation with the matter of authority. Hyrum detailed "the
commissioning of his brother Joseph, and others, by revelation and the ministering of angels, by which the apostleship and authority had been again restored
to earth."[95] Later, the church's narrative would represent priesthood authority
as descending by literal laying on of hands following an unbroken line from
Christ to his apostles, and from resurrected apostles to Joseph Smith. Like
Smith's first vision, such accounts took time to become a seamless part of
Mormonism's public self-presentation.[96] But the Book of Mormon already
existed as the most tangible evidence that Smith's authority was not imagined
or merely self-proclaimed. In the church's formal constitution, publicly
accepted at the church's first conference just months earlier, Smith represented
the word of the Lord as emphatically declaring that he had empowered Smith
to translate the Book of Mormon, "proving . . . that God does inspire men and
call them to his holy work, in these last days."[97] And on the day of organization,
April 6, a similar oracular pronouncement bestowed upon Smith the title of
"seer, a translator, a prophet [and] an apostle of Jesus Christ."[98]

Pratt had preaching appointments to get back to, but Hyrum gave him his
own copy of the Book of Mormon, which Pratt had yet to finish. As he
resumed his study of the new scripture, he became fully determined on his
next course of action. After fulfilling his preaching obligations in what must
have been an agitated condition, he hastened back to the Smith household
and asked Hyrum to baptize him. Hyrum suggested they visit the church in
nearby Fayette. Barely rested from his thirty-mile walk thrice undertaken, he
set out with Hyrum the next day for a journey of another twenty-five miles.
Arriving, Pratt found, to his delight, that he was surrounded by the people
and places that featured so prominently in the Book of Mormon's production. They arrived at the Peter Whitmer home, where the church—which
now numbered four or five dozen—had been formally organized months earlier, and where the final pages of translation had been dictated, surrounded by
family members who claimed to have personally handled the metal plates

from which Smith worked. The next day, September 1, Pratt was baptized in Seneca Lake by Oliver Cowdery, "Second Elder" of the church, and the very scribe who "wrote with [his] own pen the entire book of Mormon (save a few pages) as it fell from the lips of the prophet."[99] Up to this point, the vast majority of converts to Mormonism had been drawn from the Smiths' immediate circles; these individuals generally first encountered Joseph Smith and his revelatory claims and then read the Book of Mormon. Pratt represented a different type of convert, who became convinced of Mormonism's truth claims by reading the Book of Mormon and not through association with Smith.

The evening of his baptism, Pratt was ordained an elder. Without missing a beat, he continued his preaching tour in the Fayette area, but now with the confidence that he had full authority to do so. His first sermon as a Mormon, the Sunday after his baptism, yielded several converts. His command of the scriptures which sustained Mormon views on restoration surprised even the members, according to a later account by George Q. Cannon, a friend of Pratt's and a church leader decades later: "He brought forth from the prophecies of Isaiah, Jeremiah, Ezekiel and other prophets, abundant proofs concerning the work which the Lord had established through his servant Joseph, a great many of the Latter-day Saints were surprised that there were so many evidences existing in the Bible concerning this work. The church had then been organized some five months, but the members had never heard from any of the Elders these proofs and evidences which existed in the Bible." In fact, Pratt later told Cannon, even Cowdery and Joseph Smith "were surprised at the great amount of evidence there was in the Bible concerning these things."[100]

Satisfied he had fulfilled the purpose of his Spirit-prompted detour, Pratt next made his way to Canaan to rejoin his wife and relatives near the home of the Van Cotts. As lodger rather than son, he had here known his happiest moments of childhood there, including the care of a kind aunt, the love of a woman, and the joy of schooling opportunities unknown to him in his other childhood haunts. Now, he felt he had something to offer by way of repayment.

After reveling in the reunion with Thankful and extended family, Pratt replicated the pattern found in so many fledgling sects by embarking on what he remembered as his "first mission" and preaching to those most likely to credit his message—his parents, relatives, and closest friends.[101] Perhaps almost persuaded at the time, his parents, Aunt Lovina, and cousin John Van Cott joined in later years. But only one listener, his nineteen-year-old brother

FIGURE I.I Orson Pratt, 1849. Steel engraving by Frederick H. Piercy (1830–1891). Courtesy Church History Library, The Church of Jesus Christ of Latter-day Saints.

Orson, was moved enough to ask for baptism almost immediately. After Parley, Orson became Mormonism's most powerful and influential exponent of church doctrine. Like Parley, Orson had been on a personal quest to ascertain the Lord's will for his life's path. Parley's message, delivered with an unnamed companion, found ready soil in the young man's heart.[102] Finding no more success in his community, Pratt visited the Shaker settlement at New Lebanon, a few miles away, but met with no success there either. Feeling that further labors were futile and anxious to return to the community of believers he had joined, Parley departed with Thankful for Fayette. There he learned that Joseph Smith was visiting his parents in nearby Manchester, preparing to escape opposition in Pennsylvania by moving to the area. Pratt sped on to meet him and soon was standing face-to-face with the man whom he would come to recognize as God's earthly prophet. "A hearty welcome," consistent with Smith's "frank and kind manner," was all Pratt recorded of this first encounter.[103]

With one brief exception, Pratt would remain a loyal disciple and defender of Joseph Smith throughout his life. Many of Smith's converts and close associates fell under a spell that supporters and detractors alike strove to explain, invoking words like "magnetic" and "mesmerizing." But Pratt had been converted by the Book of Mormon, not prophetic charisma. He later described Smith with unambiguous regard ("the gifts, wisdom and devotion of a Daniel were united with the boldness, courage, temperance, perseverance and generosity of a Cyrus"),[104] but his relationship with Smith never evolved into the unalloyed adoration of Brigham Young or the fanatical attachment of Porter Rockwell. Pratt's esteem for Smith was a function of his respect for the office he held and the role he filled in the latter-day restoration. Smith would bestow favor and responsibility on Pratt almost immediately. Smith seldom waited for associates to earn his trust, allowing instead the winds of strife to separate the wheat from the chaff.

Pratt had arrived in Fayette just in time for the church's first conference, scheduled for September 26. Some sixty members attended; the church was still essentially an extended circle of family, friends, and close associates. But the church was ready to take its first major step in its transformation from fledgling sect, of which dozens littered the Second Great Awakening landscape, to church and multinational religion. At about the same time as the conference, Smith produced a revelation directed to Oliver Cowdery.[105] The immediate catalyst was the claim of Hiram Page, an in-law of the Whitmers, to having received revelations that many saw as a challenge—or at least as a confusing parallel—to Smith's own. Smith's revelation established the unequivocal supremacy he held as prophet in matters of church government. No one save he, the words declared, should receive revelations for the church. Pratt may have harbored no confusion on that point to begin with. But two other items in this revelation must have thrilled him to hear and added personal passion to his spiritual conviction. First was the directive that "the city shall be built."[106] The city referred to was no mere communitarian experiment, no secular utopia of an Owen or a feeble shadow of New Testament forms attempted by a Rigdon, but a place of literal gathering, the Zion foretold in prophecy, the New Jerusalem foreseen in Bible and Book of Mormon. This gave Pratt's millennialist expectations a tangible reality, an imminence, and the church he had joined a central role in their unfolding, all pronounced in the voice of God himself through his prophet.

Second, the revelation commanded Cowdery to journey to the Lamanites (understood to mean the American Indians), preach to them, and establish his church among them. Here was Pratt's long-standing dream about to be realized, not by self-appointed missionaries but by divinely ordained elders. The only element missing from this consummation he devoutly desired was an invitation to participate personally in the mission. Even before his conversion, his heart had been "softened towards this very remnant [of Israel]" and he "foresaw I would yet be among them, to teach them, to benefit them."[107] Nevertheless, days later, a subsequent revelation indicated that Cowdery would take as his companion not Pratt, but the young Peter Whitmer, one of eight witnesses who had seen and handled the Book of Mormon plates. Still, Pratt was already earning Smith's approbation and confidence. The Sunday of the conference, Pratt delivered a sermon, and he baptized several persons following the meeting, including Oliver Cowdery's stepmother and Ezra Thayne, who later recalled that he had seen Pratt in a vision.[108] Pratt likely shared with Smith his desire to teach the gospel among the American Indian tribes and asked to be included on the missionary venture. Newcomers to the faith typically asked the impressive revelator to obtain the mind and the will of the Lord for them personally, and Pratt later indicated that Smith did in fact make prayerful inquiry on his behalf.[109] In early October, days after the conference, Smith delivered a heavenly communication to the anxious Pratt. Together with Ziba Peterson, one of the church's earliest converts, Pratt would accompany Cowdery and Whitmer to "the wilderness among the Lamanites."[110] A new era in Pratt's life—and the life of his church—was about to begin. As events would soon reveal, his mission would catapult the church into a dynamic era of growth—just not in the way he or the Palmyra prophet expected.

2

Dreams of Zion

Beyond the Mississippi's rolling flood,
A land before ordained by Israel's God!
Where Zion's city, shall in grandeur rise....
—PARLEY PRATT, *The Millennium: A Poem*

WITH THE SPIRITUAL focus and confidence he had long sought, Pratt was about to embark on the first—and in some ways the most consequential—of his myriad missionary journeys. His travels to Indian Territory (in the area which later became Kansas) launched his own life of service to the Mormon movement, ushered in a cadre of future leaders, and laid the groundwork for the work of a literal, latter-day "gathering" that would unfold in two disparate locations. But in the combustible environment that was antebellum Missouri, his millennial expectations would find both euphoric anticipation and colossal disappointment.

Less than six months after President Andrew Jackson signed the Indian Removal Act, sparking a fierce national debate about American Indians' fate, Pratt and his companions left New York with high hopes of converting Indians to the Mormon gospel. Their mission combined the goal of Lamanite conversion with the task of Zion building. On October 17, 1830, as Pratt and three colleagues prepared to depart, senior missionary Oliver Cowdery signed a covenant committing himself "to proclaim glad tidings" to the western tribes he would visit, as well as "to rear up a pillar as a witness where the Temple of God shall be built, in the glorious New-Jerusalem." Pratt, along with Whitmer and Peterson, affixed his name to the document as one who vowed to "assist him faithfully in this thing."[1] Days later, leaving Thankful in the care of the Whitmer family, Pratt departed with the group for the West. (She would be baptized during his mission.) Their path of some eleven hundred miles (Pratt pegged it at fifteen hundred), would take them from western New York to the Missouri River, beyond which lay the Indian Territory. But several tribes were scattered along their journey's path. Approaching

Buffalo, they came upon the Buffalo Creek Indian Reservation, a fifty-thousand-acre tract inhabited by the Seneca tribe. There they found a polite reception but few Indians who could read. Leaving two copies of the Book of Mormon with some who were both willing and able to investigate the volume, they moved on.[2] A hundred and thirty miles farther west, Mormon convert John Corrill later remembered, they arrived at the village of Ashtabula, Ohio, where their tale of a Golden Bible "excited the curiosity of the people."[3] Continuing on, and not quite halfway to their destination, Pratt and the missionaries visited Campbellite congregations in northern Ohio, with consequences that would transform the young sect into a serious contender on the religious scene.

Leadership in the Mormon church was extremely young in the year of its founding. Smith was not yet twenty-five in the fall of 1830, and the four missionaries were all younger than he. Except for Pratt's brief stint as a preacher, none of the four had carried substantial responsibilities, directed or organized significant enterprises, or addressed multitudes. Pratt knew someone who had done all three, whose name and reputation resounded throughout the Western Reserve, and who could bring the wisdom of middle years, scriptural expertise, and formidable rhetorical skills to the fledgling movement. Even before they left New York, the missionaries likely anticipated visiting Sidney Rigdon and his congregation; as Oliver Cowdery stated from Kirtland, "we came to the place where we had prophesied tarrying a few days."[4]

Arriving in the Kirtland area, the missionaries divided into pairs, with Pratt and Cowdery going straight to Rigdon's home in Mentor on October 28 carrying a satchel full of copies of the Book of Mormon. With hardly more than introductions made, they spoke to Rigdon about a "new revelation from God," the Book of Mormon. "I, myself, had the happiness to present it to him in person. He was much surprised," Pratt later recollected.[5] At one juncture in the Owen-Campbell debate, a moment that Rigdon had watched and undoubtedly approved of, Owen had asked, "Are the books composing the Old and New Testaments the only books of divine authority in the world?" Campbell replied, "positively, yes."[6] Now, Pratt and Cowdery asked the erstwhile Campbellite minister to consider a novel alternative to the orthodox position on biblical sufficiency. Pratt's premillennialism, which accorded to God rather than humankind the principal role in laying millennial preparations, enabled him to see new scripture as a prime instance of such cosmic curtain raising, as a God-inspired act. And he wanted Rigdon to see it in the same light. Certainly the entire Campbellite movement had thrived in an environment that made the coming of the Book of Mormon seem inevitable, in the eyes of some. The very air, wrote a nineteenth-century historian of the Campbellites, "was thick with rumors of a 'new Religion,' a 'new Bible.'"[7]

But he already had one Bible, Rigdon replied, which he accepted as God's revelation. "With respect to the book they had presented him, he must say that he had considerable doubt."[8] Pratt beseeched his former mentor: "You brought truth to me. I now ask you as a friend to read this for my sake."[9] Over the next days, Rigdon wrestled with alternating feelings, simmering indignation contending with rising regard. One eyewitness to his struggle noted that the same themes that drew Pratt now captivated Rigdon: "It had made known the origin of the Indians," and boded well to "open the way for the introduction of the Millennium."[10] While he deliberated, Rigdon gave his pulpit over to the visiting missionaries, giving explicit approval to his congregation to ponder the remarkable story of the gold plates, angelic visitations, and apostolic authority returned to earth.

Following their visit with Rigdon, Pratt and Cowdery rejoined Peterson and Whitmer, who had preached in Euclid, near Cleveland. Some and perhaps all of the missionaries then passed through the Shaker village of North Union before returning to Kirtland. The Shakers gave the missionaries some of their distinctive hats, which prompted a local newspaper to announce that the missionaries "distinguish themselves" with a "peculiar kind of hat."[11] Arriving in Kirtland, the missionaries found a particularly fertile field in the communal group associated with Rigdon and led by Isaac Morley. Morley's daughter Lucy worked for a local woman, Abigail Daniels, "doing her house work" and assisting with "the weaving." Lucy recalled that three of the "well dressed nice looking" missionaries—Pratt, Cowdery, and Peterson—knocked on the door and began to share their message about angelic visitations to Joseph Smith and the restoration of authority to preach the gospel. Their declaration of authority enraged Daniels, who shook her "loombench shuttle ... in their faces and told them to leave her house as she would not have her children polluted with the doctrin." The missionaries quickly tried another approach, telling Daniels they were hungry and "had not had any thing to eat that day." Unmoved, Daniels replied that while she had "plenty" of food, there would be "nothing for you." But Lucy then informed the missionaries that her father lived a mile away and "never turns any one hungry from his door go there and you will be fed and cared for."[12]

Following Lucy's advice, the missionaries visited Isaac Morley, then 44, who owned substantial property and along with his wife had been on a quest

for the New Testament church. As a member of Rigdon's congregation, he
had been inspired by the primitive Christian Church's communalism described in Acts and a sense of living at the onset of the millennium. Along with
several other families he had established a communal enterprise. Cowdery
wrote that "several families had united themselves as a band of brethren and
put all their property together determining to live separate from the world as
much as possible."[13] At the time of the missionaries' arrival, Lyman Wight,
who had also been influenced by Rigdon, was preparing to establish a branch
of the communal group at Mayfield, seven miles from the Morley farm. When
he had his "goods about half loaded," however, Pratt and the other Lamanite
missionaries approached Wight with a copy of the Book of Mormon. Wight
hoped they would "hold on till I got away," as he had no time for "romances
nor idle speculators." But the missionaries were insistent, though "as good
natured as you pleased." Intrigued, Wight consented to call a meeting, where
"one testified that he had seen angels, and another that he had seen the plates,
and that the gifts were back in the church again."[14]

In the aftermath, Cowdery wrote to Joseph Smith, seventeen members of
Morley's communal group "went forward immediately and were baptized,
between eleven and twelve at night" on November 5. Two days later, the missionaries followed Wight to Mayfield, where news of a planned meeting drew
throngs. "We found the roads crowded with people going in the same
direction," a deputy sheriff later recalled.[15] The crowd included Levi Hancock,
whose brother Alvah had excitedly told him that the missionaries were
"building up the church as the apostles used to do in the days of Christ" by
preaching from the Book of Mormon, which "they call a history and record
of a people that once inhabited this land." After listening to Alvah, Levi felt
"something pleasant and delightful it seemed like a wash of some thing warm
took me in the face and ran over my body."[16] Others reacted much more suspiciously. Five miles south of Kirtland, two men asked Philo Dibble "if I had
heard the news" of the missionaries who "had come to Kirtland with a golden
Bible.... They laughed and ridiculed the idea."[17]

In Mayfield, the missionaries preached at a Mr. Jackson's home, from
which the crowd removed "a few boards" "to give the spectators a fare chance
of hearing." Pratt preached from the Book of Mormon account of the visit of
the resurrected Jesus to the Americas. He further argued that the new scripture corroborated the Bible and served as a sign "sent from God in order to
prepare the people for the glorious reign of Christ." Pratt then invited any in
the crowd to speak; Rigdon arose and "said he had bin longing to preach the
gospel for a long time and now he had done he thought he should never try to

preach again and confessed he was completely used up and advised the people not to contend against what they had heard." Cowdery spoke next, declaring his status as "eye witness to the thing declared and the Book." Pratt then invited people to come forward for baptisms.[18]

One witness recalled that there were thirty baptisms that afternoon. A deputy sheriff, John Barr, and a local lawyer, Varnem J. Card, positioned themselves above the Chagrin River to watch. Card, "of a clear, unexcitable temperament, with unorthodox and vague religious ideas," suddenly gripped Barr's arm and cried, "Take me away!" Barr recalled, "His face was so pale that he seemed to be about to faint." After they rode a mile away, Card remarked, "Mr. Barr, if you had not been there I certainly should have gone into the water." Indeed, the "impulse was irresistible."[19] After Pratt baptized one of the converts at Mayfield, John Murdock, Cowdery ordained him an elder. Murdock recalled their appeal, stating that he had been searching "many years…to not only know the truth but to also find a people that lived according to truth." Their message convinced him that not only did they possess doctrinal truths, "but also the authority to administer the ordinances of the Gospel." Like other converts, Murdock immediately began preaching himself. Over the next four months in Orange and Warrensville, he baptized seventy, "& being thronged with inquirers I quit my other business & left my own house & moved my family in with Bro C. Baldwin & gave my full time to the ministry."[20]

As converts began to step forward and ask for baptism, in early November, Rigdon, the bulldog of the Western Reserve, convened his Kirtland flock to make his announcement. According to Pratt, Rigdon "addressed them very affectionately, for nearly two hours, during most of which time, both himself and nearly all the congregation were melted to tears."[21] He explained what must have struck many as an abandonment of his faith, begged forgiveness for any offense given, and freely forgave his enemies. The day following the Mayfield success, the missionaries baptized Sidney and Phoebe Rigdon. The couple forfeited the right to their home, built by their congregation, and moved in with the Morley communal group. By November 12, Oliver Cowdery counted 55 baptisms, which ballooned to 127 by the time the missionaries left the area. Overnight, as it were, Pratt, Cowdery, Whitmer, and Peterson had almost tripled the size of the church, securing in the bargain an array of future leaders.[22] Besides Rigdon, the converts included Lyman Wight, one of the original twelve apostles called by Joseph Smith; Frederick G. Williams, who would become Smith's counselor in the First Presidency; Edward Partridge, the church's first bishop; and Morley, who would serve as Partridge's counselor.

The *Painesville Telegraph* noted with regret that many converts were "respect-able for intelligence and piety" and had nevertheless been duped by the missionaries.[23] By spring 1831, the number of members in the area would grow to a thousand.

The doctrinal messages that had fueled Pratt's own conversion proved cru-cial in the Kirtland area. The Lamanite missionaries emphasized first the Book of Mormon and, buttressed by Cowdery's firsthand accounts, told of the angelic visits to Joseph Smith and the Book of Mormon's translation.[24] They preached from the Book of Mormon, used it as evidence of the restora-tion and the coming millennium, and stated that it revealed the origins of the American Indians. The local newspaper, the *Painesville Telegraph*, had first reported on the rumors of the Book of Mormon "two or three years earlier."[25] Its editor, E. D. Howe, stated in his *Mormonism Unvailed* [sic] (the first anti-Mormon book, published in 1834) that the missionaries arrived "well sup-plied with the new bibles...which they said mostly concerned the western Indians, as being an account of their origin, and a prophecy of their final conversion to Christianity."[26]

Authority was a crucial issue for both missionaries and converts. The *Painesville Telegraph* noted the missionaries' claim to be "the only persons on earth who are qualified to administer in his [Christ's] name" and to properly baptize and to confer the gift of the Holy Ghost. Priesthood authority also enabled spiritual gifts (though the *Telegraph* reported that the missionaries had "totally failed thus far in their attempts to heal" and to prophesy). The missionaries also preached about the coming millennium, including the duty for Christ's people to gather in a "place of refuge," the "New Jerusalem," and that a "prophet" would be "raised up" among the American Indian tribes.[27]

By November 22, the four left Kirtland, taking along recent convert Frederick Williams. After the euphoria of resounding success, Pratt soon encountered his first taste of opposition and legal harassment, to which he responded with good humor; he could not anticipate the not-too-distant storms of violence these first irritating squalls foreshadowed. Fifty miles to the west, Pratt's party passed through Lorain County, where he had home-steaded as a newlywed three years before. Taking lodgings at the home of Simeon Carter, they were conversing with their host when a law officer arrived with an arrest warrant for Pratt. "A frivolous charge," Pratt wrote, implying something along the lines of disturbing the peace, a frequent pre-text for arresting unpopular missionaries. He depicted his treatment as brutish and the real motives for his arrest as a mix of religious hatred and greed. The judge boasted he would throw Pratt along with Peterson, who had volunteered to accompany him, into prison to test their "powers of apostleship." But the same judge offered to release the prisoner contingent on his paying a fine. Pratt responded with a sarcasm ill conceived to assuage his captors' anger or better his own predicament. He offered, if the witnesses would repent of their perjury and the magistrate of his blackguardism, to pray with them for God's forgiveness. He was summarily locked up for the night.

Pratt's description of the following morning is one of the most famous incidents in his autobiography.

After sitting awhile by the fire in charge of the officer, I requested to step out. I walked out into the public square accompanied by him. Said I, "Mr. Peabody, are you good at a race?" "No," said he, "but my big bull dog is, and he has been trained to assist me in my office these several years; he will take any man down at my bidding." "Well, Mr. Peabody, you compelled me to go a mile, I have gone with you two miles. You have given me an opportunity to preach, sing, and have also entertained me with lodging and breakfast. I must now go on my journey; if you are good at a race you can accompany me. I thank you for all your kindness—good day, sir." I then started on my journey, while he stood amazed and not able to step one foot before the other. . . . He did not awake from his astonishment sufficiently to start in pursuit till I had gained, perhaps, two hundred yards. I had already leaped a fence, and was making my way through a field to the forest on the right of the road. He now came hallooing after me, and shouting to his dog to seize me. The dog, being one of the largest I ever saw, came close on my footsteps with all his fury; the officer behind still in pursuit, clapping his hands and hallooing, "stu-boy, stu-boy—take him—watch—lay hold of him, I say—down with him," and pointing his finger in the direction I was running. The dog was fast overtaking me, and in the act of leaping upon me, when, quick as lightning, the thought struck me, to assist the officer, in sending the dog with all fury to the forest a little distance before me. I pointed my finger in that direction, clapped my hands, and shouted in imitation of the officer. The dog hastened past me with redoubled speed towards the forest; being urged by the officer and myself, and both of us running in the same direction. Gaining the forest, I soon lost sight of the officer and dog, and have not seen them since.[28]

The story blends the salient characteristics of the legendary Pratt: wit, hearty humor, physical robustness, and patient endurance in the face of recurrent religious persecution.

Subtle details in his account, however, do not quite add up. Of the five missionaries in the group, why was Pratt alone arrested, what was the "frivolous charge," and was it coincidence the arrest occurred in Pratt's place of prior residence? A contemporary newspaper account gave a less flattering version of the episode. The day after his commission to preach as a "Rigdonite" the previous August, the *Painesville Telegraph* reported, Pratt "ran away from a constable, and numerous creditors," heading for New York. Now in the fall of 1830, with rumors circulating of Pratt's return to the area as a Mormon missionary, "an officer was kept ready to arrest him for debt. He was accordingly arrested, tried, and judgment rendered against him." The case related to a dispute concerning ownership of the piece of land Pratt sold just prior to his departure for the east. After his arrest, the neighbor who purchased the land "requested a settlement," according to the newspaper, but Pratt responded he would not do anything "unless his Heavenly Father directed him." The two accounts—Pratt's and the *Telegraph's*—agree in describing the contempt with which the jailors treated Pratt's religious views. Pratt and his companions were "deluded mortals," the writer concluded, "now at large, to deceive and lead silly women & more silly men astray." Not surprisingly, the newspaper attributed the escape to simple deceit, not derring-do.[29] For his part, Pratt had the last word. At the time of his arrest, he left the Book of Mormon with Simeon Carter, who read it, converted, and began to preach himself. "A church of about sixty members was soon organized in the place where I had played such a trick of deception on the dog," Pratt wrote, surely feeling vindicated against those he perceived as the enemies of righteousness, operating behind legal forms.[30]

Only thirty-five miles farther along the coastline of Lake Erie, the missionaries came to the Wyandot settlement in Sandusky, Ohio. The Wyandot were the last American Indians to be removed from Ohio, not having been definitively defeated by white settlers until the 1794 Battle of Fallen Timbers. Even after subsequently ceding most of their Ohio lands, many remained behind, concentrated in the Sandusky area. Within two years, the first wave of Protestant missionaries, in this case Quakers, proselytized the tribe, followed by Presbyterians at the turn of the century. (Catholics had made inroads earlier.) Methodist preachers arrived in 1816, opening their first American mission at this very spot.[31] When the Mormons arrived in 1830, only several hundred of the tribe remained in the area, and under extreme government pressure they were exploring areas for resettlement in western Missouri. They thus received the missionaries warmly and exhibited special interest in developing a correspondence with Pratt and his companions who they learned were headed for that location. Just months later, the Wyandot sent their own delegation to Missouri. But as for Pratt's message itself, though the men of the tribe listened politely, they were not particularly impressed. When the first Methodists had appeared a few decades before, one of the Wyandot leaders, the influential William Walker (later provisional governor of Kansas), had already pronounced Catholicism and Protestantism essentially the same.[32] Mormonism apparently struck the Wyandot as one more in a series of only slightly differentiated sects. The missionaries moved on to Cincinnati but found their countrymen no more receptive than the Native Americans.

As winter broke upon them, the five took a steamer to St. Louis, traveling the last few hundred miles on foot when ice blocked the passage. Over the next six weeks, they trudged across a sparsely settled part of Missouri in unusually severe weather. The season was long remembered in the Midwest as the "Winter of the Deep Snow"; temperatures dipped regularly into the single digits and for weeks well below zero, with heavy snowfalls and bitter winds

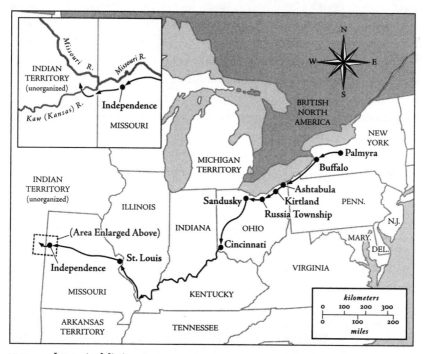

MAP 2.1 Lamanite Mission

from late December to early March.[33] They arrived in late January at Independence in Jackson County feeling they had traveled the journey of fifteen hundred miles Pratt reported. Pratt had at last reached his boyhood dream of taking the gospel to the American Indians beyond the land of the white man. They had arrived at the westernmost frontier of the United States, across the Missouri River from Indian Territory.

With funds depleted, Whitmer and Peterson secured employment as tailors in the village of Independence. Pratt, along with Cowdery and Williams, crossed over into Indian Territory. Almost immediately, their optimism and high hopes were frustrated, largely because of their inexperience and youth. Lay ministers were common on the frontier, and ministerial training was not essential. But missionary work among the American Indian tribes necessitated both political savvy and basic knowledge of legal hurdles. Isaac McCoy, a Baptist missionary to the Indians since 1817, had secured government contracts to assist in the settlement of tribes in Indian Territory. He thus had legal authority, political clout, and a personal investment in the religious indoctrination of the Indians. Then, six months before Pratt arrived, George Vashon, another authorized Indian agent, petitioned the Methodist Episcopal Church to send missionaries to the Shawnee, which they did only weeks before Pratt's arrival.[34] The American Indians in the region may have been willing to hear one more version of the Christian gospel, but Pratt's competitors were less obliging.

Initially, the Mormons proceeded without impediment, laying the groundwork for missionary work and a school among the tribes. They spent one day with the Shawnee, then crossed the Kaw, the southwesternmost portion of the Missouri River, and encountered a recently arrived group of Delaware Indians. Meeting their aged leader, Chief William Anderson, they related the story of the Book of Mormon, describing it as a record of his people's ancestors that had been providentially preserved for the Indians' benefit. Anderson listened but was reluctant to give them a fuller hearing. The next day, his resistance softened with further discussion, and he convened the tribal council of some forty men. Thus began the first of several sessions that earned the missionaries growing interest but no conversions. Cowdery wrote excitedly to Smith that "the principle chief says he believes evry word of the Book & there are many more in the Nation who believe & we understand there are many among the Shawnees who also believe."[35]

However, progress abruptly halted when word of these Mormon interlopers spread to Richard Cummins, the Indian agent with authority to deal with the Delaware tribe. He found the Mormon missionaries still flushed with their limited but happy success; according to Cowdery, Cummins was "somewhat strenuous respecting our having liberty to visit our brethren the Lamanites."[36] The missionaries responded that they "must proceed" and that if they failed to receive permission to teach the Shawnee and Delaware, they would "go to the Rocky Mountains, but what they will be with the Indians." Not yet willing to give up with seeming success on the horizon, Cowdery wrote a petition to the regional superintendent of Indian Affairs, General William Clark (of Lewis and Clark fame), for permission to continue their labors. The next day, February 15, Pratt departed for St. Louis with the petition to press his case in person. Cummins had already sent a letter to forewarn Clark against these "very strange" fellows with their tale of a "new Revelation" delivered by "an Angel from heaven."[37] Clark was absent from St. Louis during Pratt's visit and there is no evidence that Pratt received a response from any other official to Cowdery's request. Meanwhile, Cummins threatened the remaining missionaries with arrest if they refused to leave Indian Territory. "He was a man under authority," Whitmer reported, who "told us that he would aprehend us up to the garoson."[38] They complied, and with good reason. Courts could be harsh in enforcing laws about evangelizing Native Americans on government land. Only a few months later, one Methodist and two Presbyterian missionaries were sentenced to four years at hard labor for failing to obtain a permit to preach to the Cherokee.[39]

Having already traveled east three hundred miles from the frontier, it made little sense for Pratt to return after his fruitless errand. Instead, he headed for Ohio to visit the branches the missionaries had established the preceding fall, and he planned to continue to New York to make his report and receive further guidance from Smith. Delayed two weeks by a bout of measles en route, Pratt arrived in Kirtland in March, to a church that had grown to a thousand members. Fresh from his western disappointment, it must have occurred to him, as he considered that the church had grown more than tenfold in the course of his mission, that the Lord's purposes had actually been fulfilled rather than frustrated. That impression was corroborated when he learned that during his absence, Kirtland had been identified as a site for the gathering of latter-day Israel.[40]

When Smith first envisioned a literal restoration of scattered Israel is unclear, but the notion would have been met with enthusiastic support by the literalist and millennialist Pratt. Smith had intimated as far back as September 1830 that a city of Zion would be built, even stipulating that it would be built in the region of Pratt's missionary labors to the Indians.[41] About the same time, Smith had forecast the literal assemblage of a growing coterie of converts, "gathered in unto one place."[42] In December, following reports of Pratt's successes in the Kirtland area (and a visit by Rigdon and near-convert Edward Partridge), Smith received a revelation in which "the Ohio" was named as that place to assemble.[43] A month later, Smith led the advance party of the migration, departing Fayette by sleigh with his wife Emma, Rigdon, and the newly baptized Partridge. In early March, he instructed his brother Hyrum to join the Mormons in Kirtland with the several dozen members of the Colesville, New York, branch. (Hyrum hurried ahead by land when ice blocked their water passage.) Smith's mother, Lucy Mack, brought thirty Waterloo Saints and encountered the stranded Colesville members en route; Lucy rallied the group to pray for a thaw, and when the passage cleared they traveled on to Kirtland together.[44] Martin Harris soon followed with some fifty Palmyra members.

Pratt's joy at these developments included his personal anticipation that after a separation of six months he would soon see Thankful, who was expected to arrive with the Palmyra group. In the meantime, hardly had he caught his breath before Joseph Smith assigned him to a second missionary journey. A revelation dated May 7 directed Pratt, Rigdon, and Leman Copley to visit the Shaker community of North Union with near Cleveland and call it to repentance.[45]

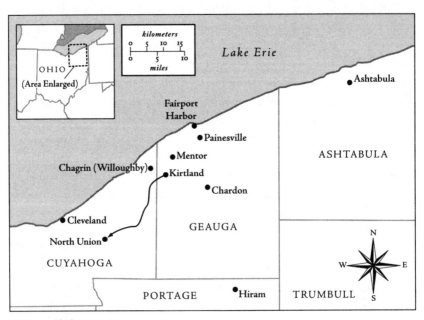

MAP 2.2 Shaker Mission

Shakers shared with Mormons a relatively recent origin, belief in modern prophecy, and millennialism; soon the Mormons would experiment with their own form of communitarianism, creating another parallel. But the revelation noted the Shakers' neglect of baptism and laying on of hands for the Holy Ghost, and it condemned many of their doctrines. The three chosen for this mission all had knowledge of and ties to Shakers. Copley had been a Shaker briefly, Rigdon had admired Shaker communalism and interacted with them, and Pratt had familial ties to Shakers and had grown up in the shadow of their New Lebanon community, which he had proselytized the previous year. Furthermore, Pratt had visited, along with Cowdery and a few others, the North Union Shakers and left several copies of the Book of Mormon with them en route to Indian Territory. For Pratt, this was most likely a return visit to see if seeds planted earlier would now bear fruit.[46] Unknown to him, a prominent Shaker leader, Richard McNemar, had read one of the copies of the Book of Mormon. Reminded of the "Persian tales which I used to read when a boy," McNemar concluded "its endless genealogies & Chronologies, afford no light to a Believer."[47]

Rigdon and Copley departed immediately for North Union, arriving on a Saturday evening. One of the last Shaker communities organized, North Union dated only to 1822. When the Mormons visited, this prosperous "Valley of God's Pleasure," as the Shakers called it, was on its way to a peak membership of three hundred members occupying some sixty buildings on more than thirteen hundred acres of fertile farmland where they raised corn, flax, hemp, and dairy cattle.[48] The able and iron-willed Ashbel Kitchell was then in his third year as presiding elder of the community. Shakers tended to have amicable relationships with other communitarians of the era, and the Mormons probably suspected that as a similarly marginalized small sect with unconventional beliefs, they would receive a friendly hearing. Kitchell met with Rigdon and Copley to discuss their doctrine, but they reached an impasse on the subject of marriage and Christian self-denial. The encounter was cordial, and, on the morrow, conversation continued "pleasantly in sociable chat," but Kitchell was clearly unreceptive to their message.[49]

The mood changed abruptly with Pratt's arrival that day. His behavior illustrates how profoundly his conversion, ordination, and mission experience had imbued him with a self-assured zeal. He was frustrated to learn that Rigdon and Copley had so timidly abandoned their efforts, had acquiesced to Kitchell's directive to silently "subject [themselves] to the order of the place," and now planned to attend the Shaker evening service as guests. Pratt protested—loudly, apparently—that Christ had authorized them to deliver their message and "the people must hear it," regardless of their leader's verdict. Cowed by Pratt's vehemence but still respectful of their hosts, Rigdon waited quietly until the end of the ensuing meeting, then received permission to read Smith's revelation to the Shakers. "Behold I say unto you that they desire to know the truth in Part but not all for they are not right before me & must needs repent," the revelation began without mincing words. Targeting some of the group's most cherished practices—including celibacy, vegetarianism, and the divine role of founder Mother Ann Lee—the denunciation continued: "Whoso forbideth to marry is not ordained of God, for marriage is ordained of God unto man...and whoso [biddeth] to abstain from meats that man should not eat the same is not ordained of God[50]...& again verily I say unto you that the son of man cometh not in the form of a woman...wherefore be not deceived."[51] To be reprimanded by outsiders before one's flock in one's own house of worship would have taxed the patience of the meekest of leaders. The fiery Kitchell restrained himself enough to simply dismiss the revelation out of hand. "I would release them & their Christ from any further burden about us, and take all the responsibility on myself," he stated.[52]

Rigdon requested that members be allowed to respond on their own account, but they were likewise unmoved. Having done his duty and been treated respectfully, Rigdon pronounced himself satisfied. Pratt, however, would not take defeat with good grace. He rose dramatically "and commenced shakeing his coattail; he said he shook the dust from his garments as a testimony against us, that we had rejected the word of the Lord Jesus." Kitchell was no milquetoast either. "You filthy Beast," he shouted before Pratt was done. "Dare you presume to come in here, and try to imitate a man of God by shaking your filthy tail; confess your sins and purge your soul from your lusts, and your other abominations before you ever presume to do the like again." As he next turned his rage on the traitor Copley, who had deserted "the living work of God," the scene concluded in farce. Pratt sat down, stunned into impotent silence. Copley sat hopelessly weeping, either in shame or disappointment of dashed hopes, while Rigdon sat smiling, perhaps feeling vindicated by the turn of events precipitated by Pratt's excessive zeal. Pratt immediately fled the room without a word and made his escape on horseback. Rigdon and Copley remained behind for a sociable Shaker supper.[53]

Upon returning to Kirtland, Pratt expressed concern about the behavior of church members in the area, many of whom he had baptized. Reynolds Cahoon, one of those converts, visited several branches with Pratt in May, including in Warrensville, Orange, and Bedford, and reported that they found members "verry far from the truth."[54] Pratt repeatedly encountered among the Saints spiritual manifestations that he considered extravagant. New Testament charismata like prophesying and speaking in tongues, which Mormonism and other newer sects frequently displayed, could frequently devolve into more disruptive practices, causing alarm within congregations and to observers without. Among the Methodists, for example, camp meetings produced widespread physical displays of spiritual awakening and rapture. One nineteenth-century historian noted that "while these extraordinary meetings were exerting a hallowed influence upon the older states,... those in Kentucky ran into such wild excesses in some instances, as to bring them into disrepute in the estimation of the more sober part of the community." Even the normally staid Presbyterians could be divided over the phenomenon. In one southern communion, the old stock Calvinists, unused to such "experimental religion," provoked the more spiritually adventuresome in their midst into leaving to form their own Springfield Presbytery in 1803. They lasted a year before splintering apart. An observer explained, "Some turned Shakers, and others ran into the wildest freaks of fanaticism. Hence originated those unseemly exercises so humiliating to recount, of jumping, dancing, jerking, barking, and rolling on the ground, by which these schismatics were at last distinguished and disgraced."[55] In the case of the more spiritually extravagant Ohio Mormons, "some would fancy to themselves that they had the sword of Laban, and would wield it as expert as a light dragoon, some would act like an Indian in the act of scalping, some would slide or scoot on the floor, with the rapidity of a serpent, which the[y] termed sailing in the boat to the Lamanites."[56]

Pratt had longed for the restoration of New Testament miracles, telling one observer before he reached the Native American tribes the previous fall, "when they [the missionaries] got among the scattered tribes, there would be as great miracles wrought, as there was at the day of Pentecost."[57] The bizarre behaviors reported by bystanders disturbed him, however, and Pratt asked Smith for clarification. After joining with the prophet and other elders in prayer, Pratt witnessed the process by which Smith received God's verdict. "Each sentence was uttered slowly and very distinctly," he recorded, "and with a pause between each, sufficiently long for it to be recorded, by an ordinary writer, in long hand." Smith's revelation, received on May 9, clearly distinguished between spiritual gifts and irrational emotional excess. In fact, the revelation invoked "reason" six times in declaring such wild extravagance not just excessive, but "an abomination," attributable to false spirits and demonic deception.[58]

Rationality is of course a relative term, especially in the context of religion, and Pratt would continue to find a harmonious coexistence in his own

ministry of intellectual disquisitions on the gospel alongside his exercise of
spiritual gifts such as healing and prophesying. The revelation also specifically
enjoined Pratt to return to his work of strengthening the churches, but now
with added authority to set things in order.[59] Accompanied by Joseph
Wakefield and Reynolds Cahoon, he spent the next weeks instilling more
decorum in the branches scattered throughout northeastern Ohio. Returning
to Kirtland, Pratt found further disappointment. Thankful did not arrive
with the Palmyra branch but sent word she had gone instead to visit her
family. Such a relatively short detour made sense, given her imminent
departure for distant parts. Still, the news must have stung. At the church's
conference in June (at which Pratt, until then an elder, was ordained to the
new higher office of high priest), Pratt received news that would ensure an
even longer separation from Thankful. A revelation through Smith directed
Pratt and others to travel to Jackson County and hold a conference, preaching
throughout the western states en route.[60] He set out with brother Orson as his
companion, holding frequent meetings along the way. Parley later said that
they "baptized many people and organized branches of the Church in several
parts of Ohio, Illinois, and Indiana." Orson, in his journal, only noted baptizing five members, in Peru, Missouri, near journey's end.[61]

Smith had declared, in God's voice, that the land they were headed for was
to be consecrated for "the remnant of Jacob." Pratt would have caught the
allusion here from the Book of Mormon, where such language prophesied the
gathering of Lamanite descendants in those same days when the Book of
Mormon should be revealed to the world.[62] Even if Jacob's remnant was slow
to respond, some of the "gentiles" in the area were not. Expelled from Indian
Territory the previous winter, Cowdery and his companions had spread their
message in the Missouri settlements instead, both before and during Pratt's
trip to the superintendent of Indian Affairs in St. Louis. A few conversions
established a staging ground for further church growth centered in that area.
Arriving in Independence in September, Pratt was surprised by developments
that continued to unfold at remarkable speed.

Almost immediately after Smith had commissioned and sent off the western missionaries, the Colesville Saints arrived in Kirtland. To their distress,
they learned that the land on which they had expected to settle was not available. Leman Copley, after his humiliation at North Union, rescinded his
donation of several hundred acres he had promised for their use, and he tried
unsuccessfully to return to the Shakers. With no place to settle the homeless
immigrants, Smith declared, via revelation, that the Colesville members
should resume their journey "into the regions westward, unto the land of

Missouri, unto the borders of the Lamanites."[63] While they made preparations for the trip, Smith journeyed ahead to scout out the area. The shocking rawness of the frontier and its settlers disheartened Smith. "Looking into the vast wilderness of those who sat in darkness," he later noted, "how natural it was to observe the degradation, leanness of intellect, ferocity, and jealousy of a people that were nearly a century behind the times, and to feel for those who roamed about without benefit of civilization, refinement, or religion."[64] Desperate for reassurance that he was not leading his people into a land of hopeless barbarism, Smith received a revelation that insisted this was indeed "the land which [God] appointed and consecrated for the gathering of the saints,...the land of promise and the place for the city of Zion."[65] That was fortunate, because five days later the sixty Colesville immigrants arrived in Jackson County, following Smith's earlier directive. They settled in Kaw Township, a dozen miles from Independence, becoming the first Saints to be resettled in the newly designated Zion. A few days later, on August 2, 1831, they ceremoniously laid the foundations for a schoolhouse with twelve men, representing the twelve tribes of Israel, placing the first log in the first building of "Zion." The next day, Smith dedicated a site for a temple. Secular learning, he seemed to be saying, was a natural and even essential preparation for spiritual knowledge. In fact, he considered such learning one of the motives of the gathering itself. "One of the principal objects...of our coming together," he wrote, "is to obtain the advantages of education; and in order to do this, compact society is absolutely necessary."[66]

When Pratt arrived a few weeks later, suffering from what was probably a malarial fever, he found the Colesville members established and a temple lot already dedicated; but he just missed Smith, who had left on August 9, taking with him the missionaries who had come from Ohio. Pratt settled in for the winter, sick and missing his wife. The Saints' material support and tender care touched him deeply, but he was determined to make his own way. During the Lamanite mission, Cowdery and Williams had done some teaching in the area.[67] And just before leaving for Missouri, Smith had commissioned Cowdery and W. W. Phelps to select books for schooling the Saints.[68] So now, sickness notwithstanding, Pratt turned to this vocation, teaching at both a Colesville school near Troost Park (in present-day Kansas City), presumably in the log building dedicated during Smith's visit, and instructing a group in Independence. In January, Cowdery, Phelps, and John Corrill were called to superintend all schools in the new settlements. Pratt, along with Phelps and Ziba Peterson, did most of the teaching.[69] A few months later, the first issue of the church newspaper reminded Saints in

Missouri that "the disciples should lose no time in preparing schools for their children" and urged parents to take matters in hand where teachers and resources were not yet available.[70]

In February 1832, Pratt, still ill, attended a conference in Independence. At the conclusion, a group of elders planned to journey to church headquarters in Kirtland. Desperate to see his wife after a year and a half apart, Pratt determined to accompany them, in spite of his weakened state. Prayed over by the elders, he received temporary respite, but he suffered from recurrent bouts of fever and chills during his long journey back to Ohio. Ever the missionary, he preached along the way. Encountering other Mormon missionaries en route who had run out of money, Pratt bragged that he had no need of purse or scrip. "We hold up our heads like honest men," he said, "go to the best houses, call for the best they have, make known our calling, pray with, or preach to them, ask for their bill on taking leave, but they will take nothing from us; but always invite us to call again."[71] He deserved such treatment as a representative of Christ, Pratt clearly believed. And when he was not so warmly received, he did not take it with good grace, as he demonstrated in North Union and would again hereafter.

Finally reaching Kirtland in May 1832, Pratt saw his beloved Thankful for the first time since he had left on the Lamanite mission in October 1830. But even now, after so many months apart, he paused only briefly before heading for southern Ohio to call the people to repentance. He groused when no converts were made that his failure was ascribable to the people's "prejudice, ignorance, and bigotry." Gone was the boastful bravado of previous weeks. Missouri, however, beckoned. The movement of the church was westward; Zion had been located there, and established members and new converts alike were streaming into Jackson County. Drawn as always to the newest frontier, Pratt in early June packed up his meager effects and with Thankful turned westward once again. She had $60, donated by her family to help the couple set up a new home, and Pratt received additional money from Lewis Abbot, the brother-in-law of future apostle Thomas Marsh and a church member in Kirtland.

The nature of Abbott's loan was not clear. Smith had declared the previous August that it was time to implement the law of consecration in Missouri, the principle by which members deeded property to the church, in a gesture toward the communal practices anticipated by many of the Kirtland converts. Implementation of the law was uneven, even chaotic. Personal investment, joint ventures, and charity often blurred, private versus public ownership was hazy, and the unclearly demarcated spiritual and financial stewardships sometimes produced confusion and ill will. In the spirit of consecration, Smith admonished members "to purchase lands in Zion" for the church.[72] Better to redeem Zion by purchase than by blood, another revelation added.[73] The former revelation appointed agents to collect members' money, but improvised arrangements took place as well. Such seemed to be the case with Pratt, but the private investor and the agent could blur. Philo Dibble, for example, said that he was "called by Joseph to purchase land in Jackson County," then added, "I paid fifty dollars for that purpose and also gave Brother Parley P. Pratt fifty dollars to assist him as a pioneer."[74] Abbott intended the money he gave to Pratt "to be expended in lands and improvements" in Jackson County—perhaps by way of a joint investment, perhaps for the general cause of Zion, or perhaps (as Pratt saw it) as a personal loan.[75] Other donors also advanced Pratt money to secure land and prepare it for Saints who would travel later in the season.

Parley and Thankful traveled most of the journey by waterway. July 4, 1832, found them steaming up the Missouri from St. Louis. Learning there was a preacher on board, passengers pressed Pratt for an Independence Day address. He thought he detected a hint of mockery behind the request and happily upset their minimal expectations. "I read a chapter," he recounted. "All was serious attention. I offered up a prayer; all was deep interest. I commenced a discourse, and nearly all were in tears." As a result of his oratorical triumph, the captain invited him into the cabin for the remainder of the trip. After changing boats in Louisville, he and Thankful received first-class cabins and complimentary board.[76]

After arriving in Jackson County, they settled among the Colesville members in Kaw Township. Though late in the season (it was August now), Pratt bought acreage, planted wheat, and put up hay and fencing. He also taught school. Weeks later, Abbot arrived and immediately quarreled with Pratt over the money he had given—or lent—to him. Pratt knew the bitterness of wasted sweat equity. He had lost the Oswego farm as a teenager and had been pressed to forsake his Amherst homestead under some confused combination of pressing debtors and the ministerial call. Now, he was forced to hand over not only his land, but his unharvested crop, his fifteen tons of hay, and even all of his cows but one to satisfy an erstwhile friend and fellow Saint. Seemingly doomed to failure in every entrepreneurial attempt, Pratt quickly resumed his missionary labors, likely seeking refuge and escape as much as fulfillment of duty. As winter fully descended upon the Missouri settlements, Pratt turned his school over to Thankful and headed eastward in late January, this time with William McLellin as his companion.[77]

MAP 2.3 Western Missions

Slightly older than Pratt, McLellin was a convert of little more than a year. He seems to have fallen under the spell of Pratt's unyielding biblical literalism, as he noted at their journey's inception, "We determined to keep all the commandments of God: Consequently we had taken no money neither two coats for our journey."[78] Only an hour into their travel, they met a ferryman who was not as New Testament oriented as they and who expected payment for his services. McLellin sat down to watch while Pratt deployed his scriptural arguments. Pratt finally wore the man down and secured their free passage over the Missouri. Traveling through northern Missouri, they found the people raw and crude but civil. Traveling eastward, McLellin worried at the prospect of crossing a deep stream just ahead in chill February weather. "Take no thought," Pratt said simply. Sure enough, the surprised McLellin recorded that at the water's edge they found a horse "saddled, as if waiting to take us across." They passed over "and went on our way rejoicing."[79] Other helpers providentially appeared to assist them, but few listened to their message. "Blindness, Ignorance, and unbelief seemed to reign," McLellin groaned. Their message of "the great things which are about to take place in this generation" and the need "to prepare for the coming of the Lord Jesus" met with indifference.[80]

These words from McLellin's journal suggest that the ambivalence of a day both "great and dreadful" spoken of in scripture was paralleled in the desire of Mormon missionaries to balance celebration of God's miraculous doings with vehement calls to repentance. The church newspaper did not always find a consistent resolution of the twin imperatives. "Warn in compassion," a church

editorial had advised a few months before Pratt's mission, "without threatening the wicked with judgments which are to be poured out upon the
world.... You have no authority... to terrify the inhabitants of America, neither have you any direction, by commandment, to collect the calamities of six
thousand years, and paint them upon the curtain of these last days, to scare
mankind to repentance." But the same newspaper regularly did just that. "In
order to give the signs of the times, we continue to glean a few of the many
accidents, troubles, calamities, &c," ran an introduction to the newspaper's
monthly catalog of "awful catastrophes." "No one can hide from the signs of
the times," ran another, which insisted that "the worst... is yet to come, and
come it shortly will, when they will gnaw their tongues for pain."[81]

McLellin and Pratt traveled along the Missouri River as far as Chariton,
teaching and testifying. When they could get appointments, Pratt usually
preached first. As lead speaker, he took the majority of time, often discoursing
for an hour and a half or more, with McLellin typically finishing up in half that
time. Even for that era, Pratt stretched the limits of endurance. "Br. Parley
arose and addressed them about 2 hours," McLellin recorded on February 9,
1833, by which time "some of them began to get very uneasy before he closed."[82]
("When I get talking I never know when to stop," he later admitted.)[83] By early
March, they had reached the eastern border of the state. Nearing the Mississippi,
they spied a majestic summit to the south. Pratt thought it the perfect place for
a sacred encounter with the divine. They climbed the peak, and "united in
prayr, meditation, and reading the prophecies and promises of the Lord to the
faithful, in which we continued about five hours. And we wrestled with our
mights but yed [yet] the veil was not rent," McLellin noted sadly.[84]

On March 9, they again received free passage from a ferryman, this time
into Illinois. Passing into Greene County, they preached to a full house and
were offered lodging by a generous Baptist minister, John Russell, "a very
learned and influential man."[85] Licensed to preach but never ordained,
Russell's sermonizing came mostly through his pen. A middling writer, he
published mostly in local papers. His greatest success would come with a temperance story, "The Venomous Worm," that became a staple of the McGuffey
readers. Russell's goodwill proved instrumental in the success of this stage of
their mission insofar as he not only lodged them but, with the approval of the
neighboring citizens, allowed Pratt and McLellin to preach some two months
in the area. When Russell visited Alton, Illinois, in April, he reported home
to his wife, "Mormonism is the main theme of enquiry," and rumors had
spread "that I had joined them & yet fortunately few believed it."[86] His
tolerance—and literary vocation—would be even more consequential several

years later. Russell's son remembered that after their expulsion from Missouri, Pratt "and a number of fugitives" again found kindness and refuge at Russell's home. "Father heard from them the heartrending stories and barbarity of the cut-throat Missourians. Hence came the story of 'Mary Maverick, the Mormoness.'"[87]

The Mormoness, a fictionalized account of the 1838 Haun's Mill Massacre, during which Missourians slaughtered eighteen Mormon men and boys, was the first published novel about Mormonism (1853). Unlike almost all of the dozens of succeeding nineteenth-century treatments, Russell's is highly conflicted, torn between disapproval and sympathy. An almost paranoid fear of seduction by these "deluded" yet wily fanatics pervades the novel. But so does the author's indignation that American institutions, "which guarantee the freedom of religion to the Jew, the Mahometan, the Pagan, and even to the *Atheist*, afforded no protection to the Mormon."[88] Undoubtedly his early acquaintance with Pratt, whom he treated as friend and colleague in spite of religious difference, allowed him to write an unusually humane portrayal of Mormons at a time when most fictional accounts demonized and vilified them.

Another Baptist minister of the neighborhood was not so obliging. Reverend Elijah Dodson became the missionaries' principal antagonist.[89] In Pratt's account, he easily bested Dodson in public forums. He probably did, because Dodson, apparently finding himself out of his league as a debater, appealed to the Baptist missionary extraordinaire, John Mason Peck, for support against Mormon inroads. Peck hurried down the sixty miles from his base in Rock Springs, Illinois. A dominant frontier figure in Baptist circles and beyond, Peck was credited with establishing nine hundred churches and founding the Rock Springs Seminary and, in the year of Pratt's mission, the American Baptist Home Mission Society. He also edited a Rock Springs newspaper that had already entered the polemical war against Mormonism.[90] In later years, he drew the rebuke of a young Abraham Lincoln for his defense of American aggression in the Mexican War.[91] At the time of Pratt's encounter with Peck, the Baptist was preparing his *Gazetteer of Illinois*, in which he lamented the lack of qualifications attendant upon a diverse and largely lay clergy: "Some are very illiterate, and make utter confusion of the word of God. Such persons are usually proud, conceited, fanatical, and influenced by a spirit far removed from the meek, docile, benevolent, and charitable spirit of the gospel."[92] Perhaps he had in mind the overmatched Dodson and overbearing Pratt as two examples of the weaknesses he deplored.

Peck sought to discredit the Mormon message by preaching against premillennialism, overreliance on prophecies, and Book of Mormon claims.

Pratt responded point by point, claiming that the "people in general...were unmoved by the exertions of Messrs. Peck and Dotson." John Russell's wife, Laura, confirmed that "Mormonism gains some they now have a church of 14 Members" and that a sermon by McLellin "did in a degree do away Mr. Pecks Sermon." McLellin "made a powerful appeal to the people asked them what testimony we had that any church was accepted a true Church and owned of God when there was no communication between earth and heaven" and declared that "the book of Mormon and the Bible must one prove the other or both fall together." While Laura Russell found this a "pretty bold assertion," she nevertheless recorded, "If this is all deception it certainly is one of the most cunningly devised things that ever entered the Human heart."[93] Pratt was disappointed in their marginal success. "We baptized only a few of the people," he noted.[94] In early June, Pratt and McLellin returned to Missouri. Soon after, Peck wrote a four-page exposé, one of the earliest anti-Mormon publications: *Mormonism, one of the delusions of Satan, exposed.*[95]

Back in Jackson County, in the midst of splitting rails and sowing crops, Pratt received what must have been his happiest church assignment to date: leader of a school of elders, modeled on the Kirtland School of the Prophets, which Joseph Smith had launched that January. In a small, second-story room of the Whitney store in Kirtland, fourteen men had assembled to study "things both in heaven and in the earth, and under the earth; things which have been; things which are; things which must shortly come to pass; things which are at home; things which are abroad; the wars and perplexities of the nations, and the judgments which are on the land; and a knowledge also of the countries and of kingdoms."[96] Another revelation added the injunction to "become acquainted with all good books, and with languages, tongues and people."[97] In this setting, dedicated to the sacralization of knowledge and the deliberate conflation of earthly and spiritual learning, Smith and other men not only studied the scriptures and theology, but also languages and a whole smattering of academic subjects. Now called to preside over a Missouri version of the school, Pratt found sixty men willing to convene weekly for instruction. Lacking an enclosed space of adequate size, they met in the open air to engage in something as much akin to charismatic prayer meetings as to scholarly instruction. Pratt depicted this era as a mini-millennium filled with "peace and plenty," devoid of crime or idleness, amid a wilderness beginning "to bud and blossom as the rose." Indeed, he asserted, "there has seldom, if ever, been a happier people upon the earth than the Church of the Saints now were."[98] In the background, however, internal dissension and conflicts with Missouri citizens were growing. Pratt wrote to Smith for counsel regarding

the school's future. He was rewarded with a revelation in August that commended him, directed him to continue the school, and promised him spiritual
gifts to expound "all scriptures and mysteries to the edification of the school,
and of the church."[99]

Peace may have abounded in the open air school, but by the time of the
revelation, the embers of conflicts both internal and external had already burst
into flame. In the previous months, internal problems had erupted out of juris-
dictional ambiguity caused by two centers of church gathering, simple personality disputes and, most potent of all, financial complications borne of trying
to implement a communal order among ordinary, frequently mistrustful, and
selfish human beings. Letters flew back and forth between Jackson County
and Kirtland, describing a spirit among members "like a pestilence" in Zion.[100]
A communication from Kirtland condemned "the Children of Zion...even
evry one" for neglecting their covenants, and chastised members for bridling at
Smith's rebukes.[101] Smith sympathized with struggling Saints trying to build
Zion under extreme circumstances but warned that their lack of unity would
nullify the Lord's protection against the looming external threats.

At the same time, Mormon behavior was increasingly antagonizing the
other residents of Jackson County. The "old" settlers—most of whom had
arrived only in the 1820s, a few years before the Saints—came primarily from
the Upper South, unlike the mostly northern Mormons. Although few of
them owned slaves, many aspired to, and support of slavery was widespread.[102]
Apprehension became alarm as the influx of dozens became hundreds, then
passed a thousand with no sign of abatement. Intimations that Mormons
would add free blacks to their burgeoning numbers pushed mutual hostility
to boiling point by the summer of 1833. The Mormons had acquired a press
and disseminated their revelations and doctrines through *The Evening and
the Morning Star*, its first issue appearing in June 1832. In July 1833, editor
W. W. Phelps published a statement of Mormon policy regarding free blacks,
indicating that the Saints sustained Missouri law, which disallowed immigration of free blacks unless they could produce proof of citizenship. Phelps
urged "great care" on this point, adding ominously (in a slave-holding state),
"as to slaves we have nothing to say." Nevertheless, he then went on to say a
great deal in a few words. He referred to "the wonderful events of this age," in
which "much is doing towards abolishing slavery."[103]

That was the gasoline the fires of Mormon opposition needed. Within
days, angry citizens circulated a draft of their grievances and called for a public
meeting on July 20. Phelps attempted to douse the flames by rushing out an
extra on July 16, which insisted no free blacks would be admitted to the church

if they came to Missouri, but imprudently repeated his fatal phrase linking abolitionism with "wonderful" developments. Aware of the impending threats, Phelps praised the U.S. Constitution for its defense of "a natural and indefeasible right to worship" and its prohibition against interference with "the rights of conscience." It was doubtless more a timid reminder than a note of praise, but the Missourians did not take the hint. On July 20, local citizens damaged the Mormon press, leveled the building that housed it, and tarred and feathered two Mormons, Bishop Edward Partridge and Charles Allen. Pratt recalled the terror inflicted by the armed mob, led by community elites and composed of "great numbers of the ignorant and uninformed." The mob went about "demolishing dwellings and stores, and plundering the contents and strewing them in the street; cutting open feather beds, breaking furniture, destroying fences and crops, whipping, threatening and variously abusing men, women and children."[104] On July 23, the intimidated Mormons signed an agreement to "remove as soon as possible" from Jackson County.[105] The terms stipulated departure in the new year, but the promised respite of several months would last only until October. While they waited for direction from Kirtland, Pratt and the others braced for further violence.

Meanwhile, in Smith's absence, the administration of the church continued to grow in complexity and efficiency. With more than a thousand saints in the area, Smith had recommended that Partridge's bishopric be split into three, with his counselors Isaac Morley and John Corrill taking charge of their own steward-ships and Pratt serving as new counselor to Partridge.[106] As events spiraled down-ward, the Missouri leaders instead apportioned ten high priests to preside over each of the ten Missouri branches, all operating under Partridge's authority. Pratt received charge of "Branch 8," probably the Colesville branch.[107] As summer passed into fall, and the Mormons delayed their preparations for departure, Missourians began a campaign of harassment that escalated to burning farms and buildings, destroying crops, and brutalizing men. In late September, Orson Hyde and W. W. Phelps journeyed to Jefferson City to petition Governor Daniel Dunklin for assistance. On October 19, Dunklin lamely claimed to be unper-suaded "that any portion of the citizens of the State of Missouri are so lost to a sense of these truths as to require the exercise of force, in order to ensure a respect for them." He instead advised the Saints to "make a trial of the efficiency of the laws" and appeal to local judicial authorities for protection.[108]

Days later, on October 31, raiders struck within two miles of Pratt's home. A large mob unroofed houses and whipped Mormon men at the settlement west of the Big Blue River. Pratt rushed to the scene, surveyed the damages and comforted the victims. He also organized an impromptu militia of sixty

men in the Colesville area to protect the settlement.[109] Shortly thereafter, he
was assaulted by two men while posting guards near the settlement, leaving a
"large gash" on his head, but reinforcements came to his aid and disarmed the
marauders. Then he did exactly as directed by the governor. Traveling with
another man to Lexington on the evening of November 3, evading mobs along
the route, he appealed to the circuit judge, John F. Ryland, for action against
the perpetrators of violence.[110] The judge refused to intercede, advising the
Mormons to defend themselves by force of arms.

Meanwhile, the struggle had been decided in his absence. Further inflamed
to learn that Mormons were not evacuating as promised but instead seeking
government intervention, locals had stepped up their violence. A mob of sixty
returned to the scene of their previous attack, but this time was met by an
armed body of Saints in a skirmish that killed two in the mobs and wounded
several Mormons, one mortally. With blood now spilt on the local citizens'
side, rumor finished the work that violence had begun; hundreds of militia
mustered to the side of the mob, and with Lieutenant-Governor Lilburn
W. Boggs at their head, Mormons were both outnumbered and politically
outmaneuvered. One Mormon reported, "We saw plainly that the whole
county were enraged, and preparing for a general massacre the next day. We
then thought it wisdom to stop the shedding of more blood; and by agreeing
to leave immediately we saved many lives; in this we feel justified. But we are
literally in a scattered, miserable condition, not knowing what we shall be
called to pass through next."[111]

As Pratt walked the twelve miles home from Lexington, a mob swarmed
the area, terrorized inhabitants, and rounded up some of the leading Mormons
as the Saints began to flee. Fearing for his own safety as a prominent leader, he
left Thankful to the mercy of God and the mob and fled into the wilderness.
He soon encountered John Lowry, a Latter-day Saint who had both a wagon
and a safe-conduct pass. He hid Pratt in the bed of the wagon and arrived
safely at the bank of the Missouri River, where Pratt took refuge in a cave.[112]
The next morning, he crossed on a ferry to the Clay County side, where he
witnessed a heartrending picture he would later describe: "Hundreds of people were seen in every direction, some in tents and some in the open air around
their fires, while the rain descended in torrents. Husbands were inquiring for
their wives, wives for their husbands; parents for children, and children for
parents. Some had the good fortune to escape with their families, household
goods, and some provisions; while others knew not the fate of their friends,
and had lost all their goods."[113] A few days later, Pratt sent a boy with a horse
for Thankful, who arrived without incident. (In Pratt's later reworking of the

story for his autobiography, he claimed to have taken Thankful with him during his own escape. Perhaps he thought the truth would suggest cowardice rather than prudence.)[114]

The religious leadership behind the Mormon persecutions especially galled Pratt. While helpless refugees huddled on the riverbank, he and other Mormons were harassed by "companies of ruffians," in at least one case headed by "the Rev. Isaac McCoy [the Baptist missionary to the Indians noted above], with gun in hand.... Other pretended preachers of the gospel took part in the persecution...exulting in [the Mormons'] afflictions."[115] Increasingly, Pratt saw preachers of religion not just as ideological adversaries, but as the source of much of the suffering, anguish, and death of his fellow Saints. The belief that Protestant ministers were the source of anti-Mormon persecution remained prominent within Mormon thought throughout the rest of the century. (This helps explain Pratt's printed outburst a few months later, that "I have preached the Gospel from Maine to Missouri, for near eight years, and all I ever received, during my whole ministry, would not amount to the yearly salary of one of the lazy, extravagant loungers, who under the name of Priests, are a nuisance to the whole country.")[116] Pratt sneaked back across the river to retrieve a few personal effects. But he found his home burned and his crops destroyed. The Saints still hoped to "return to our houses & lands before a great while," Edward Partridge wrote to Joseph Smith, "but how this is to be accomplished is all in the dark to us as yet." An overanxious Pratt, declaring that "if he ever spoke by the spirit of God he then did," prophesied that "we shall be enabled to return to our houses" by January 1 to "enjoy the fruit of our labor & none to molest or make afraid."[117]

In the meantime, most of his fellow refugees followed Pratt's example of seeking refuge on the Clay County side of the Missouri. (Several who thought they had escaped Jackson County and rebuilt crude shelters on the southern bank were driven across in January of the new year.) Pratt hired himself out as a day laborer, producing a scant income to ward off starvation. But he directed his real energies toward a project that would push his life in a new direction. Pratt was becoming a writer.

3

The Archer of Paradise

There is power in language. Power to…move upon the
spirit of nations like the spirit of God moved on the face
of the waters.
—PARLEY PRATT, *sermon, January 9, 1853*

THE LATTER-DAY SAINTS quickly recognized the power of the press.
Mormons launched their religion with the publication of a book, and they
founded their own presses to promulgate continuing revelations through
their prophet, disseminate the gospel, and rebut criticisms. People in Missouri
correctly perceived that an attack on the Mormon press struck at the movement's lifeblood. Now, with the Saints' physical survival at stake, they needed
a bold and convincing exposition of their predicament. They decided to
respond to their illegal ouster from Jackson County with a vivid, detailed
account of the violence against the Mormons, from the July destruction of the
printing office and the tarring and feathering of Partridge and Allen to a series
of December house-razings near Independence that left four elderly couples
terrorized and homeless. Pratt was principal (and likely sole) author of the
handbill, which ran to about fifty-five hundred words. Eloquent, if understandably polemical, *"The Mormons" So Called* seethed with indignation and
harrowing scenes of suffering, of "a tragedy, which stands unparalleled in the
annals of the Republic."[1] It was a modest entry into the craft of writing but
launched a new career for the twenty-six-year-old convert. Pratt had found
his voice, and over his remaining two and a half decades of life would become
Mormonism's most prolific historian, expositor, and defender of the faith.
This verbal acumen earned him W. W. Phelps's nickname, "The Archer of
Paradise," as one who always hit the mark.[2] Issued just before or after the turn
of the new year 1834, the handbill was probably printed by the firm that
acquired and repaired the Mormons' press, and it was reprinted in Kirtland a
few months later.[3] Though too late to forestall the Saints' expulsion, the piece
generated a sympathy that helped pave the way for peaceful resettlement in
adjoining counties.

The first day of 1834, leaders convened at Pratt's cabin to plot their future. Their meeting place reveals his increased prominence in the leading councils of the church. Once again, the Missouri Saints felt the need of Smith's direction, a thousand miles away in Kirtland, but no one was in any shape to make the trip. The rigors of winter travel, added to their utter destitution, discouraged all but the most intrepid. Bishop Partridge asked several men to go, but he was turned down flat. Lyman Wight stepped forward at last. Asked how things stood with his family, he replied with stoic irony, according to one account, that "his wife lay by the side of a log in the woods with a child three days old, and he had three days' provisions on hand; so he thought he could go very well."[4] Moved by his example, Pratt volunteered to accompany him, leaving Thankful behind in a "low state of health."[5] Equipped by scattered contributions from their fellow Saints, the two left Missouri on February 1. For once, Pratt resisted the itch to preach along the way. They made straight for Kirtland on horseback and arrived three weeks later. Their report to Smith captures the sense of the Saints' grief and bewilderment at their failure to realize their expected millennial joy in Zion. Only the previous June, the prophet had sent a plat to the Missouri leadership, conveying the design of the millennial city to be built in Jackson County along with plans for a temple to be built on the spot already dedicated for that purpose. Now, their hopes dashed and their plans thwarted, Pratt and Wight reported that the Saints,

> who had been driven away from their lands and scattered abroad, had found so much favour in the eyes of the people [of Clay County, Missouri] that they could obtain food and raiment of them for their labour insomuch that they were comfortable. But the idea of being driven away from the land of Zion pained their very souls and they desired of God, by earnest prayer, to return with songs of everlasting joy as said Isaiah, the prophet.

Pratt and Wight also assured Smith that, with one exception (his former missionary companion McLellin), no Saint had betrayed his or her communal enterprise by selling Zion properties into the hands of the gentiles.[6]

Presented with this most recent crisis, Smith obtained a revelation the same day, February 24, assuring the Saints that Zion would be redeemed, but the revelation was fraught with conditions and ambiguities. The Saints would begin immediately to prevail against their oppressors if they would "hearken from this very hour" unto the Lord. Eventual triumph would come, but only "after much tribulation." At the same time, if the Saints polluted their inheritance, "they shall be thrown down." Finally, the restoration of their rights and promises would come "in time." Then, invoking the precedent of the children of Israel and the need to redeem Zion "by power," the revelation promised a leader like unto Moses who would lead his people back to the land of promise. The revelation directed Pratt and Wight to raise an army and enjoined them to find "five hundred of the strength of my house" if possible, but authorized them to proceed with as few as one hundred.[7] Smith must have known that even a force of five hundred would be powerless against an aroused citizenry with militia backing. He likely hoped that by their arrival in Missouri, the governor would intervene on their behalf.

Smith's mother recorded that when he first learned of the abuse of Partridge and Allen and the dispersal of the Saints, "he bu[r]st into tears and sobbed aloud Oh my brethren my brethren said he. Oh that I had ben with you to have shared with you your trouble."[8] His grief at their distress moved him now to engage personally in the raising of an army. He prepared to accompany Pratt to the East, departing two days after their report. Others in the top leadership likewise paired up and struck out, including Sidney Rigdon, Hyrum Smith, Frederick Williams, Orson Hyde, and Parley's brother Orson.

Pratt's mission afforded him a rare, formative period of intimacy with and instruction from Smith. From February 26 until mid-March, Pratt recorded, "as we journeyed day after day, and generally lodged together, we had much sweet communion concerning the things of God and the mysteries of His kingdom, and I received many admonitions and instruction which I shall never forget."[9] Since Pratt gave no particulars of his interaction with Smith, it is impossible to know how many of his undeveloped ideas took root in Pratt's mind during the wintry days and nights of their eastern mission or, reciprocally, how many ideas expressed by the intellectually adventuresome Pratt were introduced into the mortar and pestle of Smith's religion-making imagination. Smith considered himself an inspired eclecticist as much as an innovator and revelator, though on one rare occasion he lodged a vague but angry protest against the theft of his ideas by the "great big elders" of the church, including Pratt.[10]

The mission became multipurpose from the beginning. Pratt and Smith visited and strengthened branches of the church, preached public sermons with mixed success, and recruited money and volunteers for the relief expedition soon to be known as "Zion's Camp." They traveled through Pennsylvania and western New York, passing through some fourteen communities, Pratt recorded (acting sometimes on the journey as Smith's journal keeper). The first Sunday of March, Smith and Pratt alternated speaking at morning and evening services in Westfield, New York. They passed on next to Villanova, where Reuben McBride remembered them coming to his house: "At the close of the meeting Joseph called for volunteers to go up to Redeem Zion. I volunteered to go."[11] They continued preaching, recruiting, and occasionally baptizing. In Perrysburg on March 5, they held three meetings to assembled members, with Pratt recording that Smith "prophesyed to them and the Spirit of the Lord came mightily upon them and with all redyness the yo[u]ng and mid[d]le aged volenteered for Zion."[12] They left two members in charge of preparing the recruits to assemble in Kirtland on the first of May, and resumed their journey. Success was mixed with opposition. Rabble-rousers disrupted one meeting, though on another night Smith and Pratt "preacht again to a hous crowded full to overflowing."[13] Sometimes, they even baptized converts—such as twenty-one-year-old Heman Hyde in Freedom, New York—who immediately answered the call to Zion's Camp, thus combining their two principal purposes.[14] On March 15, Pratt met up with other Kirtland elders and participated in a three-day series of meetings. He neglected to give details of the first one, held in Geneseo, perhaps because of its unsatisfactory results. Pratt's selective account of these early years celebrates the triumph of Mormon growth and gathering amid the restoration of new scripture and new doctrines. But not all of Smith's revelations were well received. Ezra Landen, a high priest and one of the church's earliest converts and missionaries, rejected Smith's "Vision," an expansive and unorthodox account of a multitiered heaven.[15] Landen had been "cut off" the previous December 31 but stubbornly refused to accept his expulsion. At the Geneseo meeting, "he continued to be rebellious" and eventually left the church.[16]

On March 17, Pratt and his companions held an elders conference in Avon, New York, meeting with Rigdon, Wight, Orson Hyde, and Orson Pratt to map out further strategy. The meeting delegated four elders to raise $2,000 for the relief of the Missouri Saints, with Hyde remaining behind to take charge of the money and preach in the interim. Smith would return with most of the traveling elders (he had been called home to testify in a court case), and Pratt would continue north with a new companion, Henry Brown, raising money, men, and the hackles of local preachers along the way.[17]

At Pillar Point, on Lake Ontario, Pratt healed a "Mrs. Cory" of an acute illness. But the consequence was a near riot when he tried to preach the next night, and he felt lucky to escape with his life. Knowing he might not return to New York in the foreseeable future, Pratt traveled 250 miles southeast to see his family in Columbia County. While there, he urged them to move to Kirtland and gave them enough money to do so.[18] His mother, Charity, made the journey the next year. Neither she nor Jared joined the church at this time, but both would later. As for Parley's other brothers, Orson baptized the eldest, Anson, in February 1832. William, the next sibling before Parley, also joined in this era, but the youngest, Nelson, never did.[19] Retracing their steps toward Lake Ontario, Pratt and Brown encountered Wilford Woodruff, a convert of three months, in Richland on April 1. Pratt sermonized till midnight, Woodruff remembered. Asked to join the expedition, Woodruff pleaded his indigence, but Pratt prevailed by insisting that God had commanded him "to gather together some of the servants of the Lord to go up to Zion."[20] Woodruff left with Brown ten days later. Pratt soon followed, bringing with him his new convert Heman Hyde.

By the end of April, a ragtag troop of more than a hundred destitute but determined Saints assembled in Kirtland. The men, mostly young, set out to cross the thousand miles of wilderness and prairie on foot. The first detachment of a few dozen left on May 1 for New Portage, fifty miles west of Kirtland, which served as the staging area; Smith followed with the main body on May 5. Recruits drifted in over the next few days, raising the number to 130. Smith organized the ranks, appointed officers, and gave instructions. On the trek, Pratt served as an outrider, visiting branches of the church along the route and helping to muster several dozen additional men, swelling the numbers to more than two hundred.[21] Once, exhausted after traveling overnight toward the main camp from a recruiting detour, Pratt fell asleep during the day. He said later that a distinct voice, "more loud and shrill than I have ever before heard," commanded him, "Parley, it is time to be up and on your journey." Feeling his body renewed, Pratt overtook the camp, where Smith, after hearing Pratt's story, told him, "It was the angel of the Lord who went before the camp."[22] Pratt sometimes traveled along with the camp. On May 12, after passing through the Sandusky, Ohio, plains, his wagon harness broke. The brethren fastened on ropes and drew it for three miles, while he rode alongside.[23]

While service in Zion's Camp forged a powerful loyalty to Smith among many of the participants, including Pratt, others grew dissatisfied with the youthful prophet. Sylvester Smith, who clashed repeatedly with Smith on the journey, once declined to share his surplus bread with Pratt, perhaps because he was not a member of his company. Joseph Smith lashed out at Sylvester, denouncing his miserliness.[24] What order did prevail was a result of strict camp discipline, courts-martial for infractions, and morning and evening calls to prayer. A staged battle along the way channeled tensions into a productive diversion and raised the men's spirits.

Arriving in Missouri the first week of June, Smith sent Pratt and Orson Hyde to the governor's office in Jefferson City. The success of the Mormons' relief expedition depended upon their reinforcement by state militia, which they had been led to expect. At the time of the expulsions from Jackson County, Missouri attorney general Robert W. Wells wrote the Saints assuring them that "if they desire to be replaced on their property, that is, their houses in Jackson County, an adequate force will be sent forthwith to effect that object."[25] And Governor Dunklin had himself fully acknowledged the justice of the Saints' petition. A few days before Pratt's visit, Dunklin had written to state militia colonel John Thornton that "a more clear and indisputable right does not exist, than that [of] the Mormon people...to return and live on their lands." While he encouraged the Mormons to settle elsewhere, he insisted that if the Mormons would not relinquish their constitutional rights, then "my course, as the chief executive of the state, is a plain one."[26] Plain it may have been, but his zeal to defend constitutional liberties was an empty boast. Faced with the specter of a local civil war, he told Pratt "he dare not attempt the execution of the laws." He advised the Saints to sell their lands and cut their losses.[27]

Pratt and Hyde returned to the camp of the Saints, now in Ray County. Smith and top leaders retired to the woods to hear the devastating report in private. Without the governor's intervention, they knew their cause was lost. Nevertheless, after a two-hour conference, the men decided "to go on, armed and equipped," hoping for a miracle and maintaining a show of bravado.[28] The contingent traveled on, unsure of what awaited them. They opened negotiations, but Mormons now gathered in Clay County balked at the dubious offer, proposed by a Jackson County delegation, to pay double the disputed lands' appraised value in exchange for a Mormon guarantee to forsake the county. In response, the Mormons offered to buy out the non-Mormon settlers in Jackson County for market value. The crisis built to a head as Zion's Camp passed into Clay County, north of volatile Jackson County, and mobs assembled to the south and east, heading in their direction. The main body of Missourians began to ford the Missouri River, crossing from Jackson into Clay County. About forty in the mob set up a cannon and sent sporadic fire toward the Mormon encampment a few miles north across Fishing River, but a violent storm arose, cutting the assailants off from the main body. Powder and men were alike soaked, horses were lost, and one man killed by lightning, whereas many of the Mormons passed a dry night in a Baptist meetinghouse. The next day, the dispirited mob returned to their homes. The episode at Fishing River was the closest the adversaries came to armed conflict. But if the

Missourians failed to disperse the Mormons, the Mormons had failed to reconquer their land of Canaan.[29]

Smith retired with his paramilitary troops a few miles farther north and sought divine guidance. The revelation he pronounced to a demoralized band stated the reason for the expedition's failure: "In consequence of the transgressions of my people...it is expedient in me that mine elders should wait for a little season for the redemption of Zion." Then, to the relief of the timid and the frustration of the more militant among them, the revelation added, "I do not require at their hand to fight the battles of Zion; for...I will fight your battles."[30] The final coup de main came not from a mob, but a bacterium. In the ensuing days, cholera brought to the Mormons the death and destruction the mob had hoped to inflict. The disease struck down seventy, more than a third of the ranks. Zion's Camp, undertaken in such exuberant hope and martial fervor, ended with fourteen burials and dispersal. Conflict within the ranks and the Saints' miscalculation of the potential for assistance from Missouri leaders had marred the expedition.[31] Smith's revelation offered the consolation that the Lord intended these travails as a "trial of their faith"; it also included the cryptic promise that "a blessing and an endowment" awaited those who faithfully endured the storms. Some did not. George A. Smith remembered that "several of the brethren apostatized because they were not going to have the privilege of fighting."[32] Pratt would increasingly vent his frustration by turning from the sword to the pen, again chronicling the abuses suffered at the hands of Missourians.

Those whose faith weathered the failure did so in part because they accepted a paradigm shift in the conception of Zion that Smith's revelation detailed. Originally hoping to inherit the land of Zion, secure possession by purchase, or repossess by force, they now learned that they could not achieve their ends until they were "endowed with power from on high." The quest for Zion, the grand project of building and sanctifying a godly people in preparation for Christ's return, could not be accomplished in isolation from the sacrifice, worship, and ordinances associated with the temple, whose walls were even now rising above the Chagrin River valley in Kirtland. The dream of building their Zion in Jackson County would never fade entirely, but the explanation for the failure of Zion's Camp initiated the Saints' transition into a more spiritually oriented strategy. Pratt's transition was effected largely by Smith's decision, the next day, to name him as one of fifteen Missouri elders to go to Kirtland to receive an "endowment" of power, accomplished in an early version of a Mormon temple ritual that included washings, anointings, covenant making, and the bestowal of spiritual powers and blessings.[33]

Before Pratt could proceed to Kirtland to claim his spiritual reward, he attended to domestic responsibilities. Returning to his home in Clay County, he found that his absence had set him further back financially. From indigence he had descended to profound indebtedness. Thankful's health had worsened; unable to sustain even her own meager needs, she had borrowed heavily on her husband's credit. He spent several months at common labor, trying to pay down his obligations, but with little success.[34] During this stay in Missouri, Pratt served as a member of the High Council, the presiding church body in the area, along with his brother Orson.[35] In October, he struck out for Kirtland with Thankful, who continued to ail. In New Portage, fifty miles short of Kirtland, Pratt found a receptive community of Saints and settled in, alternating short preaching tours with manual labor. To his dismay, he learned while there that W. W. Phelps had written Smith, sharply rebuking Pratt for fleeing his creditors and, as a consequence, suspending his license to preach.[36]

Conflicts over his financial obligations had become a pattern in Pratt's life. In this case, he felt he had been ill used. He had offered to pay his creditor, he insisted, but had understood the debt to be forgiven in light of his church service. In February, he journeyed to Kirtland to petition Smith for absolution. Hearing his account, Smith rose to his feet dramatically and pronounced, "Brother Parley, God bless you, go your way rejoicing, preach the gospel, fill the measure of your mission, and walk such things under your feet; it was a trick of Satan to hinder your usefulness; God Almighty shall be with you, and nothing shall stay your hand."[37] Vindication had come none too soon.

As if to reveal the true purpose of Zion's Camp as a great sifter of the faithful, Smith organized a quorum of twelve apostles only a few months after the completion of that expedition. In June 1829, as the Book of Mormon translation wrapped up, a revelation to Joseph Smith had directed two of the three Book of Mormon witnesses who had received angelic visitation and confirmation of the reality of the gold plates, Oliver Cowdery and David Whitmer, to "search out the Twelve," referencing the Book of Mormon (and New Testament) model of church organization based on a quorum of twelve apostles. The third witness, Martin Harris, would later be associated with this special selection panel, though Cowdery and Whitmer primarily carried out the assignment.[38] For several years, however, they made no progress on their directive. Now, at long last, Smith moved to fulfill the directive. He convened a Kirtland meeting on February 14 "of those who journeyed to Zion for the purpose of laying the foundation of its redemption last season with as many more of the Brethren & Sisters as felt disposed to attend."[39] He seated the Zion's Camp veterans in a special section, paid them homage, and then directed the three witnesses to make known the names of the Twelve. Every name that followed was one of the veterans, except for three who were living in Missouri at the time, thus having occupied the role of besieged rather than rescuers. The witnesses rose and called the first three to fill the quorum: Lyman Johnson, Brigham Young, and Heber C. Kimball. The meeting then adjourned. The next day, the meeting reassembled, and Cowdery called Orson Hyde, David Patten, and Luke Johnson, followed by William McLellin, John Boynton, and the prophet's brother William. If Pratt had knowledge or intimations that he too was to be invited to the quorum, he would have to wait another week for the formal call. On February 21, Parley Parker Pratt was named (along with inductees Thomas Marsh and Orson Pratt, absent on missions), and he rose as one of the final members called to the quorum.

Pratt, like the other apostles, was ordained to his calling in the presence of the large congregation. The recorded ordination blessings of eleven of the twelve apostles were relatively short. Pratt's was twice as long and was followed by an even longer apostolic charge (which none of the other apostles received). This was the highest church office Pratt would ever assume. This fact, added to his natural soberness of disposition and intensity of purpose, doubtless led him to weigh heavily the counsel given, to ponder the sometimes dire events the two pronouncements forecast, and to rejoice in their powerful promises. With Smith standing in for the absent Martin Harris, he and the other two witnesses invoked upon Pratt blessings of intelligence, wisdom, prudence, and understanding, both for the ministry and for the "thorny maze" of life. They prayed that "nothing shall prevail against him, that he may be delivered from prisons, from the power of his enemies, and from the adversary of all righteousness." "No arm that is formed and lifted against thee, shall prosper, no power shall prevail," they promised. Finally, they prophesied that "angels shall carry thee from place to place" and that the veil "of the Heavens shall be rolled up. Thou shalt be permitted to gaze within it and to receive instruction from on high."[40]

Then Cowdery pronounced upon Pratt an even more vivid and ominous charge. Tellingly, he warned him against pride and vainglory and cautioned Pratt never to think himself "better than [his] brethren." Twice he warned Pratt to "count the cost" carefully of what lay ahead, as he would have to "pass through many afflictions," know "the same difficulties" faced by the original apostles, "cross the mighty deep," and spend years laboring in distant countries in "great" and "incessant" toil. Finally, he would be "dragged before the authorities" for his religion and spend time in "strong dungeons and gloomy prisons." "I have spoken these things," affirmed Cowdery, "because I have seen them in visions." "But when your work is done," he promised, "your heavenly Father...will take you to Himself."[41] Pratt had already passed through a refiner's fire in Jackson County. But as Cowdery predicted, much worse was to follow.

Following these meetings, Pratt returned to New Portage to prepare for his first mission as an apostle, planned for the coming spring. In his personal recollections, he said nothing of the feelings experienced upon his call to the quorum. In his day, "apostle" was taken to mean "the ordinary traveling ministers of the church," or those who first take the gospel to a land or people.[42] For Smith to organize a group of twelve in likeness to Christ's original apostles must have been a fulfillment beyond expectation of Pratt's primitivist hopes. Still, responsibility for an ailing wife, the need to resolve his indebtedness, and the possibility of settling down for a time tempted him to postpone his mission. In addition, his aged mother had joined the household; his father, Jared, likely moved to Michigan with their eldest son, Anson, at this time, either to assist Anson with a new homestead or to divide the burden of caring for two aging parents.[43] In these straitened circumstances, and while he was calling on a sick neighbor, Parley's frame house then under construction caught fire and burned to the ground. Perhaps sensing the futility of any aspirations for stability or prosperity, he acquiesced to the mission at hand: "One [church member] gave me a coat; another a hat; a third, house room; a fourth, provisions; while a fifth forgave me the debts due to them; and a sixth bade me God speed to hasten on my mission."[44] So equipped, he headed north to Kirtland to rendezvous with his brother apostles. Finding them not yet ready to depart, he journeyed a few miles farther north, to the village of Mentor, with unnamed companions; what happened next would launch two careers at once: Pratt the apostle and Pratt the pamphleteer.

Mormonism dates its own beginning to the discovery and publication of a sacred record. Oliver Cowdery, first official church historian of the movement, traced its commencement to "the time of the finding of the plates" of the Book of Mormon.[45] Likewise, Smith dated his own enlistment in the cause not to his "First Vision" or the appearance in his room of the angel Moroni, but to September 1827, when he acquired the gold plates.[46] The Book of Mormon came off the press in March 1830. Thenceforth, the principal medium for promulgating the message of Mormonism would be distribution of this signature scripture. By fall of the next year, Smith decided that the Saints would follow the path of so many contemporary religious movements and launch a newspaper to disseminate their version of the restored gospel. (One competitor faith, Alexander Campbell's Disciple Movement, produced its first issue of the *Millennial Harbinger* almost two years earlier, in January 1830.) Beginning in June 1832, the Saints published in their *Evening and the Morning Star* Smith's revelations, spiritual counsel, and gospel-themed articles, along with occasional reprints conveying general edification or political updates. In 1833, the church attempted to publish Smith's revelations in a Book of Commandments, but a Missouri mob destroyed the print shop and most copies.[47] Two years later, the Saints discovered a vehicle they would exploit prolifically over subsequent generations: the religious pamphlet. Pratt's first published pamphlet inaugurated both his career as pamphleteer and the church's employment of the medium for polemical and apologetic purposes.

A Short Account of a Shameful Outrage chronicles an assault more mortifying than mortal occasioned by Pratt's missionary efforts in Mentor in April 1835. He had first passed through Mentor on his mission to the Indian Territory in late 1830. The village was home to a Campbellite congregation once presided over by Sidney Rigdon. But unlike Rigdon's Kirtland congregation, many of whom followed Rigdon into Mormonism, the Mentor Campbellites found Rigdon's conversion to Mormonism an unforgivable betrayal. Church members there "were furious at him" and felt "it was nonsense and a man of his knowledge ought to have known better."[48] Rather than follow his example, they found a new pastor. Five years and thousands of miles of missionary travels later, Pratt returned to a community still stinging from Mormonism's attempts to subvert its flock.

If Campbell's followers had in many cases found the Mormon message amenable to their version of the gospel, the ones who were not drawn in by that message could be especially resentful of Mormons, whom they considered religious plagiarists and poachers. Campbell himself accused Smith of simply stealing, with Rigdon's complicity, elements of his own theology. Many parallels clearly existed. For instance, Campbellite Walter Scott emphasized five cardinal doctrines of the "Gospel Restored," three of which would also be the core doctrines of Smith's "Restored Gospel": faith, repentance, and baptism for the remission of sins. To these Scott added the gift of the Holy Spirit and eternal life.[49] Smith dropped the fifth as a first principle and preferred to call the fourth the gift of the Holy Ghost.

In another critique, Campbell saw the Book of Mormon as a thinly veiled mishmash of contemporary takes on religious debates, containing

every error and almost every truth discussed in New York for the last
ten years. He [Smith] decides all the great controversies:—infant
baptism, ordination, the trinity, regeneration, repentance, justification, the fall of man, the atonement, transubstantiation, fasting, penance, church government, religious experience, the call to the ministry,
the general resurrection, eternal punishment, who may baptize, and
even the question of free masonry, republican government and the
rights of man.[50]

Rubbing salt in the wounds of a church he had so extensively pillaged for converts five years earlier, Pratt attempted to preach in Mentor's Campbellite
church. Finding the doors understandably locked against him, Pratt provoca-
tively preached on the church steps instead. He did not get very far. Resorting
to boisterous distraction rather than violence, an ad hoc band consisting of
bugles, drums, and fife marched past playing at full—and tuneless—volume.
The scene alternated between Pratt's haranguing voice and the rowdy
cacophony of the musicians as they repeatedly passed before Pratt in their
circuit of the town square. Onlookers probably found something comical in
this vivid contest between earnest missionary and musical dissonance. Pratt,
as often happened, failed to see anything at all humorous about the scene.
"To me," he wrote, "it was solemn beyond description." The protest culminated with a volley of eggs as the marchers completed their final circuit.
Dripping with yolks, Pratt bore testimony against his uncivil audience and
departed with his two companions, accompanied part of the way by a jeering
and victorious crowd.[51]

Defeated in his objective, Pratt turned to the pen to protest what he saw
as an assault on his religious freedom and to expound his sermon through a
medium no band could drown out. His *Short Account of a Shameful Outrage*
marked the first Mormon pamphlet ever printed, mixing simple narrative,
indignation, and exhortation. The finished product reflects two constants in
Pratt's ministry: his love for the Book of Mormon and his sense that the end
times of human history were already inaugurated. He found the confluence of
these themes in one of the passages most cited in nineteenth-century Mormon
discourse: 3 Nephi 29, foretelling the scriptural record's own eventual publication.[52] As Pratt explained in a subsequent article in the church newspaper,
such Book of Mormon prophecies

show, in definite terms not to be misunderstood, that, when that record
should come forth in the latter day, and be published to the Gentiles,

and come from them to the house of Israel, it should be A SIGN, A
STANDARD, AN ENSIGN, by which they might KNOW THAT
THE TIME HAD ACTUALLY ARRIVED FOR THE WORK TO
COMMENCE AMONG ALL NATIONS, IN PREPARING THE
WAY FOR THE RETURN OF ISRAEL TO THEIR OWN
LAND.[53]

Pratt's zeal in employing the Book of Mormon as a proselytizing tool was
unsurpassed by his contemporaries, who often preferred biblical passages
familiar to their audience. Pratt believed the Book of Mormon's more vivid
depiction of latter-day events, as well as its status as the tangible "ensign" of
prophecy to which the faithful could rally, made it indispensable. In the sermon he had written for the Mentor congregation, he also invoked New
Testament apocalypticism to warn the townspeople of impending judgment.
His sermon was calculated not to comfort and invite, but to alarm and alien-
ate. Even in an era rife with millennarian currents and Jeremiads, Pratt's style
was more confrontational than that of most of his apostolic peers.

Brigham Young once commented on the "want of tact" in some elders "to
know how to win the people." He used Pratt's friend Heber Kimball, a phe-
nomenally successful missionary, as an example of a softer, gentler approach.
"Come, my friend, sit down; do not be in a hurry," he would say to strangers.
Then he would "preach the Gospel in a plain, familiar manner, and make his
hearers believe everything he said.... 'Now, you believe this? You see how
plain the Gospel is? Come along now'; and he would lead them into the
waters of baptism."[54] Pratt, on the other hand, was a missionary without subtlety. Divisive Pratt could be, but he saw himself as suffering abuse and hostility with grace and dignity. He produced an affidavit, most likely his own
invention, in which a New Englander witnessed the Mentor proceedings and
remarked, "Is this the way you worship in this country?" No, the Campbellite
deacon replied, explaining that the victim of abuse was a Mormon. The
stranger observed that the Mormon "seemed to be but little disturbed by the
noise and confusion around him. O said he, he is used to it; he has been in
such scrapes before, in Missouri."[55]

Pratt was perhaps to be excused for finding no humor in the Mentor incident. Turning one's cheek in the presence of opposition may be one mark of
the Christian disciple, but when such persecution encroached on what they
saw as their constitutionally protected liberty to practice their religion,
Mormons pursued legal means of redress whenever possible. After the
near riot, Pratt therefore filed a complaint with the Mentor magistrate and

eventually received $47 for damages. Significantly and disturbingly, the verdict revealed a particularly potent form of persecution much more menacing than musical pranks or even random mob violence. The danger lurked in the subtle forms of authority that militia officers exercised over their fellow citizens on a violence-ridden frontier. During the Mentor incident, all of the band members were militiamen, and their bandleader was their captain, Grandison Newell. The unofficial reach of this kind of extralegal power—and the propensity to abuse it—was fully recognized by the judge sitting on the Mentor case, who wrote that Newell "issued orders to march, and halt, and keep time, but gave no orders to fire. The jury, however, came to the conclusion, that, holding them under military command, he was responsible for their acts."[56] The judgment foreshadowed the future Mormon expulsion from Missouri, where the lines between mob violence and militia actions blurred almost completely, with consequences vastly more tragic.

Pratt returned to Kirtland to prepare for his mission. On April 5, Orson Pratt arrived to complete the quorum, and for the next two weeks, all the apostles bore public testimony as they awaited their departure. They also met together in the temple, with Joseph Smith presiding, to receive their formal charge and instructions for a mission that had three purposes. First, they were to set in order the affairs of the Saints scattered throughout the eastern states in small, young branches. The area had already been well visited by Orson Pratt, Lyman Johnson, and others. Orson spent most of the two years from February 1832 until April 1834 teaching and baptizing throughout New York and New England, leaving several groups of converts in his wake. The apostles would now hold conferences from Ohio to Maine, instructing and correcting the church. Second, Smith instructed the quorum to raise money for the relief of the Missouri Saints and "for the purchasing of lands in Zion," since Zion's Camp had failed to provide either military or material relief for the destitute exiles now gathered in Clay County.[57] And third, the apostles would preach and baptize.

At two o'clock in the morning of May 2, the assembled apostles departed Kirtland for the trek to Fairport Harbor a dozen miles northeast. They arrived at dawn, caught the steamer just before it departed, and traveled more than a hundred miles up Lake Erie to Dunkirk, New York. They held their first conference in Westfield on May 9, preached and baptized, and then wended their way ever northward. A church conference in Freedom, New York, on May 22 gives a glimpse of Mormonism in the East in these formative years. The conference encompassed the Freedom Branch of sixty-five members (most baptized since the visit of Smith and Pratt the previous year), twenty-eight from Rushford, a number from Portage (who were welcomed in fellowship but did "not generally obey the 'word of wisdom,'" the church's health code revealed two years earlier, which banned the use of tobacco and alcohol), a handful from Aurora and Niagara, thirty from Burns, and half that number in Holland. John Murdock reported that other scattered members in the Mansfield area were "wanting instruction." Evoking the turmoil and challenges facing the primitive church of Acts, Pratt noted how one branch in particular "suffered much from false teaching by hypocrites and knaves."[58] The apostles sermonized at the conference on spiritual gifts and the Word of Wisdom.

Pratt continued north, preaching along the way. He reached Pillar Point in mid-June and passed through Kingston on his way to attending another conference in West Loborough, Canada, two weeks later.[59] In a pattern now familiar, the apostles found the members outside the normal route of traveling elders "uninformed in the principles of the new covenant." So Pratt and his colleagues gave instruction, disfellowshipped two brothers, baptized converts, and appointed a presiding elder over the congregation before returning east through Vermont. In St. Johnsbury, Pratt and his fellow apostles held a two-day conference for the area faithful, but at the public Sunday meeting found themselves facing an audience of more than one thousand curious listeners. Hyde and McLellin thought some of the community felt a deep interest. However, it was apparently not deep enough to lead to the mass conversions the apostles were always seeking. Nine persons were baptized on this occasion.[60]

Pratt took enough time out from the conference to write a letter (his earliest to survive) to Joseph Smith's uncle Asael, who lived in West Stockholm, New York. He had been baptized in June by Lyman Johnson and had hosted a number of the apostles on their journey, including Pratt. In this letter, Pratt expressed love and gratitude for the hospitality, and he included a poem dedicated to Asael on Pratt's favorite theme: the millennium. He also indulged in a bit of self-pity, saved in the end by his usual strategy of casting his travails as a literary narrative tinged with sardonic humor. "We pass from dore to dore Being refused entertainment Because we are elders of the church of Latter day saints our feet Blisterd our legs weary Our Boddyes worn down with fatigue our minds disconsolate while the dark shades of night hover round," he lamented. On one occasion, they "Calld at six houses told them we were Elders of the Church of Latterday Saints and wishd Entertainment the first had no room Being a Large 2 story Painted Building the second had no lodging the 3 had work hands the 4 did not like our doctrin the 5th had company the sixth the man was gone from home the 7th being a tavern receivd us gladly for our Money."[61]

The problem may have been Pratt's unflinching bluntness. Brigham Young boasted that he had never been turned away hungry as a missionary. He said in a sermon:

> When others would ask, we would often be refused a morsel of something to eat, and so we would go from house to house; but when I had the privilege of asking, I never was turned away—no, not a single time.
>
> Would I go into the house and say to them, "I am a 'Mormon' Elder; will you feed me?" It was none of their business who I was.[62]

Pratt shunned such tactics. He rejected the "wise as serpents" approach, preferring to be hungry and direct rather than well fed and clever.

In August, the quorum held a conference in Bradford, Massachusetts, thirty miles north of Boston. Pratt then joined the majority of the quorum at a conference in Saco, on the Maine coast, where he met a twenty-six-year-old widow, Mary Ann Frost Stearns, whom he would marry less than two years later after Thankful's death. Apostle David Patten baptized her and her mother that same month.[63] Parley left few details of the mission routine, but the journal of his brother Orson, traveling mostly in the same areas, gives a picture of an unceasing round of daily public sermons:

> Aug 23rd...preaching in the forenoon about 3 hours in the meeting house near Deacon True's upon the regularly commissioned officers in the kingdom of God....In the afternoon preached in the schoolhouse in Salisbury upon the spiritual gifts....
>
> Aug 24th...Preached in the schoolhouse near Mr. Elliots upon the prophecies....
>
> Aug 25th. Preached in the courthouse in Concord...upon the first principles....
>
> Aug 26th. Preached at the schoolhouse near Mr. Johnson's tavern. Said something about the first principles of the gospel, the spiritual gifts, ...
>
> Aug 27th. Preached at the schoolhouse near Mr. Elliots upon the...gathering of Israel....
>
> Aug 28th. Preached at the courthouse upon the spiritual gifts....
>
> Aug 29th. Preached at the schoolhouse near Mr. Johnson's tavern upon the difference between faith & knowledge....[64]

On August 28, the quorum convened its last conference at Farmington in the Maine interior. The apostles, by then having traversed the eastern United States to its northernmost border in three and a half months, received word from fellow apostle John Boynton that the quorum was to return to Kirtland.[65]

Aided by cash donations from the Maine Saints, the quorum slowly traveled back home. Pratt made a detour to Boston. In the course of his travels, he had blended his gospel zeal with his creative bent, writing several poems and hymns. These he now published as *The Millennium: A Poem to which is added Hymns and Songs*, which was not just the first book of poetry, but the first non-scriptural book of more than pamphlet size published by a Mormon. The heart of the book was a poem of several hundred lines that presented a uniquely Mormon view of sacred history, past and future. With the Book of Mormon as his guide, Pratt seamlessly wove ancient Hebrews, New World Nephites, American revolutionaries, Native Americans, and Satan bound into a comprehensive, providential narrative. An ambitious project, it gave early sign of Pratt's theological inclinations. Already a budding historian and pamphleteer, Pratt was on his way to becoming a man of letters.

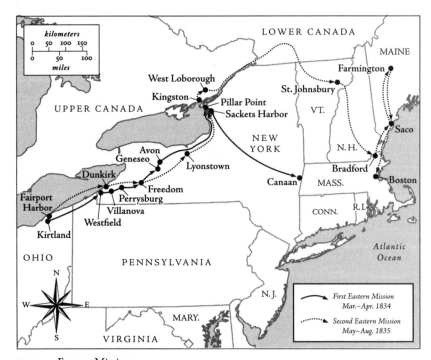

MAP 3.1 Eastern Missions

Pratt reunited with the apostles in Kirtland in October. A few days later, he retrieved his wife and mother from New Portage and settled with them in Kirtland to be nearer the prophet and the center of action. By the middle of the month, he was delivering sermons in the unplastered Kirtland Temple and attending quorum meetings with Joseph Smith and fellow apostles. He also joined several dozen other elders in the Kirtland School of the Prophets, organized into four classes that met six days a week. The first Kirtland School of the Prophets had convened in January 1833 but ceased operations that same spring. The school reopened in late 1834 in two divisions: the School of the Elders, emphasizing theology and using the *Lectures on Faith*, seven essays on church doctrine approved by Smith, as a text; and the Kirtland High School, where nearly a hundred students studied Burdick's *Arithmetic*, Kirkham's *Grammar*, and Olney's *Geography*.[66] In January, classes moved to completed portions of the temple, as befitted the status of learning in Smith's conception. This winter of 1835–1836 following Pratt's eastern mission marked the third year of the school, which soon incorporated the teaching of Hebrew under the well-qualified Joshua Seixas.

In the latter part of January, Smith began anointing and blessing the priesthood leaders in the nearly completed Kirtland Temple. Mormons recalled the time as a modern Pentecost, with several describing visions and visitations.[67] On January 22, Pratt and his quorum, along with other leaders, assembled there to receive special ordinances. Smith and the First Presidency blessed quorum president Thomas Marsh with consecrated oil; Marsh in turn blessed each apostle from "oldest to youngest."[68] Then, "in [the] presence of a large assembly of the Saints," Pratt, like the others, was "washed in pure Water by his Brethren of the twelve and Solemnly anointed to his priesthood and his Apostleship...by the hands of Joseph Smith."[69] In blessing the apostles, Smith recorded that he "pronounced many great and glorious things." As he did so, "the heavens were opened, and angels ministered unto us." Subsequently, "the gift of toungs [tongues], fell upon us in mighty power, angels mingled their voices with ours, while their presence was in our midst, and unseasing prasis [unceasing praises] swelled our bosoms for the space of half-an-hour."[70] On January 28, the Twelve returned to the temple for more instruction, and manifestations again abounded.[71] Some of these meetings followed a ritualistic pattern imposed strictly by Smith:

First part [of the meeting] to be spent in solemn prayer before god without any talking or confusion & the conclusion with a sealing prayer by Pres. Sidney Rigdon when all the quorems are to shout with

one accord a solemn hosannah to God & the Lamb with an Amen—
amen & amen—& then all take seats & lift up their hearts in silent
prayer to God & if any obtain a prophecy or vision to rise & speak.[72]

At the same time, meetings and schooling continued for Pratt and the
apostles, with some graduating to Professor Seixas's advanced Hebrew class.
Orson, more academically inclined than his brother, made the cut at the top
of the class; Parley did not. The dedication of the Kirtland Temple took place
on March 27, bringing to completion that great imperative under which the
leadership had labored for years. The apostles viewed the spiritual manifestations and rituals in the temple—before, during, and immediately following
its dedication—as the promised "endowment of power," which prepared
them for the next stage in the church's development. Two days after the dedication, the Hebrew School shut its doors, and as dedicatory services wound
down, the apostles prepared to resume a pattern in accord with the age-old
cycles of agriculture. In the cold and barren weather, missionaries and farmers
alike hunkered down to productive, but relatively sedentary, activities. As
spring returned, farmers ploughed land, worked fields, and prepared for the
harvest; missionaries and apostles likewise fanned out to sow the seeds of
faith and reap souls. But not all of them.

A revelation Smith had received three years earlier may have weighed
heavily on Pratt's mind at this time. "Let all such as can, obtain places for
their families, and support of the church for them, not fail to go into the
world," it had commanded. And "every man who is obliged to provide for
his own family," it had continued, "let him provide."[73] Noting the departure
of his colleagues, Pratt lamented, "As to myself, I was deeply in debt for the
expenses of life during the winter, and on account of purchasing a lot, and
building thereon. I, therefore, knew not what to do, whether to go on a
mission or stay at home, and endeavor by industry to sustain my family and
pay my debts."[74] Pratt had lived in indigence most of his adult life, and
Thankful was generally too sick and weak to contribute any income to the
household. He had not yet recuperated financially from the months on his
New England mission, and Thankful was ailing again with her chronic illness. Under these distressed circumstances, Pratt's friend Heber Kimball
appeared at his house. In the course of blessing the Pratts, he pronounced a
remarkable series of prophecies.

Brother Parley, thy wife shall be healed from this hour, and shall bear a
son, and his name shall be Parley; and he shall be a chosen instrument

in the hands of the Lord to inherit the priesthood and to walk in the steps of his father. He shall do a great work in the earth in ministering the Word and teaching the children of men. Arise, therefore, and go forth in the ministry, nothing doubting. Take no thoughts for your debts, nor the necessaries of life, for the Lord will supply you with abundant means for all things.

Thou shalt go to Upper Canada, even to the city of Toronto, the capital, and there thou shalt find a people prepared for the fulness of the gospel, and they shall receive thee, and thou shalt organize the Church among them, and it shall spread thence into the regions round about, and many shall be brought to the knowledge of the truth and shall be filled with joy; and from the things growing out of this mission, shall the fulness of the gospel spread into England, and cause a great work to be done in that land.

You shall not only have means to deliver you from your present embarrassments, but you shall yet have riches, silver and gold, till you will loath the counting thereof.[75]

The blessing enumerated several specific promises: a healed wife, a son, a Toronto mission, groundwork for labors in England, and eventual prosperity. Most remarkable of the promises was that of a son by Thankful, who was then thirty-nine. Parley and his wife had been married nearly a decade and had resigned themselves to their apparent infertility. Less than a year later, she would give birth to the promised son. At the present, however, without any apparent change in his material circumstances or his wife's condition, Pratt summoned the faith to act on the words of the blessing.

On April 6, in company with five others, he departed Kirtland, traveling by wagon to Erie. There, along with his brother Orson and Freeman Nickerson, who had earlier been to Canada on a mission, Pratt took a stage-coach to Buffalo.[76] The three soon separated, however, and Pratt walked alone to Niagara Falls. Crossing into Canada, he walked to Hamilton, where a stranger he befriended gave him money to continue his journey and a letter of introduction to a John Taylor of Toronto, the most important contact Pratt would make in a long life of missionary labors. Pratt arrived at the Taylor home that same evening, after a few hours' journey by steamer. Leonora Taylor received him warmly and brought her husband, a wood-turner, from his cabinet shop. Taylor had grown up in England as an Anglican, joined the Methodists as a teenager, and was soon ordained a lay minister. He had immigrated to Toronto in the early 1830s, part of a wave of

English immigrants transforming the city into a commercial center for the surrounding region. The immigration, combined with an economic boom spurred by linking the area to New York City via the Erie Canal, pushed the city's population from sixteen hundred in 1825 to more than fourteen thousand by 1841.[77] In Toronto, Taylor had associated with a loosely organized group of "dissenters." "Many of us were connected with the Methodist Society," he wrote, but "we did not believe their doctrines because they did not accord with scripture.... We rejected every man's word or writing, and took the Word of God alone. We had continued diligently at this for two years. We made it a rule to receive no doctrine until we could bring no scriptural testimony against it."[78] Taylor politely but skeptically listened to Pratt expound the gospel, exchanging views with him for three hours.

The next day, Pratt left in search of public preaching venues, but he found the city and its homes shut against him. He returned to Taylor's home to get his baggage and depart the city, but met there Isabella Russell Walton, a widow. A seeker, she found Pratt's message compelling enough to invite him to preach at her home, where he related the story of Joseph Smith, the Book of Mormon, and the restoration of priesthood authority to a receptive audience. The next day, Pratt ministered to a young widow suffering from "inflammation in the eyes" which had left her "totally blind." "She threw off her bandages," Pratt related, "with eyes as well and as bright as any other person's."[79]

The incident gained Pratt sufficient interest and opposition to prompt him to hold off on planning public meetings for a time. But when he was invited to attend a session of the group that Taylor and his wife belonged to, Pratt agreed. The topic turned to the question of authority, and whether and how such authority would be restored in these days. Taylor had until then done little to either support or oppose Pratt's preaching, but he was clearly thinking deeply about the Mormon message. Now Taylor echoed the question on the minds and lips of many in the room: "Where is our Peter and John? Our apostles? Where is our Holy Ghost by the laying on of hands?"[80] The questions were precisely what Pratt wanted to hear. As he later reported, "Some said, 'Let us be agreed and ask for God to commission us by revelation.' Others said, 'it might be that the Lord had already commissioned apostles in some parts of the world; and if he had, it must come from them.' During this time I had listened in silence: some-times crying and some-times smiling—my heart burning within me."[81] At this point, the group's leader asked if Pratt had anything to say on the subject. Pratt had so much to say that he asked for a separate meeting later that day.

That evening, to a full house, Pratt outlined not the distinctive principles of Mormonism, as he had at the Waltons. Rather, he began with familiar, Restorationist themes: the importance of apostolic authority, the principles of faith and repentance, the ordinances of baptism and conferral of the Holy Ghost, and the bestowal of spiritual gifts. On subsequent evenings, Pratt portrayed a world fully departed from the New Testament model, proclaiming Mormonism as the only true version of a Christianity fully restored at the end of the series. Consistent with his group's operating procedure, Taylor wrote down "eight sermons that [Pratt] preached and compared them with the Scriptures."[82] In the following days, Pratt baptized the Walton household and many among the small community of seekers, including John and Leonora Taylor.

Energized by his breakthrough, Pratt paused the day of the Taylor baptisms to write a letter to John Whitmer, editor of the church's *Messenger and Advocate*, for public dissemination. A little more than a week earlier, he said, he had been preparing to leave the city in dejection and failure. Now, he related, "priests and people flock to hear. Last Sunday I preached in the heart of the city, in the open air: hundreds flocked to hear, and solemnity and good order were seen through all the crowd. God gave me a voice like a trump.... There are multitudes who are expecting to be baptized, and some are only waiting an opportunity. I expect to tarry here some time."[83] Adding to his sense of holy triumph was his recognition that all was falling into place to bring about the fulfillment of one of Kimball's magnificent promises: "Many believers here are late from England, so we may have access to many names in that country: these are already beginning to express desires for their friends in that country to hear these things." In preparation, Pratt composed a letter to be sent to England in advance of his own anticipated journey there.[84] The letter outlined key beliefs but presented a rather confused and inaccurate overview of Smith's early visions.

A few weeks later, on May 20, Orson and Nickerson joined Parley.[85] Together, they ventured into neighboring communities, preaching and baptizing dozens more. Ten miles from Toronto, one of Isabella Walton's relatives, Joseph Fielding, received news that Pratt intended to visit him. However, Fielding wrote, "We had before heard some few evil Reports of some People calld Mormons," and he asked Walton and Pratt not to come. Pratt "however[,] determind that as he had expected the Invitation, he would come"; Fielding reluctantly received Pratt (in large part because he traveled with Fielding's "old Friend" John Taylor). Notwithstanding the initial "great coolness" of his reception, Fielding "soon discoverd" that Pratt "had the Spirit and Power of God, and such Wisdom as none but God himself could have given to Man." Preaching a fervent millennialism, Pratt emphasized the corrupt "present state of the Gentile Churchs," which had "all departed from the Truth" and altered God's ordinances; only a "pure Church" could restore the "very plain" truths and ordinances of the gospel before the Second Coming. "Many strongly opposed the Work, false reports were raised & sometimes our Faith was shaken," Fielding recalled. Nevertheless, he and his sisters Mary and Mercy soon converted.[86]

In spite of his hopes to tarry, Pratt abruptly broke off his missionary work to return to Kirtland. Financial obligations back home weighed upon him, and he needed a fresh supply of printed materials—his own pamphlets and the Book of Mormon—both to disseminate the gospel and to raise money. Selling one's own pamphlets would become a significant means for Mormon missionaries to fund their labors. Pratt's convert John Taylor, for example, would follow suit in a few years with an eight-page account of the Missouri violence. Often the missionaries printed one another's pamphlets for their own missions; apostles Orson Hyde and John Page reprinted a pamphlet of Sidney Rigdon's to fund their Holy Land mission, and Pratt in turn printed Hyde's letters from that mission to meet his own travel expenses.[87] In this case, generous contributions from the Toronto Saints sped Pratt's passage home and relieved many of his debts. Arriving in late May, he found his wife in good health, fulfilling another of his promised blessings, and reported on his work to Oliver Cowdery, now editor of the *Messenger and Advocate*. After a respite of a few days, he and Thankful went to Toronto. The journey to Canada, however, wearied her. Taylor recorded that when she arrived "she was very feeble and weak and could scarcely walk, she looked the most unlikely of any person to have a child, so much so that many of the sisters said if she had a son they could never disbelieve Mormonism."[88] By the end of June, Pratt found the harvest so plentiful that he asked for reinforcements from Kirtland. "Will some four or six of the first or second seventy go over and assist our brother in dispensing the words of life and salvation, and gathering souls into the kingdom of our God?" the *Messenger and Advocate* asked its readers.[89]

Orson Hyde, who had been in New York, responded to Pratt's request. In July, a Presbyterian minister challenged the pair to a public debate. Thousands came to the event, but Pratt had been called back to the States "as a witness in a[n unspecified] case at law."[90] When Pratt returned (with Hyde's wife in tow), he found an Irvingite missionary from England, William Caird, was preaching against the Mormons. (Irvingism, or the

Catholic Apostolic Church, was a Restorationist group recently founded in Great Britain.) Frustrated in his desire to engage Caird in public debate, Pratt recognized the importance of having a press to respond to attacks. In its absence, he relied upon the power of his own oratory and, when shouted down or denied a hearing, had handbills printed to make his case.[91] By the fall, Pratt felt that "the truth had now triumphed in Canada," and he and Thankful returned home to Kirtland.[92] He left Taylor in charge, ordaining and blessing him before he left. Taylor recorded that at the time, "Br. Parley prophesied concerning me in a manner that almost made my hair stand on my head: much of that prophecy has since been fulfilled."[93] Others would similarly note Pratt's gift of prophecy. David Whitmer wrote that "Joseph Smith gave many true prophecies... but this was no more than many of the other brethren did," and among those "other brethren" he singled out Pratt.[94]

Back in Kirtland, Pratt and other elders kept busy during the winter with Smith's ambitious educational agenda. This time around, Greek and Latin replaced Hebrew as the language of study in the Kirtland High School, which met in the temple attic. Pratt apparently gave Latin a try but soon gave up and sold his Latin grammar to Wilford Woodruff for a dollar.[95] As an already accomplished poet and hymnist, he may have opted instead for "instruction in the principles of vocal music," offered in the evenings by Luman Carter and Jonathan Crosby.[96]

Meanwhile, Smith preached a public sermon that made a profound impression on Pratt and was a key element in his religious education. Pratt wrote John Taylor that he had recently gone to "one of the most Interesting Meetings I ever attended." The week prior, he told Taylor, "word was Publicly given that Br J Smith Jr would give a relation of the comeing forth of the Records and also of the rise of the Church and of his Experience":

Acordingly a vast Concourse assembled at an Early hour Every seat was crouded and 4 or 5 hundred People stood up in the Aisles Br S gave the history of these things relating many Particulars of the manner of his first vissions &c the Spirit and Powr of God was upon him in Bearing testimony In somuch That many if not most of the Congregation were in tears—as for my self i can say that all the Reasonings in uncertainty and all the conclusions drawn from the writings of Others (who Could only give a small scetch of what they saw and heard) however great in themselves dwindle into insignificence when Compared with

Living testimony when your Eyes sea and your Ears hear from the
Living Oracles of God.[97]

Smith's first vision, his 1820 theophany, received little public airing in the
first decade of Mormonism. Published revelations, which gave expressive
detail to numerous other visions and visitations, were reticent about that earliest of Smith's heavenly encounters, only obliquely alluding to a prior manifestation to Smith "that he had received a remission of his sins."[98] Smith's
unpublished 1832 account cast his first vision in a similar light, suggesting the
experience held principally private, rather than public, significance. Smith's
reluctance to incorporate it in the founding narratives of Mormonism, or to
publish any details, explains why Pratt, otherwise so conversant in restoration
theology, scriptures, and Mormon history, could get the story so wrong in his
"Epistle" written from Toronto to the people of England. There, he had presented a garbled version of Smith's theophany, confusing it with the later visits
of the angel Moroni. Young Joseph, he had written, "seeing the confusion of
the churches," prayed to "assertain which was right." In response, "he was visited By a Holy Angel whose garments where [were] whiter than snow And
whose countinance was as Lightning." The angel then made known "to him
the Prophesyes concerning the Latterday glory the gathering of Israel the
Coming of the Lord. . . . The Angel also informed him that America had once
Been Peopled By a remnant of the seed of Israel" who "had left a Record
Behind them which was writen By the spirit of Prophesy and revelation. . . engraven on Plates of Precious metal."[99]

Pratt's description to Taylor of the universal excitement in anticipation of
Smith's relation of "his first vissions" must have reflected in part his own eager
desire to know, and be able to convey more accurately and authoritatively to
prospective converts, the actual details of Smith's visions and to hear in person
Smith's testimony of those events. Listening to the account certainly solidified Smith's divine calling in Pratt's mind. As he later wrote, "There was
something connected with the serene and penetrating glance of his eye, as if
he could penetrate the deepest abyss of the human heart, gaze into eternity,
penetrate the heavens and comprehend all worlds."[100] At the same time,
Smith's testimony also confirmed to Pratt that Smith did not possess some
prophetic entitlement that rendered only he eligible to behold angels and the
face of God. As he told Taylor,

For My Part I never can rest untill My Eyes have seen my Redeemer
until I have gazed like Nephi upon the gloryes of the Celestial world

until I Can Come into full communion and familiar Converse with the angels of glory and the Spirits of just men made Perfect through the Blood of Christ and I testify to All Both Small and great, Both Male and female that if they stop short of the full Enjoyment of these things They Stop Short of the Blessings freely offered to Every Creature in the Gospel.[101]

This sense of entitlement that could so easily be construed as presumption or unchecked aspiration is key to understanding what fired Pratt's mind and heart. "No more mysteries" seemed his mantra. No bondage of original sin, no depraved human nature, no jealous gods; heaven with its supernal sights and realms accessible to every man. This dual understanding of Smith as gifted prophet and visionary but also as Pratt's brother and equal would soon unleash the most conflicted, wrenching ordeal of Pratt's life.

4

"Strange and Novel Truths"

It was not with my eyes by the power of visions but by
intellectual faculties [of the] inward man; reason taught
me from the things I [do] know.... What can we reason
but from what we know?
—PARLEY PRATT, *sermon, April 7, 1853*

THE YEAR 1837 marked both Pratt's greatest spiritual trial and his greatest
theological contribution as a Latter-day Saint. During a few weeks, Pratt
emerged as a powerful dissident, spurred by the collapse of the Kirtland Safety
Society, a community bank with Joseph Smith as president, which caused
Pratt to lose his home. But if he was impetuous, he was also tractable and
capable of contrition, as he demonstrated more than once. Pratt quickly
rebounded from his disaffection, and, as if in penance or at least compen-
sation, he produced months later *A Voice of Warning*, a work that served the
church as its most powerful proselytizing tool—after the Book of Mormon—
for more than a century. It also initiated his growing role as shaper, and not
just purveyor, of Mormon doctrine.

In addition to his educational efforts during the winter of 1836 to 1837,
Pratt devoted time to a project he must have found as satisfying as preaching
about the Book of Mormon. He published the second edition of that volume,
which Joseph Smith had revised for reissue. Pratt partnered in the project
with John Goodson, one of his Canadian converts from the previous year.
(They had operated a small commercial venture together in Kirtland, likely
renting space in an established store to hawk some wares; that attempt probably ended unsuccessfully as they left their 1837 merchants' taxes unpaid.)[1]
Goodson and Pratt likely funded the publication in exchange for shares in the
profits, a typical arrangement. Pratt's participation in the project demonstrates
his ardor for the Book of Mormon. Whereas many Mormons of his generation
used the Book of Mormon primarily as a sign of a divinely sanctioned restoration (a point with which Pratt wholeheartedly agreed), Pratt was one of the

few who seriously probed the book's content and often preached from its pages. He never earned substantial amounts from any of his publishing efforts, the Book of Mormon included. But it must have been a source of the greatest pride to him that his name appeared on the title page of the volume's second edition, and that along with the eleven witnesses (three who said they saw the plates in the hands of an angel and eight who testified they had held them), his name and personal testimony prefaced every one of the copies he printed. To "the thousands whose faces [he would] never see on this side of eternity," he affirmed his "sincere conviction of its truth, and the great and glorious purposes it must effect."[2]

In March 1837, Parley became the proud father of his firstborn—a son and namesake. The most unlikely of Heber Kimball's prophetic utterances had been fulfilled. He had served his Canadian mission, found contacts to pave the way for missionary work in England, seen his wife restored to health and delivered of a child. But the same day also found him a grieving husband. Thankful had been weak and sickly for most of their marriage. Stress, poor diet, and exposure brought on through harrowing days in Missouri had weakened her both physically and emotionally. One friend in this period described her as having "very delicate health," with "severe spells of sick headache, which came upon her monthly."[3] She may have also suffered with depression, as her obituary noted that her "ill health" combined with "her peculiar anxieties for [Pratt] in his absence, to prey upon & depress her spirit." And while her health had improved sufficiently to conceive and carry the child to term, she now, in a pattern all too common in nineteenth-century childbearing, succumbed to complications hours after giving birth. "Puerperal convulsions," read the obituary, suggesting eclampsia and its attendant seizures.[4] She had turned forty just seven days earlier. "My grief, and sorrow, and loneliness I shall not attempt to describe," Pratt later wrote, a loss for words unusual for one as quick as Pratt to give utterance to his feelings through poetry or other writing. But his relationship with Thankful went much deeper than the poetic and sentimental modes of expression that he so often employed. When he recounted the details of her death just a few years before his own, and after marriage to eleven more wives across a span of years, a distinct tenderness and sorrow shone through: "Farewell, my dear Thankful, thou wife of my youth, and mother of my first born; the beginning of my strength—farewell. Yet a few more lingering years of sorrow, pain and toil, and I shall be with thee, and clasp thee to my bosom."[5]

Pratt's tragic loss was not completely unanticipated—he had spent most of their marriage apprehensive about her health.[6] His distress over Thankful's passing was slightly assuaged by intimations and dreams she had shared with Parley of her imminent death. Assured that she was going to "the Paradise of rest," he recorded, "she was overwhelmed with a joy and peace indescribable."[7] Parley gave his newborn son over to be cared for by a Mrs. Allen, who had recently lost her own child. Mary Ann Angell Young, Brigham Young's wife, served as a wet nurse for Parley Jr., alongside her own Brigham Jr.[8] Not one to wallow in grief or idleness, Pratt found distraction from his loss by abruptly departing for a return visit to Canada, this time with plans to lay the final groundwork for a momentous development in Mormon history: the first mission to overseas soil, planned for England.

In the church's infancy, Smith had a revelation that commanded him to "send forth the elders of my church unto the nations which are afar off; unto the islands of the sea; send forth unto foreign lands."[9] Although he, Pratt, and others undertook a few excursions to Canada, Smith hesitated at the prospect of sending missionaries across the Atlantic. But a natural progression from Canada to England unfolded, as first intimated in the call of the apostles in 1835 to be special witnesses of Christ "in all the world." Among the spiritual manifestations in the Kirtland Temple in January 1836, Smith "saw the 12 apostles of the Lamb, who are now upon the earth who hold the keys of this last ministry, in foreign lands."[10] A few months later, in April 1836, Kimball predicted to Pratt that a Canadian mission would lay the foundations for a greater work in England. The next year, as spring approached, Kimball raised the issue of an English mission yet again with Pratt and Brigham Young. Kimball was "deeply impressed and exercised about a foreign mission," he said, that loomed "nearer than many knew or thought."[11]

Seizing the initiative, Pratt headed to Canada the first week of April 1837, less than two weeks after his wife's burial, to "visit the Saints, and to confer on the subject of a mission to England."[12] His earlier efforts there had yielded a number of converts with English ties, including John and Leonora Taylor, Joseph Fielding and his sisters Mary and Mercy, Isaac Russell, John Goodson, and John Snider. Pratt also indicated that other preparatory steps had been taken, including letters about the church being sent to England. The Fieldings had written to relatives there, and John Taylor sent a lengthy missive to two English clergymen related to Fielding.[13] But Pratt most likely had in mind the formal epistle he had himself written and sent to England as preparation for a journey there.[14] He addressed his "Epistle Writen by An Elder of the Church of Latterday Saints" to "those In Europe who look for the glorious Appearing of our Lord and Saviour." Framing his message as the fulfillment of millennial expectations would be Pratt's consistent practice. Written before he heard

Smith publicly speak on the subject, he had related the story of the angel Moroni's visit to Smith as one in a series of "great Events which are mooving By the hand of God," bearing witness to Christ's imminent return. Pratt consistently used these events, rather than doctrines, as the principal exhibits for the truthfulness of Mormonism, thus making its history foundational to its theology. These events included the miraculous appearance and translation of the gold plates, the great work of gathering, and the persecution that he believed follows true disciples of Christ. After a brief summary of these developments, Pratt preached the simple gospel of repentance and baptism, closing with the hope that he would soon "stand on the shores of Europe" to give a fuller message "face to face."[15]

Perhaps Pratt expected to depart directly from Toronto to fulfill that very desire. If so, his ambitions and initiative were abruptly stymied by the arrival of a letter containing a stinging rebuke from the two most senior apostles, Thomas Marsh and David Patten. Writing from Far West, Missouri, in early May, they upbraided Pratt for his lack of coordination with the other apostles, expressing dismay at his plans to depart Toronto for England "in such a hasty (manner) without consulting, without exchanging with us the first word upon the subject."[16] Marsh must also have remembered Smith's promise that he would lead an English mission, and taken that to mean that he, not Pratt, would launch the church's first foray overseas.[17] But Marsh and Patten were also legitimately alarmed at the prospect of a major undertaking as the church faced its most severe internal crisis to date, with dissent in Kirtland threatening its very survival.

Having heard reports of rebellion spearheaded by apostles Luke Johnson, John Boynton, and Lyman Johnson, they asked Pratt rhetorically but anxiously, "Where is Luke and John and Lyman.... We hear much evil concerning them by letter and otherwise & will you leave while things are thus—No! the 12 must get together, difficulties must be removed and love restored." At this point in Mormon history, the apostles still functioned more as a group of semi-autonomous traveling elders, than as a tightly controlled body subject to a quorum presidency. Nevertheless, obedient to their summons but likely unhappy with their recall, Pratt sped home. He must have returned in a very anxious state himself, concerned about financial as well as spiritual matters. He had left Kirtland heavily in debt, and at the very time he was traveling to Canada the economy of Kirtland imploded. At this time of spreading turmoil, thwarted plans, and an uncertain future, Pratt attempted a return to domestic normalcy by marrying Mary Ann Frost Stearns, a convert he had met almost two years earlier at the conference in Saco, Maine.

FIGURE 4.1 Mary Ann Frost Pratt. Photograph of unknown date. Courtesy of Daughters of the Utah Pioneers.

It is likely that Pratt planned the step while in Canada, given his abrupt departure after Thankful's death and his hasty proposal upon returning. Mary Ann's first husband, Nathan Stearns, had died from typhoid fever in August 1833 after eighteen months of marriage. Mary Ann, after almost dying from typhoid herself, was left a twenty-four-year-old widow with a four-month-old daughter, also named Mary Ann. In 1834, missionaries in Maine baptized one of Mary Ann's relatives by marriage, Patty Bartlett Sessions, who later became pioneer Utah's premier midwife. David Patten baptized Mary Ann in August 1835, along with her mother; her father and sister Olive were baptized in following years. A year later, six apostles traveled to Maine and preached the doctrine of a literal gathering to Zion in her town of Bethel. Persuaded of the principle, and without consulting her parents and over the objections of a guardian appointed to oversee her daughter's inheritance, Mary Ann left for Kirtland in the middle of the night with Patty Sessions's husband, David, arriving in August 1836. Over the next ten months, the young widow, described as "an amiable, interesting woman," and her daughter boarded with several different families, including Jonathan and Caroline Crosby in a house next to

Pratt's, Brigham and Mary Ann Young, and Hyrum and Jerusha Smith.[18] Her daughter recalled how "a kind friend took me in her arms and told me I was going to have a new papa, and also a little brother. The sound of these words had quite an attraction for me, though I could not understand the full purport of them." At least, not until "Parley P. Pratt called at our house and talked with my mother."[19] On May 14, 1837, days after Pratt's arrival, Frederick G. Williams married Mary Ann to Parley in Hyrum Smith's home.

Perhaps Pratt expected to take Parley Jr. back into his home soon (though this did not happen for more than a year), which might explain the quick remarriage. In any case, the following year, Joseph Smith condemned such haste. "We do disapprove of the custom," he wrote, "which has gained in the world, and has been practiced among us, to our great mortification, in marrying in five or six weeks, or even in two or three months, after the death of their companion"[20] In any case, neither abrupt marital readjustment nor connubial bliss could distract Pratt from the factionalism tearing the Kirtland church asunder. He immediately became a vocal participant.

The Saints in Kirtland had long suffered opposition from local residents. Some enemies of the church, such as Grandison Newell of Mentor, used both the press and the legal system to harass and stymie the Latter-day Saints. By 1837, however, the problems were largely internal and fueled by two principal catalysts. First, controversy over a possible secret polygamous union by Smith with Fanny Alger created dissent. Smith perceived a duty to restore the Old Testament practice of plural marriage as early as 1831. Rumors had long been circulating about unusual sexual practices among the Saints, as they did in the case of many new religious movements. An "Article on Marriage" published in the 1835 Doctrine and Covenants referred to allegations against the church of "fornication, and polygamy."[21] Smith's associate Benjamin F. Johnson held that these whispered rumors were "one of the causes of apostasy and disruption at Kirtland, altho at the time there was little said publicly on the subject."[22] John Whitmer agreed that disunity in 1837 partially resulted from the "spiritual wife doctrine, that is plurality of wives."[23] Even Smith noted in November of that year that he was asked "daily and hourly" in his travels, "Do the Mormons believe in having more wives than one?"[24] Nevertheless, most scandalous rumors hinted of adultery, not polygamy. It was just such an interpretation that Oliver Cowdery put on Smith's relationship with Fanny Alger, openly breaking with Smith as a result.[25] In the very month that Pratt returned to Kirtland, Warren Cowdery, the editor of the *Messenger and Advocate*, issued a warning that leaders of the Seventy (a priesthood quorum established in 1835) "will have no fellowship whatever with any Elder belonging to the quorum of the Seventies who is guilty of polygamy or any offense of the kind."[26]

A financial fiasco associated with the failure of the Kirtland bank served as the second trigger as financial pressures, a spirit of speculation, national economic conditions, and internal fissures laid the foundation for bitter division and eventual disaster. Kirtland had experienced years of prosperous growth, and while huge profits could be made by the ambitious, the temple construction had incurred large debt. Its building had also functioned as a large public works project, and its completion signaled the end of ready employment for many. Warren Cowdery suggested that Saints viewed the city's sudden prosperity as a sign of divine approbation attending the gathered faithful: "The starting up, as if by magic, of buildings in every direction around us, were evincive to us of buoyant hope, lively anticipation, and a firm confidence that our days of pinching adversity had passed by."[27] Many Saints translated their optimism about the future into a rising debt load and speculative land purchases.

In early November 1836, Smith and others launched plans for a Kirtland Bank to liquidate land that had recently skyrocketed in value, as a partial solution to an acute shortage of specie. Denied a charter by the state legislature, they changed the banknote plates they had already manufactured to read, the "Kirtland Safety Society *Anti*-Banking Company." Such circumvention was not unprecedented, and they thought such a maneuver complied with the law. More egalitarian than most banking institutions in the Jacksonian era, the Kirtland institution offered stock for $50, generally purchased with an initial payment of only 26 cents a share.[28] In October 1836, Pratt purchased one thousand shares, with a face value of $50,000, for $102.[29] Sidney Rigdon served as bank president, with Joseph Smith as cashier, and thirty-two individuals—likely including Pratt—as directors.[30]

At the same time, Smith moved to curb the downside of Pratt's and others' missionary success: the influx of destitute converts was simply beyond the capacity of the Kirtland Saints to assimilate. "It becomes the duty, henceforth, of all the churches abroad to provide for those who are objects of charity, that are not able to provide for themselves; and not send them from their midst, to burden the Church in this place," read a resolution approved by Pratt's quorum. It continued by urging "that there be a stop put to churches or families gathering or moving to this place, without their first coming or sending their wise men to prepare a place for them, as our houses are all full." The resolution warned that "speculators, and extortioners" would prey on the vulnerable newcomers.[31]

The credit extended by the Kirtland Safety Society initially led to an economic boom and skyrocketing real estate prices. Church officials, including Smith, purchased property, which they often subdivided to sell to newcomers. By early 1837, some leaders, including Pratt, expressed concern about the rising speculation and worldliness among the Saints. The unraveling of the Kirtland Safety Society gave credence to their fears. Undercapitalization, unfettered speculation, and a run on the company's limited specie engineered by Grandison Newell all coincided with a national financial catastrophe: the Panic of 1837.[32] President Andrew Jackson had issued his Specie Circular a year before, requiring all purchases of federal land to be paid for in silver and gold coin. The value of federal currency had already been damaged by Jackson's destruction of the national bank. His Specie Circular created a crisis of confidence in state currencies as well. Holders of bank notes, in a panic, began a run on New York banks for gold and silver. By May 1, 1837, New York bank reserves had plummeted from $7.2 million to $1.5 million, and the banks suspended specie payments, prompting similar actions across the country.[33] If New York banks could not withstand the crisis in confidence, a small Kirtland "anti-bank" had no chance at all. For Kirtland Saints, the national economic recession did little to mitigate their feelings of disillusionment or even betrayal, given the fact that their bank had been instituted at the behest of a supposed prophet.

Discontent spread like a virus, engulfing not just the rank and file but the highest echelons of leadership. Among those who broke ranks with Smith were his second counselor, Frederick Williams; two of the three Book of Mormon witnesses; Martin Harris and David Whitmer; and five of the twelve apostles. These people joined other dissenters who objected to Smith's leadership, leading to the greatest crisis the church had yet faced. Returning from Canada, Pratt found himself suffering personally from efforts by Smith, in growing desperation and scrambling for disappearing resources, to alleviate his own plight. Pratt had purchased three lots from Smith for the extravagant sum of $2,000, which seemed justified in a time of wildly escalating land values even though Pratt believed Smith had paid less than $100 for the same lots. Pratt made a down payment of $75, and when Pratt's payments lagged, Smith turned the debt over to the Kirtland bank for collection. On May 22, a week after Pratt's wedding, bank president Rigdon informed him that Smith "had drawn the money from the Bank, on the obligation [he] held against [you] and that [he] had Left it to the mercy of the Bank and could not help what ever course they might take to collect it." In the era's legal culture, Pratt reasonably expected that Smith would take back the property in satisfaction of the note. Smith, however, had sold the note to the bank for either cash or as collateral for another transaction and left Pratt to answer to the bank. Pratt thus offered to return the lots to Rigdon, as an officer of the bank, but "he wanted my house and home also." Reeling from this unexpected demand and the specter of financial ruin, Pratt felt betrayed by both Rigdon and Smith, the men who had served as his spiritual fathers. Indeed, he wrote, Smith had given him "the most sacred promise" that he would "not Be ingured" by the real estate transactions and that "it was the will of God that Lands Should Bear such a price."[34]

That same day, Pratt found solidarity with another disgruntled member. John Johnson—one of the bank's major stockholders who feared the bank's collapse—deeded several lots at little or no cost to family members and a few others now at odds with Smith, including Pratt. The property had originally been purchased with the church's money and placed in Johnson's name as a steward. Johnson likely hoped to recoup some of the substantial money he had invested in the church's operations; it was also a gesture of conspicuous— perhaps defiant—generosity in light of Smith's actions. He sold one lot to Pratt, down Whitney Street from the Kirtland Temple and perhaps the location of Pratt's home, for a discounted price of $55.[35]

The next day, Pratt responded to Smith with a furious letter which charged that the "whole scene of Speculation in which we have Been Engaged is of the Devel; I allude to the covetous Extortionary Speculating spirit which has reigned in this place for the Last season; which has given rise to Lying, deceiveing, and takeing the advantage of ones Nabour and In Short to Every Eavle work." In Pratt's eyes, Smith and Rigdon, "Both By presept and Example have been the principle means In Leading this people astray" and had ensnared Pratt with their "false Prophesying and preaching." Following their advice, Pratt had "done many things Rong and plunged myself and family and others well nigh in to distruction, I have awoke to an awful sense of my situation, and now resolve to retrace my steps, and get out of the snare and make restitution as far as I can." Even if Smith was "determined to persue this wicked course untill your self and the Church shall sink down to hell," Pratt pleaded for mercy for himself, his family, and "others who are Bound with me for those certain 3 lots." Specifically, he asked Smith to take back the lots and return Pratt's original down payment of $75. Pratt called his spiritual mentor to repentance "or will you take the advantage of your Nabour Because he is in your Power if you will receive this admonition from one who Loves your Soul, and repent of your Extortion and covetiousness in this thing, and make restitution you have my fellowship and Esteem as far as it respects our dealings

Between ourselves." If Smith refused, Pratt would bring charges in an ecclesiastical court against him "for Extortion, covetousness, and takeing advantage of your Brother By an undue religious influence."[36]

The bitter memory of Heber Kimball's promised blessing of prosperity likely added to the sting of his financial crisis. Pratt's wife had been promised health, and she now lay buried in a Kirtland cemetery. He had been promised "riches, silver and gold," and he was destitute. Nevertheless, Pratt added a postscript, which the letter's first publisher, intent on embarrassing Pratt and Smith, omitted: "Do not suppose for a moment that I Lack any Confidence in the Book of Mormon or Doctrine and Covenants Nay It is my firm belief in those Records that hinders my Belief In the course we have Been Led of Late."[37] Others who dissented from Smith's leadership likewise avowed their continuing belief in his earlier translations and revelations. William McLellin, for example, lost all faith in Smith, but not the book associated with his name. "I have no faith in Mormonism," he wrote to defectors who hoped to enlist his support, "no confidence that the church organized by J. Smith and O. Cowdery was set up or established as it ought to have been.... But when a man goes at the Book of M[ormon] he touches the apple of my eye."[38] Another Ohio Mormon noted after the Kirtland wave of defections that "there are some that are departed from the faith," most of whom nevertheless continued to "hold on to the Book of Mormon."[39]

Pratt's letter (along with a second, of unknown details) was widely circulated, and he engaged in vocal, public denunciations of Smith as well. Because it came from an apostle, Pratt's dissent was particularly influential with those wavering in their loyalties. At the end of May, Orson Pratt and Lyman Johnson charged Smith before Bishop Newel K. Whitney with "lying and misrepresentation" and extortion. Parley likely supported the two men though he was not a formal signatory to the charges.[40] As a consequence of these cumulative actions of disloyalty, five more steadfast members of the church petitioned the High Council of Kirtland to try Parley (along with David Whitmer, Frederick Williams, Lyman Johnson, and Warren Parrish) for "behavior... unworthy of their calling." The complainants alleged that the course of the five men "for some time past has been injurious to the Church of God in which they are high officers." The council convened on May 29, in a flurry of charges and countercharges. Four members loyal to Smith appeared as complainants against Williams, Smith's second counselor; Parrish, his scribe; Whitmer, who had been presiding over the Missouri church; and apostles Johnson and Pratt. Rigdon, Smith's first counselor, presided over the meeting and began by reading the complaint. Parrish immediately protested that the version differed from the one of which they had been apprised. Williams challenged the authority of the council. Rigdon affirmed the council's legitimacy, whereupon Whitmer joined Parrish in objecting. Williams relented, but Whitmer did not and was now joined by a sympathetic member of the council. The council voted not to try Williams and Whitmer, adjourned, and then reconvened an hour later to try the others.[41]

This meeting also erupted in disorder, with objections and debates over questions of jurisdiction and procedure. Pratt objected to being tried by either Rigdon or Smith, "in consequence of their having previously expressed their opinion against him." Rigdon admitted his sentiments, defended them, and then stepped down from the stand leaving judgment to others. Cowdery arose and said that he, too, was already disposed to judge Pratt and the others guilty. This left Williams, but as he had already been implicated in the others' guilt, he recused himself and stepped down. At this point, the clerk noted, "The council and assembly then dispersed in confusion."[42]

A few days later, at the height of the crisis, Smith decided a major new initiative was imperative—either as distraction from present difficulties, to procure fresh convert blood, or merely as a strategy for bypassing the immediate obstacles to church progress and forge ahead. Heber Kimball later related, "The word of the Lord to the Elders of Israel was, go forth to the distant nations of the Earth."[43] So Smith acted decisively, calling Kimball to preside over the mission to England that Pratt had been planning to launch just weeks before. (Marsh was by now occupied as a church leader in troubled Missouri.) On June 11, Smith instructed Kimball, Orson Hyde, and Joseph Fielding regarding their English mission. That same day, Pratt publicly denounced Smith in the temple, delivering a sermon which asserted "that nearly all the Church had departed from God and that Brother J. S. had committed great sins." Pratt, however, "entirely cleared him self of all blaim." Referring to his letters against Smith, Pratt "declared he would not retract anything in them," except one of his charges against Rigdon. Unsatisfied, Rigdon, "with feelings of great disgust," dismissed "the large congregation of Saints." Mary Fielding, one of Pratt's Canadian converts who had recently arrived in Kirtland and would marry the prophet's brother Hyrum later that year, wrote with shock to her sister Mercy that Pratt's "very plausable discourse" left "some pleasd but many greatly displeased."[44]

The meeting reconvened in the afternoon; after an emotional protest against the dissenters, Rigdon left with a faction of supporters. When die-hard critic Orson Pratt took the stand, Fielding "and a great many more" also departed. Many, like Fielding, were confused, heartbroken, "destitute," and "oppressed" that the church they had sacrificed so much to gather to was on the verge of collapse. On top of it all, Smith suddenly took so sick that very evening that Fielding wondered, as she walked home past his house, "wether he [would] live till next morn."[45]

In the aftermath of the tumultuous meeting, "a great number" of anxious persons asked Fielding for details. Judging from her letter, Pratt's high standing and influence made him the special focus of public interest. Fielding further reported that subsequent to the meeting, "Elder Parley has left all his Family and set of[f] as he says for Misseurey [Missouri] without even calling upon Brother J.S. or acquainting the heads of the Church with his designs." His intentions—whether to stew in solitude or sow dissension—remain mysterious. Fortunately, although fiery and headstrong, Pratt was apparently open to mollification and reconciliation. John Taylor, who had arrived in Kirtland in March, later related that Pratt told him the grievances against Smith. Taylor reminded Pratt of the testimony he had borne in Canada of the prophet's calling, saying, "If Joseph Smith was then a prophet, he is now a prophet." Able to see past his anger, Pratt recognized the validity of Taylor's point. As Taylor charitably recounted, "he, with many others, was passing under a dark cloud."[46]

Nevertheless, Pratt persisted in his plans to leave Kirtland and moved to recoup his financial losses. On June 10, he sold his shares of Kirtland Bank stock to Lorenzo Young.[47] More important, two weeks later, he made two real estate transactions, dividing the half-acre lot he had purchased from John Johnson and selling the lots for a total of $750, nearly fifteen times the price he had paid just a month earlier.[48]

As Pratt headed for Missouri, a timely intervention paved the way for rapprochement. After a few hundred miles of travel, Pratt encountered senior apostle Marsh, hastening to Kirtland along with David Patten "to try and reconcile some of the Twelve and others of high standing who had come out in opposition to the Prophet." Marsh "prevailed on him to return with us to Kirtland" and persuaded him to make peace with Smith. In his writings, Pratt never mentioned the meeting or any details of his change of heart. Most likely, Pratt, like Smith, could be as quick to forgive as he was to anger. In early July, Mary Fielding described a church service full of reconciliation and spiritual outpouring; "the Spirit & power of God rested down upon us in a remarkable manner many spake in tongues & others prophecied & interpreted. it has been said by many who have lived in Kirtland a great while, that such a time of love & refreshing has never been known." Descriptions of bright lights, angels, and speaking in tongues recalled the temple dedication of 1836. She also reported the return of Marsh and Patten from Missouri, confident that "the difficulties between the Presidency & the twelve will very shortly be settled and then we expect better days than ever."[49] Marsh achieved his design when Smith agreed to call several of the aggrieved leaders to his home, where Marsh served as a moderator. "A reconciliation was effected between all parties," he recorded simply.[50] In Pratt's brief summation, "I went to brother Joseph in tears, and, with a broken heart and contrite spirit, confessed wherein I had erred in spirit, murmured, or done or said amiss. He frankly forgave me, prayed for me and blessed me."[51] Pratt rose in Sunday meeting and made "considerable acknowledgement" of his faults, although Fielding considered the confession less satisfactory than his brother Orson's.[52] Smith apparently considered it adequate, never mentioning the temporary estrangement thereafter.

After his reconciliation, Pratt never again wavered in his devotion to Smith or the church he led. His lapse came back to haunt him the next year when enemies of the church printed his heated letter excoriating Smith. In response, he published a statement expressing regret for his intemperate words, even as he insisted that Smith was "liable to error, and mistakes in things which were not inspired from heaven, but managed by [his] own judgment."[53] On September 3, a Kirtland High Council meeting affirmed Pratt, but not defecting apostles Luke Johnson and Lyman Johnson and the insufficiently contrite John F. Boynton, in his apostleship.[54] But Pratt had not waited around for affirmation. By then, he had already moved on to another field of labor—New York City, where he had arrived on August 5. Whether this was Pratt's long-standing intention, as his stepdaughter Mary Ann later wrote,[55] or a newly formed plan, is impossible to say.

New York in the 1830s was the nation's largest metropolis, at a teeming quarter million. Six years before Pratt's arrival, a cholera epidemic had swept the city, taking thousands of lives in the city's most crowded and unsanitary districts, ravaging Irish Catholics and African Americans especially. By 1838, improved water distribution was under way, but it would take another epidemic in 1849 before local government cleared out the tens of thousands of pigs that scavenged abundant refuse in the inner city. The 1830s would see waves of massive new immigration, ethnic unrest, and abolitionist agitation. (The young Frederick Douglass would flee to the city and freedom just weeks after Pratt's arrival.) Pratt clearly aimed to settle into this assignment, rather than pursue the missionary life of an itinerant, perhaps looking on his new posting as a time of purification.[56]

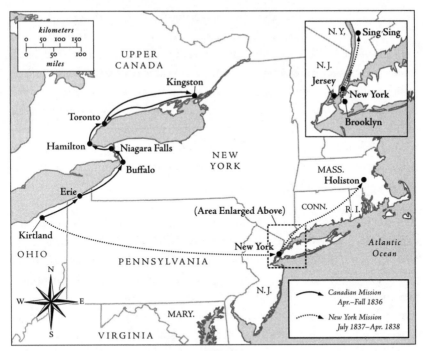

MAP 4.1 Canadian and New York Missions

Free from the fractious winds of Kirtland, and accompanied by his new wife, Mary Ann, and her daughter, Pratt launched into a new phase of his life with characteristic vigor and decisiveness. They initially lodged with the sister-in-law of a recent convert, Elijah Fordham. To economize, a few weeks later they rented a large upper room on Goerck Street, near the East River in Manhattan's lower east side, where Mary Ann cooked for the family. Pratt preached in chapels when he could, private homes when he could not, even onboard vessels in the harbor and once in a shipyard. After two months of "preaching daily," he had only four baptisms to show for his efforts. But the time turned out to be immensely fruitful in another way. For the dearth of missionary opportunities caused him to retire often to his chambers and turn to his pen instead. In those short two months, Pratt wrote the most influential book written by a Mormon in the nineteenth century. Relying only on the assistance of Fordham, who listened to his work as it unfolded and transcribed it for the printer, Pratt reeled off a 216-page volume he called *A Voice of Warning and Instruction* and printed three thousand copies.[57]

Pratt's optimism about *A Voice of Warning* was borne out. Next to the Book of Mormon itself, Pratt's book soon became the principal vehicle presenting Mormonism to the Latter-day Saint faithful and the general public alike, and it was elevated by both to near canonical status. Though Pratt's work circulated widely well into the next century, it seems to modern readers remote in its worldview, emphases, and style. Three contexts—Baconianism, millennialism, and antebellum America's oratorical culture—informed the intellectual universe that Pratt inhabited, and shed light on his rationalistic outlook, theology, and language. These contexts not only conditioned Pratt's mental world; through him and his contemporaries, they also formed the content and tone of early Mormon thinking about the meaning of restoration and Joseph Smith's role in it.

As Pratt toiled on his book, the queen of England was settling into a throne she inherited only weeks before. In retrospect, Queen Victoria's coronation would mean the transition from the Age of Romanticism to the Victorian era. The Romanticism of the preceding decades had been marked by the primitivism and pastoralism of William Wordsworth and the effusive sentiment of writers like Jean-Jacques Rousseau and poets like Percy Shelley. The new era looked exuberantly to the future rather than nostalgically to the past. Victorian England would find in the Great Exhibition at London's Crystal Palace its symbol for civilization's crowning values of industrial prowess and mechanized efficiency that were transforming the Western world.

In the intellectual culture of the Anglo-American world as elsewhere, this meant that the earlier rationalism and empiricism that had characterized the eighteenth-century Enlightenment, after a brief Romantic interlude in which passions of the heart ruled supreme, would reemerge, but this time increasingly allied with an emphasis on technological innovation, progress, and the perfectibility of humans and society. In America, Romanticism arrived later and lingered longer, as cultural rebels such as Edgar Allen Poe and Ralph Waldo Emerson celebrated the irrational, the idiosyncratic, and the radically individual. But the practical consequences of scientific achievement were becoming too conspicuous, too dramatic, not to accord the scientific worldview unprecedented esteem. "Baconianism," referring to the scientific method pioneered by Francis Bacon, is the name historians have given to the dominant strand of philosophical thought in what Americans call the age of Jackson. It entailed an exclusive focus on experimentation, facts, and the rule of experience. In this climate, if religion was not to be discarded as a regressive affair of the heart, if it was going to appeal to the new men of science, it would have to exhibit their same regard for evidence, esteem for progress, and cool embrace of sound reasoning. Under this ruling paradigm, the extension of this scientific optimism to the realm of religion was inevitable. As one scholar notes, Protestant theologians embraced Baconianism "to restore and reinforce the essential harmony between natural science and Christian faith. By this means they believed that all knowledge—whether scientific, theological, or moral—could be placed on a sure foundation."[58] Allied to this orientation was the heritage of Scottish commonsense philosophy. Timothy Dwight, one of the most influential churchmen of the era, hammered home its relevance to religious discourse: "Our Savior treats every subject in the direct manner of Common Sense," he taught. "By the first third of the nineteenth century," writes another historian, "commonsense habits of mind were axiomatic."[59]

Parley, like his brother Orson, embodied the characteristics of the era's representative intellectual: "A 'Baconian'—whether scientist or not—was a man captivated by the ongoing spectacle of scientific advance."[60] And Pratt's *Voice of Warning* epitomizes this constellation of values. He framed his presentation as a "positive demonstration" of such irresistible logic that none would be able to "gainsay nor resist."[61] (This rationalistic optimism recalls the philosopher William Godwin, who similarly insisted that "there is certainly a way of expressing truth, with ... such evidence as to enforce conviction in all cases whatever.")[62] Pratt's demonstration relied upon the facticity of ancient prophecies that have been undeniably fulfilled without making use of any "modern system of spiritualizing."[63] In other words, in Pratt's appropriation of biblical literalism to a scientific age, faith will not come at the cost of convenient language games that provide escape from the claims of supernaturalism. Revelation is as real, in this paradigm, as any other process subject to natural laws and empirical verification. Prophets, in his formulation, are as scientifically reliable as an almanac that predicts the eclipses. (His brother Orson would appropriate just that comparison, publishing *The Prophetic Almanac* in 1845 and 1846.)[64] And like astronomical predictions, revelation from God is as reasonable today as it was in the time of the Hebrew prophets.

Parley Pratt framed this scientific approach in pugnacious and apocalyptic rhetoric. The indignities he suffered in Mentor two years earlier paled in comparison with the brutality and expulsions of Jackson County, and Pratt prefaced his work with a protest at the "slanders of the foulest kind," as well as the violence and devastation his people had suffered. But Pratt made of this victimhood a cause for simultaneous pride as well as outrage. For it placed the Mormon people among the ranks of Christ's apostles contending with the scribes and Pharisees, the Reformers holding fast against a corrupt Mother Church, and even Columbus striving against the impenetrable ignorance and blindness of his age. And Pratt found, besides the blessedness of the persecuted, an unmistakable consolation in apocalyptic visions of coming vengeance. The title is, after all, *Voice of Warning*. The coming travails would be trying, but also vindicating.[65]

Pratt first laid out as evidence forty pages of prophecy already fulfilled, before moving on to his presentation of "prophecy yet future." The rampant millennialism of the era provides the most important religious context for appreciating Pratt's theological orientation and literary strategy. Influenced by the millennial fervor of the Reformed Baptists, Pratt's personal version of the imminence of the apocalyptic was heightened by his sense of personal revelation in response to his fervent study and prayer. In early 1830, he later recorded, "I felt drawn out in an extraordinary manner to search the prophets, and to pray for an understanding of the same. My prayers were soon answered, even beyond my expectations; the prophecies of the holy prophets were opened to my view; I began to understand the things which were coming on the earth—the restoration of Israel, the coming of the Messiah, and the glory that should follow.... I was all swallowed up in these things."[66] The millennialism so pronounced across the American religious scene provided Pratt with his most compelling narrative of the events surrounding him and soon, as he believed, to engulf him. Through this lens he interpreted the past, made sense of the present, and planned for the future. Mormonism fit into the pattern he had already imbibed, but it added confirmation, momentum, definition, and authority to his sense of self and mission.

Belief in the Second Coming of the Messiah to rescue the righteous from the evils of the world goes back to the generation of Christ's apostles. But that belief both alternated with spiritualized readings of God's coming kingdom on earth and varied as to the process by which a literal kingdom would be inaugurated. Third-century Church Father Origen and, later, Augustine both taught that the church Christ had founded was his kingdom; its endurance through the centuries obviated any need for a more literal kingdom. In this way, they *spiritualized* the scriptures to the point that millennialism was frequently taken as a figurative rather than historical event. This interpretation survived alongside beliefs that God would return in dramatic, triumphal glory, to usher in a thousand years of peace. Belief in the imminence of that return intensified at various times in Christian history, such as the years just before the turn of the first millennium C.E. The normative reading of scripture came to see the Second Coming as the culmination of tribulations, wars, and doomsday scenarios.[67]

By contrast, Daniel Whitby wrote a work in 1706 that built upon early allegorical interpretations to flesh out a doctrine of *post*millennialism. In his version, the evangelization of the earth would effectively extend the sway of Christ over its inhabitants, ushering in the peace of prophecy. Only at the end of this process would Christ personally return to reign. Whitby's views were popular with Jonathan Edwards and other late Puritans, but during the Second Great Awakening, more literal readings of the millennium swept across the religious landscape. These *premillennialists* saw a spiritually deteriorating world and abundant signs of prophetically described portents signaling the end-times of scripture. Christ, they anticipated, would come to intervene in history and inaugurate a new era. Such premillennialists viewed Christ's coming as rescue, not validation. He will come as history spirals out of control, not as it achieves a glorious consummation in the utopia-building of social reformers and religious zealots. Throngs of the devout split on these two fundamentally different interpretations of millennialism, though postmillennialism remained the predominant paradigm during Pratt's day. Pratt had been influenced by Rigdon, who broke with the Campbellites in part because he judged that faith to be too sanguine in claiming that humans had the capacity to lead the world to spiritual renewal. In his paper's prospectus, Campbell described the millennium as "the consummation of the ultimate amelioration of society."[68] Pratt at first equivocated in his position on the millennium, likely because his Baconian faith in progress was balanced by a competing respect for the darker side of human nature and history.

In the context of Pratt's newly discovered premillennialist zeal under Rigdon's influence, the effect of reading the Book of Mormon was electric. If Pratt had previously held sympathy for a more sedate transition into the millennial era, the Book of Mormon and events surrounding the establishment of Mormonism moved him quickly and decisively to a more catastrophic eschatology. Pratt indicated this transition into the premillennialist camp in his first literary effort, the poem "Millennium" of some five hundred lines he composed in 1835 while tramping through the eastern states preaching the Mormon message. The preface to that work noted of Pratt that "at the age of twenty three [in 1830], having searched the scriptures carefully and prayerfully, he became convinced that an overturn was at hand such as had not been known upon the earth. He saw that wickedness must have an end; the earth be sanctified, and creation cease to groan under its pollution; and this would be brought about by nothing less than an entire destruction of all who would not obey the gospel."[69] Not all Christians of the early nineteenth century were millennialists, but to Pratt and his fellow Mormons, it seemed they were. The only question was, Were they the right kind? As a church editorialist noted, "Notwithstanding all, or the most of christendom, pretend to believe, that the Millennium will soon be ushered in and cause a spiritual reign of the Savior over mankind, still, the plain fact, that he will come down in person and reign on earth....seems to be...foreign to the minds of those who pretend to believe that the bible is true."[70]

Premillennialists like Pratt saw their primary missionary responsibility as preaching the gospel and thereby saving the righteous few from apocalypse, not paving the way to social renewal and earthly bliss. In Pratt's poetic version of the immediate future,

> dire commotion[s] seize the nations all,
> While blood and war the stoutest hearts appal,
> Kingdom on kingdom, in confusion hurl'd,
> System on system wreck'd throughout the world,
> Sect against sect in bloody strife engage,
> Man against man, in single combat rage.[71]

Mormons were already millennialists before Pratt joined them, of course. Smith's initial theophany had included a reference to Christ's imminent return ("and lo I come quickly"), and the angel Moroni had immersed the young Smith in millennialist expectations. He recited Malachi's promise that "the Lord, whom ye seek, shall suddenly come" and quoted Isaiah's prophecy that an "ensign for the nations" would be set up to promote the gathering of his people, which "was about to be fulfilled." Finally, Moroni said that Peter's predicted separation of unbelievers "soon would come" and that Joel's prophesied Pentecostal renewal "was not yet fulfilled but was soon to be."[72] From its publication, the Book of Mormon was preached as that ensign, or sign of latter-day events fast unfolding.[73] Rigdon's conversion and his commanding influence solidified this focus in early Mormonism, especially evident in a series of fourteen articles he published in the church newspaper from December 1833 to May 1835. But Pratt's *Voice of Warning* proved the more influential and enduring testament to this principle.[74]

Though a premillennialist with an apocalyptic warning, Pratt recognized as well the encouraging trends of his most optimistic contemporaries and postmillennialists. Just as Thomas Jefferson and his political heirs saw the American Revolution as the initial spark of a worldwide spread of liberty, Pratt saw liberty's march as inexorable. So even in the midst of sounding the alarm regarding encroaching "famine," "earthquakes," and "pestilence," Pratt digressed to celebrate American independence, the French Revolution of 1789, the Greek war for independence (achieved in 1821), and the rebellion in Poland, where the

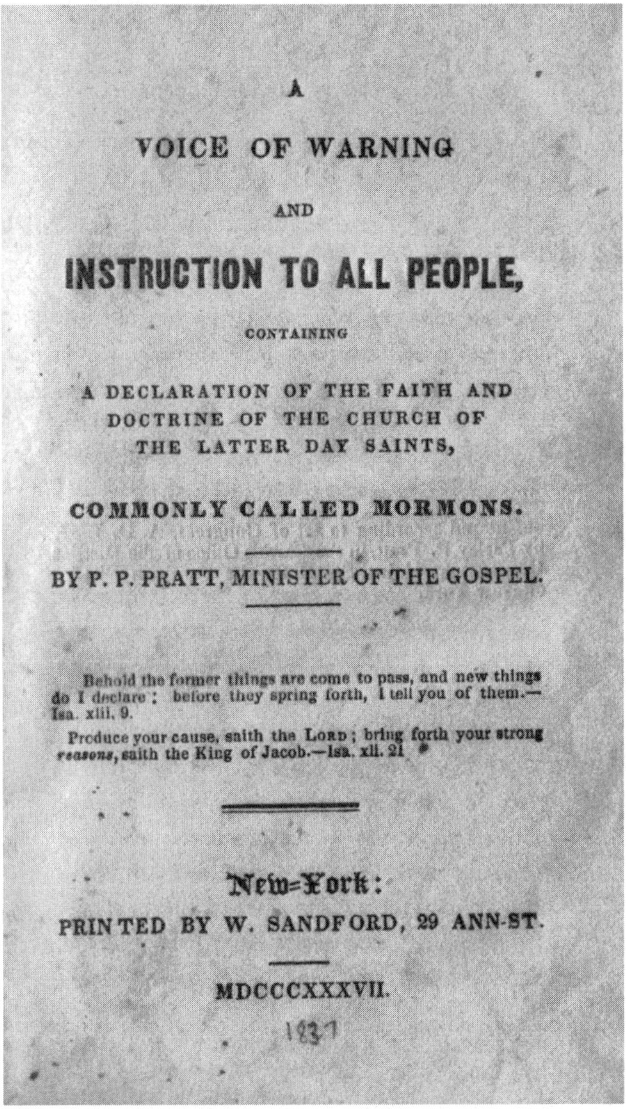

A

VOICE OF WARNING

AND

INSTRUCTION TO ALL PEOPLE,

CONTAINING

A DECLARATION OF THE FAITH AND
DOCTRINE OF THE CHURCH OF
THE LATTER DAY SAINTS,

COMMONLY CALLED MORMONS.

BY P. P. PRATT, MINISTER OF THE GOSPEL.

Behold the former things are come to pass, and new things
do I declare: before they spring forth, I tell you of them.—
Isa. xlii. 9.
Produce your cause, saith the Lord; bring forth your strong
reasons, saith the King of Jacob.—Isa. xli. 21

New-York:
PRINTED BY W. SANDFORD, 29 ANN-ST.

MDCCCXXXVII.

FIGURE 4.2 Title page to the first edition of Parley Pratt's *Voice of Warning* (1837).

pursuit of "the sacred fire" found in defeat only temporary setback (the 1830 revolution collapsed the next year). Everywhere, it seemed, "freedom's genius" swept the world in the political sphere, even as sin extended her dominions in the spiritual realm. Pratt thus initiated a scheme of world history that Mormons embrace to the present day, one in which political and religious developments alike are both providential and preparatory to the gospel's restoration.

For Pratt, the accelerating spirit of freedom was of divine provenance, not of human origins, and therefore more a call for final preparations than an occasion for self-congratulation. A gradual progression into millennial glory (the postmillennialist view) was, he emphatically insisted in the *Voice of Warning*, not to be read into these developments. He strenuously distanced himself and his church from the errors of the postmillennialists.

> Behold, ye flatter yourselves that the glorious day spoken of by the prophets, will be ushered in by your modern inventions and moneyed plans, which are got up in order to convert the Jews and heathens, to the various sectarian principles now existing among yourselves, and you expect when this is done, to behold a Millennium after your own heart.

In actual fact, he declared, "that glorious day will be ushered in by the personal coming of Christ and the resurrection of all the saints." And on that occasion, "all the wicked will be destroyed from the earth…by fire." "That burning," he added grimly, "will include priests as well as people: all but a few shall be burned."[75] Pratt's emphasis on the vivid reality of apocalyptic death and destruction may be attributable in part to a culture—and personality— that inclined to calamity howling. But he also found the "spiritualizing" mode of interpretation—especially when invoked to avoid premillennialist commitments—to be a dangerous narcotic in a time of genuinely mortal peril. To teach, as the postmillennialists did, that the words of prophecy do not mean what they say literally, although the scriptures "declare these things plainly," was a form of priestcraft he felt compelled to refute.

Pratt and Rigdon were aided in their advocacy of literalism by both commonsense rationalism and an interpretive approach conformable to the populism of the era. As one historian explains, commonsense rendering of scripture was the "common person's counterpart to the Enlightenment confidence displayed by intellectual elites."[76] Articles in the church newspaper frequently mirrored Pratt's views on spiritualizing. The *Evening and Morning Star* repeatedly affirmed literal scriptural exegesis and described "spiritualized" readings as a strategy for doubters to reject the prophesied restoration of the "order of things" while still pretending "that they are great *sticklers* for the bible."[77] Benjamin Winchester, who acknowledged Pratt's influence, repeated his views in his influential *Gospel Reflector*. From there, they were reprinted in the church newspaper, *Times and Seasons*, where they established a quasi-official doctrine of Mormon scriptural exegesis. "It is necessary to establish some definite rule for interpretation," one article ran. "The idea of spiritualizing the writings of the prophets and apostles" so that "none but the learned can understand them, is certainly repugnant to the word of God." Winchester called it an "evil practice" and argued that a literal reading, especially of prophecies of the millennium, was the proper and necessary rule.[78]

Illustrating just how immediate the preparatory scenes of the millennium were, Pratt found his own 1830 journey to the frontier smack in the middle of the penultimate drama, an instrumental episode that both clarified and enacted ancient prophecy. The prophet Amos had referred anciently to God's future mercy toward "the remnant of Joseph," meaning descendants of Ephraim and/or Manasseh, and Ezekiel had similarly intimated their eventual restoration.[79] In the Book of Mormon, Lehi referred to his posterity as descendants of Manasseh, and his people identified themselves as that remnant who would be preserved and later gathered by the Lord.[80] With the church organized and the Book of Mormon available as an ensign for the gathering of scattered Israel, Smith had launched a mission to those same children of Manasseh. Conveniently, the Lord had already begun gathering them to the Zion of prophecy, which Smith identified as being "on the borders by the Lamanites," known to contemporaries as "Indian Territory."[81] As vague as the term now sounds, the meaning was clear enough to Americans in late 1830. For in 1825, the United States government closed the area later to become Kansas to settlement and set it aside as Indian territory. The first Native Americans exiled to that area were the Shawnee, evicted from Missouri later that year. (More Shawnee joined them from Ohio in 1831.) Then in 1829, the Delaware, who had been moving west from Pennsylvania for a century, were relocated by treaty to the same general area. A few months before Pratt embarked on his Lamanite mission, President Andrew Jackson signed into law the Indian Removal Act, which speeded up the eviction of those tribes that still remained east of the Mississippi.[82]

So when Pratt crossed the Missouri River in the winter of 1830, he entered a domain that had officially been designated to sequester American Indians from the rest of the nation. Pratt saw in the political processes the gathering of the remnant of Joseph foretold by scripture. His fellow Saints widely shared that view, though Pratt was one of the most impassioned to celebrate the connection. The church paper proclaimed in 1832 that it was "marvelous, to witness the gathering of the Indians." As evidence of scripture fulfilled, it quoted a modified Psalm 80: "Give ear, O Shepherd of Israel, thou that leadest Joseph like a flock, through the instrumentality of the Government of the United States."[83] Subsequent issues enthusiastically noted developments with Shawnee, Winnebago, Sac, Fox, Choctaw, Cherokee, and Osage tribes, as they signed treaties with the government and relocated to the west. While some northerners found the forcible removal of the Native Americans morally disturbing, most Americans, including most Mormons, did not. Cowdery and Pratt saw those Delaware and Shawnee they visited as living emblems not of ethnic cleansing, but of God's mercy and providential designs. As the *Evening and Morning Star* opined, "What a beauty it is to see the prophecies fulfilling so exactly," then quoted Nephi that the Lord "shall bring them again out of captivity, and they shall be gathered together to the lands of their inheritance, and they shall be brought out of obscurity and darkness."[84] For Pratt, the American government was not breaking faith with treaty signatories inconveniently impeding American expansion, but effecting a physical gathering of scattered Israel in preparation for their spiritual conversion and reabsorption into the everlasting covenant. In his rapturous words,

> See Congress stand, in all the power of state,
> Destined like Cyrus, now to change the fate
> Of Joseph's scattered remnants! long oppressed,
> And bring them home, unto a land of rest;
> Beyond the Mississippi's rolling flood,
> A land before ordained by Israel's God!
> Where Zion's city, shall in grandeur rise.[85]

Christians and Jews alike saw Cyrus the Great as the divine instrument who paved the way for the restoration of the Jews to their homeland. In comparable fashion, Pratt suggested, the U.S. government was furthering God's providential designs for the Native Americans. But Pratt's part was equally pivotal. His appointment to the mission that fulfilled scriptural history in gathering a remnant of lost Israel, his call to be a charter member of the first quorum of twelve apostles since Christ called his fishermen and publicans, and his indispensable role as bard and theologian of Christ's restored gospel convinced him he was a chosen vessel to bring about divine purposes. When later circumstances necessitated his fibbing his way to freedom from pursuers, he compared his situation to a dissembling Rahab or David:

> Oh, yes, says one, but he was the Lord's anointed, and, therefore, had a right to save his life at all hazards to fulfill God's purposes. To this I reply, that I am also God's anointed, and have a greater reason for

living and a more worthy object to accomplish than he had, ... a greater work to accomplish than he ever had.[86]

Finally, the most relevant cultural context for understanding Pratt's rhetorical style is the antebellum contest over defining what one scholar calls "Democratic Eloquence."[87] William Wordsworth added definition and momentum to a rhetorical revolution in the English-speaking world when he promoted the use, in 1800, of "language, really used by men."[88] By the 1820s and 1830s, Romantic ideas had filtered across the Atlantic, moving written and verbal expression in the direction of a simpler, more popular style. The trend was amplified in the populist environment of Jacksonian America. In place of the Ciceronian ornateness of an Edward Gibbons or a Samuel Johnson, the plain diction and more homey expressions of pulpit preachers and popular writers increasingly drew audiences and readers.

A vast expansion of the literate public and a hugely proliferating—and suddenly affordable—print culture encouraged a more democratic public rhetoric. Pamphlet wars over theological fine points had erupted in the 1640s in England, both fueling and fueled by religious dissent and radicalism. John Milton's publisher remarked that "the slightest pamphlet is nowadayes more vendible then the Works of learnedest men."[89] But several developments in Pratt's era launched a genuinely democratic print culture. During the 1830s and 1840s, the numbers of newspapers and pamphlets, both religious and secular, in the United States exploded. The advance of public education and literacy, particularly in the North, enlarged the demand for print, as did the growth of an integrated national transportation network based on canals, steamship lines, and railroads. Cheap postage for newspapers also contributed to the expansion and nationalization of print culture. Simultaneously, technological improvements (especially the telegraph, the steam-driven rotary printing press, and wood-pulp paper) greatly reduced the price and increased the speed of printing.[90] Religious groups exploited developments by founding massive numbers of religious newspapers, and the American Bible Society and American Tract Society flooded the nation— and soon beyond—with cheap bibles and tracts. These changes created the conditions under which Pratt could publish quickly, relatively inexpensively, and in large quantities.

At the same time, however, a contravening trend emerged. Broader literacy meant a growing middle class. Increasing numbers of the educated were eager to parade a little learning. The high-flown rhetoric of public figures like Rufus Choate, Daniel Webster, Charles Sumner, and Edward Everett was both appreciated and imitated, as evident in period diaries, letters, magazines, and newspapers. These competing trends, one historian writes, provoked "a war over the soul of American life...from the 1820s and 1830s through the end of the century." The more democratically minded advocates of a raw Saxon purity blasted the attempts to resurrect an eloquence they deemed passé. "The pompous diction of the eighteenth century," they protested, "had become one of the popular styles of the day. Half-educated editors and politicians made Johnson's style their own."[91] Democratically minded religious groups, such as Methodists, Baptists, Campbellites, and Mormons, who sought to attract converts through populist language, particularly objected. For instance, the Mormon editor of the *Evening and Morning Star* reprinted an article that praised the language of scripture as appropriately "simple, unaffected, unornamental, and unostentatious."[92] The confluence of these various currents frequently created a vibrant mélange of low style bordering on vulgarity, sprinkled with displays of erudition and pomposity. Both tendencies infused Pratt's writing.

Well read, but self-educated, Pratt said of himself, "The author was an husbandman, inured to the plough—unpolished by education, untaught in the schools of modern sectarianism...reared in the wilds of America."[93] Yet he was the most prolific Mormon writer of his age, as editor, pamphleteer, essayist, historian, hymnist, and theologian. *Voice of Warning*, as in all his works to follow, contains a peculiar admixture of a blunt, common idiom, with eruptions of Ciceronian ornateness and Gibbonesque grandiosity. His dismissal of "stupid and indifferent" priests, his raw anger at "lying slanders," segues seamlessly into lofty descriptions of temples with "their foundations of sapphires, their windows of agates, their gates of carbuncles"; pedantic references to "Salmanezer king of Assyria," the "Valley of Hamon Gog," and archaeological ruins "in perpendicular attitude" alternate with his appeal to "plain examples," "plain" meanings, and "plain" prophecies. His writing is both populist and pedantic.[94]

What, then, did Pratt achieve with his *Voice of Warning*, and why did it serve such an important role in the coming century? For the first few years of the church's existence, little besides the Book of Mormon existed to ground Mormon theology or expound doctrine, and early Saints seldom used the Book of Mormon in that regard. Many of Smith's revelations were first published in the church's *Evening and Morning Star*, followed by a few dozen copies of sixty-five revelations bound as the Book of Commandments in 1833, with an expanded collection published as the Doctrine and Covenants in 1835. But for a narrative exposition, one that aspired to lay out in readable format the essence of Mormonism for member and non-Mormon alike, *Voice of Warning* had no peer and, for many decades, little competition.

In addition to clarifying the Mormon position on the paramount religious topic of the day, millennialism, *Voice* addressed an equally contentious point fiercely debated by his contemporaries: the meaning of restoration and authority. Pratt emphasized in his first chapters that the Mormon church was modeled on the Christian church "as it existed at its first organization, in the days of the apostles."[95] Not all Christians of Pratt's day believed that the church needed reform or that a return to a New Testament model was the gold standard for religious faith, but many did. Most Catholics and some Protestants believed the church changed through time under the inspiration of the Holy Spirit. But reformers since at least the sixteenth century had agitated for a return to the purity and simplicity of New Testament patterns. Such "primitivists" were an abiding presence on the religious landscape for subsequent centuries and emerged as a dominant Christian current in early-nineteenth-century America and England.[96] "Seekerism," a radical form of primitivism, comprised those who felt internal reform was inadequate to the task of establishing an authentic Christianity. Rather, they awaited the restoration of apostolic authority to perform the ordinances of the gospel. Virtually all seekers were thus primitivists, because the church they awaited would have both the form and the authority of the New Testament church. But not all primitivists were seekers, because some primitivists felt the New Testament model might be found in Christendom or achieved through reform or innovation.

Joseph Smith's 1832 account (his earliest) of his first vision reflected his immersion in Primitivist influences:

> From the age of twelve years to fifteen I pondered many things in my heart concerning the sittuation of the world.... By searching the scriptures I found that mankind did not come unto the Lord but that they had apostatised from the true and liveing faith and there was no society or denomination that built upon the gospel of Jesus Christ as recorded in the new testament.[97]

At the same time, a widely appealing element of the faith Smith founded was its dramatic satisfaction of "the quest for religious authority" that animated so many seekers.[98] Smith's position contrasts dramatically with that of Alexander Campbell, a primitivist but not a seeker, in regard to that elusive holy grail of authority: "There lives not the man on earth that can assure himself, or any one else, that there is one official in Christendom that could, by any possibility, believe, know, or rationally conjecture, that the hands laid on his head had any more connexion, lineal or direct, from Peter or any of the Apostles, than they have with Aaron or Melchisedek." And so, he concluded, "the efficacy of Christian ordinances consists not in, nor depends upon, any official virtue or power in him that does administer them."[99] Neither did Campbell take the New Testament model so far as to expect a restoration of spiritual gifts and miracles. This conservatism, along with their differing views on millennialism, contributed to Rigdon's rupture with Campbell.

When Pratt sketched the features of the Kingdom of God, he gave concrete articulation to the New Testament ideals that all primitivists ostensibly sought, but in such a way as to distinguish Mormon doctrines from their near competitors. The doctrines he emphasized included (1) the commission to preach faith and repentance and to baptize, (2) signs following the faithful, and (3) "officers commissioned, and duly qualified to administer the laws and ordinances of that kingdom."[100] In the first instance, Pratt differentiated Mormon first principles from Baptist versions: Mormons practiced baptism immediately upon conversion and promised the remission of sins accompanying baptism. In the second and third, the differences with other primitivists like the Campbellites were more stark. The Mormon emphasis on gifts such as healing and, especially, tongues, was more pronounced than in almost any other denomination. Regarding the third and most consequential criterion of the true church, Pratt argued from New Testament texts that no saving ordinances could be valid "unless those laws, and ordinances, were administered by one who had proper authority, and was duly commissioned from the King." And this requirement "brings to the test, every minister in Christendom; and questions the organization, of every church on earth."[101]

Pratt included in *Voice of Warning* a chapter on the Book of Mormon. In his exposition of the gospel, that record serves one paramount purpose. As he took Isaiah and Ezekiel to intimate, the Book of Mormon delivered by Moroni was the sign given of God "for the ushering in of that long expected day, when an angel should fly through the midst of Heaven, having the everlasting gospel to preach," as John prophesied in Revelation. Smith and others associated that angel with Moroni but also with different messengers conveying keys of the restoration; Pratt's version became the standard Mormon reading of the verse.[102] As Pratt read the scriptures, the coming forth of this "new book" brought by Moroni would happen "just previous to the gathering of Israel." Then, as Book of Mormon prophets attested, that gathering would center in the city of Zion, a New Jerusalem to be built by the American Indians (with Gentile assistance) in the place where they were even then congregating (and where he had visited them seven years previously). Thus, the Book of Mormon both physically embodied the fulfillment of ancient prophecy and provided a key to deciphering the details—and the setting—of the winding up scenes. It rendered biblical prophecies vividly concrete. Like the future state to which it bore witness, with brick-and-mortar Zions and physically reconstituted bodies, the Book of Mormon pertained "not [to] a state of shadows, and fables; but something tangible."[103]

As Pratt labored in New York City on his *Voice of Warning*, two experiences reaffirmed in his mind the key role the Book of Mormon would play in latter-day events. While he was preaching at the house of an attentive inquirer, the listener, a latter-day Cornelius in Pratt's description, was suddenly transfixed by a vision in which he saw the two "sticks" mentioned in Ezekiel 37. He immediately testified of what he had seen, spoke in tongues, and then interpreted his own words to say the stick of Joseph was a record that would soon come to the knowledge of that remnant. In addition, Pratt noted the arrival in New York of "Joseph Wolsf [Wolff]," whom he described as "a Jew, who has journeyed through all parts of the old world, from Palistine to India." A Jewish convert to Christianity, Wolff was "the nineteenth-century figure most associated with romantic missionary travel and the quest for the restoration of the ten lost tribes."[104] His quest began in 1829, when he said to his wife, "Bokhara [in modern Uzbekistan] and Balkh [in Afghanistan] are very much in my mind, for I think I shall there find the ten tribes."[105] He had spent several intervening years exploring Central Asia, Afghanistan, and India as locales where the tribes might have migrated, then he came to America to lecture on his theories. Wolff also hoped that exploring the "origin of the Indians" might help him solve the riddle of the lost ten tribes. Pratt had two personal meetings with Wolff and waxed enthusiastic. The renowned traveler's views, he wrote Joseph Smith's brother Don Carlos, "are precisely what we believe and teach, as far as prophecy & its fulfillment is concerned." Pratt took their shared views as a missionary opening, showing Wolff the Old Testament prophecies about Joseph and Ephraim and presenting him with a Book of Mormon.[106] Wolff, however, did not find his answer in the Book of Mormon or in the Americas. He visited Washington, D.C., and after conversing with a number of Native American chiefs, concluded "that they had no claim to be considered the

seed of Abraham" and forsook his project of going among the western tribes
to investigate further.[107] Nevertheless, the spiritual manifestation of the "old
Cornelious" on the one hand, and the common interest and views with a
man of Wolff's stature on the other, confirmed Pratt in believing the Book
of Mormon an unparalleled treasure and helped make him one of its most
vigorous proponents in the early church.

Pratt followed the chapter on the Book of Mormon with "A Proclamation"
of the millennium's approach, and one on the events to follow. A surprising
omission from the first edition of *Voice of Warning* is Joseph Smith's name; it
nowhere appears. Smith had not achieved the fame or notoriety he would in
following years. But in an 1837 Restoration saga with a whole chapter on the
Book of Mormon, one would expect at least a mention of his name. The omission could have been a consequence of the recent breach, mended but not yet
fully healed. It could as easily have been a function of Pratt's world vision,
which at this time saw the impending millennium as the next and final cata-
clysmic stage in a cosmic narrative. In that light, sweeping historical events
eclipsed Smith's personal role. As Pratt's feelings or his perspective changed
over the next years, he inserted Smith's name into revised editions of *Voice*. But
for the present, Pratt's purpose was to present the big picture, to capture the
scope of God's grand designs as forecast in scripture and fulfilled through historical developments beginning in antiquity and culminating in the present
moment. A sense of urgency and immediacy suffused his message, as it did
Pratt's life. This was high drama, larger and more compelling than any of the
particular characters that constituted its cast, prophets and seers included.

Although the first printing of three thousand copies of *Voice of Warning*
moved slowly at first, it sold out within two years. Pratt printed an additional
twenty-five hundred in 1839 and then issued an edition in England in 1841. By
that time, Pratt noted, the book had spread from the United States "into the
provinces of the Canadas, as well as many parts of England, Scotland, Ireland,
and Wales" and had "visited the cottages of the humble, and the parlours of
the great." Hundreds had testified to him, Pratt wrote, that *Voice of Warning*
had saved "them from infidelity—and from Sectarian error and delusion."[108]
By the time of the Saints' arrival in Utah, the book had sold thirteen thousand
copies and was in its sixth printing. Pratt supported himself in large measure
through the sale of his own publications, so he had a vested interest in pro-
moting his own work. But the book continued its prodigious sales long after
Pratt's death, proving the book's wide appeal and effectiveness as a tool both
of gospel instruction to the initiated and of proselytizing in the mission field.
In 1884, Pratt's family carefully estimated that seventy-five thousand copies

had been published in fourteen editions.[109] By the end of the century, it would be printed in more than thirty English editions, as well as Danish, Dutch, French, German, Icelandic, Spanish, and Swedish versions.[110] It was by far the most frequently mentioned book of Mormon authorship in Mormonism's early years and beyond. Mormon defector John Hyde, who felt only contempt for Pratt, acknowledged that the work was in the 1850s "the most popular" of what he called "their standard controversial works."[111]

Its preeminent role, second only to the Book of Mormon as an instrument of conversion, is typified by the experience of Sarah Studevant Leavitt. Her autobiography recounts that while living in Canada in the 1830s, her husband, Jeremiah, was given *A Voice of Warning* and a Book of Mormon; they soon converted and made plans to gather with the Saints. A few months later, the couple was living near Kirtland, renting a house from a Mr. Faulk, a man "noted for his wickedness." "I gave him the 'Voice of Warning,'" she recounted. "He took it home and read it.... Faulk joined the Church and came to Nauvoo afterward."[112]

Within Mormonism, the influence of *Voice of Warning* only increased after Pratt's death. Annie Clark Tanner, who grew to maturity in the latter half of the nineteenth century, remembered the church's emphasis on doctrinal instruction. "Belief in the theological doctrine was more emphasized in the Church, at that time," she wrote, "than practical application of ethical teaching.... We had every encouragement to read the Church publications: *The Voice of Warning*; *The Pearl of Great Price*; and *Key to Theology*."[113] That only Pratt's writings would be on equal footing with *The Pearl of Great Price*, canonized in 1880, suggests the special status his works held in the minds of early Mormon leaders and laity. His corpus was a virtual fifth scriptural volume of the church. Thomas D. Brown, in fact, claimed that Joseph Smith had pronounced *Voice of Warning* a standard work;[114] in 1864, it was one of two works that Brigham Young recommended to a correspondent for an overview of Mormon doctrine.[115] In 1875, it was the very first title mentioned (after the scriptures and hymns) in the *Deseret News* list of "Books Worth Reading" (Pratt's *Key to Theology* was next).[116]

For years after its initial publication, outside reviewers as well viewed Pratt's treatise on a par with the Doctrine and Covenants and the Book of Mormon. The *Baptist Advocate* mentioned the Book of Mormon in 1841 and quoted from both the Doctrine and Covenants and *Voice of Warning*, which it called "a standard Mormon work." The *Southern Literary Messenger* similarly grouped the three together in its sketch of Mormonism in 1848.[117] A few years later, John W. Gunnison, a federal surveyor who visited Utah and then wrote a book on the Mormons, mentioned only three "books regarded as authoritative with them": the Book of Mormon, Doctrine and Covenants, and *Voice of Warning*. In fact, he added, the Saints considered Pratt's works, "wherever found," on a par with "the writings of Joseph the Seer" and the "General Epistles of the Presidency in Deseret."[118]

At the time *Voice* was published, however, Pratt's writing success could not fully compensate for a mission that was, in its primary purpose, a vast disappointment. "Of all the places in which the English language is spoken," he complained, "I found the City of New York to be the most difficult as to access to the minds or attention of the people. From July to January we preached, advertised, printed, published, testified, visited, talked, prayed, and wept in vain. To all appearance there was no interest.... We had hired chapels and advertised, but the people would not hear, and the few who came went away without being interested."[119] There may have been some connection between his lack of success and a well-attended public debate Pratt had in these months with the redoubtable Origen Bachelor. Usual adversaries of Mormon missionaries were relatively untrained and local clergymen. Bachelor, however, was a pro. He had, for example, debated religion in ten letters with Robert Dale Owen, the freethinking son of Robert Owen, in 1831. More recently he had written articles for Alexander Campbell's *Millennial Harbinger*.[120] Bachelor soon acquired a reputation, in fact, as "the great Goliath and champion of the Cross,"[121] and he was sufficiently invested in debunking Mormonism to publish a book on the subject in 1838.[122]

Pratt did not record the results—most likely because he did not come off as well as he typically did. A much later recollection printed in the *Detroit Tribune* reported that in this "celebrated discussion," Bachelor had "proved" two contentions: first, that the Book of Mormon was a plagiarism from an earlier book; and second, that the golden plates were phony and were created to deceive. "To these various facts and charges," the journalist declared, "poor Parley P. Pratt made a feeble reply, and utterly failed to controvert the proofs produced by Mr. Bachelor."[123] Bachelor gave more details in his subsequent exposé of Mormonism. Alarmed at the "degree of public attention" that Pratt's preaching had excited, he challenged the elder to "a public discussion," which turned into a marathon debate. Pratt withstood Bachelor's attacks for three consecutive days, but on the fourth he tried to withdraw, protesting that his adversary was ridiculing the Book of Mormon. Under pressure from the audience, Pratt agreed to continue, but objected again on the sixth evening when Bachelor impugned the character of Smith, Rigdon, and others. They sparred over what constituted acceptable evidence pro or contra, but Pratt failed to win either the point or the audience's sympathy. At that moment, "in the very heat of the battle," Pratt "beat a retreat and left poor old *Mormon* to take care of himself!" Not wanting to lose his momentum, Bachelor regaled the crowd for two more evenings.[124] At least Pratt had the satisfaction of seeing Bachelor, in his printed attack, invoke Pratt's *Voice of Warning* in order to rebut it.[125] He was noticed, if not yet victorious.

Six months of hard work, and only six converts to show for it. Pratt's little family had abandoned him to the stresses of barren missionary labors, traveling to Mary Ann's parents and relatives in Bethel, Maine. In late November, Pratt had written to her of his loneliness and despondency, gently urging her to return. He complained of mounting printers' bills and weak public interest but expressed his determination to persevere. As for Mary Ann's plans, he left the future in her hands. He hoped she would persuade her father's family to join the Saints in the West, but he knew it was a hard sell. Showing unusual deference to her family ties, he assured her, "If they will not come I hope you will Not go and Leave them for I would prefer that we perish with them Sooner than go from them with Such hart rending feelings as we have once Experienced in undertaking to go without seeing them." By the end of his letter, he had sunk into profound resignation. "I see no Prospect of rest or Enjoyment, of friends or home Short of Immortal Rest," he wrote, and then—as he so often did—found catharsis in a poetic lament.

> Adieu to the Pleasures, of home and Its Joys
> To all the sweet Prospects which hope had inspired
> Our fond Expectations
> were like fleeting Toys
> Our prospects are Blighted; our hopes have Expired
> In some Lovely Cottage how oft I've Desired
> to Clasp to my Bosom the friends that I Love
> Far, far, from all Strife and confusion returned
> Together In Union and Friendship and Love
> But Still I am Doomed for to wander a lone
> A Stranger a pilgrim…[126]

By January, Pratt was preparing to depart New York for what he hoped would be greener missionary pastures in New Orleans. During his last prayer meeting with his small band of followers, "on a sudden, the room was filled with the Holy Spirit, and so was each one present. We began to speak in tongues and prophesy. Many marvelous things were manifested which I cannot write; but the principal burthen of the prophesyings was concerning New York City, and our mission there. The Lord said that He had heard our prayers, beheld our labors, diligence, and long suffering towards that city; and that He had seen our tears." Pratt felt inspired to remain in New York, as "the Lord had many people in that city, and He had now come by the power of His Holy Spirit to gather them into His fold."[127]

Pratt's spiritual intimations proved correct, and gradually his New York efforts met with greater success. Perhaps the deepening national economic crisis softened hearts, or Pratt's prior publicity had finally stirred interest. Members and interested clergy provided lecture space, and the Freethinkers invited him to speak in Tammany Hall. Within a month, he recorded, "we had fifteen preaching places in the city, all of which were filled to overflowing. We preached about eleven times a week, besides visiting from house to house. We soon commenced baptizing, and continued doing so almost daily during the winter and spring."[128] In a story that is paradigmatic of many in that generation who sought apostolic authority, Wandle Mace had been excommunicated from his own Presbyterian church and was working as a machinist in New York City while spending time as an itinerant lay preacher. Along with Mace's acquaintance Elijah Fordham, Pratt attended a Methodist meeting at which Mace lamented the lack of spiritual gifts in contemporary Christianity. Though some in the audience "declared they [gifts] were not needed in this age," the "portly" Pratt

> expressed his pleasure at my remarks in the meeting and said he would like a further conversation with me.... After partaking of one evening meal, we entered into conversation upon the doctrines taught in the New Testament. He talked of Repentance, and of the necessity of Baptism for the remission of sins, by one holding authority, and the laying on of hands for the Gift of the Holy Ghost. This kind of talk suited me exactly, but where could that authority be found? In the course of our conversation he learned from me, this, that I was waiting and watching for the gifts of the gospel as they once existed. I would no more connect myself with any denomination, unless that denomination had with them Apostles, and Prophets, Jesus Christ being the chief cornerstone.

How singular, Mace remembered him as saying, "to find a man...waiting for Apostles and Prophets and the gifts of the spirit as enjoyed anciently.... Then he began telling me about a young man in New York who had been visited by an angel."[129]

What emerges time and again from Pratt's encounters—with the latter-day Cornelius and his vision of Ezekiel's "sticks," with Joseph Wolff, and now with Mace—was Pratt's certainty that he was an agent of divine providence with a leading role in an unfolding cosmic design. The Book of Mormon proved in his personal experience to be efficient and accurate in forecasting developments before they unfolded: the apostasy of Christendom and its restoration, the gathering of the Saints to Zion, and the gathering of the Lamanites in contemporary America. He also read in the Book of Mormon that it would come forth "in a day when it shall be said that miracles are done away."[130] Once again, he stood at the center of the prophecy's dual fulfillment: the promise of latter-day miracles and apostate Christendom's skeptical response. But he also saw himself as a conduit for the continuing reality of the miraculous.

His acquaintance with Mace provided one such instance. Mace's infant son became desperately sick and was diagnosed as having inflammation of the brain. As the father recalled, "The child would be thrown into spasms, it would writhe and twist, Oh, it was enough to rend the hearts of all who watched its sufferings." His distraught wife suggested now might "be a good time to try Mr. Pratt's religion." Mace brought Pratt to his home, and upon Pratt's invitation, laid his hands on his son's head with Pratt as they "administered with all confidence in the authority he held, and *Rebuked* the *disease* in the *name of Jesus Christ*, and said the child should begin to recover from that very hour." Mrs. Dexter, "a good sensible bible reading woman" who boarded in Mace's house with her sick daughter and her daughter's infant, observed the ordinance. The next morning, Mace recorded, "I went to my shop to work. About ten o'clock my wife sent a messenger to me saying the child was well and playful. I went home immediately and found it was even so. Oh what joy swelled our hearts as we gazed upon the child, so miraculously healed."[131]

Meanwhile, Mrs. Dexter's daughter and her infant were now both on the brink of death. With the doctor expressing no hope, she sent for the Mormon apostle. He brought Fordham with him.

Together they sang a hymn to soft sweet music.... When the hymn was ended, Elder Pratt offered up prayer. He then explained the principles of the Gospel as he had done on the previous occasion, the sick woman listened attentively and at her request Elders Pratt and Fordham administered to her, and also her babe. And they began to mend from that hour.[132]

Pratt himself recorded several other instances of healings in New York. He dryly noted what he considered a typical response to the cure of a crippled woman: "Her physician was immediately dismissed, and was very angry, because we had spoiled his patronage. He even threatened to sue us."[133]

Cases such as these, which rapidly circulated as rumors attesting to either fraud or divine favor, often stirred up interest in the Mormon message. Origen Bachelor acknowledged as much when he said Pratt won public attention as he "began to reveal himself as a Mormon miracle-monger."[134] For Baconians like Pratt, a primitivism that included a return to the miraculous confirmed his view of true religion as evidentiary, supported by empirical evidence like healing. But for most Restorationists, emulating the Christianity of the New Testament stopped short of spiritual gifts such as healing. Consequently, along with the Book of Mormon, faith healing became one of the more conspicuous markers of Mormon difference on the nineteenth-century religious landscape, and Pratt adverted to many cases in his own ministry. Faith healing among American Christians was uncommon enough that authors and pamphleteers usually had to go across the Atlantic to find modern instances to denounce. The Shakers' Mother Ann Lee was one exception, and the more obscure "Mr. Austin," the "prophet of Colchester," Vermont, another.[135] But in general, disapproving clergymen associated it with past pseudo-prophets of the old world like George Fox and Emanuel Swedenborg or recent Scottish outbreaks of charismata.[136]

Pratt's long-sought success prolonged his stay in the city, but so did a gauntlet thrown down in the religious press by La Roy Sunderland, a revivalist preacher and social reformer. In 1834, he presided at the organization of the first Methodist anti-slavery society, and the next year helped found and became editor of *Zion's Watchman*, organ of the movement. Sunderland would transition from preacher to abolitionist then on to mesmerism, spiritualism, and atheism before his career ended. But in 1838, enough of the Christian apologist remained for Mormonism to arouse his ire.[137]

The increasingly wide dissemination of Pratt's *Voice of Warning* prompted Sunderland to publish a weekly series of eight installments on Mormonism in the first months of 1838. The intensity of his denunciations must have struck a sensitive chord in a man who had already suffered expulsion from his home as a result of sectarian rhetoric that rapidly escalated to violence in

Missouri. Sunderland condemned Mormonism as "a delusion...manifestly and monstrously absurd," "nonsense and blasphemy," and full of "monstrous libels upon truth and religion" and "exceeding wickedness." Such hyperbole aside, the series provides an important window into the representation of Mormonism in the popular press of Pratt's day, and emphasizes the pivotal role he had in shaping that image. Tellingly, Sunderland described Mormonism as based on three texts—the Book of Mormon, the Doctrine and Covenants, and *Voice of Warning*—and blasted Mormons for believing each to be the product of the "inspiration of God."[138] Pratt corrected a number of Sunderland's statements, but let stand his characterization of *Voice* as part of an inspired trilogy.

Outrages to Christian sensibility that Sunderland enumerated included the doctrine of "infallible inspiration," spiritual gifts accessible to all members, visitations by angels, exclusive salvation, and a New Jerusalem situated in Missouri. Pratt responded immediately with *Mormonism Unveiled; Zion's Watchman Unmasked*—the first Mormon tract published as a reply to an anti-Mormon work. Wholly intemperate in its language, at least by modern standards, Pratt's work has the verbal verve and fury of a bare-knuckled brawl. Sunderland, his antagonist, is "guilty of the most glaring falsehoods, misrepresentations, and lying slanders, that ever disgraced humanity," and is "justly ranked among dogs, sorcerers, whoremongers," not "fit to fill any place in civilized society."[139] Some of Sunderland's writings were indeed misrepresentations, while others were trivial misstatements. Most of the dispute simply hinged, as religious debates often do, on opposing interpretations of biblical passages. In his pamphlet, as in *Voice of Warning*, Pratt emphasized prophecies, gifts and miracles, and ordinances performed by proper authority as the best evidences of Mormonism's truthfulness. All of this is so much shadowboxing. Exchanging insults, quoting scripture, claiming the upper hand in authority or logic is the stuff of sectarian pamphlet wars. But this pamphlet went far beyond verbal sparring to push Mormonism in significant new theological directions.

Until Pratt, Mormon missionaries rarely responded in print to criticisms from without. They had largely replied in oral debates, as Joseph Smith and Sidney Rigdon had been enjoined by an 1831 revelation: "Confound your enemies; call upon them to meet you both in public and in private."[140] Mormon apologists who ventured into print often emphasized commonalities with Christian tradition. Even Joseph Smith, in his Articles of Faith written in 1842, would neglect to mention most doctrines distinctive to Mormons—premortal existence, God's corporeality, and theosis (human divinization)—suggesting instead a Trinitarianism and Christology shared with most Christians. Pratt, on the other hand, gave Protestant writers a target painted in florescent colors. Perhaps he had a deliberate strategy in mind. Most early anti-Mormon polemics focused on the "imposture" motif in the new faith. Critics accused Smith of fraudulent claims, sham miracles and healings, and a plagiarized book of scripture. Alleging simple deception, detractors steered the debates away from serious theological engagement with Mormon beliefs.[141]

Pratt injected doctrine into discussion in ways impossible to ignore. In his reply to Sunderland, he chose provocation over prevarication twice. First, he defended humanity's limitless potential. While Pratt's more secular contemporaries and "spiritualizing" postmillennialists put hope in the perfectibility of human society, he emphasized the literal perfectibility of the individual. Pratt, as with Smith and Cowdery, incorporated deeply ingrained political values (such as radical equality, fierce individualism, and love of liberty) into religious views. He noted that Sunderland objected to Mormons "placing themselves on a level with the Apostles." He replied unapologetically, "This, we acknowledge, of course, for they were men of Adam's fallen race, just like every body else by nature....I know of nothing but equality in the Church of Christ."[142] But Pratt pushed his point much further. Sunderland indignantly quoted the Saints as believing that they "shall be filled with glory, and be equal with [Christ]," a paraphrase of Doctrine and Covenants 7:33 (1835). While the Bible contains similar phraseology (such as the "joint heirs" of Romans 8:17), Pratt ignored the innocuous readings of precedent and pushed possible metaphor into a literal reference to theosis. Indeed, he proclaimed, "They [will] have the same knowledge that God has, [and] they will have the same power....Hence the propriety of calling them 'Gods, even the sons of God' "[143] The latter language came from one of Smith's revelations, but it had never been explicated in print to mean literal deification.[144] Other Christians may call this blasphemy, Pratt suggested, yet he would not retreat from "this doctrine of *equality*." He gave a clear intimation of Mormonism's most audacious doctrine, not taught publicly by Smith until six years later in his King Follett sermon. That Pratt had something in mind far more radical than Methodist notions of perfectionism, for instance, is suggested by the avidity with which he later expanded Smith's teachings into the planet-peopling, world-shaping, system-building model of deification known to nineteenth-century Mormonism.

Pratt's elaboration vaguely hinted at a Neoplatonic concept of preexistence coupled with theosis. The concept may have connection to revelations dating to 1832 and 1833. In the first, one of the most esoteric and cryptic of any he produced, Smith identified the "name of God in pure Language" as Awman, "the being which made all things in all its parts." Christ is called the "Son Awman" and "the greatest of all the parts of Awman," while members of the human family are "the greatest parts of Awman Sons" [Awman's Son?].[145] A year later, Frederick Williams recorded a revelation according to which Enoch "saw the begining the ending of man he saw the time when Adam his father was made and he saw that he was in eternity before a grain of dust in the ballance was weighed he saw that he emenated and came down from God."[146] Pratt faintly echoed this language to Sunderland: "The redeemed return to the fountain, and become *part* of the great *all*, from which they emanated."[147] The two revelations and Pratt's response to Sunderland represent in embryo the collapse of the ontological distinction between God and man that would result in Pratt's later succinct declaration that "God, angels and men are all of one species."[148]

Pratt took Mormon blasphemy a step further a few pages later, when he implicitly introduced an emphatically non-creedal conception of God, without Sunderland even having referred to the belief. Pratt mocked the Methodist Episcopal Church for believing (as did all who subscribed to the Westminster Confession of 1646), in "a God without body or parts." Why worship a God, he wondered, "who has no ears, mouth, nor eyes," adding with humorous sarcasm, "that we do not love, serve, nor fear your God; and if he has been blasphemed, let him speak and plead his own cause: but this he cannot do, seeing he has no mouth. And how he ever revealed his choice of La Roy Sunderland, as a 'Watchman' for his Zion, I am at a loss to determine." On the other hand, Mormons, he affirmed without apology, "worship a God, who has both body and parts; who has eyes, mouth, and ears, and who speaks when he pleases."[149] Pratt was not asserting a God with a body of flesh and blood, a doctrine he explicitly denied in a tract written a few years later. ("The Father is not composed of such gross materials," he wrote there.)[150] Still, he was moving decidedly in the direction of a corporeal deity. In any case, the fine distinctions between physical bodies and spiritual bodies seem to have been lost on some outsiders. Like Pratt, Warren Cowdery had criticized the God "without body or parts" in an article in 1836.[151] While Cowdery wrote in a Mormon periodical for a Mormon audience, others seem to have been listening. Anthropomorphism would naturally be associated with physicality, and in that same year, a Presbyterian minister from Kirtland wrote that Mormons believed in a "material being."[152]

In any event, Pratt's explicit pronouncements in his 1838 pamphlet were forcing Mormonism's most heterodox teachings into the public arena. He excelled in emphasizing radical difference, not commonality. And yet, he insisted, those doctrines were nothing new. In spite of charges that he was teaching "strange and...novel truths," he later told an audience, "I know nothing new, nothing wherein we are innovators."[153]

5

"Strong Dungeons and Gloomy Prisons"

You will be dragged before the authorities for the religion
you profess; and it were better not to set out than to
start, look back, or shrink when dangers thicken upon,
or appalling death stares you in the face. I have spoken
these things, dear brother, because I have seen them in
visions. There are strong dungeons and gloomy prisons
for you. These should not appall you. You must be called
a good or bad man. The ancients passed through the
same.

—OLIVER COWDERY, *1835, quoted in Parley Pratt's*
Autobiography

IF 1837 AND the Kirtland conflicts gave Pratt the severest test of his spiritual
mettle, the next year proved the hardest to his physical and mental constitution.
In 1838, Pratt and thousands of his coreligionists suffered devastating losses,
exile from their homes, and occasionally death at the hands of Missouri mobs.
Already a proven writer, Pratt would transform his experience of long imprisonment in a squalid cell into the century's most influential narrative of
Mormon persecution.

Spring 1838 began auspiciously enough. In April, he wrapped up his work
in New York. His success in the city had been relatively meager, though proselytizing sallies from the city had resulted in branches in Sing Sing, Brooklyn,
and other nearby towns, and members had been baptized as far away as
Holliston, Massachusetts. Departing with a band of converts, he journeyed
not back to Kirtland, but to Missouri. For several years, Mormon gathering
had been divided between the Ohio headquarters and sites in Missouri, but
the bulk of the population was shifting to the latter as early as July 1831, when
a revelation positively identified it as "the place for the city of Zion."[1] It was
not until April 1838, however, as Pratt wended his way west, that the church
hierarchy unanimously resolved to build a temple in the new Missouri
Mormon headquarters of Far West, Caldwell County, which was identified as

consecrated land and the place of gathering.[2] Joseph Smith had moved there in January 1838, fleeing Kirtland with Sidney Rigdon in the dead of night, their lives in peril from dissenters. Defections resulting from the previous year's strife had stripped almost half the apostolic quorum away. At a conference on April 7, David Patten said he could affirm only Marsh, Young, Hyde, Kimball, and the Pratt brothers "as being men of God whom he could recommend with cheerful confidence."[3]

On May 7, Pratt and his family arrived in Caldwell County and were warmly greeted by Smith. As in Kirtland the year previous, Pratt showed a knack for showing up on the very cusp of acute crisis. Although Missourians had forced the Mormons to retreat from their homes in Jackson County in 1833 and in Clay County a few years later, this time the Mormons were more recalcitrant. Pratt, remembering the land he lost in the earlier expulsions, was determined to put down stakes again. Immediately upon arriving, he wrote, "I again commenced anew; built a house and made a farm."[4] With the laying of the cornerstone for the Far West temple just weeks away, a date decreed by revelation as July 4, Pratt must have felt divine intervention would secure the Saints in their homes this time, in spite of gathering clouds that indicated a coming tempest. As in Kirtland, the problems involved the dissent of former stalwarts; this time the opposition was led by the Whitmers, W. W. Phelps, and Oliver Cowdery. David Whitmer had until recently presided over the church in Far West. John Whitmer, his brother and counselor, and Phelps, his other counselor, had largely been responsible for laying out and administering the city—"without asking or seeking council," reported Thomas Marsh. Indeed, Marsh alleged they had "purchased land with Church funds, in their own name, for their own agrandisement."[5] This seemed a conspicuous instance of ecclesiastical leaders profiteering from their positions, though here as in Pratt's experience, the financial pressures on a self-supporting clergy could blur the venal and the entrepreneurial. Nevertheless, wherever converts poured into gathering places, greed and exploitation of latecomers tempted the weak, or so it seemed to onlookers. With the return of Smith to Far West, personality clashes and jealousy over ecclesiastical jurisdictions and differing visions of church-state separation added to the ill feeling, as did lingering bitterness over the Kirtland Bank and suspicions by some that Joseph Smith was a polygamist. Along with Cowdery, the Whitmers and Phelps were charged with attempting to sell their Jackson County holdings, a display of unbelief in God's promises. All four were removed from their leadership positions in January, then cut off from the church a few months later.

The situation became more precarious when these dissenters spread allegations against Smith and others among a larger public. Missourians had not been tolerant of Mormon ways in other counties, and the mix of vocal dissent and hostile "gentiles" was especially volatile. Mormons exacerbated Missouri suspicions of their motives with their militant language. Smith may have associated his mission, as early as 1823, with the kingdom building described by Daniel.[6] During the Missouri years, the project of establishing Zion was colored increasingly by the Old Testament prophet's image of a stone that "became a great mountain, and filled the whole earth."[7] Pratt had devoted considerable attention to the Daniel passages in his *Voice of Warning*. "A greater *blunder* could not exist," he wrote, than to believe the prophesied kingdom had reference to the church organized by Christ. "When we speak of the kingdom of God," he said, "we wish to be understood as speaking of his organized government on earth." This kingdom entails "first, a king ['the Lord Jesus']; second, commissioned officers,...thirdly, a code of laws,...and fourthly, subjects who are governed. Now, where these exist in their proper order and regular authority, there is a kingdom." Based on those criteria, he declared, "we have at length discovered the kingdom of God, as it existed at its first organization." But its present incarnation, centered in Missouri, had one difference from its New Testament predecessor, he wrote portentously. According to Daniel, the latter-day version "is never to change masters, like all kingdoms which have gone before it. It was never to be left to other people. It was to break in pieces all these [other] kingdoms and stand forever....All the powers of earth and hell will not impede its progress."[8] By 1838, the Saints' public invocation of Daniel 2:44–45, with its reference to a kingdom that should "break in pieces and consume" all other kingdoms, was common enough—and threatening enough—to be invoked at a court of inquiry as evidence of nefarious Mormon designs.[9]

Rigdon exacerbated tensions with an inflammatory sermon on June 17 in which he ominously warned dissenters they would be "trodden under foot," then followed up with a rousing July 4 tirade in which he invoked the specter of a "war of extermination" against mobocracy. In this round of harassment, he thundered, with an approving Smith on the stand, that the Saints would stand up for their rights "until death." Even other Mormons came to recognize that Rigdon's words were catastrophically ill conceived.[10] In a further and fatal development, Mormon "Danites" intimidated dissenters into leaving the area. The Danites have long been viewed by many scholars as a secretive, militant group of vigilantes operating with Smith's approval or knowledge and modeled on the warrior Old Testament tribe of Dan, but the best evidence suggests a different genesis. Contemporary Mormon Albert Perry Rockwood described an open organization based on the Book of Daniel, which oversaw defense of Mormon settlements as well as provisioning, construction, and communications. Along with many of his comrades, Sampson Avard, an officer in the Danite organization, grew exasperated at the depredations of the anti-Mormons, and began to reply with equal aggression. Most likely, Smith initially approved of the Danites' intention to "clense the Church" but withdrew support and disavowed Avard when they grew more violent. Once captured, Avard defected and turned state's evidence against the Saints.[11]

As the crisis deepened, Smith and his counselors chose four new apostles—John Page, George A. Smith, and future church presidents John Taylor and Wilford Woodruff—to replace those who had been ejected. In addition to the previously excommunicated apostles John Boynton and Lyman and Luke Johnson, William McLellin was dropped in May. Pratt was told to write his brother Orson, on a mission in New York, and inform him to gather with the full quorum in Far West immediately.[12] At this critical moment, La Roy Sunderland's newspaper *Zion's Watchman* published Pratt's earlier, intemperate tirade against Smith and Rigdon, adding to public unrest and Pratt's embarrassment. Meanwhile, reports of Rigdon's speeches circulated in the press, inflaming old settlers' suspicions and antagonisms. A compounding factor was the Missourians' understanding that when the Mormons fled Clay County in 1836, they would confine their relocation to Caldwell County, newly created for that purpose. But they soon spilled over into Daviess and other adjoining counties in a growing influx. Added to alarm at the growing threat of Mormon political domination through sheer numbers—some eight thousand Mormons were now in northern Missouri—these factors sparked a brawl at a polling site in Gallatin, in Daviess County, when Mormons tried to vote in state elections on August 6. The fracas left more bruised and bloodied Missourians than Mormons, and with exaggerated tales of violence spreading on both sides, the conflict spiraled out of control. Communities met in emergency councils and passed resolutions, and armed vigilantes were soon riding down on Mormon settlements, assaulting and terrorizing Mormons. Mormons for their part engaged in their own raids of retribution, but the odds were lopsided, with mobs and state militia working in concert, well armed and even possessing artillery.[13] At this critical time, Pratt was called away on church business, leaving pregnant Mary Ann and their daughter in a half-completed, unroofed cabin. Her plight was dreadful, but not atypical. From 1830 to 1899, almost thirteen thousand Mormon missionaries were called, most of them leaving behind families for service afield that lasted for a few months up to six years.[14] Family friend Isaac Allred checked on Mary Ann and her daughter after a heavy storm and, finding them half inundated, moved them to his farm. "My mother had her bed in a smoke house," daughter Mary Ann recalled, "and on 31 August 1838 my little brother Nathan was born."[15]

The Saints continued to act in defiance of the writing on the wall, enlarging farms and holdings into the fall. On October 7, Mormon settler Warren Foote recorded, "we have bargained for 80 acres of…land," even as he observed in the next sentence, "we heard today, that the mob commenced firing on the 'Mormons' at De Wit, in Carroll county."[16] Days later, those besieged Saints fled Carroll County and moved west to Caldwell County, but most of that region erupted in violence as well. In mid-October, a mob destroyed Pratt's unfinished house. With Nathan only six weeks old, they moved to Far West, into a crude log hut only nine feet square.[17] In Daviess County, where the violence originated, raiders pillaged outlying Mormon homes and farms, and the Mormons retaliated in kind. Hearing of mob depredations in a Mormon settlement there, Adam-ondi-Ahman, Smith asked for volunteers to assist the Saints, with county judge Elias Higbee, a Mormon, issuing the orders. Pratt headed north to the settlement with a Mormon militia unit on October 15, as David Patten's second in command. Ebenezer Robinson, serving alongside Pratt as second lieutenant, captured the mood of the times when he recorded that "there were large numbers of armed men gathering in Daviess County, with avowed determination of driving the Mormons from the county, and we began to feel as determined that the Missourians should be expelled from the county."[18] Increasingly, Mormons took the offensive, losing much of the moral high ground as they did so. On October 18, they attacked the village of Gallatin, pillaging and burning. One hostile witness put Pratt at the scene, ordering men to remove goods from a house before setting it afire.[19]

A third front in the war opened when defecting Mormon leaders, including Thomas Marsh, visited Ray County to the south and swore out affidavits that Mormons were contemplating action against Liberty and Richmond, seats of Clay and Ray counties, respectively. David Atchison, a major general in the state militia, authorized a militia unit to patrol the border area between Ray and Caldwell. Ray militia leader Samuel Bogart instead ventured into Caldwell County, harassing Saints and taking three prisoners, in what was supposed to be the Mormon county of sanctuary. Back in Far West, the alarming news came to Pratt and others "in the middle of a dark and gloomy night of October." To the south, they learned, "a party of the enemy were

plundering houses, carrying off prisoners, killing cattle, ordering families out
of their houses, on pain of having them burned over their heads."[20] In the early
morning hours of October 25, Pratt joined a rescue posse that began with
about forty and gained twenty more men en route. As on the Gallatin raid,
Patten, the senior apostle with Marsh's defection, led the troops. Rumors that
the mob planned to execute three Mormon prisoners at dawn added to the
sense of alarm and urgency.

Years later, Pratt cast the episode as a chivalric rescue by a band of brothers
worthy of a tale by Sir Walter Scott. In his retrospective, romanticized description, Pratt may have been recalling Missouri Mormonism's last heroic gasp,
before treachery and overwhelming force replaced armed resistance with igno-
miny, imprisonment, and expulsion from the state. "The thousand meteors,"
he recalled of the posse's night march toward Crooked River,

> blazing in the distance like the camp-fires of some war host, threw a
> fitful gleam of light upon the distant sky, which many might have mis-
> taken for the Aurora Borealis. This scene, added to the silence of mid-
> night, the rumbling sound of the tramping steeds over the hard and
> dried surface of the plain, the clanking of swords in their scabbards, the
> occasional gleam of bright armor in the flickering firelight, the gloom
> of surrounding darkness, and the unknown destiny of the expedition,
> or even of the people who sent it forth; all combined to impress the
> mind with deep and solemn thoughts.[21]

After proceeding for two hours, Pratt's party dismounted to seek out the
enemy. Dividing into three groups, they converged on the supposed site of the
mob's camp, but found the terrain unoccupied. They then struck out together
for the banks of Crooked River. Hundreds of yards from the riverbank, they
were detected by a picket, who hailed them and ordered them to lay down
their arms. Instead, a Mormon musket misfired, and the sentry returned fire,
mortally wounding Patrick O'Banion, a non-Mormon serving as militia guide
for the Saints. The sentry and his companion guard retreated to the encampment, with the Mormons following close behind. Attacking a defensive
position without the element of surprise worked to the Mormons' fatal disad-
vantage. Patten, aptly nicknamed "Captain Fearnought," led a charge that
routed the defenders, but at the cost of his own life and that of several others,
including Gideon Carter, who died the next day. Only one Missourian
perished—Moses Rowland, shot from behind as he fled. Five others were
bloodied but survived.[22]

Contradictory accounts and mistaken identities utterly confused other particulars of the melee and its immediate aftermath. Pratt left out of his autobiography details that suggest just how vicious and desperate both sides became in the white heat of the conflict. Two Mormons reportedly intercepted a fleeing Missouri militiaman, Samuel Tarwater, and savagely slashed his face and head with corn knives, even after he fell into unconsciousness.[23] After the skirmish, Mormons took Missourian Wyatt Cravens prisoner but apparently released him hours later. Cravens suspected a plot to kill him, which he attempted to evade as he made his way to safety, but was shot and wounded from behind. Cravens testified of Pratt's presence at Crooked River but did not identify him as the assailant. However, an account written by Mormon John D. Lee forty years later, while facing execution for his role in the Mountain Meadows Massacre, accused Pratt of shooting Cravens. The lack of contemporary allegations against Pratt suggests the unreliability of Lee's statement. When a Missouri court charged Pratt with murder for his participation at Crooked River, his alleged victim was Moses Rowland, not Cravens.[24]

Besides the cultural and religious clashes between Mormons and Missourians, two historical circumstances contributed to the conflagration known as the Missouri War. One was the context for Pratt's reference to the "common boast that, as soon as we had completed our extensive improvements…they would drive us from the State, and once more enrich themselves with the spoils."[25] Preemption rights, based on laws first passed in 1830, allowed impoverished settlers to acquire unsettled land, with no payment required until a survey was completed and the land went on sale at a specified date. If they improved and inhabited the land they settled on, it gave them preferred status to buy it. By 1838, most of the land in Caldwell had been fully surveyed and was not eligible for preemption purchases. But the land in Daviess County had not been. Hence thousands of impoverished Mormons settled across the county and immediately began improvements. Months later, as surveys in those areas neared completion and the date of public sale (November 12) neared, the very preemption rights that had attracted the Saints became, in the words of one legal scholar, "an impetus for non-Mormon land speculators to force Mormons out of Missouri." As he explains, "The imminent vesting of those property rights further explains the frantic efforts to dislodge Mormons from their lands in Missouri altogether in late 1838."[26] Even observers who found the Mormons to be a "weak and credulous people" recognized those motives in the expulsions:

The Anti-Mormons were determined the Mormons should yield and abandon the country. Moreover the land sales were approaching, and it was expedient that they should be driven out before they could establish their rights of pre-emption. In this way their valuable improvements—the fruit of diligence and enterprise—would pass into the hands of men who would have the pleasure of enjoying without the toil of earning.[27]

The ploy was successful. Those who played key roles in the Mormon expulsions immediately swept in and bought up nearly eighteen thousand improved acres in Daviess County alone.[28]

The second important element was the role and behavior of state militias. The federal Second Militia Act of 1792 had mandated the conscription of able-bodied white male citizens ages 18 to 45 into state-sponsored militias under the command of each state's governor. By the 1830s, most citizens resisted or ignored mandatory militia service, and volunteer militias generally replaced the common militia.[29] Volunteers who organized themselves into units of sufficient size, equipping themselves and electing their own officers, could apply for a state charter under names they chose. Militia service was particularly popular in Missouri, partly as a consequence of American Indian unrest; three times in the 1830s, the governor called out the militia to deal with Indian disturbances. In addition, it reflected a frontier ethic that tended toward rough-hewn independence and violence. Militia units had been notoriously ill trained and unreliable dating back to Revolutionary times, and Missouri's Black Hawk war of 1832 revealed the same weaknesses. As a result, men were required to muster with the militia four times a year, though the occasions generally took the form of diversion and public spectacle rather than serious military training.[30]

On the Missouri frontier in antebellum America, the line between mobs and these militia units was sometimes fluid or nebulous. The operative principle seemed to be that anything public opinion considered a threat to American values was fair game; depending on the moment and setting, that could mean Irish shanty towns, Catholic convents, abolitionist newspapers, or Mormons. In New York in 1835, two years before the height of the Missouri conflict, a Democratic congressman led a mob that destroyed an abolitionist newspaper office. One year earlier in 1834, armed Democrat Party loyalists chased Whigs from a polling place in New York, foreshadowing the Gallatin polling violence that launched the last stage of the Missouri War.[31] In fact, the 1830s have been called the high point of extralegal violence in America with dozens of public riots, some of which involved volunteer militias.[32] In the Jacksonian era generally, political and economic leaders, "gentlemen of property and standing," led both mobs and the local militia—and sometimes both, rendering distinctions almost meaningless.[33] In Missouri, Mormons repeatedly identified prominent leaders at the head of mobs and militias alike. The blurring raised a crucial legal question: Did the call to action formally originate in state authority? This was the implicit question recognized by the judge in the case of a group led by Grandison Newell in Mentor, Ohio, that disrupted Pratt's preaching. Since on the Missouri frontier the modus operandi of mobs and militia turned out to be the same, uncertainty as to the legal status of an armed group could confuse both sides. Missouri militia often behaved against the Mormons like mobs, and Mormon militia reprisals gave little appearance of being within the law.

In the Battle of Crooked River, the blurred boundaries between mob and militia had especially tragic repercussions. The Missouri men attacked by Patten's company operated as a unit of state militia, even if their actions were more vigilante than soldierly. On the other side, Patten was a captain in a different unit of the state militia, and his men acted under authorization of Elias Higbee, Caldwell County judge. Mormons thought themselves legally constituted as a militia unit to defend themselves against lawless aggressors. State officials saw the Mormons as lawless fanatics operating against authorized militia units. Weeks later, when John B. Clark, major-general in command of the Missouri militia, prepared to court-martial Mormon leaders in Richmond, he seemed astonished to learn they had themselves been acting as part of a militia unit. In a discussion with Pratt, he referred to Mormon George M. Hinkle as "your commanding officer." Pratt replied in dismay,

> "Colonel Hinkle, our commanding officer! What had he to do with our civil rights? He was only a colonel of a regiment of the Caldwell County Militia."
>
> "Why! was he not the commanding officer of the fortress of Far West, the headquarters of the *Mormon forces*?"
>
> "We had no '*fortress*' or '*Mormon forces*,' but were part of the State militia."
>
> At this the general seemed surprised, and the conversation ended.[34]

Nevertheless, in the eyes of Missouri officials, Mormons had attacked state militia at Crooked River, thereby crossing a line that put them squarely outside the law and made them enemies of the state. That perception, added to exaggerated reports of the Crooked River casualties, led to the famous

FIGURE 5.1 C. C. A. Christensen (1831–1912), *The Battle of Crooked River*, ca. 1865. Tempera on muslin, 78 x 114 inches. Courtesy of Brigham Young Museum of Art, gift of the Christensen Grandchildren.

extermination order of Governor Lilburn Boggs dated October 27. The dénouement to the Missouri tragedy followed quickly.

Rigdon had earlier invoked extermination in his fiery July 4 sermon. Three months later, on October 4, Major General Samuel D. Lucas, a Jackson County nemesis of the Saints, wrote Boggs, predicting hopefully that Mormon perfidy would lead "those base and degraded beings [to] be exterminated from the face of the earth."[35] The night after Crooked River, Judge E. M. Ryland of Lexington wrote to Ray County leaders that citizen volunteers must rise up "with the full determination to exterminate or expel the [Mormons] from the State enmasse."[36] That report reached Boggs on October 27, and he officially endorsed its sentiments and language. "The Mormons must be treated as enemies," he wrote to Atchison's replacement, General John Clark, "and must be exterminated or driven from the State if necessary for the public peace—their outrages are beyond description."[37]

As militia and mobs gathered, most Mormons consolidated their positions in Adam-ondi-Ahman in Daviess County and Far West in Caldwell County. Residents of Haun's Mill, a small settlement in the eastern part of the latter county, chose to dig in there. Three days after Boggs's order, but probably acting without knowledge of their license to "exterminate" Mormons, 250 militiamen rode into Haun's Mill. The Missourians attacked Mormon men and boys barricaded in a blacksmith shop, killing eighteen with guns and corn knives. That same day, Joseph Smith was looking for a way to avoid the anni-hilation of his people massed in Far West. Mormon leaders only now learned that they had attacked a state militia unit at Crooked River, rendering their position hopeless. Some twenty-five hundred state troops under General Lucas were already beginning to encircle the town. The next morning, a rider brought word of the massacre at Haun's Mill, confirming the utter despera-tion of their situation. Smith authorized Colonel George Hinkle to sue for peace with the troops on the morning of October 31. In the meantime, fearing that the Crooked River participants would be "tried by a court martial and shot," leaders urged them to flee the area immediately.[38] Some three dozen escaped the state over the following days.[39] Pratt, however, would not leave.

Lucas stalled for several hours. He had received the governor's extermina-tion order and knew he held all the cards. Meeting the afternoon of October 31 with the Mormon negotiators, Lucas read them Boggs's order and imposed draconian surrender terms: the surrender of all their leaders, responsibility for full monetary restitution of war costs, confiscation of all their property, and expulsion from the state.[40] When Hinkle asked for time to consider the terms, Lucas demanded five hostages by sundown: Joseph Smith; his counselor Sidney Rigdon; Lyman Wight, leader of the Daviess County militia; George Robinson, clerk to the First Presidency; and Pratt. Pratt's fate was virtually sealed, not only because as an apostle he was a senior leader, but also because Lucas stipu-lated that participants in the Crooked River battle would be tried as criminals. Nevertheless, Pratt, Smith, and the others gave themselves up to Lucas that evening, understanding they would discuss surrender terms. Instead, they were immediately taken prisoner, treated harshly, and pressured to order the sur-render of Far West at peril of the destruction of the city and its people. Pratt, like most of his colleagues, insisted that they had been duped by Hinkle into giving themselves up to Lucas. In reality, they willingly surrendered, but appar-ently were led by Hinkle to believe there was still room for negotiation of terms. Given their immediate reduction to powerlessness and imprisonment, they naturally felt betrayed and blamed their chief "negotiator," though Hinkle could only listen impotently to the unconditional surrender terms dictated by Lucas. Under the circumstances, including an undisciplined militia bent on pillage and revenge, the carte blanche for punitive action issued by Boggs, and the lack of the Mormons' own legal or moral standing in their enemies' eyes, the treatment of the captives was not surprising.

Five years later, in a legal deposition, Pratt testified that the prisoners "were continually surrounded with a strong guard whose mouths were filled with cursing & bitterness blackguardism & blasphemy who offered us every abuse & insult in their power both night & day, and many individuals of the army cocked their rifles and taking deliberate aim at our heads swore they would shoot us." The soldiers bragged of "having the previous day disarmed a certain man in his own house & took him prisoner & afterwards beat out his brains with his own gun in presence of their officers they told of other individuals laying here & there in the brush whom they had shot down without resistance & who were laying unburied for the hogs to feed upon." Furthermore, "one or two individual females of our society" had been "forcibly bound & twenty or thirty of them one after another committed rape upon." (Pratt later confirmed one case of rape with the woman's family.)[41]

The next morning, November 1, Smith sent word for the defenders of Far West to submit to surrender terms. Many of the Mormons bristled at the decision, but the Saints gave up their weapons as ordered. The day's last development, however, was too much even for one of the militia generals to countenance. "We were informed," recalled Pratt, "that the general officers held a secret council during most of the night, which was dignified by the name of court martial; in which, without a hearing, or, without even being brought before it, we were all sentenced to be shot. The day and hour was also appointed for the execution of this sentence, viz: next morning at 8 o'clock, in the public square at Far West."[42] The death sentence included the five Mormon leaders previously taken (Joseph Smith, Rigdon, Wight, Robinson, and Pratt), as well as Hyrum Smith, Joseph's brother and second counselor, and Amasa Lyman, a Mormon militiaman and spy, who had been arrested the day previous. Lucas justified the proceedings because, knowing the Mormons had acted as a legally recognized militia, he considered them subject to military law and jurisdiction. However, the Smiths and Rigdon claimed a clergyman exemption from militia service. As one of General Alexander Doniphan's militiamen recognized, "These men [the Smiths and Rigdon] never belonged to any lawful organization, and could not, therefore, have violated military law."[43] Doniphan, who had earlier acted as Joseph Smith's attorney and was ever after revered by Mormons for his intercession, protested the planned executions, swearing he would withdraw with his brigade rather than countenance the decision, and that he would hold Lucas legally responsible if he proceeded. Even though the other four prisoners, including Pratt, belonged to a militia and fell under the jurisdiction of the court-martial, Lucas backed down.[44]

Throughout the ordeal, Pratt and the others reasonably expected the worst. Even so, Wight remained as fierce and defiant as a mad bull. Offered clemency if he defected, he declined the offer. Told he would then be shot with the others, he replied, "Shoot, and be damned."[45] Instead of the planned execution, on the morning of November 2 the men of Far West assembled in the town square, signed over all their property to militia commissioners, and then took oaths that they did so voluntarily.

Meanwhile, the Mormon leaders were trundled off more than forty miles southward to Jackson County. Lucas delegated Brigadier General Moses Wilson, with three hundred troops, to escort the prisoners. Before they set out, they were permitted brief farewells to their families. Pratt found his wife in bed with a fever and their infant son, Nathan, at her breast, young Mary Ann at her side, and an indigent neighbor taking shelter at the foot of the bed. Overcome by his family's pathetic circumstances and his own impotence, Pratt recalled, "I stepped to the bed; my wife burst into tears; I spoke a few words of comfort, telling her to try to live for my sake and the children's; and expressing a hope that we should meet again though years might separate us. She promised to try to live. I then embraced and kissed the little babes and departed."[46]

Pratt pleaded with Wilson to allow him to stay with his family but was summarily herded with his brethren in the direction of Independence, the Jackson County seat. Wilson's conduct over the next days proved bizarrely at odds with the militia's prior behavior. According to Pratt, Wilson confessed to the prisoners as they camped at Crooked River that night that "we know perfectly that from the beginning the Mormons have not been the aggressors at all.... We mob you without law; the authorities refuse to protect you according to law; you then are compelled to protect yourselves, and we act upon the prejudices of the public, who join our forces, and the whole is legalized, for your destruction and our gain. Is not this a shrewd and cunning policy on our part, gentlemen?" At the same time, he promised there were no hard feelings for their resistance: "No blame, gentlemen; we deserved it. And let a set of men serve me as your community have been served, and I'll be damn'd if I would not fight till I died." Then he insisted, protectively, that "I'll be damn'd if anybody shall hurt you."[47]

Whether or not Wilson was quite that forthcoming in acknowledging the injustices which he had helped conduct and oversee over five years, he clearly saw political benefits for himself in putting the prisoners on display. A few years later, Pratt bitterly recalled that the prisoners "were exhibited like a caravan of wild animals on the way & in the streets of Independence & were also kept prisoner for a show for several days."[48] At the time, however, in a letter to Mary Ann, Pratt lauded the actions of the "oficers and troops" of Jackson

County, for showing them "that Respect, honor and kindness towards us, which we would have Expected from Brethren." Pratt even stated that a few days of kind treatment "has in a great measure attoned for their former trespasses, and has restored the Best of feelings Between us and them." Given the circumstances of earlier oaths "freely undertaken" at the point of a bayonet, one wonders if Mary Ann doubted the veracity of a tale in which Pratt's company were feted as curiosities rather than as despised traitors doomed to the gallows:

> We fared Even Better on the way than their own troops. Our Meals were served to us In the Best Manner with Plenty of Coffee and Shugar. We had the privilege of Sleeping In a tent with the officers, while Many of the troops Slept In the Open air; No person was suffered to Insult us or treat us with disrespect in the least; Crowds of Gentlemen and Ladys Thronged the way side to see us, and General Wilson often halted the troops to Introduce us to them. Many of Both sexes Shuck us warmly By the hand; and when we Arive In Independence we were provided with a Comfortable house, and a Noble fire, as the storm was very severe. There we spent the time In Conversation with the throngs who flocked to see us untill Supper, when we were guarded to a hotell and a Splendid Supper was Set Before us.[49]

Assuming that the harsh circumstances of the surrender and the surreal experience of their initial day in Independence had not distorted Pratt's sense of reality, he most likely understood that his letter to Mary Ann would be read by his captors. Indeed, in the same letter to Mary Ann, he counseled her, "If your Cows, Corn, or Other Property Is taken By the Soldiers, or If they offer any Insult or abuse, you Must Inform the officers of the guard And State to them that you are sick and your husband a Prisoner and no Doubt they will restore or Protect you." Hoping a show of deference and civility would improve their prospects, the prisoners similarly wrote a letter of thanks the next day, soon published in a local newspaper, to General Lucas and General Wilson (whom Pratt retrospectively condemned, without irony, as a "hardened murderer") along with the Jackson County citizens. They thanked them for being "friends at a time when we most needed them," and expressed prayers for their "prosperity in this life, and rest eternal in that which is to come."[50]

Their unexpected respite did not last long. The ranking officer, General John Clark, who had been preempted by Lucas in their rivalry to apprehend the "Mormon royalty," arrived in Far West with his troops on November 4. He sent a subordinate to Independence to escort the seven prisoners to Richmond, the county seat of Ray County, where the battle of Crooked River took place. While the prisoners were busy expressing their appreciation to their hosts in Independence, Clark rounded up almost fifty additional Mormons for prosecution. At this time, Pratt and his brethren were kept under a loosely enforced house arrest. Learning that Clark's troops were on their way to take them to Richmond and trial, Pratt decided he would "try an experiment."

> I arose one morning when it was very snowy, and passed silently and unmolested out of the hotel.... I passed on eastward through the town; no one noticed me.... Obscured by falling snow, my track was covered behind me, and I was free. I knew the way to the States eastward very well, and there seemed nothing to prevent my pursuing my way thither; thoughts of freedom beat high in my bosom; wife, children, home, freedom, peace, and a land of law and order, all arose in my mind; I could go to other States, send for my family, make me a home and be happy.

The experiment failed by the work of Pratt's conscience. Though tempted to escape, Pratt resolved, "never, while brother Joseph and his fellows are in the power of the enemy. What a storm of trouble, or even of death, it might subject them to." He returned to prison.[51]

On November 7, Pratt wrote to Mary Ann, he and the others were preparing for what they believed was a journey back to Far West "by way of Richmond, under a Strong Guard."[52] Richmond, however, twenty-five miles northeast, was clearly intended all along as their destination. Before they arrived, Clark sent a detachment to escort them into the town. In his first meeting with the prisoners, Pratt reported, Clark wanted to try the accused in a court-martial, as enemy combatants under the command of Mormon colonel George Hinkle. Circuit Court Judge Austin A. King thwarted Clark's hopes and ordered him to turn the men over to the local authorities for a court of inquiry, which began on November 12.

Once confined in Richmond, conditions for the seven prisoners went rapidly from humane to hellish, with a strong guard and heavy chains. Damning testimony against Smith and the others by high-level Mormon defectors such as Sampson Avard dampened any potential sympathy from local citizens. In a dangerously volatile decision, Samuel Bogart, whose men had been attacked

by Pratt and his colleagues at Crooked River, was given charge of the prisoners. Subjected to the mockery and abuse of hostile guards, the prisoners
suffered the further torment of listening to their captors boasting of "defiling
by force wives, daughters, and virgins, and of shooting or dashing out the
brains of men, women, and children."[53] In the midst of these conditions, Pratt
would famously recollect, Smith struck his persecutors silent with righteous
fury:

> On a sudden he arose to his feet, and spoke in a voice of thunder, or as
> the roaring lion, uttering, as near as I can recollect, the following
> words:
> "SILENCE, ye fiends of the infernal pit. In the name of Jesus Christ
> I rebuke you, and command you to be still; I will not live another
> minute and bear such language. Cease such talk, or you or I die THIS
> INSTANT!"
> He ceased to speak. He stood erect in terrible majesty. Chained,
> and without a weapon; calm, unruffled and dignified as an angel, he
> looked upon the quailing guards, whose weapons were lowered or
> dropped to the ground; whose knees smote together, and who,
> shrinking into a corner, or crouching at his feet, begged his pardon,
> and remained quiet till a change of guards.
> I have seen the ministers of justice, clothed in magisterial robes,
> and criminals arraigned before them, while life was suspended on a
> breath, in the Courts of England; I have witnessed a Congress in
> solemn session to give laws to nations; I have tried to conceive of kings,
> of royal courts, of thrones and crowns; and of emperors assembled to
> decide the fate of kingdoms; but dignity and majesty have I seen but
> once, as it stood in chains, at midnight, in a dungeon in an obscure
> village of Missouri.[54]

The passage, perhaps the most famous in Pratt's autobiography, has become a
prime ingredient in the hagiographic tradition surrounding Joseph
Smith. Written years after Smith's death, the account describes a hero of
inspiring proportions; if Pratt did not express such veneration during Smith's
lifetime, distance and the aura of martyrdom made it easier for Pratt, as his
disciple, to describe such a moment of mythic splendor. With his tendency
toward Victorian grandiloquence, his Manichean worldview, and sense of
poetic license, Pratt perhaps embellished the scene, which first appeared in
print almost two decades later. However, there is no reason to doubt the

FIGURE 5.2 Danquart Anthon Weggeland (1827–1928), *Joseph Smith Rebuking the Guard*. Courtesy Church History Museum, The Church of Jesus Christ of Latter-day Saints. Pratt was depicted kneeling immediately behind Smith.

essentials of the account.[55] On other recorded occasions, Smith subdued critics and won over enemies with his undeniable charisma, if not with thundering righteous indignation.[56]

The preliminary hearing before Judge King lasted more than two weeks and involved sixty-four defendants, most of them housed in the town's large, unfinished courthouse. Pratt remembered King as intensely hostile to the prisoners, telling one Mormon witness that if the Saints remained in Missouri past April 1, "the citizens will be upon you, they will kill you every one, men, women & children, leave you to manure the ground without a burial."[57] At the conclusion, four of Pratt's high-profile companions—Joseph and Hyrum Smith, Sidney Rigdon, and Lyman Wight—were charged, along with Caleb Baldwin and Alexander McRae, with treason and sent to Liberty Jail in Clay County. Pratt was held under murder charges for the death of Moses Rowland, killed at Crooked River. Also bound over for trial were four other Mormon participants in the battle who had been apprehended: Luman Gibbs, Morris Phelps, Darwin Chase, and Norman Shearer. King transferred these five and a dozen others to the Richmond Jail. Within a few days, all those aside from the Crooked River five were allowed to post bail and leave. Pratt and the rest settled in for a gloomy stay, as winter approached. Initially they had been housed in the debtors cell above the dungeon; with their numbers reduced, they were confined to the more squalid—and cramped—cell at ground level, with a kettle for a latrine, no windows, and coarse though plentiful food.

In his autobiography, Pratt spoke of the "cold, dark dungeon," a small, damp room accessible by a trap door from the floor above, where they spent months enduring the insults and abuse of the guards. But although they did sleep in the dungeon initially, they were allowed the freedom of the upper floor on most days, and they came to spend nights there as well.[58] The more humane conditions, though not a constant, were a welcome relief, as Pratt wrote to Mary Ann in early December: "The Jail Is somewhat Open and cold; But the Sherif has promised to furnish us with a good Stove and plenty of wood, and we have plenty to Eat,—and drink."[59]

Such close proximity under duress can forge powerful bonds—and equally potent tensions. The disposition of the group's oldest man, Luman Gibbs, drove the others to near desperation. He "greatly added to our affliction," Pratt remembered, "as if to complete our hell." He was "quarrelsome and noisy,... full of jealousy, extremely selfish" and "very weak minded."[60] But even in the most oppressive conditions, or especially in those, men seek a release from tension in humor, however dark. Gibbs sometimes provided such moments of comic relief, welcome to all his cellmates save Pratt, whose seriousness could frequently morph into dourness. Humor was well and good, as seen in his many pamphlets, if employed to unsettle a rhetorical foe. But in some contexts he could out-Calvin the Puritans, as Ebenezer Robinson recalled:

> A considerable snow had fallen, and the weather became severely cold by the first of December. An amusing scene occurred one cold night. Brother Luman Gibbs...lodged in the same bed with the writer, and after retiring for the night, he put his feet out of the bed and said: "Stay there and freeze, it serves you right; bring me here all the way from Vermont to be in prison for murder and never thought of killing anybody in all my life." The act was so unexpected and so ludicrous, it convulsed his fellow prisoners with laughter, except Parley P. Pratt, he seemed to get out of humor, and gave him a good scolding.[61]

From his cell, Pratt wrote Mary Ann and, reflecting a practice common in the Anglo-American world of the nineteenth century, invited her to soften his prison hardships by enduring them with him. In England and America, imprisoned debtors frequently brought their entire families into confinement with them, as Charles Dickens's father did in Marshalsea debtors prison just a decade earlier. Such a move not only gave comfort and companionship to the debtor but also sometimes provided better living conditions than those confronting a destitute and fatherless family outside. In Pratt's case, Mary Ann and the children faced poverty but also a community of fellow suffering Saints, and she had family in Maine where she could find refuge. Since she and Parley had spent less than eighteen months of married life together, and much of that in rented lodgings or a crude cabin, he was understandably timid about asking her to take up residence in a jail cell with several other prisoners. Still, he was not above playing upon her fears and guilt. His letter provides a glimpse of the freedom prisoners had to set up elaborate housekeeping; it is also a poignant portrait of a husband doing the best he can to lure his wife into the squalor of imprisonment with romanticized visions of a curtained boudoir and cozy domesticity.

It is now at your own Choice to come and spend the winter with me; Or to Live a lonely widow on a desolate prairiee, where you are not sure of a Living, or protection; If you Choose to come and winter with me, you will please Bring your other Bed and great Plenty of Beading So that we can hang a plenty of Curtains all round our Bed. Bring a Chest of Clothing Such as you need; Bring our table and 2 or 3 plates, a few Basons and a wash Bole; Bring all my Interesting Books and Espesially my Big Atlas; Bring all the wrighting paper and my Steel pens; In Short Bring Every thing you think we Shall need; I can pay your Board; and mine Is found me; You will have nothing to do but to Sit down and Study with me and Nerse your Little one;…I think it will Be much cheeper, and Easyer, and more comfortable for you to winter In jail with me than to Live where, you do; as you have none to help you: But take your own Choice.…If you do not come, you will please Send the Books paper and pens; you need not Be a fraid of the old jail for it is better than the hut where you now live.[62]

Pratt obviously anticipated a long stay, given the list of amenities he requested. With a curtained-off bed chamber and his personal library, Pratt would be comfortable and equipped to write. And his ultimate intention as a writer was to author a major history of the Mormon persecutions. To his sense of aggrievement at the hands of Mormonism's opponents was now added the sting of acute betrayal and misrepresentation. The authorities had captured the leader of the Danites' most militant wing, Sampson Avard, and in a portentous coup persuaded him to supply information against his fellow Mormons. Other disaffected members assisted the prosecution with little or no prodding. Learning of their damning testimony, Pratt lamented in a letter to Ruth Haven Rockwood (whose husband had described less sensationally the more mundane organizational scope of the Danites) that "the apostates have sworn to murder & Treason & almost evry thing against us which never entered our hearts to say or do but we are in the hands of God."[63]

Meanwhile, moved by loyalty, destitution, or both, Mary Ann joined Pratt in Richmond in early December with Nathan and Mary Ann, where they would spend three months at his side (Parley Jr. remained in the care of Mrs. Allen). Luman Gibbs's wife also came, but the quarrelsome pair provided more amusement to their cellmates than comfort to each other. Mary Ann, on the other hand, lifted Pratt's spirits, given her steadfast cheerfulness in the face of sorry circumstances. "I am Glad that I am Counted worthy to suffer afflictions for the Gospel sake," she wrote her parents from the jail. "I never lost one minuts sleep."[64] Parley described her as "all kindness and goodness and…a pattern of patience enduring all her afflictions with a cheerful meekness and resignation and acting as an angel of mercy."[65] Undoubtedly, both put the best face on events to allay the distress of her parents at Mary Ann's predicament. At the same time, initially at least, conditions were tolerable. Pratt spent his time writing to family and friends, composing poetry and hymns, and penning his account of the persecutions in Missouri.

Religious persecution has long existed uneasily alongside American rhetoric about religious freedom. By Pratt's day, the history of religious violence in America encompassed American Indians, Baptists, Jews, Shakers, Catholics, Quakers, black Christians, and others; violent outbreaks persisted against religious minorities, often tinged with racial or ethnic prejudice, well into the nineteenth century. Violence against Catholics, who were mostly new immigrants, was prevalent from the 1830s to the 1850s. Priests were assaulted, churches vandalized, Irish-Catholic shanty towns destroyed, a convent in Baltimore attacked and, in the most famous incident, a convent in Boston burned to the ground—not as a spontaneous act of violence but as the result of premeditated, coordinated action.[66]

Wherever religious persecution flares, the celebrated martyr is not far behind. The cult of the Christian martyr extends back to St. Stephen, but Protestants also learned to parley the violent demise of their faithful into mythologies both edifying and unifying.[67] First published in English in 1563, John Foxe's luridly anti-Catholic *Book of Martyrs* shaped generations of European and American Protestants and was a standard fixture in personal homes and village libraries in Pratt's day—including the Manchester Library of Joseph Smith's youth.[68] A vividly illustrated American edition of 1833 offered itself as "an antidote to the insidious poison [of the] professors of popery," who, it warned, were already invading and corrupting North America. The book kept alive not just a virulent strain of anti-Catholicism, but a vocabulary and template for a heroic type of suffering that still had contemporary relevance. The 1833 edition, for example, had an updated section on attacks on the Protestant churches through 1820. Suffering for Christ at the hands of a corrupt Christianity, in other words, was not relegated to a distant past captured in wood engravings of stoic saints. "The future," editor Charles Goodrich warned, "is not without its dangers, and the condition of the persecuted may fluctuate with the slightest political alteration."[69] American Protestants took such rhetoric seriously. Methodist itinerant preachers of the era, for instance, often spoke of the "unparalleled persecution they faced." Francis Asbury, America's leading Methodist until his death in 1816, claimed, "Mine are apostolic sufferings."[70]

Pratt likewise saw himself in the tradition of apostles and martyrs. Like Paul, he considered himself a prisoner for Christ, writing letters full of faith and testimony. From his Missouri cell he chronicled a new generation of embattled saints. With Paul in mind, he introduced his work as written "in a cold, dark, and dreary prison."[71] Just as Paul had set all of Thessalonica in an uproar, turning the world upside down in the alarmed words of disbelieving Jews, so Pratt considered himself a gospel revolutionary, suggestively titling one of his own pamphlets, "The World Turned Upside Down."[72] In addition to Pratt's personal motivations, Smith had provided more immediate catalyst for his persecution narrative. From his prison in Liberty, Smith was urging "all the saints" to gather

> up a knoledge of all the facts and sufferings and abuses put upon them by the people of this state...and present the whole concatination of diabolicalil rascality and nefarious and murderous impositions that have been practiced upon this people that we may not only publish to all the world but present them to the heads of government in all there dark and hellish hugh.... It is an imperious duty that we owe to God to angels with whom we shall be brought to stand and also to ourselves to our wives and our children who have been made to bow down with greaf sorrow and care under the most damning hand of murder tyronny and appresion.[73]

Pratt probably had already initiated his own work, but Smith's injunction gave an enormous boost to the spotty attempts to chronicle the persecutions

already begun. Ephraim Owen, a victim of the Missouri expulsions, had petitioned members of Congress months earlier for redress, and they ordered his
five-page account of the troubles published in December 1838. Perhaps the
first to respond directly to Smith's pleas was Francis Gladden Bishop, a
Mormon missionary in North Carolina during the last stages of the Missouri
troubles. He gave a more detailed, if less accurate, account of what was tran-
spiring to his coreligionists ("it was extremely difficult to obtain confirmed
facts," he acknowledged). On his own initiative, he published a fourteen-
page pamphlet "for the purpose of correcting the misrepresentations, which
had prejudiced the public against the Latter Day Saints, and then circulated
this pamphlet gratis by mail in almost every direction."[74] Weeks after Smith's
Liberty letter, a committee began to gather affidavits and documents pertaining to the Missouri experiences. John Portineus Greene incorporated the
committee's work into his forty-three-page *Facts relative to the expulsion of
the Mormons*, published that summer.[75]

Meanwhile, Pratt began his own account while still imprisoned as a legal
casualty of the persecutions he narrated. Completing a first draft, and knowing the guards intended to confiscate or destroy it, he devised a plan to get
the manuscript safely out of prison. He hid it in his wife's petticoats, and a
timely accident involving his stepdaughter provided the perfect distraction.
As she was climbing the ladder linking the dungeon to the main floor, a
falling trap door struck her head. In great alarm—greater than the injury
merited—Mary Ann rushed the hurting child outside and into the fresh air.
In the panicky commotion, the guards did not search mother or child. She
subsequently delivered the manuscript safely to nearby friends, the
Stoddards, who kept it safe until Pratt's release.[76] When completed, the
eighty-four-page treatise was widely reprinted and incorporated into
subsequent works, and it was partially serialized in the church's Nauvoo
newspaper *Times and Seasons*. It long served as a principal vehicle for publicizing the Saints' version of the most protracted episode of religious violence in American history.

While Pratt self-identified with the Christian martyrs of the past, he
found his particular predicament more galling because he lived in a modern
democracy rather than the Roman Empire. This sense of outrage not just to a
moral sensibility, but to a political ideology, suffused Mormon writing of this
era, and was clearly intended to appeal to a public still basking in the after-
glow of two wars fought for independence against unrepublican oppressors.
These "horrid scenes" transpired in "our renowned Republic," Pratt lamented.
How could citizens countenance the actions of mobs who acted to "hush the

impulse of freedom in the bosoms of Americans—silence the voice of Liberty in the free born sons of Columbia?"[77]

As so often in his writings, Pratt's hyperbole threatened to undermine his credibility. It is unlikely that he was actually "daily in danger of being assassinated while prisoner" or that he had truly "no prospect of ever living to publish his work." Still, he was astute enough not to rely on his own interpretation of events alone to garner public sympathy. He allowed the Missourians to incriminate themselves, by beginning his narrative with an astonishing document that some Jackson County citizens published in 1833. There, they publicly announced their intention of ridding themselves of the Latter-day Saints by extralegal force. And they openly acknowledged that the Mormon "evils" eliciting such recourse to violence were in part religious ones: "They pretend...to hold personal communion and converse, face to face, with the most high God—to receive communications and revelations direct from Heaven—to heal the sick by laying on hands—and in short, to perform all the wonder working miracles wraught by the inspired Apostles and prophets of old."[78] Nevertheless, the antagonists largely cast their objections, as they had in the case of anti-Catholicism, in political rather than religious terms, to maintain the fiction of supporting Jeffersonian ideals of religious toleration.[79]

Pratt then chronicled five years of house burnings, pillaging, beatings, and shootings directed against the Saints as they experienced serial expulsion from a number of Missouri counties. He was less than forthcoming when it came to the Mormon response in the latter stages of the conflict. "It is said that some of our troops," he wrote, "exasperated to the highest degree, retalliated in some instances by plundering and burning houses....I am rather inclined to believe it was the case," he granted, omitting to say he may have participated in at least one raid. The narrative made for gripping reading, and while newspaper reports had relayed many of the details at the time they transpired, the effect of gathering into one account the long saga of bloody violence that grew to include thousands of militia, the razing of whole villages, and the largest expulsions of American citizens in national history was dramatic. Further confirming his people's role as victims of mob oppression, Pratt included accounts from Missouri politicians and common citizens, alarmed at the prospects of Missouri's reputation as "the most lawless invaders of religious and civil rights," and lauded Major General David Atchison for his refusal to "carry on a war of extermination against defenceless women and children." Illinois newspapers, Pratt noted, condemned "the cold blooded murder, by the mob of Missouri, of Mormon men and children, the violation of females, the destroying of property [and] the burning of houses." As far away as New York, he wrote, the editor of the *New York Sun* had protested Missourians' "primitive mode of administering justice."[80]

Pratt's work climaxed with the narration of his own escape and trek to freedom, and concluded with his testimony of the work for which he felt himself persecuted, and a copy of his fruitless petition to Judge Austin King, after seven months' imprisonment, for either trial or banishment. As the post-script, he added a poem he wrote while imprisoned, a lyrical denunciation of tyranny and plunder, which ended with his irrepressible confidence that "though they should hang me, or keep me in jail,/The spirit of Freedom and Truth will prevail."[81]

Through *History of the Late Persecution*, Pratt became the most prolific and persuasive Mormon voice on the Missouri experience; his writings reinforced a Mormon collective identity forged in persecution and indelibly shaped Latter-day Saint memory. Throughout the nineteenth century, and in some ways until the present, Mormon memory of their victimhood at the hands of fellow Americans has created an oppositional identity between the Saints and the larger culture.[82]

Though Pratt's account and the martyrological tradition within Mormonism have forged a Latter-day Saint identity, he primarily wrote it for a broader audience. His appeal to culturally powerful narratives of reli-gious liberty, persecution, and suffering attempted to reshape the image of Mormonism in the American mind. Although most Americans consid-ered Mormonism fraudulent and fanatical, a threat to religion and republi-canism, Mormons could also be depicted as a persecuted religious minority, exiled from their home because of their sincere convictions, in a replay of the archetypal American story of the Puritans.

On March 12, while Pratt labored on his history, fellow Saint King Follett was indicted for robbery and incarcerated with the other five. He came into the prison as Mary Ann was preparing to return to Far West, where she found only the most destitute Saints had remained in the largely abandoned town.[83] About this time Pratt's colleague Heber Kimball planned to visit Smith and his companions at Liberty Jail, but all visits were disallowed after they had made an escape attempt in early February and again the first week of March.[84] Perhaps in response to the alarm raised in Liberty, conditions in the Richmond prison rapidly deteriorated. By March, Pratt bitterly described his incarceration in a letter to his father-in-law as "a lothesome filthy jail in the midst of darkness and dirt Such as I cannot discribe, suffise it to say that a state prison would be a pallace of pleasure compared with it; our food is only fit for dogs to eat; or for soapgrease; and as to Insults we are allmost dayly told that we will be hung, Sacrifised, or Shot, and verry frequently we are told of getting fat against killing time as if they would kill and eat us."[85] Denied access to the Liberty prisoners, Kimball went to Richmond to see Pratt instead and managed to speak with him through the cracks. "If I had been a Sampson the Prisoners should go free," he wrote in impotent sympathy.[86]

In mid-April, a few weeks after Mary Ann's arrival back in Far West, a mob pillaged the stragglers in that city and ordered them out of the state. The fastest route out of Missouri—and mortal peril—was in a line almost due east from Far West, toward the major ferry crossing of the Mississippi at Quincy Bay, across from the town of Quincy, Illinois, with its population of some fifteen hundred. Most Missouri Saints had taken this route of exodus, but travel in the winter of 1838–1839 had been grueling. Ice on the Mississippi would neither melt enough for ferry passage nor freeze solid enough for wagons, so thousands of refugees huddled on the western shore. "Some had sheets stretched to make a little shelter from the wind," observed Wandle Mace, "but it was a poor protection, the children were shivering around a fire which the wind blew about so it did them very little good. The poor Saints were suffering terribly."[87] Threats of Missourians against those who failed to get out of the state added to the trauma. (As late as the summer of 1840, at least one party of Missourians raided the Illinois side, returning to Missouri with four Mormons whom they beat almost to the point of death.)[88] David Rogers, one of Pratt's New York converts, took charge of Mary Ann and her children and several of Brigham Young's dependents. Crossing the Mississippi River, little Mary Ann fell off the wagon. "As I drove up the bank out of the water," Rogers reported, "I looked back and saw something in the water about the middle of the slough, which I thought was some bundle of clothes that had fallen off the back end of the wagon and called out there is something lost off in the water upon which Sister Pratt cried out it is Mary Ann." Leaping out of the wagon, he saved the child, who was "nearly drowned but we soon brought her to again."[89] In one of the greatest humanitarian manifestations in frontier history, the townspeople of Quincy aided, sheltered, and sustained the refugees, who exceeded in number their own population.

Meanwhile, on April 2, Parley was formally indicted for the murder of Moses Rowland. Ten days later, he lamented his predicament with wry humor:

> This is the day that gave me birth
> In eighteen hundred seven

From worlds unseen I came to earth
Far from my native heavn
Thirty and two long years have passed
To grief and sorrow given
And now to crown my woes at last
I am here, confined in prison....

Then, on April 16, Joseph Smith and his fellow prisoners escaped from the authorities (with the complicity of their guards) while being transported to Boone County, where they had obtained a change of venue. Pratt and his companions felt doubly abandoned and alone as a consequence. "I have neither wife, nor children, nor friends, to administer to my comfort, or necesities While in Jail," he wrote Mary Ann, "nor witnesses to attend my trial."[90] Conditions worsened in response to Smith's publicized escape. Kimball came to visit again, but guards turned him away, threatening him with death. Pratt sent him a frantic warning through Morris Phelps's wife that a mob was assembling to tar and feather him, as an alleged accomplice to Smith.[91] Days later, on April 22, Pratt and his colleagues appeared before the grand jury. "The town is quite thronged this morning to attend the court," he noted. The court released the two youngest prisoners, seventeen-year-old Norman Shearer and twenty-two-year-old Darwin Chase. Of all the dozens of Mormons arrested, from Joseph Smith to members of the rank and file, only Pratt, Gibbs, Phelps, and Follett remained in custody. Though release had not come, the promise of liberty did, in a vision Pratt experienced at this time. As he lay in bed pondering his future, "a heaven of peace and calmness pervaded [his] bosom," and he saw the form of his first wife, Thankful. She assured him he would again be reunited with his family and the other Saints, and preach the gospel as he had before, though she could not tell him how or when.[92]

By May, Pratt's resilience was fading. He poured out his heart to Mary Ann in a letter that combined heartrending pain, impressive selflessness, and gentle humor. She had been gone two months and had not written him until two weeks previous. "I had almost concluded that you would never write to me," he lamented. He could see no prospect of liberty, and even his attorneys appeared to have given up hope or interest, for "none of them come near us." He insisted that he wished no friends to risk their own safety in coming to give moral or legal support, even though he knew he could mount no defense without witnesses. In the same spirit, he asked her to "tell my quorum to not delay their mission to the East on my account."[93] In the lighthearted guise of a prophet, he tried to buoy up his flagging spirits while casting his love for

Mary Ann as Jacob's love for Rachel: "I will venture to predict that…all our affairs will be amicably settled in one hundred years from Last october. I shall then, only be a lad of the age of a hundred and thirty two: And you will be my own sweet Mary, a matron of the age of a hundred and thirty, and we will then spend the remainder of our days in peace, and be assured that the hundred years will seem but a few days to me." For the present, however, the anguish was the severest test he had known. "In my night visions I often See you and my little babes, but it is allways at a distance, and Some [barrier] between us; to prevent us from converseing togather; Either you are buisily engaged; or in Some other room, or Something which forever disappoints me in my dreams. O Mary, why do you forever fly from my visionary persuit."[94]

On May 13, the day after writing Mary Ann, Pratt penned a petition to Judge Austin King. He outlined yet again the long chain of miseries visited upon himself and his people. He protested the judge's own prejudices, the miscarriages of justice, and the impossibility of finding impartial judgment in Missouri. Accordingly, he requested a change of venue—with the innovative twist that this be effected by banishing him from the state altogether, according to the terms of Boggs's extermination order.[95]

King visited the prisoners four days later to discuss their petition. Pratt described him as ridden with guilt and misery, unable to meet the steady gaze of men who were haggard and sallow, probably malnourished and sickly, but convinced of the rightness of their cause. The recent defection of "the apostate" Luman Gibbs, who according to Pratt had turned state's evidence and remained incarcerated to spy on the others, only hardened them in their resolve. Additionally, Pratt had given himself to days of fasting and prayer, genuinely uncertain if he would ever again know freedom and family. The four prisoners presented King with a formal request for a change of venue, more conciliatory than Pratt's letter a few days earlier, simply stating that local residents "are so much prejudiced" that they could not receive "a fair and impartial trial."[96] King granted the appeal for a change of venue to Boone County, in the central part of the state.[97] Along the journey, initial exuberance at traveling in springtime, free from the dungeon's squalor, collapsed under the burden of incessant rain, muddy roads, ill treatment, hunger, and thirst. During the change of venue, Amasa Lyman and three other Mormons returned to Missouri in disguise in hopes of helping the prisoners escape, but another Latter-day Saint inadvertently revealed their identities.[98] Instead, after a journey of several days on wagon, canoe, carriage, and foot, Pratt and his companions arrived in Columbia, the county seat, on May 28.

Conditions for the prisoners improved quickly in Columbia, which was more developed and urbane than the raw western Missouri towns. The citizens of Columbia furthermore lacked the intense hostility toward Mormons which western Missourians had honed over half a decade of sustained animosity.[99] The prisoners were lodged above ground, visited by the jailor as if they were friends and boarders, and fed generously. Still, the prospects looked grim. Virtually all Mormons in the state had fled at the point of a militia gun, meaning it would be impossible to find witnesses to testify on their behalf. Without exaggeration, Pratt wrote Mary Ann that he had no reason to hope "I Shall be at Liberty Short of several months or years." His loneliness and his impotence in the face of Mary Ann's own travails almost overwhelmed him. Timidly, he hinted at the comfort a renewed stay on her part would bring him. "Dear Mary," he wrote, "I Know not how to Express my feelings Concerning this Long abscence from you and our Little ones. I hardly dare to trust my fingers with a penn to write on the Subject Lest I should Express feelings which would Increase your sorrow—or Lest I Should ask that of you which would Influance you to again suffer with me In prison." He would never have asked for her hand, he told her, if he had known what sufferings awaited them. But his solitude in suffering was becoming unbearable: "[I] am doomed to Languish out Long Months and perhaps years deprived of your Sosiety while My Little ones grow, and change their Sise and appearance without one Sweet Kiss or fond Embrace from a father who Loves them Dearer than Life. for what then do I live? It is more than I can endure."[100]

He described an all-too-familiar domestic arrangement that would provide as much comfort and stability as she had yet known in her marriage to Pratt:

> If you Come here, you Can Come into the upper room of the prison which Is Large, airy, well Lighted, and has a good floor; and you can visit with me as Long as you please, and I can help you take care of the children. you Can board with us for one dollar and fifty cts per week, and we Live as well as farmers In General. The Jailors family Live under the same roof and you Can go out into their apartment to do your washing &c. they are kind and good to us and to mrs Gibbs.[101]

Mary Ann declined to subject herself and her children to a second imprisonment. So while he languished in loneliness, Pratt's thoughts turned to the written legacy he would leave behind. He had earlier written Mary Ann that he was "very buisy with my penn, most of the time, and...somewhat weary with studdy, and writting."[102] In his poignant missives to her, he urgently directed her to see some of his poems into print, and "such other of my writings as the Brethren may think advisable."[103] In the relative security of his new confinement, at least he did not need to worry about his work being confiscated or destroyed. He exulted in a near freedom he expressed through new writing projects and resuming old ones. He turned again to one he called "The Journal of my Life and Sufferings," an early anticipation of his autobiography. But even as Pratt enlivened in the less restrictive atmosphere of the Columbia Jail, he predicted "It will take a number of months at least to give full vent and exersise to the Smuthered feelings of Liberty and patriotism which have so Long Slept in my bosom."[104]

In Quincy, Illinois, Mary Ann found the new security and the camaraderie with thousands of fellow refugees preferable to married life in a prison. She rented a house and managed a frugal existence with her two children and stepson, Parley, who was brought to her in Quincy. In June, Pratt wrote more poetry, decried mobs and tyrants, and lamented his three months apart from family. "Most gladly would I say," he wrote his father-in-law, Aaron Frost, who had joined the church the previous year, "that My dear wife, and our little Mary ann, Stand looking over my Shoulder, telling me to send their love, to all their old friends and acquaintance. But Allas I am a lone. I only see them in the visions of the night when deep sleep falleth upon man. It is then that I enjoy their smiles, and hear the musick of their voices. But I awake in hartsickening and Lonely disapointment Only to hear the greetings of Locks and Bars."[105]

Pratt retained some optimism that a trial scheduled for July 1 would free him. After eight months in captivity, he longed not only for hearth and home, but also to "preach the fulness of the gospel more faithful than ever I have done."[106] A letter he received at this time must have caused him extreme vexation even as it offered a glimmer of hope. Pratt had missed out on the first English mission, but a second, larger one was in preparation. Heber Kimball wrote him of the Quorum's determination to "go forth into the world to preach the gospel" and assured Pratt that "the Presidency feel well towards the Twelve, and especially towards you, they say you must come out of that place, and so I say, for I do not feel as though I can go to England until I take you by the hand, when this takes place, my joy will be full." And then the prophecy-prone Kimball said, "Be of good cheer, brother, a few days more, and you shall see the salvation of God; and I shall see you in other lands." He added presciently, "Whatever you do, do quickly."[107]

Pratt's trial, however, was postponed for months in the future. Orson braved the hostile climate of Missouri to visit his brother, and both were convinced that they would need to rely upon their own devices, rather than legal process, to secure his freedom. Parley was passionate about what he called republican principles and he had more than a touch of the theatrical. Those traits coalesced around an escape plan to be executed on Independence Day. With spirited cheek, Pratt and his fellow prisoners advertised their plans with a crude flag they fashioned of a white shirt, on which they sewed a red flannel eagle, beneath which they emblazoned the single word "Liberty" in large letters. Pratt wryly attributed the obliviousness of their keepers to their plan—also announced in lyrics they sang repeatedly on the night of their escape—to the same sectarian tendency that led men of the age to "spiritualize" clearly worded prophecies, rather than interpret scripture in the plain sense of the words. According to their plan, Phelps's wife, Laura, along with her brother John Wesley Clark and Orson, would station three horses in a thicket behind the jail. At the dinner hour, she would ask the jailor to open the prison door to pass through a pot of coffee. King Follett would then pull the door open, and the "athlete and wrestler" Morris Phelps would overpower the jailor allowing all to flee. Gibbs was by default allotted the role of passive spectator, which he happily fulfilled.[108]

Near dusk, as the jailor opened the door to deliver coffee, Follett yanked the door wider and the others forced their way. "We all rushed out and down the stares," Pratt wrote, "and cleared for the woods, over fences and through fields for about 100 rods." Finding the horses, they "instantly mounted them and fled" as "men with dogs and guns were within Pistol Shot." The plan came off perfectly initially, but notwithstanding the chaos and confusion of darkness, the Missourians quickly fanned out to recapture the escapees, and a company of horsemen soon came across Phelps.[109] As a writer, Pratt excelled when his flair for melodrama, biting wit, and gift for dialogue merged in set pieces that were tinged with satire. His later account of these "thrilling scenes," particularly the attempted recapture of Phelps, combined all of those elements.

> They immediately hailed him, and cried out, "Say, stranger, G—d damn you, what is your name?" He replied in the same rough and careless manner, "You damned rascals, what is yours?" On finding he could damn as well as themselves, they concluded he could not be a Mormon, while his bold and fearless manner convinced them that he was not a man who was fleeing for his life. They then begged his pardon for the rough manner in which they had accosted him, "Oh, you are one of the real breed. By G—d, no damned Mormon could counterfeit that

language, you swear real natteral; hurrah for old Kentuck. But whar mought you live, stranger?" He replied, "just up here; you mout a kno'd me, and then agin you moutn't. I think I've seed you all a heap o' times, but I've been so damned drunk at the fourth of independence, I hardly know myself or anybody else, but hurrah for old Kentuck; and what about the damn'd Mormons?" "What about 'em? egad, you'd a know'd that without axin', if you'd a seed 'em run." "What! they are not out of prison, are they?" "Out of prison! Yes, the damn'd rascals raised a flag of liberty in open day, and burst out, and down stars right in the midst of the public celebration, out rassling the damn'd jailer, and outrunning the whole town in a fair foot race. They reached the timber jist as they war overtaken, but afore we could cotch 'em they mounted their nags, and the way they cleared was a caution to Crockett. We tuk one on 'em, and seed the other two a few feet distant, rushin' their nags at full speed, but we couldn't cotch 'em nor shoot 'em either; I raised my new Kentucky rifle, fresh loaded and primed, with a good percussion, and taking fair aim at one of their heads only a few yards distant, I fired, but the damn'd cap burst, and the powder wouldn't burn." "Well, now, stranger, that's a mighty big story and seems enemost onpossible. Did you say you cotched one on 'em? Why I'd a tho't you'd a kilt him on the spot; what have you done with him?" "They tuk him back to prison, I suppose, but it was only the old one. If it had been one o' them tother chaps we would a skinn'd 'em as quick as Crockett would a coon, and then eat 'em alive without leaving a grease spot."

This interview over, the horsemen withdrew and left Phelps to pursue his way in peace.[110]

The "old one," fifty-one-year-old King Follett, was recaptured and languished in jail several more months before being released. Laura Phelps had bravely remained behind at the jail, where the fury of the mob at her role in the escape prompted a sympathetic young man to rescue and shelter her until, two weeks later, she made her way to Illinois.

As to Pratt, shortly after mounting his horse he was accosted at gunpoint, but he turned his horse and rode for the forest. There he dismounted, climbed a tree, and rather strangely—considering the tumult surrounding him—collapsed in slumber for several minutes. Upon awakening, he climbed down, found his horse had escaped its tether, and traveled northeast on foot for the better part of the night, beginning a trek of more than 150 miles. The next day, he journeyed through sodden forests, asked directions as he passed through scattered settlements, and arrived at last, drenched and exhausted, at an expansive prairie. As night approached, a storm drove him to risk his freedom by seeking refuge at a cabin he saw in the distance. There he assumed the character of a visitor from Indiana, spying out possible land to settle, who had lost his way in search of a horse that had wandered. The couple living there fed and lodged him for the night. Hospitality was the norm on the frontier, but it was enhanced by the custom of paying for the room and board. Pratt settled his bill and tipped the wife a quarter. Another day or two of travel took him well into eastern Missouri and a neighborhood he knew to be inhabited by a family alienated from the church. Pratt approached the house and found not the owners but a sympathetic Mormon, who took Pratt to the home of a nearby relative.

Pratt was now in the vicinity of the Mississippi, the last barrier to his escape from Missouri. Word had spread of the Mormon breakout from jail, and he knew the ferry crossings would be watched. Exhausted, weak, and fearful of recapture, Pratt hid in a deep ravine until it was dark and entirely safe. Then he went into the home of his guide's relatives, took some refreshment, and passed time with the children of the family while he awaited their father's return home. Tense moments passed when a stranger dropped in, also hoping to call upon the man of the house. When the cottage's owner at last arrived, he and Pratt feigned ignorance of each other, and the visitor soon left. His anxiety heightened by exposure to a stranger, Pratt decided not to spend the night with the family, but he asked, in a feeble gesture of disguise, to exchange hats with the man, who then led him along a little-traveled route toward the great river.

Months without exercise, marathon days working through thickets and traversing prairies, and days and nights of incessant rain had worn Pratt down to the limits of his endurance. Resting intermittently, he forged ahead until the Mississippi was less than ten miles distant. On a broad, flat expanse, two armed riders approached him, eyed him suspiciously, but passed him by. Pratt walked to the next town without being seen and pushed on in hopes of finding an untended boat or canoe. Finding himself hopelessly mired in swampy terrain and completely blocked at last by a substantial river, most likely a branch of the Mississippi, he backtracked to the town and asked the way across. Fortunately, he aroused no suspicion, was directed to a mill dam, and made his way to the other side. Fording another small river, he arrived in the small river town of Saverton as night fell.

The next morning he found a boy ten or twelve years old who was, unbeknownst to his parents, willing to take Pratt in a family canoe to an island

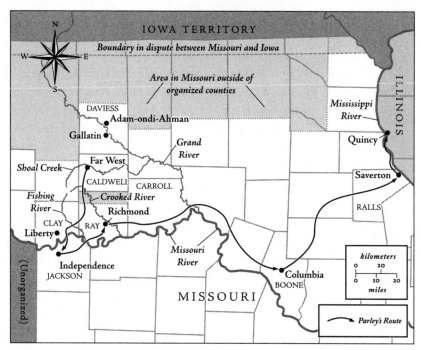

MAP 5.1 Imprisonment and Escape

midway between the shores for a fee. From there, the boy said, Pratt could hail a boat from the far side. He rowed Pratt across, and Pratt made out for the other side of the island. Whether the boy's strategy was a ruse, or whether the weary Pratt was simply not up to the arduous trek through briars and across yet more watery obstacles, he felt himself deceived, returned to the Missouri-facing shore, and called the boy to return. Fearful of defying his parents' prohibition on crossing to the Illinois side, the boy was persuaded by a combination of Pratt's vehement insistence and the bribe of a whole dollar. The boy navigated the mile or two around the island and to the far shore, and Pratt stepped out of the boat and onto Illinois soil, a free man eight months and a week after his initial incarceration.

Pratt made his way through swamp and woods to a house, where a young boy admitted him. When the boy's mother returned, she shrieked with delighted recognition. Pratt, with mock solemnity, admonished her to "be not afraid—handle and see, for a spirit hath not flesh and bones as you see me have." The woman, Sabre Granger, had been a neighbor of the Pratts for many years in Ohio. She fed Pratt, washed his blistered feet, and animatedly brought him up to date on mutual friends. She then took him out to her husband, who

was clearing land. So close to his final destination, Pratt was anxious to immediately continue his journey. So Granger's husband led him some five miles
through marshy, grassy bottomland to the nearest settlement of Mormon refugees. Almost within hailing distance, his strength at last gave out. Desperate
for relief from the blazing sun and overcome by thirst, he sheltered under the
sparse shade of a fence before fainting entirely away. Granger went for help
and returned with water and camphor to revive Pratt, who rose to meet him
only to collapse again. They assisted him into a house, where he washed and
refreshed himself, then gave himself up to sleep until the next day. That evening he recovered enough to mount a horse and ride the twenty-five miles to
Quincy, arriving in the early morning hours.

Word of the three Mormons' escape had reached the town days before.
Phelps had made his way to Illinois on horseback in just two days, according
to plan, and it was known that Follett had been retaken. Pratt's fate was a mystery, and by now Mary Ann was sick with worry. "She had watched for four
successive nights and most of the fifth," Pratt recorded, "and had now just lain
down and given up all for lost." At this moment he located her cabin by his
two Missouri cows lying in front of it. He gave a light knock, upon which "she
sprang from bed and opened the door, and in another instant I had clasped
her in my arms."[111]

6

Apostle to the British

Now, "In the days of these kings (or kingdoms represented
by the feet and toes,) the God of heaven should...
break in pieces all these kingdoms and stand forever...."
Of course, then the government of England is one of
the toes.
—PARLEY PRATT, *"A letter to the Queen, touching
the signs of the times"*

PRATT'S PIONEERING MISSION of 1830 had catapulted the fledgling sect
into a competitive new church, adding a strong core of members and leaders
to Smith's followers. His *Voice of Warning* provided one of the most important vehicles for spreading the Mormon message through the printed word.
While his dreams of converting the "red man" and building a Missouri Zion
were on indefinite hold, his writing and preaching skills would now come
together to lay the foundations for an international church.

The man Pratt revered as his prophet had a penchant for curious timing.
At the height of the 1837 Kirtland crisis, rather than consolidate his forces and
surround himself with allies, Smith inaugurated the British mission, sending
some of his most loyal supporters abroad. Few remained at his side to face
down the lions. Then, in July 1838, days after Rigdon's inflammatory July 4
sermon, as conflict with Missourians reached boiling point, he again turned
in the direction of England. He declared, by way of revelation, that the Twelve
were to be reconstituted, with the vacancies of the defectors filled, and depart
for another mission to England from the Far West temple site on April 26,
1839, almost a year thence.[1] As April 1839 approached, however, virtually the
only Mormons still in Missouri were in the Richmond Prison with Pratt or in
Liberty Jail with Smith. The last few, destitute exiles in Far West were soon
forced out at gunpoint.

The Twelve met to consider the looming deadline given in the revelation.
As Smith's only revelation that included a specific date for its fulfillment, it

lent itself especially well to disproof, and enemies of the church in Missouri were determined to see it fail. On April 15, Mormon nemesis Samuel Bogart approached Theodore Turley, who was in Far West overseeing the removal of the remaining indigent saints, and mockingly asked him to read aloud a copy of the revelation. When Turley refused, Bogart reminded him that the Twelve were scattered far and wide, adding, "let them come here if they dare; if they do, they will be murdered."[2]

Smith's father counseled the Twelve and new quorum president Brigham Young that under these circumstances, "the Lord would accept the will for the deed." Neither Young's implicit faith in the prophet nor his pugnacious pride would permit such a tactical retreat. Woodruff remembered the apostles agreeing: "The Lord has spoken and it is for us to obey," adding, "we felt that the Lord God had given the commandment and we had faith to go forward and accomplish it, feeling that it was His business whether we lived or died in its accomplishment. We started for Missouri."[3]

Young, Woodruff, Orson Pratt, John Taylor, and George A. Smith met up with Heber Kimball not far from Far West. They ran into John Page, who was fleeing Missouri, but persuaded him to join them instead. In the early hours of April 26, the date stipulated in the prophecy, a majority of the quorum convened. They rolled an enormous stone to the southeast corner of the temple lot as a symbolic cornerstone, ordained Smith and Woodruff to the apostleship, and designated the official commencement of their British mission from that date and place.[4]

Even with the prophecy fulfilled, none of the apostles immediately departed for England, though preparations soon began. Pratt would certainly have learned about these events almost immediately upon his return, if not while in prison, and he doubtless determined not to be left behind this time around. He arrived too late, however, to participate in the preparatory meetings and formal leave takings. While Pratt was hatching his escape plan, Joseph and Hyrum Smith were giving instructions and blessings to the other apostles. On July 7, while Pratt made his way across Missouri and into Illinois, apostles Young, Page, Taylor, Woodruff, and Orson Hyde made their farewell addresses in anticipation of a yet-to-be-named departure.[5]

When Pratt arrived a few days later in Quincy, one of the first to greet him was Kimball, who mere days later helped move Pratt and his family the fifty miles upriver to Commerce, soon to be renamed by Joseph Smith as Nauvoo. Pratt was never one to hover in the wings while the events of the Restoration played out around him. His immediate relocation to the very geographical center of the new gathering place reflected his keen desire to reassume his pivotal role in church affairs without delay. A few days later, Woodruff noted, "I had the happy privilege of once more taking Elder PARLEY P. PRATT by the hand.... I was truly glad to see him. In a short time Joseph & Hiram & others Soon rode up to see Parley & in fine it was a happy meeting. I returned home to Montrose feeling thankful to God for his deliverance."[6] Smith's parents also welcomed the near martyr, Pratt remembered, and "they wept like children as they took me by the hand."[7]

Pratt immediately set to work, buying a five-acre lot next to Kimball's land. Together they erected 14-by-16-foot log houses, assisted by "a few of the old citizens" since most members were prostrate with malarial fevers. Kimball got the walls raised on his, a fancy puncheon floor put down (slabs as opposed to simple dirt), added a shake roof, and personally built a rock chimney to the roofline before fever laid him low.[8] Pratt said only that he "toiled a few days" on his, perhaps mindful of the looming mission to England.[9]

On July 22, Smith asked Parley, Orson, Page, Taylor, and Kimball to accompany him across the river in a skiff to Montrose, Iowa. The miasmic swamps, not yet drained, harbored malarial mosquitoes that were infecting and sickening large numbers of Saints, many of whom had yet to fully recuperate from the rigors of the previous autumn's expulsions, and Smith was on a mission of healing. Wandle Mace remembered that Smith and his associates "went first to the house of Brigham Young...then to others of the quorum of the Twelve who lived here, and all were healed." The group, including Pratt, then visited Elijah Fordham, Pratt's faithful New York assistant, who lay at the point of death. Smith took him by the hand and commanded him in Christ's name to rise and walk, which he did. They then continued from house to house, ministering to numerous others, with enough similar results that this day became enshrined in Mormon memory as the "Day of God's Power."[10]

The last Sunday of July, Pratt spoke to a Sunday congregation on the gathering of Israel, alongside Joseph Smith. The quorum had now agreed to depart as soon as possible, and the next Sunday, he was probably one of the apostles who gave witness to those assembled of "their willingness to proceed on their mission to Europe without either purse or Scrip."[11] Woodruff and Taylor left first, after visiting Pratt and Kimball to ask for assistance. Woodruff found Pratt, destitute after his months in prison, "barefooted, bareheaded, without coat or vest on." Pratt had no money to give, but offered an empty purse. Kimball then said, "as Parley has given you a purse, I have got a dollar I will give you to put in it."[12]

Pratt delayed only long enough to sell his recently acquired and improved lot. Then, without a recorded word of murmur, he departed on August 29.

But after the long loneliness of Missouri prison walls, he was not about to leave his family behind. When he entered his carriage, it was in the company of Hiram Clark, his brother Orson, and his wife and children. Other apostles were still laid low with sickness, the day of healing notwithstanding. On September 18, the desperately ill Young and Kimball, barely able to stand, heaved themselves into a wagon and also headed for New York, the port of departure. The most recently called apostle, George A. Smith, began his journey three days later, nearly blind from illness. Of the other apostles in the depleted quorum (consisting of ten at this time), John Page changed his mind about serving, and William Smith declined the call. Orson Hyde sailed instead for Palestine, which he dedicated for the return of the Jews to fulfill millennial prophecy.[13]

Pratt planned to join his quorum in New York, but he and Orson detoured to visit family along the way, preaching frequently. Near Cuba, Illinois, they visited their brother William. They continued on to Detroit, where their brother Anson now lived, together with their father, Jared. Parley lingered there two weeks, probably sensing his father's death was imminent (he died a few weeks later in early November, at age seventy). He also put the finishing touches on his prison manuscript about the suffering of the Saints in Missouri and secured a Detroit printer. He obtained a copyright the last day of the month, and saw the first books off the press ten days later.[14]

Pratt's *History of the Late Persecution*, alongside other accounts of the Mormon expulsion from Missouri, succeeded in creating an alternative image of the Latter-day Saints and generating widespread indignation at the Mormons' sufferings. Indeed, Pratt's history arrived in the hands of an already sympathetic public. The *Quincy Argus*, for instance, had proclaimed that the "injustice" the Mormons had "received from the People, Authorities, Executive, and Legislature of Missouri" should "concern *every Freeman* of these States."[15] Pratt wrote to the Mormon leadership on October 12, 1839, "The news papers, for the last three weeks have teemed with our sufferings and the outrages in Missouri. Every part of the country feels indignant at these unparalleled outrages. You have doubtless heard of the Large meetings on the subject, in N.Y. and other places."[16]

With his book now in circulation, he sold his carriage and took a steamer to Buffalo, the Erie Canal and railroad to Albany, and steamer again to New York, where he continued his writing.[17] At the conclusion of his New York mission two years earlier Pratt had left behind not only several converts but dear friends. Now, he learned from Addison Everett that on the evening of the previous July 4, Saints of the city united in prayer for his release from captivity. Everett told Pratt that he had dramatically declared on that occasion that he knew by the spirit of prophecy that "brother Parley goes at liberty" in the very hour of their praying.[18]

After four weeks in the city, Pratt exuberantly reported to Smith in Kirtland that church membership in the area was approaching two hundred, with branches firmly established "in Philadelphia, in Albany, in Brooklyn in N York in Sing Sing, in Jersey, in Pennsylvania [and] on Long Island and in various other places." Mormon debaters "frequently confounded" opposing preachers, and interest in the Book of Mormon far exceeded supply. They needed hundreds of copies but could not find them "in this part of the vineyard for love or Money." "Attentive listeners," Pratt enthused, filled the thousand-capacity Columbian Hall, "one of the best places in the City," three times a Sabbath.[19] On one typical Sunday, Pratt sermonized on "the authenticity of the Book of mormon and the origin of the American Indians."[20] The phrasing affirms the peculiar role the Book of Mormon played in his—and most Mormon—minds. Few clerics would preach on "the authenticity of the Bible," but rather on some message taken from it. The Book of Mormon, by contrast, was important because—if authentic—it was an emblem of larger events unfolding outside it.

Pratt settled in for the next six months, preaching and revising his *Voice of Warning* for a new edition.[21] The first edition had proved an effective missionary aid and had been widely distributed (the first print run was three thousand copies, an ambitious undertaking given that it sold at the not inconsequential 37 and a half cents a copy). Just three days after Pratt's departure from Commerce in August, Joseph Smith had publicly spoken "concerning some errors" in Pratt's published work, no doubt referring to *Voice of Warning*, which Smith may have read for the first time only after his escape from prison a few months earlier.[22] Pratt now prepared a second edition, making relatively minor changes. Those made with Smith's criticisms in mind probably concerned either Pratt's remark that the ten tribes would be assembled from the four quarters of the earth (they would come "from the land of the north," Smith believed),[23] other interpretive references to ante-millennial events involving Gog and his armies, or the status of Joseph's remnant in the latter days.[24] Pratt also expanded a chapter on the Book of Mormon (introducing Smith into the story of its publication), and discussed parallels in works by Elias Boudinot and Josiah Priest, who had published books that placed the American Indian into the history of the lost tribes of Israel. Pratt thereby launched a distinctive kind of Mormon apologetics, one that invoked the science of the day in support of Book of Mormon authenticity. Following Pratt's lead, the church's *Times and Seasons* referenced or excerpted Priest's 1833 *American Antiquities and Discoveries in the West* five times. The first sustained attempt to connect the Book of Mormon to North American antiquities, Charles Thompson's 1841 *Evidences in Proof of the Book of Mormon*, also drew on Priest.[25] Perhaps to compensate for the additions, Pratt deleted a chapter called "A Proclamation," which read more like a Jeremiad than the reasoned argument and proof-texting of his other chapters. Pratt arranged for twenty-five hundred copies of this second edition to be printed.

Pratt also confronted in print an accusation about the Book of Mormon's origins, the Spaulding theory, which became the dominant explanation for the book throughout the nineteenth century. Six years previously, Doctor Philastus Hurlbut (Doctor was his given name, not a title) was excommunicated from Mormonism for "an attempt at seduction" and had threatened to kill Smith. In seeking to discredit his former faith, Hurlbut learned of a manuscript written by Solomon Spaulding, who died in 1816, that purportedly bore resemblances to the Book of Mormon. When Hurlbut found the manuscript in the possession of Spaulding's widow, it contained only the most superficial similarities to the Book of Mormon. Rather than renounce his theory, however, Hurlbut argued that Spaulding had also written a second manuscript, which had been lost. He sold the affidavits and manuscript to Eber D. Howe for his 1834 *Mormonism Unvailed*. Howe suggested that Spaulding had given the second manuscript to a Pittsburgh printer, who then provided it to Sidney Rigdon. Rigdon allegedly either then wrote the Book of Mormon and surreptitiously gave it to Joseph Smith or collaborated with Smith in the book's authorship.[26] In his 1838 *Mormonism Unveiled*, Pratt complained that the "ignorant and impudent dupes or knaves" who edited religious newspapers in New York had characterized the "Spaulding lie" as "*positive, certain,* and not to be *disputed!*"[27]

In a letter published in New York newspapers, as well as the Saints' *Times and Seasons*, Pratt dismissed Hurlbut as "one of the most notorious rascals in the western country," denounced the Spaulding theory, and denied that Rigdon had any connection with Smith prior to the Book of Mormon's publication, as "Rigdon embraced the doctrine through my instrumentality. I first presented the Book of Mormon to him."[28] Pratt's repudiation convinced a Unitarian paper to republish Pratt's letter "in justice" to the Mormon position.[29] The Spaulding theory, however, refused to die, and Pratt was himself soon implicated in it as the shadowy link between Rigdon and Smith in the late 1820s. Perhaps, some opponents wildly suggested, Pratt's wanderings in New York and Ohio had simply been pretext for religious mischief-making.[30]

In its first decade, Mormonism primarily appealed to the familiar. Missionaries invoked Old Testament prophecies of the last days and claimed the spiritual gifts and church organization described in the New Testament. Mormon millennialism played into attitudes and expectations so prevalent they spawned a whole generation of prophets and movements. The first doctrinal exposition published by the church, the "Lectures on Faith" in the 1835 Doctrine and Covenants, "treat only the most general Christian principles." Most earlier theological publications "could just as well have been published in the magazine of any Christian denomination."[31] All this changed with Pratt's "Treatise on the Regeneration and Eternal Duration of Matter," which he wrote in his Missouri prison and appended to a new edition of his collection of poems, first published as *Millennium* in 1835. His essay's significance was out of all proportion to its length and its placement as an apparent afterthought to a middling array of poems. It went even beyond his response to La Roy Sunderland in elaborating and defending some of Mormonism's most radical and distinctive doctrines, encompassing cosmology, the nature of God, and original sin.

Against the more general, conservative Christian background, Pratt's work—like that of his contemporary Thomas Dick—stands in sharp relief. No Mormon thinker, Pratt included, would exceed Joseph Smith's own audacity as a Christian iconoclast. Positing heavenly councils, preembodied spirits, Gods who were once human, and humans who could attain to godhood—these and other doctrines blasted asunder the creedal conceptions of God and humans alike. But Pratt assembled these ideas for the first time in something like a systematic form, the prime instance of Pratt acting the part of Paul to Smith's teachings. If Smith instigated Mormonism's essential beliefs, Pratt organized, elaborated, and defended them in a manner that gave them the enduring life and complexion they have in the church to this day. Pratt was, in this sense, the first theologian of Mormonism.

In this essay, Pratt began by challenging a Christian fundamental. "The Bible does teach that God is the Creator of matter, the material or substance, as well as the order, of the *kosmos*. Creation was the absolutely free act of God, unconditioned by any preexisting thing. Matter, with its properties and forms…; spirit, with its life and feeling…these all had their origin in the creative word of God."[32] So pronounced a nineteenth-century cleric, confident his formulation would find no opposition in the Christendom of his day. Pratt utterly rejected the doctrine of creation ex nihilo with his pronouncement that "matter and spirit are of equal duration; both are self-existent,—they never began to exist, and they can never be annihilated."[33] God is not the source of all existence;

rather, a universe filled with self-existent material abides independently and eternally. Here propounded by Pratt in 1838, this material eternalism was explicitly taught by Joseph Smith only years later, though he had suggested the idea earlier.[34] This is one of several points where Pratt seems to have taken the nucleus of an idea from Smith, or found in Smith's germinal pronouncements corroboration of his own notions, and then enthusiastically developed and promoted those doctrines before Smith had traced their implications. Smith first used Pratt's expression "eternal duration of matter" only in 1840.[35]

The principle of creation ex nihilo is inseparable from a particular conception of God's sovereignty and omniscience. To make God the mere manipulator of matter, as the Christian Gnostics argued, seems to "exclude the idea of the almightiness of the creator."[36] But it is precisely a conception of God's nature and power that Pratt was reformulating. Although he did not assert the evolution of God from man, as Smith would, Pratt emphatically stated that God is himself subject to law. It is impossible, he wrote, "for God to bring forth matter from nonentity, or to originate element from nothing," because "these are principles of eternal truth, they are laws which cannot be broken, ... whether the reckoning be calculated by the Almighty, or by man."[37] Not only laws of self-contradiction demarcate the limits of divine power, but scientific laws of the type Antoine Lavoisier propounded in laying the foundations of modern chemistry on the law of conservation of mass.

For Pratt, God's perfect compliance with eternal law both constitutes his own supreme power and indicates that path whereby humans can become his full heirs and genuine "partakers of the divine nature."[38] These eternal laws or "principles" thus become empowering and liberating rather than confining.

> What a glorious field of intelligence now lies before us, yet but partially explored. What a boundless expanse for contemplation and reflection now opens to our astonished vision. What an intellectual banquet spreads itself invitingly to our appetite, calling into lively exercise every power and faculty of the mind, and giving full scope to all the great and ennobling passions of the soul.... All the virtuous principles of the human mind may here expand and grow, and flourish, unchecked by any painful emotions or gloomy fears.[39]

Pratt captured the euphoric sense of boundlessness that progressive, Baconian-influenced theologians like Thomas Dick so enthusiastically promoted. Like Pratt, Dick had been consumed by the spectacle of a scientific juggernaut that was already opening worlds immense and minute to human knowledge, and would leave in its wake any theology too timid to follow.[40]

Contemporary developments in astronomy in particular led the era to increasingly unfold as what one scholar labels "the age of wonder." As recently as 1781, William Herschel had discovered Uranus, doubling the size of the solar system with one intellectual leap. This greatest astronomer of the age also thought he had detected signs of civilization on the moon. And why not? James Ferguson had written in a textbook twenty-five years earlier that the universe teemed with life: "Thousands upon thousands of Suns...attended by ten thousand times ten thousand Worlds...peoples with myriads of intelligent beings, formed for endless progression in perfection and felicity."[41] So Dick had respectable scientific precedent for his view on a richly populated universe. "Consider the boundless extent of the starry firmament," he rhapsodized, "the scenes of grandeur it displays, the new luminaries, which, in the course of ages, appear to be gradually augmenting its splendour, and the countless myriads of exalted intelligences which doubtless people its expansive regions."[42] Dick felt ennobled rather than diminished by the titanic scope of creation involved. So Pratt was not on entirely new terrain when he, similarly, named the organization of this earth as one event "in the progress of the endless works of Deity," with hints of a celestial diaspora of intelligent life he would explicitly describe a few years later.[43]

In addition to novel ideas concerning the nature of godliness, Pratt broke sharply with Christian notions of human depravity. The doctrine of original sin is not clearly reflected in New Testament writings or taught in the earliest Christian era ("obscured by other preoccupations in the age of the Apostolic Fathers and the Apologists," writes one scholar).[44] However, original sin had become an integral aspect of creedal Christianity long before the nineteenth century, though it had also increasingly come under assault by Pratt's day. The Book of Mormon stated that Christ's atonement redeemed mankind from the Fall, and it condemned the baptism of infants.[45] Smith reiterated the principle in an 1832 revelation.[46] But Pratt gave it formulation that would make its way into Orson Pratt's version of church principles (in his 1840 *Interesting Account of Several Remarkable Visions*) and then into Joseph Smith's 1842 Articles of Faith. Christ's atonement redeems all infants from original sin, Pratt wrote, and situates them "in a state of salvation, and not of depravity." Therefore, "after all men are redeemed from the fall and raised from the dead,... they are to be judged according to their own individual deeds done in the body; not according to Adam's transgression." They are therefore "condemned...not for Adam's fall, but for their own sins." Or in Smith's later language, "Men will be punished for their own sins, and not Adam's transgression." Then Pratt continued, again in language that Smith would adapt as an Article of Faith, that through "the blood of Christ," men will be redeemed "on the conditions of faith, repentance, and obedience to the gospel."[47] Or, as Smith recast it, "through the atonement of Christ, all men may be saved, by obedience to the laws and ordinances of the gospel."[48]

The genesis of all these ideas found in Pratt's pamphlet is hard to trace. Smith did not always publicly preach the doctrines of the kingdom as fast as he received or formulated them. Pratt enjoyed Smith's intimate association at a number of periods in his life, including their initial confinement together in Missouri, shortly before Pratt wrote this treatise of speculative theology. On such occasions, Smith may have shared ideas that he would only later promulgate to a mass audience. He first conceived of plural marriage, for example, in the early 1830s but only slowly divulged the doctrine to an inner circle that expanded over time. Other doctrines he seems to have withheld out of frustration with the Saints' incapacity for novel ideas. He complained that "I have tried for a number of years to get the minds of the saints prepared to recieve the things of God, but we freequently see some of them after suffering all they have for the work of God will fly to peaces like glass as soon as any thing Comes that is Contrary to their traditions. They cannot stand the fire at all."[49] It is also possible that Pratt propounded his highly unorthodox notions to Smith, who later embraced them and confirmed them. Though some of Pratt's contemporaries and predecessors (like Dick) matched his theological iconoclasm, Pratt's work differed from them in at least two consequential regards. He wrote on the basis of what he believed was authoritative revelation rather than simple inference. And he wedded his system to a young but flourishing institution, which assured its dissemination and survival.

Pratt's revised *Millennium*, with the appended theological treatise, came off the press in early January 1840. At the same time, Pratt was finishing revisions to a third work. Mere months after he had published in Detroit his work on the Missouri persecutions, he began work on a second edition. Pratt's immersion in the doctrinal material of his revised *Voice of Warning* likely led him to prepare a summary of Mormon belief for inclusion. This he added as an introduction, enumerating the first principles of the Restored Gospel in language that would later find a close echo in several of Joseph Smith's 1842 Articles of Faith.[50] He affirmed Mormon belief in God, Christ, and the Holy Ghost, and outlined the four principles of faith, repentance, baptism, and gift of the Holy Ghost along with a series of other tenets, including proper authority to perform ordinances, gifts of the spirit, the validity of the Bible and of the Book of Mormon. To this he added, as also found in the current Articles of Faith, belief that God "will continue to reveal" important truths, that the House of Israel will be literally gathered, and that Christ will inaugurate a millennial era. Whereas the first edition was published as an eighty-four-page pamphlet, the new edition was published as a 216-page ribbed-cloth book with gilt lettering.[51]

Pratt intended his publications for missionary work, but he also hoped his efforts would fund his own mission and provide support for his family. In a letter to Joseph Smith, Pratt noted the lack of resources for major publishing projects in Nauvoo, pleaded the need ("there is a great call for our Books"), and asked permission to publish the Book of Mormon on terms that would benefit both of them while advancing the cause of Zion. Speaking for himself and two partners, he wrote, "We will give you one hundred dollars on each thousand coppies for the right of publishing, or we will give you one hundred Books on each thousand. Or we will publish it on commision and return you all the profits after defraying the expences of the same together with a reasonable charge for our time. Or, we will publish it on any other conditions which you can reasonably propose." Then he added hopefully, "any Hymn Book which Sister Smith or the church will favor us with shall also be published on similar conditions."[52]

Pratt's persistent poverty, combined with his passion for Mormonism, blurred evangelistic and economic motives, but the difficulties of a full-time call to a lay ministry left him no alternative. Before Pratt's departure, the impoverished church had passed a resolution to support the apostles' families during their absence, but Pratt would have recognized this as more a show of solidarity and wishful thinking than sound economic assurance.[53] Unlike the other apostles, Pratt had brought his family on his missionary journey, rendering his usual method of traveling without purse and scrip impractical.

By the time Pratt had written Smith in November 1839, asking for permission to publish the Book of Mormon, Smith had already left Nauvoo for Washington, D.C., to seek redress for the Missouri sufferings. Along with Sidney Rigdon, Smith then traveled to Philadelphia for a branch conference and to speak to large non-Mormon audiences (three thousand people on one occasion, according to Pratt).[54] Pratt paused in his publishing endeavors long enough to take a side trip to Philadelphia in January 1840, where he spent days under Joseph Smith's personal instruction.

Pratt prized his private conversations with Smith. "From [Smith and Rigdon] I received much precious instruction, in which I shall always rejoice," he wrote later that year.[55] Some of this instruction related to Smith's evolving ideas about marriage. Side by side with Smith's doctrine of plural marriage, there evolved in his mind an understanding of the marriage relation's eternal duration. As with plural marriage, it is unclear when Smith first conceived the eternity of marriage relationships. The first records of Smith teaching the doctrine do not appear until 1843, when he explicitly made marriage a prerequisite to full celestial glory.[56] The year after Smith's death, the church newspaper trumpeted "the irresistible conclusion, that the love and union of a man and his wife should extend into, and even be more perfect in eternity."[57]

But Smith was clearly teaching the principle in private much earlier. In 1835, just months after taking up temporary residence with Smith, W. W. Phelps made one of the first public references to the idea. "New light is occasionally bursting in to our minds," he wrote in the *Messenger and Advocate*. "We shall by and by learn that we were with God in another world... that we came into this world and have our agency, in order that we may prepare ourselves for a kingdom of glory; become archangels, even the sons of God where the man is neither without the woman, nor the woman without the man in the Lord: A consummation of glory, and happiness, and perfection so greatly to be wished."[58] And Pratt wrote that it was during their shared time in Philadelphia, in early 1840, that Smith taught him "the heavenly order of eternity. It was at this time that I received from him the first idea of eternal family organization, and the eternal union of the sexes."[59] He wrote rapturously of an idea he would later develop and defend passionately.

> Till then I had learned to esteem kindred affections and sympathies as appertaining solely to this transitory state, as something from which the heart must be entirely weaned, in order to be fitted for its heavenly state.
>
> It was Joseph Smith who taught me how to prize the endearing relationships of father and mother, husband and wife; of brother and sister, son and daughter.
>
> It was from him that I learned that the wife of my bosom might be secured to me for time and all eternity; and that the refined sympathies and affections which endeared us to each other emanated from the fountain of divine eternal love. It was from him that I learned that we might cultivate these affections, and grow and increase in the same to all eternity; while the result of our endless union would be an offspring as numerous as the stars of heaven, or the sands of the sea shore....
>
> I had loved before, but I knew not why. But now I loved—with a pureness and intensity of elevated, exalted feeling, which would lift my

soul from the transitory things of this grovelling sphere and expand it as the ocean. I felt that God was my heavenly Father indeed; that Jesus was my brother, and that the wife of my bosom was an immortal, eternal companion; a kind ministering angel, given to me as a comfort, and a crown of glory for ever and ever. In short, I could now love with the spirit and with the understanding also.[60]

Pratt brought his publishing zeal with him to Philadelphia, hoping to secure permission to publish a new edition of the Book of Mormon in New York. He had already begun to put such plans in motion, earlier writing Smith for permission to publish "two or three thousand" copies. (He further suggested an ambitious initiative to publish it "in Europe in English, French, German, and other languages.")[61] Hyrum Smith recognized the "famine" of the book, both in New York City and the nation, but he vetoed the plan, saying the publication of a new edition should happen at Nauvoo, "where it can come out under the immediate inspection of Joseph and his Counselors."[62] In Philadelphia, Pratt pressed his suit in person at the conference, but fared no better. Rigdon vocally opposed the plan and agreed with Hyrum on the advantages of a Nauvoo printing. Benjamin Winchester, one of Pratt's most prolific contemporaries on the subject of the Book of Mormon, sided with him in arguing for an immediate New York printing. Finally Joseph Smith directed that the project should be executed from Nauvoo. Pratt, stubborn as always, asked for the matter to be referred to the High Council of the Church, which the brethren voted to do. Smith may have had Pratt's zeal in mind when he urged, minutes later in the same conference, that "travelling Elders should be especially cautious of incroaching on the ground of stationed & presiding Elders and rather direct their efforts to breaking up and occupying new ground."[63] Pratt was still grousing months later that in the English mission copies were "verry much wanted" and not available.[64]

Smith left Philadelphia to return to his lobbying efforts in the capital at the end of January. His journey to the nation's capital and audience with a sitting president was no simple public relations venture. At this moment, nothing was more important to Smith than prosecuting the church's case for redress from their Missouri expulsion. A few months later, Smith halted the great enterprise of the "consecration law," the blueprint for a Zion society, in deference to what he saw as the more pressing matter of temporal salvation, stating that "the affair now before Congress was the only thing that ought to interest the Saints at present."[65] To further this objective, he charged Wheeler

Baldwin, Lyman Wight, and Abraham Smoot with collecting affidavits on the Missouri experience for forwarding to Washington.

Pratt now accompanied Smith to Washington to lend his pen. Smith had earlier appointed Elias Higbee as his own aide and traveling companion for the Washington effort. Now returned to Washington, Smith gave a favorably received public sermon on February 5.[66] To continue the momentum of the church's public relations effort, three days later Higbee and Pratt published an address under their names, giving a "sketch of our faith and principles" as background to their lobbying efforts. Higbee's name was attached alongside Pratt's because he would continue serving as the church's official representative, but the pamphlet was largely Pratt's reworking of his *Late Persecution*'s introduction. Like Smith's public address, the four-page pamphlet sought to allay suspicions, dispel misinformation, and establish the commonalities between Mormonism and mainstream Christian belief. Addressed to "the citizens of Washington, and to the public in general," it began by affirming a loose paraphrase of the Apostle's Creed, and faith in the Holy Scriptures. In unusually temperate terms for Pratt, the piece said that the Saints "have endeavored to restore the ancient doctrine and faith" and insisted they were not calling "in question the morality, the sincerity, or the spiritual enjoyment of individuals belonging to any religious system."[67] Pratt thus followed in the ecumenical spirit of Smith's public sermon, which declared twice that "all who would follow the precepts of the Bible, whether Mormon or not, would assuredly be saved."[68] Pratt acknowledged that the Saints were millennialists but insisted they were not alarmists like William Miller or Joseph Wolff, both of whom courted ridicule by stipulating dates for Christ's return. He also introduced the Book of Mormon, but in defensive rather than his typically bold tones, insisting it did not negate the Bible, "as some have falsely represented," and asking rhetorically if the discovery of an ancient record should not elicit interest rather than insult.[69]

Feeling confident he had done his duty in warning his own nation and government, Pratt returned to New York to make final preparations for his family's continued stay in New York and for his own departure to England. Elders Woodruff and Taylor had set sail in late December. Now the other five apostles assembled, gathered donations and provisions from local members, and booked passage on the packet ship *Patrick Henry*. On March 4, they held a final conference with the New York Saints, singing a hymn composed by Pratt for the occasion, "When Shall We All Meet Again?"[70] Five days later, they set sail for Liverpool, to the cheers and singing of a farewell party of well-wishers. The sea journey took four weeks. Brigham Young and George

A. Smith were sick most of the time; Pratt said only, "We had a rough passage."[71] On exactly the tenth anniversary of the founding of the church, the ship landed in Liverpool. A majority of the quorum were now prepared to assist in the most fruitful era of missionary work that Mormonism had yet known.

At the end of his first day in England, Pratt wrote Mary Ann, full of enthusiasm for what lay ahead. He related details of their harrowing passage and diverse companions ("some of the filthyest Lousyest caractors I ever saw But all verry generous and kind to us"). When not hanging to their bed rails for dear life, they enjoyed "fiddleing, fluiting, dancing, Singing, (mostly Love or war Songs, some Religious) togather with Blasphemy, Swearing Continding, Laughing, Courting and vomiting." Once on dry land, he reveled in the sights of a "new world to us, and yet the very world of our fore fathers," where the faces looked familiar, though the ladies "not as Beautiful as ours." Seeming to realize the size and scope of the missionary challenges ahead for the first time, he made an important decision regarding his family's future: "Here all the Kingdoms of Europe are before us on every side. Here is a boundless harvest for the next 15 or 20 years, or as long as God holds forth the arm of mercy: and here if the Lord will I expect to spend five or ten years at least." Anticipating such a long mission, he advised her "to sell every thing except beding and wearing apparrel, and fill two chests and a trunk, and get ready to come to England the first opportunity." His detailed instructions for settling his printing and financial affairs reveal a pragmatic as well as spiritual interest in his writing success:

> Collect all that is due for Books, sell all you can, Pay the seventy five dollars to the printer, Mr. Harrison; and Leave the Book Buisness with Eld[er] [Lucian] Foster.…I will allow Eld[er] Foster a good percent For his trouble, if he will take Charge of this Buisiness and now I say to you and to [h]im in particular Do not let the Books go without the pay in hand, for they have cost me much money and I owe for them; and I need the remainder after the debt is paid, to support my family.[72]

If she showed herself a shrewd negotiator, he advised, she would be able to purchase second-class rather than steerage fare ("it will not be so crouded with filthy vagrants of the rougher sort"). Then, perhaps considering the rigors of the voyage, he advised borrowing enough money to purchase her own cabin: "You will then be in a clean, warm, well fernished place" with "a chambermaid to wait upon you." And she could then depart immediately without waiting for an Elder to accompany her.[73]

Pratt was an indefatigable missionary, but he was also a compulsive writer. A little more than a week after landfall in Liverpool, he received an assignment that gave him formal sanction to blend his two passions. In Preston, the apostles convened a general conference of thirty-three branches of the church, a prodigious number given the mere three years since the first missionaries visited England. Willard Richards, who had been serving as a counselor to British Mission president Joseph Fielding, was ordained an apostle. Then, "Brigham Young, Heber C. Kimball and myself were appointed a publishing committee for the Church," Pratt recorded, no doubt with great satisfaction. Pratt realized earlier than most the possibilities of a vastly expanded Mormon print culture. Newspapers had issued from church centers of gathering since 1832, but Pratt had urged Smith to establish one in New York City months earlier, and now "craved the privilege" of editing a periodical in England, according to Young.[74] Thus at the Preston conference Pratt was appointed editor and publisher of a monthly periodical."[75]

He set up offices in Manchester, where he would write, edit the paper, and oversee distribution of church publications. Pratt was already the most prolific writer in the fledgling church, having enormous influence on how the gospel was presented, explained, and interpreted. The day before the conference, local member William Clayton purchased three books, all authored by Pratt: *Voice of Warning, History of the Persecution*, and *Millennium* (likely brought by Pratt to England).[76] Except for the scriptures and the church newspapers, little else was available to Saints who wanted to study the principles—or enjoy poetic celebration—of their new faith. This new position as editor of a periodical (which would end up surviving more than a century) consolidated and expanded Pratt's influence. The prospectus for the paper went out that same month of April, and Pratt's imprint was immediately evident in the very title—*The Latter-day Saints' Millennial Star*, reflecting his abiding sense of urgency and millennial fervor.[77] The title was perhaps inspired by the journal of the movement in which he received so much of his religious training; the Campbellites had been publishing since 1830 *The Millennial Harbinger*. As Pratt described his emphasis in the inaugural issue, launched just weeks after receiving his new assignment:

> Its columns will be devoted to the spread of the fulness of the gospel—the restoration of the ancient principles of Christianity—the gathering of Israel—the rolling forth of the kingdom of God among the nations—the signs of the times—the fulfilment of prophecy—recording the judgments of God as they befall the nations, whether signs in the heavens

or in the earth, "blood, fire, or vapour of smoke"—in short whatever is shown forth indicative of the coming of the Son of Man, and the ushering in of his universal reign on the earth.[78]

He also filled the pages with minutes of church conferences, abundant excerpts from the Book of Mormon, and letters from missionaries and members. The tone of his Washington *Address* published months earlier had been temperate, even conciliatory toward other faiths. The restrained tone suited that moment of political precariousness and vulnerability surrounding Joseph Smith's petition to the government. Now, freed from such considerations, Pratt reverted to form. His writing for the *Millennial Star* was once again rhetorically rich ("the following volume [is sent] to the world, as a flaming arrow of truth through the startling nations"); imbued with his dramatic flair ("in 1830 ... a church of six members rising from obscurity, and coming forth from the wilderness. The curtain falls, and opens upon 1838, and what is then beheld? Ten thousand people disinherited, robbed, plundered, driven, and all fleeing before their enemies"); and wryly sardonic ("A printed circular was lately put into our hands, ... holding out a warm invitation to men to become members of the Church of England, from which we extract the following, ... which, until satisfactorily answered, will prevent us from availing ourselves of the reverend gentleman's generous offer").[79] Young urged the publication of twenty-five hundred copies of the first run. Pratt feared the number was excessive, but within days thirteen hundred were sold.[80]

As an essayist and theologian, Pratt shaped the content and language of early Mormon self-understanding. Few Latter-day Saints today read Pratt's treatises, though his imprint pervades the theological spectrum they have inherited. Equally significant and more recognizably enduring was his influence on the words Mormons sing in worship. Pratt contributed three hymns to Emma Smith's original 1835 compilation. And along with Young and Taylor, Pratt was delegated to produce a hymnal for the British Saints. Smith had not approved an English hymnal, expecting to publish in Nauvoo an updated version of the 1835 hymnal. While work on that revision stalled, Pratt and his collaborators forged ahead on their own initiative, as they "found the brethren had laid by their old Hymn books, and they wanted new ones."[81] As Young took care of the business arrangements, Pratt composed at a feverish pace, producing some fifty hymns to contribute to the collection, considerably more than any other writer, though he had hoped to have one hundred in time for the edition.[82] The hymnal opened with Pratt's celebration of the restoration, first published on the cover of the inaugural issue of the *Millennial Star*:

The morning breaks, the shadows flee;
Lo! Zion's standard is unfurled!
The dawning of a brighter day
Majestic rises on the world.

Though Pratt's contributions were winnowed down to thirty-eight in the 1927 Mormon hymnal, and to eight in the current edition, his "Morning Breaks" still opens the collection. Like other Mormon hymnists, Pratt wrote on an array of gospel themes, but he focused on those premillennial events in which he gloried. Foremost in this category is one of Mormonism's most beloved anthems about the Book of Mormon:

An Angel from on high,
The long, long silence broke—
Descending from the sky,
These gracious words he spoke:
Lo! in Cumorah's lonely hill,
A sacred record lies concealed.
Sealed by Moroni's hand,
It has for ages slept,
To wait the Lord's command,
From dust again to speak;
It shall come forth to light again,
To usher in Messiah's reign.

Millions of non-Mormons have heard the tune to yet another of Pratt's hymns: "As the Dew from Heaven," the Mormon Tabernacle Choir's weekly signature signoff tune, which contains his most lyrically concise and elegant work:

As the dew from heav'n distilling Gently on the grass descends
And revives it, thus fulfilling What thy providence intends,
Let thy doctrine, Lord so gracious, Thus descending from above,
Blest by thee prove efficacious To fulfill thy work of love.
Lord, behold this congregation; Precious promises fulfill.
From thy holy habitation Let the dews of life distill.
Let our cry come up before thee, Sweetest influence shed around,
So the people shall adore thee And confess the joyful sound.[83]

The Manchester hymn book was off to the printer almost as soon as the first issue of the *Millennial Star* rolled off the press in May 1840. By July, three thousand copies had been published. The new Nauvoo hymnal finally arrived the next year, but the "Manchester Hymnal" emerged as the favorite among English-speaking Saints. While the Nauvoo version retreated to a more conventional Protestant hymnody, the Manchester Hymnal, inspired by Pratt's millennialism and restorationist fervor, was redolent with themes more calculated to resonate with a Mormon congregation, such as gathering, priesthood, and the Book of Mormon.[84] As a consequence, it remained the standard well into the twentieth century, going through twenty-five editions.[85] Smith praised the apostles' effort: "I highly approve of it and think it to be a very valuable collection."[86]

Meanwhile, Smith had finally resolved the debate over a British Book of Mormon by printing a new Nauvoo edition of two thousand, even as he authorized Pratt to proceed with a British edition. After negotiating with printers for an ambitious five thousand copies, Pratt and Young signed an agreement in mid-June 1840.[87] Amid these larger publishing projects, Pratt in May also reprinted with minor changes ten thousand copies of his *Address by Judge Higbee and Parley P. Pratt* as *An Address by a Minister of the Church of Jesus Christ of Latter-day Saints, to the People of England*, most of them "distributed gratis among the people."[88] For three months, Pratt squeezed what preaching duties he could into rare respites from his exhausting editorial responsibilities. Both were immensely successful and satisfying, but he felt overwhelmed. "I am confined entirely at home as Editor of the 'Star' and publisher of the Hymn Book, B. of Mormon, and all our other Books," he wrote Mary Ann. "I have not been gone from home Save 24 hours Since I Came here 3 months ago."[89]

Mormon missionary work in England had begun when, building on the contacts resulting from Pratt's Canadian mission, apostles Heber Kimball and Orson Hyde; and Willard Richards, who would later be ordained an apostle; along with Canadian converts Joseph Fielding, Isaac Russell, John Snider, and John Goodson arrived in Liverpool in July 1837. The religious landscape of England, to a significant though lesser degree than in America, was a scene of vigorous competition and innovation. Catholic emancipation and the repeal of the Test Act (which restricted most public offices to Anglicans) were less than a decade in the past. Two-thirds of the English belonged to the established Church of England, but the time had never been more propitious for the growth of genuine religious pluralism, including

Catholics, denominations known collectively as Dissenters (scattered Baptists, Presbyterians, Quakers, and Congregationalists), Methodists, and seekers. Many of the same religious trends that proved persuasive to Mormon converts in the United States also existed in England, including a vibrant millennialism that cut across many groups and a movement toward Christian primitivism. Methodists proved particularly receptive to the Mormon message; recognizing this, Pratt claimed common ground by reprinting a John Wesley sermon in the *Millennial Star*: "JOHN WESLEY A LATTER-DAY SAINT, in Regard to the Spiritual Gifts and the Apostasy of the Church!!"[90]

At the same time, acute economic distress, political liberalism, and evangelical fervor fueled a volatile mix of social agitation, labor unrest, and reform movements. Chartism, a working-class movement for political liberalization, began its period of greatest influence in 1838, the same year the Anti–Corn Law League was founded to protest tariffs on grain that kept prices artificially high. Temperance movements proliferated throughout the 1830s; Luddite riots had abated, but labor conflicts arose with waves of Irish immigration, massive unemployment, and plummeting wages; trade unionism was on the ascendant, often provoking violent clashes. Religious fervor was often allied to social reform, but just as often displaced by more pressing economic and political agendas. The disparity in social classes' living conditions in Liverpool shocked the Mormon missionaries. "We wandered in the streets of that great city," Kimball recorded, "where wealth and luxury, penury and want abound. I there met the rich attired in the most costly dresses, and the next moment was saluted with the cries of the poor, without covering sufficient to screne them from the weather; such a distinction I never saw before."[91]

Kimball and his companions immediately struck out for Preston, thirty miles to the north, where Fielding had extended family. Fielding's brother James, pastor of a Baptist congregation, opened the doors of his church to the missionaries. A week later they baptized their first converts, to the reverend's chagrin, and soon organized the first branch in England. Visits to the surrounding villages yielded fruit as well, and on Christmas Day, more than three hundred Saints from throughout Lancashire attended the mission's first conference.[92] Within four months, fifteen hundred converts had been baptized. Hyde and most of the missionaries then departed for home, leaving Fielding, Richards, and newly baptized William Clayton in charge of the British mission.

Spearheading the 1840 mission to England, apostles Woodruff and Taylor arrived three months ahead of the others. They found the mission presidency had just managed to maintain a constant membership base, offsetting defections with occasional new baptisms.[93] With their arrival, the work surged ahead again, and hundreds of converts poured into the church. Woodruff achieved phenomenal success in Herefordshire, particularly with a group of primitive Methodists called the United Brethren. He was soon baptizing so many that he grew weary and summoned Richards to assist. "I cannot do the work alone," he happily complained the last day of March. "I am called to Baptize 4 or 5 times a day."[94] With Richards's arrival, the need only increased. "There has been in these two weeks about 112 baptized.... There are many doors open which we cannot fill; calls for preaching on almost every hand which we cannot answer," he wrote Pratt, who also was in England, in mid-May.[95]

Jubilant apostles and missionaries from across England and Scotland sent Pratt regular progress reports for publication in the *Millennial Star*, requesting impressive numbers of copies of the Book of Mormon and the church paper. From the Potteries in the north of Staffordshire, an elder reported "a great call for...the *Voice of Warning* and also for the *Star*. We sent him one hundred of the *Star*," Pratt reported proudly in June. From Herefordshire, Richards requested 250 copies of the *Millennial Star* after already receiving that number previously. Similar tidings poured in from Paisley, Scotland, from Edinburgh, from Stockport, and from other regions; missionaries also headed for Glasgow.[96] In Manchester, they rented the Carpenter Hall, with a capacity of two thousand, to preach in.

As the church grew in England, so did clerical resistance—along with misinformation and pamphlet attacks. If the religious print culture produced a sea of pamphlets in antebellum America, in England it created an ocean. The New England Tract Society distributed nearly eight hundred thousand tracts by 1823. In England, by contrast, the London Tract Society had distributed fifty-eight million by 1824.[97] In this environment, Pratt realized it was not enough to distribute Mormon scriptures and doctrines—he would have to respond to the attacks using the power of the press. In February 1840, the Reverend C. S. Bush, the Anglican minister of a Peover parish, published *Plain Facts, Shewing the Falsehood and Folly of the Mormonites*. Bush's title reflected his double critique of Mormonism: it was predicated on fraud, since the Book of Mormon was allegedly plagiarized from a novel by Solomon Spaulding; and it was based on doctrinal error, since the Bible was complete and sufficient. A few months after his arrival, Pratt wrote a rejoinder, which parroted the title, but substituted "Rev. C. S. Bush" for "Mormonites" as the perpetrator of falsehood and folly, marking the first entry of a Mormon author into the pamphlet wars of Victorian England. Pratt responded to the second criticism by pointing to the many extra-canonical works referred to with implicit approval by the Bible itself, such as Jasher and the Acts of Solomon. Citing proof texts in support of "continual and universal revelation," he somewhat disingenuously implored Methodists, Quakers, and the Christian world at large to join him in condemning "this atheism in new dress—this religion which shuts heaven, and cuts off all communication between God and his creature."[98] He then refuted the Spaulding origin of the Book of Mormon by introducing evidence that the letter on which the theory was largely based was a forgery, and by attacking the time line on which the alleged forgery depended. It was a technical, legalistic refutation, effective if not exactly riveting.

The Manchester Hymnal arrived just in time for the second General Conference, held on July 6, 1840, a mere three months after the apostles' arrival. The apostles appointed Pratt to preside over the Manchester meeting, which drew almost three thousand members. Pratt was expecting the arrival any day of Mary Ann and the children. During the conference, he received a letter which he opened anxiously, only to learn that all his family were dangerously stricken with scarlet fever. (Fifteen to twenty percent of cases were fatal; odds of losing his wife or at least one child were therefore better than even.) Pratt was understandably shaken, his emotions a chaos. "This is more than I can bear," he wrote to Mary Ann, thinking first of his own predicament. "Here must I live alone, my Chamber dessolate." The fault was hers: "Why did you not come with me when I pressed it upon you last winter?" he chided, then immediately apologized. "Do not for a moment suppose I blame you, for not coming, it is only my feelings which I cannot help expressing in the anguish of my heart." He wanted to share news of his successes, but his "feelings will not suffer me to write it." He wanted to be with her, to comfort her, and would "gladly lay down his life" for her and the little ones, but the press of work meant it would be "months or years" before he could leave.[99]

If Pratt momentarily forgot where his obligations lay, his brethren in the quorum did not. They persuaded him to return to New York, and he set off immediately. Arriving in New York he learned that the crisis had passed and that all his family members were recovered. Realizing it might be years before opportunity again permitted, he went with Mary Ann to visit her family in Maine. While at the home of Mary Ann's sister, Pratt received confirmation, if any was needed, that he had a special calling as a literary John the Baptist, ushering in with his writings the new dispensation and its scriptures:

Mrs. Bean had a dream a few days previous to our arrival, in which she dreamed that I came to her and gave her a key to the Bible. As she related the dream to me, I presented her with my *"Voice of Warning."* It seemed to her and her husband as they read it as if it was indeed a key to the doctrine and prophecies of the Holy Scriptures. They rejoiced with exceeding joy, and promised to be baptized, and to gather to Nauvoo.[100]

Enlisting one of his wife's other sisters, Olive Frost, as an au pair, Pratt returned to New York, packed up his family, and embarked once more for England. He returned with exciting new information, preached by Joseph Smith, about the importance of their work in England. America was "guilty of Blood" for its role in the Missouri expulsions, he wrote brother Orson. The country was consequently "near desolation," but the Lord's servants were to spread throughout the earth, gathering the righteous to constitute "a mighty army!!!!!!" Thus spiritually strengthened by the infusion of the elect, America would become "an asylum for the remnant of all nations." The millennial zeal behind Pratt's missionary urgency was now combined with the need to redeem Zion, newly defined by Smith as North and South America.[101]

Pratt and his family arrived back in Manchester in October. His commodious lodgings in the city were probably the most comfortable he had yet enjoyed with a family that now numbered five dependents with another on the way: "I had hired a House consisting of a Shop in front, for my office and Book Store, and two more rooms below and 3 rooms above, it is an airy and healthy pleasant place."[102] Pratt settled back into the work of writing and editing, taking frequent trips to preach and visit the branches. In addition to his work on the *Millennial Star*, Pratt continued to be the principal player in the pamphlet wars swirling around the Mormon missionary effort in England. "The country is flooded with pamphlets, tracts, papers &c. published against us," Pratt complained to Sidney Rigdon. "Some of them have *bear* & *wolf* stories in them, some of them, have *snake* stories, and others *gander* stories. I must say that 'Jonathan' is far behind 'John Bull' in ingenuity in regard to inventing lies; all the foolishness ever published in the United States against the truth, would be considered sober earnest, compared to the follies which are being made manifest here."[103] Reuben Hancock seconded Pratt's lament, writing from Scotland that "the priests cry 'false prophets' from their pulpits,—they generally take their text from the newspapers and pamphlets that are published against us."[104] Woodruff called the print campaign a "deluge" of misinformation, and George A. Smith complained that England "is as much flooded with false reports concerning us, as ever America was."[105]

Pratt was determined to reply in kind—and in bulk. Woodruff estimated that in their single year in the British Isles, the apostles published fifty thousand tracts. Orson Hyde published the first missionary broadside in England in 1837. In the years before the apostolic British mission, however, the temperate Joseph Fielding, who presided there from 1838 to 1840, had chosen the path of dignified indifference. "It appears they want to provoke us to Controversy," he wrote of two anti-Mormon authors, "but we have washed our feet against them all so they may talk and write until they are tired, or till the Lord puts a stop to them."[106] Or until Parley Pratt arrived in England, he might more accurately have forecast.

As 1840 drew near to a close, he entered the lists again. The first anti-Mormon tract in England, preceding Bush's attack by more than a year, was Methodist minister Richard Livesey's twelve-page *Exposure of Mormonism* (1838, reprinted in Manchester in 1840). At the same time, Thomas Taylor "of the Mason Street Sawmills," made hay out of a catastrophic public relations ploy that gave the Mormons substantial notoriety. Taylor challenged a young English convert, James Mahon, to demonstrate the gift of tongues before a panel of judges at a public meeting. Foolishly agreeing, Mahon was unable to interpret Hebrew when read to him. According to the *Annals of Manchester*, Mahon "then spoke what he declared to be Hebrew, but the teacher of languages, who was the referee, declared that there was not a word of Hebrew in his jargon."[107] Taylor gleefully wrote up the fiasco as *An Account of the Complete Failure of an Ordained Priest of the "Latter Day Saints"*.

Pratt responded to the two pamphlets simultaneously. Taking the Mahon bull by the horns, Pratt chastised the young convert for improperly catering to sign-seekers. If Taylor denied spiritual gifts, Pratt wished to do no more than invoke New Testament precedent. If Taylor was unrepentant of demanding a sign before he would believe, then he was part of the "evil and adulterous" generation condemned by Christ. Turning to Livesey's pamphlet, Pratt methodically refuted criticisms of Mormon gathering, the Book of Mormon, and Joseph Smith's character. Then turning the tables, he reproached Taylor for his Methodist beliefs, which he rather intemperately called "a bundle of nonsense, contradiction and absurdity."[108] He referred most particularly to the creedal "God without body or parts." Even before he or other Mormon thinkers had fully worked out their conception of the Godhead, Pratt declared that he was no "idolater," like other Christians.

While he did not yet articulate a physically embodied Father, he emphasized that Christ, God the Son, "arose from the dead, and took upon him his body," and would return in like form.[109]

Pratt rounded out the year by publishing a thousand copies of *An Answer to Mr. William Hewitt's Tract Against the Latter-day Saints*. In a rare step, Pratt distanced himself from doctrines he entertained but did not insist upon. Accused of believing "there is nothing which had a beginning, but what will have an end," Pratt rather disingenuously stated that in his ten years in the church, he "never heard that doctrine before." In fact, he had insisted as much in Regeneration and Eternal Duration of Matter only months earlier: "Matter and spirit…never began to exist, and they never can be annihilated."[110] Charged with believing in a God in human form rather than a God of spirit, Pratt hedged. A spirit, he argued, does indeed have "eyes, mouth, ears, &c." Nevertheless, a divine body is "not composed of such gross materials as flesh and bones."[111] Pratt may have sincerely believed that was the Mormon position, since it would be another year before Smith would state in public that "there is no other God in heaven but that God who has flesh and bones."[112]

Perhaps realizing that plodding rejoinders to theological critiques were not convincing many readers, Pratt hurled one more volley against the church's antagonists, this time employing satire. At the close of 1840, he published "An Epistle of Demetrius, Junior, the Silversmith." He based it on the account in Acts that describes the uproar created by Paul's teachings in Ephesus, when he threatened the livelihood of the idol-makers. A sly and effective satire, it pretends to mock the Latter-day Saints for teachings that in the mouth of "Demetrius" sound eminently reasonable, and implicitly but pointedly compares the clergy of England to merchants more concerned about their gate receipts than the pearly gates. Mormons, Demetrius warns his audience, are simple enough to believe "the Bible as it reads," rather than as it is "spiritualized." They take Jesus at his word when he sent them to preach without purse or scrip, and naively embrace the spiritual gifts seen in the New Testament church. Finally, they believe that their God, in contrast to theirs of silver, can reveal his will through revelation to the faithful. Pratt ended by imagining the frustration the professors of false religions like Demetrius must have in the face of Mormonism's onward march. Invoking the recent Missouri persecutions especially, he combined righteous outrage, an appeal to sympathy, and his personal sense of vindication:

> The deadly rifle has laid them low in the dust: their leaders have been
> dragged to prison, and bound in chains and dungeons; their houses

burned, their property robbed, their women and children driven from their homes by thousands, to seek shelter where they could find it; and then we fondly hoped it was overcome and put down, but alas! we were disappointed still. The chains were rent, the dungeons were burst. The prisoners and others are again abroad in the earth, and their system is spreading with tenfold rapidity.[113]

The intrusion of Missouri memories into his satire may have been prompted by word that had just come to Pratt that the last round of appeals to Congress, like the first, had fallen on deaf ears. Pratt must have felt at times that his vaunted land of liberty he so loved fared poorly in comparison with England. Opposition and physical harassment followed the quorum to England, but on balance the apostles fared well in the ecclesiastical and civil courts. Alarmed at the Mormon successes in Herefordshire, ministers petitioned the Archbishop of Canterbury to intercede with Parliament to stay the hand of the missionaries. The archbishop and his council declined, blaming the ministers for the defections. Later, when Pratt preached in Bolton, a minister and his associate in his audience became so disruptive and violent that police were called in. At the ensuing trial, the rabble-rousers were found guilty and fined.[114]

Everywhere the work surged forward. With a strong base of converts, abundant hymnals, scriptures, and pamphlets, the apostles asked Smith about the possibility of a return to their homes and families in the coming spring. In December, Smith commended them for their "diligence and faithfulness," and declared "the propriety of [their] returning in the spring." Pratt's case, he continued, might be different.

> If Elder P. P. Pratt should wish to remain in England some time longer than the rest of the Twelve, he will feel himself at liberty to do so, as his family are with him, consequently his circumstances are somewhat different to the rest; and like wise it is necessary that some one should remain who is conversant with the rules and regulations of the church, and continue the paper which is published.[115]

Finding the field so ripe, ensconced comfortably with his family, and with the supreme satisfaction of being able to publish his own work at will, Pratt was content to stay. That same month, the elders rented the largest hall in Liverpool (the Music Hall) to accommodate the growing numbers of members and throngs of the curious who came to hear John Taylor preach. "The work is smashing all before it as it rolls and the poor Ignorant Editors are losing what little sense they had, and actually going mad," Pratt told his brother Orson with hope and hyperbole.[116] To Sidney Rigdon in Nauvoo, he excitedly reported the deep interest in Mormonism among a congregation of Campbellites and remarked: "Tell friend Campbell to go ahead and prepare the way, the Saints will follow him up and gather the fruits."[117]

In January 1841, Pratt took enough time off from writing to hold conferences, with Brigham Young and Willard Richards, in Liverpool and Preston. One of the subjects of the conferences was the principle of gathering. It was not at first clear if foreign converts would be expected to comply with the command to "go up to Zion." There were concerns about financial feasibility, and the effect on the morale of those left behind. Days after his 1840 arrival, Pratt gave "the first general discussion of the gathering" to British Saints. His support was unequivocal, marked only by concern that the emigrants should make "no noise about it" and that the fortunate help the destitute.[118] The first emigrant ship of converts, led by John Moon, sailed that June. A few months later, the First Presidency issued a statement titled "To the Saints Scattered Abroad" that confirmed Pratt's judgment: "The work of the gathering spoken of in the scriptures," the letter declared, "will be necessary to bring about the glories of the last dispensation." And that project required "the hearty co-operation of the Saints throughout [America], and upon the islands of the sea."[119] At the Preston conference, Pratt added to the spiritual imperative to gather in Zion an economic one. It simply made sense for a "dense and hungry Population" to seek opportunity elsewhere, he told the Saints.[120] Weeks later, a group of 240 converts embarked for Nauvoo.

As spring approached, the long-awaited Liverpool edition of the Book of Mormon was almost ready, and Pratt's work continued to be fruitful. The only serpent in the grass was his old nemesis, penury. Sales from Pratt's printing office suddenly dried up, leaving him and his family especially vulnerable, as he informed Young in a letter verging on desperation:

> I would inform you that My buisiness is entirely done.... We get little or no reterns from any of our Agents abroad;—indeed we have not got *any* for some weeks, and as to the trade at home it would not Buy our Bread.....I think of closing up the Shop in a few weeks, and moving in to a private house, (what the English call retiring from buisiness!)—If you have any council for me please give it.—I have tryed to Borrow 10 or 20 pounds—but I find no prospect of obtaining any.[121]

He followed this up with a letter to George A. Smith, pleading for help in his financial embarrassments. "From all my Agents I have Rec'd but 2 returns of cash, for Many Weeks.—I have rec'd none of late from the Poteries either on the old account or the late Numbers. I have never Rec'd one *penny* for the 1,000 Replies to Hewit Which I got printed allmost entirely for the poteries," he complained. "Will you be so kind as to Stur up the conference of Staffordshire and their officers to the dilligence in Supporting the *Press*."[122] Aware of his distress, other elders scrambled to collect overdue payments. George Simpson asked Smith "to get me as much Money for the Stars" as possible. "I want to send all I can to Elder P. P. Pratt," he explained, "for he wants it."[123]

Clearly, Pratt's earlier circulation estimates had been overly optimistic, even with so many "agents" scattered abroad. Pratt's practice of using missionaries to drum up subscriptions for the *Millennial Star* was based on long-standing practice. The second issue of the church's Independence newspaper had noted, "Our Elders abroad, may do much good by obtaining subscribers for the Star"—a good both pecuniary and spiritual.[124] But collecting payment was a good deal harder than distributing the papers and pamphlets. By March, Pratt's situation had not perceptibly improved, and he grew despondent over what had been such a promising enterprise, both financially and spiritually. "Br. Pratt…has got over all his feelings about Books," wrote Young, with little need to elaborate.[125] The editor of the *Millennial Star* found it necessary to trade in his spacious office for more humble accommodations on Oxford Road. Apparently lacking clearly defined guidelines separating his personal business from the church's, Pratt's plight prompted Young to propose altered business arrangements. To Willard Richards, he wrote, "What say you to Br. Pratt's taking the Books to pay the Herefordshires debt & having the prophets [profits] himself." Young also fretted that the binder contracted to finish the five thousand copies of the Book of Mormon that had come off the press in January would not "due his duty" given the church's financial predicament.[126] Then, on April 3, the quorum voted to divest the church of any financial interest in the paper, agreeing to make Pratt the "Editor and Sole proprietor" of the *Millennial Star*. They gave him rights over the hymnbook as well.[127]

Somehow, Pratt scraped together enough resources to keep himself and the press afloat. Woodruff, feeling either pity or optimism for Pratt, wrote a few days later, "We left [Pratt] with a Store of Books of Mormon Hymn Book voice of warning, Poems, tracts, & Stars for sale."[128] Even as this solution offered some hope, the publisher of the Liverpool Book of Mormon declined Pratt's request to alter their agreement. "We cannot be accountable for the loss you have sustained," he informed Pratt, and "it is out of our power therefore to accord to the terms of your request."[129] With time, sales of his pamphlets and the *Millennial Star* increased, and Pratt optimistically subscribed $500 for the Nauvoo Temple and another $500 for the Nauvoo House. Somehow, over the course of his English mission he found the "many thousand dollars" to "support a numerous family, and to feed the hungry and clothe the naked, and aid the poor to emigrate, and the missionaries on their journeys."[130]

Financial problems notwithstanding, the mission continued to prosper, and Pratt's shop was a nexus of activity and sociability, which lifted his spirits considerably. Nine apostles converged on Manchester in early April for a conference, the first time in four years so many had been gathered together. "We had a happy time together," Woodruff noted on April 1. "Unity prevailed." A few days later, he called on Pratt at the bookstore, "& found his house full of Elders."[131] On April 6, 1841, one year from their arrival, the conference was held. Even subtracting the eight hundred converts who had emigrated, the church in the United Kingdom now numbered almost six thousand (only half that number populated Nauvoo, Joseph Smith related to them).[132] The Twelve declared their British mission officially over. Pratt and his brethren celebrated by spending an afternoon at the zoological gardens. Pratt enjoyed it well enough that he returned weeks later with a different group, to see the magnificent gardens, but also "Loyans Tigers Lepards Helephant Rynostious Camel" as well as "2 Sea Bear" and "munkeys."[133]

Pratt was now reappointed president of the Manchester conference and named president of the British mission. Designating American missionaries Lorenzo Snow and Levi Richards to assist Pratt in their absence, the other members of the quorum prepared to depart. Pratt wrote to his father-in-law, Aaron Frost, of the burden he now felt:

> The care of the Churches in England, Scotland, Wales, Ireland and the Isle of Man are left for me to Superintend, with the aid of the presiding officers. This throws under my Charge, some thousands of Members, and some six or Eight hundred Ministers of the fulness of the Gospel. I trully feel that My Responsibilities are great indeed, and I feel to Say with Soloman, O! Lord, give me wisdom, that I may Go in and out among thy people and Clear my Garments of their Blood.

His family remained steadfast at his side, but he hoped to entice his in-laws to migrate to Nauvoo, suggesting to Frost in the same letter that his two daughters, Mary and Olive, "would soon be there with you."[134]

Editing the *Millennial Star* and administering the affairs of the British mission occupied Pratt's time in the subsequent months. In May, before his departure, Brigham Young directed Lorenzo Snow to present Queen Victoria and Prince Albert with a Book of Mormon. Pratt wrote a formal letter to the queen to accompany the gift and published ten thousand copies.[135] With typical impetuosity, Pratt sent the letter to press before Snow could make the presentation. It was a brash proclamation, even provocative—not exactly calculated to win regal favor for the church. Against a background of social agitation and violent upheaval, Pratt assured the royal couple "that the world in which we live is on the eve of a REVOLUTION, more wonderful in its beginning—more rapid in its progress—more powerful in its operations— more extensive in its effects—more lasting in its influence—and more important in its consequences, than any which man has yet witnessed." He quoted Daniel's prophecy of the "stone cut without hands," warning that this kingdom not of this world would soon supplant their dominions, with consequences both religious and political.[136] Victoria and Albert did not need a Mormon missionary to alert them to the volatility of their realm. Less than a week after Pratt published his letter, the English Anti–Corn Law League mustered fifty thousand citizens at a Manchester meeting even as the more militant Chartists demonstrated for expanded suffrage. The two erstwhile allies clashed on June 2. "Blood is shed...& great excitement prevails," Pratt reported to Woodruff.[137] Amid the social tension, Pratt preached one night and then debated a female socialist lecturer on the topic of resurrection for two additional evenings in Manchester's Hall of Science, the city's largest lecture hall, seating three thousand, which had been established by Robert Owen in 1840 to encourage working-class education. A Latter-day Saint observer commented, "I have heard that many of them were pleased with Br. Pratt."[138]

The mission continued to progress rapidly under Pratt's direction. A conference in Manchester in May drew a thousand participants and reported that there were seventy-two hundred church members "in good standing" throughout Great Britain; Levi Richards described Pratt's preaching as "very free and powerful."[139] The next month, Pratt presided at another church conference, where he was reported to be "well and in good spirits."[140] All the while, streams of converts departed the mission field, bound for Nauvoo under Pratt's direction. Six months later, he gave a report to Smith so overflowing with optimism that even defections had their silver lining:

New branches of the church are rising in many places, and great additions made to the old ones. Manchester and vicinity has poured forth a stream of emigration for the last 18 months, and still we numbered at our Conference, two weeks ago, near sixteen hundred members, and between one and two hundred officers, all these with in one hours journey of Manchester. There has been a general time of pruning, we have cut off upwards of 100 members from this Conference in a few months; this causes the young and tender branches to grow with double vigour.

He also sent Smith some money toward the construction of the Nauvoo Temple and detailed construction advice he had picked up from English converts.[141]

Months later, Pratt wrote again to Smith, having migrated to the opposite emotional extreme of despondency and heartache. In late 1841, England was in the last throes of a severe trade depression. Spurred by the rapid growth of the cotton mills, Manchester had emerged as one of the critical centers of British industrialization. Visitors to the mills and the squalid slums expressed shock at the plight of the working class. In 1835, Alexis de Tocqueville captured the paradox at the heart of Manchester's advance: "From this foul drain the greatest stream of human industry flows out to fertilize the whole world.... Here humanity attains its most complete development and its most brutish; here civilization works its miracles, and civilized man is turned back almost into a savage." Three years later, Charles Dickens wrote that the city "disgusted and astonished me beyond all measure." He resolved to "strike the heaviest blow in my power for these unfortunate creatures," which he eventually did in his 1853 novel *Hard Times*.[142] Friedrich Engels's experience in Manchester from 1842 to 1844 compelled him to write *The Condition of the Working Class in England*, which described in graphic detail this "Hell upon Earth." He wrote of the workers' living conditions, "The race that lives in these ruinous cottages, behind broken windows, mended with oilskin, sprung doors, and rotten doorposts, or in dark, wet cellars, in measureless filth and stench...must really have reached the lowest stage of humanity."[143]

No wonder that with the growth of the British mission, the euphoria of convert baptisms had become the burden of an indigent membership. "O! Br. Joseph," Pratt lamented. "Millions of Laborers are out of employ, and are starving in this country, and among others hundreds of the most faithful Saints, and hundreds more are laboring like slaves on about half what they can eat. This pains my heart, and I sometimes feel as if I could take them all on my shoulders and upon my arms and carry them to Zion; but allass, the means is

Wanting." Gladly would the men indenture themselves out in return for passage to Zion, he wrote, "but no one will *buy* them." Cut off from the brotherhood of the quorum, the burden of office heightened his sense of isolation, and he pleaded with Smith to send him "a word of encouragement, and advise, for I get no letters from America."[144]

Pratt then followed with several questions regarding administration of the mission. How could he make provision for the Saints' care after his departure, which he hoped to take in the spring? When would the gospel go to other nations? How could he better effect the emigration of British Saints? Two questions in particular carried special poignancy, revealing as they did the fading of those hopes that had inspired the initial, heady days of his devotion to the Restoration of the gospel: "When Will The 'purchased possession' be Redeemed and the temple and city commence in Jackson Co. Mo." and "When Will the ungodly, lying, Gentiles begin to loose their Power and ceace to Rule; and We who have now spent half of our lives for them, be privaledged to turn from the Gentiles and go in full power to the Remnants of joseph"?[145] Pratt was far from alone in refusing to relinquish faith in an imminent return to Jackson County. Two more generations would come and go before Saints ceased to clamor for their delayed inheritance. And it was more than a century later before Mormon leaders would finally pronounce that the "day of the Lamanite" had arrived with the explosive growth of the church in Latin America.[146]

Early in 1842, Pratt relocated to Liverpool, to better superintend the exodus of converts. By the spring, with no help from church headquarters forthcoming, Pratt had devised a trade arrangement to fund further emigration. He told Smith he was sending $2,000 worth of cloth goods and $3,000 in gold advanced by merchants to purchase flour and wheat in Nauvoo. The foodstuffs would sustain further emigration of British converts and presumably allow enough for sales to repay the loan. (Provisions were forbiddingly high in England—six times their price in America, according to Pratt.)[147] The need was acute, since Pratt ambitiously anticipated sending another five thousand to six thousand converts to Nauvoo the following season.

Pratt continued to preach as occasion permitted, but the scope of past success left him dissatisfied with incremental gains. In late April he rented a large amphitheater in Birmingham for a series of three lectures. When audiences failed to materialize in numbers sufficient to fill the cavernous space, he cancelled the third meeting to the dismay of one "looker on," who chided Pratt for apparently believing 120 souls were not worth saving.[148] Meanwhile, Pratt's schemes to maintain an active emigrant pipeline were working. In June,

Lorenzo Barnes reported that "Br Pratt & [Amos] Fielding have established an excellent lione [line] of emigration ships to N. Orleans and emigrants can now be taken from Liverpool to Nauvoo including all expenses for 25 dollars a peace & perhaps less." Chartering the ships, Pratt boasted, cut the price per emigrant in half.[149]

At the same time, Smith acquiesced to Pratt's entreaties for a show of recognition and support and sent a letter by Amos Fielding, the trade agent Pratt had sent to Nauvoo in the spring. Smith's letter attempted to solve Nauvoo's immigrant problem as much as Pratt's emigrant one. The problem at both ends was Saints relocating without sufficient provision for either those leaving or those left behind. "The gathering is not in haste," Smith said, hoping to rein in Pratt's ardor as much as that of his converts. "Prepare all things before you," he continued, then zeroed in on the consequences of precipitous gathering: "There are poor men who come here and leave their families behind in a destitute situation, and beg for assistance to send back after their families. Every man should tarry with his family untill Providence provides for the whole, for there is no means here to be obtained to send back." If the advice solved few of Pratt's problems, he found some solace in Smith's few words of approbation. "We assure you that you have our best feelings, and our prayers, and [we] have no fault to find. Believing every man has done the best he could, that is—the Elders, such as have remained in England."[150]

In September, Pratt wrote to Smith that economic conditions in England remained bleak ("Distress is unparalleled in the whole Country") but that the church was drawing more people as a consequence ("the Saints are geting out we send 3 ships this month Crowded with emigrants for Nauvoo").[151] By now, Pratt was longing to be on board with them. His former colleague in the English mission Wilford Woodruff had written him just a few months previous that "the whole world is in a hubbub except Nauvoo we have peace & quietness here."[152] For more than a year, Pratt had been pining for his old friendships. The previous fall, Pratt wrote that often while "gazing upon the congregation of rejoicing hundreds, (who were strangers to me but yesterday, but who are made nigh by the blood of Christ,)" he momentarily saw old friends: "One looks like Newel Knights, another like John Murdock, a third resembles Lyman Wight....Alas! the illusion vanishes as a dream of the morning."[153] And so he wrote in September to Smith that he planned to come back to America the next spring. Within weeks, however, he had changed his mind. Exhausted by his labors and yearning for his home country and fellow Saints, he prepared to depart almost immediately. Bidding goodbye to the English members at an October 1842 meeting, he then published a farewell in the *Millennial Star*. Formal in tone, he gave an account of his successful stewardship, appointed Thomas Ward as his successor, and noted with pride that the Saints in Europe (meaning essentially England and Scotland) had surged in numbers from two thousand at the commencement of his labors to nearly ten thousand as he prepared to relinquish the presidency.[154]

The passage on the *Emerald*, with about 250 emigrants, took ten weeks. Pratt was accompanied by wife Mary Ann, who again was pregnant; sister-in-law Olive; nine-year-old Mary Ann; five-year-old Parley Jr.; four-year-old Nathan; and daughter Olivia, born in England the year before. In early January 1843, they docked in New Orleans. Pratt and his family then took a steamer only as far as Chester, Illinois, deliberately disembarking before the boat reached St. Louis. He gave bitter memories as the reason for avoiding Missouri, but it made legal sense as well. As recently as the past September, a sheriff arrived in Nauvoo to arrest Pratt and others, in response to an extradition demand made by the Missouri governor of Governor Thomas Carlin of Illinois. But as the *Times and Seasons* reported, "Through the tender mercies of a kind Providence, who by His power has sustained, and once delivered them from the hands of the blood-thirsty and savage race of beings in the shape of men that tread Missouri's delightful soil; they were not to be found—as the Lord would have it, they were gone from home, and the sheriff returned, of course without them."[155]

In Chester, Pratt waited with his family for the frozen river passages to Nauvoo to clear. Uncharacteristically, Pratt attempted for two weeks to blend into the population as a common citizen, even going so far as to attend a Presbyterian church service. Perhaps he hoped for a respite from the burdens of his office; perhaps his wife—weary after a taxing voyage and far along with another child—needed an especially focused and solicitous husband. Or perhaps he was confident the mountain would come to Mohammed if he bided his time. If the latter, he was correct. "After all my endeavors to be quiet," he claimed, "it is noised abroad, through all parts of town and surrounding country for twenty-five miles, that a 'Mormon' is here.... [I] commence my public ministry tomorrow."[156] And so he was back to the schedule of a circuit rider, speaking to congregations and curious parties in homes and churches.

But it wasn't enough for Pratt. Too restless and anxious to remain idle and icebound, on January 27 he left his family in Chester County and headed out on horseback for Nauvoo.[157] After a few days, having reported to Smith and caught up with family and friends, he returned to his family to await the spring thaw. In April, they embarked on the *Maid of Iowa* from Alton, captained by Dan Jones, a Welsh immigrant and recent Mormon convert. Pratt entered Jones's "state room" and told him by way of prophecy "that the king of Kings had condescended to offer me [Jones], through his *holy prophet*, an Embassy, containing deliverance—the freedom, happiness, eternal life & exaltation of my nation." As Pratt predicted, Jones afterward became a legendary missionary to his native land.[158] Mary Ann gave birth to her fourth child, a daughter, Susan, onboard. Upon their arrival, the sight of Mary Ann and her infant daughter, "only 3 or 4 days old," left Smith "melted in tenderness."[159] Daughter Mary Ann remembered the moment:

> Brother Joseph came down to the landing at the foot of Main Street to meet the company. He came in the cabin, shook hands with our family, took my two little brothers on his knees, and said, "Well, well, Brother Parley, you have come home, bringing your sheaves with you," and the tears rolled down his cheeks. Brother Pratt answered, "Why Brother Joseph, if you feel so bad about our coming, I guess we will have to go back again." Then a smile went all around. Brother Joseph arose and said, "Come, bring your folks right up to my house."[160]

Triumph and Tragedy in Joseph's City

For my part, I want to see a gathering in earnest....If the
saints would do this with all their might and means;
Nauvoo, in one year would be the largest city in the
west—in ten years the largest in America, and in fifteen
years the largest in the world.
—PARLEY PRATT, *March 19, 1843*, "To the
Publishers of the Times and Seasons"

PRATT MARVELED AT Nauvoo's transformation during his absence in
England. After returning, he recounted to the church's newspaper *Times and
Seasons* that he "searched out the cottage which my hands had once reared in
the wilderness....But O! how changed the scene! Even my cottage had been
removed to open one of the principle streets." Perhaps the name of that street
offered some consolation: Parley Street. Pratt continued, "Hills had been leveled, blocks, streets, houses, shops, gardens and enclosures were now extending in every direction; scarce a vestige remained by which I could realize that
I had ever been there before." He soon found reassurance amid the changed
landscape, as he encountered his brothers William and Orson and their families, his mother, and "many of my old acquaintances of Europe and America."[1]
Although Pratt emphasized the physical changes, the social and theological
transformation of Nauvoo Mormonism was even more striking. Over the
next year, Pratt began practicing Mormonism's most radical social doctrine,
plural marriage, and published a series of short pamphlets elaborating
Joseph Smith's dramatic doctrinal innovations. A little more than a year after
his arrival from England, however, external opposition and internal dissent
over these changes led to Smith's death, the end of Nauvoo's utopian dream,
and the splintering of Mormonism.

Pratt settled into Nauvoo by beginning construction on a large brick
home, the first house he would own since the financial disaster of Kirtland.
In April, during a meeting in which Smith sent the majority of the apostles

on a mission to the eastern states to raise funds for the Nauvoo Temple and the Nauvoo House, Smith exempted Pratt to "stay at home & build his house."² In early May, he purchased a lot one block north of the partially completed temple. He encountered a large labor force needing work, partly the result of the success of the English mission, and he quickly employed immigrants to assist in his home's construction. British convert Nicholas Silcock, a talented carpenter who came from England with Pratt, supervised.³ In the interim, the Pratts moved into a cabin that Mary Ann purchased across the street from their future home.⁴ To his cousin John Van Cott, Pratt described his family—"wife and her sister, 5 children, hired girl, and hundreds of goers and comers"—as "huddled into one small room which we use for kitchen, parlour, diningroom, bedroom and publick office." The cramped cabin contrasted sharply with the new home under construction, a "two story store and dwelling house 32 ft. by 56 [feet]," which Pratt hoped to finish within three months, "and then I am ready for another mission."⁵

Pratt and Silcock first built a large barn, which included a spacious basement room to serve as a temporary store. Pratt saw a promising business opportunity in the rapidly growing city and had purchased goods along the

FIGURE 7.1 Drawing of Parley P. Pratt's house in Nauvoo, Illinois, in the 1880s. Courtesy Church History Library, The Church of Jesus Christ of Latter-day Saints.

> DRY GOODS, PROVISIONS &c.
> *Good news—100 per cent. reduction on*
> *the necessaries of life.*
> MR. PRATT wishes to call the at-
> tention of the inhabitants of Nauvoo
> and vicinity to his stock of Dry Goods,
> Groceries, Hardware and Provisions,
> of which he has a constant supply
> on hand, and may be had at his store,
> Young Street, one block north of the
> Temple. Mr. P. would take this oppor-
> tunity of thanking his numerous friends
> for the patronage he has already received
> and feels confident that his prices and
> the quality of his goods will ensure a
> continuence of their favors and therefore
> he offers no other inducement.
> May 24th, 1843, tf.

FIGURE 7.2 Advertisement in the *Nauvoo Neighbor* for the dry goods store of Parley
P. Pratt.

Mississippi River before arriving in Nauvoo. In June, he advertised his "stock
of Dry Goods, Groceries, Hardware and Provisions."[6] Parley's stepdaughter,
Mary Ann, remembered the "thriving grocery business"; residents of Nauvoo
brought "butter, corn meal and eggs to exchange for sugar, molasses, dried
fruit, etc."[7] During a trip to Massachusetts in September, Pratt partnered with
Erastus Snow, who used an inheritance received by his wife to purchase
goods.[8] In November 1843, the firm of Pratt & Snow advertised in the *Nauvoo
Neighbor* a shipment from Boston, which represented "the largest supply of
Dry Goods ever opened in this city, consisting principally of good staple articles for fall and winter, such as Broad-cloths, Casimera, Sattinetts, Flannels,
Shirtings, Sheetings, Calicoes, Boots, Shoes, &c." Customers could either pay
cash or barter "country produce," but not buy on credit.[9] Perhaps remembering the disastrous results of mixing religious authority and finances in
Kirtland, Pratt would not even extend credit to his fellow apostles Heber
Kimball and Brigham Young. Years later, Kimball still resented that Pratt did
not allow him and his wife, in "destitute" circumstances, to "have a little
domestic and a few yards of print." Kimball "went home and cried like a
child."[10] Pratt had hurt his friends, but the store's success paid for the
construction of homes for both Pratt and Snow.[11]

In late June, Mary Ann's parents, Aaron and Susan Frost, and her younger
sisters, Sophronia and Huldah, came from Maine to live with the Pratts.

Aaron's carpentry skills were especially welcome as work on Pratt's home progressed. Stepdaughter Mary Ann described the finished two-story house, with a full basement, as "brick with white stone base caps and window sills, and four-foot square-stone pillars at the front of the store, supporting a stone cornice at the first story. There were twenty-seven large windows in the building, and the cost when finished was $3,500." The family moved in, likely in mid-July, "before the roof was quite finished...and kept going from one part to the other until it was all completed." During construction, young Nathan fell through the partially constructed floor into a "deep cellar," "breaking his leg between knee and hip."[12] Silcock, whose craftsmanship earned him one of the few full-time positions as a construction worker on the Nauvoo Temple, painted the home and added the finishing touches such as "hand-made decorative moldings, handcrafted paneled doors...and elegant handrails on stairs."[13] It all made for a dramatic contrast to Pratt's long years of penury. On August 17, 1843, before the home's completion, Pratt, along with Orson Hyde, left Nauvoo for Boston via Chicago on a brief mission.[14] Along with six other apostles, Pratt directed a conference of the New England Saints at Boston's Boylston Hall on September 9 to encourage gathering to Nauvoo and donating money for the temple. Pratt returned to Nauvoo by early October.[15]

As Pratt constructed his home and established his business, he also confronted the fallout from the expanding practice of plural marriage among church officials. While in England, he was likely unaware of the extent of Smith's doctrinal and marital developments and the resulting tensions within and outside the church. Brigham Young had detailed a particularly explosive situation involving Smith and Orson Pratt's wife, Sarah, in a letter to Parley dated July 17, 1842: "Br Orson Pratt is in trubble in consequence of his wife, his feelings are so rought up that he dos not know whether his wife is wrong, or whether Josephs testimony and others are wrong and due Ly and he decived for 12 years or not; he is all but crazy about matters." Young vowed, "We will not let Br Orson goe away from us he is to good a man to have a woman destroy him."[16] Two days earlier, John C. Bennett, former assistant president of the church, mayor of Nauvoo, and major general of the Nauvoo Legion, had charged in the *Sangamo Journal* that Smith had proposed marriage to Sarah Pratt during Orson's 1841 mission to England. According to Bennett, Sarah had rejected Smith's advances, a statement Sarah repeated decades later. Smith, however, accused Bennett and Sarah of being romantically involved, a position supported by affidavits of Nauvoo residents, including non-Mormon Jacob Backenstos, who declared that Bennett had "illicit intercourse with

Mrs. Orson Pratt." Young captured the crux of Orson's awful dilemma: either the prophet to whom he had dedicated his life had proposed marriage to his wife, or Sarah had committed adultery with the philanderer Bennett. Orson disappeared for several hours on July 15, leaving behind a note to Sarah that provoked fears of suicide and led Smith to organize a search until the distraught Orson was found.[17]

The silver-tongued Bennett had quickly impressed Smith and risen swiftly into the top ranks of Mormon leadership in the early years of Nauvoo. Even when Smith received word that Bennett's first wife had left him because of serial adultery, Smith accepted Bennett's pleas for forgiveness. However, in May 1842, Smith discovered that Bennett had used his positions of authority to seduce women in Nauvoo, telling them that Smith had authorized extramarital sexuality as long as it was kept secret. Furious at the distortion of plural marriage, Smith gradually removed Bennett from his leadership positions and then excommunicated him. Bennett struck back by publishing a series of letters alleging infidelities on Smith's part and various evils on the part of Mormons in general. After the letters were published in the *Sangamo Journal*, Bennett collected them in a book, *The History of the Saints; or an Exposé of Joe Smith and Mormonism*. While many outsiders believed Bennett to be, in the words of Illinois governor Thomas Ford, "probably the greatest scamp in the western country," his widely publicized charges nevertheless darkened the national mood against the Saints.[18]

In response to the reports involving his wife, Orson Pratt temporarily distanced himself from Smith and Mormonism, declining at a meeting on July 22 to vote for a resolution praising Smith's character. Smith maintained his innocence and told Orson that "if he did believe his wife and follow her suggestions, he would go to hell." Though Young had vowed to Parley that the apostles would save Orson, after a month of repeated attempts to persuade Orson, they excommunicated him on August 20 for apostasy and dropped him from the apostolic quorum. During fall 1842, Orson refused to associate himself either with Smith or his enemies. In October, he rebutted a public report that he would abandon Nauvoo and Mormonism. In January, Bennett addressed a letter to Sydney Rigdon and Orson, inviting them to join a conspiracy to entrap Smith and take him to Missouri to face criminal charges. Orson gave the letter to Smith and was quickly reinstated as an apostle, with Smith declaring that his excommunication had not followed official procedures and was therefore void.[19] Soon after his arrival in Nauvoo, Parley wrote his cousin John Van Cott, who was then considering joining the church, "Orson Pratt is in the church and always has been and has the confidence of Joseph Smith and all good men."²⁰ But the episode sowed seeds of discord between the two brothers. Parley remained suspicious of Sarah, and Orson complained in 1846 of Parley's description of Sarah as "an apostate" for "speaking against the heads of the church"²¹

The furor involving church leaders, Sarah Pratt, and other purported targets of polygamous proposals resulted from the secrecy surrounding the practice of plural marriage in Nauvoo. Smith had likely entered into a clandestine, short-lived plural marriage with Fanny Alger before 1836 and then resumed the practice by marrying Louisa Beaman in April 1841. Gradually, he taught members of his inner circle about plural marriage and authorized their participation. He introduced most of the apostles to polygamy when they returned home from England in 1841. The new doctrine shocked them. Young recalled, "It was the first time in my life that I had desired the grave, and I could hardly get over it for a long time."²²

Pratt had learned some details of a new marriage doctrine from Smith himself during their time together in Philadelphia in 1840, but apparently on that occasion Smith taught him of marriage's eternity, not its plurality.²³ Soon after the Pratts' arrival in Nauvoo, Smith taught Parley the principle in its fullness. The first occasion may have been on May 9, 1843, when Parley and Mary Ann, along with her sister Olive, accepted Smith's invitation for a steamboat trip on the *Maid of Iowa* up the Mississippi to Burlington, Iowa. The entertainment included the Nauvoo Band, comic songs by a professor of "natural magic," and an address by Pratt, who spoke for an hour on the reality of a material heaven: "He wanted his eyes saved so that he might behold the beauties of the other world and tongue saved that he might taste its sweets. He spoke of inteligence and affection as the fountain for the manifesting of happiness. He ramarked that the powers of the mind was infinite."²⁴ At some point, according to the much later recollection of Parley's stepdaughter, Mary Ann, Smith commented to Parley in reference to his wife Mary Ann and her sister Olive, who were "dressed alike and were standing a little distance off," that it was "'the will of the Lord that those two sisters should never be parted' (meaning that they should both belong to one man)." Stepdaughter Mary Ann stated, "I heard Brother Pratt tell it on his return home, and my mother also told me about it, and remembered it all her life, and frequently spoke of it."²⁵ Pratt may have been confused when, a few days later, in a public meeting at the Nauvoo temple site, Hyrum Smith called plural marriage an "abomination in the sight of God" and exclaimed, "If an angel from heaven should come and preach such doctrine some would be sure to see his cloven foot and cloud of darkness over his head."²⁶ Soon after, Brigham Young, now reconciled to polygamy, persuaded Hyrum to speak with his brother Joseph about plural marriage, which led to Hyrum's acceptance of the doctrine.

Pratt left no record of his initial reaction to plural marriage, though he and Mary Ann both objected to it. According to one reminiscence, Parley "walked the streets saying that strange things had happened in Nauvoo in his absence."[27] In mid-July, Willard Richards reported to Brigham Young a sermon in which Joseph Smith had denounced internal enemies, citing Matthew 10:36, "a man's foes shall be they of his own household." Richards speculated on the target: "was it Bro Marks?...bro Cole? or bro P.P.P.?" The first two men—Nauvoo Stake president William Marks and his counselor Austin A. Cowles—emerged as key opponents to plural marriage. The inclusion and then strike-through of Pratt's name suggests that rumors placed Pratt in the ranks of those disaffected over polygamy, though perhaps Richards then received information of Pratt's reconciliation.[28] A Pratt family story, recorded by a great-granddaughter, held that Pratt "begged Joseph not to insist upon his entering into polygamous marriages, but Joseph was adamant" and instructed him to pray about the practice: "All night he prayed, and in a vision Thankful came and told him that by taking other wives he would be adding to his own glories in the next world and thus would make her queen over the other wives, who would become her handmaids."[29] Mary Ann had also "been rageing against these things" but accepted polygamy as well, telling Vilate Kimball in late June "that the devel had ben in her until within a few days past, she said the Lord had shown her it was all right."[30]

The Pratts' acceptance of polygamy apparently occurred in mid-June and, since Joseph Smith had left Nauvoo on June 13, they turned to others to obtain further information. Prior to leaving, Smith had told Parley "his privilege, and even appointed one for him."[31] (Even before the Pratts returned from England, Smith had suggested to one English convert, Mary Ann Price, that she marry either Pratt or Orson Hyde; she chose Hyde.)[32] Pratt's acceptance of plural marriage was evident in his decision to participate in an eternal marriage ceremony (a sealing) with Mary Ann, since Joseph Smith made the former a prerequisite to the latter.[33] They approached Hyrum Smith, who himself had recently accepted polygamy and who, as assistant president of the church, presided in Joseph's absence. On June 23, Hyrum sealed Parley and Mary Ann at his home "for time and all eternity."[34]

In late June, the Saints in Nauvoo learned that Joseph Smith had been arrested near Dixon, Illinois, and might not return to Nauvoo for some time. Anxious to learn more of plural marriage, the Pratts visited Vilate Kimball, whose husband, Heber, had entered into polygamy the previous year.

According to Vilate, Mary Ann "wants Parley to go ahead, says she will do all in her power to help him." Once persuaded that the principle was from God, Parley switched from incredulous resistance to anxious haste. Vilate worried, "They are so ingagued [engaged] I fear they will run to fast." Parley and Mary Ann asked her "many questions," but Vilate demurred, telling them, "I did not know much and I rather they would go to those that had authority to teach." Parley replied that he and Joseph Smith had been "interrupted before he got what instruction he wanted, and now he did not know when he should have an opportunity." Vilate perceived that Parley was "unwilling to wate [wait]," though she told him "these were sacred things and he better not make a move until he got more instruction."[35]

Mary Ann was also "unwilling" to wait. On June 27, Parley sent a letter to England to Mary Wood, a seamstress and convert who had known the Pratts on their English mission, "Mrs. Pratt wishes me to say particularly that she wants you to live with us and have one of our upper rooms to follow your trade, which she thinks will be good here; and I think myself that it would give me great pleasure to see two spirits so congenial, so like each other, live so near as to enjoy other's daily society."[36] He would marry Wood after her arrival in Nauvoo the following year. While he awaited her reply, he made preparations to marry a young English convert, Elizabeth Brotherton. Joseph Smith returned to Nauvoo on June 30, learned of Hyrum's sealing of the Pratts in his absence and rebuked him for performing the ordinance without explicit authorization. Brigham Young told William Smith in 1845, "The sealing power was not in Hyrum legitimately," and he could only act as "dictated by Joseph." "This was proven," Young continued, "for Hyrum did undertake to seal without counsel, & Joseph told him if he did not stop it he would go to hell and all those he sealed with him."[37] Joseph's revelation on celestial marriage, written for the first time soon afterward, reiterated that only Joseph held such authority.[38] Joseph thus annulled the sealing between Parley and Mary Ann, though he quickly approved Hyrum to perform another sealing. On July 24, 1843, Hyrum, after reading the revelation on polygamy to the Pratts, sealed Parley to Thankful Halsey for eternity, with Mary Ann acting as Thankful's proxy. Hyrum then sealed Parley to Mary Ann and then to his first plural wife, Elizabeth Brotherton. The ceremonies occurred at the Youngs' home with only Brigham and Mary Ann Young as witnesses.[39] Parley and Mary Ann became the tenth couple to receive an eternal marriage sealing, and Parley's sealing to Thankful by proxy was likely the eighth proxy marriage performed.[40]

Born in Manchester, England, in 1816 and raised a member of the Wesleyan Methodist Church, Elizabeth Brotherton later recalled that she "often regretted that I had not lived in the days of our Savior and His Apostles and as I pondered over these things I became dissatisfied with that faith [Methodism] and mode of baptism." In 1840, she read a Latter-day Saint pamphlet "which told of a Prophet being raised up and of angels appearing that the true gospel was restored in the fullness with all its gifts and blessings." Brigham Young baptized her on September 4, 1840. Elizabeth wrote, "I received a powerful testimony of the truth which was a great blessing to me in the opposition I had to meet with from my relatives and past friends." Heber Kimball blessed her that she "should receive the gift of tongues which I did that night, and [that] by my faithfulness my father's family should all come into the Church" which they did within within three months.[41]

Along with her parents and younger sister Martha, Elizabeth sailed for the United States in September 1841 with a large company of English converts. She nearly died on board ship, "but was healed by the administering of the Elders, and the prayer of faith." In March 1842, Brigham Young approached Martha about becoming his first plural wife. Martha rejected Young's proposal and soon claimed, in sensationalized allegations that John C. Bennett publicized and church leaders disputed, that Young and other leaders had locked her "in a room for several days" in an attempt to persuade her to accept polygamy.[42] Martha and her parents quickly left Nauvoo and Mormonism, but Elizabeth denounced her sister's allegations as "falsehoods of the basest kind."[43] Remaining in Nauvoo, Elizabeth "worked around from place to place; and nursed the sick, waiting on them for my board, for all were too poor to pay wages." Joseph Smith taught her "the law of Celestial marriage." Elizabeth recorded, "I never doubted its truth and I felt in time to come I should enter into the holy order."[44]

Elizabeth did not live with Parley and Mary Ann immediately. In October 1843, Parley wrote her, "I am Glad you have not left here for Warsaw," suggesting that she had considered joining her family in that city. He encouraged Elizabeth, "Stay here and enjoy the Society of the Saints, and be useful to them, instead of serving the Gentiles.... You can be employed in doing good to the poor, and nursing the Sick, and, when you can Get wages do So, and when you cannot get wages, be buisy in doing good." Recognizing the taxing secrecy of polygamy, Parley promised a future in which she would "have a house and home, and enjoy more and more of the Society of those you love." He continued, "Perhaps I may not See you to night because of other matters. If not I will see you tomorrow night at the same place at Six O Clock or between that and nine."[45] Meanwhile, on August 20, William Clayton recorded in his journal that Parley "has through his wife made proposals" to

FIGURE 7.3 Parley Pratt and Elizabeth Brotherton Pratt. Photograph likely taken in September 1854 in San Francisco. Courtesy Daughters of the Utah Pioneers.

Mary Aspen (whom Clayton hoped to marry as a plural wife and who had accompanied the Pratts home from England), "but she is dissatisfied." According to Clayton, "Sister P[ratt] is obstinate" and told Aspen that the "Twelve would have more glory than" Clayton. Though Clayton "tried to comfort her and told her what her privilege was," Aspen married neither Clayton nor Pratt.[46]

In the midst of the tumult over plural marriage, Smith introduced Pratt to another of the dramatic doctrinal innovations advanced during Pratt's extended stay in England, the reconceptualization of the temple. The Kirtland Temple had been the site of a long-promised "endowment of power," a pentecostal experience of spiritual gifts combined with Old Testament–inspired washings and anointings and New Testament-inspired foot-washing. During fall 1840, Latter-day Saints began proxy baptisms for their deceased relatives in the Mississippi River; with the completion of a font in the basement of the Nauvoo Temple, the ordinances moved there in late 1841. In May 1842, Smith gathered nine men in an upstairs room in his brick store and introduced them to a new endowment, a ritual "reenactment of the Creation, the Fall, and the establishment of a priesthood order among humans."[47] While initially given to a select group, Willard Richards recorded, "there was nothing made known to these men, but what will be made known to all the Saints of the last days, so soon as they are prepared to receive, and a proper place is prepared to communicate them, even to the weakest of the Saints."[48] Most Saints awaited the completion of the Nauvoo Temple to receive the temple rites. But, as Heber Kimball, one of the original men to receive the new endowment, made clear in a letter to Pratt in June 1842, a select group of church leaders had been taught "pressious things...on the preasthood that would caus your Soul to rejoice." Kimball could not share them with Pratt in a letter "fore they are not to be riten. So you must come and get them fore your Self."[49]

Kimball also informed Pratt about the rapid growth of the Nauvoo Masonic Lodge, part of a vast expansion of Masonry across the nation in this era as the fraternal movement recovered from the anti-Masonic political fervor of the 1830s.[50] While Pratt was in England, all of the apostles in Nauvoo, with the exception of Orson Pratt, had become Masons, as had Joseph Smith and Sidney Rigdon. Orson will "wake up soon," Kimball predicted, because "thare is a similarity of preast Hood in masonary. Br Joseph ses masonary was taken from preasthood but has become degenerated, but menny things are perfect."[51] Consistent with Smith's vision of inspired eclecticism, he took bits and pieces of Masonic ritual and incorporated them into the new temple ceremonies.[52] Parley became a Mason in July 1843.

Those initiated into the endowment ceremonies before the completion of the Nauvoo Temple called themselves the "Anointed Quorum" or the "Holy Order." As Kimball told Pratt, Smith now felt "he has got a Small company that he feels safe in thare hands."[53] Nevertheless, the controversy over plural marriage instigated by Bennett suspended the activities of the Anointed Quorum from 1842 to late May 1843, when activities again began, including the first sealing of couples for eternity. During fall 1843, women, beginning with Emma Smith, began to enter the Anointed Quorum. On December 2, 1843, Pratt was inducted into the Anointed Quorum and received his endowment. He met frequently with the Anointed Quorum to hold prayer circles, participate in temple rituals, and listen to instructions from Smith and other leaders.[54]

At a meeting of the Anointed Quorum in January, Wilford Woodruff noted that confusion existed over Pratt's marital status. He recorded, "Joseph said Concerning Parley P Pratt that He had no wife sealed to him for Eternity and asked if their was any harm for him to have another wife for time &

FIGURE 7.4 William Major (1804–1854), *Joseph Smith and Friends* (1844). Courtesy Church History Museum, The Church of Jesus Christ of Latter-day Saints. From left: Hyrum Smith, Willard Richards, Joseph Smith, Orson Pratt, Parley P. Pratt, Orson Hyde, Heber C. Kimball, and Bringham Young.

Eternity as He would want a wife in the Resurrection or els his glory would be Cliped." Woodruff then added a few more sentences, though he crossed them out in his journal: "Br Joseph said now what will we do with Elder P P Pratt? He has no wife sealed to him for Eternity.... [Mary Ann] had a former Husband and did not wish to be sealed to Parly for Eternity. Now is it not right for Parley to have another wife."⁵⁵ For some reason, unless Woodruff misunderstood the situation (a possibility, since he crossed out the latter half of the explanation and because other accounts indicate Smith was not present on that occasion), the earlier sealing between Parley and Mary Ann was now considered void. Had Mary Ann, remembering with fondness her first husband, decided she would rather remain his monogamous wife in the eternities than one of Parley's plural wives? After all, Parley had been sealed to the wife of his youth, Thankful. Should not Mary Ann and Nathan Stearns inherit a comparable eternal union? Alternatively, did Smith himself intend to marry Mary Ann? By this time, probably in fall 1843, Smith had married Mary Ann's sister Olive.⁵⁶ As Smith had previously told Parley, "It is the will of the Lord that those two sisters should never be parted." Notwithstanding the speculation of several historians, Mary Ann did not marry Smith during his life, though she was sealed to him, not Parley (Nathan was not viewed as an option), in January 1846. Some historians have suspected that Mary Ann's son Moroni, born on December 7, 1844, was Smith's son, though recent DNA testing on Moroni's descendants conclusively demonstrated that Parley fathered him.[57]

Less than three weeks after Pratt's endowment, tragedy struck his family on December 21, 1843, when five-year-old Nathan succumbed to "fever of the brain."[58] Following his accident during the home's construction that summer, Nathan had been confined for several weeks but had recovered. Then "he was seized with his last illness which was very severe until his death." In eulogizing his son for the *Times and Seasons*, Pratt placed Nathan's life within the narrative of persecution: he had been born in the midst of the Missouri troubles, was made homeless at the age of six weeks, joined his father in prison, and was driven from Missouri at nine months.[59] Joseph Smith visited the Pratts to mourn with them, and Eliza R. Snow wrote a poem to "Mrs. Mary Pratt on the Death of Her Little Son."[60] The Pratts buried Nathan in their backyard rather than the Nauvoo Cemetery.

Perhaps it was Nathan's death, along with the new temple rituals, that led Pratt to another outburst of speculative theology in the ensuing months. In early 1844, he published three essays, "The Fountain of Knowledge," "Immortality of the Body," and "Intelligence and Affection." Pratt included in the collection his 1841 letter to Queen Victoria, warning monarchs that a kingdom not of this world would soon supplant their dominions.[61] Also written in this mournful winter, and read to Joseph Smith and a general council of the church, was a dream vision Pratt titled "Angel of the Prairies."[62] Standing on the western borderland from which he had been led into captivity five years earlier, Pratt the narrator saw through a seerstone an expansive future empire where now was only wilderness. Then he witnessed, with the lapse of time, a new empire of millennial glory. Denied possession of the city of Zion in his lifetime, Pratt found comfort in the panoramic vision which unfolded the building of the New Jerusalem, the glorious destiny of the American Indians, and the establishment of a heavenly government that would rule the earth for a thousand years. In the months since his anguished question to Smith—"When Will The *'purchased possession'* be Redeemed and the temple and city commence in Jackson Co"—Pratt had apparently reconciled himself to a deferred inheritance. Zion, if it was to blossom like the rose, would do so on the far side of American expansion, with its populous millions filling out the farthest reaches of the continent.[63]

"The Fountain of Knowledge," a small pamphlet, was vintage Pratt. With elegant metaphor, he made a few simple points: Scriptures resulted from revelatory process and are thus the product of revealed truth, not the other way around. As a consequence and not a source of revelation, scriptures should not be assigned foundational status. People would do well to look to a stream for nourishing water, but do better to secure the fountain. That fountain, Pratt proclaimed, is "the gift of revelation," which "the restoration of all things" heralds.[64]

With another essay, "Immortality and Eternal Life of the Body," Pratt elaborated points made earlier in his "Eternal Duration of Matter." In the latter, Pratt had affirmed the eternity of matter and celebrated a resurrection fully physical. Now he finished the work of collapsing the spiritual and the physical into the same ontology. Gone was the equivocation he had shown in his tract in England to Hewitt. It helped that Smith had declared months earlier that "there is no such thing as immaterial matter. All spirit is matter but it is more fine or pure."[65] The resultant vision of the cosmos, Pratt asserted, will reveal as "errors of the grossest kind" two staples of Christian belief: "the idea of a 'God without body or parts'... and a heaven beyond the bounds of time and space." As to the former, he bluntly stated, "a God without body or parts as described in the Church of England Confession of Faith, in the Presbyterian Articles, and in the Methodist Discipline, and as worshipped by a large portion of christendom, is not with me an object of veneration, fear, or love." As the resurrected Christ appeared as a being of flesh and bones, so is the Father, he argued. Any retreat into immateriality was the true heresy: "What say ye, my readers, who is the infidel? Is it the materialist who believes in the eternal existence of matter in union with mind? Or is it he who, like the heathen, only fancies to himself an immortality in some fairy world of spirits, some heaven without substance?" The world of "realities and tangibility," to which the embodied Christ returned, *is* the world inhabited by God. And this "God the father has a real and substantial existence in human form and proportions," though "of a more subtle and refined nature than we are prepared fully to comprehend."[66]

The second "gross error" embraces not just the physicality of the heavenly, but its temporality as well. Neoplatonic conceptions of eternity, which took hold in early Christianity and still inform the idea in most theological circles, define eternity not as time without a beginning or end, but as the simultaneous presence of the future, present, and past; not the infinite succession of time, but of duration without any succession at all. Eternity, in sum, is held to be atemporal. Therefore, as an eternal being, God is outside of time.[67] For Pratt, a corporeal God inhabits both spatial and temporal dimensions, and those parameters inform all that is heavenly.

Where then is heaven?...earth, and the other material creations which spangle the firmament with a flood of glory, are all heavenly kingdoms, together with the inhabitants thereof....Heaven then, is composed of an innumerable association of glorified worlds, and happy immortal beings, beaming with an effulgence of light, intelligence, and love, of which our earth, small and insignificant as it is, must form some humble part.

As for humans, they will participate in the ongoing work of eternal creation. Man "will by no means be confined, or limited in his sphere of action to this small planet; but will wing his way, like a risen Saviour, from world to world.... While the continued and ceaseless exertions of creative goodness will, by the acquisition of new creations, form a sufficient field for the exercise of his priestly and kingly powers."[68]

Pratt further developed these intimations of human theosis, or divinization, in his most eloquent piece of theologizing to date. If the glory of God is intelligence, as Smith preached, but God is love, as John held, then those two master attributes have to find a synthesis, and that is what Pratt worked to achieve with his aptly titled "Intelligence and Affection." Nineteenth-century Mormonism was conspicuous in the way it addressed, through both theology and institutional practice, the realms of intellect and heart. From the School of the Prophets to the University of Nauvoo, Smith made education central to Mormonism. The most visible social dimension of Mormonism, the Saints' geographical dislocation to achieve literal gathering, directly resulted from this emphasis. "Intelligence is the great object of our holy religion," Smith declared, and "is the result of education, and education can only be obtained by living in compact society; One of the principal objects, then, of our coming together, is to obtain the advantages of education; and in order to do this, compact society is absolutely necessary."[69] At the same time, Mormonism's most prominent social institution in Nauvoo and after the exodus to Utah was plural marriage, a practice that turned marital relationships into eternal dynasties and godly parenthood. Though on the surface "Intelligence and Affection" concerned monogamous marriage, it likely represented Pratt's reconciliation of plural marriage with his religious sensibility, to persuade his audience that Mormon marriage was about love, not lust; it grew out of a desire to eternalize and expand relationships, not sacralize sexuality. While modern Mormonism distills celestial marriage into a primarily monogamous arrangement of eternal duration, it continues to situate conjugal attachment at the heart of the religion.

Pratt made the two principles of "Intelligence and Affection" interdependent. God "loves because he knows; and in proportion to the extent of his knowledge, or intelligence, so is the extent of his love." And love or affection "can only be increased by an increase of knowledge." This essay represents the fullest flowering of Mormonism's celebration of divine physicality. Proceeding from the premise that God—like all divine entities—is embodied (one conclusion of his essay "Immortality of the Body"), Pratt argued that the prejudice of Platonism and Puritanism against the bodily was groundless. Ascribing our natural affections to a fallen and corrupt nature as creedal Christians do ("wholly defiled in all the parts and faculties of soul and body") mistakes "the source and fountain of happiness altogether."[70] Those true mainsprings are, first, our natural affections and, second, our social nature. Asceticism does not transcend the carnal but, rather, rejects what is inherently godlike. The direction and cultivation of the passions, not their repression, is God's intention for humans. And foremost among these human affections is the reciprocal sexual desire of a man and his wife. There is, in fact, "not a more pure and holy principle in existence than the affection which glows in the bosom of a virtuous man for his companion." The union commanded—and thus commended—by God in the Garden of Eden is the wellspring of all other relationships, and in heaven we shall be "capable of exercising all those pure emotions...which fill our hearts with such inexpressible delight in this world." As men were made to "govern this world" and people it "with myriads of happy, free and social intelligences," so is their eternal destiny to participate in "the organization of new systems of worlds...over which we may reign as kings."[71] Pratt implied, but left unstated, that such celestial stewardships will include siring posterity to people those worlds. Smith had been more explicit on this topic in his revelation on plural marriage, which confirmed that righteous couples would "bear the souls of men" in "the eternal worlds."[72] Smith's words and actions on marriage were crucial ingredients in the combustible mix of doctrine and behavior that made 1844 a turning point in Mormon history. Pratt's essays helped secure those doctrinal foundations that would soon expand a secretive, limited practice into churchwide institution.

Pratt appended these theological pamphlets to his "An Appeal to the Inhabitants of the State of New York," written in response to Smith's request for petitions in support of Missouri claims still pending. Similar to Smith, in his *Appeal to the Green Mountain Boys* (drafted by William Phelps) of his home state of Vermont, Pratt contrasted his patriotic heritage and own love of country with the religious persecution he had suffered. Like other advocates for religious, racial, or ethnic outsiders in nineteenth-century America, Pratt argued that the treatment of the Mormons mocked the legacy of the American Revolution and the country's reputation as an asylum for the oppressed. He asked, "Must *we* because we choose to worship God according to the dictates of our own consciences, be killed, robbed, plundered, driven and banished from a State of this union, and the government find the weapons and pay the murderous wretches for committing these crimes?" If the Mormon claims went unaddressed, Pratt wrote, "then farewell to the glory of Columbia; farewell to the peace and security of the citizens of this once happy Republic." Apocalyptically, he warned that if earthly justice failed, divine wrath awaited: "Remember the flood of Noah,—remember Sodom and Gomorrah,—remember Pharaoh and his hosts...remember there is a God in Heaven who will avenge the blood of inocence, and especially of his own elect."[73]

As the 1844 presidential campaign approached, Latter-day Saint leaders sought to obtain assurances from the leading candidates of the rights of Mormons and the validity of their claims in Missouri. John Tyler, who had assumed the presidency upon William Henry Harrison's death in 1841, had quickly alienated the Whigs who had elected him. Since the Whigs would not renominate Tyler, no incumbent would run, and the race seemed wide open. In November 1843, Joseph Smith wrote five leading potential candidates—Democrats Martin Van Buren, John C. Calhoun, Lewis Cass, and Richard M. Johnson; and Whig Henry Clay—and asked, "What will be your rule of action, relative to us, as a people?" Only three responded, and they offered no commitments and little sympathy; Calhoun lectured Smith that the Mormons' treatment in Missouri was a state, not a federal, issue. Smith responded, "If the General Government has no power, to re-instate expelled citizens to their rights, there is a monstrous hypocrite fed and fostered from the hard earnings of the people!"[74]

Repelled by the contenders' responses, Pratt and the other apostles nominated Smith for president on January 29. *General Smith's Views of the Powers and Policy of the Government of the United States*, written by William Phelps under Smith's direction, spanned the agendas of both Whigs and Democrats. Smith announced his support for federal power to "suppress mobs," a national bank (though one restricted to hard-money practices), the annexation of Texas and Oregon, prison reform, and the emancipation of slaves by compensating their owners.[75] Smith may have thought he had a chance in the absence of a clear front-runner. He boasted to the Twelve, "There is oretory enough in the church"—thinking particularly of Hyrum Smith, Brigham Young, Parley Pratt, and John Taylor—"to carry me into the presidential chair the first slide."[76] More likely, he knew the platform would aid him in publicizing the Mormon message and their mistreatment in Missouri.

As they prepared for Smith's campaign, Mormon leaders sought to quell the growing disquiet within the church and looked for respite from the increasing opposition from without by turning their eyes toward the West. The West already figured in the American imagination as a place of refuge and redefinition, a role it had played within Mormonism since Pratt's mission to the Lamanites in 1830. A year before newspaper editor John L. O'Sullivan proclaimed it the "manifest destiny" of the United States to spread across the continent, the Saints looked toward new western settlements in Texas, California, or Oregon. Smith commissioned the apostles on February 20 to explore the possibility of Mormon settlement in California or Oregon, not as an abandonment of Nauvoo, but as an expansion of Latter-day Saint influence where they could "build a city in a day and have a government of our own in a healthy climate." The apostles appointed eight scouts to begin preparations.[77]

To oversee the western plans, Smith, acting on a revelation he had received two years earlier, organized in March the Council of Fifty, composed of members of the Mormon ecclesiastical elite, including Pratt, and three sympathetic outsiders. The revealed name of the council suggests a mix of political purpose and religious symbolism: "The Kingdom of God and His Laws with the Keys and Power thereof, and Judgment in the Hands of His Servants, Ahman Christ."[78] Pratt called it "the most exalted Council with which our earth is at present dignified."[79] He and other participants may have seen it as the beginning of a government that would rule the earth during the anticipated millennium.

The council gave some substance to Smith's vision of a "theodemocracy," in which "God and the people hold the power to conduct the affairs of men in righteousness." On April 11, the Council of Fifty voted Smith as their king, revealing how far Mormon conceptions of "theodemocracy" diverged from the world of mid-nineteenth-century American electoral democracy. Revealing their ambitions, the council unsuccessfully petitioned Congress for Smith to be authorized to raise a private army of one hundred thousand men to protect western settlers from threats by Indians, criminals, and foreign governments.[80]

At the April 1844 church conference, Pratt answered Smith's call for volunteers to canvass the United States for his campaign.[81] Brigham Young stated that the missionaries, whose numbers eventually approached four hundred, would both preach and campaign.[82] With the exception of Willard Richards and John Taylor, the entire quorum of apostles participated in the campaign,

as did Parley's younger brother William. The apostles scheduled a series of
conferences throughout the United States, which were to culminate in a
national convention scheduled for Baltimore on July 13. Since both Pratt and
Erastus Snow accepted the call, they shut down their store, which had not yet
been open a year.[83] In mid-April, Pratt left Nauvoo for New York and
Massachusetts. He first passed through Chicago to sail to Buffalo. Like
Nauvoo, Chicago was in the midst of a population explosion. From a
population of about four thousand when it was chartered in 1837, Chicago
blossomed to almost thirty thousand in 1850 and 109,000 by 1860.[84] Pratt
encouraged Smith to establish Mormon settlements between Nauvoo and
Chicago, citing the city's accessibility to eastern cities by the Great Lakes,
canals, and railroads, and the benefits of its harbor and its economic markets.
"By enlightening the present inhabitants, and poring in a flood of Emigration
from the East," the Saints could "Commence the Immediate Ocupation" of
the region, he said.[85]

Crossing Lake Erie en route to Buffalo, Parley complained to Mary Ann
of "sea sickness, nose bleeding, toothache, gloom, and home sickness."
Succumbing to self-pity, he contrasted Mary's situation—"in the midst of
the society of parents, children, sisters, kindred and friends"—with his
own "gloom and loneliness." Frustrated by those who "do not understand...nor will they aid, those who would fain be their benefactors,"
Parley stated, "my heart is on my kindred and my friends, the aged parents
and the helpless Infants, on the tender wife of my Bosom." Indeed, he
wrote, "Aside from them and the Saints the world to me is all a dreary
waste, a confused wilderness of bewildered human beings very few of
whom are in a situation to be benifited by the Light of Truth." His youthful optimism in the cause of Zion was a distant memory. After years of
missionary labor, he now desired to "retire for ever, from this wilderness—
this sea of confused, and Deranged Inteligences who neither know nor can
be taught, and to Devote my principle attention to my family, my kindred,
my Ancestors and my offspring, and to those who love the truth." As such,
Pratt planned to "deliver my political and doctrinal message" in
Massachusetts and New York before quickly returning to Nauvoo. The new
doctrines of the sealing power and eternal families consumed Parley's
future plans. He wrote, "I believe that the duties I owe my family, and the
ordinances and duties encumbant on me in preperations for my heavenly
kingdom and that of my kindred and friends, will require a great portion
of my time even if I should live to the age of man." He hoped it "will not be
required of me to travel much more."[86]

Pratt found some solace by satisfying his itch to write. He had flirted with fiction in his 1840 "Epistle of Demetrius," then returned to that mode with his unpublished dream vision, "Angel of the Prairies." Now, he tried once again, employing the satirical tone of Demetrius in a set piece called "A Dialogue Between Joe Smith and the Devil." He seemed to be working his way up to a substantial work of dramatic fiction; in 1854 he wrote the first act of a play, "The Mormon Prisoners," based on the 1838 Richmond hearing before Judge Austin King, but Pratt was too emotionally invested in the project, and it lacked any subtlety or artistic grace. The satiric dialogue, however, was a perfect medium for Pratt. From Juvenal to Swift, satire has combined caustic wit with moralistic outrage—both of which Pratt exercised regularly. "Joe Smith and the Devil" was Pratt's most successful foray into fiction, published on the front page of the *New York Herald* that August and reprinted by Pratt several times.[87]

His dialogue cleverly pairs Smith and Satan (they even drink to each other's health with spruce beer at the end), exploiting the religious press's coupling of the two. The twist is in the discovery that they can treat each other civilly as colleagues because their goals are divergent rather than competing. Satan, it turns out, is very "liberal minded" and "decidedly in favor of all creeds, systems and forms of Christianity, of whatever name and nature," with one caveat: they must steer clear of the one abominable principle with the power to bring his whole kingdom to ruin, namely, "direct communication with God, by new revelation." Smith, of course, teaches this very principle. But in doing so he is a religious innovator, and since "tradition and custom, together with fashion and popular clamor, have in all ages had more effect than plain fact, and sound reason," the Mormon system will have little sway over the devil's dominions. Still, the devil warns Smith he will take measures to ensure that he will never become a threat. With eerie prescience, he pledges to "excite jealousy, fear and alarm, till all the world is ready to arise and crush you."[88]

In May and June, Pratt promoted Smith's candidacy in "Jeffersonian" conventions in Boston and New York City. At the New York meeting, Pratt "called for the people to awake from their lethargy and begin to attend to the *weightier matters of justice, judgment, right and protection*." The Mormon expulsion from Missouri, Pratt asserted, was only the most egregious violation of civil liberties during a decade in which "white men have been shot and hung, and negroes burned without trial, judge or jury; abolitionists have been mobbed and shot; Catholic churches, dwellings and convents burned." In an argument used effectively by abolitionists, Pratt warned that the loss of civil liberties to minority groups threatened the rights of all Americans: "The Catholics may be the sufferers to-day; the Mormons to-morrow, the Abolitionists next day, and next the Methodists or Presbyterians. Where is safety if a popular mob must rule, and the unpopular must suffer?" The partisan disputes over "minor" issues like tariffs and banks paled in importance to this fundamental question. Ignoring the Saints' suffering under the guise of states' rights, Pratt thundered, meant that Congress, the presidency, and government officials, "with a few exceptions, stand with their skirts stained and their heads dripping with the blood of innocent men, women and *children*, the saints and martyrs of this nation." Smith, by contrast, would protect the rights of all citizens: "He is not a Southern man with Northern principles; nor a Northern man with Southern principles. But he is an Independent man with American principles, and he has both knowledge and disposition, to govern for the benefit and protection of ALL."[89]

But Smith's presidential aspirations, combined with his theocratic control of Nauvoo and its thousands-strong militia, served only to confirm widespread suspicions of his power and ambition. A proliferation of damning rumors of sexual impropriety—extending now well beyond Nauvoo—added to the volatile mix. Pratt wrote to warn Joseph Smith and Orson Spencer, a Baptist minister who had converted to Mormonism in 1841 and who, like Pratt, was a leading writer on theological topics, of a plot by Spencer's brother Augustine. He was "a snake in the grass, a base traitor," circulating a letter around Richmond, Massachusetts (the Spencers' home area), "with the most Infamous slander and Lies.... It affirms that Joseph Smith is in the habit of Drinking, Swearing, Carousing, Dancing all night, etc, etc, and that he keeps six or seven young females as wives etc." Augustine had further cautioned the recipients of his letter to keep it secret, so that he could remain "on Intimate terms and confidencial friendship with the 'prophet Jo' and the mormons."[90] Internal opposition in Nauvoo, particularly over Smith's polygamy, had been mounting through the early months of 1844. In January, Smith dropped William Law as one of his counselors in the First Presidency because of Law's rejection of plural marriage. After efforts at reconciliation failed, Law was excommunicated on April 18, along with his wife, Jane; brother Wilson; and Robert Foster, surgeon general of the Nauvoo Legion and a justice of the peace. Joined by other dissidents, they formed a reform church a few days later, headed by William Law, to save Mormonism from the excesses of its fallen prophet. In late April, Augustine Spencer was arrested for attacking his brother Orson, and several dissenters physically threatened Smith. Opponents of Mormonism outside of Nauvoo gleefully noted the rising internal dissent within the city.[91]

As Pratt stumped for Smith's presidential campaign, events quickly spiraled out of control in Nauvoo. The Nauvoo dissidents moved against Smith not only religiously, but also legally and politically. In May, they brought several charges against him, including perjury and polygamy, in courts in the county seat of Carthage. Smith disputed the accusations, denying involvement in adultery, polygamy, or spiritual wifery, drawing a distinction in his own mind (which Pratt and others followed) between these unauthorized practices and plural marriage under priesthood order. On June 7, the dissenters published the first and only issue of a newspaper, the *Nauvoo Expositor*, designed to purge Smith's "vicious principles"—polygamy and some of the doctrinal innovations of the Nauvoo era—from Mormonism. Furthermore, the *Expositor* argued for the repeal of Nauvoo's expansive city charter and the restriction of Mormon political power. Smith and his followers retaliated quickly. Arguing that the *Expositor* was a "nuisance," a threat to public safety because it would encourage an anti-Mormon mob to march against Nauvoo, Smith persuaded the Nauvoo City Council to order its destruction. Ironically, the perceived trampling on the freedom of the press by Mormonism's theocratic prophet ignited the mobs that Smith had hoped to avoid, and Warsaw newspaper editor Thomas Sharp called for Smith to be killed and the Mormons to be expelled. Over the next few weeks, Illinois governor Thomas Ford frantically attempted to negotiate a settlement between Smith's supporters and his opponents. Ford persuaded Smith to face legal charges in Carthage related to the press's destruction. Meanwhile a siege mentality settled over Nauvoo, with constant reports and rumors of attacks on outlying Mormon settlements, oncoming mobs, and planned assassinations. On June 27, a unit of the Illinois militia stormed the jail, killing Joseph and Hyrum Smith and severely wounding John Taylor.[92]

The murder of the Smiths left the Saints in Nauvoo, including Pratt's family, crushed and terrified. Mary Ann's sister Olive, a plural wife of Joseph, "went entirely mad," according to one observer, and died the following year.[93] The night of the Smiths' funeral, many in Nauvoo feared that a mob might ravage the city. One Mormon woman recorded, "A thousand men, we were told, were on their way bent on our destruction." Fearing that her home and those of other church leaders would be targeted, Mary Ann gathered women and children from the neighborhood, including the families of Orson's wife Sarah, Mary Ann's parents and sisters, and neighbor Jane Silcock, in the Pratt's cellar, which was concealed by a trap door and carpet. Mary Ann told them, "If we have to be killed, let us all die together." "The women were assembled in groups, weeping and praying," another woman wrote, listening to the "noise of war" in the preparations of the Nauvoo Legion to defend the city.[94] Around midnight, a ferocious tempest hit Nauvoo. The "awful thunderstorm and lightning" ensured the "mob did not come as they intended." Parley's step-daughter, Mary Ann, later recalled, "Everything seemed to stand still.... Fear escalated to alarm at the sound of labored footsteps in the soggy street. A hollow clutter of boots on the wooden porch produced terrible panic," until they recognized the voice of Jane's husband, Nicholas, which "broke the spell of terror that had consumed the night." Nevertheless, the "fright of the mob" induced premature labor in Jane, resulting in a stillborn son.[95]

Not only mobs threatened Mormonism in the aftermath of the Smiths' death. Riven with internal strife, the succession undefined, and the apostles scattered, the immediate future looked bleak. The excitement Pratt had felt since his return to Nauvoo only a little more than a year earlier—over the rapid growth, the building of the temple, the dramatic doctrinal innovations such as family sealings and plural marriages, the resulting burst of theological writing, the bold promise of the presidential campaign—had now evaporated into the tragedy at Carthage. Warren Foote captured the mood of thousands of his coreligionists: "We all felt as though the powers of darkness had over-come and that the Lord had forsaken His people. Our Prophet and Patriarch were gone! Who now is to lead the Saints! In fact we mourned 'as one mourneth for his only son.'"[96]

8

Many Mormonisms

THE EAST

The public are particularly cautioned against imposters
and counterfeiters of the doctrine and authority of the
Latter-day Saints. As several persons have dissented and
been regularly excommunicated from our society in this
and other cities.... These have no priesthood, or authority
from God, angels or inspiration.
—PARLEY PRATT, *New York Prophet, April 5, 1845*

IN LATE JUNE 1844, as he proselytized for Mormonism and Joseph Smith's
presidential campaign in the eastern states, Pratt recalled in his autobiography, he was "constrained by the Spirit to start prematurely for home,
without knowing why or wherefore" and boarded a boat on the Erie Canal
near Utica, New York, to start for Nauvoo. By chance, his brother William,
also on a mission, embarked on the same boat. As they spoke, Parley sensed
"a strange and solemn awe...as if the powers of hell were let loose."
"Overwhelmed with sorrow," he paced silently along the boat's deck until he
told William, "This is a dark hour; the powers of darkness seem to triumph,
and the spirit of murder is abroad in the land; and it controls the hearts of
the American people, and a vast majority of them sanction the killing of the
innocent." That same day—even the same hour, Pratt suspected—a mob
broke into Carthage Jail and murdered Joseph and Hyrum Smith.[1]

Pratt learned of the Smiths' deaths aboard a steamer from Buffalo to
Chicago on the next leg of his journey. He remembered, "Great excitement
prevailed on board, there being a general spirit of exultation and triumph
at this glorious news." Passengers "tauntingly inquired what the Mormons
would do now, seeing their Prophet and leader was killed." In his retelling,
Pratt silenced the critics by affirming that Mormonism would prosper and
that "a MAN never triumphs and exults in the ruin of his country and the
murder of the innocent." As he mourned while traveling from Chicago to

Nauvoo, Pratt sought spiritual guidance and later recorded that the "Spirit said unto me: 'Lift up your head and rejoice; for behold! it is well with my servants Joseph and Hyrum." Pratt's revelation instructed him to counsel the Saints in Nauvoo to "pursue their daily duties and take care of themselves, and make no movement in Church government to reorganize or alter anything until the return of the remainder of the Quorum of the Twelve. But exhort them that they continue to build the House of the Lord."[2]

As Pratt recognized, Smith's death created a crisis of authority within Mormonism. The death of a charismatic founder is typically a time of great danger to the survival of new religious movements. Since its beginning, Mormonism had contained competing impulses. In the words of one scholar, "Mormonism was both mystical and secular; restorationist and progressive; communitarian and individualistic; hierarchical and congregational; authoritarian and democratic; antinomian and arminian; anti-clerical and priestly; revelatory and empirical; utopian and practical; ecumenical and nationalist."[3] Smith had used these polarities to create a dynamic religious movement; indeed, part of the strength and appeal of early Mormonism derived from the balancing of these paradoxical impulses. Following his death, however, confusion over the process of succession united with these underlying tensions to create many Mormonisms.

Most scholarship on the competition among various claimants to be recognized as Smith's legitimate successor has focused on the Mormon center of Nauvoo, demonstrating how Brigham Young and the apostles consolidated their authority over most Mormons in that region. But the succession battle raged as well in the periphery of Mormonism, where perhaps a majority of Saints lived. Two areas were of particular importance: the large eastern cities, with relatively few Mormons but with access to the nation's publishing centers; and Great Britain, with its large population of Mormon converts. Rumors of polygamy, aggressive proselytizing by rival claimants, and lack of control over Mormon publishing threatened the apostles' claims in the East. In England, a failed joint stock company, which had intended to assist the English converts in emigrating to the United States, posed the largest obstacle to the apostles' efforts. Pratt played the key role in both critical regions, helping to consolidate the apostles' authority by imposing new controls over Mormon publishing, quieting rumors of plural marriage, and retaining the loyalty of the English Saints. But first Pratt had a role to play in the events unfolding in Nauvoo. At various points in his life, Smith had indicated at least eight possible successors.[4] Nauvoo Mormons considered two possibilities immediately following his death. First, Sidney Rigdon, who had long served as a counselor to Smith but had been estranged from him for much of the 1840s, argued that he should serve as "guardian" of the church. Second, Pratt, Young, and the other apostles argued that Smith had designated the apostolic group as his successor.

Pratt arrived in Nauvoo on July 10, joining apostles Willard Richards and the injured John Taylor, both of whom had been with the Smiths at Carthage Jail.[5] Pratt and Richards immediately asserted the apostolic prerogative to govern the church. William Marks, the president of Nauvoo's stake, argued on July 12 that the priesthood quorums should "appoint a trustee under civil law to manage church financial affairs." Pratt and Richards, joined by Bishop Newel K. Whitney and W. W. Phelps, countered that the appointment of a trustee (or a group of trustees) should occur only "when a majority of the Twelve returned." After Pratt, Phelps, and Richards argued this in a council meeting on July 14, William Clayton, who had been Joseph Smith's secretary, wrote, "These three brethren seem to keep matters very close to themselves and I and several others feel grieved at it. After meeting I informed Emma [Smith's widow] of the proceedings. She thinks they don't use her right."[6] During this critical month, Pratt repeatedly met with other leaders, preached publicly (using a Book of Mormon text on mourning), and helped organize a company of fishermen to "supply the city" with fish.[7]

As the Saints in Nauvoo awaited the arrival of the other apostles, rumors swirled about possible candidates, including Pratt, who might assume Smith's place as church president. A Mormon in Rock Island County, Illinois, James Blakesley, recorded the speculation: "if I have been correctly informed, some of the members of the church at Nauvoo, want Stephen Markham for their head, and others Sidney Rigdon, and others President Marks, and others Little Joseph, and others B. Young, and some others P. P. Pratt." The fact that Pratt had no particular ecclesiastical position (as did William Marks, Young, or Sidney Rigdon), blood filiation (as did William Smith or Joseph Smith III), or reputed commission (as did James Strang or Lyman Wight) on which to base a claim suggests how prominent he was in his contemporaries' eyes by sheer dint of his authoritative voice and writings. Blakesley understood the dangers to Mormonism's future posed by the problem of succession: "if they can all have their choice, we shall soon have a multiplicity of churches of Latter Day Saints."[8]

Rigdon arrived in Nauvoo on Saturday, August 3, and moved quickly to resolve the succession issue in his favor before most of the apostles had returned from the eastern states. Though he agreed to meet with Pratt and the other apostles in Nauvoo the next morning, he did not do so. Rather, in a public meeting on Sunday, Rigdon proposed that he serve as a guardian for the church. In a millennially themed address, Rigdon prophesied that "he would personally lead a militant church to a triumphant victory over the nations of Babylon."[9] One Saint later remembered that Pratt dramatically intervened to delay a vote on Rigdon's guardianship proposal. When he learned Rigdon would call for a vote, Pratt, who had been working in his garden, "dropped his hoe and came to the meeting Walked on the stand Barefoot his pants roled up above his ankles and his shirt sleeves half way to his Elbows" and "soon put a stop" to Rigdon's plan.[10]

That Sunday afternoon, following Rigdon's discourse, stake president William Marks, sympathetic to Rigdon's guardianship proposal, called for a conference on Thursday, August 8. Rigdon initially acquiesced to Pratt's proposal to hold only the regularly scheduled prayer meeting because of the absence of the other apostles, but Rigdon subsequently transformed it into a business meeting to vote on his guardianship proposal. After this maneuver, Pratt stated, "I then saw that this was a deep and cunning plan laid to divide the best people that ever lived."[11] Jedediah M. Grant recorded that the apostles in Nauvoo, particularly Pratt, "insisted with great earnestness that no action of the kind [election of a guardian] ought to be taken before the Church until a majority of the Twelve could be present."[12] Fortunately for Pratt's position, two days prior to this conference, Brigham Young, Heber Kimball, Orson Pratt, and Wilford Woodruff arrived in Nauvoo (George A. Smith had returned somewhat earlier). On August 7, the apostles met with Rigdon to hear his case. Woodruff dismissed it as "a long story" and a "kind of second Class vision"; Young seconded Woodruff, saying that there "could not be any one before the Twelve."[13]

At the August 8 conference, Rigdon preached a lengthy sermon in the morning, again asserting the need for a church guardian. That afternoon, Young spoke for the apostles, arguing that Rigdon's station as Smith's counselor had ended with the prophet's death. He asked, referring to Rigdon's disaffection, "Who has stood next to Joseph and Hyrum? I have, and I will stand next to him. We have a head, and that head is the Apostleship.... No man has a right to counsel the Twelve but Joseph Smith."[14] Many Saints later recalled that during his sermon, Young appeared or sounded like Smith, miraculous evidence, they affirmed, that Smith's prophetic mantle had fallen on Young and the apostles.[15] Following Young's speech, Amasa Lyman, who had also served as a counselor to Smith, affirmed his support for Young, as did William W. Phelps (whom Rigdon had asked to speak on his behalf) and Pratt.[16]

When Young called for a vote, the assembled Saints overwhelmingly rejected Rigdon and accepted the leadership of the Twelve Apostles. Just as Pratt's preaching to his former religious mentor Rigdon and his Campbellite congregation in 1830 had marked a critical juncture in Mormon history, his intervention to delay a vote on Rigdon's guardianship proposal fundamentally changed the course of the Latter-day Saint movement by allowing the apostles to assemble in Nauvoo before the crucial vote.

While the August 8 meeting and the apostles' subsequent arguments resolved the issue of succession for large numbers of Latter-day Saints, especially in the Nauvoo area, it was only the beginning of a long, hard-fought battle. In the months and years immediately following Smith's assassination, two principal alternatives to apostolic leadership emerged. First, Rigdon denounced the apostles, threatened to "Expose the Counsels of the Church and Publish all he knew," and began to organize followers who believed that the doctrinal developments of Nauvoo indicated that Smith had been a fallen prophet in the last years of his life.[17] In early September, the apostles "met together with Elder Rigdon to investigate his course." Rigdon "came out full against the Twelve and said he would not be controlled by them."[18] A few days later, the apostles and the Nauvoo High Council excommunicated Rigdon at a trial that he refused to attend, with Pratt testifying against Rigdon extensively.[19]

In addition to Rigdon, James J. Strang, a recent convert to Mormonism, claimed that Smith had sent him a letter nine days before his death designating Strang as successor. Many Saints saw in Strang's charismatic claims to prophetic status and revelatory power echoes of Smith's own actions.[20] Like Smith, he would, for example, claim to translate records uncovered from the earth. Followers of Strang seized on a popular song that Pratt had composed: "[A] church without a Prophet, is not the church for me/It has not head to lead it, in it I would not be." Strang's followers mocked believers in apostolic authority for dropping the song "like a hot potato."[21] Notably, both Rigdon and Strang concentrated their efforts on Mormons outside of Nauvoo; Rigdon established his headquarters in Pittsburgh, and Strang designated Wisconsin as the new gathering place for the Saints. They appealed to Mormons dissatisfied with the leadership of Young and the apostles and their intention to move to the West. (The most successful of the groups to claim succession, besides the apostles, did not appear until the 1850s—the Reorganized Church of Jesus Christ of Latter Day Saints, which claimed a lineal succession to Joseph Smith III and is now called the Community of Christ.)

Rigdon and Strang also attracted followers by denouncing the apostles for practicing plural marriage, even though both would eventually embrace a form of polygamy. Indeed, rumors of the apostles' involvement in polygamy explain much of their difficulty in asserting leadership over the Mormon movement. During the succession crisis, most Mormons, particularly those outside of Nauvoo, did not know that Smith had sanctioned polygamy. Allegations that the apostles practiced polygamy (and had thus, many Mormons thought, scandalously corrupted Smith's teachings and Mormonism) proved persuasive to large numbers of Saints.

After the dramatic August 8 conference, Pratt continued to meet privately with the apostles and preach publicly, even as cholera struck his family. Testifying at a Sunday meeting in late August, he declared "that Joseph the Prophet and Seer had ordained, anointed, and appointed the Twelve to lead the Church. Had given them the Keys of the Kingdom of God for that purpose."[22] Three days later, his sixteen-month-old daughter, Susan, died "of Disease of the bowels."[23] His other children likely were ill as well; Parley Jr. and stepdaughter Mary Ann attended school only three days between August 12 and September 20.[24]

In September, the apostles solidified their claim to succession by dramatically expanding the quorums of the seventy. Joseph Smith had established this priesthood office in 1835 at the same time as the apostles' own calling. But while the apostles' role within the church had increased over the previous decade, the seventies' position had atrophied, in part because of internal rivalries between the seventies and the high priests. Creating new quorums (an increase from four at Smith's death to thirty-five by early 1846) aided missionary work, the seventies' central responsibility, but it also organized some twenty-five hundred Mormon men within priesthood organizations staunchly loyal to the apostles. This helped undercut the succession claim of a potential rival, Nauvoo's influential Stake president William Marks, the leader of the Nauvoo high priests and the twelve-member Nauvoo High Council. Many Saints, including Emma Smith, initially saw Marks, a fierce opponent of plural marriage, as a possible successor to Joseph Smith. Pratt and the other apostles also clarified the relative position of the seventies and the high priests. Smith had intended, Pratt preached, that the seventies occupy a third tier of Mormon leadership, only after the First Presidency and the apostles. However, "the jealousies that began to arise in the minds of the High Priests" in Kirtland "prevented [Smith] from doing so." If the "Quorum of the Twelve should by any means become disorganized," Pratt taught, the seventies, not the high priests, "held the Jurisdiction and authority of [the] Presidency of the church in all the world."[25]

As the apostles moved to consolidate their authority, they simultaneously expanded the practice of plural marriage, both taking new plural wives themselves and authorizing others to do so.[26] Though counterintuitive from a public relations standpoint, the apostles believed they were honoring and extending Joseph Smith's legacy. That fall, Pratt married three additional women. (He eventually married ten plural wives, eight between 1843 and 1847.) On September 9, 1844, Brigham Young sealed Pratt to Mary Wood, a twenty-six-year old native of Glasgow, Scotland. Mary became acquainted with Parley and Mary Ann during their English mission and had been one of the women they originally considered for plural marriage. She accepted their invitation to come to Nauvoo, arriving on March 1, 1844.[27] Mary joined the Latter-day Saints in 1839 while living in Manchester; according to her son, Mary's father gave her an ultimatum: "This night you must choose between the Mormons and your home, and all that the word home implies." Mary replied, "Father, if I must make such a choice, I cannot go back on what I know to be true, even if it should mean the loss of home and kindred and all else. I know the Latter-day Saints have the true gospel, and I cannot sacrifice what I know to be true." Her father retorted, "Then, there is the door and you must never darken it again."[28]

Two months after his marriage to Mary Wood, Pratt married Hannahette Snively, a thirty-two-year old woman from Woodstock, Virginia, with Young performing the ceremony on November 2. Two days before, Pratt had married Young to Hannahette's sister Susan. The Snively sisters had joined Mormonism and moved to Nauvoo, where they built a house near the Pratts with money from their father's estate.[29] Hannahette and Susan helped nurse the Pratt children during the cholera outbreak. A year later, Parley wrote that he would never forget Hannahette's "coming to the house and kindly taking care of the sick.... It opened an acquaintance and laid the foundation of a friendship which will be as durable as the throne of Jehovah."[30] When Parley left for the eastern states a month after their marriage, Hannahette was pregnant.

Shortly before he left for the East, Parley married Belinda Marden on November 20, in a ceremony performed by Young in the home of Erastus Snow with only Snow as witness.[31] Marden, the youngest of fourteen children raised in a strict Congregationalist family, had earlier married Benjamin Abbot Hilton in New Hampshire. Belinda described Hilton as "an infidel" and herself as a religious seeker, hoping "to find the right kind of religion never feeling assured that those I was acquainted with were right." The Hiltons moved to Boston where, in the winter of 1843, they attended a Mormon

FIGURE 8.1 Parley Pratt and Belinda Marden Pratt, daguerreotype of unknown date. Courtesy Church History Library, The Church of Jesus Christ of Latter-day Saints.

meeting. During the opening prayer, Belinda felt "the light of heaven rested down upon me, for the joy and peace I experienced was unexpressible." They attended two other meetings that day and Belinda received "an overwhelming testimony" of the religion's truth and "was so rejoyced that I seemed to myself light as air." Hilton thought his wife "was too enthusiastic" but saw Mormonism as a "splendid doctrine to whip the secterians." Belinda's extended family likewise opposed conversion. Much to her relief, Hilton "one day in March...came home at an unusual hour and told me he was so wrought upon that he could not work or sleep, and he would have to go and get baptized." Though both were soon baptized, "it was not long before my husband began to doubt and feel ill towards the church and the brethern" and soon opted for the "Odd-Fellows" rather than the Mormons.[32]

Parley met Belinda during his visit to Boston with other apostles as part of Joseph Smith's presidential campaign in June 1844, though by this time Belinda "did not mingle much with the Saints for fear of displeasing my husband." Brigham Young urged Belinda to obtain a letter of recommendation from the Boston branch to other church branches for possible use on upcoming travel to visit family. As the clerk gave her a recommendation, Lyman Wight counseled Belinda to travel instead to Nauvoo, telling her "in the name of the Lord God of Israel if I would leave I would never see the day I would be sorry for it." Wight arranged for Belinda to travel to Utica, New

York, where she could stay with a Mormon family in preparation for traveling to Nauvoo. Under the pretense of visiting relatives, Belinda left her husband and went to Utica, where she remained for two months, making dresses and satchels to earn travel money. Belinda then traveled along with another Mormon woman to Nauvoo, arriving in late September.[33]

Once there, she came to accept "all the revelations of God, Polygamy included. But on account of the sayings and doings of some of the brethren and sisters I suffered the temptations of Satan nearly overcome me so far that I thought I would have nothing to do with it, I mean Polygamy." After Young taught Belinda the doctrine, however, she felt that the "holy Spirit of God rested down upon me and it was made plain to my understanding that it was a divine principle." Belinda married Parley in a secret ceremony because of her existing marriage to Hilton, though she considered that marriage over and likely saw divorce as an impossible proposition. (A year earlier, Young had likewise married an upper-class Boston convert, Augusta Adams Cobb, who had left her husband without obtaining a divorce; when her husband filed for divorce in 1847, Boston newspapers exploded with stories of the scandal.)[34] Belinda stated that Hilton "obtained a divorce from me by the false swearing of apostates," though this likely occurred after her marriage to Pratt.[35] This type of informal separation and remarriage without a legal divorce occurred relatively frequently during the nineteenth century.[36] Nevertheless, Pratt was likely sensitive over charges that he had married Belinda before she obtained a formal divorce. A few months later, he warned missionaries to encourage the "harmony of husbands and wives" and instructed that separated spouses could not remarry "unless they are lawfully free" by a formal divorce.[37]

As Pratt married these three women in fall 1844, the controversy over polygamy was proving especially potent in the eastern branches of the church, inflamed by three of the most colorful figures of early Mormonism: Apostle William Smith, Joseph Smith's erratic younger brother; George J. Adams, a talented orator and writer with a flair for the dramatic; and Samuel Brannan, editor of the church's New York newspaper, the *Prophet*. Their later histories were merely the playing out of the chaotic conditions Pratt confronted upon arrival in the eastern states: William Smith later passed through Strang's movement before eventually joining the Reorganized Church; Adams became a leading Strangite and later established a religious colony in Palestine that Mark Twain satirized in his *Innocents Abroad*; and Brannan accompanied a group of Saints in 1846 to California, where he soon left Mormonism and became one of San Francisco's wealthiest and most controversial citizens.[38]

Serious problems in the East emerged just months after Joseph Smith's death. Wilford Woodruff, traveling through the eastern states en route to a mission in England, warned Brigham Young in October 1844 that William Smith, Adams, and Brannan were preaching the "Kissing Women spiritual wife" doctrine. Using Smith's apostolic authority and the claim that Adams "was the great Apostle to the gentiles as Paul even was the 13th Apostle," the men were "crowing their spiritual wife claims, visiting the Churches, Uniting together in Begging money, running all over rights of [local] presiding Elders." Not only had they mixed Mormonism with Democratic Party politics, but they had also taught "the Lowell girls," female members who worked in the Lowell textile mills, "that [it] is not wrong to have intercourse with the men." The church in the East, in short, existed in a "vortex of recklessness."[39]

Soon, an explosive feud between local leaders and Adams, Brannan, and William Smith—involving accusations of illicit polygamy and sexual immorality—threatened to tear apart Mormonism in the East. William Smith believed that "any Elder" could seal "a man to his wife for Eternity," whereas the other apostles believed the sealing power rested with the apostolic quorum.[40] Smith sealed together Brannan and Sarah E. Wallace after Brannan allegedly seduced her.[41] When John Hardy, president of the Boston branch, called Adams, Smith, and Brannan "licentious characters" for teaching and practicing polygamy, they excommunicated him in October 1844 for slander. Hardy published a pamphlet, excerpted in newspapers, that detailed his excommunication trial and contained credible accounts of seductions taking place under the guise of the "spiritual wife" doctrine and hasty sealings performed to conceal adultery. The pamphlet brought the divisions within the church to the attention of a scandal-hungry public.[42] The situation deteriorated further when Brannan's newspaper accused Benjamin Winchester, an influential Mormon pamphleteer who had affiliated with Rigdon's movement, of participating in Joseph Smith's death. Winchester sued for libel, and Woodruff worried that the "character of Joseph & Hiram & the Twelve will be made as black through falsehood as the Lawyers can make them & all Hell is raked over to get testimony against the Twelve." As he prepared to depart for England, Woodruff warned that Brannan, Adams, and William Smith worked to build up themselves, "instead of the Temple the Twelve & Nauvoo" and that he did not "feel like sustaining them in their practice until they reform." He called for "one of the Twelve from Nauvoo" to "take charge" in the East.[43]

Young thus dispatched Pratt to take control of this chaos. The *Times and Seasons* described his responsibility as to "go to the city of New York, to take charge of the press in that city, to regulate and counsel the emigration that may come that way from Europe, and to take the presidency of all the eastern churches."[44] Pratt made the impolitic decision to take his new polygamous bride, Belinda, with him. It was ill advised for two reasons. First, since most eastern Saints did not yet know of the apostles' polygamy in Nauvoo—or other doctrinal innovations such as the new temple endowment—traveling with Belinda (even secretly and cautiously) had the potential to lessen Pratt's moral authority among them. Second, his decision to take Belinda had personal repercussions. He left Nauvoo a few days before Mary Ann gave birth to their fourth child, Moroni, on December 7. He wrote Mary Ann, "I never left home with more intense feelings, Nor under more trying Circumstances than the present," with the exception of his time in prison, when Mary had been left "Sick of a fever with a babe 3 months old and to the mercy of Savages." "I was Sorry to Go," he told Mary Ann of his recent departure, "and your tears quite over Came me."[45] Belinda followed Pratt by a few days, traveling on her own. Joining up in St. Louis, they journeyed first by boat to Pittsburgh and Wheeling, Virginia, by stage to Wilmington, and finally by railroad to Philadelphia and New York.

From Wheeling, Parley wrote Mary Ann of his concern for her and their infant: "I suppose you have Long e're this had to pass through a trial which I would fain Never had you endure *without my presence* but we have a God who is able to be more to us than earthly help or comfort. To him I have often Cried in your behalf while silently reflecting on your trials." He continued, "The time will Soon pass with you, Surrounded as you are with Mother, Children, and friends. But with me it is far different. I not only have to part with one but all." Pratt referred to polygamy only obliquely, promising a letter soon to "Sister Wood and Others": "My Love to them and God bless them and he knows what is in my big heart though only expressed in those few words." In closing, Pratt hoped that the rewards of eternity would compensate for the sufferings of mortality: "you Shall ever be with me and all I have is thine and I am thine for ever and you Shall forever Reign in Glory and in a fullness of Joy with those you love."[46] Pratt's lofty rhetoric provided little comfort; his departure with a new bride as Mary Ann suffered the travails of childbirth alone marked a crucial rupture in their relationship. Also left behind in Nauvoo were plural wives Elizabeth, Mary, and the newly pregnant Hannahette. Once in New York, Belinda rented a separate "boarding place among strangers, for it was not known that the sealing power was practiced except by few of the Saints." "After a short time," they rented a home together; Belinda paid expenses by making dresses and knitting baby socks.[47]

Shortly after his arrival in New York, Pratt published an important notice to the eastern Saints in the church's New York City newspaper, the *Prophet*. Timed to suggest the dawn of a new era, the New Year's Day proclamation asserted apostolic control over the Mormon church in the East. Pratt congratulated the eastern Saints on their "peace, union, and prosperity." Nevertheless, he acknowledged the "desertion, apostacy and traitorism" that had occurred, as the church had "been in perils among false brethren...betrayed and wounded in the house of her friends." Pratt emphasized that the government of the church was a theocracy, directed by the apostles. In his writing, he developed what became the standard defense of the apostles' right to lead the church, arguing that before Joseph Smith's martyrdom, their prophet had been inspired

> to call the Twelve together from time to time, and to instruct them in all things pertaining to the kingdom, ordinances, and government of God....Having done this he rejoiced exceedingly, for said he, the Lord is about to lay the burden upon your shoulders and let me rest awhile; and if they kill me, continued he, the kingdom of God will roll on, as I have now finished the work which was laid upon me, by committing to you all things for the building up of the kingdom according to the heavenly vision.

Smith had also conferred on Young, as president of the Twelve, the "keys of the sealing power...this last key of the priesthood is the most sacred of all." In comparing the roles of Joseph Smith and the apostles, Pratt wrote:

> He has organized the kingdom of God.—We will extend its
>   dominion.
> He has restored the fullness of the Gospel.—We spread it abroad.
> He has laid the foundation of Nauvoo—We will build it up.
> He has laid the foundation of the Temple.—We will bring up the
>   top-stone with shouting....
> In short, he quarried the stone from the mountain; we will cause it to
>   become a great mountain and fill up the whole earth.

According to Pratt, Smith's death had even been necessary: "While the Testator lived, the testament was not of full power; all that was done was preparatory."[48]

After laying the theological foundations for apostolic authority, Pratt established regulations to restore order to the church. The church would be divided into presidential districts presided over by high priests and under the general jurisdiction of the apostles. Local officials would have authority only within their own district; Pratt restricted them, for instance, from appointing missionaries who would go beyond their own area. Only the apostles possessed authority that was universal rather than local. "These regulations," he wrote, "will save the church from imposition, fraud and also false doctrine; endless calls for money to support the moving to and fro of elders, and from ten thousand snares, troubles, difficulties, jarrings and confusions, to which they are now exposed." Pratt suggested that this would undercut attempts by people like Adams—whom he referred to not by name but as the "Great apostle of the Gentiles"—to gain authority. Finally, Pratt emphasized the importance of completing the Nauvoo Temple, as all Saints "will stand in need of an endowment in the Temple." As such, Pratt called on eastern Mormons to "bring all your tythings into the storehouse" (and to pay tithes only to agents he appointed).[49]

The targets of Pratt's proclamation were clear to eastern Saints and knowledgeable observers. Henry Rowe, who had written for the *Prophet* before his disaffiliation with Mormonism, wrote a series of articles on Mormonism for the *Boston Investigator*. He described Pratt as the "Golia[t]h" and "Autocrat of the Mormons," and "one of the very few scientific men that the church can boast of." Pratt's proclamation, Rowe correctly perceived, targeted George Adams, among others, for his practice of polygamy (and for unauthorized soliciting of funds from the Saints). According to Rowe, "the Rev. President Pratt condemns in Elder Adams what he and his brothers, the Twelve, openly call for.... They are jealous of Elder Adams's success at the same game, and want to turn it into their own coffers." Indeed, Rowe exclaimed, polygamy was "being most scandalously and unblushingly practiced in Boston, Lowell, New York, Philadelphia," and Nauvoo.[50] Suspecting the proclamation was also directed at him, William Smith defended himself in a letter to the *Prophet*. Following the death of his brothers, Smith suggested, "the church has had to undergo almost an entire revolution of things and those away from Nauvoo have had to guess their way, or get along the best they could, and if errors have been committed, they have been of the head, and not of the heart."[51]

The same day as his proclamation, Pratt issued another statement with even more momentous ramifications. His "Regulations for the Publishing Department of the Latter-day Saints in the East" further consolidated the authority of the apostles by placing all church publications under their control. Until this time, the world of Mormon publishing was made up of freelance editors, authors, and publicists, many of whom naturally gravitated to the large eastern cities with their publishing houses and printing presses. Joseph Smith had boasted that "the Latter-day Saints have no creed, but are ready to believe all true principles that exist."[52] Accordingly, he exercised little control over the marketplace of Mormon ideas; now, as versions of the gospel were proliferating and a succession crisis had yet to play out fully, it became more imperative than ever to manage Mormonism's message. Pratt explained, "Are you not all aware that very many, if not all, of our men, women and children are turning authors, and publishing works purporting to be illustrative of the doctrine of the saints." Many problems marred these works, Pratt complained, including poor writing, doctrinal errors, too much copying from other works (including the scriptures and his own pamphlets), and a waste of scarce resources. Furthermore, competition limited the ability of those, like himself, "whose business it is to write and publish the truth," to produce works that "pay for themselves." In the future, only works published by church presses in three locations (Nauvoo, New York, and Liverpool), all under the direct supervision of apostles, would be sanctioned by the church. Pratt thus warned members "not to patronize, purchase, or support any publication pertaining to our cause, except they emanate from one of these offices." The *Times and Seasons* supported Pratt's directive: "There is nothing like order in the kingdom of God."[53] The importance of centralized control was dramatically emphasized when the dissident Strang established his own newspaper, perhaps the key element in forging his movement into the most successful initial alternative to apostolic leadership.

Pratt next sought to strengthen the loyalty of the eastern Saints, many of whose faith had been shaken by the claims and actions of William Smith, Adams, and Brannan, as well as the efforts of Rigdon to discredit the apostles by publicizing their polygamy. He used both short preaching tours in several states and his writings in the *Prophet* to strengthen the apostles' authority. On January 11, he reported on a "visit to Boston and vicinity" describing "a spirit of light and truth prevailing in the branches generally" which contrasted with the "troubles and trials to which they have been subjected of late on account of persecution and apostasy." Though Pratt publicly disdained Adams, he showed atypical restraint in not condemning Smith, his fellow apostle, or Brannan, whom he considered an effective and frugal editor. In fact, he praised Smith, as well as local leaders, "in relation to the apostacies and dissensions with which they had to grapple." They had "taken a decided stand against rebellious, wicked, and corrupt men."[54]

To Young, however, he wrote that "there has been Some Curious doings such as Sealings, etc. by Elders Adam Brannan, etc. But I shall be Silant on the subject till I see you."⁵⁵ Then privately, Pratt directed Brannan to "repent, with all his heart, and do so no more, if he had been Guilty of acting upon, or holding to certain principles, or he could no longer Stand in his place."⁵⁶ After Young excommunicated Adams and Brannan in late spring, Pratt (much to his later regret) successfully urged the reinstatement of Brannan, believing he was "only one of the Branches" of the evil that had infested the eastern church.⁵⁷ Pratt also obtained a promise from the troublesome dissident Benjamin Winchester to "neither write nor preach against the church any more" and to "stop all suits and bury the hatchet" if Pratt arranged for Reuben Hedlock, a church leader in England, to settle an outstanding debt.⁵⁸

Having sorted out the disharmony and dissension in the ranks, Pratt moved to implement the new publishing regulations by writing Young that the eastern Saints needed books, in particular a thousand copies of the Doctrine and Covenants and two thousand hymnals. He requested that Young either "publish them there in sufficient quantities to supply us" or send him the "Stereotype Plates" to publish in New York. This would allow the Saints to "dispense with Hardies Edition [a hymnal] and all other unauthorized works." Pratt pledged to undertake the publishing without any "personal Considerations or proffits."⁵⁹

Probably happy for the opportunity afforded by the new regulations, Pratt now assumed the editorship of the *Prophet*, though Brannan continued to manage the newspaper, which issued two thousand weekly copies. (In early summer 1845, signaling the new regime, the paper was renamed the *New-York Messenger*.) In April, Pratt told Young that he kept "very buisy as you will see by Reading the Original matter that pours forth weekly in the Colums of the Prophet."⁶⁰ Though Pratt was tempted to use his platform to attack the rivals to apostolic authority, Young directed Pratt not to wage battle against Rigdon in the paper, as there was already "sufficient published [material] on Rigdonism to show every honest man his corruption." Rigdon and his followers should be allowed "to fester and die in their own corruption like all other Apostates."⁶¹ Even before reading this letter, Pratt had already instructed the eastern Saints to not actively oppose "Rigdonism" as it "would have been dead and buried and almost forgotten e're this time, but for the exertions of our Elders." Rigdon, who "seems in his old age to have become a little deranged," should be pitied, not hated.⁶²

Rather than attack Strang or Rigdon, Pratt's newspaper writings explicated, often in bold and even brash essays, key Mormon principles. In "The Bible and the Book of Mormon contrasted," Pratt declared that the Book of Mormon "is of more importance to Americans than the other bible" because it described the "history of a larger, a better and more important country" and contained "much more plain" doctrinal teachings and prophecies about America. Pratt also defended the Book of Mormon on archaeological grounds.[63] By this time, Pratt had developed a highly significant shift in his exegesis, expanding the category of Lamanites to include not only Native Americans in the United States but all of the "aboriginal inhabitants of North and South America," which he numbered at between ten million and twelve million.[64] In an important editorial, Pratt also further elaborated the Mormon doctrines of materialism of spirit and a domestic heaven, favorite themes of his.[65]

Pratt also defended specific Latter-day Saint practices, such as bloc voting, which had been widely condemned. In so doing, he argued that Mormons should work within the American democratic system to obtain their political aims: "Thus united, we become at once a powerful people, though small and few in number. We are able to maintain a balance of power in this nation, and to say which of the two great parties shall hold the administration of government." Like nearly all religious, social, and political movements in nineteenth-century America, Mormons claimed to be the heirs of the American Revolution. But Pratt went further, arguing that Mormon "revolutionaries" were

> of far more importance than were our fathers or the founders of the nation. They fought for liberty, and independence of a foreign power. We, for life and existance, in our own country. They fought to establish a country, laws, and constitution. We fight to restore its surpemicy [supremacy], or to preserve it in existence.... Their weapons were the merciless cannon, and sword. Ours, are, the TRUTH and the BALLOT BOX.[66]

Just as the Book of Mormon was more relevant to nineteenth-century Americans than was the Bible, the Latter-day Saint movement was more important than was the American Revolution.

Recognizing the unique challenges facing eastern Saints who did not follow the general summons to gather, Pratt urged that while they should work within the American political system, they should separate themselves socially. To avoid contamination in a non-Zion society, Pratt instructed the Saints to remove "all sectarian books, tracts, pictures, paintings" from their homes.[67] Reflecting his own Puritan bent more than Mormon doctrine, he also cautioned the Saints not to participate in "music, dancing, feasting and merriment," as they were "of too sacred and holy a nature in themselves, to be enjoyed for vain and trifling purposes and occasions, or by persons who are unworthy and disqualified to enjoy them in their original purity." Mormons should thus avoid them "at present" as "we are not sufficiently separated from corrupt society to indulge in such enjoyments without min- gling with the idle, foolish, vain, and impure, not only around us in the worldly circle, but in our own society." Within the church lurked both "abandoned and designing knaves and villains" (an inevitable situation given that the "gospel is for sinners") as well as potential apostates, who would eventually "publish all that is said and done" and "make the most innocent words or actions appear both wicked and ridiculous." Pratt declared, "I have not come to play with, or to amuse this generation," and "none need expect me to join in dancing, plays, public kissing parties, or other public amusements."⁶⁸ At least part of Pratt's antisocial bent was likely more a function of his ineptness than his theology. Orson Hyde later recalled that when "dancing was first introduced into Nauvoo...I observed brother Parley standing in the figure, and he was making no motion particularly, only up and down. Says I, 'Brother Parley, why don't you move forward?' Says he, 'When I think which way I am going, I forget the step; and when I think of the step, I forget which way to go.'"⁶⁹

Far removed from the turmoil and vulnerability of post-martyrdom Nauvoo, Pratt found some comfort in recourse to occasional sallies of wry humor directed at the church's detractors. In one editorial romp he provided a glossary of terms helpful to understand "the science of anti-Mormon Suckerology" ("suckers" was slang for Illinoisans). Some of his entries included: "Mormon—A believer in revealed religion," whereas "Gentlemen of High Respectability" he defined as "those who have been indicted by an impartial Grand Jury of their country, for the most cruel, cold-blooded and cowardly murder known upon the annals of history, and those who justify them." And, he continued, in entries worthy of Ambrose Bierce, "Mormon Fortifications: A garden fence; a common city enclosure of public grounds"; "Mormon Tyranny—Any attempt on the part of civil officers to bring mob- bers to justice"; "Mormon Treason—To emigrate to the west; to settle in one place or neighborhood; to build a city or temple."⁷⁰

Besides his frequent writings for the newspaper, Pratt penned "a procla- mation to all the Kings, Presidents, Rulers, and people of the world" on behalf of the apostles, in part to fulfill a commandment given to Joseph Smith in January 1841 to send a "solemn proclamation" to world leaders. Pratt had it "stereotyped in most beautiful large type, and ready for press" and sent a few copies to Nauvoo for approval by the other apostles. He stated, "I think some such publication is necessary as a *Standard*, and as a *warning* to go forth to the nations Spedily, as there is a General wonder and expectation every where in relation to the Latter day Glory."[71]

The proclamation returned to the canonical Mormon vision of the end-times, emphasizing the nearness of the Second Coming and explaining the future destiny of the indigenous peoples of North and South America, the Jews, and the Gentiles. Pratt called on the "kings, rulers, and people of the Gentiles" to repent, accept the Mormon gospel, and contribute their riches for the work of God. In his vision, neutrality was impossible, as "all nations and creeds" would be reduced "to *one* political and religious *standard*," taking supremacy over the "courts of Rome, London, Paris, Constantinople, Petersburgh, and all others" as well as over the "priests, bishops, and clergy, whether Catholic, Protestant, or Mahomedan." Pratt urged American leaders, though by now with little real hope, to protect the Saints, compensate them for their financial losses, punish their persecutors, and allow American Indians to be gathered, civilized, and taught their destiny from the Book of Mormon. If American leaders assisted the Mormons, they would realize their vision of Manifest Destiny, of "one great powerful and peaceful empire of Liberty and Union."[72]

Pratt envisioned a wide circulation for his proclamation, encouraging newspaper editors to print it and instructing Mormon leaders throughout the world to publish it. He boasted that he would publish "one hundred thousand copies of this work, to circulate in this country, *gratis*."[73] Young gave his approval of the proclamation in May 1845.[74] That fall, Wilford Woodruff published twenty thousand copies to distribute in the British mission, and Dan Jones printed four thousand in Welsh. The *Millennial Star* advised missionaries to circulate the brashly millennialist pamphlet with discretion, "so as not unnecessarily expose themselves to difficulties and persecutions."[75]

By June, Pratt despaired of progress in his assignment, suffering the dual burden of personal debts outstanding in the West (he received news of "an Old Judgment...from Ohio against me") and economic difficulties with the *Prophet*. He initially intended that Mary Ann and Mary Wood would join him in New York, but financial problems (as well as the logistical challenge of traveling with three wives) quickly stymied this plan.[76] Arranging to publish an almanac that Orson had compiled, he hoped it would enable Orson to pay off some of Parley's obligations while freeing up a few hundred dollars so Mary Ann could resolve others.[77] Adding to his worries, Elizabeth Brotherton fell seriously ill during early 1845. Parley asked Hannahette to "go and see" her "Immediately if She is yet alive and sick and devote your time and attention faithfully in comforting and nourishing her, and see that she lacks for nothing, that the country affords, and I will repay the money you will spend."[78]

During a preaching tour in Boston and again via the *Prophet*, Pratt was reduced to asking for donations to cover his expenses. He received some help but was stung by criticism from eastern Saints who complained that he asked for money even though he had "a good house in Nauvoo." Lashing back publicly, Pratt protested that he had "already spent some half dozen houses" in God's service and that "I seldom beg, in the pulpit or out of it, except for others than myself."[79] While the eastern Saints had contributed to "Wm. Smith, G. J. Adams and many others," Pratt explained to Woodruff, he refused to "whine nor plead necessity, nor beg." "I now want to go home," he wrote, "but I can neither Borrow nor beg the means at present as I know of, or at least I shall not try the Beging part." The *Prophet* would also halt production, Pratt warned, for "want of support."[80]

Nor was consolation forthcoming from a populace that was, Pratt lamented, "entirely Indifferent" to his preaching. "As to the City of New York," he told Young, "I have become Convinced that I Can do no good in it.... The Saints are few, say about fifty of them attend a Sunday meeting in a large hall, and perhaps half a dozen strangers come in and out to Gaze and gape, and wonder and perish." His yearnings had ever been westward—to the wilderness as a youth, to the Lamanites as a missionary, and to Zion with the Saints. He bridled at administration, inaction, and the thought of further dissipating his energies in a futile endeavor. Pratt informed Young that he would return soon and "follow that spirit which draws me to Nauvoo with the rest of the Children of the Kingdom," where he would "bow at your feet and humbly ask for the liberty of staying in Nauvoo, or of Going to the Chocktaws, Creeks, or Cherokees—in short any where but to a Nation of Proud, blind, Gentile Murderers, who have rejected the fulness of the Gospel, and put to death the prophets."[81] In the *Prophet*, Pratt counseled the eastern Saints to gather to Nauvoo, participate in the temple ordinances, and "take away the fullness of the gospel" from unbelievers. "Run after them no more," he continued, "but let them, if they will be saved run after you ... until then, they shall never have the blessings of it—No—NEVER-NEVER-NEVER."[82] The pregnancy of his plural wife with him in New York—Belinda would give birth to Nephi in January 1846—also likely spurred his decision to return to Nauvoo.

In his farewell letter to the eastern Saints (published in the *Prophet* in July 1845), Pratt struck a more positive tone, praising them for "hearkening to the counsel of those who were sent among you, bearing the keys of the kingdom

for the government and direction of the church in all things." He predicted
that, within a decade, Nauvoo might be "the largest and most wealthy city in
America," and he again urged the eastern Saints to gather: "We must be the
Noahs and the Lots of the age." But in the meantime he also cautioned them
to remain loyal to the apostles and not "be led away by the influence of some
'great man' who may chance to come among you with great swelling words,
and fair speech, who is not sent here by the Twelve."[83]

Pratt visited Boston and Philadelphia before returning to Nauvoo in late
August 1845. In his last months in the East, he continued to battle Mormon
factions opposed to the apostles' leadership. In a conference in Philadelphia,
he attended an ecclesiastical trial of Elder M. B. Helverson, who had gone
"from house to house...denouncing the Quorum of Twelve as corrupt men
rejecting their authority."[84] He also informed Young that one Joseph Ball, a
close ally of William Smith's and George Adams's, had claimed "pretended
revelation," but was in reality "a very Corrupt Man, and guilty of Adultery,
fornication, or attempts at seduction and crime of the gravest kind."[85]

Pratt wrestled with the question of how to denounce unauthorized plural
marriage, which he believed unscrupulous men like Smith and Adams had
exploited out of lust, without condemning sanctioned polygamy. The
"'SPIRITUAL WIFE' doctrine," Pratt wrote in an editorial, was "but another
name for whoredom, wicked and unlawful connection, and every kind of
confusion, corruption, and abomination." Those advocating such a system, he
warned, would be "expelled from the church." Continuing with an ambiguity
of language that could cover both monogamous and polygamous marriage
sealings, Pratt explained the difference between spiritual wifery and authorized sealings:

> If a man has a wife according to the law of God and the regulations of
> the church, she is his REAL wife, body, soul, spirit, heart, and hand,
> and not his "SPIRITUAL WIFE," she is bound to love, honor, obey
> him as her lord, head, and master, and to devote all her energies to the
> mutual welfare of her husband, herself and family....On the other
> hand the husband of a woman is bound to be her REAL husband; to
> provide for his wife and children, and to be their head and father, and
> bring them up in the fear, and love, and truth of God, as did Abraham,
> Isaac and Jacob of old.

The "holy and sacred ordinances" of sealing, Pratt stated, bore no resemblance
to the chaotic and lustful practices of spiritual wifery; rather, they "have laws,

limits, and bounds of the strictest kind, and none but the pure in heart, the strictly virtuous, or those who repent and become such, are worthy to partake of them." Pratt had not performed sealings in the East because such ordinances awaited the completion of the Nauvoo Temple.[86]

The problems with the William Smith–Adams faction, however, followed Pratt to Nauvoo. By the time he arrived, tensions between Smith and the other apostles had heightened considerably. Already by May 1845, at the same time the apostles ordained William Smith as church patriarch, William Clayton recorded that Smith was "coming out in opposition to the Twelve and in favor of Adams.... Wm. says he has sealed some women to men and he considers he is not accountable to Brigham nor the Twelve nor any one else. There is more danger from William than from any other source."[87] Believing that Smith "aspires to uproot and undermine the legal Presidency of the church, that he may occupy the place himself," Pratt objected to Smith's continued offices in the church in the October 1845 church conference, leading to his excommunication.[88]

When Pratt had encouraged the eastern Latter-day Saints to emigrate to Nauvoo, he had done so anticipating it would be a prelude to a western exodus. He wrote Young that the eastern Mormons "want the Kingdom of God, and its righteousness, and an end to everything else—and so do I."[89] Pratt likely minimized in his report to Young the success enjoyed by both Rigdon and Strang in recruiting followers from among eastern Mormons, exploiting the confusion and bitterness caused by William Smith, George Adams, and Samuel Brannan. Nevertheless, Pratt's mission to the East had largely accomplished its purpose. He articulated the theology of apostolic succession, established church control over an unwieldy Mormon print culture, and brought partial order to the chaos created by Brannan, Adams, and Smith.

9

Many Mormonisms

EXODUS AND ENGLAND

If people want to follow Strang go...follow a new thing
hatch it up for we have only the old thing. It was old
in Adams day it was old in Mormons day & hid up in
the earth & it was old in 1830 when we first began
to preach it.
—PARLEY PRATT, *comments in an April 25, 1847, meeting*

FOLLOWING HIS RETURN from the East, Pratt joined his fellow apostles in their vision for the immediate future. To solve the dilemma raised by the succession crisis and the multitude of Mormonisms that resulted, it was imperative to confirm Joseph Smith's legacy. This would entail completing the Nauvoo Temple, allowing all faithful Saints to participate in the endowment ritual, and establishing a new gathering place in the West. But even with the temple completed and the exodus under way, the question of succession would remain unresolved in the minds of many Saints. As the threat posed by Rigdon's movement began to subside, Strang's influence only increased among Mormons in far-flung areas. Exploiting rumors of the apostles' polygamy, the suffering of their followers during the expulsion from Nauvoo, and a failed church joint-stock company in England, Strang targeted the richest area of Mormon converts, Great Britain. Along with fellow apostles John Taylor and Orson Hyde, Pratt hastily traveled to Britain during fall 1846 in an effort to retain the loyalty of the large numbers of English Saints to the Quorum of the Twelve.

During fall 1845, Pratt and his fellow apostles were consumed with planning for the trek west and finishing the Nauvoo Temple, so the Saints could receive their long-awaited endowment. In a September letter to Isaac Rogers and his wife, a prosperous Mormon couple in New Jersey, Pratt discussed both of these tasks, writing with almost anticipatory nostalgia that the Nauvoo Temple "far exceeds my expectation both in Beauty and in progress.

The view from the top of the tower is Sublime beyond discription." Though the apostles remained vague in their public declarations of a possible settlement site in the West—generally referring to somewhere in the Rocky Mountains—Pratt knew that they had decided to move somewhere between Utah Lake and the Bear River Valley.[1] He told the Rogerses, "We have decided on Sending from one to 3 thousand Men to that place next spring…I expect to go also if I live and the Lord will." Specifically, Pratt believed the pioneers would "Stop near the Rocky mountains about 800 miles nearer than the Coast…and there make a stand, until we are able to enlarge and to extend to the coast." Pratt saw two key advantages: "When we arrive there we will have land without buying it. And we will have liberty without asking a set of corrupt office holders for it." But for Pratt and other Saints, the trek west did not yet mean the abandonment of Nauvoo. Rather, Pratt stated, "Our intention is to maintain and build up Nauvoo, and Settle other places too." He encouraged the Rogerses to come to Nauvoo that fall and help the Pratt family cross the plains, as it "will Cost a Great deal to fit out."[2]

Young and other Mormon leaders had been investigating possible sites for relocation since spring 1845, and the plans became more specific as Pratt arrived back in Nauvoo. On August 28, they opted for the plan that he described to the Rogerses. Vigilante attacks and house burnings in Mormon settlements outside of Nauvoo during September, evidencing the depth of hostility to the Saints even after the Smiths' murders, however, forced revisions to the plan. The apostles also feared that the federal government might interfere with the exodus if they delayed too long. After negotiations with local and state political authorities, the apostles agreed to a complete evacuation of the church from Nauvoo and the surrounding area by spring 1846, rather than the earlier partial exodus they had envisioned.[3] Pratt plunged into the preparations for the exodus, preparing a report on the supplies needed to support a wagon company to the Pacific Coast. Initially, he assumed that the wagons in the advance company would carry five men, but as plans changed, he modified the supply list to include women and children.[4] Pratt also worked on a "schedule for a pioneer company of 1,000 men, to preceed the body of emigrants, find a proper location, & put in seed early in the summer."[5] Along with other church leaders, he pored over recently published books on the West, particularly John C. Frémont's report of his 1842 to 1844 expedition and Lansford Hastings' *Emigrants' Guide to Oregon and California.*[6]

The whirlwind of activity in Nauvoo—constructing wagons, selling off property (seldom successfully), procuring supplies, planning for the emigration of the poorer Saints—occupied much of the fall. Continuing harassment by mobs, as well as false accusations against the apostles, complicated the preparations. In December 1845, a Springfield grand jury indicted several apostles, including Pratt, and other Mormon leaders on counterfeiting charges. On December 29, Pratt and fellow apostles George Smith, John Taylor, and Orson Hyde "disguised themselves to avoid suspicion of their [departure] and went home" from the temple.[7]

Pratt and the other apostles sought, aside from physical preparations, a theological justification for the exodus. In the October General Conference, Pratt answered the question on every Saint's mind—why had God commanded them to build up Nauvoo and the Temple "and then [we] are called to leave it"? He responded, "The people of God always were required to make sacrifices":

> The Lord has another purpose to bring about and to fulfill. We know that the great work of God must all the while be on the increase and grow greater.... The Lord designs to lead us to a wider field of action, where there will be more room for the saints to grow and increase, and where there will be no one to say we crowd them, and where we can enjoy the pure principles of liberty and equal rights.

Within five years, Pratt thought, they would "build a larger and better Temple" than the one they were struggling to complete.[8]

Pratt and the other apostles believed the Saints also required the spiritual preparation that the temple ordinances would provide. They thus continued to divert scarce resources of time and material to the temple, even as they prepared to abandon it. Throughout the fall, they met repeatedly in the nearly finished temple, to supervise the construction, conduct prayer circles, and plan the emigration. On December 10, the apostles opened the temple for ordinance work. From then until they left Nauvoo in early February, they focused on administering the temple ordinances—ritual washing and anointing of bodies, a reenactment of the creation and mortal life known as the endowment, and the sealing of husbands and wives—often working deep into the night. Heber Kimball commented on Pratt's dedication: "Were Parley and Orson Pratt officiating in the ordinance of washing, you would not see them until they were through their day's work, except to go down to their meals."[9]

Pratt participated in several ordinances and sealings with his plural wives. On October 15, 1845, he had married Sarah Houston, a twenty-three-year-old

native of Ohio. Sarah's parents had converted to Mormonism several years previously and had moved to Nauvoo.[10] Sealings that had been performed earlier
outside of the temple were now repeated in the temple. Thus, on January 10,
Brigham Young sealed Parley to his first wife, Thankful, with his first plural
wife Elizabeth acting as proxy. Young also sealed him that day to Elizabeth and
Mary Wood, both of whom had been endowed on December 23.[11] Over the
next three weeks, Parley was sealed to three more wives—Belinda, Hannahette,
and Sarah—each of whom also received their endowment.[12]

Pratt's experience in the Nauvoo Temple salved some wounds, such as
Thankful's early death, but caused others to erupt into public view. On
January 1, Belinda gave birth to her first son, Nephi, Parley's second child
born to a plural wife (Hannahette's Alma had been born on July 31, 1845).
Even Parley's closest family members, including Mary Ann and Orson, had
most likely been unaware of his marriage to Belinda. Her pregnancy and
Nephi's birth, however, made it impossible to completely conceal their
union. Orson, who had replaced Parley as presiding apostle in the eastern
states the previous year and had arrived back in Nauvoo in mid-December,
had heard rumors of Parley's relationship with Belinda in the East and saw
their relationship as adulterous rather than as sanctioned polygamy. Apparently
Orson's wife, Sarah, shared his views. Ten days after Nephi's birth, Parley
confronted Sarah in the temple "in the presence of a large assembly" and
rebuked her for "whispering against him all over the temple." The brothers
erupted in violent argument, with Orson defending Sarah and accusing
Parley of "false accusations and lying." The other apostles sided initially with
Parley and expelled Orson from the temple.[13]

Stunned by his expulsion when he viewed Parley as the culprit, Orson
wrote the following day to Young and the other apostles of his repeated
"injuries…from that man" over the previous three years, which were "of such
an aggravating nature as to be past endurance without some complaint."
Parley, Orson fumed, had accused Sarah of apostasy (over her alleged relationship with John C. Bennett) and of "influencing his wife [Mary Ann]
against him, and of ruining and breaking up his family." Such ideas had "originated in his own corrupt heart," Orson declared, and were "wicked and
malicious lies." Orson and Sarah had not said "the least disrespectful word
concerning him or his family," nor had they meddled in Parley's family affairs,
even though, referring to the rumors of Parley's relationship with Belinda, he
had gone "into the city of New York or elsewhere…[to] seduce girls or females
and sleep & have connexion with them contrary to the law of God, and the
sacred counsels of his brethren." (While he was at it, Orson also accused

Parley of stealing "a large fat hog that runs in the street which may belong to some poor widow or saint" the previous week, though admitting that he "may have been misinformed.")[14]

Orson particularly complained about his eviction from the temple. Had Orson made such accusations against the wives of other apostles, he wrote, "I should have been very thankful if I escaped without getting my head broke." Nevertheless, while he considered the apostles' actions misguided, Orson offered to make any confession they required, even if he "should be required to kiss the foot of the wretch who has for the last three years slandered & belied my family in the most hellish manner." "As for Parley," Orson concluded, "I consider him my avowed enemy, until he make restitution for the multiplied injuries which he has wickedly & maliciously inflicted upon his brothers family."[15] Orson's defense persuaded the apostles to quickly restore him to fellowship within their quorum, and within two weeks he and Parley were officiating together in the temple.[16] Nevertheless, tensions remained between the brothers until the early 1850s.

The rift between Parley and Mary Ann proved even more intractable. On February 6, the day before ordinance work in the Nauvoo Temple ceased, Mary Ann, who had frequently administered ordinances in the temple to other women, told Parley that she wanted to be sealed in the temple. The relationship between Parley and Mary Ann had been deteriorating for the last few years, but Belinda's pregnancy had apparently brought it to a crisis point. In November, Heber Kimball had met with Parley and Mary Ann and reported matters as "rather dismal and unhappy."[17] Parley later recalled that she had become "Alienated from her husband and Sought by all manner of falsehoods to distroy his Infleuence and Caracter."[18] At the temple, according to Mary Ann's son Moroni, Parley "told her it was her privilege to make a choice, and that she could be sealed to any one she chose." Mary Ann replied that Parley "would be her choice but she wanted to know the mind and will of the Lord." They consulted with Young, who stated, "If Joseph [Smith] had lived he would have had Mary Ann sealed to him."[19] Parley additionally stated that Mary Ann asked him for forgiveness for her "words of falsehood," for which he "frankly" forgave her.[20] Young told Parley, "Take Sister Mary Ann and her children, take good care of them and take them to Joseph and it will do more for your exaltation than any thing you can do in this matter."[21] Kimball then sealed Mary Ann to Joseph Smith for eternity and to Parley for time.[22]

Two days later, after Young had closed the temple to ordinance work, John Taylor married Pratt to Phoebe Soper, a native of Long Island, New York, whom Pratt had first met on his recent eastern mission.[23] In September

1845, he had asked Isaac Rogers to bring Phoebe to Nauvoo "for I promised her that you [would] do so," and she arrived on February 6.[24] Young likely considered the sealing as unauthorized; in 1851, he resealed Parley and Phoebe in the Endowment House.[25]

The advance company of the Mormon emigration began leaving Nauvoo on February 4, crossing the frozen Mississippi River and traveling nine miles to Sugar Creek in Iowa Territory.[26] On February 14, Pratt and his family loaded their wagons, went down Parley Street, and crossed the Mississippi. His family consisted of Mary Ann and her three children, Mary (then twelve), Olivia (four), and Moroni (one); Parley Jr. (eight); and his plural wives and their children—Elizabeth; Mary Wood, then pregnant; Hannahette with six-month-old Alma; Belinda with one-month-old Nephi; Sarah; and Phoebe. Pratt later stated, "I left a good house, lot and out buildings, worth about seven thousand dollars, and several lots and houses of less value, besides a farm in the country worth near two thousand." But he also had substantial debts and authorized an agent to "sell the property, settle up my business, and take care of such of my family or friends as might be left in his care," particularly his mother, Charity, and his Frost in-laws. Any surplus, Pratt explained, would go to the general church emigration fund.[27]

The Pratts huddled together in a tent the first night before finding a vacant log cabin about four miles from Nauvoo (near the church's Iowa tithing office) and about four miles from the main encampment at Sugar Creek. George Whitaker, an English convert who served as Pratt's teamster, recalled, "Everyone seemed to be cheerful, although complained a little of the cold." The Pratts had one "good new milk cow" which allowed them to live "on milk and cornmeal." During the days, Pratt counseled with Young and other leaders at Sugar Creek before returning at night. Whitaker recalled that Pratt "would then begin to talk to us and teach us a great many good things," particularly recounting for a private audience, including his new wives, the persecution narrative he had honed for the public: the Jackson County expulsion, Zion's Camp, Boggs's Order of Extermination, Haun's Mill, Crooked River, and his own imprisonment. He also "told about the Rocky Mountains and California and spoke of the prospects of the future." Whitaker recorded, "I thought he was the best man I ever saw. I felt that I would like to stay with him all my life." Isaac Rogers, his wife, and their two children also accompanied the Pratts and helped outfit them with "horses, oxen, wagons, and provisions." Pratt's brother William initially worked as one of his teamsters.[28]

While at this encampment, Mary Ann returned to Nauvoo with her children to assist her parents, indicating she would soon return. When she did not, Parley followed her to Nauvoo, "but she would not come; she said she would come along in the spring with her parents." Mary Ann, who had lost two children and two sisters to death in the previous two years, likely worried about the dangers to her surviving children, particularly her infant, Moroni, who was then sick. In addition, living in close proximity with Parley's six plural wives, at least some of whom she had not known about until very recently, likely proved extremely difficult for her. This marked the final rupture in the marital relationship of Parley and Mary Ann, though they would not be divorced for six years.[29]

After a few weeks, the Pratts traveled through the snow to Sugar Creek. Whitaker captured the camp's mood: "Some were singing, some were dancing, some were playing music, everyone seemed full of life and joy. We felt as though we had been released from bondage and were free, where there was no one to make us afraid."[30] Leaving Sugar Creek on March 1, the Saints made painfully slow progress across the Iowa plains; the loss of valuable time meant that the goal of arriving at the Rocky Mountains that year would be unattainable. Disorganization, lack of provisions for some emigrants, overburdened wagons for others, and the persistently wet and cold weather (Young termed the trek "a great mud hole") slowed the march to a crawl.[31]

Impatient, Pratt and some others, including Bishop George Miller, struck out ahead of the main group. As they slogged across the muddy roads of Iowa, enduring nearly daily rain, they struggled to obtain sufficient corn for their animals and had to stop to earn money or trade household goods along the way. Pratt's wives particularly lamented that he traded away, now that the weather was improving, a "small cooking stove" which had kept "the children from freezing." Pratt, on the other hand, was energized by the vigorous demands of the trail, after the sedentary life of past months. Notwithstanding their constant work in the rain, Whitaker recalled, Pratt "was always in a good humor and would be singing and talking and encouraging us all he could" (even though some of the other men "kept in their wagons as much as they could to keep out of the rain").[32]

Pratt's impetuosity in traveling ahead of the main company of Saints soon led to a clash with Brigham Young. On March 20, Pratt wrote to Orson, Young, and other leaders from Shariton Ford, explaining that his group consisted of thirty-five wagons that were daily awaiting the arrival of the "Main Body." He reported that they could purchase corn at 20 cents a bushel (paid for through cash, work, or household goods) and had traded horses and household property (such as "cookstoves, carpets, chests, trunks, Beds, crockery") for oxen. They also obtained "some fine fish, deer, turkey, geese, ducks, prairie hens, wild hunney, etc."³³ Two days later, Parley's group had been joined by his brother Orson as well as George A. Smith and John Smith; camped on Shoal Creek, they pressed on, leaving "vacant Grain for you, and plenty of Corn in the nabourhood," he told Young. They would go on "so as not to eat up the Corn in this place, which may all be needed, also to keep out of your way so as not to hinder in traveling."³⁴ It was a plausible explanation, though perhaps a rationalization for his relentless haste.

Young responded the next day, advising the forward group to await their arrival rather than continue on so that they could properly organize the emigration. He singled out for chastisement Orson, who had been instructed to give his excess flour to the camp, but who had instead "sold it to the citizens of Bloomfield." His patience wearing thin, Young wrote, "The Lord is not well pleased with his servants inasmuch as they wish to withdraw from each other and there awaiteth a scourge for them.... Hearken to council before the anger of the Lord is kindled against this people." If they had already traveled ahead, Young wanted their officers to "return and meet us at Shoal Creek so that we can organize without further delay."³⁵

The Pratts and Miller did not immediately attend the council because of swollen creeks in the area and because Parley had fallen ill.³⁶ On their way to meet with Young on March 26, they received an angry letter that Young had sent that morning. While the main body had "labored dilligently to overtake your division of the camp so as to organize, but just so sure as we come within a few miles of you, we find you off again, seemingly determined to keep out of our reach." The course pursued by the forward group (and particularly Miller) had already cost "hundreds of dollars which might have been saved." Ever the pragmatist, Young emphasized that a properly organized camp would allow the Saints to emigrate in the most efficient manner and better provide for the poor. Young threatened ecclesiastical sanction if he did not receive a satisfactory response.³⁷ After the Pratts and Miller arrived in the main camp that afternoon, Young chastised them for their "spirit of dissension and of insubordination," while they "plead that the charges in the letters were unjust" as they "had done all for the best." It would not be the last time Young clashed with Parley over organization of the trek west. Reflecting on the situation a decade later, Pratt wrote that while he silently protested that he had acted from the "purest motives," he later realized that "it was the true Spirit which reproved and chastened us," citing Miller's later apostasy as evidence.³⁸

In late April, the Saints arrived at Garden Grove, where Young instructed them to build a large farm to assist those who would follow. After Pratt helped "fence this farm and build some log houses," Young sent him ahead with a small group to scout for another farm site.[39] Whitaker recalled, "Brother Pratt was a 'go ahead' man, and he was very glad when the word came out to start." Pratt's group found a suitable location near the headwaters of the Grand River where a farm of several thousand acres was established; reminded of the biblical mountain from which Moses first saw the promised land, Pratt named it Mt. Pisgah. Mary Wood gave birth to her first child, a son named Helaman, at the new settlement on May 31. Leaving several hundred Saints behind to tend the farms at Garden Grove and Mt. Pisgah, the main camp, including Pratt's family, reached the Missouri River on June 14.[40]

Young still had not abandoned his goal of reaching the Rocky Mountains that year with an advance company. Fearful of rumors that the U.S. military might impede their emigration, Young revived the idea that an express company led by the apostles and numbering between two hundred and five hundred men would go "to Bear River Valley in the Great Basin, without families, forthwith." That very year, Young declared, they would go "over the mountains to set up the Kingdom of God or its Standard." Young dispatched Pratt and Solomon Hancock to return to Mt. Pisgah and Garden Grove to recruit pioneers.[41] On July 1, Pratt hurried to Pisgah in hopes of raising five hundred volunteers who would immediately leave "to go to the mountains without there families to pick out A location And put in spring & fall Crops."[42] By this time, however, Captain James Allen of the U.S. military had already been to Mt. Pisgah to recruit the same number of volunteers for the Mexican-American War.

Allen's arrival in the camps in late June had generated much controversy. At Mt. Pisgah, Wilford Woodruff initially believed Allen and his men "to be spies." After meeting with Allen, Young realized that the federal government had accepted an earlier Mormon proposal made to President James Polk. Jesse C. Little, with the assistance of a young and politically connected non-Mormon Thomas L. Kane, offered to provide troops for the war, an attractive proposition for the government given the Mormons' location on the western frontier. Accordingly, Pratt, Young, and the other apostles now began a strong recruitment drive for troops; to skeptical Saints, Pratt argued, "it is the mind and will of God that we should improve the oppertunity which a kind providence has now opened for us to secure a permanant home, in that country, and thus Lay a foundation for a territorial or state Government" where they would be "the first Settlers and a vast majority of the people, and thus be independant of Mobs, and be able to maintain our Rights and freedom."[43] Young added, "The outfit of these five hundred men costs us nothing, and their pay will be sufficient to take their families over the mountains."[44]

While Mormon leaders recognized the value of a battalion of Mormons, many rank-and-file Saints, those who would bear the burden of the battalion, still suspected a government conspiracy to destroy the Saints. One Mormon thought the federal government ordered the enlistment for "our destruction" and so that the wives and children of the soldiers would be "in an indian country left to mercies of the savage and the cravings of hunger." Nevertheless, by mid-July, the battalion had successfully been raised. Pratt's instructions to the soldiers contrasted with the jingoistic American rhetoric about the War with Mexico. He told the battalion to neither "misuse their enemies" nor "spoil their property" as the Mexicans were "fellow human beings to whom the gospel is yet to be preached."[45] The battalion soon left on the longest infantry march in U.S. history, traveling through Santa Fe and on to California. Money from their salaries helped fund the emigration, and their service to the U.S. government quieted talk of Mormon disloyalty.[46]

With the battalion raised, the apostles turned their attention to another challenge, securing the loyalty of the English Saints. The reverberations of the succession crisis crossed the Atlantic as the various claimants battled for the allegiance of the thousands of English Mormons. In this confrontation, the apostles had significant advantages over Rigdon and Strang, particularly since their joint mission to England in the early 1840s meant that many English Saints were acquainted with the apostles and had already experienced a church under their direction.

Nevertheless, Wilford Woodruff, who had arrived in Council Bluffs on July 9 after returning from a mission to England, brought troubling news that imperiled the apostolic leadership in England.[47] In 1842, Brigham Young had first suggested American Saints and the English Saints cooperate to fund emigration of the latter. In April 1845, Woodruff wrote to Young, describing the worsened economic climate and unprecedented number of impoverished Saints. "In the days of Brother Parley," Woodruff stated, "when he had thousands of dollars worth of books, & Emegrants enough to load down a ship at a time with their gold in hand not carrying Saints without pay, He could heap up gold readily."[48] As such, Woodruff endorsed a plan to create a joint stock company which would sell stock to English Saints and use it as capital "to establish manufactories in Nauvoo or elsewhere, in America, for the employment of the poor" and to raise funds for the emigration of English Saints.[49] It would charter ships to carry poor emigrants to America (along with "articles of trade suitable to the South American trade, and necessaries for the Saints in their new home") and return with "a cargo" of American goods to sell in England.[50] Reuben Hedlock, the British mission president, argued that the joint stock company would unite the Saints in England and America as well as the rich and the poor.[51] Dan Jones similarly proclaimed, "It is the Joint Stock Company or nothing. Every one must see that their temporal and spiritual salvation depend on this and the gospel."[52] The English Saints supported the scheme in large part "because it was sanctioned by Bro. Woodruff" and thus, they reasoned, by the apostles.[53]

Simultaneously, an economic depression hit England, fueled in part by the devastation of the Irish potato famine, heightening the desire of converts to emigrate while further limiting resources to do so. A young American missionary in Liverpool, Oliver B. Huntington, recorded in his journal, "Near half the people in the Streets were Beggars, and some the most pittiful looking objects I ever saw. Bare footed, Bare headed and a little better than bare bodyed, and principally Irish, for there was great distress in Ireland, for The Potatoes were nearly all rotted there." The crisis had also "overrun England in a great measure," Huntington explained, "for Cotton was scarce and many Factories stoped, others run 1/2 and 3/4 of the time, thus throwing hundreds and thousands of the poor into hunger for want of work."[54]

Notwithstanding these economic catastrophes, Hedlock and a few close associates raised substantial money for the joint stock company only to squander it, in Pratt's words, "in any and every way but to do good."[55] In October 1845, Woodruff wrote to Young that the situation in England "has caused me tears and sorrow by day and night. I have grown old under it." He particularly complained that Hedlock had "manifested a spirit to gain all the influence possible" and would not consult with him. "Taking all things into consideration," Woodruff stated, "I do not think things will go right until Bro. Hedlock is called home."[56] The company lost money through unwise loans, officers' salaries, and overpayment to obtain a charter from Parliament (for the British and American Commercial Joint Stock Company).[57] Most critically, Hedlock had partnered with dubious businessmen in attempts to charter ships. Hedlock's counselor, Thomas Ward, explained that "his transacting business with the rascally brokers of Liverpool was the entire cause" of the company's downfall.[58]

Young and the apostles learned fully of the situation only with Woodruff's arrival. Alarmed, in mid-July, Young commissioned three apostles—Pratt, John Taylor, and Orson Hyde—to leave the Saints' camps and travel to England to disfellowship Hedlock and Ward and to reinforce the loyalty of the Saints to the apostles.[59] Sensing his opportunity, Strang belittled the corruption of the joint stock company in his newspaper and similarly dispatched three missionaries to England, including Martin Harris, whom all

Mormons knew as one of the three Book of Mormon witnesses. Strang wrote that the English Saints were "in great confusion in consequence of the... oppressions of the Brighamites" and he hoped to reap the benefits from a "general apostasy" from the apostolic leadership.[60]

Pratt, Taylor, and Hyde had other reasons behind their journey to England. The forced exodus from Nauvoo left the Saints in a deeply precarious financial situation, leading the apostles to attempt unsuccessfully to sell the Nauvoo Temple (another development publicly exploited by Strang). Though the funds from the Mormon Battalion helped considerably, Young hoped that donations from the English Saints might further alleviate the financial woes. In addition, the Saints had heard rumors of a plan by the English government to subsidize the emigration of thousands of impoverished British citizens to Vancouver Island to strengthen the British claim to the disputed Oregon territory.[61] The apostles decided to propose to the English government that Mormon emigrants accomplish this purpose.[62]

Pratt left his family—consisting now of six plural wives, including newly pregnant Sarah, and three infants under the age of one—under the care of his cousin John Van Cott and George Whitaker.[63] The three apostles traveled first to Fort Leavenworth, where Mormon Battalion soldiers, who had been issued government money for clothing, donated "several hundred dollars" for the mission and wanted to send between $5,000 and $6,000 for "their families and friends at the Bluffs." Pratt agreed to deliver the money, separating himself from Hyde and Taylor. Fulfilling his errand at Council Bluffs, Pratt purchased a light buggy and drove to Chicago, where he "immediately sold my horse and buggy, and then took steamer the same evening across Lake Michigan, thence by railroad to Boston; thence to New York." In his autobiography, Pratt referred only to travel details: cities visited, miles traveled, modes of transportation.[64] The controversy over polygamy on the Mormon margins, however, shaped his journey.

Arriving in Boston with Jesse Little, Pratt faced accusations about polygamy in general and his marriage to Belinda in particular. Learning of a meeting of Mormon dissidents in Boylston Hall, they "hurried thither" and interrupted the gathering. Pratt jested to Belinda, "had a good time," though he also reported more seriously the charges: "Sister '*Hilton*,' P. P. Pratt and the rest of the twelve are terable Creatures. Some excitement here, but we Came in the Nick of time."[65] The coded reference to Belinda's first married name—"Sister Hilton"—made clear the root of the accusations against Pratt, which forced him to flee Boston in haste. The Strangite newspaper savored his discomfiture: "What has become of P. P. Pratt? He advertised to preach in Boston, but writs, warrants, and policemen are getting too thick after him. The Archer shot himself—out of Boston."[66] According to the paper, Pratt barely escaped the city without being arrested: "Between notes for borrowed money, writs for seducing wives, and warrants for adultery he would have stood but a slim chance of getting any more spirituals if the officers had caught him."[67]

In New York, Pratt found, Strangite dissenters continued to exploit the issue. The charismatic George Adams and Lucian R. Foster, the former Nauvoo Temple recorder, had been decrying the apostles' polygamy to alarmed Mormons, including the father of Pratt's newest plural wife, Samuel Soper. After visiting Soper on Long Island, Pratt reported that Foster had told "the Old gentleman and Others that I have got Phebe and have now come for" his other daughters. Soper responded that "he cant think how it is that I want them all." Pratt "Beged his pardon for not asking his Consent Owned up to every thing, and finally the Old gentleman Laughed, and said I might have them all, if I would take him also, So it all passed off verry well." Pratt did not pursue the offer, only telling Phoebe's sisters about the "Gathering, and that Phebe wanted to have them come." Pratt told his wives, "I do not feel the least desire to seek any covenants, promises or encouragements with any person, touching Eternal things while abroad. I have Learned by experience that such things, are often broken and disregarded by females which is sin, or at least it is trifleing with affections which are sacred."[68]

Hyde and Taylor had sailed from New York in early September, just before Pratt's arrival. Lack of money delayed Pratt's departure; the relentless Strangite editor ridiculed him for "begging money."[69] Church member Alexander Badlam helped pay Pratt's passage across the Atlantic. Along with three other missionaries, Pratt departed on September 22, with him in the main cabin and the others in the second cabin. He told Belinda, "We fair well in the Cabbin,—have roast beef—roast Goose, all kinds of meat and fish—Sweet potatoes—Cucumbers, onions—green corn—pudings, pies, every thing that heart can wish. But Still I am not satisfied. I lack the Tin Cup, the Milk, the Dager, the prairie—the Camp, and the Social and domestic Circle for which I live, and without which life would be an intolerable burthen." Indeed, he joked that he, "used to a quick, yankee way of Eating," felt ill at ease at the elaborate meals served in the cabins.[70] Pratt was often too ill to enjoy them, apparently. One of his companions, Cyrus Wheelock, wrote that with Pratt and Franklin D. Richards seasick, he and another missionary were "able to eat our and their allowance."[71]

Hyde and Taylor dissolved the joint stock company after arriving in England. They reported to Young that they "found that money was daily coming in to the Joint Stock Co. and that it was received by a set of men who ate and drank it up and squandered it away about as fast as it came in." The "poor Saints" had scrimped and sent "their pennies, their sixpences, their shillings" to "lay by a little money to emigrate with." However, with no checks on the officers of the company, "nearly every pound had been squandered and lent to irresponsible favorites." They attempted to explain their actions, but Hyde and Taylor were unconvinced. "We heard their tales, and after their yarn was all spun, we opened our batteries upon the nice breast work they had thrown up and poured a deadly fire upon them." After Pratt's arrival, a conference on October 19 formally dissolved the joint stock company. Oliver Huntington recorded, "Throughout the Conference, a spirit of Peace and union prevailed; and everything went right ahead just [as] the three of the Twelve wanted, and there was but one dissenting voice in all. I can say truly, that from the time they landed on this land, things took a change for the better."[72]

The English Saints, however, were still "nearly all…too poor to emigrate." As planned, the apostles arranged for the Saints to petition the English government "to cede to us as her subjects a part or the whole of the Island of Vancouver, on the western coast of America; and also ship us there."[73] Early in 1847, the British Saints thus delivered a 168-foot petition, containing more than thirteen thousand signatures, to Queen Victoria. Huntington thought the request would be granted as the queen was "willing to do anything to relieve the distress of the Nation, and that seemed a favourable plan for it." The British government, however, quickly rejected the petition and dashed Mormon hopes of gathering the British Saints on the queen's dime.[74]

Leaving Hyde in Liverpool to edit the *Millennial Star*, Pratt and Taylor embarked on a preaching tour to encourage the loyalty of the English Saints. In Birmingham, for instance, Taylor "addressed about two thousand, five hundred people at the waters edge, previous to Baptising Some 70." That evening, Taylor and Pratt preached to a "house full of joyful and Loveing Saints." Pratt wrote a letter to his family in blank verse which he published as a broadside, lectured at a tea party in Birmingham, and traveled to Sheffield, where he and Taylor advertised in "large bills" their Sunday sermon at "the Music Hall, the best place in town." That Sunday, Taylor and Pratt "preached 3 times…had good attention and at evening Every part was crammed with attentive hearers; Galery, Stand, and every knook and Corner." Pratt wrote home, "The Spirit of the Lord Came mightily upon us; we poured forth our testimony as if heaven and earth was Coming togather. The people Listened for hours, and when we were through they seemed loth to leave their Seats, so astonished and convinced were they."[75] At the Town Hall, Pratt preached on "resurrection and salvation of the body...making manifest the inconsistent and absurd notions entertained by modern Christians respecting Deity, Heaven and the world to come."[76]

The English Saints received Pratt and Taylor as "the Apostles and prophets of old.... they strive who shall wash our feet—comb our hair, or any other kindness. And I must say of Late they have thined my hair considerably in begging locks of the same to keep as memorials." He had high hopes for them: "a more simple, unaffected, humble, childlike, social, Loving, virtuous, and joyful and happy people I never saw. They Could be Governed and Moulded into a Millennium Kingdom without any difficulty, if they were out of Babel."[77] One young convert recalled Pratt's electrifying preaching, "I remember hearing Parley P. Pratt speak one Sunday evening, and of loving the words he said so much that I felt as if I could lay down my life for him."[78] Pratt and Taylor continued their preaching tour through December, traveling as far as Glasgow. Feeling by late December that they had achieved their purpose, the three apostles made plans to return to the United States.[79]

Though Pratt relished the warmth of the Saints and the fertile mission field, he constantly lamented his separation from his family. Earlier, on board ship in October, he wrote a revealing missive. Driven by duty to long years of service, Pratt had exhausted both native wanderlust and his taste for novelty. Now, he found spiritual respite only in Zion and his own domestic circle. Even though accompanied by three missionaries, he wrote Belinda,

> I am *Alone!—Alone!—Alone!* O Horable!—Yes—Alone—the Punishment—the Hell I always dread—and the one to which I am often doomed. How oft has it been my lot to Spend wearysome days, weeks and even months, Confined to the Society of those whose Spirits, ways, Manners, tastes, pursuits, hopes and destiny are so different from mine, that not a single cord, or nerve beets in unison. This is Hell to me.
>
> I pray the Lord to Deliver me from such torment, and to Grant me one thing above all others, and that is: the privaledge of enjoying the Society of *kindred Spirits*. I Should then be happy in heaven, earth or else where. Its Oposite I Could not long endure.[80]

Only the power of the Spirit and the joys of the ministry, which "thrills through every extremity of our Spirit and Body as it were with a throb of Immortality," Pratt assured his family, compensated for his "feeling of Lonliness and desolation" at his "Long separation" from his "Lambs."[81]

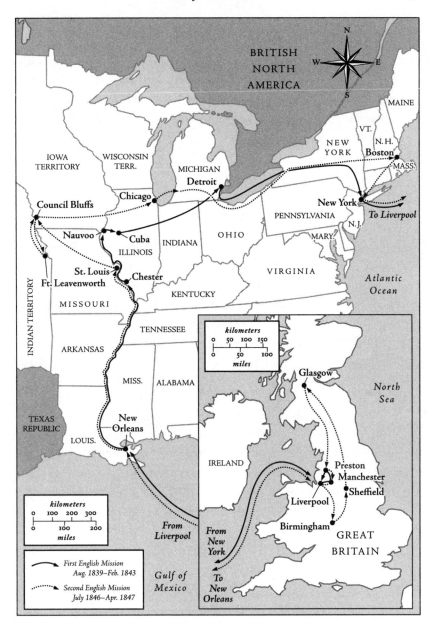

MAP 9.1 English Missions

Pratt also worried that his plural wives might abandon him, as he believed Mary Ann had done. In October, he expressed his fears to Belinda: "Should you be tempted more than you can bear; and go away, to forsake him who Loves you and I have no Clew to your retreat; O do not be so Crewel, it would kill me—I would ransack Creation Over—I would Search every Secret Corner of the earth if posible, and find you, and forgive, and bless you." He immediately rebuked himself for his "wicked and Childish" thoughts, as he had "no Intimation, or whispering of the Spirit that any such thing will happen." Nevertheless, he wrote, Belinda had "some times Intimated to me that you have had such thoughts for a moment" and he warned her "in the Hour of trouble and darkest temptation, beware of desperate Steps."[82] In late November, he wrote his family that he often dreamed of them, but "one of my dearest lambs," Mary Wood, "is allways missing." He plaintively told Mary, "I Cannot think you would ever forsake me. The thought would break my heart. Thou art My own dear '*Mary*.'"[83] The constraints of polygamy also intruded in his sleep in December, when he dreamed that he and Belinda were "in the House of some good brethren and Sisters who were strangers" and "did not know what we were to each other and therefore I was about to sleep alone." Pratt, however, "ventured to tell them, and they Said we might arrange as we liked for Lodging," though as "we were about arranging these Matters," he awoke to what he described as "a full sense of my loneliness."[84]

Even as the difficulties of plural marriage troubled his dreams, controversy over polygamy hovered over Pratt's preaching tour. Charles Miller, an English Mormon leader, remembered that during Hedlock's presidency, "The Knowledge of Plurality of Wives was at this time whisperd among a few Saints." Some Mormons, "not knowing the Laws," left their spouses and "felt to make Covenants with others thus many of the Saints got entangled & a spirit of Lasciviousness brooded over the Churches."[85] Orson Hyde accused Pratt of fostering such teachings: "The Spirit whispereth me that you are preaching things in Manchester which you ought not." Specifically, Hyde accused him of teaching that if men and women were "dissatisfied with their present companions they are not bound to be united for Eternity, but are at liberty to choose others." Such teachings would "lead every little upstart, both male and female to desire another Companion It is opening the very floodgates of sensuality and lust." Hyde continued, "It is the spirit of lust that teaches the above doctrine in *this country* and not the spirit of God, for such principles gender evil and create anxieties that cannot be relieved without going into an explanation of things that ever has been forbidden.... It is casting pearls before swine and giving holy things to dogs." If Pratt did not desist, Hyde warned, he would publicly chastise him through the *Millennial Star*.[86]

Pratt replied to Hyde's apostolic rebuke with a call to repentance of his own: "Your railing accusations, and insults against that Priesthood…alltogather manifest a spirit so false—so foreign from the true spirit of your high and responsable office that I am Constrained to Exhort you to repent and Return again to the Spirit of Charity and truth." If Hyde continued in his accusations, Pratt, with the help of Taylor and the English Saints, would have Hyde "removed out of your place, and sent home, to answer for these things before the Council." Hyde's statements were not only false, Pratt averred, but had ignored apostolic procedure, as only a "united quorum" could judge Pratt, and then only "by testimony." Pratt denied teaching anything "about Marriage, Wives, Covenants, or Choosings either for time or eternity, in England." Thus, he continued, "I Care not a fig for your dreams, nor for the whisperings of the Spirit about me, or my teachings." Additionally Pratt charged Hyde with passing off gossip as whisperings of the spirit: "Let me tell you that the Spirit that whispered to you had *Lips*, of flesh and Blood, and a tongue to '*Set on fire of hell*.'"[87]

While Hyde accused Pratt of teaching that individuals could leave their current spouses if "dissatisfied," the misunderstanding likely stemmed from a dispute over authorization of new plural marriages. In his proclamation to the eastern Saints in January 1845, Pratt had asserted that Joseph Smith had given Young the sealing power. Before the three apostles had left Iowa in July, Young instructed them, "No man has a right to Attend to the ordinance of sealing except the President of the Church or those who are directed by him so to do And that ordinance should be confined to Zion or her stakes." Hyde evidently believed that only Young could authorize sealings, the position that later became standard. Pratt and Taylor, however, interpreted "or those who are directed by him to do so" to give them latitude.[88]

On January 19, Pratt and Taylor sailed from England, leaving Hyde to supervise affairs in England until Orson Spencer arrived to preside over the British Saints. In a farewell address, Pratt praised the Saints for their "spirit of confidence and obedience to the instructions we had to impart," as well as for their hospitality: "We have been lodged, fed, comforted, and cheered as if we had been angels of glad tidings."[89] Oliver Huntington appraised their mission: "They loosed the bands of Jointstockism which held the Church from prospering, and set all parts to rights." He concluded, "I often heard the saints say 'what a good thing it was that the 12 and other American Elders came to this land just as they did, for they saved the Church from seeming destruction.'"[90]

Another missionary concurred, "They have saved the Church in this land from being sunk in ruin by the wicked conduct of those who stood at the head and moreover they have set on foot a misure [measure] for the temporal deliverance of the Saints in this land."[91]

The effective preaching of Pratt, Taylor, and Hyde, the trust they carried with them from years of labor with the British Saints, and their timely oversight of publishing operations in England combined to blunt any success the Strangites or other dissenters might otherwise have enjoyed. Martin Harris's Strangite mission failed; one missionary noted that a quarterly church conference declined to listen to him and that police removed him when he insisted on preaching outside the conference.[92] The British Saints remained overwhelmingly loyal to the apostolic quorum.[93]

Pratt's activities from 1844 to 1847 demonstrate key lessons about times of transition in radical religious groups. Mainstream Mormon memory focuses on the events in Nauvoo, particularly the supernatural passing of the mantle from Smith to Young in August 1844 and the spiritual witnesses the Saints received of apostolic succession. Pratt's experiences, by contrast, are an ideal lens through which to understand the messiness and contingency of the battle to succeed Smith. They indicate the importance not only of the center but also of the margins. In the case of Mormons and other similar groups, maintaining the loyalty of individuals who had not yet joined the center community was vital to the future of the movement. In addition, Pratt's actions in the eastern states illustrate the importance of controlling the press, as the consolidation of power by the apostles depended on this. By dissolving the English joint stock company, supervising the press, and suppressing the reports of their participation in plural marriage, the Twelve Apostles became leaders of the largest branch of the many Mormonisms that emerged after Joseph Smith's death.

10

Pioneering Westward

Let us join in the dance, let us join in the song,
To thee, Oh! Jehovah, new praises belong;
All honor, all glory, we render to thee,
For here in the mountains thy people are free.
—PARLEY P. PRATT, *song, recorded in Gatha*
[Ann Agatha Walker Pratt],
"Personal Reminiscences"

BETWEEN 1844 AND 1846, Pratt's main agenda was to establish the supremacy of the apostles in the chaos of the Mormon succession crisis. In 1847, following in the wake of the pioneer company, he and John Taylor led the first large group of Mormon immigrants to the Salt Lake Valley. Questions of authority, however, did not end with the trek west. Though Brigham Young had consolidated his position as head of the largest body of Saints, the exact nature and extent of his authority were still years in the working out. During 1847 and 1848, Pratt clashed with Young and local church and civil authorities over an array of issues: What was the balance of power between Young as senior apostle and the other apostles? Who could authorize new plural marriages? What was the relationship between local ecclesiastical and civil authorities and the Quorum of the Twelve? With the establishment of the First Presidency in late 1847, Young no longer needed to fight running battles with Pratt on these questions. To the presumable relief of them both, in 1849 and 1850 Pratt increasingly turned his attention from presiding over Saints and missions to exploring and developing the resources of the Great Basin. He became an entrepreneur, constructing a toll road that opened a new route into the Salt Lake Valley, and a colonizer, leading an expedition that found sites for settlements in central and southern Utah. Writing and preaching had defined Pratt's public identity and leadership within Mormonism throughout the 1830s and 1840s. Now, his leadership took on a more pragmatic dimension, and he added the role of explorer to his public persona.

Apostles Pratt and John Taylor departed England together in January 1847, journeying as far as St. Louis. There, still leery of his reputation in the state, Pratt separated from Taylor because he did not want to "come up the River lest it should cause the Missourians to go to the truble of feeding him on State expense." Fortunately, he "found one of Brighams horses in St. Louis" and rode overland to Council Bluffs, arriving on April 8, five days ahead of Taylor.[1] Young and the vanguard company of pioneers had already left Council Bluffs to begin their journey west. Hearing of Pratt's arrival, Young and other leaders backtracked, eager to hear his report on the English situation. Pratt and Taylor also brought important, though disappointing, cash resources (469 gold sovereigns, about $2,500) and expensive astronomical, meteorological, and engineering equipment for the trek.[2] Young instructed Pratt and Taylor to immediately leave with the pioneer company, but both refused, wanting to remain with their families rather than immediately push across the continent. Pratt's family was certainly not anxious for him to leave again. During the previous winter, Elizabeth recalled, "We suffered with cold, hunger, and sickness. Our bread was corn meal ground on a hand mill and not much to go with it." While they had a "log room built to cook in and crowd into in the daytime," they slept in their wagons at night. Furthermore, in Parley's absence, many of their cows and horses died or were lost.[3] Sarah bore her first child, Julia, a few days before Pratt's arrival back.

If Pratt did not teach plural marriage during his recent English mission, as he insisted, he apparently did on the trip home. Weeks before his departure, John Taylor had written him that that seventeen-year-old Ann Agatha Walker had received parental permission to accompany Pratt to America to be a servant in the Pratt household.[4] Be "happy and useful in Bro. Pratt's family," her mother counseled.[5] Agatha had been born in Leek, Staffordshire, in 1829 to William and Mary Godwin Walker, a well-educated and refined couple. Mary worked as a prosperous milliner, an occupation she passed on to Agatha, and William was a schoolteacher and bookkeeper. After a move to Manchester, the Walkers converted to Mormonism about 1840, even though William worried he would lose his teaching position at a denominational children's school.[6] When Pratt and Taylor sailed from England, they were accompanied by Walker, Martha Monks, and Mary Elizabeth and Sophia Whitaker, sisters of Pratt's teamster George Whitaker.[7] Three weeks after his arrival in Winter Quarters, a Mormon settlement on the west side of the Missouri River across from Council Bluffs, Parley was married to Martha Monks and Ann Agatha Walker, his ninth and tenth wives, by Taylor. Pratt married Sophia to Taylor. Soon after, Mary Parker Richards, a British convert whose husband Samuel was then on a mission in

England, visited Pratt "and saw all his ladys." Homesick, Martha told Richards, "I do love you Sister Richards because you came from My Country."[8]

Ceding to the wishes of Pratt and Taylor, Young and the vanguard company departed without them on April 14 planning to travel quickly to the Salt Lake Valley and prepare for the large emigration expected that season. As the only apostles remaining at Council Bluffs, Pratt and Taylor confronted two major issues: resolving tensions among Mormons, American Indians (the Omaha and the Otoe), and federal Indian agents; and preparing the emigration company. The American Indian disputes focused on the Mormon settlements on the west side of the Missouri River, as the Saints had received government permission to settle temporarily only on Potawatomi lands on the river's east banks. Complicating matters, both the Omaha and the Otoe claimed the land on which the Saints had built their settlements on the Missouri's west banks. The Saints had negotiated agreements with both tribes that permitted them to settle on the land in exchange for the Mormons' protection and assistance in hauling corn to the Indians. However, the poverty-stricken Omaha were stealing Mormon cattle.[9] Concerned about the "destruction of timber [and] Range Game" by the Saints, federal Indian agent John Miller had advised Young "that the best service you can render the Omaha's in my opinion, will be as soon as practicable to leave the Indian country."[10]

After Young's departure, continuing Omaha raids on Mormon cattle increased tensions. Pratt, Taylor, and the High Council met to consider solutions. Pratt advised the Saints to cease hauling corn for the Omaha unless they returned the cattle; if the Omaha refused, the Mormons should put the "whip to them."[11] A Mormon delegation met with the Omaha chief Old Elk, and both sides agreed to abide by their earlier agreement. Pratt and other Mormons subsequently met with Otoe leaders, who demanded that the Saints transport corn for them rather than the Omaha. Pratt and other Mormon leaders decided to haul corn for both groups, reasoning that "$60 to $80 is nothing to get peace for we lose that amount in two or three days by their killing our cattle!!"[12] At a public meeting on April 25, Pratt repeated his counsel to "whip the Indians with a hickory but don't kill them" if the Omaha attempted to steal more cattle.[13] He further encouraged the Saints to remain united and prepare for the journey west. Of particular concern to Pratt, many Saints were leaving Winter Quarters, either to settle on nearby land or to follow schismatic leaders such as James Strang, George Miller, and Lyman Wight. John D. Lee described the river ferry as "thronged continually with waggons to cross."[14] Pratt fretted that the Saints could ill afford disaffections or dispersion at such a time. The departure of the Mormon Battalion and of the pioneer company meant "we are weak having so many men drawn from among us." To discourage this scattering, he required that all Saints seeking to cross the Missouri River on the ferry obtain a certificate from Isaac Morley.[15]

Remembering his expulsion from Indian Territory fifteen years earlier, Pratt was also worried lest federal Indian agents, suspecting a Mormon intention to settle permanently at Winter Quarters, force them to leave the Omaha and Otoe land. To assuage their fears, Pratt encouraged large numbers of Saints to prepare for the trek west that year. Meanwhile, the "stupidity" and "dullness" of the Saints "in observing the council & instructions of the Twelve & their heedlessness about their cattle in exposing them to the Omaha" was driving Pratt to exasperation. Notwithstanding the efforts of Pratt and others, tensions with American Indians bedeviled Mormon leaders until they abandoned Winter Quarters.[16]

During the winter of 1846–1847, Young and the other apostles in Winter Quarters had organized the Mormon emigration along the theological principle of adoption, with the emigration divided into two adoptive families, those of Young and Heber Kimball. In the Nauvoo Temple, couples were sealed to church leaders and their wives as their adoptive children. Nearly all these adoptions involved first wives of the adoptive fathers. Pratt's rift with Mary Ann was likely the explanation for his nonparticipation, unusual for an apostle, in these adoption ordinances. The ritual had both spiritual and temporal significance, with the Saints believing that it created heavenly networks of extended kin and eventually an unbroken bond of priesthood succession to Adam. It also established a web of reciprocal responsibilities between the adoptive parents and children; some of the children even took the last names of their parents. While Pratt was in England, a form of the practice rapidly expanded at Winter Quarters. In the absence of a temple, church members organized themselves into family networks around prominent leaders. Adoptive families joined together for spiritual meetings and social events; Young even organized a farm north of Winter Quarters for his family to work.[17]

As Pratt and Taylor oversaw final preparations, it became increasingly clear that Young's organization had not prepared a cadre of leaders qualified to lead the Saints west. Reorganization was imperative, and in the absence of Young and the other apostles, they felt authorized to make alterations based on the facts on the ground. As Taylor publicly explained, "Elder Young, some say, said so & so. But I tell you Bro. Young never set up stakes that cannot be drawn up according to circumstances." While this caused confusion and

grumbling, Pratt justified the changes by pointing out that "Captains of hundreds, of fifties &c appointed last winter, are not here."[18] Pratt may not have
supported or understood the vast expansion of adoptive families that took
place in his absence. In 1850, a Latter-day Saint queried Pratt about the practice, asking, "Is it the duty of a man who comes into this church (and who has
no parents or relatives in the church,) to be adopted into the family of any
other man?" Rather than endorse the practice, Pratt answered simply, "I do
not know."[19]

Young had appointed Patriarch John Smith, Joseph Smith's uncle, to preside over the emigration company, assisted by Isaac Morley, the oldest of
Young's adoptive sons. Young left detailed guidelines for the emigration,
instructing each family to bring enough provisions to last through the next
winter and each company to bring as many of the poor and Mormon Battalion
families as possible. In Young's mind, the company should "follow the pioneers as soon as the grass is sufficient to support the teams" and assemble at
the Elkhorn River for departure by May 25. Companies of no more than a
hundred wagons would then proceed across the plains. Notwithstanding
Young's designation of Smith and Morley to lead the emigration, Pratt later
stated that he and Taylor, because of their ecclesiastical rank, "were appointed
and invited to take a general superintendency of this emigration."[20] Under the
direction of Pratt and Taylor, Smith would oversee spiritual affairs, and
a presidency of John Young, Edward Hunter, and Daniel Spencer would
supervise temporal issues.[21] The Saints were divided into companies of one
hundred men, fifty men, and ten men, with captains over each.[22]

The relatively small number of emigrants envisioned by Young soon ballooned as Pratt and Taylor were unable or unwilling to restrict those who
wanted to go. One historian comments, "The result was a rising tide of the
most adequately provisioned and best-prepared families but fewer of the
poor and Battalion families than originally anticipated.... It became the
departure of the fittest." Pratt pressed for a timely departure—remarking,
"I mean what I say when I talk of the 25th of May"—but delays inevitably
occurred as Saints, weary of the sickness at Winter Quarters and hopeful to
migrate to their new Zion, pushed to be part of the 1847 migration, even if
they did not have adequate provisions. Pratt did not leave Winter Quarters
with his own family for the Elkhorn River until early June. Other delays,
including the "late arrival of a nine- and a six-pound cannon, a leather skiff,
and the rescued 700-pound Nauvoo Temple bell," further pushed back the
start.[23] In August, Taylor explained the late start to Young: "It takes a little
time and labor to start a large wheel."[24]

The scene at the Elkhorn was a whirlwind of preparation. Agatha recalled that Parley "was busy mending wagons, hooking up yoke-bows, making bow-keys, or pins to hold the bows in the yokes, hunting up the cattle, mating them, finding chains." The Pratt wives and other Mormon women "were busy making and mending wagon covers, making crackers, and in every way aiding and assisting to prepare."[25] The Saints also experienced spiritual manifestations while preparing for the trek. On June 16, Eliza Snow visited the Pratt family and "sang a song of Zion" in tongues, which another woman interpreted.[26]

Six hundred wagons rolled out from the Elkhorn in mid-June, two months after the pioneer company and three weeks behind their anticipated departure. The wagons eventually stretched out over ten miles and were accompanied by 1,448 Saints, "2,213 oxen, 887 cows, 716 chickens, 358 sheep, and 124 horses."[27] Dissension soon arose over the order of travel and the leadership of the emigration. Jedediah Grant, a captain of one of the one-hundred-men companies, refused to accept directions from Taylor that contradicted earlier instructions given by John Young. Furious, Taylor charged Grant with insubordination. At a council that evening, Pratt "gave a full history of the Mod of government of the Church & Camp to the entire satisfaction of the Camp." On Pratt's advice, Grant asked Taylor's forgiveness, and "all was amicably settled," with the supremacy of apostolic leadership now established.[28] Pratt's group followed the route blazed by the original pioneers, traveling first along the north bank of the Platte River, reaching Grand Island on July 6, Chimney Rock on July 29, and Fort Laramie on August 5. Because of a number of factors—"better feed, little Indian interference, less time spent in hunting, easier river crossings, and the very clear instructions left them by the pioneer camp"—the company traveled nearly as rapidly as had the much smaller advance group.[29]

The Pratts traveled in Daniel Spencer's company of one hundred and Perrigrine Session's company of fifty. The contingent consisted of roughly four hundred people, including Pratt's aunt Lovina Van Cott and her son John and his family, who had helped provision Parley's family. Women drove more than a third of the wagons because of the lack of a sufficient number of men.[30] Recently arrived from urban England, without ever having seen "cattle yoked together," Agatha volunteered, along with Belinda, to drive one of the wagons. Decades later, Agatha proudly recalled how she "learned to put on the lock-chain instantly at the top of a steep hill, and would jump out quickly while the cattle were going, to take it off, so that the impetus afforded by the end of the descent would aid them in starting up the other side." While jumping out of the wagon once, her skirt "caught on the tongue bolt, and threw me down," and the front wagon wheel ran over her leg. Providentially, in Agatha's eyes, she received no bruise, and the pain soon dissipated.[31] Agatha also remembered that Parley was

> one of the busiest and hardest working men I ever knew. When we were crossing the Plains he drove the largest wagon we had with three yoke of cattle; he would walk along side of them, and the first thing you knew you would see him three or four rods ahead. The slow walk of the team could not keep pace with his active mind. Often he would recollect, turn back to his team, see that all was all right, hurry them up, and do the same thing again. When it came near camping time, he would go ahead and look up a good place for camping. His mind was ever on the alert for the benefit of the company.[32]

In the early part of the trek, Sessions's group led the entire train; he and Pratt traveled ahead of the camp to scout the trail and find fords across rivers. One day, Sessions and Pratt discovered two "fine horses," including one with a saddle and bridle, which Pratt and Taylor captured. (Sessions's mother, Patty, recorded that Taylor took one of the horses even though her son "was the first that saw them.")[33] Pratt saw this as a "very timely providence," since he had "lost all my horses the previous winter, and was now pioneering for the company without any horse, and on foot."[34] On another occasion, Pratt and Sessions discovered and buried a man recently killed, presumably by Indians, whose corpse had been partially eaten by wolves. While they saw this as a reminder of the potential danger from Indians, Sessions recorded that they "met with the Lamanites allmost daley but they seamed friendley and glad to see us."[35] In late July, a group of American Indians, including "many Squaws," entered the camps to "sing dance and ride around." Pratt and Taylor "feast[ed] and smoke[d] with the Cheif."[36] The Saints understood that their migration would take them outside the boundaries of the United States, though the land would quickly pass into American hands as a result of the Mexican-American War. On July 4, the Saints did not "feel to Celebrate it as the Birthday of the Independence of the united States As we have been Driven from her because we worship God according to his laws." Rather than a traditional July 4 celebration, Pratt and Taylor both preached, delivering "very good teaching" on the "laws of God."[37] The men, including Pratt, hunted for meat en route; in mid-July, Pratt killed a buffalo for his company.[38]

The experiences of Pratt's children suggest the alternating excitement, monotony, and danger of life along the trail. Parley Jr. remembered that crossing the plains as a ten-year-old was difficult but also provided moments "of interest, novelty and pleasure": "Daily, new scenes burst upon our view, and now and again we would meet the hunter and the trapper or a band of Indians decked with beads, ornaments and feathers." His father gave him a "good Indian pony" with which, along with other "boy companions," he "drove cows most of the way across the plains."[39] While the trek thrilled Parley Jr., his younger brother Helaman, barely a year old, almost perished on August 6. Left asleep in the wagon while it was double-teamed "through the quick-sand of the Black hills," Helaman awoke, looked over the wagon's side, and "fell right between the wheels, the hind one passing over his limbs." Parley rushed to him; Agatha turned away, fearing the wagon might have severed Helaman's limbs. However, "owing to the soft sand, and the great mercy of God," Agatha recalled, "all the hurt was a red mark made by the iron tire across his limbs." After a blessing from his father, Helaman quickly recovered. Perrigrine Sessions considered Helaman "one among the many that was healed by the Ordinance of laying on of the hands" during the trek.[40]

The Pratts suffered a range of other hardships, including sickness, broken wagons, and dead oxen.[41] Agatha recorded that "the first part of the journey I enjoyed much, being young, and having good health, I did not mind the driving and the labor." However, as they neared the Salt Lake Valley, "our journey became wearisome and full of toil. Grass became scarce, cattle began to give out, often, when an ox gave out, a cow was put in its place. The roads were rough, wagons had to be pitched up."[42] By late August, Taylor warned Pratt that the camps in the rear had lost "great numbers of the cattle" because of "want of feed" or poisoning.[43]

In early September, shortly after Pratt sent a letter to the Salt Lake Valley requesting assistance, Young and the other apostles, returning to Winter Quarters with a company of thirty-three wagons, met the large emigration company west of South Pass in what is now southwestern Wyoming. In a meeting of the apostles on September 4, which Wilford Woodruff called "one of the most interesting Councils we ever held together," the apostles shared news of the Salt Lake Valley with Pratt.[44] George Smith extolled the "sweet little valley in midst of hills," commenting that "with ind[ustry], economy & prudence it will be one of the most bles't places in the world." The Saints had begun to build houses of adobe, or sun-dried bricks, and Smith estimated that the Salt Lake Valley, along with the promising Utah and Cache valleys, could support a "million" inhabitants. "We all feel first rate," he concluded, "& you will all feel first rate." Young testified that the pioneers had received divine guidance, informed Pratt of their irrigation efforts, and instructed him to divide, rather than sell, the land in the valley.[45]

Most of the council, however, dealt not with future settlement but with the conduct of Pratt and Taylor at Winter Quarters and on the trek. Young harshly rebuked them for reorganizing the large emigration company in violation of his explicit counsel and his revelation on the subject. Pratt and Taylor had dismissed the original organization based on adoptive families, had crossed the plains with a company far larger than envisioned, and had allowed the company to swell with the better prepared while leaving behind too many of the poor and the Mormon Battalion families. He thus "reproved Sharply" Pratt and the absent Taylor "for undoing what the majority of the quorum had done in the organizing of the camps." Notwithstanding their "good work" in England, they had "done wrong by disorganizing the two divisions & Companies that the quorum of the Twelve had spent the whole winter in organizing & which was Also governed by revelation." Woodruff fingered Pratt as the main culprit, as he "took the lead in the matter & entirely disregarded our organization & mixed the companies all up." According to Young, Pratt had violated a principle of ecclesiastical government, as "when one or more of the quorum interfere with the work of the majority of the quorum they burn their fingers & do wrong." By contrast, if an individual apostle exercised discretion on a mission under his own jurisdiction, he "would be blessed in doing that & the quorum would back up" his actions. The other apostles concurred that Pratt "had committed an error."[46]

Pratt initially defended himself, manifesting a "hard spirit," in Woodruff's opinion.[47] Pratt argued that he and Taylor had been nominated to take over the leadership, based on their apostolic status, and that necessity had forced the reorganization. In the absence of Young's presiding authority, Pratt rebutted, he and Taylor had the jurisdiction to act independently using their best judgment: "We hold the keys as well as yourself and will not be judged by you but by the Quorum."[48] Before leaving Winter Quarters, Pratt had reflected the still coalescing views about Young's authority, when he had publicly taught, "I do know about 12 men who hold the keys of this kingdom & are Presidents & one of them by reason of age is the President of the Quorum and of the church…[but] all the 12 are alike in keys power might majesty & dominion."[49] Young retorted that their companies "were perfectly organized" and that the meddling by Pratt and Taylor had "set at naught" their "whole winter's work." Appealing to a plurality rather than his seniority, he argued that "when the Quorum of the Twelve do a thing it is not in the power of two of them to rip it up.… When we got the machine a moving it is not your business to stick your hands among the cogs to stop the wheel." The adoptive family organization, he explained, had sought to "get the poor, the halt, the lame, and the blind" to the West.[50] Pratt correctly sensed that Young was also angry over his and Taylor's refusal to travel with the original pioneer company. Young had long been considering the reorganization of the First Presidency and had hoped that a united apostolic quorum on the trek west could take such action. However, their absence from the pioneer company had made this impossible.[51]

Pratt was strong-willed but not obstinate. After defending himself, he soon "repented & Confessed his fault." He told Young, "I've done the best I could. You said I could have done better.... I am guilty of an error and am sorry for it.... I am willing that the camp should know that I've done wrong and that I repent.... Am I forgiven and in fellowship?" Young responded, "I forgive you but I'll swear to you I shall whip you and make you to stick to me."[52] As Young proceeded to teach the quorum, Woodruff recorded, "the power of God rested upon us & our hearts melted & our eyes in tears." Previous apostolic apostasies loomed over the conversation. Woodruff summarized Young's sentiments: "If he did not tell us our faults we would be destroyed but if he told us of them & reproved us we would live in love & our hearts be semented together." Indeed, Young stated, he would "Chastize Br Parley or any one of the quorum as much as he pleased when they were out of the way & they Could not help themselves but He done it for their good & ownly done it when Constrained to do it by the power of God." Heber Kimball responded, "If I or my Brethren do wrong tell us of it & we will repent." Young commented, "There was not a better set of men on the earth than the Twelve."[53] Young also made clear the line of authority within the apostolic quorum: "I look upon myself as a weak, poor, little man who is called by the providence of God to preside.... I want you to go right into the Celestial Kingdom with me.... God bless you [Parley] forever and ever. Don't think any more about it."[54]

Nevertheless, Young would not let the matter rest. A few days later, Young's group held a council with Jedediah Grant's company, in which "Grant related the circumstances of the organization of the companies," and Young replied that "He was more & more Convinced that there was A wrong with P. P. Pratt & John Taylor in these things."[55] In November and December 1847, after the apostles except for Pratt and Taylor had traveled back across the plains to Winter Quarters, Young proposed to reorganize the First Presidency and again addressed the insubordination of Pratt and Taylor. One observer recorded that Young "raked down very hard on the conduct of Parley & Taylor last Spring while they were here."[56] Some of the apostles, including Orson Pratt, objected to Young's rebuke of apostles without action by the entire quorum.

Young, however, was by now consolidating his authority and vigorously defended his right to criticize other apostles without the permission or guidance of the entire quorum.[57] He cemented his position at Winter Quarters, when those apostles present accepted his proposal to reorganize a First Presidency, with Heber Kimball and Willard Richards as his counselors.

In these Winter Quarters meetings, Young also charged that Pratt and Taylor had entered into unauthorized plural marriages—with Phoebe, Agatha, and Martha in Pratt's case (though Young did not name them specifically). Young claimed that Pratt's "adultery" was "shewn to me in the valley" and that both he and Taylor had thus "committed an insult on the Holy Priesthood."[58] That same week, the Twelve excommunicated William W. Phelps for unauthorized plural marriages, but they did not discipline Pratt or Taylor.[59] The question over who could authorize plural marriages had been at the center of disputes between the apostles and William Smith as well as in Pratt's clash with Orson Hyde in England. The reorganization of the First Presidency ensured that Young's view—that he alone could give permission for new plural marriages—would prevail. Pratt acquiesced to it; in 1851, he was resealed in the Endowment House to Phoebe and Agatha (Martha had left him by this point). If Young forgave Pratt's independent-mindedness, he never forgot. That same year, he used Pratt and Taylor as an example of how individuals who try to "govern out of their place...do not prosper."[60]

Pratt arrived in the Salt Lake Valley roughly three weeks after his meeting with Young. Reflecting upon the Pratts' arrival, Agatha recalled that her wagon was almost broken down—"the front wheels wabbled about"—but it "held together and when my eyes rested on the beautiful entrancing sight—the Valley; Oh! how my heart swelled within me.... My soul was filled with thankfulness to God for bringing us to a place of rest and safety—a *home*." Parley immediately began exploring the nearby canyons, planting a crop of wheat, and building a makeshift home: "In a very short time a log room was up, a rough fireplace was built, what few chairs we had brought with us, our trunks and boxes were brought in, and a few rough seats were improvised." The Pratts added more rooms throughout the fall and winter, though they "slept in our wagons far into the winter." Pratt also carefully surveyed their provisions and determined that if they ground their wheat into "unbolted flour, we would have from half to three quarters of a pound a day to each person" until the next harvest. "This might seem ample," Agatha explained, but since they had "no vegetables, milk or butter, and hungry winter coming on, it was but short allowance." They subsisted primarily on "lean corned beef and a little Graham bread," reserving their few "groceries" for times of illness.[61]

That winter, Pratt explored the nearby region, traveling as far south as Utah Lake, where he "launched our boat and tried our net, being probably the first boat and net ever used on this sheet of water in modern times," and as far west as Tooele Valley.[62] (In March 1848, the High Council authorized Pratt to take a small company to Utah Valley to "take possession of the Valley and make a treaty with the Indians," but this expedition did not materialize.)[63] Along with his family, he also participated in the ritual of rebaptism as a display of renewed spiritual dedication. Following the example of Young and the other apostles, who rebaptized each other after arriving in the Salt Lake Valley and urged other Saints to do likewise, Pratt was rebaptized by Taylor on November 28 and then performed the ordinance for his wives, Parley Jr., and Isaac and Mary Rogers, whom he considered "members of his family." Taylor also confirmed Pratt "anew in the Gift of the Holy Ghost, and in all his blessings Covenants, promises, Ordainations, Washings, Anointings, Sealings, Priesthood, Apostleship."[64]

During the first year in the Salt Lake Valley, Pratt again wrestled with conflicts arising out of contested ecclesiastical jurisdiction. In September 1847, Young had appointed a Stake Presidency and High Council for the Salt Lake Valley, charging them with executive, legislative, and judicial authority; they enacted statutes, provided for their enforcement, and judged disputes.[65] Taylor and Pratt quickly found themselves at odds with leaders they considered Young's surrogates. On October 6, Willard Snow wrote to his brother Erastus that Pratt and Taylor "appointed a committy to seek out farming land & presented their doings to the council & was rejected," as the High Council maintained that the apostles had overstepped the bounds of their authority. "Rumour says," Snow continued, "that they feel as though this place belonged to Brigham & Heber...& they are at liberty to locate in the Piute valley the Utau or some where else." Snow attributed these feelings to "the effects of Pres Youngs whipping" as they "both feel keenly as though they were disarmed & shorn of a great portion of their power." Nevertheless, Snow thought "they will act in consert."[66] Indeed, they abandoned their scheme in deference to Young's plan for all of the pioneers to concentrate their initial settlement in the Salt Lake Valley.

The ambiguous governmental structure—stake leaders alongside two apostles—led to a series of further clashes. One pioneer remembered, "Father John Smith was looked on as President of the Camp; but Taylor and Pratt took the lead and in fact were in charge."[67] For example, Perrigrine Sessions took to the High Council his dispute over the horse that Sessions and Pratt had discovered and Taylor had caught on the trek west. After the council sided with Sessions, Taylor unhappily reported that he would "appeal to the Quorum of the Twelve."[68] Even so, Pratt and Taylor worked well on many occasions with the High Council. In October, Pratt advocated the surveying and division of the land, using the organization of the trek west to accomplish this, which the council accepted.[69] He also served on a committee in late December that drafted the settlement's first laws, including ordinances against vagrancy, disorderly conduct, theft, arson, indecent language, and firing weapons unnecessarily in or near the forts.[70] Dissension among the Saints made the new laws necessary. Stake leaders explained to Young in March 1848, "We found it somewhat difficult to establish order, peace, and harmony among the saints; after so much mobbing, robbing and traveling through such a dreary country, the minds of many became restless."[71]

When discontent morphed into threatened provocation, the persecution-weary Pratt struck preemptively. Some Saints, particularly a group of disillusioned Mormon Battalion veterans, made plans to leave for California with fur trader Miles Goodyear, from whom the Saints had purchased land in Ogden; one bitter veteran expressed his hope to "destroy every Mormon on the earth," and another promised to denounce the Saints publicly in California. Pratt persuaded the High Council to direct the marshal, his cousin John Van Cott, to halt the planned exodus.[72]

The High Council overlooked its battles with Pratt long enough to recompense him for his long life of unremunerated service and unstinting sacrifices, allotting him fifteen acres of plowed land for public service, exempting him from taxation, and allowing another pioneer to donate to Pratt a pair of boots as part of his labor tax.[73] The poverty implied by the latter gesture was a sore spot. Patty Sessions recorded in February 1848 that she had heard that Mary Pratt had told others "that we thought we stooped very low to visit her," which was "false."[74]

Still, Pratt seemed incurably conflict prone. In early January, the High Council met with the stake president "to learn whether he wood [would] have them and his own counsil to assist him in governing the afares, or P. P. Pratt."[75] Another incident reveals the continuing tensions. The council adopted an ordinance in March that individuals who brought charges against violators of the law would receive half of the fine levied. On April 1, Ira Eldredge accused Pratt of violating a ban on cutting green wood. One pioneer recalled, "We were required to use dead timber for fuel, and there was plenty of it, but some would not do it."[76]

Though notified of the charge, Pratt refused to appear before the High Council when summoned in April. On May 6, he came to the council meeting, not as a "transgressor," but "by way of teaching them." Pratt argued that his apostolic status gave him the authority to "preside over the presidency and high council and people at this place." All apostles except Young possessed equal power, he explained, and the apostles had the authority to preside anywhere in the church. He continued, "There had been more jarrings this winter than he had ever known," which would not have occurred had the "Spirit of the Lord" governed the council and if they had listened to Pratt and Taylor. The spirit of resisting apostolic authority, he claimed, evoked memories of apostates such as James Strang and Sidney Rigdon. In his strongest assertion of apostolic authority, Pratt stated that "Young decided in my hearing that wherever any one of the twelve was, he was king." As such, he declared, "I have a right to pre- side over every living being except Brigham Young, Heber C. Kimball and Orson Hyde who are older than myself and this council shall respect me." He admitted to violating the ordinance against cutting green wood but stubbornly insisted that he would continue to do so as he had only two small boys to help him collect firewood. He "acknowledged that he was subject to the law but felt that the timber law should be altered." Taylor affirmed Pratt's declara- tions.[77] Under Pratt's onslaught, the High Council put the charge against him "under the table" and agreed to "Receive Instruction" from Pratt and Taylor.[78] News of the council "excited some feeling" among the Saints.[79] The situation remained largely unresolved until Young's return from Winter Quarters in fall 1848. Not surprisingly, he affirmed the status of the stake presidents, not the apostles, as the "ruling authorities" in "all the affairs in the stake, spiritual and temporal, under the direction of the First Presidency." Even the apostles were thus subject to "the authorities of the Stake and the High Council."[80]

More pragmatic concerns eclipsed ecclesiastical squabbles, as a rainy spring and food shortages increased the Saints' suffering during the first year in Utah. Agatha remembered that the winter had been pleasant: "We held meetings, visited each other and were comparatively happy and contented." However, in mid-March, it rained continuously for a week. As Agatha recounted,

We were told that there was no rain to speak of in this country, so, in building our roofs, they were made nearly flat. They were constructed of—first poles put as closely together as possible, then dried grass and weeds, then a good layer of earth, which made a warm roof, but alas! not impervious to rain. So we had rain out of doors and a mud-fall in the house, for the continued fall of rain so thoroughly soaked the earth over head that the downpour was mud, *good-honest-mud*.

Hannahette, whose baby, Lucy, was only nine days old, "stayed in bed till it was soaked through, then she was placed in a chair before the fire with an umbrella over her head."[81]

During spring and summer 1848, the Pratts "suffered much for want of food." Parley remembered that his family was in particularly bad shape because "we had lost nearly all our cows, and the few which were spared to us were dry." Along with his wives and older children, he planted forty acres that year "in grain and vegetables." They "toiled incessantly," and Parley and some of the others worked without shoes, "reserving our Indian moccasins for extra occasions." Until the first harvest, they subsisted on "a few greens and on thistle and other roots," as well as "sometimes a little flour and some cheese" and perhaps some "sour skimmed milk or buttermilk" from neighbors. A frost in May, combined with a "terrible drought" that summer, imperiled the Saints' crops.[82] Agatha also recalled the threatened destruction of their crops because of crickets. The crops were rescued, she affirmed, by the famed "Miracle of the Gulls": "The gulls came, gorged themselves with the crickets, flew to the lake, disgorged themselves, came again, till the plague was stayed, and we harvested more wheat to the acre than seemed possible."[83]

In a letter to Young, then returning to Utah with another emigration company, Pratt reported positively on the first agricultural year, writing that his family had "Lived on the fruits of our Garden in a great measure since the early part of May, And now we have some green corn, Squashes, Cucumbers, Mellons, bean, etc." They also succeeded in raising sixty bushels of wheat, "a few bushels rye and Oats, tollerable flax," and corn.[84] When Young arrived in September, Pratt proudly exhibited the bounty of the first year by hosting him and George Smith at a "vegitable dinner" featuring "green corn, green peas, green beans, cucumbers, beets, parsnips, carrots, onions, potatoes, turnips, squashes, pumkin pies, cabbage, mush melons, water melons, cantelope, corn bread, wheat bread, corn stalk, molaces, and Roast beef."[85] Nevertheless, as Pratt acknowledged, "Many have Lost their crops, some for want of a proper selection of soil, some for want of good cultivation, and some because of insects, especially Crickets."[86] The Saints again faced a "scarcity of bread-stuffs" the next year, since the harvest overall was less abundant.[87]

With Young's arrival, governance passed to the Council of Fifty, which was dominated by the First Presidency and the apostles. In December 1848, aware that the United States would soon officially annex the area as part of the Treaty of Guadalupe Hidalgo ending the Mexican-American War, the council decided to petition for a territorial government and slate of officials, including Young as governor, Willard Richards as secretary, Heber Kimball as chief justice, and Newel K. Whitney and Pratt as associate justices. Remembering their experiences in Missouri and Illinois, the Saints desired self-determination with their own leaders in positions of political power. The council proposed to call the territory Deseret, after a Book of Mormon word for honeybee.[88] Over the next several months, Mormon leaders gathered signatures for their territorial petition and, in March 1849, replaced Pratt's name with Taylor's, perhaps anticipating that Pratt would shortly serve a mission to the Pacific. An election unanimously supported the slate and, on May 4, John M. Bernhisel, a gentlemanly Mormon doctor, left for Washington, D.C., with a twenty-two-foot petition containing 2,270 signatures.[89]

Mormon leaders quickly shifted course in July 1849, after the arrival of letters from the East. Thomas L. Kane, a trusted non-Mormon adviser with substantial connections in Washington, learned that President James Polk would likely appoint his own officials, rather than Mormons, as the territory's officers. Foreseeing the tensions that would arise between outside officials and Mormons, Kane urged the Saints to seek statehood instead. In response, Mormon leaders hurriedly drafted a constitution for a planned state of Deseret and even fabricated the existence of a convention which had supposedly met in March 1849 to approve the constitution. Pratt participated in the ruse in his *Autobiography*, claiming that he had helped draft a constitution "for the Provisional State of Deseret" in mid-March.[90] Their petition for statehood reached Congress during debates over the organization of territories and states from the land acquired in the Mexican-American War, when sectional disputes about the future of slavery crescendoed and swept aside Mormon ambitions.[91]

As part of the Compromise of 1850, Congress admitted Utah as a territory, though stripped of its Mormon name and with its borders curtailed (though still including present-day Utah and portions of Nevada, Colorado, and Wyoming, as opposed to the Mormon proposal that extended into present-day California, Arizona, Oregon, Idaho, and New Mexico). The failure of this statehood campaign profoundly shaped the history of the Saints, the American West, and the nation. The nature of territorial governance—supervision by Congress with officials chosen by the president rather than the populace—guaranteed battles between Mormons and the federal office-holders. Mormons gained some consolation for their efforts, as President Millard Fillmore appointed Young as governor, while balancing the rest of the appointments between Saints and outsiders.[92] Before they received news of Congress's decision, Mormon leaders organized a legislature of the provisional state of Deseret. Pratt and other legislators met for three separate sessions between December 1849 and March 1851.[93]

During the winter of 1848 to 1849, Pratt and other Mormon leaders also reorganized ecclesiastically. On February 12, the First Presidency and apostles in the Salt Lake Valley ordained four men—Charles C. Rich, Lorenzo Snow, Erastus Snow, and Franklin D. Richards—to vacancies in the quorum of the Twelve to replace Young, Kimball, and Willard Richards, now members of the First Presidency, and the excommunicated Lyman Wight, who had maintained that the gathering place for the Saints should be in Texas. The four new apostles, combined with the three in the Valley (Pratt, Taylor, and Amasa Lyman) now constituted a majority of the apostles and could therefore "act as a quorum." (Three apostles—Orson Hyde, George A. Smith, and Ezra T. Benson—remained in Winter Quarters, and Wilford Woodruff and Orson Pratt were serving missions elsewhere.) Pratt assisted in dividing Salt Lake City into nineteen wards with a bishop to oversee each, helped organize other wards in outlying areas, and took part in reorganizing the Salt Lake Stake Presidency and High Council.[94]

While participating in civil and religious governance, Pratt also attended to the needs of a rapidly growing family. During the first year in Utah, five of his nine wives were pregnant. Hannahette gave birth to her second child, Lucy, on March 9, 1848. That was followed by the birth of Belinda's twins, Belinda and Abinadi, on May 8; Agatha's Agatha on July 7; and Mary's Cornelia on September 5. "Though I had not scarcely a full enjoyable meal through the nine months" of pregnancy, Agatha recalled, little Agatha "was a plump healthy child."[95] Even though polygamy was an open part of early Utah society, Mormons still officially denied the practice to the outside world, even to converts in far-flung areas. When Agatha's parents, still in England, inquired in 1848 if she was married, she carefully responded that she was "still living" with the Pratts, whom she described as "the same kind friends they always were." Parley encouraged the Walkers to immigrate to Utah (which they soon did), praised Agatha's "noble, generous and amiable disposition," and assured them, with more truth than they knew, that she "will never be separated from us."[96]

All five of the children born in 1848 survived to adulthood. However, on January 30, 1849, Martha gave birth to a son, Ether, who died a month later. Two of the three children born in 1850, Sarah's Mormon and Phoebe's Mosiah, also died before their first birthday, both of "consumption" (perhaps malnutrition or tuberculosis).[97] Agatha's second daughter, Malona, born on April 15, 1850, survived. Martha, having buried her son while the other wives who bore children in 1848 cared for their healthy infants, left Parley in July 1849 and headed for California. But disillusionment with polygamy, Pratt, and Mormonism preceded her son's death.[98] Parley wrote in his family record that Mormon Jesse Turpin "seduced her from her home, led her into bad company at his house which finally resulted in her prostitution and elopement to the gold mines with unprincipled men."[99] During these years, Mormon leaders worried constantly that non-Mormons passing through Utah—particularly gold miners and soldiers—would "seduce" plural wives or teenage daughters of the Saints.[100] For some Mormon women, especially those unhappy with the faith and polygamy, California offered an alluring escape.[101]

Martha's disappearance provided grist for rumor mills as extravagant, false, and imaginative as any nineteenth-century anti-Catholic exposé. Elizabeth Ferris, who wrote a book about Mormon polygamy after a brief stay in Utah, claimed that before Parley's mission to Chile, he had been unable to raise sufficient funds, as he "had borrowed so often, forgetting to pay, that his exceedingly bland manner had lost its influence." Recognizing that his "house was somewhat over-stocked with wives," he traded Martha, "a good-natured English girl," to Walkara, an American Indian leader, for "ten horses." After Parley cruelly informed her of the exchange, Martha prematurely aged: "Her cheeks became sunken and pallid; her countenance exhibited the deep-drawn lines of unmistakable agony." After Walkara saw Martha, he rebuked Pratt, saying, "me no want old white squaw."[102] Another author offered a version only slightly less colorful: "One or two of the Mrs. Pratts mysteriously disappeared, and the elder immediately came out with a fine stud of horses" from Walkara.[103]

The rumors about Martha's disappearance linked Pratt's poverty with his supposed decision to sell her. For the second time in his life (the first being his Nauvoo store), however, Pratt appeared to be on the verge of financial success, thanks to his shrewd decision to build a new road into the Salt Lake Valley. The pioneer route followed a path blazed by the ill-fated Donner-Reed Party in 1846 from Fort Bridger, which descended down Echo Canyon and Emigration Canyon into the Salt Lake Valley.[104] Several obstacles marred this route, including two mountains, windy canyons, steep descents, and frequent crossings of streams.[105] The Mormons hoped to find an easier way. In June 1848, Pratt, along with Jacob Workman, explored Big Canyon, traveling to the future site of Park City and to an area they named Parley's Park (now Snyderville Basin). Pratt extolled the canyon to the High Council, noted the existence of valuable timber and limestone, and encouraged the council to commission more investigation and possibly construct a road through the canyon.[106] The council thus appointed Pratt, John Van Cott, and Daniel Spencer to explore further in early July. After three days, they returned "weary and worn, and some of us without shoes, and nearly without pantaloons, the Kenyon haveing Robbed us of these in a great measure, and of much of our flesh and skin." Nevertheless, they reported that a road through Big Canyon bypassing the original pioneer route could be built for $800.[107]

The discovery of gold by James Marshall at Sutter's Mill in January 1848 (where former members of the Mormon Battalion were working) transformed the situation. Within a year, thousands of the hopeful and the desperate were passing through Salt Lake City en route to California. The Gold Rush provided a critical boost to the Mormon economy, as the travelers purchased supplies at inflated prices and sold valuable and heavy merchandise at bargain prices to the Saints. Pratt recalled, "Money and gold dust was plenty, and merchandise of almost every description came pouring into our city in great plenty."[108] The infusion of cash into the Utah economy allowed the Saints to begin ambitious immigration and colonization projects.[109] Pratt moved quickly to capitalize and received a commission from the Legislative Council of Deseret to build a private toll road up Big Canyon; the council gave other prominent Saints similar rights in nearby canyons. The council also granted Pratt rights to build a sawmill (which he sold to Samuel Snyder) and sell wood lots in the canyon.[110]

Pratt began work on the road in July 1849, driven both by the economic opportunity of Gold Rush migration and financial necessity, as the crop he planted that spring and early summer had failed.[111] He hired some forty-niners, who "arrived in Salt Lake, utterly worn out, and teams and wagons in bad condition," who hoped to "make a little means wherewith to prosecute their journey." Agatha, along with Parley Jr. and her infant daughter, went along to cook for the camp. She recalled, "The food consisted mostly of bread baked in bake kettle, meat, coffee and a little butter. We had a small tent and a wagon to sleep in.... We would make camp in a shady place near the creek. We would stay there till about two miles of road was made, then move camp and make another mile or two." On one occasion, as a group of men "were busy chopping down trees about a mile above the camp," a large grizzly bear approached, forcing the men to climb trees for safety. By November, when they ceased work for the year, the road was completed to the Weber River. As they journeyed home, Agatha proposed that she "get out and walk over the bad places," but Parley asked her to ride the entire way, so that he could "say that a woman and baby came down in safety."[112]

The next spring, following the southern Utah expedition, Pratt again "commenced working on my road in Big Canyon Creek, and in getting out timber and wood from the same." This time, Elizabeth accompanied him as cook, and Mormons John Pulsipher, Rufus Allen, and perhaps others "worked considerable" on the road. Pulsipher described Pratt as "a strong healthy man and a very hard working man, one of the best men I ever worked with. He was full of the gospel. His conversation was instructive and exalting." As they worked that spring near the Weber River, full and rapid from the melting snow, the men left Elizabeth and Parley Jr. to look for a suitable ford. They soon heard cries for help and rushed back. Pulsipher found Elizabeth "in the water, hanging to a bush with one hand and little Parley holding to the other." She had been picking berries when the riverbank collapsed under her. The men came just "in time to save her, [as] just head and arms [were] above water, [and she had] nearly lost hold of the bush." "Scared and chilled," Elizabeth "trembled for hours."[113]

In the recently launched *Deseret News*, Pratt announced that his new road, named the "Golden Pass," would open about July 4, 1850, connecting the Weber River and the Salt Lake Valley, "avoiding the two great mountains, and most of the Kanyons so troublesome of the old route."[114] From Echo Canyon, the road passed "present Coalville, Hoytsville, and Wanship, traveled up Three Mile Canyon to the present Silver Creek Junction on I-80," then descended through Big Canyon into the Salt Lake Valley.[115] The toll station was in southeast Salt Lake City (near 3300 East and 2100 South).[116] Pratt boasted, "If a road worked by the most persevering industry, and open country, good feed and fuel, beautifully romantic and sublime scenery, are any induce-ment, take the new road, and thus encourage public improvement." Wagons cost 50 cents if drawn by one animal and 75 cents if drawn by two. Furthermore, an "additional draught, pack, or saddle animal" cost 10 cents, "loose stock" was a nickel, and sheep were a bargain at a penny apiece.[117]

In his advertisement, Pratt said, "The road is some what rough and unfinished: but is being made better every day."[118] Travelers agreed with at least half of his sentence. In August 1850, Mary Ann Weston Maughan, a Mormon immigrant from England, called it "the most dreadfull road imaganable." She wrote, "Some places we had to make the road before we could pass it is full of large rocks and stumps." She grumbled that they paid for the privilege of "passing over the road we had made."[119] Pratt earned $1,500 in tolls that year, serving travelers to California, Mormon emigrants, and local Saints seeking timber and stone in the canyon. On the cusp of financial success, missionary duty once again trumped an elusive prosperity.

Called to California and Chile, Pratt would sell his interest in the road "to several individuals" in early 1851 to finance his mission.[120] Nevertheless, the route became known as Parley's Road and the canyon as Parley's Canyon. The road soon fell into disrepair, though appropriations by the territorial legislature continued to make it passable in the 1850s and it became the preferred route into the valley by the 1860s. The road eventually became the site of Interstate 80.[121]

In late 1849, following his first summer of work on the toll road, a mission of another kind turned Pratt's attention from the road before it even opened. Since their arrival in Utah, Mormon leaders had thought about expanding Mormon settlement southward and westward to link the Great Basin with Southern California. In March 1849, Brigham Young told Orson Pratt, "We hope soon to explore the valleys three hundred miles south and also the country as far as the Gulf of California with a view to settlement and to acquiring a seaport." The November 1849 session of the Legislative Assembly, which included Pratt, commissioned him to raise fifty men to travel through southern Utah to the site of present-day Las Vegas, going over the rim of the Great Basin into the Virgin River country.[122] Isaac Haight, one of the participants who later became infamous for his role in the Mountain Meadows Massacre, described the intention "to find a vally for another settlement of the saints in the south part of the Mountains of Israel."[123] The company's exploration and its detailed reports would set the agenda for the Mormon settlement of central and southern Utah over the next few decades.

Pratt immediately recruited men with varied skills and solicited donations of money and supplies. The company was organized on November 23 with forty-seven men between the ages of eighteen and seventy-one. They elected Pratt as president with William W. Phelps, a fifty-seven-year-old printer and engineer, and David Fullmer, the forty-six-year-old first counselor in the Salt Lake Stake Presidency, as his counselors. The company included Dimick Huntington, a talented Indian interpreter; Robert Campbell, a twenty-three-year-old who served as clerk and secretary; Ephraim Green, a gunner in charge of the expedition's cannon; and three men, John Brown, William Henrie, and Joseph Matthews, who filled the role of hunters, as they had for the original 1847 pioneer company. Dan Jones, a native of Wales and prolific baptizer of his countrymen, likely went because of a Mormon belief that a group of Welsh Indians lived somewhere in the region. Three of the men—Phelps, Joseph Horne, and Huntington— had explored the Sanpete Valley in August and thus had experience with the first part of the route.[124] Pratt organized the expedition on the pattern of the westward trek, creating divisions of ten in the company of fifty. The captain of fifty, John Brown, noted that the company was "fitted up with ox teams, having also quite a number of riding and pack animals to enable us to explore the country where we could not take our wagons. We were all well armed and [had] quite a quantity of Indian trade."[125]

The decision to explore the territory during the harshest winter months suggests the Mormon sense of urgency to colonize the Great Basin as well as the pragmatic recognition of the necessity of keeping men close to home during the spring and summer growing season. Almost immediately, heavy snows impeded the company's progress, as they would throughout the expedition; roughly a foot fell as they drove their wagons to Fort Utah (Provo).[126] During a brief stop there, Pratt conferred with local residents about the increasing hostilities with the Utes led by Walkara. Initially, Mormons in Provo and the American Indians who were clustered around Utah Lake had interacted amicably, but tensions were rising and would soon explode into a cycle of violence. Traveling through frigid weather, the explorers next arrived at the Sandpitch (Manti) settlement, then only two weeks old, in the Sanpete Valley. At Sandpitch, Pratt became "very sick" and "vomited all day."[127] Throughout the rest of the expedition, he was intermittently ill with a complaint of "stomach and bowels," making the physical stamina displayed by the forty-two-year-old Pratt even more striking.[128] Pratt recruited five more men at the settlement, bringing the total to fifty-two, and learned that Walkara "and his Indians are 70 miles from here up the Sevier river on our way."[129]

A meeting with Walkara's Utes two days outside of Sandpitch demonstrates the exchanges—of goods, spiritual power, and geographical knowledge—between Mormons and American Indians. The tensions in Utah Valley made Pratt and his men apprehensive when Walkara "Rode up on horse back Just as we had Left our Camp." To the chagrin of many of his company, Pratt complied with Walkara's request and ordered the men to return to their campsite. That evening, Walkara arrived with his "Camp...Consisting of Men Women and Children, Cattle Horses and Dogs." Huntington interpreted a letter to Walkara from Brigham Young, and the Mormons gave "coffee and provisions" to the Indians.[130] Measles had struck the band, and on Walkara's request, "Parley, Dan Jones & Dimic goes & prays for Indians...rebukes their meazles, by laying hands on them in the name of Jesus." They also witnessed the Indians' own measures of "making medicine, see them sucking one anothers feet, forehead &c."[131] Pratt confronted, perhaps for the first time, American Indian slavery; the Utes participated in Spanish slave-trading networks, a practice that repelled him. Walkara shot and killed a young Paiute slave boy "as a Sacrifice that the sickness may stop" and Pratt's intervention likely prevented Walkara from killing other Paiute children.[132] "Like an experienced geographer," Walkara also gave advice on the route, directed his brother Ammomah to serve as guide (but soon afterward, he became sick and left the company), and stated that he "wished all to come American and Mormon & live in peace."[133]

Continuing south along the Old Spanish Trail, a horse route which ran from Santa Fe to Los Angeles through Utah, the company encountered frigid temperatures and heavy snows. On December 10, Campbell noted a temperature of "21 below zero, extreme hard frost, river froze over hard." The men often lost sight of the trail because of the heavy snows; John Armstrong wrote, "We are making a new road all the way."[134] Nevertheless, the company remained in high spirits. With the help of Campbell and others, Pratt composed several hymns and songs along the way. The company routinely gathered at night to sing, dance, tell jokes and stories, discuss doctrine, and even prophesy.[135] One evening, Campbell described a "discussion till late on Gods, Angels, Prophets &c."[136] On another occasion, Phelps, who had converted to Mormonism in 1831, "conversed freely about the coming forth of the plates of the Book of Mormon and the translating of them by the Prophet Joseph Smith."[137] Another night in early January, "Parley gets round fire, talks good things to the Brethren, gave his ideas, his experience & answered questions."[138] Notwithstanding the camaraderie of the camp, Pratt deeply missed his family. He wrote them in poetic lament,

> O Solitude! What is it? who Can feel it? Where is it known? it is only known and felt in its extreem by one who has a fireside, kindred souls, kind, Lovely, faithful, trusty, tried friends who have suffered everything for their Love to him, who always smile at his approach and comfort and nurse him when weary and cast down—One who has Little Children to caress him and Clime about his nees when he returns from the Cares and Toils of the day. Such an one Cast fourth, after the buisy toils of summer to spend his winter evenings in Solitude and eat heavy pancakes amid the wild and Lonely desarts of the Rocky Mountains. In his heart is Solitude.[139]

As they continued south along the Sevier River, the men soon faced their greatest challenge, crossing the southern end of the rugged Tushar Mountains to arrive in the Little Salt Lake Valley (now known as Parowan Valley).

Throughout the expedition, Pratt often rode ahead of the company, generally with another scout or two, to explore the path. As they approached the
Tushars, he scouted on several days to find a pass through the mountains.
After a day of scouting with Pratt, Armstrong wrote, "When we got back to
camp I was so tired I cant stand nor sit down. I could not lift my leg up to
step in the wagon."[140] As they searched for a pass through the mountains on
December 15, Pratt "road out some ten miles to the left to find a pass but did
not succeed the mountains were very high on either side."[141] By this point,
lacking their Indian guide, the explorers were confused and frustrated; they
bypassed some possible passes, including the Old Spanish Trail. On
December 16, John Brown reported an "impracticable but barely passible"
route, "rocky road all along for 6 miles, winding over a succession of kanyons,
steep ascents and descent, cobble stones all the way, nearly perpendicular in
places."[142] After Brown's description, the "cry was we can go it. It was a great
undertaking and a very hazardous one to cross so large a mountain at this
season of the year."[143]

Brown was not exaggerating. The next five days, December 17–21, as the
company endured bitter cold and deep snows, were the most difficult and
perilous of the journey. The experience of John C. Frémont's expedition in
crossing the Tushar Mountains four years later illustrates the challenges the
Pratt expedition faced. Even though they traveled without cumbersome
wagons, Frémont's expedition barely traversed the pass. They suffered the
death of one man and would have lost several others if they had not received
assistance at the young Mormon settlement at Parowan.[144] Pratt's men mustered "all the courage and united exertion possible" as they understood their
"severe job on hand." Sickness notwithstanding, Pratt "led the way being followed by all the men who were not driving teams or loose cattle armed with
axes, picks, shovels, spades &c." After a relatively easy four miles, the company
confronted both "deep ravines" and steep hillsides, forcing them to leave half
the wagons and double-hitch the other half and then return to repeat the process. In the ravines, the explorers, in groups of at least twelve, lowered the
wagons by rope before pulling them up the other side. On the hillsides, the
men pulled their oxen up, "then the oxen pulling the wagons." Fierce winds
blew off the wagon covers and snowdrifts "as high as the oxen" obscured the
path.[145] Armstrong described the road as covered "with cobbled stones and
large rocks" and the "feed mostly all covered by the snow," which stood "in
places from 2–4 feet deep."[146]

After a night of nearly constant snow, the company continued their slow
ascent up the mountain. Brown recorded, "Some were almost ready to dispair,

the snow was now one foot deeper than before half of the wagons were in the midst of the pass and the others just entered, however, discouraging as it was we hitched to the wagons and moved on." That night, after managing only two and a half miles of progress, Pratt huddled in a carriage with a few others and prayed that God would "forgive the camp for their vanity, folly, & wickedness," pleading "with the Lord not to hedge up our way, but to enable us to get out of these Mts & to find a pass." Some men were at their breaking point. Schuyler Jennings "swore & dam'd Captn Jones in Gods name to take his horse away from near his waggon & threat[ened] him with club in hand."[147] Alarmingly, the company's animals were also breaking down "for want of feed and water." The next night, after an arduous day of double-teaming their wagons up and down ravines and hillsides, Pratt "made a long exhortation" to the men, lamenting that "the Lords spirit grieved on account of the folly, nonsense, & vanity in camp." Perhaps Pratt remembered how the initially promising Zion's Camp had descended into disputes and finally a cholera epidemic which Joseph Smith had interpreted as God's rebuke. Unrepentant, Jennings muttered "that he'd a good mind to black his mind, &c using the word damd."[148]

The next day, December 20, the company began its descent, traveling five miles. Concerned for their provisions, Pratt sent hunters to find thirteen lost cattle and to hunt deer. Along with Brown, Pratt traveled ahead, going "down a little narrow canyon which led us into the upper end of the Little Salt Lake Valley," returning "after dark."[149] Pratt's initial report on the Little Salt Lake Valley incorrectly stated that the rivers in the valley emptied into the Colorado River, an indication of his geographic confusion, particularly surprising because informed individuals, including the Mormons, understood that the region was a Great Basin, with only interior drainage. Relieved, exhausted, and triumphant, the explorers completed the mountain pass on December 21 and descended into Little Salt Lake Valley. Armstrong boasted, "we have fought with the storms and tempests and it must have been by and thru the divine interposition of providence of God who led Nephi of old, that we were brought over these mountains. To look at them it would be said that no white man could do it or be rash enough to undertake it or have enterprising spirit enough to attempt it. The Mormons are the boys for such expeditions."[150]

Pratt now divided the company, leaving thirty men under Fullmer's leadership to guard the wagons and explore the vicinity while Pratt led twenty men "over the rim of the Basin" into the Virgin River region.[151] He assured those who remained that they would have an "equal share in the glory."[152] He also dispatched two men, including the troublesome Jennings, to Salt Lake with mail. In a letter to the First Presidency, Pratt confidently predicted that the region they had traveled "will admit of a continuous line of Settlements" and described the Little Salt Lake Valley as "well adapted to the sustenance" of a "small settlement."[153] (He more pessimistically told his family, "All the good soil and Water we have seen in one hundred and fifty m.s. would not amount to ten thousand acres.")[154]

Pratt's advance group passed through the future sites of Cedar City, Harmony, and St. George. They soon encountered Southern Paiutes, who had been devastated by disease and the Indian slave trade and who had been informed by the Utes of the Mormons' impending arrival. Huntington invited a small group of Indians to stay with the camp, telling them "we were Mormons not Americans." Campbell described them as "mean, dirty almost naked creatures," who told the Mormons, "the land is all ours if we come & settle among them, glad to av [have] us." Brown noted that they "had no women no children they said they had sold them to the Spaniards." After the Paiutes indicated that the route ahead down the Virgin River included "many kanyons, Red Knolls, high Red bluffs perpendicular like Mts no timber, for a long way South East nothing but barren land," Pratt decided to begin the homeward journey. The Paiutes spoke accurately, as the Virgin River Gorge cannot be traversed on horseback.[155]

Turning north, the expedition traveled by way of the future Santa Clara settlement and then Mountain Meadows, a well-established campsite on the Spanish Trail and California Road. At Mountain Meadows, they camped near a "large company of about 50 wagons" headed to California, with whom they traded (acquiring enough whiskey to get one member of the expedition drunk).[156] Along with Dan Jones, Pratt rode ahead of the rest of the group, arriving back in the Little Salt Lake Valley on January 7. As they approached the camp, Pratt and Jones fired a gun to signal their arrival, interrupting an evening when "the boys were dancing cotillions." After Jones shared a "canteen full of whiskey" with the camp, they ate dinner and then "some went to boxing some to singing, some dancing to amuse them." Pratt instructed the camp to prepare "a large dinner for the whole camp tomorrow, Put up a liberty pole and have Jubilee."[157]

The following day's jubilee gives a glimpse of how the explorers perceived themselves, their mission, and Pratt. Some men awoke at 3 A.M. to begin preparations. They "erected a liberty pole about 40 feet high, hoisted a white flag," on which they inscribed, "Great Basin, meeting of Rough & Ready club this even[ing]." They also made a banner borrowing the slogan of the 1848 Free

Soil Party—"Free soil, Free speech, free labor"—but adding, "& freedom of the Saints." Cannons, gunfire, and "loud huzzahs" greeted the rest of the explorers as they came in. A wagon cover spread on the ground provided the table for an "excellent Dinner" of "Plenty coffee, roast Beef, Pumpkin & Squash, with pies, minced, apple &c little Sugar, and butter handed round while eating." Pratt then gave a speech rejoicing that the isolation of the Great Basin guaranteed the Saints' liberty. He stated that "he has read of the sunny climes of fair Italy, he had trod Europes shores heard of the fertile & productive countries in France, but all these things were, where neither the soil, the elements nor the air, the light of heaven was free, but here is 'free soil free speech free labor free Saints' & free Pumpkin pies." After lauding the mineral resources they had discovered, he proclaimed, "we have the best defence the most rocks, the best women, most beautiful children & more of them than any ppl [people] on the earth in proportion to our number, therefore boys the Great Basin for me." At the conclusion of Pratt's speech, "cannon fired amid three cheers—long & loud by the Fifty," and Phelps praised Pratt as "vigilant & persevering neither the snow, the rain, the bad road, the thunder nor the lightning had prevent[ed] him from going a head & finded passes." Singing of the company's new hymns followed, as did so much firing of the cannon and guns that Pratt eventually "said enough ammunition wasted for to day." The day ended with boxing, bowling (on a "ten pin alley"), "prayers & singing & Dancing" along with "some wrestling."[158]

Leaving Little Salt Lake Valley, the explorers headed north toward home, taking a more western route (through contemporary Beaver and Fillmore) rather than returning through Sandpitch, bypassing the Tushar Mountains. Heavy snows, high winds, a lack of provisions, and fatigued and dying animals soon contrasted sharply with the jubilee celebration. On January 15, they "remained in camp snowed and blowed all day and night," and Pratt felt "quite unwell."[159] Four days later, it snowed an additional ten inches, and the company found it "very difficult finding the road" under the two-foot drifts.[160] Near present-day Fillmore, after scouts reported that deeper snow lay ahead, Pratt separated the company, leading a group of twenty-four mostly married men on horseback to Provo, about a hundred miles away, while leaving most of the provisions with the other men. He "spoke on the expediency & necessity of part of the Camp going ahead, & reporting our situation, & if necessary sending us teams back, that they might see to their families & not stay here & all eat up the Provision."[161] Before leaving, Pratt dictated his report of the expedition for the legislature to Campbell, using Campbell's extensive journals. Pratt told the remaining men, "God bless you

Brethren, you have my good feelings....Don't be idle because you have nothing to do, but inform yourselves & see to the cattle and do as you are told."[162] Those left behind organized dancing lessons as well as a "Ute Indian school" to learn the native language before traveling home in March.[163]

Pratt predicted that those leaving would "have the worst of it." Indeed, the stretch home to Provo proved one of the most difficult of the journey. Before departing, Pratt became "very sick, of a bilious attack, and was confined to my bed." When the group departed on January 22, he "had not eaten one mouthful for a day or two, but vomited many times very severely." Nevertheless, he "mounted a mule" and "commenced our wallowing in the snow." Fortunately, Pratt felt better the following day as the company struggled along "waist deep in snow." Their animals exhausted, the men took turns breaking a path through the snow on foot; each man could continue in the exhausting work of "breaking the track" for only a "few moments" before "giving place to another" and taking a place at the rear.[164] The frigid conditions left some men with frostbite, and the animals "so tired they could not hunt the grass that night but stood among the cedars and ate bark, a thing I never saw before."[165] Several of the debilitated animals had to be left behind on the trail. On the morning of the fourth day of travel, the men awoke to find themselves "completely buried in snow." As some men "began shovelling the others out," which Pratt "found too tedious," he "raised my voice like a trumpet and commanded them to arise, when all at once there was a shaking among the snow piles, the graves were opened, and all came forth." They lightheartedly dubbed the spot "resurrection camp." The storm subsided that day, and on the following day, January 26, the company traveled "16 or 18 miles." However, the men were growing desperate, still "50 miles from any settlement" and with their "provisions almost exhausted." They moved slowly because of their weak animals and their own ailments: two men suffered with frostbite, and another was "snow blind."[166]

Calling on his reserves of physical strength notwithstanding his illness, Pratt announced that he, Chauncey West, and Dimick Huntington would "take some of the strongest animals and try to penetrate to Provo," where a relief party could be raised to rescue the other men. Huntington "soon gave out and fell back into the rear company." Pratt and West heroically pressed on from daylight to 11 o'clock at night, "breaking the way on foot and leading the mules in our track, and sometimes riding them." They stopped for the night "extremely hungry and feet badly frozen, we built a small fire, it being the coldest night we had ever experienced, and after trying in vain to thaw out, our frozen shoes stocking and the bottoms of our drawers & pants, we rolled ourselves in our blankets, and lay trembling with cold a few hours" as the thermometer plunged to 30 below zero.[167] Pratt and West awoke "long before day" and ate "a few mouthfuls" from their last piece of food—a "black frozen biscuit" smaller than a fist. "After another laborious day," they arrived in Provo "at dusk," where they "raised a posse of men and animals with provisions, and sent back same night." The posse saved one man that night, an English convert who had wandered ahead of the rest and had "sunk down in the snow in a helpless condition" eight miles from Provo. They rescued the other men, who had eaten the remainder of their food that day, "somewhere in the southern end of Utah Valley."[168] The expedition likely would have been lost but for Pratt's courage and fortitude. His men realized that they had escaped a calamity. Isaac Haight recorded, "Our hearts burned with gratitude to God for delivering us from starvation and death."[169] After resting for a "day or two," Pratt returned to Salt Lake to deliver his report.[170]

Pratt's expedition took a heavy toll in pain and hardship, but it bore fruit commensurate with its cost. His discoveries, both of settlement sites and natural resources such as the rich iron deposits, advanced Young's plans to colonize the region. In January, before the expedition had even returned, Pratt's initial reports led the legislature to include Little Salt Lake Valley among the six counties it created throughout the territory. Within a week of his return, Pratt presented his report to the Legislative Council of Deseret, identifying at least twenty-six sites of eventual Mormon settlements. Young moved rapidly. Within a year of the report, the first waves of pioneers began to fan out through central and southern Utah. A large group of about 450 settled in Parowan, and many moved the next year nearer the iron ore at Cedar City, both areas that Pratt had enthusiastically endorsed.[171] Settlers soon arrived as well in Fillmore, which briefly served as territorial capital because of its central location. Pratt's assurance that the Southern Paiutes welcomed Mormon settlers prompted Young to establish missions among the Indians of southern Utah. In 1852, Young designated John D. Lee and a few others to establish an outpost, the first over the rim of the Great Basin, at Harmony. The missionaries to the Native Americans later founded Fort Harmony and Santa Clara.[172]

Between 1847 and 1851, Pratt remained in Mormonism's center place longer than at any other period in his life. Before this time, missionary journeys had continually pulled him away from home, as they would for the rest of his life. Indeed, a year after completing the expedition to southern Utah, Pratt again traveled through southern Utah, but this time toward a much more distant destination: Chile.

11

Lamanites in the Pacific

Red men of the forest; Peruvians, Mexicans, Guatimalians,
descendants of every tribe and tongue of this mysterious
race, your history, your gospel, your destiny is revealed.
— PARLEY PRATT, *Proclamation! To the People of the Coasts
and Islands of the Pacific; of Every Nation, Kindred and Tongue.
By an Apostle of Jesus Christ.*

DURING ITS FIRST two decades, Mormonism operated primarily within
the English-speaking world bordered by the northern Atlantic Ocean. Pratt's
own missionary travels throughout the eastern United States, Canada, and
Great Britain had been instrumental in establishing the movement throughout
Anglo-America. Nevertheless, Mormon leaders always dreamed of a much
more expansive outreach, a gospel message that would flood the world prior
to the millennial return of Jesus Christ. In the early 1850s, Mormon eyes
turned westward and southward toward the Pacific and Latin America. In
1851, Brigham Young designated Pratt to preside over an ambitious missionary
program in the Pacific. The First Presidency wrote, "Pratt's mission circum-
scribes the Pacific, & all lands surrounded by & bordering on the same," and
they hoped he might "open the door of life to Japan & China, Bornea &
Chili," and eventually to "every country, & Kingdom, city & village on the
Pacific."[1] Pratt described the scope of his mission as "a world of itself," "nearly
one-half of the globe," encompassing a "vast field of labor among unnumbered
millions of East Indies and China" as well as the Pacific coast of South
America.[2]

A few Mormon missionaries had been sent to islands in the Pacific in the
1840s. The renewed effort was partly a response to the California Gold Rush,
which transformed religious competition throughout the Pacific as large
numbers of forty-niners, not only from the United States but from nations
such as Chile and Australia, converged on California shores. In focusing on
the Pacific, Mormons entered contested religious terrain as they confronted
Catholic nations, indigenous religions, and Protestant missionaries who had

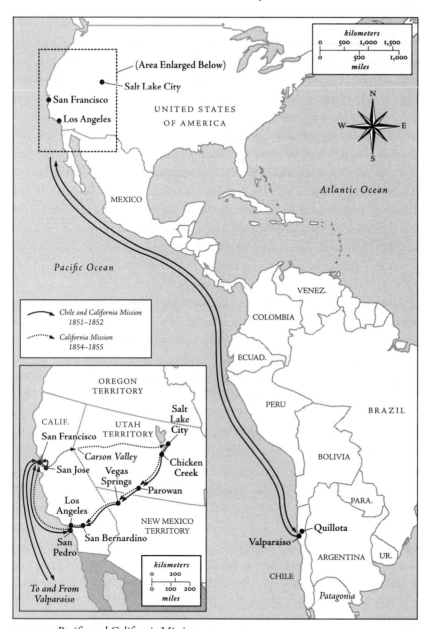

MAP 11.1 Pacific and California Missions

arrived on some Pacific islands a few decades earlier. For instance, the interdenominational American Board of Commissioners for Foreign Missions sent missionaries to the Sandwich Islands (Hawaii) in 1820. King Kamehameha II welcomed the missionaries, who converted large numbers of native Hawaiians. American traders and whalers, displeased in part by the new discouragement of prostitution, complained that "religion is cramm'd down the throats of these poor simple mortals while certain famine and destruction are staring them in the face." Indeed, the Hawaiian population was in the midst of a precipitous decline in this era, a result of exposure to European and American diseases.[3] In these decades, Protestant ministers also tentatively entered Latin America, though because of restrictive laws, they did not proselytize among Catholics but served the growing population of Protestant foreigners in the region. Latter-day Saints had first contemplated mission work in South America in the early 1840s, even designating Joseph Ball to go to the continent in 1841, though he did not fulfill the mission.[4]

Mormon missionaries' operations were different from those of their Protestant contemporaries in the Pacific. Unlike Protestants, American Mormons had a relationship of animosity with their own government, ensuring problems with federal government officials and negative press. The complexities of imperial politics, however, meant that the Mormon tensions with the U.S. government could also prove attractive to native peoples. The Mormon doctrine that converts gather to Utah also distinguished their efforts, as did their sacralization of many native peoples of the Pacific, whom they saw as descendants of the Book of Mormon civilizations.[5]

Mormon attention on the Pacific coast slightly predated the Gold Rush. Led by Samuel Brannan, more than two hundred Mormons arrived in San Francisco in 1846 from New York on the ship *Brooklyn*, and some former members of the Mormon Battalion joined them in 1847.[6] The Gold Rush accelerated Mormon interest in the region. In March 1849, Pratt offered, at Young's suggestion, to go "to the Islands or to Chili with a view to establish the Gospel in South America, Australia, New Zealand, China, Japan, [and] the various groups of the Pacific Islands."[7] Pratt subsequently began to study Spanish.[8] In 1851, Young also commissioned apostles Charles C. Rich and Amasa Lyman to supervise a settlement in San Bernardino in southern California to serve as a Mormon outlet to the Pacific Ocean and as a gathering place in a temperate climate for converts from the Pacific islands.[9] Young envisioned a string of Mormon settlements that eventually would stretch from locations scouted by the southern Utah expedition to sites in California. California would also be a source of tithing in cash, which might alleviate the

Church's "heavy" debts and the Salt Lake Valley's "scarcity of cash."[10] In early 1851, Young called Pratt to preside over the Pacific mission and personally visit Chile; he also designated seven missionaries to accompany Pratt to northern California and then continue on to their own fields of labor in Hawaii, Australia, and Chile.

On March 16, 1851, Pratt left Salt Lake City along with two wives, Elizabeth Brotherton and Phoebe Soper, and the missionaries (as well as wives of three missionaries and infants of two).[11] The poor health and childlessness of both Elizabeth and Phoebe (whose infant son, Mosiah, had died the previous year) contributed to the decision for them to accompany Parley to California. Phoebe commented that San Bernardino had "a lovely climate, warm and very healthy.... As my health is not good I am advised to go."[12]

Pratt left the rest of his family in an unfinished home and in a precarious financial position—as usual. The five wives who remained in Utah headed a household that included a multitude of children: Parley Jr., now thirteen; Pratt's niece Jane (fifteen) and nephew Joseph (twelve), who had been orphaned when Parley's brother Anson died of cholera in 1849; and ten children under the age of six. At least four of these wives, and perhaps the fifth, were pregnant. On June 9, Belinda gave birth to her fourth child, Lehi. On October 26, Hannahette gave birth to her third child, Henrietta. Three weeks later, on November 15, Sarah's son Teancum, her third child, was born. Agatha's third daughter, Marion, arrived later that month, on November 28. While the first three of the 1851 babies survived to maturity, Marion died on October 6, 1852, a few weeks prior to her father's arrival back home, of "Disease of the Bowels."[13] Mary was also possibly pregnant and may have miscarried. In a letter from Chile, Parley suggested naming Sarah's baby Teancum, Hannahette's Limhi, and stated, "I hope Mary and Agatha will not Send for names, till I have time to read the Book [of Mormon], because P[hoeb]e, being a little covetous wishes to retai[n so]me of the best of them against [a] time of need."[14] When he learned that Mary had either miscarried or had never been pregnant, he wrote, "Tell Mary not to be discouragd. it will be her turn next, and She shall have a great boy, as hansome as a picture, and the verry Image of his father and mother."[15]

Pratt's missionary letters reflect deep concern for his family and a sharpening resentment against those Saints who would not assist them financially. Soon after he left, Pratt wrote a letter to his five wives in Utah praising their faithfulness and speaking of his abiding love. To Belinda, Parley wrote, "Let your heart be Comforted, you shall be safely Carried through every trial, and have Joy in your Children, and they will keep you So buisy that time will seem short." He asked Hannahette (or Etta, as he called her), "How do you get on in farming and raising Chickins and Children." To Sarah, he queried, "Are you as Good Looking as Ever?... Be diligent in the garden and in the house, and in the care of Julia, and kiss her for me and you will not be lonesome." To Agatha, he wrote, "Last, youngest, But not forgoten... take care of the Children, help to build and improve the premices and educate and comfort the family and you shall be blessed and not be very lonesome."[16]

Traveling toward southern Utah, Pratt re-created his role from the southern Utah expedition and spent his "time on horse back during traveling hours searching out the Recources of the Country," even carrying a large telescope to view the "vast Country before me."[17] Pratt supplemented his earlier expedition's report by describing to Young additional settlement sites throughout central and southern Utah.[18] Pratt proposed that Young establish a string of towns along the Virgin River, the Vegas springs (the future site of Las Vegas), and the Colorado River, stretching some three hundred miles southwest from Iron County. At that point, he hoped the Colorado River would be "Navagable for steamers, to the gulf of California," allowing the Mormons to "forever avoid the dessart, save two or 3 hundred miles of travel by Land between this and the Paciffic Coast, and keep free from the throng, Confusion, and Corruption of the gold mines."[19]

Pratt's missionaries and the San Bernardino emigrants reached the newly settled fort at Parowan, one of the first fruits of Pratt's earlier expedition, on April 10. Under the leadership of apostle George Smith, the first settlers had reached Parowan (also called Little Salt Lake) in January; by the time Pratt arrived, they had built a fort, held elections, laid out the city, and begun construction on homes and public buildings. It seemed "like the work of years," Pratt thought, rather than "about 2 months."[20] Smith hosted "a sumptuous repast" to celebrate Pratt's forty-fourth birthday on April 12.[21] At Parowan, Pratt added another missionary, Philo B. Wood (along with his wife), and asked William Dame to survey a 130-acre tract for him in the foothills south of Parowan, appropriate for rangeland but not farming. Pratt likely saw the acreage as a potential investment and a reward for his earlier exploration.[22]

Pratt left Parowan on April 14 and traveled south to Summit Creek, where the San Bernardino company held a conference at which several church leaders, including Pratt, urged some settlers bound for California to remain in southern Utah. Young had thought initially that twenty families would accompany Lyman and Rich, but the company had ballooned to 437 people, including many relatively prosperous Saints. Believing that many left for the wrong reasons, Young exclaimed that he was "sick at the sight of so many of the saints running off to California."[23] Pratt wrote that Smith "and Others spoke with power in the Spirit and testimony of Jesus, Rebuking Iniquity, worldly mindedness, unbelief, profanity and all manner of Iniquity and exhorting the people to Obey the Servants of the Lord."[24] Pratt also tried to dissuade those who were leaving "against the counsel of the [First] presidency," but none of the settlers seemed particularly willing to give up their California dream for what they had seen at Parowan, though nearly all of the adult men covenanted to obey the counsel of Lyman and Rich.[25]

The journey from southern Utah to Southern California, according to a historian of the overland trails, "stands as one of the most challenging in the annals of American pioneering." The four-hundred-mile route "traversed some of the most difficult desert passages ever attempted by wagon trains." Pratt's journal and letters vividly describe the difficulties encountered through southern Utah, over the Great Basin divide, and across the deserts of southern Nevada and California. The company endured long stretches between oases, scrapes with Native Americans, and the loss of many animals to exhaustion and lack of water.[26]

The route between southern Utah and the oasis of the spring and meadow at the Vegas, Pratt wrote, was a "dreary and monotonous desert; Gravel, Sand, Rocks, thorns and thistles, and a parched and dreary waste." Minor brushes with American Indians occurred on the Santa Clara and the Virgin Rivers, and in one raid Pratt lost a cow which would have "Calved in a day or two," thus depriving him and his wives of milk. They lived on "a little dried meat and Bread and a little sugar and coffee." "Many of the Camp have Milk and Butter," Pratt complained, "but Cash we have none, and love will not pass for Currency, or exchange." The inadequate provisions and the "daily labours and exposures" worsened Phoebe's and Elizabeth's health, leaving them unable "to do any portion of the domestic duties, or hardly to Crall out of the waggon without fainting."[27]

Just as troubling to Pratt as the desert heat was the spiritual apathy of the San Bernardino settlers, at least some of whom were disaffected with Utah Mormonism. Pratt painfully noted how attempts to gather for "Religious worship or instruction on Sundays" attracted few congregants. The playing of the fiddle, on the other hand, "is well attended, although I have not been to see."[28] In addition, missionary Morris Miner had a "falt finding Spirit" and requested that he be "released from the Mission" but "remain a member of the Church," which Pratt agreed to. Morris quickly left with a "set of packers...mostly profane and wicked unprincipled men," Pratt grumbled.[29]

After leaving the present site of Las Vegas (which Pratt thought could hold a settlement of a hundred to two hundred families) on May 13, the terrain became even more difficult and arid, and Pratt measured time in the "worthless dessart" between the few oases along the route, noting their arrival at Resting Springs on May 19.[30] After leaving Resting Springs, he encountered the "Lowest Hell" he had yet seen. The American Indian tribes consisted exclusively of men, Pratt wrote, as they had "bartered, sold, or gambled away" their women and children to Spanish traders or other Indians. He commented, "The beings who are left are without Natural affection, Without Caractor or morals of any kind, Without union or national feeling" who in their "beastial features...seem to resemble the Munky or the Orang Outang."[31]

Pratt's views on American Indians oscillated between his lofty hopes for them as descendants of the Book of Mormon peoples and a baser view of their nature similar to that held by many nineteenth-century Americans. Indeed, his frustration with American Indian failure to live up to his millennial expectations partly explains his interest in the natives of Latin America, which would soon turn into a new missionary initiative. The stretch after Resting Springs also proved difficult, as some of Pratt's oxen "had given out entirely,...and 15 or 20 miles still intervened between us and water, and without grass sufficient to feed a goat," including "6 or 8 miles" uphill. "This was the most trying time of all," Pratt recorded, the "hardest times I ever saw." The group traveled "without much intermission 2 days and 2 nights," and "Women and children young and old, and old men walked on foot day and night." After fervent prayer, Pratt wrote, "a Myraculous strength seemed to inspire the cattle," and they reached Bitter Springs, "saved from the Horrors of the desart" by God.[32]

The company soon arrived in the settlements of Southern California, where Pratt's first objective was to raise money to pay debts and to obtain passage for himself and the other missionaries to their fields of labor. Along with Philo Wood, he traveled ahead to Los Angeles to "purchase and send back Supplies" to sell to the San Bernardino emigrants.[33] He and the other missionaries also sold cattle, wagons, and other property.[34] The missionaries sought to renew themselves spiritually after they separated from the larger emigration group. On May 31, they conducted a prayer meeting at which they "offered themselves in Prayer, Acknowledgeing their falts and imperfections, seeking the Remission of the same, Renewing their Covenants with God, and with each other and giving thanks to Him for deliverence from the perils of the desert, and praying that God would Gratiously open the way for the further prosicution of the appointed Mission."[35]

In Los Angeles, where they arrived on June 17, the missionaries hoped to earn money "in keeping boarders, in Washing or in diging"; failing that, they would "be compelled to go up to Francisco to Seek employment till such times as we can pay our debts and obtain means to Sail to the Islands."³⁶ Pratt reported that the American residents of Los Angeles spoke to him "in a friendly manner" and "seemed much interested in the Mormon Settlement about to be made" as it would add "additional security" for the local inhabitants.³⁷ Nonetheless, Pratt scathingly wrote about the lawless nature of Southern California society and lamented that the few Mormons in the region had fallen away from the church: "On enquiry for Br So and So the answer is—Keeping a gambling house, a monte table, Cheeting, Lying, Swindleing, Swearing, Stealing, horsracing, Keeping a house of Ill fame, Living in Whordom with some abandoned female, a Squaw, a Spanish girl, or an abandoned American, Rotten with disease, the fruits of vice, or begging from one grog shop to another as a drunken Sot."³⁸

In Los Angeles, Pratt and the missionaries also attended the Catholic celebration of "Corpus Christi," which honors the Eucharist. His mission to California and Chile represented his first sustained engagement with Catholicism. At the celebration, they "witnessed, perhaps 500 people of all ages, sexes and collours, the Indian Blood prevailing." Fascinated and repelled, he described the ceremony: "In these costly Robes Every female kneeled or Sat on the filthy floor of Earth in the old church, for hours, No Seats, Carpets or spreads of any kind, While various Images were exibeted in turn and were worshiped in humble postures." The men, equally "dressed in their best, and Kneeled in a devout manner, or Stood in a reverent posture" for the services, which "lasted for hours."³⁹ While in Los Angeles, Pratt preached at public meetings, helped bury the infant child of one of the missionaries, baptized an Englishman, taught an "inteligent Gentleman from Connecticut who Recieved the word with Joy," and visited with a Latter-day Saint woman "married to an unbelieving husband, but Who still retained the Spirit of the Gospel."⁴⁰ When describing a visit with a former Baptist preacher, Pratt referred to Phoebe and Elizabeth as his "Wife and Sister," suggesting the problems of traveling with two plural wives in an era before Mormons' official acknowledgment of polygamy.⁴¹ After traveling to San Pedro, they sailed for San Francisco on July 7, arriving after "four days rather rough passage."⁴²

In San Francisco, Pratt found a thriving city that bore little resemblance to the former village of Yerba Buena, which at the time of the discovery of gold possessed a substantial Mormon population.⁴³ During the Gold Rush, San Francisco quickly became one of the most cosmopolitan cities in the world as argonauts poured in not only from the United States, but from Europe, South America, Asia, and Australia. Pratt noted that in San Francisco, he heard Chinese, Spanish, French, German, and "almost every other language" and associated "with people from every one of the remotest corners of earth."[44] Before the Gold Rush, only about fourteen thousand non-Indians, mostly Californios, resided in California. By 1852, however, California had 255,000 residents, which increased to 380,000 by 1860, 40 percent of whom were foreign born.[45] San Francisco—which experienced a proportional boom, growing from one thousand residents in 1848 to thirty-four thousand in 1852 to about fifty thousand in 1856—served as the economic, intellectual, and religious center of this demographic explosion.[46] Pratt wrote, "We find a great city here and perhaps one thousand vessels in port, a more Central point for spreading the Gospel, and communicating with all nations I have not found."[47]

Of particular interest to Pratt, tens of thousands of Chileans, mostly miners but also many experienced merchants, joined the Gold Rush between 1848 and 1852. The fierce competition for gold claims sparked racial and ethnic animosity, much of it directed against Chileans, whose prior mining experience in Chile made them among the more successful gold seekers. In 1849, Persifer Smith, the U.S. military commander of California, issued a proclamation banning foreigners from mining for gold. This prohibition, combined with resentment against the Chileans' success, prompted widespread vigilantism against them. As American miners forced Chileans off of their claims, many Chileans fled the mining areas for the relative safety of urban San Francisco. In July 1849, riots against Chileans, especially targeting prosperous merchants, raged in San Francisco. Violence against Chilean miners and appropriation of their mining claims by legal means continued over the next few years. These actions enriched many American miners but threatened the entire state, which relied heavily on food from Chile, by jeopardizing trade relations.[48] In 1851, a Vigilance Committee, led in part by Mormon Samuel Brannan, took extralegal actions, including hanging four men and deporting others, to defend Chilean merchants and miners, protecting them in San Francisco but not in the gold mining camps. By Pratt's arrival, many Chileans had returned to their country with stories of American depredations.[49]

The concentration of single young men, weak government institutions, and the presence and prospect of easy money led to a culture in which violence, gambling, and prostitution flourished. Missionary John Murdock noted, "The state of society here is very bad theving robing Murdering

Drinking Gambling Whoring Burning and Debauchery of every kind is the most common character of the place."[50] Another Mormon missionary described northern California's "depraved condition of society," charging that in Sacramento "gambling and carousing is the chief pursuit of the male sex" and "there are scarcely a dozen virtuous women in the City."[51]

Religious societies relished the conspicuous need for soul saving, and Protestants, Catholics, Jews, and Spiritualists staked their spiritual claims. In this highly fragmented society, no single religion attained majority status, a fact particularly lamented by evangelical Protestant missionaries seeking to re-create the culture of the eastern United States.[52] As a result, minority groups such as Mormons and Catholics, while not unopposed, were tolerated more in San Francisco than in the East.[53] Mormonism even attracted favorable notice in the San Francisco press. Pratt wrote, "The people here and Every where are geting unbounded Confidence in 'Mormon Government,' 'Mormon Industry,' 'Mormon Enterprise.' "[54]

Following his arrival in San Francisco, Pratt plunged into preaching, holding public meetings at the Adelphi Theater and in the homes of local Mormons, seeking both to reclaim lapsed Mormons and to attract converts.[55] He and the other missionaries rebaptized many of the *Brooklyn* Saints, some of whom Pratt had known in the East, including both those who had "fallen into transgression" and those who wished to rededicate themselves to Mormonism. They also baptized "several new members," including the children of *Brooklyn* Saints and "strangers from different countries."[56] He wrote home, "The spirit has been poured upon me greatly in this place. We have a good little branch here of more than 50 members. We add to it by baptism almost every week."[57] For instance, Pratt visited the home of Caroline Augusta Perkins Joyce, one of the *Brooklyn* Saints, who had loaned a copy of the Book of Mormon to Colonel Alden A. M. Jackson, a veteran of the Mexican-American War. After talking with Pratt through the night, both Joyce and Jackson accepted his invitation to be baptized. Joyce stated, "Ten years ago last night I was baptized in the Atlantic at midnight; to-morrow I will be baptized in the Pacific." Jackson and Joyce later married and moved to Utah.[58]

Pratt also presided at a meeting which disfellowshipped the flamboyant Brannan, whom Pratt had earlier saved from excommunication and whose entrepreneurial talents were quickly making him the richest man in California. The meeting unanimously endorsed cutting Brannan off from the church "for a general course of unchristianlike conduct, neglect of duty," and, in a reference to the Vigilance Committee, "for combining with lawless assemblies to committ murder and other crimes."[59] Pratt commented to Agatha, "S. Brannan is never seen among us. He is any thing but a man of God."[60]

Mormons in the area were concentrated in San Francisco and in San Jose, where John M. Horner, one of the *Brooklyn* Saints, had made a fortune selling vegetables and other crops to gold miners. In August, Pratt crossed the bay to San Jose to meet with Horner and the Saints who had congregated in that region.[61] The following year, Pratt reported that the San Jose branch had "30 members or more generally in good standing" and that the San Francisco branch had "30 or 40 members all in good standing."[62] Pratt also continued his writing, working on a new manuscript he ambitiously titled "Key to the Science of Universal Theology."[63]

Besides "making some noise" in San Francisco, Pratt was anxious to send the missionaries to their fields of labor. While he expected the imminent departure of those headed for the Sandwich Islands, the other missionaries were experiencing financial difficulties and were working to raise money for their passage. William Perkins and Rufus Allen had "been Compelled to go to the mines," where Allen earned $100 per month. Philo Wood found employment "superintending a vegitable depot" for Horner on the Sacramento River to "obtain means for Our South American Mission." John Murdock was "out of Cash to go further," as was Pratt, who was also struggling to repay a debt of $500 he had left behind in Utah. Within the next month, Pratt found a way to serve his God and his creditors both; he "baptised a man and Borrowed five hundred dollers of him."[64] Before his departure for Chile, Pratt raised an additional $1,435 from California members, including $500 from Horner, $240 of it in "Gold Coin" which he sent home to help his family, and $400 from Barton and Rhanaldo Mowry, *Brooklyn* Saints.[65] The financial demands placed upon the northern California Saints were substantial, as Lyman and Rich visited San Francisco in July seeking funds for their San Bernardino settlement, which had been purchased for $77,500 with Gold Rush interest of 3 percent a month.[66]

From his base in San Francisco, Pratt launched a missionary initiative among "all the Islands and Coasts of the Pacific." Readers of Pratt's autobiography see in him the zealous convert, the feisty pamphleteer, the jokester who outsmarts bulldogs. This phase of his life adds a new dimension to that portrait. Just as he saw himself in the midst of a dramatic—and rapid—unfolding of premillennialist history in the 1830s and 1840s, he viewed the supervision of this new pan-Pacific work as the next great phase in kingdom building, and one in which he again would play a pivotal role. One senses in his urgency a tremulous, anxious excitement to get the ball rolling and cover the vast stretches of the earth now placed under his stewardship. In July, he wrote Addison Pratt (no relation), a former whaler who served Mormon missions in the Society Islands (a French protectorate including Tahiti) from 1843 to 1847 and from 1850 to 1852, and urged him to "push the gospel to every people as fast as possible."[67] By July 1851, the French government was imposing new restrictions on Protestant and Mormon missionaries, and Addison Pratt sent fellow missionary Thomas Tompkins to California to "collect means for our sustinance here as the French had forbid us receiving any directly from the native brethren, unless we paid them for it."[68] Pratt's discussion with Tompkins convinced him to not send more missionaries there due to "french Oppression and Misrule."[69] In 1852, the French government expelled the remaining Mormon missionaries, leaving behind between fifteen hundred and two thousand local Tahitian members.[70]

As restrictions increased in the Society Islands, Mormon missionaries turned their attention in Polynesia to the Sandwich Islands, where the government appeared more accommodating.[71] Ten missionaries had arrived in Oahu in December 1850, though half quickly left their mission and returned home. Those who remained gradually began to acquire the Hawaiian language and to find success among native Hawaiians. Three of the missionaries who accompanied Pratt to California—Philip B. Lewis, Francis A. Hammond, and John S. Woodbury—arrived in Hawaii in August, carrying a letter of introduction from Pratt to King Kamehameha.[72] Soon after, one of the original missionaries, George Q. Cannon, wrote Pratt, "Upon these lands I think the work will be a mighty one." Already, nearly two hundred Hawaiians had joined the church, and the missionaries had "demands for preaching upon almost all hands."[73] "Many natives are holding back," Hammond, a former sailor who had earlier lived in Hawaii, reported to Pratt, to see "what he [the king] will do with" the growth of Mormonism.[74] Nevertheless, Hammond noted deep interest among the "natives, & some among the foreigners." While in Chile, Pratt would receive "several letters" from missionary leaders in the Sandwich Islands. He wrote his family, "They are doing wonders there Having Baptised hundreds of the natives and some of the whites."[75] By 1854, four thousand Hawaiians had converted to Mormonism, and the Book of Mormon was published in Hawaiian the following year.[76]

Though some Mormons had preached in Australia in the 1840s, Pratt launched the church's official work there by sending John Murdock, whom he had baptized in 1830, and Charles W. Wandell. Murdock had been called to a mission in Australia by Young and had accompanied Pratt to California. In San Francisco, they rebaptized Wandell, a lapsed Mormon, who had been "in sorrow and in a backward State as to faith and righteousness."[77] Pratt assigned Wandell to accompany Murdock, and he wrote *Proclamation! To the People of the Coasts and Islands of the Pacific of Every Nation, Kindred and Tongue* to publish when they arrived. Pratt expected the proclamation would eventually "be translated and published by especial messengers, in due time, in every language and tongue included within the bounds of the Mission."[78]

Emphasizing familiar themes of restoration, authority, and spiritual gifts, Pratt's proclamation announced the arrival of a "New Dispensation, *a new Apostolic Commission.*" In separate sections, he made targeted appeals to pious Christians (including the "sincere, zealous, and devoted missionaries" of other denominations in the Pacific), wicked and wayward Christians, pagans, Jews, and the "red men of the forest" of Latin America. In this last category, he encouraged indigenous Latin Americans to accept their Book of Mormon heritage and explore the "prophetic telescope of that book." The Book of Mormon, he promised, "will soon be published among you in English, in Spanish, and in every written language in use among your various tribes and tongues," and missionaries would arrive to "read, recite, and interpret the contents." Perhaps thinking of the problems with French officials in the Society Islands, Pratt assured government officials that missionaries would not "intermeddle with the civil, political, or domestic institutions, established by law," except if they clashed with "liberty of conscience" or the "commandments of Jesus Christ."[79]

Carrying Pratt's proclamation, Murdock and Wandell sailed for Australia a few days after Pratt left for Chile. The day after their arrival, they contracted with a printer to publish two thousand copies of Pratt's *Proclamation*, making it the first Mormon work published outside of Europe and North America. Pratt's reach as the premier pamphleteer of Mormonism was now worldwide. (The pamphlet later appeared in the *Millennial Star* as well as in editions in Scandinavia, France, and partially in India.)[80] Murdock and Wandell arrived in Australia during a gold rush there; Murdock complained to Pratt (in a letter from Sydney to Valparaíso) that Melbourne was "nearly destitute of mail [male] inhabitance" as a result. Nevertheless, they succeeded in creating a small branch in Sydney. Murdock left Australia in June 1852, and Wandell remained until the following April, when he sailed for California with a group of emigrating Saints.[81]

As he coordinated missionary work throughout the Pacific, Pratt prepared to sail for Chile. He initially hoped first to "go to N. Y. per steamer, to print a book," possibly *Key to the Science of Theology*, but he apparently could not raise money for the trip.[82] In any case, he would continue working away at the manuscript for the next few years. Meanwhile, he continued "studying Spanish with all diligence," hoping to "master it in the course of a few months."[83] Pratt probably chose Chile because of political problems in Mexico and Central America, as well as his belief that the Book of Mormon prophet Lehi had landed in Chile, a supposition that some early Mormons attributed to Joseph Smith and which Pratt stated as fact in his *Proclamation* to the Pacific and his *Key to the Science of Theology*.[84] The recent Mexican-American War, including the well-known participation by the Mormon Battalion, made Mexico an unlikely target. Political chaos in Central America, combined with negative reports from Americans who had traveled through the isthmus of Panama, rendered that region unattractive. In South America, three nations—Colombia, Peru, and Chile—bordered the Pacific coast and thus were part of Pratt's jurisdiction.[85] Colombia lacked port facilities, and Pratt opted for Chile rather than Peru, to his later regret, likely because of his belief about Lehi's landing.

In addition, Pratt likely interacted with Chileans in San Francisco and other California Mormons who had some experience with Chile. The *Brooklyn* Saints had intended to stop at Valparaíso on their way to California, but a storm forced them instead to the island of Juan Fernandez, 360 miles off the coast of Chile; one of the *Brooklyn* Mormons, Origin Mowry, had visited Chile in 1848 to buy produce to sell to the miners in California and likely gave Pratt firsthand insight into the country.[86] While Pratt demonstrated no doubts about sailing to Chile, Brigham Young may have been ambivalent about Pratt's plans. After Pratt left, the First Presidency wrote, "You are at liberty to remain on the Coast, or in California, at present; and send missionaries, where you will, unless the Spirit shall *press* you to go."[87]

For Pratt, the mission represented a continuation of his fascination with indigenous peoples that predated his conversion to Mormonism. He connected his Chilean mission to his youthful immersion in Book of Mormon prophecies, particularly concerning the restoration of the descendants of Lehi. Subsequent to his return from Chile, he recalled that after his conversion in 1830, "I began to look into geography more fully and into history travels and into every thing that would give me any information on this great land of promises and of its several nations." Within the United States, Pratt concluded, "there was only a few scattered remnants," only a "mere handful," and those were in the "last stages of debauchery [and] disease brought on them by wicked white people." Pratt then cast his gaze toward Spanish America, where the inhabitants were Spanish "in name, in language, in geography, in history, in religion," but the "great mass" of them were "in countenance, in color, in language, the sons and daughters of Lehi and the other people of the Jews." "They are in fact," he declared, "Lamanites," though they varied from "pure blood of Lamanites" to "all the stages of European blood."[88] In a letter to fellow apostle Franklin D. Richards, he calculated that of the forty million inhabitants of Latin America, "more than two-thirds" descended from Lehi.[89]

Accompanied by Phoebe (Elizabeth remained in California) and Rufus Allen, Pratt departed San Francisco on September 5, taking economical passage on the *Henry Kelsey*, a small cargo ship without passenger accommodations.[90] Allen, who turned twenty-four the next month, had been a member of the Mormon Battalion, the southern Utah expedition, and helped construct Pratt's Golden Pass.[91] Pratt characterized their sixty-four-day passage as "most tedious and disagreeable." Their "miser for a captain," he complained, would not allow the steward "to cook potatoes, bread, pies, puddings, or any other holesome or palitable food; but keeps us on mouldy, hard bread full of bugs and worms; and on salt beef and pork, the pork being rotten. He has flour, potatoes and good pork in plenty, but will not allow it to be used." The passage was particularly difficult for Phoebe, then in an advanced stage of pregnancy; Parley worried that she "eats but little, vommets continually, and is getting verry poor in flesh." In October, off the coast of Peru, they were nearly shipwrecked, but after "much labour we got under weigh [way] and stood again to sea." The Pratts and Allen planned to pass their time on the ship by studying Spanish. Pratt confidently if condescendingly commented, "It is a beautiful Language and wonderfully adapted to the simplisity of the Lamanites. I hope to master it during the passage and a few months residence among the Chilanos." However, after a month on board, Pratt wrote, "We have not been able to read, write or studdy much."[92]

While traveling, Pratt's thoughts often turned to his family; he had not received letters from them since his departure from Utah. He wrote home to his family in Utah: "O how lonesome! Just imagine the monotony Sky and Sea!—Sea and Sky!—Night and day!—Day and night!—Infinitude of space!—Boundless waste!—Emblem of eternal silence!—Eternal banishment!—Eternal loneliness...Where the holy music of childrens voices in Joyous merryment falls not on the ear." He often prayed for each wife, child, and "dear friend...He calls each by name, over and over again before the altar of remembrance. When this is done for all on earth he remembers those in heaven:—calls their names:—communes with them in spirit.—wonders how they are doing! whether they think of him!"[93]

Soon after arriving in Valparaíso on November 8, Pratt was gratified to receive seven letters from his family, one from Elizabeth in California and the others from his wives and Parley Jr. in Utah, which he and Phoebe anxiously read "three or four ti[mes] over." In a letter to his wives and children, Parley praised Sarah's letter as "excelent and well writen, She has improved much in Education and in Spirit." Parley Jr.'s letter was "good, and gave me much joy in recieving a first Letter from a son." To Mary Wood, who had written an "excellent" though short letter, Parley wrote that he had dreamed of her: "O Could I get my mouth as near her lips as I did in a dream, I would immediately snatch one good Long hearty kiss, Lest in stoping to smile into her eye I should awake with my mouth within about an inch of hers and go without a kiss as I did in my dream." He had also "dreamed of seeing" Belinda "several times but she would not speak freely, for her soul was vexed, and I knew not the cause. But the Last time I saw her she was seting in my lap with her arms around my neck in a meak and humble spirit and she said: 'comfort me.' And I did comfort her, with kind words while I enfolded her in my arms and pressed her to my heart." Agatha's letter "was Like yourself, all Love and affection for me." He wrote,

> I sometimes think, and I am now inclined to believe that our father in heaven never associated in this Lower world of fallen nature, spirits more conjenial, Lovely and happy in each other, than we are as a family. Nor do I believe that a greater Lot of hapiness ever fell to the Lot of mortals than we have, and do enjoy. Others have had riches, Luxuries, and the pleasures of the world, with the honors thereof. But we have learned to endure poverty with cheerfulness, and affliction and crosses with joy. And in these circumstances we have learned to love, and bear with each other, till we feel a union, which links us to each other and with all good beings.[94]

Parley's family letters provide a rare and vivid window into the complicated dynamics of plural marriage. While Parley sometimes wrote and received love letters to and from individual wives, he also included intimate expressions of love and physical longing (such as in his comments to Mary) in family letters, suggesting that he did not consider these relationships essentially private.

A few months later, Pratt received the discouraging news that his wives had been unable to borrow money to finish their home. Pratt condemned those who did not share with his family and promised his wives eternal, if not temporal, blessings. He wrote, "I am glad from the bottom of my heart that you cannot get in debt. Not that I am glad that men a[r]e faithless, and afraid to do good, not that I want you to suffer. But, I am glad to prove men, for that

is part of my calling, as I expect also to Judge some of them." Pratt often displayed an Old Testament sternness of character, an affinity for the God of
justice more than the God of mercy, which erupted in conflicts with enemies
of the faith and in frustration with colleagues in the faith. Nevertheless, he
wrote encouragingly to his family, "Be of good cheer, I have suffered poverty
much longer than any of you. Nor do I expect to find the end of Poverty and
want this side of the grave. If the Lord gives us something to eat we will not
much covet Buildings nor furniture nor fine close [clothes]. for we are
strangers and pilgrims." He would finish the house when he returned "and do
it tolerably well." He further promised his family, "The god who has sustained
us thus far will still be the *one* to *care* for my family and will be a good *father*
to my children and will make Nations of them, even if I were to be swallowed
in the sea or dye on the Desart. But I expect to Live and to see them again."[95]

In Valparaíso, Pratt found a vibrant and cosmopolitan city, the busiest
Pacific port in the Americas and the main stopping point for U.S. and
European ships sailing around Cape Horn for California. Of the city's
population of around thirty thousand, a third were foreign. The cosmopolitan mix supported an English newspaper, a Church of England, and a
Protestant Union congregation.[96] Pratt and his fellow missionary and wife
initially stayed at a "Hotel 'de France'" in Valparaíso where they had "a great
variety of good eating, and a front parlour to ourselves" at the cost of $4 a day.
Pratt commented, "The proprietor speaks french, the Bar tender french and a
few words of broken english: the landlady German, and the waiter Spanish.
ourselves speak English with a little Spanish, so you see we have a little babel
of our own." They soon purchased furniture and rented a one-room house.
Pratt painted an idyllic portrait of their initial time in Chile. The rented
home, in a tidy, middle-class section of town, was surrounded "with beautiful
trees, such as orrange, fig, peach, Pear, etc., togather with roses, pinks, and a
variety of flowers and srubs [shrubs]." He found their landlord and neighbors
"kind and sociable," and they lent the missionaries "tables, stands, Cooking
utensils, flat Irons, etc." He noted, "We divide our time between reading, and
studying our Spanish Lessons, and chatting, visiting, reading Spanish, hearing
them read, etc., and playing with the Little ones."[97]

Signaling his hopes for missionary work in Chile, Pratt asked in a
November letter to Franklin D. Richards of the British mission for a shipment of Books of Mormon and a subscription to the *Millennial Star*. Of their
progress in Spanish, Pratt wrote, "We are already beginning to understand
and speak it a very little. We also read and partly comprehend the Spanish
prints and Bible." Within a "year or two," Pratt hoped to translate "the Book

of Mormon in their own liquid '*Lengua*' if the Lord will." Pratt expected Philo Wood to sail for Chile soon and, in a letter to Amasa Lyman, suggested that he would remain in Chile for up to two years, admitting it might take that long to master the language.[98]

Pratt's attempts to preach Mormonism in Chile, however, were foiled by an inflationary economy, anti-American sentiment, civil unrest, and the religious restrictions of a Catholic nation. The voracious California demand for grains, fruits, and vegetables led to a boom in Chilean agriculture but also caused prices to soar. Their presence in a foreign country where they spoke little of the native language rendered the usual mode of missionary travel—without purse or scrip—impossible, and their inability with the language made finding temporary employment, another common missionary tactic, improbable as well.[99] Pratt wrote, "There has been no employment for neither of us. We have picked up gold and silver coin in the street, but even that is becoming scarce, and is now poor picking."[100]

The missionaries arrived in Chile during a period of intense civil conflict between the conservative regime and liberal dissidents. Ever since Chile gained independence from Spain in 1818, political tensions had simmered between conservatives, who desired independence but few other social or economic changes, and liberals who supported broader structural reforms. After elections in the summer of 1851 reinforced conservatives' power, liberals charged electoral fraud and, in September, revolted against the government. According to Pratt, the liberals fought for "Universal Suffrage, and absolute Liberty of Concience, of the press, and of Speach. The mass are warm Revolutionists, but they hate to fight." While the Pratts were in Valparaíso, conservative forces won a major victory against the liberals in southern Chile on December 8 at Barros Negros, in which approximately eighteen hundred soldiers died. Hostilities in northern Chile ended at La Serena on December 31, but a rebellion at a penal colony in the Magellan Straits extended the climate of civil unrest until early spring.[101] Even after the war ended, Pratt reported, "the people are sanguine in their hopes and purposes to accomplish their Liberties in the course of a few years. they are by no means crushed, or broken in their feelings on the subject." Though the actual battles raged outside of the area where the Pratts and Allen lived, they perceived that the civil war had impeded their progress. As a zealous partisan of freedom, Pratt felt profound sympathies with the liberals and saw developments as part of a providential plan.[102]

In addition, Pratt arrived at a particularly rocky moment in the relationship between the United States and Chile. The Gold Rush increased economic and cultural ties between the nations but exacerbated tensions. While California's prosperity stimulated the Chilean economy, it created problems for the country's shipping industry. More than half of Chile's commercial ships were essentially stuck in California when their crews abandoned them for the gold fields, distressing Chilean legislators and allowing foreign ships to capture a share of the Chilean market.[103] News of the mistreatment of Chileans in California, emphatically emphasized by returning miners, embittered Chileans. Seth Barton, the divorced and Protestant American ambassador to Chile from 1847 to 1849, had also infuriated the local Catholic hierarchy when he married a Chilean. The mutual recriminations between Barton and Chilean religious and governmental elites further damaged relations before Pratt's mission.[104] In addition, a commercial treaty between the United States and Chile ended in January 1850, leading American officials to demand that Chilean ships in California pay higher duties, further creating ill will.[105]

Finally, for the first time in his years of missionary labors, Pratt found himself in a Catholic nation with limited religious liberty. While some Chilean liberals advocated religious toleration, the Chilean constitution, like the constitutions of almost all Latin American nations of the era, declared Catholicism the state religion and denied freedom of worship to other denominations, including the right to publish religious literature and hold services. The Chilean government by this time tolerated Protestant churches that catered to foreigners and did not seek Chilean converts, but religious freedom was not guaranteed until the Chilean constitution of 1925. David Trumbull, an American Protestant minister who arrived in Valparaíso in 1845 and remained until his death in 1889, informed Pratt "there was no difficulty in landing religious books and papers, and circulating the same, although the press is not free to print or publish any Religion but the Catholic."[106] Nevertheless, restrictions frustrated Pratt and precluded his normal missionary tactics of publishing tracts and holding public meetings.[107] Pratt believed that the indigenous population of the Americas had been forced into Catholicism by the conquistadors, whom he saw as having about "as much motives of Christianity in their hearts" as did those engaged in the "California gold digging." For the past "3 hundred years the original Lamanites of Mexico Peru and Chile" had "groaned under the oppression of Spanish yoke."[108]

Nineteenth-century Protestant authors often saw Catholics and Mormons alike as un-American because of their perceived bloc voting, politically ambitious clergy, secret and sinister rituals, reliance on immigrants, and the exploitation of women in convents and polygamy. Nevertheless, Mormons like Pratt from the church's earliest days described Catholicism in language nearly indistinguishable from that used by Protestant America.[109] Largely drawn from the ranks of disaffected Protestants, early Mormon converts lived in a world inundated with anti-Catholicism, promulgated by sources as diverse as John Foxe's *Book of Martyrs* and lurid contemporary best-sellers depicting priests' unparalleled appetite for political power and sex. Since the Reformation, Protestants had associated the Catholic Church with the imagery in Revelation of "Babylon the Great, the Mother of Harlots and Abominations of the Earth."[110] The Book of Mormon contains similar statements about the whore of Babylon, which early Mormons identified as Catholicism, including a prophecy of a millennial battle between the "mother of abominations" and the Saints of God.[111] The narrative of Mormon sacred history, particularly of the "Great Apostasy" in which corrupt Catholicism replaced the primitive Christian Church, further reinforced early Mormons' anti-Catholic tendencies.[112] Pratt and early Latter-day Saints thus viewed Catholicism as a unique evil.

In January, Pratt wrote a pamphlet that summarized his disagreements with Catholicism and explicitly equated it with the biblical whore of Babylon. Titled *Proclamacion! Extraordinaria, para los Americanos Espanoles,* or *Proclamation Extraordinary! To the Spanish Americans*, the sixteen-page pamphlet contains Spanish and English text side by side and was published after his return to San Francisco.[113] In the pamphlet, Pratt discussed John's dream of the "mother of harlots and abominations of the earth," which he confidently identified as "the city of Rome; and the mystery of her religion." While praising the South American revolutions for independence, Pratt declared that "the work of freedom is far from complete. You have retained 'Mystery Babylon,' sustained her Priests by millions from the public treasuries." He encouraged Latin Americans to ensure freedom of religion, speech, and press, and to adopt separation of church and state and a system of public education, reforms that, he believed, would prepare the way for the acceptance of Mormonism. Pratt also reaffirmed his view that Latin Americans were descendants of the Book of Mormon civilizations: "Spanish Americans! a vast majority of you are the descendants of the ancient race of the Mexicans, Peruvians, Chilena and other nation of original Americans. The origin of that entire race is now revealed by Angels, and by the discovery and translation of their *ancient records*."[114]

The *Proclamacion* reveals Pratt's difficulty with Spanish. The pamphlet's first eight pages were competently translated by someone other than Pratt, but the quality of the translation then "drops dramatically to the level of a beginning student."[115] Nevertheless, Pratt worked incessantly to improve his language skills and "soon became able to read [Spanish] with a degree of understanding." During his mission, he "read nearly through the Spanish testament" and copied "in writing many of its most important passages," memorizing several. Pratt also read secular works, including Chilean, Argentine, and Peruvian newspapers and a history of Chile.[116] By January, Pratt wrote, "We Cannot yet understand general conversation. But we are able to converse in simple sentences, spoken slowly, and with care. We also recognise many words when they talk fast, and sometimes get the run of their subjects." Pratt even read from the Bible to illiterate Chileans in his imperfect Spanish.[117] The next month, he sent Agatha his "first effort to write to any person in Spanish," promising to "translate it for you when I return": "Yo amo V. con todo mi corazo y con toda mi alma. Yo he conocido V. por muchos anos. V. ha ido siempre un amiga a me en verdad. Si V esta cerca yo quiero dar V. un Besita." ("I love you with all my heart and with all my soul. I have known you for many years. You have always been a true friend to me. If you were near I would give you a kiss.")[118]

On November 30, three weeks after their arrival in Chile, Phoebe gave birth to a son, Omner. According to Phoebe's great-granddaughter, who had access to family letters no longer available, "No doctor could be found when her labor started, and two native women acted as midwives. Since Phoebe was making no headway with her pains the two women lifted her by the armpits and shook her violently up and down until they literally shook the baby into the world. Such treatment not only permanently weakened Phoebe but injured the baby."[119] Over the next thirty-eight days, the baby "pined away and finally died" of "consumption" on January 7 and was buried in the "Protestant Burying Grounds" in Valparaíso.[120] Pratt wrote, "He was a beautiful Child.... During all the s[c]enes of his birth, life, death, and burial no female friend was near except his mother, except strangers who knew not our language.... His mother is in her usual health, or, rather better than, in years past."[121]

Two weeks after they buried Omner, concerned for Phoebe's health and frustrated by the high costs of Valparaíso, the Pratts and Allen moved to Quillota, a small town forty miles northeast on the route between Santiago and Valparaíso. Pratt described the city as situated in a "large well watered, well cultivated valey: with streets, caves, farms, Water ditches, shady groves of tall poplar, Gardens, vinyards, and orchards, with fruit of every variety." They rented a house, including "fuel and all expences" for between "75 cents and one dollar a day," in the hills surrounding the city and lived with a "widow Woman and her two daughters"; Pratt and Allen daily went up a nearby hill "at sundown, or, in the twilight of early evening, to pray for all our friends, and for Zion." From Quillota, Pratt wrote Agatha that he was "verry well, and as fat as you ever saw me in England. I live mostly on ripe figs, which with other causes will, I hope remove that bilious costiveness [constipation] which has troubled me for so many years."[122]

Though impressed by Quillota, Pratt looked longingly toward Peru, which he learned had recently guaranteed freedom of religion, press, and speech and allowed non-Catholic churches to conduct marriages and burials. By allowing these freedoms, the Peruvians had "enraged the pope of Rome," which delighted Pratt.[123] The Peruvian government also had signed a "special treaty with Great Britain, in which all these Liberties are guaranteed to british subjects in Peru," a significant enticement to sending British Mormon missionaries there. Pratt excitedly noted the writings of Francisco de Paula González Vigil, a Peruvian liberal who "came out against the pope in the Colums of the public print" for interfering in government affairs.[124] Pratt thought, "All these things go to show that the press and the mind is begining to exert its freedom in the countries where for 3 centuries all intelect has slept and all freedom of thought been crushed—buried, under the incubus of the Horid institutions of the Great mother of Abominations." If Peru guaranteed religious liberty, he wrote, "a field is opened in the heart of Spanish America, and in its largest, best informed and most influencial city and Nation for the Bible, the Book of Mormon, the fulness of the gospel to be introduced." Pratt hoped to visit Peru, "but an empty purse, an imperfect tongue...togather with the want of Books, or the means to print them," made that impossible.[125]

Pratt's attempts at proselytism in Chile were more anti-Catholic than pro-Mormon. He talked about Mormonism sparingly, having "generally felt to hold my peace, till I can talk fluently, and understand their replies." Perhaps the response of the "first Chilana" to whom he "explained our manner of Baptism" discouraged him, as she "actually Laughed herself into histerics." An educated Jewish refugee from Hungary expressed more interest, Pratt reported. "He has read the Book of Mormon, and preaches it in German, Spanish and English" and talked of "Coming to the valey, But He has not faith enough to repent and be Baptised."[126] Pratt found more interest when he commiserated with Chileans about the "abominations of their Priests, who openly administer all the Ordinances, for money." Even "remission of sins," wrote a disgusted Pratt, could be purchased, for "25 cents up to probably hundreds of dollars adapted to all classes and conditions that all might have it within their reach." Pratt built common ground with the Chileans, who were eager to talk with an American once he learned "a little broken Spanish," by emphasizing how he believed in "purgatory," a "middle place, a prison place of departed spirits," while Protestants preached a sharp dichotomy of heaven or hell. Otherwise, he did little to temper his fierce denunciation of "abominable" practices, like purchasing the release of a spirit from purgatory, infant baptism, and a celibate and paid clergy.[127]

His reaction to the Chilean culture was similarly mixed. He found the country a "hundred years behind the empires, nations of America and Europe in arts, sciences, institutions." And the people's sexual openness shocked him: "Educated females ask us the english, or tell us the Spanish names of things that are never named in the family circle, or between the sexes in other countries." More positively, he wrote that Chileans had "many good traits of caracter," being a "sociable, kind, peacible and affectionate people." Though some Chilean customs puzzled or repelled Pratt, he found their practice of spending "the evening siting, or standing in groops outside of their doors" to engage in "social and lively conversation" as "pleasingly sociable."[128]

Frustrated by the political, religious, social, and economic obstacles, Pratt decided further efforts were vain. With Allen and Phoebe, Pratt returned to Valparaíso in late February and on March 2 embarked for California on the *Dracut*, advertised as a "fine fast sailing American brig."[129] The principal cause of their early departure, Pratt admitted, was their lack of "sufficient [knowledge] of the Language to turn the keys of the gospel as yet to those nations," though they had "sought and prayed diligently for our way to open." While on the ship, Pratt reflected on his Chilean mission and the future of Mormonism in Latin America in a letter to Brigham Young. He described his mission as having been "devoted by us to the Study of the Spanish language, and the Laws, Constitutions, Geography, History, Caractor, Religion, Manners, Customs, revolutions and events of Chile and peru in particular and of Spanish America in general." Fact-finding, not proselytism, had occupied their time. Notwithstanding his setbacks, Pratt advocated sending more missionaries to Latin America, as ongoing developments, like the expansion of religious liberty in Peru, would make the work more fruitful. Since in his mind the vast majority of Latin Americans were descendants of Lehi, their conversion was crucial in the restoration of Israel that must precede the Second Coming. Still optimistic, Pratt proposed that the Book of Mormon, as well as "some small cheep publications" be published in Spanish. After he improved in the language, he hoped to translate the Book of Mormon and write "some in Spanish." The other apostles, Pratt wrote, should follow his example of language training to promote the global spread of Mormonism: "If the Twelve Apostles will divide the European languages between them and each become thoroughly versed on *one*, so as to translate the fulness of the

Gospel and turn the Keys in the same, it will be a very great step toward the consummation, for a host of fellow laborers would soon be raised up in each to cooperate with them."[130] Notwithstanding Pratt's hopes, Mormon missionaries did not return to South America until 1923 and Chile until 1956, though Chile is now the only major nation in the world where over three percent of its population has been baptized Mormon.[131]

The journey home was even worse than the voyage to Chile. The time "passed like a dreary imprisonment to us," Pratt wrote, "with but little to eat." Even though they paid "a good price for cabin passage," they were only given "a little poor hard bread, probably baked some two or three years since, and some beans and verry poor damaged salt meat and pork." Weather also conspired against the *Dracut*. They had "not had one day of good sailing in a month," Pratt complained, and though they had prayed "for fair wind and speed, we find our prayers are not answered, and we have given it up, and have asked our Heavenly Father to give us patience and reconciliation to His will."[132] Among Phoebe's descendants, a legend circulated that the ship ran out of food and the crew opted for cannibalism rather than starvation, forcing all aboard to draw lots. Phoebe drew the shortest lot, but before her execution she received a vision as the Pratts and Allen prayed: "There was salt beef in the hold." Though the sailors initially disbelieved Phoebe, she led them to the lost beef, and her life was spared.[133] Though the cannibalism story exceeded even Pratt's capacity for melodrama, Pratt confirmed that the sailors "spurned and hated" the missionaries (with the exception of a young American who requested baptism "as soon as we land"), and the voyage was marred by the crew's "most horrid blasphemies...gambling and blackguardism." They finally landed in San Francisco on May 20, after a harrowing journey of seventy-nine days.[134]

While Pratt was in Chile, a national furor erupted over Mormon loyalty to the federal government and over plural marriage when a handful of federally appointed territorial officials abruptly left Utah after clashing with Governor Brigham Young and other Mormons. Although a concerted public relations effort by Latter-day Saints and their ally Thomas Kane largely discredited the "runaway" officials, the incident popularized allegations of Mormon polygamy and revealed the impossibility of keeping it secret any longer. In August 1852, Orson Pratt, in a discourse in the Tabernacle in Salt Lake City, officially acknowledged the practice. A month earlier, Parley defended polygamy without explicitly admitting its practice by the Mormons; his arguments foreshadowed those used by Orson and later defenders of Mormon plural marriage.[135] Following the publication of Pratt's Spanish proclamation, a San Francisco editor, according to Pratt, lamented "our neglect of our countrymen, the Americans, in our religious instructions" and asked about "Gov. Young's family matters, and whether 'Mormonism' allows a man more wives than one!!!" In response, Pratt published a broadside, "'Mormonism!' 'Plurality of wives!' An especial chapter, for the especial edification of certain inquisitive news editors."[136]

In stating that "'Mormonism' is not in a corner, nor its light under a bushel," Pratt broke ranks with the Saints who continued to deny polygamy and revealed again his deep-seated preference for confrontation to evasion. He wrote that he "never had the curiosity to inform" himself about "Young's family matters," though he defended Young's morality and stated, "we presume the number of his family does not exceed the late estimates, which have been the rounds of the American Press," a tacit admission of plural marriage. He juxtaposed Old Testament polygamy with the current repudiation of the practice by the Christian world, who would "exclude Abraham, Isaac, and Jacob, and the kings, patriarchs, and prophets of old from the kingdom of God." Current laws would thrust Jacob into prison and "turn his four wives, twelve sons and a daughter into the street," though they did not sufficiently criminalize adultery, which Pratt argued was rampant in contemporary society. Within the Mormon system, he stated, every woman would have the opportunity to "answer the end of their creation; to be protected in honor and virtue; and to become a happy wife and mother." Mormon family arrangements, he concluded, would revolutionize the world: "And thus adultery, and fornication, with all their attendant train of disease, dispair, shame, sorrow and death will cease from our planet, and joy, love, confidence, and all the pure kindred affections, and family endearments be cherished in every bosom of man." Characteristically, Pratt led the charge to defend polygamy before the war had even been officially declared.[137]

While Pratt remained in San Francisco, Phoebe and Elizabeth—still faring poorly—worked, "one in San Jose and the other in the mission 2 ms. [miles] from town." Allen traveled "above Sacramento" where he found work "for 100 dol. per month." For himself, Pratt wrote, "I wander where ever I can find a lodging, or a dinner."[138] He soon raised money from local Saints ($1,200 plus mules and a wagon) to travel home.[139] After recruiting a few men to accompany him on the potentially dangerous route from Southern California to Utah, Pratt left San Francisco with his wives, stopping first at the church colony in San Bernardino from mid-August to mid-September. Pratt saw San Bernardino as a potential gathering site for converts from South America and the Pacific islands. While he preferred the "climate upon the rim of the Basin, where the cool winds of Summer keep the milk and butter cool, and 2 feet of snow in Winter," he thought the climate of Southern California would be "necessary for the inhabitants of South America, Asia, the Tropical portions of Europe, and the Islands of the Pacific."[140] Before leaving San Bernardino, Pratt, along with Rich and Lyman, appointed "certain young men to study the Spanish language, with a view to a mission hereafter," with William Stout, a Spanish-speaking Mormon, as instructor.[141]

Shortly after Pratt's arrival in Salt Lake City on October 18, he made his report in a tabernacle discourse. He explained the significance of his mission and his abiding interest in Latin America while defending what to all appearances was a failure. Pratt did not "officially open" the "keys of kingdom to that nation" because he "was not fully prepared to do it neither [did the] spirit of [the] Lord lead me to do it." His hopes for the future resided in the one impregnable foundation to his faith: he hoped to "translate the Book of Mormon if my brethren think proper" and "then unlock the door of [the] gospel" to the Latin American peoples. Until then, the Saints should "consider Brother Parley on [a] Spanish mission."[142]

12

Parley and Mrs. Pratt(s)

Dear Mary, and Belinda, and Sarah, and Hannahette,
and Kesiah, and Agatha, and Phebe, and Parley, and
Alma, and Nephi, and Helaman, and Julia, and Belinda
Jun'r, and Abinadi, and Cornelia, and Lucy, and Agatha
Junr and Malona, and Teancum, and Ette, and Lehi, and
Mary Jun'r, and Phebe Junr, and Moroni, and so many
more as there be.... Br. Morris sais it is a long catalogue
of names for one family circle. I say; the Lord increase it
a hundred fold while I yet Live.

—PARLEY PRATT, *letter to his family, July 29, 1854*

SAILING HOME FROM Chile, Pratt reflected on the suffering of his family
during his latest absence. He knew his wives had sold their personal belong-
ings, including clothing and shoes, in an unsuccessful attempt to raise money
to finish their home, and he hoped to bring them a "few nessessary" things—"a
little Leather and a little plain humbly clothes," perhaps a "little sugar and
tea"—to compensate in small part for their "noble sacrafice." Pratt promised
they would "never go hungry more" even if he had "to earn the means by
washing Shirts for Gamblers." Knowing that he might be sent on yet more
missions, he placed one large caveat on his promise: "this is dependent on one
if—if—the Lord will." Pratt found solace in the long view, and hoped his
wives did too: "With my posterity and that of my Brethren," he would "take
the earth, and live in it, and multiply, till there is not room enough upon its
serface and transplant my seed on other planets, and set down and rest and
look on, and up and at it again."[1] After arriving home in October 1852, Pratt
spent the next eighteen months in Utah, which turned out to be the most
stable period of his family life after the introduction of polygamy in Nauvoo.
He occupied his time, he told Orson, in "building, farming, gardening,
Preaching, studying Language, Writing Theology, Spiritual philosophy, sermons, and letters."[2] He partially fulfilled his promises to his family; he finished

their main home as well as two others and placed his family on a firmer financial foundation. In addition, he completed his most expansive book, *Key to the Science of Theology*, and participated in an ambitious attempt to reform the English alphabet. His time in Utah allows a unique view into the complex dynamics of the Pratt family and the daily reality of polygamy among the Mormon ecclesiastical elite.

Parley's divorce from Mary Ann Frost soon after his return from California resulted from the rocky transition into polygamy of the later Nauvoo years. Upon arriving in Utah, Pratt saw his children Olivia and Moroni for the first time in more than four years. In 1850, he inscribed in his family record a history of his estrangement from Mary Ann. Stung by "falsehoods which are circulated in the Church," Parley charged that Mary Ann "has now been Willfully absent about four years from her husband, squandering his property, scattering his children, and never communicating with him by Letter." He bitterly wrote, "These things are writen that the two children thus seperated by a perverse and wicked mother may read them and come to the knowledge of the true circumstances and be restored to the full confidence and affections of their father, who Loves them with an everlasting Love and will seek them even to the ends of the earth should his circumstances ever permit."[3]

After returning to Nauvoo in early 1846, Mary Ann had resisted overtures from Parley to rejoin him and his plural wives on the trek across Iowa. In April 1846, Parley sent her a letter by his brother William, along with a wagon to take her across Iowa, but Mary Ann declined to go.[4] She remained in Nauvoo until she was expelled, along with her children and the families of William and Anson Pratt, in September 1846 during the Battle of Nauvoo, when Illinois vigilantes forced the remaining Saints in the city across the Mississippi River and into refugee camps. Brigham Young offered Mary Ann the services of a church agent to arrange her travel to Winter Quarters. Learning of the harsh conditions there, however, Mary Ann declined the proposal and returned to a largely deserted Nauvoo, where she spent the winter with her children in John D. Lee's abandoned house along with the family of church agent John Fullmer.[5] In June 1847, she traveled to Winter Quarters and informed Parley that she and the children were returning to her birthplace in Bethel, Maine. One observer described her health as "very poor" and commented, "I think she is a very unhappy Woman and a very good one also."[6] Parley again urged her to come on the trek west, but when she declined his offer, he provided clothes and money to her. She received further funds the following year, when, in March 1848, Parley's principal Nauvoo property, his brick home, sold for $850 (though Parley

valued it at $7,000) to a Catholic leader. (Till this day, the home remains a
residence for Catholic priests.) The Winter Quarters High Council directed
that, after paying debts, the proceeds should be split, with half ($200) to
Anson Pratt, likely to assist in the care of the Pratts' aged mother, Charity,
and half to Mary Ann. She stayed in Maine for three years, remained in
contact with church members, and then journeyed to Utah over the objections of her relatives in 1852.[7]

After his arrival from California, Parley wrote an accusatory letter to Mary
Ann, begrudgingly offering to support her financially if she acquiesced to his
guidance. The money he had given her in 1847, Parley wrote, had been squandered "in traveling about the world." Although she had come to Utah, Parley
disdainfully wrote, "I suppose your next move would be to California, and
then to Maine, and so on." He continued, "I will never consent for my dear
children Olivia and Moroni to leave me more, beyond the Reach of my dayly
care guidance and government from this time fourth and forever I wish to
educate them in the Branches of industry Science, and Religion." If Mary
Ann rejected these conditions, Parley would repudiate further financial obligations to her, though he would "not consent to part with their [his children's] society except by the providence of God."[8]

Mary Ann's response was to obtain a divorce on March 5, 1853, from
Brigham Young, who routinely granted divorces to plural wives who requested
them, though he generally denied divorce petitions from husbands.[9] She then
moved to Battle Creek, Utah (now Pleasant Grove), where her daughter Mary
Ann had previously settled with her husband. Notwithstanding Parley's desire
to have Olivia and Moroni live with him, they went with their mother. In
1854, on the way to a second mission in California, Parley visited Olivia and
Moroni, whom he had not seen for fifteen months. "They were glad to see
me," he recorded, "and I made them some presents." Parley saw Mary Ann "at
meeting" but "did not speak" to his "enemy."[10]

Their marriage in 1837, uniting a young widower with an infant son and a
widow with a daughter, had met their practical needs of help with child care
and financial support (though the Missouri expulsion and Parley's imprisonment made this difficult at times). In the early years of their marriage, before
the introduction of polygamy, the union also provided emotional, spiritual,
and intellectual companionship for both, dramatically revealed by Mary's
decision to join Parley in a Missouri jail. The strains of polygamy and the dissolution of her marriage to one of Mormonism's leading men did not destroy
Mary Ann's faith. She had been a believer before her marriage to Parley and
died in the faith decades after their divorce. Mary Ann worked as a midwife

and later participated in advocacy by Mormon women for their rights against national anti-polygamy crusaders.[11]

The tensions originating in the Nauvoo practice of polygamy had also strained the relationship between Parley and Orson, culminating in their dramatic confrontation in the Nauvoo temple in 1846. Since then, Parley "could never obtain a line" from Orson "or even an acknowledgment of the Receipt of any of my letters." He finally gave up, telling Orson their correspondence was over "forever unless, recommenced by yourself." In March 1853, Orson was in Washington, D.C., editing a periodical called *The Seer* that was largely devoted to the public defense of plural marriage. That month, he at last broke the impasse, motivated by a project that united religious fervor with their family heritage and would, Orson hoped, heal the breach between the brothers. Orson excitedly told Parley about Frederick W. Chapman, a Congregational minister from Connecticut, who was compiling a book on the descendants of William Pratt, the brothers' earliest ancestor in America.[12] The treasure chest of family history that Chapman opened to Orson's eyes prompted him to weep "like a little child." He wrote Parley,

> Now my dear brother, there are none among all the descendants of our Ancestor, Lieut. William Pratt, who have so deep an interest in searching out his descendants as ourselves. We know that the God of our fathers has had a hand in this. He it was who brought our ancestor William from England and established him in this choice land of promise, given to us by virtue of the covenant made with our ancient father Joseph, the son of Jacob. The Lord God of our fathers has multiplied them in this land & made them almost a nation within a nation.[13]

Orson was one of the first Mormons to see fully the connection between ordinances of salvation, vicarious work for the dead, and the logically entailed imperative to search out and compile detailed family histories. Chapman's discoveries prompted not only Orson's own family history research, but also his personal reconciliation with Parley.[14] "I will beg pardon for having been so backward in writing to you," Orson wrote. "I hope you will forgive me."[15]

He then solicited Parley's assistance in the family history project as well as an autobiographical sketch for inclusion. In response, Parley sent Orson details pertaining to the siblings of their father, Jared, presumably obtained from his aunt, Lovina Pratt Van Cott, who lived in Salt Lake City.[16] Orson's enthusiasm for Chapman's project was unbounded; he contacted numerous relatives throughout the country and even researched William Pratt's heritage in England.[17]

In a discourse, Parley urged the Saints to likewise compile genealogical records, insisting the dead "not only live, move, and think but might hear the gospel." Joseph Smith propounded the redemption of the unevangelized as early as 1836 and introduced vicarious temple ordinances in the Nauvoo era.[18] Yet Pratt went beyond Smith's formulation in envisioning a vast missionary work in the spirit world. In 1918, church president Joseph F. Smith announced a vision (now Doctrine and Covenants 138, canonized in 1976), which described postmortal missionary work in vivid detail. But Pratt anticipated him by more than half a century. "We reason from...what we know," Pratt matter-of-factly said. In the "spirit world societies are made up of all kinds." Many presumably "have lived in part of [the] spirit world...where the key has not yet been turned nor the gospel preached." The sinful, "being left in their darkness," wait in a hell of uncertainty, "without even a clear idea of hope of resurrection....Yes, they [are] waiting." Identically with Joseph F. Smith's subsequent description, Pratt announced that faithful "modern saints that have departed this earth clothed upon with...priesthood [have] gone to the world of spirits not to sorrow but as joyful messengers with glad tiding of eternal truth anointed to preach the gospel."[19]

Although committed in principle to linking family history with vicarious salvation, Parley was privately suspicious of Chapman's endeavor. In a letter to Orson, he accused Chapman of mercenary motives; implied that a Congregationalist would not be open to Parley's faith-filled story; and peevishly complained that the majority of Lt. Pratt's descendants rejected the restored church and that others were corrupt members of the hated English nobility or Church of England clergy. Probably, Pratt was unable to see beyond the clerical affiliation of Orson's collaborator. It was perhaps also too sensitive a time for him personally, so soon after Mary Ann's request for divorce, to bring up visions of vast family dynasties united by love, spanning space and time. Later, Pratt relented enough to submit a sketch of his life, but in the larger project of a Pratt family history he played only a small role.[20] Orson forged ahead without him, and, following the publication of Chapman's book in 1864, he and his family performed vicarious ordinance work for twenty-six hundred relatives.[21] In 1881, Orson also established a family organization to meticulously track the descendants of Jared Pratt, who likely now number in the range of a hundred thousand.

After his divorce from Mary Ann, Parley had seven wives—Elizabeth, Mary Wood, Hannahette, Belinda, Sarah, Phoebe, and Agatha. Most

Mormon polygamist families consisted of two or, at most, three wives; only a few men, most of them religious leaders, married numerous women. Mormon polygamous families maintained a matriarchal order of sorts by endowing the first, initially monogamous wife, with supervisory authority over the household. Parley's estrangement and then divorce from Mary Ann left this role vacant. On March 25, 1848, Parley gathered his family to celebrate Parley Jr.'s eleventh birthday. He recounted to the assembled family his first son's birth and gave "a scetch of his History, the death of his Mother Thankful" and "exhorted him to prepare to fill the Steps of his father, or to succeed him in the service of his God and his fellow men, by a well Ordered life, and by laying hold of Knowledge and a good education." Parley then instructed his son to choose from among the plural wives "who should be his mother untill he should meet his own mother in the next life." Parley Jr. selected Belinda, and the two "made a solem covenant before God and all present that they would be to each other as son and mother through life, that she would care for, love, and Educate him as her own son; and that he would love, Respect, obey and sustain her through life as a son."[22] With this ceremony (and because of her strong-willed personality), Belinda became the de facto head of the wives.[23]

Relatively few Mormon plural marriages occurred between the exodus west in 1846–1847 and 1855, when the Saints finished the Salt Lake Endowment House (which functioned as a site for temple ordinances before the completion of the Salt Lake Temple). Pratt followed this pattern: he married his first eight plural wives between 1843 and 1847, then took an additional wife in 1853 and 1855. His two later wives, Keziah Downes and Eleanor McComb, also signaled a shift in the type of women he married, as he selected older, previously married women to join his household. The average age of his first eight plural wives was 24, whereas Keziah and Eleanor were 41 and 38 at the time of their marriages to Parley. In addition, the final two wives both stood out for their intellectual abilities.

His marriage proposal to Keziah Downes gives a glimpse of the courtship dynamics of polygamy during this era. In December 1853, he requested Brigham Young's permission to propose to Keziah. Men anticipating marriage sometimes mitigated the emotional strains of shared intimacy by rhetorically desexualizing and deromanticizing the plural relationships. Pratt, for instance, frequently invoked the terms of friendship and companionship. On this occasion, he more imaginatively wrote to Young, "I have in my own mind selected another assistant missionary to assist me in my mission for time and all eternity. It only requires *your sanction*, the *Lady's Consent*,—and the *Seal of*

God to complete the appointment. The candidate is a sister from Manchester Eng. heretofore known as Sister Hill.—What say ye?"[24] After Young gave his permission, Pratt proposed in a letter to "Sister Hill" (he added in a postscript, "excuse the name of Hill. your [first] name I do not know"):

> I hope you will excuse the Liberty I have taken in presenting the above to Prest. Young. He gave his ready sanction, to the selection, and it now remains for you to say whether you will undertake such a mission, of your *own free will and choice.*
>
> Count well the cost I can promise you nothing but Poverty, hard work, and many burthens in this work which but few can bear.
>
> And be assured your decision either way will never lessen our friendship.[25]

Keziah accepted his proposal. Six days later, Young married them.[26]

The formality of the correspondence and Parley's unawareness of her full name suggest a lack of acquaintance between the two. In reality, they had known each other for more than a decade, since 1842, when Keziah was baptized into the Manchester branch. In a pattern common to many female converts, her husband, William Hill, was not a member, and, perhaps as a result of a family rupture precipitated by her baptism, Keziah lived with her brother Samuel next to the British mission headquarters, where Pratt and his family lived while in Manchester.[27] In 1845, Charles Miller, a British church leader, wrote Pratt, "Having called on sister Hill in Oldham [nearby Manchester] one day she told me that some time ago when you was in Oldham preaching she felt by the Spirit to give you some money for your nessesities she was bashful & did not do it & since then she has been condemnd in her mind." She thus gave Miller a "crown piece" worth five pounds, "desiring you will receive it from an handmaiden of the Lord she is poor or she would have done more."[28]

After their marriage, an exchange of letters during Parley's second mission to California demonstrates how Mormonism's doctrines framed their relationship. In October 1854, Keziah excitedly informed Parley that her "sister Hannah and her husband and children, together with my dear old mother" were headed for Utah. She wrote, "I rejoice much in my present associations, and privileges as a member of the Kingdom of God.... I am desirous of walking humbly and acceptably...so that I may become worthy of a crown and place in the Celestial Kingdom, which favorrs I ask not only for myself, but for you, and every wife and child which the Lord has given unto you."[29] In response, Pratt cast their marriage in terms of religious mission, as he had in his marriage proposal. He stated, "Continue to be diligent in your mission, & remember you are doing all you do—to assist one of the twelve in a mission. how Many women would have Desired such a Mission as yours, but they died without even seeing such blessed days." Keziah's duties, Pratt suggested, included helping with the Pratt children: "You have the honor of training & assisting to educate young princes & princesses—heirs to the Eternal Priesthood." He assured her, "As to Love—I have an eternal fountain Laid up for you—I love you a little now, & I expect to grow in it forever." Repeating the connection between love and intelligence he had formulated in his Nauvoo pamphlet, he wrote, "As to the eternal affections—giving does not impoverish, the more I increase in intelligence the stronger & more Lasting is my love."[30]

Keziah, along with Belinda, Mary, Hannahette, Elizabeth, and Phoebe, resided in the main Pratt house. The living arrangements in large Mormon plural households took a variety of forms, with wives in some families living under the same roof, while other families used a type of duplex arrangement (wives in homes next door to each other). In yet other families, wives lived in completely separate households or even in different towns. The Pratt family used a mix of living arrangements. Agatha lived and established a millinery business in a small house behind the main Pratt residence, while Sarah lived in another house near the Pratt farm, which she supervised.[31]

The challenge of avoiding jealousy and insecurity in such a polygamous household must have been daunting. In 1849, Pratt sought Brigham Young's advice on "what was strictly right as to the association and connection" of a man and his plural wives. He received counsel that recognized a principal distinction between first wives who had never expected to share a husband and subsequent wives who did. Husbands, Young said, should give more attention to the "wives of our youth, who dwelt in our bosoms while we and they knew not the things of God's more perfect law; for the others, who never enjoyed that constant society, could better endure the distant association than if they had enjoyed the greater familiarities."[32] After his divorce from Mary Ann, Parley was no longer wedded to a wife who had married in expectation of monogamy, perhaps easing the tensions within the household.

Nevertheless, even in prosperous times and a well-administered household, communal living could create financial difficulties. And Pratt's household was seldom prosperous. While Pratt was on his second California mission, Agatha defended herself against an accusation by Belinda that she was making "money like smoke" and spending it improperly. Agatha's millinery skills enabled her to earn money more easily than Parley's other wives, but she argued that she contributed to the family economy. She had "been

very busy all summer at my trade," which had allowed the family to purchase butter and cheese during Parley's absence.[33]

Other wives had recourse to less skilled means of supporting the family:
"The mothers of my little children have to leave them, and go out at days
works, take in washing, or leave their house to camp out in the distance to
cultivate the earth for food, to pick greens, or to save the milk of two or three
cows to keep the family from actual hunger." He was not speaking figura-
tively. In May 1853, Parley told Orson that his family lacked money to buy
bread. Furthermore, he wrote, "I toil early and late, six days in a week, and on
the seventh, I go to meeting 3 times, and fill up the interstices by writing
Letters, and other necessary writing reading, conversing etc. so that I hardly
have time to speak to my family."[34] Nevertheless, they raised sufficient crops
during summer 1853 "to nearly feed us till next summer."[35] Within the family
duties, Hannahette served as the nurse, and Keziah acted as the secretary and
schoolteacher. In his letters to his wives, Pratt often resorted to expansive
and abstract rhetoric about the power of love, but he also understood the
pragmatic side of family life, telling Agatha that love was "takeing care of
hogs and getting a living."[36]

Pratt's material circumstances sometimes surprised newcomers to Salt
Lake City. When Francis Hammond, who converted to Mormonism through
Voice of Warning, first arrived in Utah following a mission to Hawaii, he
dressed in his "best bib and tucker" to meet Pratt, whom he revered as his
"father in the Gospel." He found Pratt "threshing beans before his door...bare-
footed, in shirt sleeves, and [with] a home made straw hat." Surprised to find
his "ideal Apostle in such a plight, and forced to labor in such a manner for his
support," Hammond soon found himself listening as Pratt sat on a fence
and spoke about the Hawaiians as part of the house of Israel. Hammond concluded, "Never in all my life had I heard such a discourse so full of inspiration
and prophecy concerning the great work of the Lord in the latter days."[37]

Poverty notwithstanding, Pratt managed this same year to finish a major
construction project. Before departing for his Chile mission, he had begun
work on a new home directly south of Temple Square, to replace his original
simple "adobe house" on the same lot. He hoped his wives would oversee its
completion by his return. The First Presidency informed Pratt in October
1851, "The walls of your house are up, and the joiner work progressing."[38]
Progress stalled, however, and Pratt advised his wives to "not run in debt
much" to finish their house, as he would "finish it when I come" and would
"try and bring some glass, nails, Trimings, Puty, Paints Oils, etc." By May 1853,
Parley boasted to Orson that he had "built with my own labours, without

capital or church assistance a substancial house, 1 ½ stories high, upon a good cellar, 26 feet square, which is now Recieving a roof." Furthermore, he described his garden as "among the best."[39] By that fall, Parley had "nearly fin-ished" a second, smaller home, "and all this by the blessing of God on the Labours of my own hands and that of my family." During 1853, he had "fenced to the amount of 4 or 5 hundred dollars more," totaling $2,000 "worth of improvment" that year. Prosperity still eluded him, but he could at least assert that he now owed "less than I have owed for many years."[40] (Parley had earlier complained about his financial difficulties to Orson, hinting that Orson might loan him a few cows; Orson explained that he was too heavily in debt himself to help.)[41] While Parley at times complained of his poverty, he tried, with varying degrees of success, to convince himself and others that he was resigned to it. He wrote Orson, "I do as I am directed by my president, whether to stay at home or go abroad, to dig potatoes, study, write, or publish. If I Live it is all well. If I die, or wear out it is all the same."[42]

Parley learned about this same time that his newly completed house threatened his recently mended relationship with Orson. After the pioneer company arrived in the Salt Lake Valley in July 1847, Orson surveyed the city site and chose an "inheritance" (a plot of land) for himself directly south of the temple site.[43] The following September, while Orson was in England on a mission, Brigham Young and Heber Kimball reapportioned the city lots, giving single men no property, married men one lot, and polygamous men one lot for each wife. They also allocated five-acre lots for each family unit in the "Big Field," designed for farming.[44] Parley received eight of these five-acre lots, which made for a forty-acre farm between State and Main streets at 1300 South. His residential lots were located between 800 and 900 South and between West Temple and First West, with an additional lot on the southeast corner of 400 North and 300 West.[45] In addition, on Young's instructions, Parley assumed ownership of Orson's lots directly south of Temple Square, though he reserved the "choisest corner Lot" for his brother.[46]

Now, in August 1853, after Parley completed the house on land his family had occupied for five years, Young stated that Parley had "entirely misunder-stood" the situation and that the property belonged to Orson. Parley pro-tested the injustice to Orson, writing that Young's statement came "after toiling with my wives and children for so many years, and going hungry and destitute and, even selling our clothes, to make improvements, fence, build and set out trees." Nevertheless, he offered to abandon the lots to maintain peace.[47] Orson generously refused his offer, writing that he considered Parley the rightful owner. Had they "been reserved for me," Orson wrote, "I should

probably have built upon them according to my means, and located the
different branches of my family a little more compact than what they are at
present." Nevertheless, he wrote, "sooner than I would hold any feelings
against you for the occupancy of those lots, I would resign the one which is
left me, and seek for an inheritance elsewhere."[48]

During 1853, three more children were born into the Pratt family:
Phoebe's daughter, Phoebe Soper, born on May 19; Mary's daughter, Mary
Wood, born September 14; and Agatha's son, Moroni Walker, born October
10. (Agatha's sister recorded that Moroni was "a twelve and a half pound"
baby.)[49] The Pratt household swarmed with children. By the end of 1853, the
family (not including Mary Ann Frost's Olivia and Moroni) consisted of
sixteen-year-old Parley Jr.; eight-year-old Alma; two seven-year-old boys,
Helaman and Nephi; six-year-old Julia; five five-year-olds—Cornelia, Lucy,
Belinda, Abinadi, and Agatha; three-year-old Malona; three two-year-
olds—Henrietta, Lehi, and Teancum; and the three infants. In all, Pratt
fathered thirty children, twenty-three of whom lived to adulthood. Besides
five-year-old Nathan and one-year-old Susan, the children of Parley and
Mary Ann who died in Nauvoo, five infants under the age of one died in the
early Utah years. The other children lived an average of sixty years, ranging
from Sarah, thirty-five at her death, to Mathoni, the last surviving child
who died at eighty in 1937.

At times, the children tested the wives' patience. In May 1854, shortly after
he had left for California again, Parley advised his wives, particularly Belinda,
on childrearing: "Dont fret at 'siss' so much, nor at any of the Rest...they are
the best Children in the world: but there is Life in them, and they must give
it vent in some way."[50] Agatha described Parley as a "kind and gentle" father
and remembered that he "hailed each newcomer with as much pleasure and
delight as if it were the only one." She continued, "One of the greatest plea-
sures of his life was to gather them around his knees, holding as many as he
could, and have them sing their sweet childish songs, often trying to join in
with them as he dearly loved music and singing and always when possible he
would have his family gather together for family worship."[51] Parley envisioned
his children's education as a mix of practical, religious, and cultural teaching.
He hoped to instruct his sons "not only to plow and reap and drive teem and
chop wood, but also to be carpenters, Joiners, Masons, readers, writers,
preachers, Prophets, schoolmasters, governors and even Kings and Patriarchs."
His daughters' "education should consist in reading, writing, etc. and in
cooking, housework, milking, Churning, Baking, Sewing, etc. and to make
coats, pants, vests, dresses, Bonnets, etc. while music, the fine Arts, Medicine,

the sciences, and above all faith, hope, and charity must not be neglected by either sex."[52]

Elizabeth Cordelia Ferris, wife of Utah territorial secretary Benjamin Ferris, visited the Pratt household in 1853 and gave a rare outside assessment in a published exposé of Utah polygamy. Ferris portrayed Pratt as a particularly proud polygamist. At a dancing party hosted by Young at the Social Hall, Ferris expressed shock at the open polygamy of Mormon leaders. For her, the "crowning incident of the evening" occurred when Pratt "marched up with four wives, and introduced them successively as Mrs. Pratts. The thing was done with such an easy, nonchalant air, that I had difficulty in keeping from laughing outright." She wondered, "Did the man do this to show what he could do, or because he thought politeness required it of him?" By contrast, Ferris appreciated the sensitivity of some leaders who "only introduced the first wife."[53] Benjamin Ferris added that while "most of his brethren exhibit a kind of hang-dog look...and seem to feel like a culprit caught in depredating upon a hen-roost" when introducing several wives, "Parley puts a bold face upon the matter, and in this is certainly consistent with his professed principles."[54] A polemicist such as Pratt, who celebrated rather than shied away from Mormonism's most radical religious beliefs, was not likely to conceal his embrace of Mormonism's most radical religious practice. In addition, the incident also likely expressed Pratt's attempt to treat his plural wives on an equal basis.

Notwithstanding her shock at Pratt's manners, Ferris accepted an invitation from Zerubbabel Snow, a Mormon territorial judge, and his wife to "spend an evening with them, at Parley's house, and hear him read from a manuscript work on theology." "This was too good an opportunity to look into a Mormon harem," Ferris commented, "to be neglected." When they arrived, Pratt, with "much suavity of manner," introduced them to "five Mrs. Pratts in succession; one of whom assumed the office of mistress of ceremonies, taking our shawls, and inviting us to seats near the fire. The rest remained demurely seated after the ceremony of introduction, busily plied their knitting, and were as whist as mice while the cat is foraging for supplies." She identified the head hostess as "a Boston divorcée" (Belinda), three others as English (Elizabeth, Mary, and Agatha), and the final as a "fair looking American girl" (probably Phoebe).[55] Ferris described the "burly" Pratt:

Parley seated himself at a candle-stand, in the centre of the room, and entertained us for some time with conversation in regard to the Chilians.... The man has a very even flow of language, and converses with great ease. He read from his manuscript for nearly or quite half an hour, and certainly until I got heartily tired of it. The style was much like his conversation; but the matter was devoid of vitality, consisting of the most external and lifeless misapplication of scriptural texts to the support of his peculiar notions.

As the Ferrises left, Pratt proudly showed them a painting of his family, identifying the seven wives depicted along with various children.[56] William W. Major, a Mormon artist, painted the family portrait, which one observer termed "splendid," in 1851. Pratt commissioned another family painting of "about twenty person" in 1854; unfortunately, neither painting has been located.[57] Ferris commented disparagingly, "We were compelled, of course, to give the same degree of polite attention that would have been expected by a farmer at the East, in exhibiting a favorite flock of Shanghais, or litter of pigs."[58]

Pratt—and his fellow polygamous husbands—were not alone in proudly defending "the principle." Young assigned Orson Pratt to publicly announce polygamy in 1852, only one year before the Ferris's visit. The status of women immediately became central to the ensuing decades-long national furor over plural marriage. Anti-polygamy religious crusaders and fiction writers alike depicted Mormon women as victims of patriarchy who had been duped, forced, or coerced into plural marriage.[59] By the 1870s, Latter-day Saint women lashed back, assembling in mass "indignation" meetings, rebutting in writing such allegations, and denouncing anti-polygamy legislation aimed at saving them; they objected to their portrayals as victims and insisted that they were willing participants in polygamy, motivated by their religious beliefs.[60]

In January 1854, Belinda became the first Mormon woman to enter the national debate by writing a pamphlet defending the practice. She framed the pamphlet as a response to a letter her sister Lydia Kimball, living in New Hampshire, had sent her about polygamy. Kimball had called polygamy "licentious," "abominable," and "beastly," "the practice only of the most barbarous nations, or of the dark ages; or of some great or good men, who were left to commit gross sins." Belinda's response, intended for publication, defended polygamy on both biblical and natural grounds, stating that "a man of God...is more worthy of a hundred wives and children than the ignorant slave of passion, or of vice and folly, is to have one wife and one child." Belinda focused not only on the biblical male participants, such as Abraham, but also the wives, such as Sarah. In praising the biblical matriarch, she noted that this "wife of a polygamist, who encouraged her husband in the practice of the same, and even urged him into it, and officiated in giving him another wife, is named as an honorable and virtuous woman [in the New Testament], a pattern for Christian ladies, and the very mother of all holy women in the Christian Church."[61]

Furthermore, Belinda reasoned, biological differences between the genders also justified polygamy. She enumerated several benefits that women derived from plural marriage. Since sexual relations were "mainly for the purpose of procreation," they should not be indulged in during pregnancy, as doing so might "disturb, irritate, weary, or exhaust" the female body. A man, however, "has no such draw back upon his strength." Belinda reasoned, "Polygamy then, as practiced under the Patriarchal law of God, leads directly to the chastity of women, and to sound health and morals in the constitutions of their offspring." Furthermore, polygamy allowed all women to marry "virtuous men," rather than "a drunkard, a man of hereditary disease, a debauchee, an idler, or a spendthrift." Belinda described the Pratts' own family life:

> I have a good and virtuous husband whom I love. We have four little children which are mutually and inexpressibly dear to us. And besides this, my husband has seven other living wives, and one who has departed to a better world. He has in all upwards of twenty-five children. All these mothers and children are endeared to me by kindred ties,—by mutual affection—by acquaintance and association; and the mothers in particular by mutual and long continued exercises of toil, patience, long-suffering and sisterly kindness. We have our imperfections in this life; but I know that these are good and worthy women, and that my husband is a good and worthy man; one who keeps the commandments of Jesus Christ, and presides in his family like an Abraham.[62]

With the publication of *Defence of Polygamy, By a Lady of Utah, In a Letter to Her Sister in New Hampshire*, Belinda acquired a reputation as the "foremost female advocate of polygamy."[63] One of the few pro-polygamy pamphlets by a woman, her work was widely reprinted, appearing in the *Millennial Star, Zion's Watchman* (a Mormon newspaper in Sydney, Australia), various non-Mormon American newspapers, Jules Rémy's *A Journey to Great Salt Lake City* (1861), Richard Burton's *City of the Saints* (1861), and Edward Tullidge's *Women of Mormondom* (1877). It thus "reached a wider audience in the nineteenth century than any other Mormon work on the subject with the exception of Orson Pratt's works."[64] While in California in 1854, Parley wrote Belinda, "Your Printed Letter is of world wide notoriety.... It convinces or shuts the mouths of all. It is one of the

Little entering wedges of a worlds Revolution." An educated Spiritualist characterized it as a "great treasure," and the California governor's brother, after reading the pamphlet, "remarked that the whole foundation of society was wrong, and needed revolutionizing."[65] Parley commissioned missionary William McBride to contract with a printer in San Francisco to publish a run of a thousand, and he sent copies to missionaries in Hawaii.[66]

Most of Parley's wives echoed Belinda's contentment in plural marriage and her positive assessments of the dynamics of the Pratt household. In 1853, Parley told a non-Mormon childhood friend, "We generally live in love and harmony, and I have very seldom a wife who would be willing to live aside from the society of the others. They love and mutually assist each other and so do the children."[67] Agatha later recalled of their relationship:

> He had an innate reverence and respect for women as the mothers of the souls of men. He loved his wives, not only as the beloved of his bosom but as mothers of his children, whom he loved very dearly.... Amid all our poverty, toil and care, and the difficulties and perplexities and experiences, he would sometime have occasion to reprove or admonish. He would do so in a manner to touch the heart, make a lasting impression, but never leave a humiliating sting. His wives always knew that he respected them and cared for their feelings.[68]

Elizabeth wrote, "I married into polygamy and believed it to be a divine principle, and those who enter into it with this knowledge and are faithful to its requirements will inherit the same kingdom and glory that Abraham does, the friend of God and the father of the faithful."[69] Phoebe added:

> I am blest with a husband of a noble and generous turn of a kind and affectionate heart, one that delights in good acts and kindness and discharging every known duty.... I have one of the best men that ever graced this earth or ever will in my humble opinion.... I know that my husband is capable and will exalt me and what more do I want.[70]

Certainly Pratt's wives wanted to put on the best public face in defense of a contentious religious practice. Still, the evidence suggests his household was generally as happy and harmonious as they depicted. Most of Pratt's adult children, both sons and daughters, entered into polygamous families as well.[71]

During this time in Utah, Parley devoted time to writing. In his letters, Orson expressed his deep admiration for Parley's works and encouraged him to continue in his vocation. At this point, Parley had not published anything of significance in years, whereas Orson's missions in England and Washington, D.C., had vaulted him into the role of most visible public defender of Mormonism, replacing his older brother. Orson commented, "Writing always was tedious to me, but seeing the good that may be accomplished, I have whipped my mind to it, till I am nearly bald-headed, and grey-headed, through constant application."[72] Orson regretted that Parley "had to toil, and labor hard, and live poor; and I have anxiously desired that the way might be opened for you to occupy your time and talents in writing, publishing, preaching &c. wherein millions might be benefitted instead of being obliged to toil with your own hands all the day long." Orson also suggested that Parley should be receiving royalties from *Voice of Warning*, which "sells well" and should be affording Parley a "handsome profit on each successive edition, by the Church publishing office in Liverpool." Orson sensed that the brothers, then in their forties, needed to take full advantage of the years that remained to them.[73]

Even before he received Orson's advice, Parley finished *Key to the Science of Theology*, portions of which he had read to the Ferrises. Pratt had commenced work on his magnum opus in August 1851, while presiding over the Pacific mission from San Francisco. His usual practice was to write under the ferment created by contending for the gospel in the mission field, so he possibly labored away on the manuscript while spending the next fourteen months in Chile and California. Benjamin Ferris noted that since his return, Pratt "has been busily engaged in another work, which is to furnish the key to all religious knowledge."[74] Upon completion, Pratt offered the copyright to the Perpetual Emigration Fund Company, but Brigham Young told him, "You need the means you receive from that work for the support of your own family." (By 1884, *Key to the Science of Theology* had gone through nine editions and sold thirty thousand copies.)[75] In May 1853, Parley reported to Orson that his "volume of Theology" was "Ready for the press." He described it as "the choicest, and most perfect specimen, from my pen."[76] The *Millennial Star* soon published an extract from the book, but publication of *Key* did not occur until early 1855.[77] The final product was the most cerebral, temperate, and comprehensive of Pratt's writings, and it would become paired with his *Voice of Warning* as the most influential non canonical volumes in nineteenth-century Mormonism.

The key to understanding Pratt's work is in what he found to be Mormonism's most peculiar, and doctrinally pregnant, pronouncement: that "Jesus Christ and his Father [are] in possession of not merely an organized spirit but also a glorious immortal body of flesh and bones." Such extreme anthropomorphism originated with Joseph Smith. But the inference that follows is what shatters the boundaries of traditional theologizing. If the Father and Son have physical tabernacles, Pratt reasoned, then they are "subject to the laws that govern, of necessity, even the most refined order of physical existence." Because "all physical element, however embodied, quickened, or refined, is subject to the general laws necessary to all existence."[78]

By so naturalizing Deity, Pratt furthered Smith's work of collapsing the entire universe of God and humankind, heaven and hell, body and spirit, the eternal and the mundane into one sphere. The paradigm to which this stands in opposition was neatly formulated by the most famous amateur theologian among Pratt's contemporaries, Samuel Taylor Coleridge, who stated the matter simply: "The very ground of all Miracle is the heterogeneity of Spirit and Matter."[79] On that distinction, rooted in a dualism both Platonic and Pauline and continuing to the present, stands the entire Christian understanding of a bifurcated reality, split into two realms, two ways of knowing, and two sets of laws. Pratt contested thousands of years of philosophical theology with one elegant, economical summation of Mormon metaphysics: "Gods, angels and men, are all of one species, one race, one great family widely diffused among the planetary systems."[80] In his sweeping vision, first enunciated in 1845, "men are the offspring or children of the Gods, and destined to advance by degrees, and to make their way by a progressive series of changes, till they become like their father in heaven, and like Jesus Christ their elder brother. Thus perfected, the whole family will . . . continue to organize, people, redeem, and perfect other systems which are now in the womb of Chaos."[81] As God took preexistent matter and shaped it into the earth, so does he take primordial intelligences, father them into spirits, and mentor them into divinity. As the chaos of matter becomes earth, planets, and star systems, the scattered children of God are assimilated into eternal marriages, families, and heavenly dynasties. This is the project Pratt's *Key* details.

In a universe so conceived, in which the physical and spiritual are one, it follows that the entirety of reality is governed by laws fully conformable to and accessible by human reason. In the aftermath of Sir Isaac Newton's momentous decipherment of the laws of the universe, the French scientist Pierre-Simon Laplace famously told Napoleon, in his philosophical euphoria, that he no longer had need of God to make sense of creation. Secular science could henceforth exile God from his universe. In Pratt's theological euphoria, God was reinscribed in the universe, but as a part of it, rather than outside it. For this reason, it would be more accurate to say that for Pratt, science encompassed theology rather than simply coexisted harmoniously with it. That is the sense in which Pratt's title must be understood: "Key to the Science of Theology."

Even before he had fully articulated his vision of divine—or human— anthropology, Pratt was collapsing the distance between the two. In his earliest work of speculative theology, "Regeneration and Eternal Duration of Matter" (reworked into *The World Turned Upside Down* in 1842), Pratt had not yet reinterpreted all theology within the construct of a kind of scientific materialism, but he fully elevated matter to an eternal role and equity with spirit. "Matter and spirit are the two great principles of all existence," he had written in that work, which was composed in a Missouri prison at a time when the fear of death and physical dissolution "stared me in the face."[82] Both constitute the eternal—and material—constituents of the universe. His hope of subsuming all processes and principles within one set of laws, valid in heaven and earth alike, was evident in his discussion of atonement. Just as the physical universe was directly affected by the Fall, he had written in that essay, so must Christ's atonement be seen as entailing "the salvation and durability of the physical world, the renovation and regeneration of matter, and the restoration of the elements, to a state of eternal and unchangeable purity."[83] With his *Key*, he was simply expanding that methodology. Man's spirit and the physical components of the earth, laws of motion and of priesthood power, the parenting of children and the siring of gods in embryo, all conform to one set of laws. Therefore, "to a mind matured, or quickened with a fulness of intelligence…there is no use for the distinction implied in such terms" as "Physical and Spiritual," "because all things which do exist are eternal realities, in their elementary existence."[84]

Pratt laid his groundwork methodically and scientifically. The general laws that govern earth and heaven alike sound like a blend of Aristotle and Aquinas with Newton. Each atom occupies a space, which cannot be simultaneously occupied by other atoms. Organized intelligences must possess the power of self-motion. Voluntary motion implies an inherent free will, and motion implies time. Therefore, God cannot be omnipresent. Nonentity is the negative of all existence. This nothingness has nothing on which the creative power can operate. Hence, the elements are eternal, and creation ex nihilo a sectarian myth. Reminiscent of Plato's description of god in *Timaeus*, Pratt outlined the meaning and purpose of life in one eloquent paragraph:

Wisdom inspires the Gods to multiply their species and to lay the foundation for all the forms of life, to increase in numbers, and for each to enjoy himself in the sphere to which he is adapted, and in the possession and use of that portion of the elements necessary to his existence and happiness.[85]

Thus, conditions are created favorable for the endless advance of God's progeny "through every form of life, and birth, and change, and resurrection, and every form of progress in knowledge and experience." This great work of God, like the universe itself, will be

> endless or eternally progressive.... While eternal charity endures, or eternity itself rolls its successive ages, the heavens will multiply, and new worlds and more people be added to the kingdoms of the Fathers. Thus, in the progress of events, unnumbered millions of worlds, and of systems of worlds, will necessarily be called into requisition, and be filled by man, and beast, and fowl, and tree, and all the vast varieties of beings and things which ever budded and blossomed in Eden.[86]

No Mormon writer had plumbed the heady heights of human potential so unabashedly. One of the most surprising aspects of Mormon culture was the ease with which early members, most from evangelical backgrounds and reared in strict Methodist and Reformed Baptist traditions, segued into a faith that demolished some of Christendom's most cherished precepts. "An immortal man...perfected in his attributes in all the fulness of celestial glory, is called *a God*," wrote Pratt without apology. And then, without blinking, "It may then consistently enough be said, that there are, in a subordinate sense, a plurality of Gods."[87] Anglo-Saxon Protestantism had shown, since England's Toleration Act of 1689, a remarkable effort to allow dissent and heterodoxy in Christian faith—within a few non negotiable parameters, particularly the creedal definition of the Trinity. But here Pratt unblinkingly professed Mormonism to be, in an essential regard, polytheistic, while simultaneously monotheistic in the sense that mortals in this sphere worship God the Father in the name of Christ. But Pratt did not pause to offer that clarification, because he was not interested in passing muster with the guardians of Christian orthodoxy. It would have sounded too apologetic, and Pratt never condescended to apologies for Mormon heterodoxy.

Another great principle that animated Pratt's cosmology was dynamism. The heavens were for him, as for Jewish thinker Philo and church father Origen, seething with activity, populous with humans, spirits, and gods, all going and coming, ascending and descending, like the angels on Jacob's ladder. The differences among them derive from "the varied grades of intelligence and purity, and also in the variety of spheres occupied by each, in the series of progressive being."[88] This is theology that comes fittingly out of the age of Malthus and Hegel, conformable to Darwin's universe of flux and conflict. If by Pratt's day the dour face of Puritanism had long been in retreat, and Calvinism was fast becoming a "one-horse shay," the Christianity of yester-year was not receding quickly enough to suit him. The gospel he taught and embraced was, like the age of progress, one of unfettered optimism and boundless possibilities, not one of guilt, rules, and hellfire. He urged upon his contemporary religionists the importance of "ceasing to teach and impress upon the youthful mind the gloomy thoughts of death, and the melancholy forebodings of a long slumber in the grave." The "wayward and buoyant spirits of youth," he continued, were already too "weighed down and oppressed," and he hated to see "the more cheerful faculties of the soul...thus paralyzed."[89]

His embrace of human theosis, this "doctrine of equality," his more general application of the appellation "gods"—all are susceptible to the charge, if not of blasphemy, then of a dangerous collapse of sacred distance, a risky diminution of the grounds for awe that constitute reverence before God's transcendent holiness. Such concerns never occurred to Pratt. He was too swept up in what he took to be the invitation to fellowship with the gods. No other writer in early Mormonism so elaborated and celebrated this doctrine of human deification.

Besides writing theology, Pratt often preached in the newly constructed tabernacle near the site of the future temple.[90] Assessments by outsiders of Pratt's mature preaching abilities differ widely. Elizabeth Ferris attended one of Pratt's sermons before an "immense" crowd, perhaps two thousand, among whom she noted were "a few intelligent countenances, interspersed with sly cunning and disgusting sensuality; in both male and female, a large mass of credulity, and an abundance of open-mouthed, gawky stupidity." She found Pratt to be little better than his audience, as his discourse "was made up mostly of a rambling and disconnected glorification of the saints."[91] "As an intellectual effort," Ferris wrote, "it was beneath contempt." She noted the populist nature of Pratt's preaching style: "He resorted to the same kind of clap-trap common in political assemblages, which excited the boisterous mirth of his audience; and somehow it did not strike me as out of place in such a gathering."[92]

Most observers found more to praise in Pratt's oratory. Ferris's husband, Benjamin, described Pratt as one of the Mormons' "ablest men" and "most plausible sermonizers": "He is evidently above mediocrity in point of talent, and, with proper cultivation, and under any other than a system of imposture, would be noted as a good speaker. He has a subtle and seductive genius, is very self-possessed, and wears a candid and friendly appearance."[93] A Mormon dissident, John Hyde, favorably contrasted Pratt's "calm reasoning" with the "ringing voice and fluent 'talk' of Young, the nonsensical trash of Kimball, the enthusiastic declamations of Hyde" and the "abstractions of his brother Orson, swayed by every thought, and eagerly gulping all down as gospel inspiration to this wicked age."[94] Likewise, Frenchman Jules Rémy contrasted the preaching of the "two brothers Pratt, who made sensible and eloquent discourses before us," with the "insanity" of other Mormon speakers, such as Young and Kimball, who though possessing a "natural eloquence...did not observe the bounds of modesty in their speech, nor did they abstain from indecent pleasantries and buffooneries."[95] Another non-Mormon observer stated that in speaking to a tabernacle crowd of three thousand, Pratt "did not bellow but talked in an easy familiar voice, making his great audience all hear without effort."[96]

During this time in Utah, Pratt also participated in various civic and ecclesiastical affairs. He told Orson, "I have been verry buisy in the Legeslature, in the Regency of the University, and in the spanish school. We are about commencing to administer the holy ordinances of Endowment which will keep me buisy 2 days in a week."[97] Pratt served in the Legislative Council (the upper chamber) of the territorial legislature from 1852 to 1854; the composition of the council dramatically demonstrated the "theodemocracy" earlier envisioned by Joseph Smith, as it consisted of apostles and other high church officials. Church leaders chose the slate of officers, which was then approved in noncompetitive elections. Pratt's legislative committee assignments reflected long-standing interests (including committees on education and on engrossing, printing, and library) and newer concerns (such as on roads and bridges). As a member of the committee on petitions, Pratt helped draft petitions to the federal government for territorial needs as mundane as increasing the legislators' per diem and as consequential as receiving statehood. Petitions also focused on integrating Utah more tightly with both East and West, including a weekly mail from Salt Lake City to San Diego and both a transcontinental railroad and a telegraph connecting the Mississippi River with the Pacific Coast and running through Salt Lake City.[98]

The Spanish school indicated Pratt's hope that he might return to a Spanish-speaking area or help translate the Book of Mormon into Spanish. In October 1853, Parley informed Orson, "We are instructed to study Spanish, 'Yout,' [Ute] and 'Shoshone;' and all other American languages as fast as we can get at them." Pratt served on a committee charged "to prepare a first book in two or three of those Languages."[99] He described himself to Orson in May 1853, rather too generously, as "nearly as well versed in Spanish as in English and Ready to translate our works as soon as I have time."[100] During the winter of 1853 to 1854, Pratt taught Spanish to a class of roughly twenty students, including Wilford Woodruff and a group of missionaries preparing to teach American Indians in southern Utah who spoke some Spanish. Mexican traders, passing through Salt Lake City from New Mexico, participated at times.[101]

Pratt also engaged in an even more ambitious linguistic task, the reformation of the English alphabet. Earlier reformers, including Benjamin Franklin and Noah Webster, had attempted to simplify and rationalize English orthography. Brigham Young moved in the same direction after the establishment of the Board of Regents of the University of Deseret in 1850. The State of Deseret legislature had mandated the creation of a university governed by a chancellor and twelve regents. Though the University of Deseret closed temporarily in 1852, the Board of Regents, including Pratt, continued to supervise education in territorial Utah. Believing that a phonetic alphabet would allow foreign converts to assimilate more rapidly, Young instructed the Regents to create a system designed to eliminate English's idiosyncratic spelling. George D. Watt, an English convert central to the effort because of his knowledge of Pitman shorthand, explained the basic concept: "An alphabet should contain just as many letters as there are simple-pure atoms of sound."[102]

While the regents discussed alphabetic reform sporadically beginning in 1850, they seriously approached the subject in early 1853. After rejecting one possible alphabet in April, the regents commissioned Pratt, Watt, and Heber Kimball in late October to create a new proposal. Parley informed Orson that they intended "to prepare a more simple sistem of orthography for the English language, and to prepare books of the same."[103] On November 7, Parley presented an alphabet comprising forty characters, with each letter representing a distinct sound, based on Pitman's phonetic alphabet. At a regents' meeting the following week, Pratt stated that he had begun work on a children's textbook with the new alphabet. A revised version, designed primarily by Watt and announced in January 1854, consisted of thirty-eight letters, with many altered Latin and Pitman characters. The *Deseret News* explained, "After many fruitless attempts to render the common alphabet of the day subservient to their purpose, they found it expedient to invent an entirely new and original set of characters." To illustrate the new alphabet's efficiency, the *News* pointed out that the word "eight" "requires two letters instead of five to spell it, viz: AT."[104]

Pratt advocated for the Deseret alphabet in a public meeting in January and often signed his letters or wrote brief messages using it.[105] He excitedly explained to Orson that the new alphabet "will write Spanish, hebrew, greek, and with the addition of a few more Leters, all the Languages of the Earth. We shall put it out as a standard as soon as we get the type."[106] A *Deseret News* editorial similarly stated that the Deseret alphabet would enable "every nation and language" to understand the apostles.[107] With church leaders pushing for widespread use of the Deseret alphabet, some Saints learned it and even used it in their journals. Eventually the system was employed in an edition of the Book of Mormon and a few school readers, but it died a few years later.[108] Like the logical but utopian Esperanto language, devised in the late 1800s to create an international language, the Deseret alphabet improved upon a system that it could never dream of displacing.

In some ways, the experiment served as an allegory of nineteenth-century Mormonism. The Deseret alphabet, millennial hopes, the United Order, and perpetually refashioned dreams of Zion appealed to those Saints who yearned to transcend a corrupt society and its defective institutions. But such aspirations seldom survived the exigencies of life on this side of the River Jordan.

13

Prospecting for Souls in San Francisco

> Our light is now on a hill, and our candle lit, and placed
> on a candlestick in the centre of the Pacific House. Its
> light is so brilliant and unlooked for that it seems to
> dazzle the eyes of many, so I fear they will "wonder and
> perish."
>
> —PARLEY PRATT TO FRANKLIN D. RICHARDS, *March 24, 1855*

IN THE MIDST of his second term as president of the Pacific mission in
March 1855, Pratt proudly wrote from San Francisco to Brigham Young,
"Courthouses, schoolhouses, churches, and other Buildings have been opened
to us, and all our meetings have been well attended. Judges, Lawyers, leading
spirits, and many others have Listened with attention, and many are reading
and enquiring with deep interest."[1] Besides his preaching success, Pratt's
writing and publishing plans fueled his optimism; during this mission, he
wrote the bulk of his autobiography, sparred with San Francisco newspapers,
and received news of the publication of his most ambitious work, *Key to the
Science of Theology*. His mission followed the Mormon acknowledgment of
plural marriage, which made public defense of the Latter-day Saints even
more controversial, difficult, and dangerous. Even so, Pratt boasted, he had
succeeded. "Polygamy meets us everywhere," he told Young, "so we have met
it in press, and pulpit, and the Spirit of Truth has almost struck [our oppo-
nents] dumb with amazement & wonder."[2] And yet, Pratt's jubilant assessments masked disappointment with the pace of the missionary work,
frustration at publishing delays and impediments, and the beginning of a dispute over polygamy that eventually led to his death.

In April 1854, Young called Pratt on a second mission to San Francisco as
part of a strategy of selecting "new gathering places for the Saints" outside of
the Great Basin. Young directed Pratt to establish a "stake" and "lay out a
City" near San Jose, where John M. Horner, a Latter-day Saint who had
become California's first large-scale agriculturalist and had amassed assets

worth approximately a half-million dollars, had a large ranch.[3] Young hoped that Horner would "donate land for the purpose"; if he would not, Pratt could "go to San Diego or else where."[4] Pratt would again preside over the Pacific mission, supervising the church in northern California and throughout the Pacific, and gathering Saints to the new location or to "other places of gathering, on the Shores of the Pacific."[5] Young also called twenty missionaries to the Sandwich Islands (Hawaii) who would accompany Pratt to California, including fifteen-year-old Joseph F. Smith, Hyrum Smith's son and the church's future president.[6]

In preparation for his mission, Pratt collected donations, carefully noting each in his journal, ranging from $2 to $50 from a man who "is to supply the family meat" (and also grousing that a prosperous shoemaker "would give nothing").[7] On May 5, Pratt departed Salt Lake City with another missionary in a "small waggon drawn by 2 small Mules."[8] Pratt and the Sandwich Island missionaries initially accompanied a much larger caravan, including Young and five other apostles, traveling south to negotiate a peace treaty with Walkara and to visit the central and southern Utah settlements. In all, the company numbered nearly one hundred people; along with John Taylor, Pratt served as chaplain. Simon Carvalho, a Jewish artist and photographer from South Carolina who had spent the winter in Utah after leaving one of John C. Frémont's expeditions, described it as "an imposing travelling party." The Saints often sang, Carvalho recorded, "sometimes ending with 'I never knew what joy was Till I became a Mormon.'... Certainly, a more joyous, happy, free-from-care, and good-hearted people, I never sojourned among."[9]

Their "free-from-care" attitude belied the serious nature of the journey and the threat posed by Native Americans hostile to the Mormon settlements in central Utah. Young, who served as both territorial governor and federal superintendent of Indian affairs, hoped to end the so-called Walker War (named for Ute leader Walkara). Walkara had initially been friendly to the Mormons, even accepting baptism in 1850; however, the rapid growth in the Mormon population and new settlements such as Provo increasingly led to conflict. Disease, the disruption of the Indian food supply, and an 1853 territorial law banning the slave trade commonly practiced by the Utes caused further tensions. Beginning in July 1853, clashes between Utes and Mormons in central Utah led to the temporary abandonment of smaller settlements amid retaliatory violence, which resulted in the deaths of twelve whites and many more Native Americans. In early 1854, Walkara signaled to a federal Indian agent that he would agree to end hostilities and, on May 1, sent Young a letter offering peace in exchange for gifts and the end of restrictions on Native American trade.[10]

On May 11 and 12, Young, Pratt, and other Mormon officials met at Chicken Creek near present-day Nephi with about fifteen Indian leaders. According to Wilford Woodruff, Walkara initially "appeared dogish & was not disposed to talk," but Young "manifested great patience with him even after the patience of most men was exhausted. He went to him & lifted him out of the dirt & finally got him to talk some." Young presented the assembled leaders with "sixteen head of cattle, blankets and clothing, trinkets, arms and ammunition." Walkara allowed the other chiefs to speak first; several berated the Mormons, whereas others expressed a desire for peace. The following morning, Young proclaimed that "he wanted to be friend with all the Indians; he loved them like a father, and would always give them plenty of clothes, and good food, provided they did not fight, and slay any more white men." Walkara accepted the Mormon proposal, though the underlying issues—Mormon possession of American Indian land and interference with traditional trade (including slavery)—remained unresolved. Nevertheless, he stated, "Wakara love Mormon chief; he is a good man ... If Indian kill white man again, Wakara make Indian howl." Afterward, the "calumet of peace was again handed around, and all the party took a smoke."[11]

Pratt's youthful visions of restoring to the Indians a knowledge of their Israelite origins and glorious destiny had morphed into the more modest project of helping establish a peaceful coexistence. Although the federal government never formally approved the treaty, both sides respected the peace. Walkara and other American Indian leaders accompanied Young's party on their journey to the southern Utah settlements.

Young's caravan traveled during the day and preached at night in Mormon settlements which had been founded partly as a result of Pratt's southern Utah expedition. Because of the size of the traveling party, which had "accumulated Like a rolling snow ball all the way," Pratt grumbled, "Lucky is the man who gets invited to a Lodging or meal of victuals." The "visiting party," he complained, had "Largy Roomy Waggons, good beds and provisions, every convenience, and some of their wives to help them," but he and the missionaries only had "small waggons, and blankets, without beds." Pratt complained of bitterly cold nights shivering in his wagon, though he had also been hospitably entertained in some settlements. At Parowan, for instance, he had been given "3 pair of good summer stockings and other Little etceteras; and some wheat" for his animals.[12]

Nevertheless, Pratt's resentment of his physical and financial hardships when contrasted with the comforts of other Mormon officials continued throughout his mission. Many of his fellow leaders "stay at home and ride in carriages," he carped, and would not "afford me a horse for such a journey. But that is their business and not mine. all will be Rewarded according to their works and it is mine to do all I can, and Let God be Judge of other mens Labours." While he had tried to be "Cheerful" on the journey, he told his family, "I have felt a Loneliness, a sollemn Gloom, or Melancholy which I cannot wholly shake off. In short, it is contrary to my nature to Live away from home, and absent from the endearing scenes, and the joys and comforts of the family Circle. but duty to the world, and even to my family Requires it; and why should I repine?"[13] His long years of toil and separation from family were wearing on him. Zion had not been redeemed, the Lamanites remained in his mind a quarrelsome and difficult race, and Mormon solidarity under persecution was giving way to the bickering and stinginess of the prideful and affluent. It was his sense of duty as a veteran apostle, not the feisty zeal of a young millennialist, that would see him through this mission.

A few months later, Pratt remarked that he was "far below the youngest members of the quorum in point of means, and of houses, lands, Cattle, food and Clothing." He comforted himself and his family by recalling that God "has counted me worthy of Laboring in his cause for a Quarter of a century" and had allowed him to marry "some of the choisest spirits of this fallen sphere" and to father "some noble souls."[14] He envisioned that in the future, when a man blessed "a faithful and virtuous woman, or faithful and virtuous sons and daughters," he would state, "The Lord make thee fruitful, and multiply thee, and make thee as the house of *Parley, of old*; who were faithful in all things...and the Lord multiplied them; and delighted to Honor them. there fore is their House, and name and Lineage established in the earth, and known among all nations and tribes."[15]

As Pratt and the missionaries prepared to leave Young's company behind in southern Utah, Heber Kimball prophesied, as he had done before Pratt's 1836 mission to Canada when he had promised that Thankful would bear a son, that his work in Canada would open the way for the preaching of Mormonism in England, and that he would one day have "riches, silver and gold, till you will loath the counting thereof." Cognizant that the third blessing had gone unfulfilled and perhaps discerning Pratt's ill-concealed resentment at wealthier church leaders, Kimball reiterated the promise, stating that Pratt's family would have "every good thing" and that his posterity would be "as numerous as the stars of heaven."[16] (Pratt's twenty-three children who survived to adulthood produced 266 grandchildren for him; today, Pratt's living descendants are estimated between thirty thousand and fifty thousand.)[17] Nevertheless, as during his other missions, Pratt's family suffered during his absence. In June 1855, as drought and crickets ravaged the Mormons' crops, a "scarcity of bread stuff existed in many families" in Salt Lake City, including Pratt's, who had "commenced to ration themselves at half a pound a day each."[18]

Before parting with Young's company, Pratt visited Mormon missionaries to American Indians in Harmony, a new settlement under the leadership of Rufus Allen, his companion in Chile, and Thomas D. Brown. He noted that many "Lamanites" had been baptized, and "one of their children was Raised from the dead." Pratt interpreted the American Indians' current state of "human degradation," including the nakedness of women and children, as a result of the rejection of Jesus Christ by the Book of Mormon Lamanites. He wrote, "I wept to think that even a chosen Linage could be thus Reduced." In the condition of the Indians, he saw a lesson for the Latter-day Saints: if they rejected God's priesthood, they would experience a similar fate. He groaned, "How would we feel to see our Sons and daughters or their descendants, going wild in the dessarts, naked, Living on grass and Roots, filthy in body, deformed, and idiotic in features and minds with no sentiments, of feeling, sympathy or delicacy—no sense of Modesty or propriety to distinguish them from the wild beasts." Nevertheless, the visit rekindled Pratt's hope of the American Indians' future. The Saints, Pratt believed, "are Called upon and keys given us to deliver them from this Hell." Besides spiritual teachings, they had a responsibility to assist the Indians materially, and he encouraged his wives to seek the support of other women and Young's sanction in preparing clothing for converted Indians.[19] He encouraged the missionaries working with Native Americans to "feed, clothe and instruct them" and to "Learn their Language as fast as you can…. They have suffered hell enough here."[20] At Cedar City, Pratt preached "upon the subject of their being kind to the Indians, to feed them, clothe them and learn them how to labor."[21]

The plight of captive slaves, many as young as his own small children, particularly disturbed Pratt: "Think of children the age of Lehi, took prisoners, to be sold or killd, see them squat round the fire naked in a Cold day rosting and eating grass as their only food, with no one to Care for them."[22] After the negotiations with Walkara, Young purchased two Snake Indian toddlers, whom he found "on the open snow, digging with their little fingers for grass-nuts, or any roots to afford sustenance." He sent these "living skeletons" to Salt Lake City to "have them cared for and educated like his own children."[23] Two years later, in June 1856, Pratt similarly agreed to care for a six-year-old "Lamanite girl," who had been purchased by William Dame in Parowan. Pratt gave her to his childless wife, Elizabeth, "to be brought up as her own daughter" and named her Abish, after the only female Lamanite named in the Book of Mormon.²⁴

Pratt separated from Young's caravan with his missionaries, Carvalho, and an additional Mormon woman en route to San Bernardino. They traveled along the Old Spanish Trail through the deserts of southern Utah and Nevada.²⁵ As in his trek four years earlier, the desert crossing proved excruciating. On May 28, the company departed its campsite at 3:30 P.M. to travel the fifty to sixty miles of desert to reach the relative oasis of the Vegas Springs. They arrived, much fatigued, at about 10 o'clock the following morning after an arduous night of travel. Pratt told his family that their "little mules are failing so fast" and that "19 hours without ceasing to travel...was hard on me. But it will all help wear me out and make an old man of me."²⁶ On June 3, at Bitter Springs, they were "in a weary and exhausted condition," traveling a road littered with "dead animals" and "waggons and household things left on the desert by companies who had gone before us."²⁷ Silas Smith complained, "The air was strongly impregnated with stench from the dead cattle that lay in great number along the plain."²⁸ As they struggled toward San Bernardino, they consumed all their supplies, eating the "last of our provisions"—"the dust of some crackers that was left in the bottom of the sacks"—for breakfast on the day of their arrival on June 9.²⁹

In San Bernardino, Pratt counseled the missionaries to sell their possessions and earn money for their further travel.³⁰ He went ahead to San Pedro, where he arranged for the missionaries' passage on a steamer to San Francisco. He sailed on June 24, and the missionaries followed a few weeks later. Pratt then traveled to San Jose, where he found his wife Elizabeth, who had earlier returned to California.³¹ The news that local Saints had forced her to be a "servant till her health was to poor to work" infuriated Pratt. In addition, likely because of her status as a plural wife, "she had been insulted, or shunned by most, while a secret influence was afloat against her and me, and all who were governed by the holy order of God." Some Mormons in San Jose resented Pratt for both his financial solicitations and his practice of plural marriage; Pratt complained that these "snakes in the grass continued to insinuate that I was allways a begging, etc., and that we were no better than *whores— whoremungers*." Livid at this reception, Pratt refused to return to San Jose. Indeed, he "would as soon go to hell" as to the site Young had envisioned as a gathering place for Mormons in northern California.³² With the help of local Mormons, Parley and Elizabeth rented a home in San Francisco in July, before finding another in the city in August in which they could live and hold church meetings. They later moved to cheaper lodgings in Santa Clara.³³

Throughout their stay in California, Elizabeth suffered from ill health. In September, Pratt wrote that Elizabeth's work was "fast killing her" as she "does the house work for, from 6 to 8 persons," notwithstanding being "afflicted continually with spinal complaint, inflamation of the Wo'b."[34] He told Agatha that Elizabeth was "never well," and was "only a sister to her husband and is a wife to nobody."[35] Her sufferings drove her into "a dreadful state of gloom," suggesting possible endometriosis combined with depression. As a result, Elizabeth remained primarily in Santa Clara and San Francisco while Pratt traveled throughout northern California.[36] Years of arduous travel had begun to take a toll on Pratt's health as well. In June 1855, at the age of forty eight, he wrote after walking five miles, "this wearied me very much as I am heavey and fleshy and somewhat disabled by the enduring of much hardship, by means of my former sufferings and extreme exhaustion in the cause of Truth and in settling new counties."[37]

Pratt, who in his travels often relied on the generosity of faithful Mormons, arrived in San Francisco in the midst of a business depression caused by overspeculation and diminished returns from gold mining. The depression worsened during his stay and became a full-fledged banking crisis. Local members—who numbered about 120 scattered among five branches—could scrape together very little to give him.[38] The crisis ruined even the fortune of John Horner, a supporter of earlier missionary efforts. In August, Pratt wrote his family, "As to money in this country, it is out of reach. The saints at San Bernidino, and Br. Horner and others in this part, are worse off for money than I ever was—or ever expect to be. I pity them from my heart."[39] With donations from church members heartfelt but entirely inadequate, Pratt and other missionaries struggled to support themselves.[40]

Throughout his stay in San Francisco, Pratt was almost utterly dependent on the generosity of a "few sisters and a brother or two" for his "daily sucor."[41] Pratt asked Young if money collected as tithing could be used to support him and other missionaries and to pay for printing expenses.[42] Young granted permission only to "use small amounts" if absolutely necessary.[43] Pratt lacked even enough money to mail letters regularly to Salt Lake, and he once stated, "I have not even one dollar either to pay my house rent, (35 dol. per month) or to go to market."[44] In November, Pratt told his family that he was "several hundred dollars" in debt, not including $2,000 worth of books he had ordered from England on which he would have to pay "several hundred dollars" in duties.[45] His obligations, which climbed to $1,500 by January, included debts he had incurred in his first California mission "to get means to get home." His clothes were by then "old and shabby, though I mannage to keep up a tolerable appearance," he wrote with resignation. His living arrangements were often appalling. When he visited San Francisco in January, while Elizabeth stayed at Santa Clara, he rented for $12 a month a "small dark cluttered, unfurnished bedroom in a little back shed, or shanty."[46] He even auctioned off a broach given him by Phoebe to raise funds for his family.[47] The financial crisis offered the occasional consolation; it led to a deflationary cycle and allowed Pratt to purchase millinery supplies for Agatha on deep discount.[48]

An ill-advised boat purchase compounded his financial problems. His principal concern during his first few months in San Francisco was to secure passage for the Sandwich Island missionaries. Nathan Tanner, a missionary returning from Hawaii, had been commissioned by missionaries still in Hawaii to buy a boat to transport missionaries and members between Hawaii and California.[49] Before Pratt arrived, Tanner purchased a 271-ton brig, the *Rosalind*, for $2,600; Tanner estimated the boat would need $500 of repairs to make it seaworthy.[50] Since the ship promised to solve the problem of missionary transport to Hawaii, Pratt "lent his council to the enterprise, & my credit & my influence to help it out." He tried to salvage what was emerging as a financial misstep by having some missionaries take lodging on the *Rosalind* and work on its repair, while he directed others to find local employment to raise additional money. The missionaries did not share Pratt's enthusiasm for the project. Silas Smith groaned, "If one was to judge it from its dilapidated state he would readily come to the conclusion that it was built at or near the time that the American Pilgrims landed on Plymouth Rock." Compounding the failure, the captain hired by Tanner to repair the boat, an "apostate Mormon" named Thomas Moss, turned out to be inept, and his insulting manner alienated the missionaries. Tanner was forced to pay Moss an exorbitant fee to get rid of him, after which the missionaries submitted a bill for their work as well.[51] The financial misstep had become a full-blown disaster, and Pratt eventually decided that Tanner had defrauded him and other local Saints. At long last, the missionaries left San Francisco in small groups for Hawaii that fall, but not before Pratt rebuked one for drunkenness and changed the assignment of another from Hawaii to California for "having made himself most free with the sisters."[52]

Financial problems also complicated the establishment of a gathering place. While Young wanted converts from the Pacific mission to settle in Utah, he believed a Mormon community in northern California would "operate as a screen" by ensuring that those who immigrated "will be ready, and cheerfully willing to walk up to their covenants, and build up the

Kingdom of our God."[53] Pratt, however, told Young that he saw little possibility of establishing a stake in northern California, as they had "no land to put it on," "no body to put on it," and "no means of raising children there."[54] By late October, Pratt had abandoned the idea of a Mormon colony in northern California and decided instead to organize an emigration of the California Saints to Utah.[55] Notwithstanding his original instructions, Young concurred: "If the whisperings of the Spirit are to come to the valley of the mountains it is a happy whispering to you and them and very satisfactory to me."[56] He further wrote that Pratt should perhaps "go out and bring up a company every year" from California, suggesting a long-term role for Pratt in the state.[57]

Pratt and Young also debated the location for a gathering spot for Hawaiian Saints. Francis Hammond, one of the missionaries to Hawaii, had advocated "either a gathering place prepared for these saints on their own lands" or one in California. Without a centralized gathering, Hammond worried, converts would be "surrounded with all manner of influences that are calculated to draw them away from the truth, to serve other Gods again." Young had directed the Hawaiian missionaries in 1853 to "obtain a fitting island or portion of an island where the brethren can collect in peace and sustain themselves unmolested," in preparation for a later gathering to Utah. In October 1854, Hammond suggested the sparsely populated island of Lanai as a possible gathering site.[58] Pratt evidently agreed and informed Young, "At present there is no means to gather them to this coast, so they are being gathered, and are commencing to farm, etc. on a certain Island."[59] Though the settlement on Lanai eventually failed, it established a precedent for a more successful settlement at Laie on Oahu in 1865, which remains the center of Mormon life in Hawaii and a center for other Pacific islands.

Since his arrival in San Francisco, Pratt had been holding meetings, generally on Thursdays and Sundays, as well as "circulating Books and tract; and every thing we could to notify and warn the people."[60] Missionary work focused on converting new members and on reclaiming lapsed Mormons. Pratt told his family, "*Mormons* turn up under every toad stool as it were. Some are coming to life—some are frostbitten like a soft Potatoe, and some are the worst enemies we have."[61] George Q. Cannon, a talented missionary returning from a Hawaiian mission who would eventually become one of Mormonism's most prominent leaders, recorded, "Parley has held meetings all the time at his house and has preached every opportunity—the people are hard hearted and careless and the truth has no charms for them."[62] Pratt's preaching topics ranged from the "state of the human family after leaving this state of probation, and going to the world of spirits" to "instructing the saints...to influence men and means" to build up the "Kingdom of God."⁶³

Pratt's responsibilities included supervising missionary work throughout much of the Pacific, which now included fledgling Mormon efforts in the Pacific islands, Asia, and the West Coast of the United States.⁶⁴ To spread the Mormon message more effectively across such far-flung areas, Pratt hoped to acquire a printing press to publish a newspaper and pamphlets. In August, Young approved purchase of a press, though he suggested that perhaps Pratt should instead use one that had been acquired by the Hawaiian Saints. In San Francisco, Young wrote, the press would "be in a central and influential position, and can print for the islands as well."⁶⁵

Pratt, however, could not immediately acquire a press and, frustrated by the debacle of the *Rosalind* and the animosity in San Jose, he turned to his writing. He explained, "As I have no land on which to lay out a city: and no funds by which to print, I can only buisy myself with writing and in the work of the ministry as the way opens."⁶⁶ He first plunged into a project he termed his "history." During his correspondence with Orson in 1853–1854 over Frederick Chapman's Pratt family history project, Orson informed Parley that Chapman had learned they were "prominent men in this Church" and had asked them to write autobiographical sketches for his volume. Parley replied that "a mere sketch of the outlines of [my] truly eventful life would occupy several hundred pages" and speculated that Chapman would not publish it if it "contained the truth as it is in Jesus." Praising his brother's "interesting, easy, flowing stile," Orson encouraged Parley to "Try them and See." Working together and with the "dictations of the Holy Spirit," Orson hoped they might "write something that shall hereafter prove a blessing to our brethren." Parley eventually acquiesced to Orson's entreaties, and Chapman's book, published in 1864, contained short biographies of the brothers.⁶⁷

In July 1854, a few months after this correspondence, Parley embarked on a project to narrate his "truly eventful life" in "several hundred pages." Within a month, he had written 250 manuscript pages, bringing the story "up to the prison, in Boon Co. Mo. 1839" (roughly half of the published autobiography).⁶⁸ He described the project to Church historian George Smith as "a Lean, megre sketch of Church History. As my hurried life, and hurried manner of writing, prevents my branching out on many interesting items." He further told Smith, "I am determined to complete it now if the Lord will. If I miss this opportunity I have my doubts whether it will be writen at all." Perhaps, Pratt thought, his autobiography might be published in California.⁶⁹

To accomplish this goal, Pratt hired George Q. Cannon as his scribe. Cannon, who copied three hundred pages over the next six weeks for $50, relished the work (perhaps because while he transcribed and went with Pratt to the "theatre to hear the world renowned violinist Ole Bull and the pianist M[aurice] Strakosch," his three companions dug potatoes to earn money for their trip home).[70] By mid-November, Pratt had completed an additional hundred manuscript pages, bringing his history "up to the begining of the year 41. it is neetly revised and chapters and headings all finished up to that time ready for the press, or to leave to my children; or to the archives of the church."[71] Without Cannon's assistance and with mounting responsibilities in California, Pratt's pace slowed, though he continued to write intermittently.

For Pratt, the autobiography represented an opportunity to spread the Mormon message not in a doctrinal tract or combative pamphlet but in a narrative of the lived experience of an early Latter-day Saint. It also allowed him to relive the excitement of early Mormonism when he had played a central role in so many pivotal events: the Lamanite mission, Zion's Camp, the Missouri troubles, the apostolic mission to England, the trek across the plains. In the late 1830s and early- and mid-1840s, Pratt had been Mormonism's leading voice to the world and a central player in the faith's major dramas. By 1854, Pratt's status as Mormonism's preeminent writer had been challenged and perhaps surpassed by Orson, who wrote a series of tracts in England that were published by the tens of thousands. Indeed, it had been nearly a decade since Parley had published anything significant (*Key to the Science of Theology* was printed the following year), though his earlier works continued to be read and exert a profound influence on Mormon thought. In addition, Pratt's missions to California placed him on Mormonism's geographic margins; the Pacific mission was thrilling in its possibilities but disappointing in its short-term results. His autobiography returned Pratt to a time when he had been at the center of the action and allowed him to reclaim his role.[72]

Pratt may have also seen publication of his autobiography as a partial solution to his financial woes. Though many nineteenth-century Mormons produced autobiographical accounts, few wrote, as did Pratt, with publication explicitly in mind.[73] A year earlier, Orson had encouraged him to write more extensively, both to benefit the church and support Parley's family:

There are no writings in the church with the exception of the revelations, which I esteem more highly than yours; and I think were you to

FIGURE 13.1 Parley P. Pratt. Engraving by J. C. Buttre from a daguerreotype from mid 1850s. Courtesy of Ben Parkinson.

give your time more to writing and publishing it would not only be a blessing to millions, but would render great assistance to you in a temporal point of view.... Oh, my dear brother, do, in some way, burst these shackles and send forth your theological Works by thousands among all languages and nations till the whole earth shall be enlightened with the light thereof.[74]

Pratt had good reason to hope his autobiography would produce a profit. Nineteenth-century Americans purchased biographies and autobiographies in such quantities that periodicals reported a "Biographical Mania" had swept the nation.[75]

Pratt was able to write so quickly because he relied heavily on his previous writings. Almost 90 percent of the text is based on or copied from earlier works, which he generally revised and condensed. Pratt drew especially from his books about the Missouri *Persecution* and articles from the *Millennial Star*.[76] The autobiography also includes selections from his book of poetry, *The Millennium*; his earliest pamphlet, *Shameful Outrage*; his manuscript family record; various letters and journals; and newspaper articles. For instance, perhaps the most famous episode of the autobiography—Pratt's account of Joseph Smith's rebuking of the guards in Richmond Jail in November 1838—first appeared in the *Deseret News* in 1853. Pratt generally avoided or minimized controversial subjects, confining his dissension from Smith in Kirtland, for example, to a single paragraph, with a second discussing their reconciliation. The published autobiography also contains little information on his wives and children.[77]

After completing his San Francisco mission, Pratt would continue working on his autobiography, assisted by his wife Keziah. He completed his narrative to 1851 and then inserted his journals for the later years. When he left for his last mission, he hoped to arrange publication with an eastern press, as he had earlier in Detroit and New York. Before he left, he preached on the necessity of recordkeeping, particularly of writing a man's "official acts in the priesthood." Pratt expressed regret that he had "not kept more of a Journal" as he wished he "had written evry mans name" he had baptized or blessed in his ministry.[78] Isaiah Coombs, one of his traveling companions to the East, recorded, "Br Pratt has read 13 chapters of his history to me.... It is very interesting; so much so that I could have listened to it all day without tiring. I am sure no saint will be without a copy of it when it is printed."[79] A lack of financial resources, however, prevented Pratt from publishing his autobiography in the East. By January 1857, he lamented that it likely would not be "published in my days," and he instructed his family, "Should any thing happen to me, & the record be preserved I wish it Carefully Compiled, Coppied & taken Care of."[80] A month before Pratt's death, he entrusted his autobiography manuscript to George A. Smith while the two were in St. Louis in March 1857, with instructions to return it to his family.[81]

In late May 1857, Smith delivered the manuscript to Parley Jr., then twenty years old. Between 1872 and 1874, John Taylor assisted Parley Jr. in preparing the autobiography for publication. Taylor minimized their role, claiming they made few changes "and preserved intact" Parley's original manuscript "so far as possible."[82] Because the manuscript has not survived, it is not clear to what extent Taylor and Parley Jr. edited the autobiography, particularly the pre-1851 section. Some information on the amount and type of editing done can be gained from a comparison of Pratt's journals in the 1850s with his published autobiography. For the last six years of Pratt's life, the autobiography contains journals, letters, and newspaper articles. In preparing the autobiography for publication, Pratt's journals were first copied (in a document known as the "After Manuscript") and then edited. In general, passages about Pratt's family, both positive and negative, as well as references to financial difficulties and controversial events were excised. (Parley Jr. was also apparently conscious of his own image. His father's journal recorded that on August 18, 1855, Parley Jr. met him riding on a mule. In the "After Manuscript," Parley Jr. crossed out "mule" and inserted "horseback," though the section was eventually cut from the autobiography.)[83]

In seeking subscriptions for the forthcoming book, published in 1874 by the New York firm Russell Brothers, Parley Jr. promised that his father had not emphasized "dull, stale, and uninteresting events," but had written on "the most noted and striking incidents of, as he says himself, a truly eventful life...with an originality, a force and beauty of style peculiar to himself."[84] At the end of his short editor's preface to the autobiography, Parley Jr. quoted his father's *Voice of Warning*: "Should the author be called to sacrifice his life for the cause of truth, he will have the consolation that it will be said of him, as it was said of Abel, 'He being dead yet speaketh.'"[85]

Pratt's voice in the autobiography is in the tradition of Jonathan Edwards under the influence of Benjamin Franklin, rather than in the idiom of the romantic autobiographers of the era. Modern autobiography is generally traced to the romantics, beginning with Jean-Jacques Rousseau's *The Confessions* (completed in 1769 and published in 1782) and including figures such as William Wordsworth and Percy Shelley, who used autobiography as a form of introspection, a revealing of the inner man and a journey toward self-knowledge.[86] Like other religious autobiographers, Pratt was concerned more with divine knowledge than self-knowledge and spoke with a certainty and assurance that was foreign to the romantics. Edwards's *Personal Narrative* (1740), which traces his pilgrimage toward God's grace and love, exemplified the tradition of spiritual autobiography of the English and American Puritans. Widely reprinted in the nineteenth century, it served as a model for generations of spiritual autobiographies.[87] Mormon autobiographies before Pratt's— most notably Joseph Smith's autobiographical statements and his mother Lucy Mack Smith's *Biographical Sketches of Joseph Smith*, first published by Orson Pratt in 1853—combined "providential history and autobiography" in the Puritan style. For the Puritans, as for the Smiths and Pratt, "biography and autobiography were simultaneously scripture as well as history."[88]

Pratt's religious quest, his spiritual yearnings and conversion to Mormonism, thus dominate the early portions of the autobiography. And in the remainder, he prominently featured the central themes of his ministry, particularly his quest for authority, the reality of spiritual gifts, and his millennial hopes. Early Puritans lived in a "world of wonders," seeing continual divine intervention into their world through everything from miracles to deformed babies to astronomical events.[89] Pratt's autobiography clearly demonstrates that early Mormons likewise lived in a world of wonders, as he described visions, healings, dreams, revelations, and God's vengeance on the wicked. Soon after his conversion to Mormonism, for example, while Pratt walked alone on a country road, he witnessed a "brilliant light" in the night sky that traced the outlines of a compass. He immediately "fell upon my knees in the street, and thanked the Lord for so marvelous a sign of the coming of the Son of Man."[90] To the Puritan emphasis on conversion and the reception of God's grace, Pratt added the persecution narrative, which he had honed since his publications in the late 1830s. Roughly one-fourth of the entire autobiography focuses on his imprisonment in Missouri in 1838–1839, and the motif of the persecution of the Saints runs throughout his book.

But Pratt presented himself not merely as religious seeker, preacher, and martyr. He portrayed himself also as a trickster and self-made man more in the guise of Franklin than Edwards. Franklin's autobiography, recounting his rise from obscurity to international stature, was even more popular than Edwards's *Narrative* in nineteenth-century America and established the era's other major autobiographical tradition: the rise of the self-made man. Like Franklin, Pratt described his ascent from poverty to prominence through hard work, self-education, ingenuity, and wit. Pratt's autobiography still stands as the most widely read autobiographical account of Mormonism's early years.[91]

While working on the sweeping narrative of his life, Pratt also found outlet for his writing in combative essays published in the San Francisco press. The initial lack of a press and his financial problems precluded Pratt from publishing large numbers of pamphlets, a system he had relied on in earlier missions, and he turned to the free publicity of newspapers to advance his cause. The Gold Rush attracted a highly literate population to San Francisco, creating a climate in which journalism thrived. During the 1850s, San Francisco boasted more newspapers than London; over the course of the decade, 132 papers appeared (and most disappeared) in the city. Representative of the city's ecclesiastical pluralism, San Francisco boasted eighteen religious newspapers between 1848 and 1865, which by the time of Pratt's visits included sponsorship by Baptists, Congregationalists, Presbyterians, Methodists, Catholics, and Jews.[92] San Francisco journalism tended to be sensational and highly personal, and unflattering articles often inspired duels or other violence. In 1856, the most infamous incident of newspaper violence occurred when the editor of the San Francisco *Tribune*, James Casey, shot and wounded James

King, editor of the San Francisco *Evening Bulletin*; the dispute helped insti-
gate the Vigilante Movement of 1856.[93] In the hard-hitting world of San
Francisco journalism, Mormonism quickly became a hotly debated issue.
Pratt, one of Mormonism's most literate and combative figures, was in the
right place at the right time.

The mid-1850s proved to be a crucial transitional period for the public
image of Mormonism. Although the Saints were ostracized by much of the
press even before the 1850s, the martyrdom of Joseph and Hyrum Smith in
1844 and the subsequent forced exodus from Illinois had evoked some
sympathy. However, after the announcement of plural marriage in 1852 and
the rampant rumors of Mormon defiance of federal authority in the years following, Mormon stereotypes hardened and became nationalized through
extensive reinforcement in regional and national periodicals.[94] Nevertheless,
the Mormon elite such as Pratt primarily saw the press in optimistic terms.
For example, John G. Chambers, a Mormon journalist, stated in 1855 that
while the press had worked against Mormonism in "propagating falsehood,"
its true purpose would be realized as a "powerful means in disseminating
truth."[95] That year, the Mormon press included ten newspapers—three in the
United States (Salt Lake City, St. Louis, and New York City) and seven overseas. The number of Mormon papers caused apostle Franklin D. Richards,
editor of the *Millennial Star*, to celebrate the press for advancing the "principles of righteousness and eternal life" throughout the world.[96]

Pratt had publicly announced his return to San Francisco in a letter to
John S. Hittell, an assistant editor of the *Daily California Chronicle* who
had advertised a series of lectures against Christianity.[97] The *Chronicle*
published the letter along with a circular printed by Pratt that missionaries
and local members, including "the sisters," distributed in the city.
Missionary Henry Richards wrote that he "distributed some notices that
Bro Pratt had got published some tore them up as soon as they saw what
they were, others said they did not want any and some refused to look at
them at all."[98] Pratt confirmed to Young that "few will buy or read" his
tracts.[99] This first letter established the tone of Pratt's relationship with the
Chronicle, which published nine letters from Pratt and numerous articles
on him over the next ten months.[100] Established in 1853 by a group of
reporters led by Frank Soulé, a newspaperman from Maine who soon
became embroiled in local politics as a Whig and then a Republican, the
Chronicle quickly became one of the city's most important papers. Like
many of San Francisco's newspapers in the 1850s, the *Chronicle* enjoyed a
relatively short life, but proved uncommonly influential during the five

years of its publication (1853–1858); at the time of Pratt's correspondence, it claimed the largest circulation in the city.[101]

Pratt's fiery letters generally elicited sarcastic, humorous, and often mocking responses from the *Chronicle*. In his introductory letter, Pratt suggested that Hittell need not give the public any "uneasiness" over the corrupt forms of traditional Christianity, and in his circular, he promised to baptize the penitent, heal the sick, preach a pure religion, and accept any donations. In response the *Chronicle* noted that it had given Pratt "all the publicity we can, by publishing his circular gratuitously," and remarked on the futility of Pratt's mission, characterizing California as "the very h-ll on earth of the Mormons."[102]

Pratt's tone became scathing in a September 1854 letter to the *Christian Advocate*, a Methodist paper, which had printed excerpts from a book by Benjamin Ferris, a former federal official in Utah, which Pratt did not consider "decent to be read in a brothel." Bristling with anger, Pratt told his family, "He represents the Daughtrs of Zion as, being divourced, and being married again every few days till the same woman goes the whole round of the priesthood, and begins again."[103] Pratt's letter, reprinted in the *Chronicle,* warned the editors of the *Advocate* to "*tremble*—for God will not suffer such lies to be published with impunity much longer" and condemned its readers to the "lowest hell."[104] In response, the *Advocate* mocked Pratt: "to have a man possessed of divine authority, and capable of raising the dead, threaten us so, is truly awful.... A few more such will cause us to retire to private life."[105] Young, without knowledge of Pratt's letter, cautioned him not to discuss Ferris's book, stating the "let alone policy is the only one to be pursued in this matter both publicly & privately," because additional publicity would spur greater sales.[106] This warning arrived well after Pratt's attack, but it may have shaped Pratt's later articles, which concentrated on positively portraying Mormon doctrine rather than responding to specific attacks.

Pratt's letters, in reality short essays, published in the *Chronicle* covered a variety of subjects. In "What is Mormonism?" Pratt provided a brief insight into the expansive view he held of the church. For him, it consisted of "an emanation of Divine light," which embraced "all the elements of a renewed and renovated system of social, moral, political, and spiritual order." "In short," Pratt concluded, "it is the reign of Heaven commenced on the earth."[107] In "Spiritual Philosophy," Pratt reprised major themes of his forthcoming *Key to the Science of Theology* including the materialism of spirit.[108] In "The Bible!" Pratt decried the "arrogance and infidelity" of the Protestant world's abandonment of biblical doctrine for modern principles. He declared that the congruence of the Bible and Mormonism on subjects such as "its laws of marriage, [and] its theocratic institutions" would cause the world to either reject the Bible or embrace Mormonism.[109] Pratt reiterated this argument privately to Young: "The public are forced to see that the Bible & "*Mormonism*" must stand or fall together.... Editors, Clergy, & lawyers spern the Bible as barbarous, Its Patriarchs, prophets & apostles are looked upon as children of darkness, or at best as children of the twilight—far less moral, virtuous, & enlightened than 'this christian age.'"[110] In two letters, Pratt traced the calamities that would occur before the Millennium and the ultimate triumph of Christ's people. Denouncing the wickedness of the American people, he singled out their "treatment of the Mormons, the Indians, and the negroes" for condemnation.[111]

Throughout Pratt's correspondence with the *Chronicle*, nearly all of his letters were preceded by critical editorial statements. The paper compared the zeal of the Mormons with that of the Spiritualists, who were influential in the city. "Enthusiasts in any 'ism,'" the *Chronicle* opined, fail to see the "irrational, inconsistent, impracticable and ridiculous aspects of their hobby." Furthermore, they focus on "certain fancied bright sides, which their heated brains rub and polish till the sight dazzles and confounds cold, pure reason."[112] The *Chronicle*'s sarcasm reached its zenith in the paper's commentary on Pratt's millennarian prophecies: "Is there a devil or a god among us? Is he inspired or does he rave only and is mad? Is he forthwith to follow Elijah of old or to be quietly translated to a cell at [the insane asylum in] Stockton?"[113] After the publication of Pratt's first apocalyptic letter, which had freely interspersed phrases from Zechariah 14 with his own prose, the *Chronicle* accused him of plagiarism "for palming off as his own what Zechariah had already given as his, or rather as the Lord's."[114]

Even the manner in which the *Chronicle* referred to Pratt was steeped in sarcasm, as it referred to him as the Right Reverend Archbishop, the High Priest of San Francisco, Saint Parley, and "Prophet, Apostle, Elder, or whatever else he calls himself."[115] Further, it identified him as Peter Parley Pratt (linking him to a popular figure in children's fiction by Samuel Griswold Goodrich), then correctly as Parley Parker Pratt, then Parley Peter Pratt, and finally, given Pratt's propensity to sign his letters "P. P. Pratt," as Pee Pee Pratt. In supposed exasperation, the paper named him as "Mr. Parley-Peter, or Patrick, or Prattle, or Parson, or_____ Pratt (we have forgotten the gentleman's middle name)."[116]

Why did Pratt subject himself to the open mocking the *Chronicle* heaped on him and his cause? And why did the *Chronicle* continue to publish his submissions? In an article titled "Rattles and Bubbles," the *Chronicle* answered these puzzling questions by comparing Mormonism to a pleasing rattle and a beautiful bubble, enjoyable to see and hear, but containing no substance. While noting the "humorous impudence in the patriarchal polygamist's manner" and conceding the "good deal of common sense and truth in his observations," it published Pratt's articles "only to amuse the public." It was a canny public relations ploy to feed the flames of public controversy over the new religion and sell papers (much as was the case with James Gordon Bennett's earlier *New York Herald* coverage on Mormonism). Furthermore, the *Chronicle* suggested that any publicity pleased Pratt, as "he thinks the seed he scatters may fall on what he considers good soil."[117] The *Chronicle* praised Pratt's sensibility in recognizing, in its cynical calculation, that "it is better to be laughed at, than not to be talked of at all."[118]

The consistency of Pratt's correspondence suggests the truth of the *Chronicle*'s remark: for Pratt, any publicity, especially that over which he could exercise partial control, was better than none. To Young, Pratt happily reported that the "news paper channels have been opened to us a little—and we had Laid some truth before the public through their collum."[119] Later in his mission, he wrote Young that he was "still able to work upon the public mind more or less through the public press." Without mentioning the mocking introductions that preceded his articles, he exulted, "The 'California Chronicle' has never failed to publish any article from my pen," which caused other newspapers to be in a "stew and chafe continually."[120] Church leaders encouraged Pratt to continue to use the press to his advantage.[121]

Even with the generally negative tone of the San Francisco newspapers, both the national and the Mormon press perceived that the Mormons in San Francisco, led by Pratt, enjoyed somewhat greater respect there than in other areas. The *St. Louis Luminary*, a Mormon paper, republished an article from the *St. Louis Intelligence* that lamented that Mormon elders commanded enough respect in California that "Christian ministers there cannot afford to meet them with contempt, but are compelled by force of public opinion, as well as by a sense of duty, to meet them in public debate and attempt the serious refutation of errors, which five years ago, were met by a smile of pity or a sneer of contempt."[122] Several factors—including the diversity and relative tolerance of Gold Rush San Francisco, the prior involvement of the *Brooklyn* Saints and the Mormon Battalion, and the preaching and writing of Pratt and other missionaries—contributed to this situation. Even so, the *Chronicle*'s biting commentary suggests that the church could claim little admiration in the city and that the newspapers used Pratt for their own objectives.

Nevertheless, the exploitation was reciprocal; Pratt used the mainstream San Francisco press to present the Mormon side of the debate.

References to plural marriage constantly appeared in Pratt's letters, as well as in the *Chronicle*'s responses. In a letter to Young, Pratt wrote that "plurality is a choker," the major obstacle to Mormonism's progress in San Francisco.[123] Pratt's frequent discussions of polygamy resulted not only from his sincere belief in the principle but also from a pragmatic recognition that to win converts, he needed to first "satisfy their minds" on polygamy "before they can possibly be satisfied with our preaching."[124] In a city where men greatly outnumbered women, polygamy must have been an especially tough sell.[125] Tired of the barrage of attacks, Pratt printed a public challenge for others to debate him on the subject, using the "Old and New Testaments, the constitution and laws of the United States, and the laws of Utah" as the standard to determine whether plural marriage was a "crime, a transgression of law, or an immorality."[126] Rather bravely, he agreed to take on all comers in a debate at the Oakland Lyceum.[127] Even though "some say they threaten to mob me," Pratt debated in the Lyceum in December before "a large assembly of both sexes" and recorded that "truth was triumphant, and my adversaries confounded."[128] A reporter described the event: "The chairman having taken his seat, Elder Pratt was called upon to open the debate in the affirmative. Having done so, and after concluding a forty-five minutes speech, the word-firing became general. The Elder brought down his assailants at every discharge, evidently because he used fact-cartridge, while his opponents only used blank.... The Elder is in high feather, and crows lustily at his triumph."[129]

San Francisco's Mercantile Library Debating Society also accepted Pratt's challenge. While the official topic was the question of whether Brigham Young should be reappointed Utah governor, the debate centered on polygamy. Leading the charge against Pratt was M. C. Briggs, a crusading Methodist minister who had sparred with Pratt as editor of the *Christian Advocate*. Pratt argued that the Mormons were the spiritual heirs of the Old Testament patriarchs and bristled at Briggs's insinuation that no differences existed "between Polygamy and adultery; between a house full of wives and children and a house full of harlots." Plural marriage, Pratt asserted, led to the "highest order of physical, moral and intellectual development," which would stand in stark contrast to the "degenerate" race produced by the "whoredoms in modern Christendom." Finally, Pratt argued that constitutional right of religious liberty protected the "most sacred rights of conscience in regard to marriage relations or family ties."[130] Briggs was followed by some "Lawyers & Editors" and two missionaries who spoke after Pratt for the Mormon position.[131] In its treatment of the debate, the *Alta California*, one of San Francisco's largest newspapers, stated that they had "considerable respect [for Pratt] as a man and as a teacher," and declared that by "wheeling and charging his squadron of Polygamic arguments," Pratt had emerged as the clear victor, proving that "there really appears to be no law to prevent polygamy." The *Alta* called for a David to go "forth against this Philistine to meet him on either point of law, morality, or religion" to preserve the honor of Christianity in San Francisco.[132] In his report, Pratt claimed victory and stated that one-third of "a crowded house, of Lawyers, priests, Editers, [and] Merchants" supported Young's reappointment and that others had defended polygamy as constitutional.[133]

Pratt's ability to attract attention in the San Francisco press through his articles and debates contributed to a more optimistic assessment of Mormonism's prospects in California than he had expressed earlier. In October 1854, Pratt predicted that Mormonism would attract many converts in California, but cautioned that "so great a revolution of mind is not the work of a moment."[134] Preaching tours in outlying towns, both to strengthen church members and to find potential converts, affirmed Pratt's optimism. He traveled throughout northern California in October, staying primarily in Santa Clara and Santa Cruz, where he gave a series of well-attended lectures on prophecy fulfilled, prophecy yet to be fulfilled, the Book of Mormon, and spirits in prison.[135] Perhaps because of his youthful association with the Campbellites, he held a joint public meeting with a Campbellite preacher. Pratt recorded, "God blessed me, prejudice gave way, and many hearts were touched."[136] Pratt was clearly a man like Luther, born to strife. As an administrator, he sank into gloomy despondency. Placed in the middle of the fray, he returned to life, to spiritual and intellectual vigor. Fractiousness within the ranks disheartened him. Opposition from without enlivened him.

Pratt saw additional grounds for optimism in California's heterogeneous culture, and he reported that immigrants from Europe, China, and Latin America had shown interest. In August, Pratt wrote, "A chinese Interpreter here is reading the Book of Mormon."[137] Pratt, who continued to study Spanish, baptized a Spanish-speaking native of Sweden and his Argentine wife in October.[138] His language efforts bore other fruit as well. "A Learned frenchman and his son, who also speak Spanish, have become convinced by reading the works, and hearing; they give up their Catholicism," he wrote.[139] In December, Pratt expressed even greater optimism, as "many leading minds in town, and country are considering 'mormonism' with deep attention, and some of the best embrace it."[140] The election of Mormon missionary

M. Devalsen Merrick as chaplain of the California Legislature demonstrated the relative acceptance of Mormonism in the region and led the "press & Clergy" to be "exceedingly Chafed, & piqued." Pratt linked his interaction with the press to the renewed success of the missionary efforts. The newspapers, "though very corrupt, [have] been a providencial means of agitating Mormonism." A church conference on New Year's Eve, which erupted into a modern Pentecost, further thrilled Pratt: "All were filled with the spirit—and all, or nearly all prophecied, and testified in power and demonstration of the spirit. a stream of Life & light & joy seemed to thrill through each of us, as it were fire, and a pillar of fire seemed to rest upon our heads—all felt it—& some said they saw it." While converts were relatively few—about twenty in the first three months of 1855—Pratt described them as "very precious & noble ones."[141]

Even though Pratt had turned journalistic ridicule to his own advantage, he chafed at having to disseminate his message subject to the constraints of mocking, self-interested newspapermen. In February 1855, Pratt wrote to Young, excitedly anticipating the arrival of a printing press secured in Hawaii. Henceforth, the Mormons in California could control the terms of their print culture and Pratt hoped to establish both a bookstore and a newspaper, the *Mormon Herald,* a project he had envisioned as early as 1853. He told Young, "A *Book Depot—Press—*& a well conducted Periodical in this central Position will, by the aid and blessing of God, be a blessing, & a help to the cause of Zion."[142] However, the paper's prospectus elicited little excitement from local members, who argued that San Francisco was already saturated with newspapers and that a Mormon paper, with its extremely limited audience, would surely fail.[143]

Frustration with the bookstore, the pace of missionary work, and the lack of support for his proposed newspaper led Pratt to spiral again into pessimism. In February 1855, he stated that "there are but few in this country who feel interested in the Gospel, and but few who obey it." He received a shipment of thirty-four hundred books from the church publishing office in Liverpool that month. After he had sold few books in the first month of his store, Pratt wrote, "The sheep are so wild, that they hardly dare venture to lick the salt."[144] He sent some of his unsold inventory to his family on his forty-eighth birthday on April 12, 1855. He shipped copies of the Book of Mormon, Doctrine and Covenants, a hymnal, *Voice of Warning,* Lucy Mack Smith's *Biographical Sketches of Joseph Smith*, and John Lyon's book of poetry *Harp of Zion* to each of his wives and each of his older children (younger children received other books and candy).[145] He reiterated to Belinda in May, "None seek after truth, & none feel interested, in my mission except a very few. I long to leave them & devote my time where my presence is needed."[146] According to the *Chronicle*, the "Right Rev. Archbishop" Pratt gave a discourse in May in which he delivered "this wretched city into the hands of the enemy of mankind" and denounced the materiality and spiritual apathy of San Francisco. "We are a lost people; we are 'gone-ers,'" the *Chronicle* noted wryly, though it declared itself exempt from Pratt's condemnation, having graciously given him free publicity.[147]

Discouraged and eager to return home, Pratt prepared to leave in June, and even the arrival of the printing press, shipped from Boston and paid for with money raised by missionaries in Hawaii, failed to change his mind. By May, he had abandoned his proposed newspaper and stated that the press "awaits the actions" of George Cannon, whom Pratt had asked Young to send to assist him.[148] (Cannon was the scribe Pratt had used for his autobiography; now twenty-eight years old and well familiar with Hawaii from his missionary work there, he was commissioned by Young to print a Hawaiian translation of the Book of Mormon in San Francisco.) Not even the news of the publication of his magnum opus altered Pratt's intentions. In March, Pratt requested from the church's press in Liverpool two thousand copies of his newly published *Key to the Science of Theology*, the culmination of decades of assimilating, synthesizing, and expanding Mormon doctrine.[149] Franklin Richards told Pratt in May that printing problems had delayed publication, but that he had sent Pratt twenty-six hundred copies, five hundred to Utah and twenty-one hundred to California.[150]

Even as he prepared to leave San Francisco, with its fractious members, newspaper wars, and polygamy debates behind him, Pratt became embroiled in a more serious controversy. Early in his San Francisco mission, he had met a recent convert, Eleanor Jane McComb McLean, then 37 and described as a "woman of more than ordinary intelligence and refinement," whose troubled marriage had initially prevented her baptism.[151] Born in Wheeling, Virginia, in 1817, Eleanor was raised by staunch Presbyterians who moved while she was young to Greenville, Louisiana (near New Orleans). In 1841, Eleanor married Hector McLean, but her husband's alcoholism led to a separation three years later. After receiving advice from her father and brothers, Eleanor sent McLean an ultimatum: "Having used every persuasion in my power to no effect, I see but three alternatives all ending in misery if not in crime. First, to live the victim of the vice to which you have became a prey 2nd to seek a home among strangers, or shall the smoothe current of the Mississippi be the last page that any may read of my 'Ill Fate?'"[152] McLean's pledges of reformation led to a reconciliation and the couple, along with their three children and one of Eleanor's brothers, moved to San Francisco, where McLean worked as a customs clerk and bank cashier. Gold Rush California, with its celebrated hard-drinking culture, however, was a poor choice for a man seeking to escape alcoholism.

Out of curiosity, the McLeans and Eleanor's brother attended a Mormon meeting in San Francisco. Eleanor soon wanted to be baptized into the church, but McLean and her brother violently opposed her decision. According to Pratt, they "raged, foamed, cursed, railed, stormed," and even held a "large *sword cane*" over her head, threatening to kill her "and the minister who dare baptize her."[153] Nevertheless, Eleanor attended Mormon meetings, though church officials refused to baptize her without her husband's consent. On one occasion, McLean discovered his wife singing from a Mormon hymnal; enraged, he beat her and locked her out of their home. With the help of her family doctor, Eleanor found lodgings at a hotel and filed a charge of assault and battery against her husband. At this point, Eleanor thought of leaving her husband and moving to the church colony at San Bernardino, but her doctor and local Saints dissuaded her, counseling her to "treat her husband with kindness and submission, and by that means, if possible, obtain his consent to her being baptized."[154]

Pursuing this plan, Eleanor abandoned the legal charges, moved back into her home, and continued her church attendance. In April 1854, Caroline Crosby, one of the San Francisco Saints who had once boarded with Parley and Thankful in Kirtland, recorded that Eleanor "attends our church and wishes to be baptised, but is prevented by an unbelieving husband." At one meeting, Eleanor hoped to speak with John Horner "with regards to her proceedings in that respect, but he was so late that she said she dared not wait longer as she wished to be at home before her husband."[155] McLean finally gave written consent for her baptism, though he forbade her from mentioning Mormonism in his presence. She was baptized on May 24, 1854, more than a month prior to Pratt's arrival in San Francisco.[156] Eleanor's situation was not unique; Pratt stated that the "few Saints" in San Francisco were "mostly Sisters who had either apostate or unbelieving husbands."[157]

Eleanor quickly became an active member of the San Francisco Branch, speaking "very zealously" in meetings, donating to the missionaries, visiting ill church members, and inviting the "sisters to meet at her house."[158] At a fast meeting in late July, at which Pratt presided, there was an outpouring of spiritual manifestations. Crosby recorded, "The good spirit was with us, and rejoiced our hearts exceedingly. Sister Jones spoke in tongues, br Curtis prophesied to Sister McLean, that her husband would yet come into the church, but that she would first have great troubles with him, but her prayers would eventually prevail."[159] Pratt soon became deeply involved with Eleanor's situation. In August 1854, he baptized Eleanor's two sons at her request.[160] She later recounted her role as one of Pratt's benefactors: "I have often sought his door at the dawn of day, when his wife was sick, to take some *meat, bread, and fruit,* upon which they might subsist until the following morning."[161] Eleanor also recalled that once she "was coughing and spitting blood not long before I left California, and to appearance I was going in a speedy consumption as all my mother's sisters have died." At a fast meeting, Pratt blessed her and "declared in the name of Jesus that I should cough no more, but be made whole from that very hour, and I have never since had a cough."[162] Pratt attempted to intervene directly in the McLeans' troubled marriage. "He visited Mr. McLean, and tried to soften his prejudice against the principles which his wife had embraced, and did what he could to make things agreeable" between them.[163] Steeped in the Southern culture of patriarchy and honor, McLean was likely infuriated by the meddling of a Mormon polygamist in his domestic affairs.

Eleanor's devotion to Mormonism despite McLean's opposition deeply impressed Pratt. In January, he first mentioned Eleanor to his family, suggesting that Belinda name her newborn daughter Eleanor after a "kindred spirit of that name now in the world, which you will become acquainted with & love as you love your own soul." He described Eleanor to Belinda as the "very counter part of your self—& ought to have been your twin sister." Both women were strong-willed and literate and left husbands who opposed their embrace of Mormonism. And both married Pratt without obtaining a formal divorce from their husband. He continued to Belinda:

> Pray for her with all your might, for she is groaning under a bondage tenfold more terrible, & hard to break than yours once was. For twelve Long years has she been in dread of her life or that of her children, & at Last she has sworn the peace against a tyrant who rules with a rod of Iron. She has lately joined the S[aint]'s and is a very spirited enerjetic & noble hearted woman. Her children tye her, where she would otherwise break her chains. She lives in a well furnished pallace, but sighs for a log hut with quiet. A pious, genteel, proud, "titotaler" who drinks to hard in secret, & hates truth, is her tyrant.[164]

The McLeans' marriage continued to unravel over her Mormonism and his alcoholism. Apparently revoking his permission after her baptism, McLean threatened to place Eleanor in an insane asylum, a real threat in an era in which members of radical religions were sometimes institutionalized by family members on charges of religious enthusiasm or monomania (insane on only one subject).[165] To protect her, Pratt assigned a pint-sized fifteen-year-old missionary, Brigham Young's nephew John R. Young, to "keep McLain from doing this thing." Decades later, Young remembered that he obtained employment as a cook in the McLean home without revealing his status as a missionary. When McLean convened an examining committee to decide upon Eleanor's possible institutionalization, Young testified on Eleanor's behalf and insinuated that the couple's problems stemmed from Hector's drinking. Soon after the examining committee ruled in favor of Eleanor, McLean discovered Young's identity. Furious, he threatened to kill Young, but then relented and merely fired him (even paying him his month's wages).[166]

Convinced of Eleanor's devotion to the Saints and believing that Mormons had targeted his family, McLean sent their three children—without Eleanor's knowledge and without a chaperone—by boat to her parents in New Orleans, via Nicaragua. Afterward, he locked Eleanor in her room and taunted her, but he soon capitulated to Eleanor's distress and agreed "to help her off in the next steamer, to follow them."[167] Pratt explained to Amasa Lyman in San Bernardino that Eleanor had "been Called suddenly away to New Orleans—& never expects to see this Country again, But to make her way to Zion with her Children, if she can get the means."[168]

After Eleanor's departure, which signaled her marriage to McLean was irrevocably shattered, Pratt may have thought that he might marry Eleanor if and when she arrived in Salt Lake City. Months earlier, he told Belinda, "As to other candidates for family membership; I have neither seen, thought of, or sought any; nor do I feel inclined to. My whole mind, strength, and desires are to do my duty, magnify my calling,—and take good care of the Sheep and Lambs which God has given me."[169] In May 1855, however, in response to a letter from Belinda instructing him to "love any body who is *worthy of it*," Pratt replied, "My Noble hearted sister, you will have to wait till I can find the first one in this country who is worthy to be loved with the love wherewith I love you." He added, in a reference to Eleanor, "There *was one* soul here that is worthy to be loved by some good Son of God—But she is now far away in tribulation deep. I hope & pray for her deliverance, & safe arrival in Zion, & so would you if you knew her."[170] Eleanor remained in contact with Parley, sending him a letter from New Orleans that reached him in June 1855.[171]

That month, Pratt left San Francisco to return to Utah along with a small company. In April, he had organized a larger group of fifty-one people, including some returning missionaries and many converts, who traveled from California to Salt Lake.[172] Before returning home, Pratt sought to "set in order some things" among the local Saints.[173] At a church meeting in early June, he noted that the "Holy Ghost rested on me in power" and he preached to a "full meeting," testifying of the divine calling of Joseph Smith but also chastening members "for their neglegence and indifference to the Priesthood and their wards; and because they loved and fellowshipped iniquity and abominations." At a service that evening, six people were baptized, followed by confirmations the next morning.[174] Pratt also called a church conference that disfellowshipped several Saints for offenses ranging from adultery to drunkenness to apostasy to Nathan Tanner's defrauding of local Saints and Pratt in the purchase of the brig *Rosalind*. Pratt ordained Jonathan Crosby to succeed him as president of the San Francisco branch.[175]

The only outstanding business was orienting George Cannon on taking charge of the new printing press.[176] Pratt waited for him awhile but then decided to leave. Cannon, along with his wife and two assistant printers, arrived a few days after Pratt's departure; "quite disappointed," Cannon quickly caught up with him, however.[177] Pratt ordained Cannon to preside over the Pacific mission and instructed him to "obtain a suitable building" in San Francisco and to publish the Hawaiian edition of the Book of Mormon and a newspaper.[178] Cannon would publish the *Western Standard* for a period of nineteen months beginning in February 1856. The newspaper's motto expressed the Mormon desire to defend itself through the press: "To Correct Mis-Representation We Adopt Self-Representation."[179]

Rather than take the southern route, Pratt's company traveled across the Sierra Nevada Mountains, reaching Carson Valley on July 15, where they encountered a group of Saints, newly arrived to settle the valley, led by Orson Hyde. Pratt was weary, and he longed for home and the journey's end. "Dear Belinda & family," he wrote in his journal, "I am now within 457 m.s. of you by the traveled road & every day brings me 20 m.s. nearer. O how slow. But can you not sense and realize that I am drawing sensibly & feeling near."[180]

14

Murder and Martyrdom

One Mormon Less! Nine More Widows!! Alas for the
Mormon Prophet!!! If thou hast power to raise the dead,
Parley, raise thyself!!!!
—FORT SMITH HERALD, *quoted in "Tragic End of a*
Mormon Patriarch," Farmer's Cabinet, June 4, 1857

One more good man has gone to assist brothers Joseph
[and] Hyrum...in another sphere.
—BRIGHAM YOUNG TO ORSON PRATT AND
EZRA T. BENSON, *June 30, 1857*

IN AUGUST 1856, Agatha later recalled, Parley "came to my house one
day...and said to me, 'Agatha, I have bad news for you.'...His words and
manner sent a strange thrill through me. I said, 'What is it?' He replied, 'I am
called to go on a mission.' I said, 'Why do you call it bad news, you have been
on missions before.' He said, 'Because I feel as if I shall never come back.'"[1]
Quite apart from any premonitions he may have had, Pratt had legitimate
reasons to fear his mission to the East. First, as he prepared to leave, national
attitudes against Mormonism were darkening. The 1856 presidential campaign
featured the newly formed Republican Party, which targeted polygamy and
slavery—the "twin relics of barbarism"—for elimination. By the next spring,
the election's victor, Democrat James Buchanan, prepared to send a federal
army to Utah to quell a reported rebellion of the Mormons against federal
authority. Hostility to Mormonism was becoming a national moral crusade.[2]
Second, Pratt would be accompanied by his twelfth wife, Eleanor. Following
her failed attempt to regain her children from her parents in New Orleans,
Eleanor had traveled to Salt Lake City, where Brigham Young married her to
Pratt in November 1855. Eleanor would travel with Pratt in a second attempt
to retrieve her children, a course of action they had reason to believe might
cause Eleanor's estranged husband, Hector McLean, to seek vengeance.

During the previous year, since his return from California, Pratt had
served "several home missions or preaching tours" throughout Utah Territory,

part of an effort known as the Mormon Reformation which aimed to inspire renewed fervor in the Saints. In November 1855, he spoke at a conference in Ogden, urging consecration and the "necessity of the young men and maidens' receiving their endowments" at the recently completed Endowment House "and obeying the instructions to marry and raise up a righteous posterity."[3] He was continuing to do his part; though no longer young, Pratt fathered three children in 1856: Sarah's Sarah Elizabeth, born on May 31; Mary Wood's Mathoni Wood on July 6; and Agatha's Evelyn on August 8.

In December 1855, Pratt traveled to Fillmore in central Utah to serve as chaplain of the legislative session. In front of the legislature, he delivered a New Year's Eve lecture on "Marriage and Morals in Utah," which proclaimed the superiority of Utah polygamous society and was later published as a pamphlet in English, Danish, Welsh, and French. Unlike other pro-polygamy pamphlets, but reflecting the anti-Catholicism of his earlier proclamation to Latin Americans, Pratt blamed Christian opposition to polygamy on Catholicism, the "mother of harlots and abominations of the earth." He argued that while Christ and the New Testament apostles did not explicitly endorse polygamy out of respect for Roman law, they had not altered the

FIGURE 14.1 Eleanor Jane McComb Pratt. Photograph of unknown date, first published in the 1938 edition of the *Autobiography of Parley P. Pratt*.

marital laws of the Old Testament. By contrast, Catholicism (and, later, Protestantism) had banned polygamy and enshrined the "monogamic law" with its "attendant train of whoredoms, intrigues, seductions, wretched and lonely single life, hatred, envy, jealousy, infanticide, illegitimacy, disease and death."[4] During this final year in Utah, Pratt also served as a regent of the University of Deseret, participated in a convention that drafted a constitution for a proposed state of Deseret, and completed his autobiography.[5]

The First Presidency gave Pratt only vague instructions for his eastern mission, telling him to "travel and preach the gospel in different places, as you shall be led by the spirit of the Lord." They suggested he visit "a large number of Saints" in southwestern Virginia and write for Latter-day Saint newspapers the *Mormon*, edited by John Taylor in New York City, and the *Luminary*, which Erastus Snow was hoping to revive in St. Louis. Since he would return in spring 1857, Pratt should not assume the presidency of the mission.[6] In Pratt's farewell discourse in the Tabernacle, he stated that after his numerous years of travel he had hoped "to stay at home and minister among the people of God, and take care of my family." But he was resigned: "If it is the will of God that I should spend my days in proclaiming this Gospel and bearing testimony of these things, I shall think myself highly privileged and honoured."[7] As Pratt prepared to leave, Brigham Young blessed him "with the gift of the Holy Ghost and power over sickness—and over death—and over the elements—and over devils and unclean spirits,—and to triumph over my enemies and wicked men." Furthermore, Young promised Pratt he would return to the Saints and "be numbered among those that are faithful to the Priesthood, both in this life— In the world of Spirits—And in the Resurrection."[8] Wilford Woodruff recorded, "I never heard a better blessing given to man."[9]

In preparation for his mission, Pratt resigned his seat in the territorial legislature, gave Parley Jr., then nineteen, instructions on his business affairs, and attempted to clear his financial obligations.[10] He asked Young to assess his indebtedness to the church and appoint representatives to "select, among my property and possessions" appropriate payment. For personal debts to Young, he offered "four China Shawls."[11] The president clearly thought Pratt's family sacrifices were compensated by the larger good his missionary gifts served. "I feel that some men ought never to be called upon to do anothers day work," he told a small group of church leaders, "but they should spend there time in preaching the gospel. They should have a man to take care of their Families. This should be the case with P P Pratt."[12]

On September 11, 1856, Pratt left Salt Lake City accompanied by Eleanor and "several Elders and friends" headed for Europe and the eastern states, a total of "15 wagons 47 men & some women & children."[13] As they traveled east, they passed pioneer companies journeying to Utah, including "several hand cart companies," the first Mormon emigrants to cross the plains inexpensively by pulling their possessions in carts. A traveling companion described the scene when Pratt's group met the first handcart company near Green River, Wyoming: "As the two companies approached each other, the camp of missionaries formed a line, and gave three loud Hosannahs, with the waving of hats, which was heartily led by Elder P. P. Pratt, responded to by loud greetings from the Saints of the hand-cart train, who unitedly made the hills and valleys resound with shouts of gladness."[14] Pratt clearly admired these pioneers, whose "faces were much sunburnt and their lips parched; but cheerfulness reigned in every heart, and joy seemed to beam on every countenance." He attempted to speak to the handcart pioneers, "observing that this was a new era in American as well as Church history; but my utterance was choked, and I had to make the third trial before I could overcome my emotions."[15] Taking a slightly different route, Pratt's group missed encountering the ill-fated Willie and Martin companies, which were stranded on the Wyoming plains the following month; more than two hundred people died.[16]

In letters home, Pratt expressed a melancholy to which he was increasingly prone: "I feel lonesome, but I am reconciled to my fate—that of a poor wanderer. I have ceaced to anticipate any thing better in this life, & I try to think myself as well off as I have any reason to expect." Nor did he have much hope that his mission would improve his family's material condition. He told them, "If I can honor & magnify the Priesthood—do good—save *some* souls—and get back alive I shall consider myself blessed."[17] Initially, he managed to conceal his despondency. Missionary Isaiah Coombs described Pratt as "not only a man of God but a very agreeable companion.... We rode or walked side by side almost the entire distance and the time was spent in the most interesting and instructive conversation possible." To the admiring Coombs, he "was like unto an everflowing fountain—his conversation always interesting—always full of intelligence." However, after they passed Fort Laramie, he noticed "a great change" as Pratt became "very much depressed and moody." Surveying the passing landscape, he "would sigh heavily and exclaim: 'Soon the scenes that know me now will know me no more forever.'" Pratt specifically feared returning to Missouri, telling Coombs that the "spirit forbade" him from doing so and "that if he went on to Missouri soil he would get into danger and likely lose his life."[18]

On October 14, his moodiness erupted in a sharp rebuke of "the boys for growling and said if they did not stop muttering the Lord would scourge them with a greater scourge than they ever met with before." If they were dissatisfied with him or the company's other leadership, he told them, they should leave the camp.[19] Coombs could excuse Pratt's mercurial disposition in light of his scintillating intellect and magnanimous spirit. Toward Eleanor, Coombs was less forgiving. "I wish never to travel with her again," he declared bluntly. On one occasion, one of the travelers "killed 7 wild turkeys." Coombs bitterly wrote in his journal, "Oh! what a kind & generous woman is sister Elenor Pratt. She has been keeping some Elk meat untill it has spoiled & as she has a good, large fat turkey she has really been so kind as to offer me the spoiled meat. Really such kindness will meet with its reward."[20]

By mid-October, Pratt's group had arrived at Fort Kearney, where they heard confirmation of the murder of Almon W. Babbitt, a controversial and politically connected Mormon killed by Native Americans while traveling from Utah to Washington. Though Fort Kearney's commanding officer informed Pratt that he "had an account of Babbitt's death from the Indians themselves," the eastern press largely blamed the Mormons for his murder, further heightening tensions between the Saints and the nation. The company arrived in Florence (formerly Winter Quarters), Nebraska, on October 28, where Pratt was perturbed that the missionaries escaped the cold by staying in the homes of local church members, but Parley and Eleanor "still Slept in one carriage, no person offering us a bed." At times, the couple paid for the "privalege of going into the house to warm & cook breakfast" or to sleep indoors.[21] Traveling through Illinois, Pratt "saw Nauvoo and the ruins of the Temple in the distance," which prompted him to reflect on his "once happy but now fallen country" and console himself that eventually "justice would triumph and righteousness reign."[22]

In Iowa, Pratt composed his first letter to John Taylor for publication in the *Mormon*. Taylor, who had been charged to defend Mormonism in the East, had established the *Mormon*'s offices between those of the city's leading newspapers, the *New York Herald* and the *New York Tribune*. Noting the worsening public climate over Mormonism, Pratt responded to an article in a New York periodical, *Brother Jonathan*, which denounced polygamy, accused Mormons of colluding with Native Americans against the federal government, and favored the building of a transcontinental railroad to break the Mormon hold on Utah. Pratt satirically agreed that the nation should spend $100 million to build a railroad to Utah and that *Brother Jonathan* be placed in "some impregnable asylum…where he may consider himself safe in case the Mormons of Utah should happen to overthrow the poor, unprepared people of the United States."[23] Pratt also reported to Taylor his willingness to serve under Taylor's ecclesiastical jurisdiction. Taylor, who considered Pratt his "Father in the gospell," encouraged Pratt to write for the *Mormon* and told him to "come when you please go where you please return when you please & do as you please."[24]

After departing Fort Kearney, Parley and Eleanor left the main group of missionaries and continued east with a smaller group, from whom they departed in turn to go to St. Louis, in spite of Pratt's fears about Missouri. Arriving in St. Louis on November 18, Pratt found apostles George Smith and Erastus Snow; he remained for nearly a month preaching, "writing history, and writing for *The Mormon.*"²⁵ Pratt also attended the theater with Smith and Snow, viewing Shakespeare's *Merry Wives of Windsor*.²⁶ Days before, he had to pay to lodge with members. Now, according to Eleanor, they jointly visited "a number of families in St. Louis who thought it a greater honor to entertain him than they would to entertain any king."²⁷ At this point Eleanor borrowed $100 from Snow and headed to New Orleans to regain custody of her children.

On December 16, Pratt left St. Louis to travel further east by railroad, stopping to preach in Cincinnati (where he spent "4 days Drawing full houses") before passing through Philadelphia and reaching New York on New Year's Eve.²⁸ At the conclusion of the year, Pratt was "among strangers, and yet in my own native State—a pilgrim and almost a stranger in the very city where, twenty years ago, I labored, toiled, prayed, preached, wrote and published the message of eternal truth." His feelings about the city had not changed. "Oh, how darkness prevails!" he lamented. "How ignorant, blind and impenetrable are the minds of men!" On New Year's Day, Pratt attended a party of some four hundred people in the Latter-day Saints' Hall, which included preaching by Pratt, Taylor, and George Smith, as well as "songs, recitations, speeches, and amusements of various kinds, refreshments, etc."²⁹ News of the arrival of a shipload of English Mormons provided a happy interruption to the festivities. The next day, the three apostles visited the newly arrived Saints. A New York newspaper described Taylor giving a welcome speech as the "two other parsons [Pratt and Smith] fat and sleek sat and smiled approval."³⁰

Pratt fell comfortably into his role as Taylor's editorial assistant, writing several articles for the *Mormon*. In one, he described a recently discovered "gold plate" shown to him by Benjamin E. Styles in Cincinnati, which contained "ancient raised letters, beautifully engraved upon its surface." Rabbi Isaac Mayer Wise, a leader of Reformed Judaism, had "pronounced the characters to be mostly ancient Egyptian."³¹ Given its echoes of the Book of Mormon gold plates and script, the plate held great interest for the Mormons. In reprinting his brother's correspondence in the *Millennial Star*, Orson Pratt stated that it "gives corroborative evidence in favour of the divine authenticity of the Book of Mormon."³² In another article, Pratt condemned Spiritualism, a movement that had exploded in popularity since 1848, when two sisters, Margaret and Kate Fox, claimed to communicate with spirits through knockings and rappings. Pratt, incensed that critics often compared the supernaturalism of Mormonism with Spiritualism, sharply differentiated between the visions and revelations promoted by the Saints and the "mysterious knockings, table tippings, trances, swoons, cramps, convulsions, contortions, fits, and many other unseemly, disgusting, and even horrible, or trifling manifestations of the other system."[33]

Meanwhile, finances hounded Pratt in his eastern mission, as they had most of his life. He despaired to Orson that he would publish his autobiography "in part or in full if Gold was plentiful. But there is no prospect whatever, in a pecuniary Line."[34] He complained to his family in early January that while he had been in New York for three days, "no person in the place has invited me to eat drink or lodge, though God has opened my way to obtain sufficient funds for traveling expences."[35] Exasperated, he lashed out in print at eastern Saints for their failure to support the missionaries, comparing them to the followers of Noah who did not assist in the construction of the ark. He particularly chastised some eastern Saints for rejecting the doctrines of the gathering and tithing, for asserting that church leaders possessed only spiritual authority, and for allowing their children to marry non-members. The Kingdom of God, Pratt thundered, was an all-or-nothing proposition: "If a person has any interest at all in the Kingdom of God, all his interests are in it. He cannot consistently have any interests outside of it."[36] Hardened in the fires of Missouri, Zion's Camp, and Nauvoo, he had little patience for those unwilling to pay the price of gathering and of building Zion.

Throughout his stay in the East, Pratt's communications continued to be ominous. He told Orson, "This Country is no place for me, the darkness is so thick I can litterally feel it." Nevertheless, he wrote with dubious encouragement, "Orson be of good courage, our pilgrimage will soon be over & our personal history in this world will naturally come to the word: Finis."[37] To his family, he wrote more hopefully but not without foreboding, "I have no doubt but I shall return in safety & live to a good old age: But still I must acknowledge that I do anticipate with a great deal of pleasure the change [of worlds.] And every day I work on my history I naturally think that the word, "*Finis*," will soon be added to the end." He sought escape in imagining a new beginning, haunted by the images of the handcart immigrants passed earlier: "The darkness which broods over this country can be felt. It is no place for me. I feel like going to the frontiers, & fiting out as soon as grass grows & water runs, even if it must needs be with a hand Cart." The "whole country," according to Pratt, "is being overwhelmed with the most abominable lyings & mockery & hatred of the saints." Feeling like an "intruder" and a "stranger" in the East, he exclaimed, "O God, Let me retire from such a generation."[38]

In January and February, Pratt traveled to New Jersey and Pennsylvania to preach and visit local church members, and also to Hanover, Ohio, to call on his youngest brother, Nelson Pratt, the only sibling who had not converted to Mormonism and whom he had not seen in twenty-one years. He remained with Nelson, his wife, and three children for a week and "talked, read, reasoned" with them, reporting hopefully to his family that Nelson "is trying to sell & go to the vally."[39] After Parley's visit, Nelson and his family "read the Book of Mormon through.... [They] think it very plain as a mater of history and prophecy much more so than the Jewish scriptures; [and] are now searching the prophecies of the old and new testements."[40] They never joined, however. Pratt then traveled to Cincinnati, where he met up with George Smith, visited local members (who numbered "less than fifty" and were "poor men from the old World"), preached, and wrote an article for the *Cincinnati Gazette*, copies of which he mailed to members of Congress and the *Mormon*.[41] On February 22, Pratt and Smith traveled to St. Louis by train, where they encountered Erastus Snow. Pratt recorded, "The spirit of reformation is abroad in the St. Louis branch, but the adversary also has a great hold here."[42]

As Pratt preached in the eastern states, Eleanor arrived at New Orleans, where she found her youngest two children "in tolerable health." Her oldest son had been sent to a boarding school in Ohio. In early January, Pratt reported to his family, "I have heard from E once since she sailed from St. Louis....She is living there in quiet with them. She may make a break soon."[43] By late January, he learned that after a week at her parents' home, she took her children "by stratigem & cleared for Texas," where she found assistance from a missionary and hoped to join a company of Saints emigrating to Utah.[44] Eleanor's father immediately reported her escape to her former husband, Hector McLean, who began to track Pratt doggedly. McLean's cross-country pursuit of Pratt and the homicidal rage behind it were rooted not only in his internal psychology, but also in nineteenth-century cultural traditions that justified his revenge.

As a Southerner, McLean was deeply influenced by notions of honor and manhood. Historians use the term "culture of honor" to describe a cultural system that emphasized the importance of an individual's public reputation. A man sought to preserve not only his personal honor, but also his family honor, being careful to ward off even the taint of disgrace, particularly sexual scandal involving the family's female members.[45] In the eighteenth century, the culture of honor had been shared by both North and South, but Northern mores changed rapidly in the late eighteenth and early nineteenth centuries, spurred by the integration of Northerners into a market economy and the expansion of evangelical religion. Honor in the North came to mean respectability, defined as freedom from illicit vices. Southern attitudes shifted much more slowly, and the culture of honor, with its most celebrated feature, the duel, continued to be central to Southern culture.[46]

An extralegal tradition that upheld the right of a husband to kill his wife's seducer also impelled McLean's vendetta. In theory, two conditions restricted the husband's right: he had to catch his wife and her lover in a compromising situation, and he had to act immediately, out of the "heat of passion." "Otherwise," explains a legal historian, "if he dawdled, if he planned…he became a premeditating murderer." In practice, however, juries generally acquitted a husband even if he had obviously planned the killing.[47]

Though this unwritten law held sway across the nation, the South's tradition of extralegal violence made it especially potent there.[48] (In the coming decades, this tradition together with the region's virulent anti-Mormonism led to hundreds of incidents of threats or actual violence against Latter-day Saints and their property in the South.)[49] But most Northerners—generally less favorable to extralegal violence—also accepted this tradition. In Pratt's Utah, the territorial legislature had codified it (known as "mountain common law") after two incidents in 1851.[50] A whole series of notorious cases came to national attention between the 1840s and 1880s. In a celebrated 1859 incident, U.S. Rep. Daniel Sickles of New York killed his wife's lover, Philip Barton Key, U. S. attorney for Washington, D.C. (and son of Francis Scott Key, whose poem became the lyrics of the "Star-Spangled Banner"). The resulting trials generated an enormous amount of media attention because they served as symbols for a larger social debate over marital prerogatives in an era when the legal rights of wives were expanding.[51]

Eleanor's attempt to retrieve her children became national news in December 1856 when the *New Orleans Bulletin* published a widely reprinted story titled a "Sad Story of Mormonism—The Mother and Children."[52] The *Bulletin* did not name names, but it clearly referred to Pratt, Eleanor, and McLean. The article narrated how a "gentleman" and a lady of "more than an ordinary share of intellect" had moved to the "golden shores of the Pacific." Out of curiosity, they attended a Mormon meeting. "Fatal curiosity! Inconspicious day!" the paper roared. The woman soon converted and was persuaded to abandon her husband if he refused to join the "grand rendezvous of the Latter Day Saints" in Utah. Resolving "to save the children," the husband sent them to his in-laws in New Orleans.[53]

The mother followed, "chafing like an enraged tigress, whose young had been taken from her," but her parents were determined that "she should not drag her innocent babes down into the foul abyss with her." Her character could be ascertained by her choice not to "relinquish joining the wild horde which contaminate the air of Great Salt Lake by their abominations" but to leave her children and travel alone to Utah. However, she soon returned to New Orleans and told her parents that "she had been mad, had now left the Mormons and had come to live with her parents and children, and to do what she could to make them happy," though she did not renounce Mormonism. After requesting "permission to take her children into town" to shop, she and the children disappeared.[54]

The *Bulletin* integrated its portrayal of Parley and Eleanor into the well-established public narrative of the evils of Mormonism, which portrayed the movement as a threat to evangelical religion and American republicanism, a product of fraud and fanaticism.[55] Depictions of Mormonism generally rested on a sharp dichotomy between unscrupulous leaders (like Pratt) and the deceived rank-and-file members (like Eleanor), who, though innocent, would unquestioningly obey their evil superiors. Thus, the *Bulletin* concluded that Eleanor intended to take her children to Utah, "to be thrust into the opening throat of the grim visaged and horrible monster, who sits midway upon the Rocky Mountains, lapping his repulsive jaws, and eager to devour new victims as they become entangled in his foul, his leprous coils."[56] Such incensed writing gave cultural sanction to McLean in his manhunt.

The widespread attention given the article from the *New Orleans Bulletin* prompted Pratt to respond. Writing under the pseudonym "A Friend of the Oppressed," he wrote his own narrative of his relationship with Eleanor and Hector McLean in the *Mormon*, titling his article "Sad Story of Presbyterianism: The Mother and Children." Pratt reframed the history of Eleanor and Hector to blame religious intolerance, not Mormonism, for the breakup of the family (which had already been marred by abuse and alcohol). Eleanor obtained Hector's consent to be baptized and "remained a faithful and obedient wife and mother," though he remained "harsh and tyrannical." The McLeans continued in an uneasy truce for a few years, with Eleanor "utterly forbidden to mention any point in her religion in presence of her husband." One day, after she sang two lines of a Mormon hymn, Hector flew into a "violent rage" and threw her out of the house at night. He then sent their children away to his in-laws—but to punish her, rather than to save them.[57]

Pratt placed Eleanor's experience within the larger Mormon narrative of religious persecution, which the Saints, led by Pratt, had honed since their expulsions from Missouri in the 1830s. The Saints portrayed themselves as sincere devotees of religious truth who had endured violent persecutions and been driven into exile in a land of supposed religious liberty.[58] Pratt exclaimed,

"Talk not of Rome, of Nero, of the dark ages, or of the Spanish Inquisition. All these combined could scarce form a parallel worthy to compare with the heartless, unfeeling, inhuman, savage and worse than fiendish tyranny of the nineteenth century. And all this enacted by Protestants in a land of freedom!" When she arrived in New Orleans, Eleanor "found her bigoted and hard-hearted Presbyterian parents and brothers and sisters in the same plot" and traveled to Utah only after she found herself "sinking under the accumulated wrongs and oppressions of those who should have been her friends." Only then did she leave her children "for a season…promising to return to them in due time." After teaching school in Salt Lake City for a year, she heroically traveled back to her children. If intolerant Christians had reacted to Mormonism differently, Pratt concluded, or if Hector had been "a kind and dutiful husband, instead of an unfeeling tyrant, religious differences would not have separated the family."[59] Nelson Pratt wrote Parley after reading his account, "Facts are sometimes stranger than fiction; if you should ever happen to see that Lady pleas give her our best respects tell her it is our most ardent desire that she may live to see her children grow up a blessing to her and the world."[60]

But Nelson was the exception. The *Bulletin*'s portrayal reached a much wider audience and assisted McLean in his search for Pratt. Clearly aware of the danger, Pratt asked Thomas Sirls Terry, a missionary in Philadelphia, to meet him in St. Louis and act as his bodyguard on his way home. Terry arrived on time, but Pratt had been forced to leave.[61] Possibly assisted by dissident Mormons, McLean almost caught Pratt in St. Louis. On March 1, Pratt—fearing such collusion—told George Smith "that there were persons in the church who wished to kill him."[62] Expecting the worst, Pratt entrusted his manuscript for his autobiography to Smith, who later returned it to Parley Jr.[63]

Fellow apostles Snow and Smith reported to Brigham Young in mid-March on McLean's pursuit of Pratt in St. Louis. The public attention aided McLean in attracting the "sympathies of the Mayor, Police and the Apostates of this City" who subsequently helped him "in searching the Saints Houses and keeping up a general watch."[64] In addition, Pratt had "been hunted by the police," and a reward had been offered for his "apprehension" on charges of adultery with Eleanor.[65] Snow added that the search for Pratt extended to St. Louis, Cincinnati, and Boston, where McLean and his associates had enlisted the help of police and railroad conductors.[66] As McLean zeroed in, local Mormons secreted Pratt out of St. Louis. After a friendly ex-Mormon woman informed Snow and Smith of McLean's pursuit, Pratt disguised himself and hid overnight in the Belfountaine Cemetery. The next morning, missionary

Andrew Sprowl came with a "satchel of clothes and some $100.00 expense money" and accompanied Pratt twelve miles out of town, traveling a "circuitous route" and "avoiding the roads."[67] Anticipating an indefinite future in hiding, Pratt sent Smith a message "that I should not feel uneasy concerning him, if I did not hear from him in a year."[68]

Church leaders in St. Louis believed that Pratt had successfully eluded McLean. Perhaps fearing that his letter might be intercepted (a common concern among Mormons in the era), Erastus Snow wrote Young in code language that Pratt had escaped and that Eleanor was on her way to Utah with her children, indicating that Young knew of Pratt's assistance to Eleanor. Snow wrote, "The Hare however escaped narrowly but silently by a way they knew not and the blood hounds have lost every scent of his trail. The Bird with her Young had flown over the Gulf and her beak headed towards the high places of the Mountains. *Selah!*"[69]

Heading south, Pratt searched for George Higginson, a twenty-six-year-old missionary to whom a local church leader in St. Louis had provided Pratt a letter of introduction, eventually finding him in Indian Territory (now Oklahoma) with some Native American converts. Pratt's demeanor led Higginson and the Native Americans to suspect Pratt was a U.S. marshal who would expel Higginson from the territory as "some Methodist Ministers had Threated to have me turned out." Still in disguise, Pratt whispered his identity to Higginson and convinced him by producing the letter. Pratt informed Higginson he "was flying from 'death' and was seeking shelter in these Nations." Higginson and Pratt initially stayed with a secluded family of Latter-day Saints who knew Pratt as "Elder Parker from New York." On April 6, Pratt attended a conference of missionaries, most of whom recognized him, though he continued to be introduced as Elder Parker.[70]

Pratt attempted to make contact with Eleanor so they could travel together to Utah, writing her on April 11 that McLean was in St. Louis and had "offered a reward for your discovery, or your children or me. The apostates have betrayed me and you. I had to get away on foot, and leave all to save myself." Pratt gave instructions for how she could find him and stated, "Do not let your children or any friend know that I am in this region...except it is an elder from Texas who is in your confidence, and even him under the strictest charge of *keep you it*." Pratt also warned that "all the frontiers are watched."[71] On Pratt's instructions, Higginson traveled to the "Frontiers of Texas" to look for Eleanor, who was expected to be traveling north with Mormon emigrants from Texas. Discovering that the Texas company was still three hundred miles distant, Higginson returned to report to Pratt.[72]

McLean, however, intercepted Pratt's letter to Eleanor and persuaded a
U.S. deputy marshal, a Mr. Shivers, to help him find Eleanor and the children.[73] He had also enlisted a "dozen of my Masonic friends, who gathered
from all parts of the territory to aid me should the government not take any
notice of my grievances."[74] On May 6, McLean caught up with Eleanor and
the two children in Creek territory west of Arkansas. They were in a wagon
accompanying a non-Mormon family traveling from Texas to Nebraska.
Along with a companion, McLean rode up to the wagon, grabbed the children, twelve-year-old Albert and nine-year-old Ann, "threw one on each
horse in front of their saddles," and quickly rode off. Three hours later,
Shivers, accompanied by McLean's companion, arrested Eleanor on the
charge of stealing the children's clothing (valued at $10). The warrant for
Eleanor's arrest also charged Pratt. Fearing that the wagon train, reportedly
consisting of three hundred to four hundred people, might rescue Eleanor,
Shivers and McLean petitioned help from U.S. Army officers at nearby Fort
Gibson, who "promptly dispatched Capt. Henry Little" along with eleven
men.[75] One of McLean's associates "happened to ascertain that Pratt, or a
person calling himself Parker" had crossed the Arkansas River two miles
from the fort, and he persuaded Little's soldiers to pursue him.[76] The army
patrol soon overtook Pratt and Higginson and detained them until the
marshal arrived to arrest them.[77] The crowd debated whether Higginson
should also be arrested; a Native American objected futilely that preaching
to Native Americans was not a crime. Pratt's right ankle was tied with a
thick rope, and both prisoners were marched toward Fort Gibson, twenty-
five miles away.[78]

McLean exulted to his friends, "I have just arrived from a *sore* tramp, in
which I *succeeded* in coming up with Eleanor and the children, and have taken
the children from her by force." He boasted of the arrests and indicated that
the marshal would march the prisoners to Van Buren, Arkansas, the next day
while McLean took a different route with the children. McLean knew that
the legal ruse of arresting Pratt and Eleanor for "stealing the clothing on the
children," the "only way I could arrest them in these Territories," would likely
be dismissed by the U.S. commissioner in Van Buren. At that point, he hoped
to "have Pratt arrested for having fled from justice in St. Louis, Mo., and get a
requisition from the Governor of Missouri for him." He concluded, "Thank
God for his goodness."[79] McLean and his children proceeded to Van Buren
escorted by his Masonic brethren as well as prominent local citizens.[80]

After her arrest, Eleanor was taken to a "kind of hotel" in the Creek town
of North Fork, where she saw "twelve armed men who appeared to be in a
state of great excitement." She spent that night in the "private room" of the

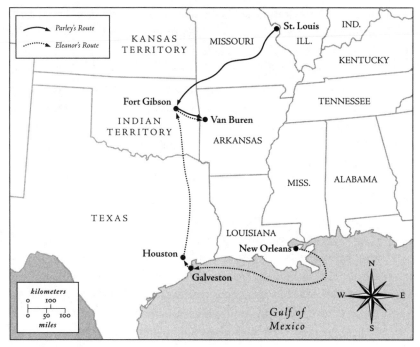

MAP 14.1 Final days

Native American hotel keeper, sleeping in the same bed as his eighteen-year-old daughter. The following morning, Eleanor was placed on a horse, and the "crowd set off all on horse back at an early hour." After about fifteen miles of riding, one of the men inquired if she "would like to see Mr. Pratt" who was "not 40 miles from here." Eleanor had not yet realized that Pratt was also in the region. She replied, "Not in tribulation such as I am in. He is a good man and I know his family and would be sorry to see him as a prisoner!" When the entourage stopped for lunch, Eleanor noticed that the "excitement greatly increased" as did the "number of men." She recounted, "They brandished their weapons, rode to and fro, and spoke to each other in a subdued voice, as if planning some fearful and deadly combat." Eleanor learned that McLean and the children were nearby. Shivers also told her, "They have arrested Pratt, and McLean is *determined to kill him, but he shall not do* it while he is a prisoner! I told Cap Little of the millitary to protect him and McLean shall not molest him while in my custody." After riding a half a mile after lunch, Eleanor "came in sight of the military troops, who had arrested Mr. Pratt." She soon saw Pratt himself, surrounded by "many armed men...Indians and white men old and young"; she contrasted "his calm penetrating look" with the "*pale, trembling fiendish looking* beings" who surrounded him.[81]

In Eleanor's estimation, Parley "looked in excellent health, and perfec[t]ly free from all agitation." Shivers allowed her to speak to Pratt, and she asked, "How do you do brother Parley"? He replied, "Very well madam how is your health." Eleanor responded, "I am well in health, but that Demon who has been in my pathway these thirteen years has again crossed my way He has torn my children again from me! and he says I shall never see them again!" Pratt told her, "Well my sister never mind. These things are all in one short life time and life is but a speck of eternity and will soon be over." Eleanor responded, "Brother Parley I rejoice in one thing Mormonism has taught me how to live, and taken from me all fear of death and the grave." She then spoke to the crowd, "You civil and millitary officers and soldiers you can only kill the body and after that you have no power over the soul, do what you please I am as ready and willing to die as to live."[82]

Eleanor arrived at Fort Gibson so "bruised and mutilated with the ride and McLean's violence the day before" that she had to be lifted off her horse. The next day, the prisoners remained "closely guarded" at the fort. Pratt later told Eleanor that he had been "really amused at the manner of the officers," as they had demonstrated their authority by alternately commanding Pratt and Higginson to remain on "opposite sides of the room" and to sit side by side. Meanwhile, "officers, me[r]chants, & clergymen" visited Eleanor, and the "Ladies sent me d[r]esses and different kinds of clothing." Her visitors were particularly curious about Mormonism, especially given reports that President Buchanan might send an army to Utah. A military officer asked Eleanor if "the mormons could meet 8 or 10 thousand U.S. troops." Eleanor affirmed that God would protect His people, notwithstanding the size of the opposing force, and stated that she would rather die among the Saints than live among her enemies: "Surely you do not think I wish to stay in this Land, where a woman's own children can be torn from her, on account of her religious faith, and she dragged without mercy as a prisoner before the populace and the court, simply because she dared to seek to retain her own flesh." Notwithstanding Eleanor's bravado, the officer advised her to "stay this side the mountains untill the fate of that people is decided."[83]

The next morning, Shivers and two soldiers escorted Pratt, Eleanor, and Higginson from Fort Gibson to Van Buren for trial. Eleanor started on a horse but soon fainted and was placed in a carriage driven by the soldiers. Pratt traveled with his right wrist chained to Higginson's left wrist as the group rode toward Van Buren for the next two days. After traveling about forty miles, they stopped for the evening at "an Indian house," where they "had a fine supper and all slept in one room." Pratt "proposed to the Marshall that he would give him his hat, boots, and coat if he would let them sleep without the chain[,] to which the Marshall agreed." Eleanor wrote, "The Man of God appeared very weary and his countenance heavy that night, and I do not believe he slept." Parley confided to Eleanor, "Light has burst upon me and I know this thing is all of the Lord, there will yet be dark spots in it, but it will work great things." He told her later that night, "I feel like a little child that is led by its father, it knows not whither: but is sure father will lead it right. I am as happy as I have ever been any day of my life."[84]

When the three prisoners arrived in Van Buren, after crossing the Arkansas River from Indian Territory, Shivers released Higginson, sent Pratt to jail, and took Eleanor to the office of Judge John B. Ogden, who interviewed her in the presence of lawyers. At first "severe in his tone and manner," Ogden soon sympathized with Eleanor's account. She convincingly placed the blame for her marriage's breakdown on McLean's alcoholism and abuse. "It was not Mormonism that desolated McLean's house," Eleanor avowed, "but that spirit that comes in bottles, prepared his heart and him for deeds of desperation, and at last he found a pretext in my religion."[85]

Following Eleanor's statement, Ogden informed her that the district attorney wanted to drop the charges against her and call her as a witness against Pratt. She replied, "I am in your power and you can do as you please. But I hope to be protected from insult or personal injury." Ogden promised that she would be "taken to the best hotel and all your wants attended to, and no one shall molest you." The lawyers then asked her many questions about the status of women in Utah society. To the question, "Are there not many discontented women there?" Eleanor retorted, "Yes, but I do not believe quite as many as there are here." Using a typical Mormon argument, she insisted, "The difference in your customs & the people of Utah is in the fact that *there* every man who has a plurality of women, has a plurality of wives and honors them as such, and the result is purity of life, and increase of healthy, and gifted children."[86]

Outside the courtroom, McLean charged Pratt with destroying his marriage. In the presence of a chained Pratt and Eleanor, he "mounted a dry goods box and made an inflammatory speech to the populace, produced and read some of Pratt's letters to her, he all the time claiming her as his wife and pointing to Pratt as the whole cause of the disturbance of the domestic relations and pointing to him as a Mormon and a wife stealer." Pratt replied: "I only did for this woman what I would have done for any lady." Unfortunately for Pratt, the crowd believed he meant "he would take any woman from her husband if opportunity offered," and the judicial authorities had to take him to jail for his protection. Eleanor defended Pratt before the "leading men of the place, doctors, lawyers and preachers interrupted her and it is proverbial even now how she showed her knowledge of law and justice and also of the scriptures and their testimony was that none could cope with her."[87]

The following morning, Eleanor again appeared in court before Ogden. Approximately five hundred people packed the courtroom to overflowing. Eleanor recounted that the "rabble rushed in of course eager to see not only the lady prisoner, but that much greater curiosity[,] a living Mormon woman from Salt Lake City!"[88] Pratt soon came into the courtroom, accompanied by his counsel Henry Wilcox, a local lawyer. Ogden first dismissed the charges against Eleanor and instructed her to leave the court. She described Pratt as "weary but not sad." This was the last time Eleanor saw Parley alive. After McLean read the charges against him, Pratt stood to reply. "McLean drew his pistol and pointed at him," but an officer grabbed McLean's arm and declared, "You cannot do that in the court." Facing a large crowd sympathetic to McLean, both inside the courthouse and outside the building, Ogden postponed the case until the next morning, claiming that he was awaiting the arrival of defense witnesses.[89]

That night, fearing that McLean and his followers would break into the jail and kill Pratt, Ogden summoned McLean and advised him to leave Pratt alone, since he had already recovered his children and had "failed to prove one thing against him." Ogden kept McLean talking with him in his office until "2 o'clock in the morning" and "told him I did not wish violence done to the prisoner, and I hoped he would not incite men to take his life." McLean told Ogden he "did not wish any man to touch him, that *that* was a privilege he wished to reserve to himself."[90]

Early the next morning, Judge Ogden, along with a few other men, secretly released Pratt, offering him his own pistol and knife to "defend himself if attacked," but Pratt refused. "Gentlemen," he said, "I do not rely upon weapons of that kind. My trust is in my God!" Pratt then shook hands with the men, mounted his horse, and "rode off quietly like a man leaving his friends to go upon a journey."[91] McLean's friends, who "kept a watch all night on the jail," quickly told McLean that Pratt had escaped.[92] Though closely followed, Pratt succeeded in eluding the mob after a few miles. However, someone who crossed Pratt on his path soon alerted his enemies as to his direction. Along with two others, James Cornell and a Mr. Howell, McLean caught up to Pratt roughly twelve miles northeast of Van Buren. As his associates cut off Pratt's routes of escape, McLean began shooting at Pratt, the bullets striking his saddle and five passing through the "skirts of his coat," and then followed Pratt into a thicket of trees. Catching up to Pratt, McLean tore him from his horse and stabbed him three times near his heart. After leaving the thicket, McLean obtained a derringer and then returned about ten minutes later and shot Pratt in the neck at point-blank range, the bullet glancing off of Pratt's collarbone.[93]

The attack occurred near the home of a local blacksmith, Zealey Wynn, who witnessed McLean force Pratt into the thicket. Thinking Pratt dead, Wynn spent the next hour alerting his neighbors. When they finally approached, Pratt asked, "Sir will you please give me a drink of water for I am very thirsty; and raise my head if you please." Pratt identified McLean as his murderer, stating that he "accused me of taking his wife and children I did not do it they were oppressed, and I did for them what I would do for the oppressed any where!" Pratt stated that he had not known his other assailants.[94] A crowd soon gathered, including the local justice of the peace, who asked "more than once if he wanted a doctor and he answered no, no, but asked for water which I had brought to him." As the men "consulted about sending for Doctors," Pratt said, "I want no Doctors for I will be dead in a few minutes."[95]

In his final hour, Parley's thoughts turned to his family. He told the assembled men, "I have a family in Salt Lake City Utah Territory and that is my home. My gold is in this pocket (pointing to his pants) and my gold watch in this and I want them with all my effects sent to my family in Salt Lake."[96] One witness stated that Pratt asked the crowd "to communicate with the Mormon [wagon] train and have some of them return and take his body to Utah, and he desired us to send his dying statement to Brigham Young and the Church." The observer remembered Pratt's declaration:

> "I die," said he, "a firm believer in the Gospel of Jesus Christ as revealed through the Prophet Joseph Smith, and I wish you to carry this my dying testimony. I know that the Gospel is true and that Joseph Smith was a prophet of the Living God" and then added, "I am dying a martyr to the faith."[97]

According to Wynn's wife, Pratt had not "groaned or appeared to suffer much," but he "lay still and complained of nothing but thirst and his last breath was like a man going to sleep."[98]

James Orme, the local justice of the peace, inspected the murder scene and Pratt's body, finding $72, some gold coins, a gold pen, glasses with gold rims, and a "new pocket knife in his pocket closed and unused." McLean's borrowed derringer still lay near Pratt.[99] Also nearby was a "bunch of paper about as large as a common egg bloody on one end," which Pratt had likely used in an attempt to stop his bleeding.[100] The crowd moved Pratt's body to Wynn's home, where a Van Buren coroner inspected it, and Orme held an inquest into the murder. Though everyone believed McLean had murdered Pratt, no witness had actually seen him kill Pratt; Wynn was not acquainted with McLean and therefore could not testify that it was McLean who had chased Pratt into the thicket. Thus, the jury ruled that "he came to his death by the hand of some unknown person." Orme was given custody of Pratt's belongings, including his money and horse, which he used to pay for the funeral expenses; the excess proceeds "went to the public treasury," instead of to Pratt's family, as the dying Pratt had hoped.[101]

On the morning of Pratt's murder, Eleanor was informed of Pratt's release and soon heard that "many men on horseback were in close pursuit, and that some had stated what they meant to do, which was to my mind far worse than death, and I prayed earnestly to my father in heaven that he would not suffer them to mangle the body of his faithful servant, and leave him to linger in pain in a land of strangers." Shortly after noon, a lady in the hotel told Eleanor of the news that Pratt had been shot "all to pieces," though another report arrived "that he was wounded but not dead." A few minutes later, "McLean with his party were drinking in the bar room of the Hotel in which I was." The hotel keeper asked McLean, "What have you done?" McLean responded, "Well I've done a good work." Eleanor soon saw McLean cross the Arkansas River and his companions leave. About an hour later, a man arrived from the scene of the murder and confirmed Pratt's death.[102]

That evening, a different marshal, Mr. Hays, spoke with Eleanor "a considerable time" and said "he regretted exceedingly the deed that had been done." He also related that the public sentiment "had greatly changed" and "there was a disposition to punish the murderers, not so much McLean as the citizens of Van Buren who were equally guilty." At Eleanor's request, Hays promised protection for her and Higginson to "go and clothe the body for the grave." Hays "spoke with apparent emotion of the quiet uncomplaining manner of the deceased. Said he 'I never saw a man like him!'" Furthermore, Hays believed, "McLean failed to substantiate any thing against him." Eleanor responded, "'Tis better for the state of Arkansas to have suffered seven years famine, than to have the blood of this man upon her soil!"[103]

The next morning, Hays came with a carriage to drive Eleanor to the "place of the murder." Approximately a hundred men had "gathered to see me come out," but Eleanor left through a back way to avert the "crowd of idle gazers." The wife of a Methodist minister drove Eleanor's carriage, while Hays and Higginson rode on horseback. Entering Wynn's home, she saw "the body of the man of God, upon a board. He had on the same blue check shirt, but other pants, and the blood was still dripping from his side.... There was no rigidity or congealed look to the skin or flesh, and he was limber, yet warm about the heart. There was a great deal of blood on the floor and a vessel about two thirds full in the midst of it." At Wynn's house, there was also a "grand jury" and a "number of respectable looking women.... They all appeared to feel that a terrible thing had been done in their neighbourhood."[104]

By the time of Eleanor's arrival, Parley's body had been "cleanly washed and nicely shaved" and a "handsome shirt and material for a shroud" had been gathered. Higginson and Hays dressed Pratt's body in clean garments, and then Eleanor wrapped Pratt's entire body in "a long winding sheet," a fine piece of linen provided by the hotel keeper. Eleanor also placed "an envelope in his bosom addressed to Joseph Smith." She left that evening, as she depended on Hays to take her back to town, before Pratt's burial.[105]

Local residents buried Pratt in the Wynn family cemetery after a short public service. William Steward, a local resident who had known Pratt as a young man in New York, gave his own coffin for Pratt's burial. Higginson later gave a very different account of Pratt's burial. He wrote, "After his martyrdom I rode through the homes of the mobocrats and obtained possession of his corpse and buried it with a mob all around me at 10 o'clock of the night of the 14 of May, AD 1857, without the presence of a brother or sister."[106] Perhaps both burials occurred: a public ceremony during the day and then a private reburial by Higginson to protect Parley's remains (as the bodies of Joseph and Hyrum Smith had been secretly reburied). Eleanor worried that Parley's grave and body would be desecrated by local citizens and wrote Erastus Snow in St. Louis, asking, "Can you send for the body of Brother Parley" for removal to the West?[107]

Then, with renewed fears both of McLean's continued violence and the possibility that her family might commit her to an insane asylum on the grounds of "religious insanity," Eleanor left Van Buren on a steamboat down the Arkansas River on May 18. The only woman on board aside from a black stewardess, Eleanor asked the captain for "special protection" but instead was "grossly insulted" by him. She stopped a few hours from New Orleans to await a response from a letter she had written to her father. After hearing nothing for three days, she continued on to New Orleans, where she stayed in the home of an "old friend" and again wrote her father, "my feelings towards you and my dear mother are unchanged, and I feel a desire to see you. But I do not wish to encounter McLean.... I am entirely alone, and my heart is desolate." Rebuffed by her father ("The moment you accepted the

name of Mr. Pratt *you* cut the last cord of sympathy that bound me to you")
and rejected by friends (one wrote, "You had better keep away from this
place! You have brought sorrow suffering, shame & disgrace into your family
here"), she turned her face to the West instead. She also soon learned that her
fears of commitment were well founded. By testifying that Eleanor "was a
maniac," McLean and her eldest brother persuaded a New Orleans court to
issue a warrant for her arrest. Eleanor fled the city, traveling by boat to St.
Louis, where two brothers and a brother-in-law lived and had alerted the
police to her potential presence, though she managed to elude them.[108] As
she made her way to Utah, Eleanor encountered Orrin Porter Rockwell, the
controversial Mormon gunfighter and lawman; she then traveled with
Rockwell and a few others who were hurrying Utah with news of the decision
of the federal government to send an army to Utah along with a new governor
to replace Brigham Young.[109]

As Eleanor struggled to reach Utah, the news of Pratt's death raced across
the United States. In widely reprinted articles, local newspapers set the
national tone by portraying McLean as Pratt's victim. The *Van Buren
Intelligencer* wrote that while it regretted the murder, "More than all do we
deplore the melancholy affair that led to its commission."[110] The *New Orleans
Bulletin* presented McLean as "stung to phrenzy, maddened beyond the power
of endurance, under the grievous outrages he had endured, leaped upon a
charger and as with the wings of the wind, overtook the destroyer of his peace,
and slew him."[111]

Before leaving Van Buren, Eleanor had moved quickly to protect Pratt's
legacy from defamation. On May 18, she wrote a lengthy letter to the *Arkansas
Intelligencer* describing Pratt as "a fountain of light and intelligence, at which
thousands might drink, and yet the stream flowed, *clear, pure, and free.*"[112] Her
article was reprinted throughout the country, often accompanied by biting
commentary.[113] Eleanor influenced the coverage of Pratt's murder in the
Mormon press by writing similar accounts for the *Mormon* and for the
Millennial Star, under the editorship of Orson Pratt. The Mormon press also
republished Eleanor's account to the *Intelligencer* as well as her poem, "The
Orphans' Lamentation, on Hearing of the Martyrdom of Their Father." The
narrator "heard a wail from out a distant mountain home....

> It was the voice of wives and children wild with grief,
> Who sought to heaven, with prayers and tears, for kind relief;
> For they'd learned, by a paper from a distant place,
> The news that they no more could see a father's face.

Their cry soon "reach'd the throne of God," who promised to avenge the "blood of Parley." God's wrath would fall not only on the perpetrators, but also on the nation.[114] Eleanor's emphases on Pratt's martyrdom and God's vengeance upon the wicked set the tone for the Mormon response.

In a letter published in San Francisco's *Alta California*, by contrast, McLean cited widespread public approval for his action. He matter-of-factly stated, "I killed him." Regarding the murder, McLean concluded, "I am not able to say how you will view the act but I look upon it as the best act of my life. And the people of West Arkansas agree with me."[115] Most Americans concurred. While the national debate over the "Mormon Question" simmered throughout the nineteenth century, it was probably never more volatile than at this moment. President Buchanan, inaugurated two months before Pratt's death, immediately faced a crisis in Utah, as federal territorial officials charged Mormon leaders with disloyalty amounting to insurrection. As the complaints of these officials captured the attention of the press and public, politicians of both parties flocked to the anti-Mormon standard. Senator Stephen Douglas of Illinois, a former ally of the Mormons, called for Congress to "apply the knife and cut out this loathsome, disgusting ulcer."[116] William Appleby, an experienced Mormon observer of Eastern perceptions of the Saints, said he had "never perceived such an acrimonious spirit prevailing against the Mormons, as appears to be gathering at present."[117] By the time of Pratt's murder, Buchanan had decided to dispatch an army which would install an outsider to replace Brigham Young as governor of Utah and compel the Saints' submission to national power.[118] One newspaper helpfully suggested that Buchanan appoint McLean as Utah's governor, since he would bring the "old Brigand" (Young) to "have a sudden weakness in his knees."[119]

The competing versions of the Pratt-McLean episode fanned the flames on both sides of the debate. For Mormons, Pratt's killing proved that the murderous spirit of the Smiths' assassins was still alive and well. If anything, it steeled them in their resolve to resist federal tyranny. For most Americans, the alleged seduction of Eleanor was one more example of the depravity of the Latter-day Saints in general and the evils of the polygamous hierarchy in particular. The *Alta California* used the incident to argue that "Mormonism is ripe for dissolution—ripe and ready to fall and putrefy with its own innate rottenness."[120]

Pratt's polygamy powerfully reinforced the tale of seduction. Mormon missionaries of the era were often accused of being seducers, and Pratt's actions appeared to confirm this suspicion. The extralegal tradition of violence against seducers assumed that women had no will of their own, that they were always the victims of seduction rather than active participants. In Eleanor's case, this assumption was heightened—notwithstanding her protests—by the common notion that a woman would never freely choose polygamy and Mormonism. She must have been duped, forced, coerced, or even mesmerized, a belief constantly reinforced in the era's popular anti-Mormon literature. The national press erased Eleanor's agency by emphasizing either her victimhood or insanity.[121]

At least one non-Mormon newspaper dissented from this chorus by using her story to rail against abusive husbands and the hypocrisy of anti-polygamy rhetoric in a land of prostitution and sexual abuse of slaves. The *Chicago Weekly Ledger* lamented that "McLean is almost canonized as a hero for the deed. Pratt is treated as would be the death of a beast of prey. Mrs. McLean is looked upon as the denizen of a brothel." The *Ledger* came to Eleanor's defense—not because of any affinity to Mormonism, which it repudiated— but to protect womanhood. Indeed, the paper viewed polygamy (which it disdained) as a "great deal better" than "the licensed brothelism" of America's "Christian cities" and a "million times better than the open, shameless, ravishing all over the land of slavery."[122]

While most of the nation cheered and jeered, Mormons on the trail west learned of Pratt's death. Philip Margetts, along the Missouri River with a group of handcart missionaries in June 1857, wrote that his associates "felt like young lions and almost as savage in consequence of hearing of the assassination of our beloved P. P. Pratt."[123] When news of Pratt's death arrived in Salt Lake City on June 23, apostle Wilford Woodruff recorded, "This was painful news to his family. The papers of the United States are filled with bitter revileings against us. The devil is exceding mad." Young asked George Smith, who had returned to Utah, "if it was not hard to acknowledge the hand of God in the death of Parley P. Pratt by as wicked a man as McLain."[124] For Young, the lesson of Pratt's death was "if we live our religion we shall have all the world upon us." Indeed, he continued, "the day has come when the Elders have got to take care of themselves, for the people will publish a lie and shoot them if they are not careful."[125] In informing other Saints, Young wrote of the "lamented death of our old friend and true and faithful Brother."[126] The news quickly raced around Mormon country. One Saint wrote, "I cannot yet believe that bror Parley P. Pratt is dead," an event which reminded him "of the power of the destroyer, and the fatal effects of fiendish enmity."[127] Such enmity was echoed as far away as England. From Liverpool, Orson Pratt wrote, "The journals of the day are filled with the most barefaced & malicious lies…and so violent is their hatred, and great their prejudice, that we cannot get a single word in one of them in self defence."[128] A crowd in London taunted apostle

Ezra Taft Benson, "Where's your brother Parley and where's Joe. Smith? We'll serve you the same as they were served."[129]

The Mormon press immediately cast Pratt in the role of martyr. In the *Millennial Star*, Orson described his brother as a martyr who "fell in a righteous cause…in the defense of suffering innocence, while endeavouring to aid by his letters a helpless female with her little children, to escape the fury of her savage persecutors." Following his brother's lead, Orson recounted the story of the marriage of the "brutal monster" McLean to Eleanor, her sufferings, and their later separation, without mentioning Eleanor's marriage to Parley. The reluctance of the Pratt brothers and Eleanor herself to refer publicly to the marriage between Parley and Eleanor illustrated that they recognized the public relations disaster latent in the whole episode.[130] The events surrounding Pratt's death gave at least some leaders pause before integrating him into the larger Mormon martyrology narrative. In January 1858, a group of church leaders discussed Pratt's death at a prayer meeting. Apostle Woodruff recorded that while Pratt was in St. Louis in March 1857, George Smith told him "not to go to Arkansaw but to go diret to Salt Lake & take care of himself. He told Parly if he went to try to protet Eleanor & her Children He would loose his life. But He did not take Care of himself or take G. A. Smith Council."[131] Other Saints seemed to agree, remarking, "Died Parley as a fool dieth."[132] Even Young later charged that Pratt's "blood was spilt" as punishment for his earlier disputed plural marriages (with Phoebe, Agatha, and Martha).[133]

In general, though, the Saints easily integrated Pratt into the pantheon of martyrs. At a mass meeting in Lehi, Utah, in February 1858 to demonstrate support for Mormon leaders during the Utah War crisis, the resolutions asserted that the Saints had "been cruelly persecuted,…[and] some of our best men murdered in cold blood," singling out for mention Joseph and Hyrum Smith, David Patten, and Pratt.[134] Woodruff affirmed Pratt's status as a martyr, as did the *Deseret News* when in 1888 it commemorated the "martyrs to the truth of this dispensation," including victims in the "Missouri Wars," the Haun's Mill massacre, Joseph and Hyrum Smith and Pratt, murdered "in cold blood."[135] Long after the rest of the nation forgot Pratt, Mormon authors and leaders continued to hail him as a martyr to the truth. In 2001, Gordon B. Hinckley, president of the Church of Jesus Christ of Latter-day Saints, stated that Pratt "died a martyr to this great work and kingdom."[136]

A complicating episode in the saga of Pratt's death unfolded on a horrific September 1857 dawn. The Mormons viewed Buchanan's decision to send a federal expeditionary force against Utah as a repetition of their government-approved expulsions from Missouri and Illinois; this time they pledged to resist. Four months after Pratt's death, as the rhetoric of defiance soared, a branch of the Mormon militia in southern Utah—acting without orders from leaders in Salt Lake City and assisted by local Indians—attacked a wagon train of Arkansas emigrants headed for Southern California and slaughtered more than 120 people, sparing only small children.[137]

The bare facts are certainly suggestive, and commentators at the time linked Pratt's murder in Arkansas with the massacre of Arkansans in Utah. When news of the Mountain Meadows Massacre arrived in California in October 1857, the California press attributed the bloodshed to retribution for the death of the "Sainted Parley."[138] In the wake of John D. Lee's execution for his participation at Mountain Meadows in 1877, a new round of national news stories asserted that Pratt's murder had been a primary cause of the massacre.[139] Certainly, the Saints' reaction to Pratt's death demonstrates their intense bitterness over the crime, the national celebration of the deed, and the failure to prosecute McLean. Nevertheless, Mormons' public and private commentary suggests that they expected God—not them—to take vengeance upon Pratt's murderer and the nation which lauded McLean. Pratt's murder probably contributed to the mentality of persecution that helped spur the perpetrators at Mountain Meadows. But it ranks low in the scheme of causation of that crime, a conclusion Juanita Brooks reached in her classic history sixty years ago.[140]

The drama of Pratt's death, combined with the contemporaneous furor over the Utah War, ensured that it would interest, perhaps even gratify, the general American public. As the most despised religion of nineteenth-century America, Mormonism tested the boundaries of tolerable religious dissent. The mainstream narrative of Pratt as evil seducer thoroughly trumped the alternative narratives of Pratt as victim or Pratt as martyr in the American press and mind. Likewise, the dominant narrative of Latter-day Saints as malicious fanatics easily beat back the Mormon counternarrative of themselves as the objects of religious persecution.

The nearly unanimous voice of the American press in either condoning or celebrating Pratt's murder demonstrates the profound depths to which American opinion of Mormonism had plummeted in the wake of plural marriage and the tumult over governance in Utah in the 1850s. While Mormonism had inspired heated opposition since its beginnings, sympathetic voices could be found in the national press following the Mormons' Missouri expulsions, the death of Joseph Smith in 1844, and the later murders of Mormon missionaries in the South in the last decades of the nineteenth century. The praise for Pratt's murder resulted both from the heated historical atmosphere against Mormonism in 1857 and because he, with his "seduction" of Eleanor, appeared to confirm the worst stereotypes about the Mormon hierarchy. The coverage—both by the national and Mormon press—suggests how thoroughly both sides considered the Latter-day Saints to be outsiders in American society.

As the nation debated the larger meaning of Pratt's murder, his family coped with his loss. The day the news of Pratt's murder arrived in Salt Lake, apostles Wilford Woodruff, Orson Hyde, George Smith, and Amasa Lyman went to "visit the family & to comfort them on the Death of their Husband & Father. They were calm & composed."[141] Parley's death left nine widows and twenty-three children without a father; he had been preceded in death by his first wife, Thankful, and seven children. His oldest child, Parley Jr., was twenty years old; his next oldest, Olivia, was fifteen; and his twenty-one other surviving children were twelve and under. According to his son Teancum, Parley's death brought "grief to a large family of widows and Orphans as well as to all the Latter day Saints who knew him, for few men have had as many warm friends in the church as had my Father."[142]

His widows ranged in age from twenty-seven-year-old Agatha to forty-five-year-old Keziah. They all outlived Parley by decades; Eleanor died first in 1874 and Agatha last, in 1898. Three of Pratt's widows—Belinda, Sarah, and Agatha—remarried following his death (though all of their subsequent marriages ended unhappily), while the other six—Elizabeth, Mary Wood, Hannahette, Phoebe, Keziah, and Eleanor—did not.[143] Mary received several marriage proposals, but she rejected all; according to family accounts, she always saw Parley's face as she contemplated another marriage. All of the widows stayed in Utah and remained committed to Mormonism.

Parley's death left his family in a precarious financial position, and his widows worked a variety of jobs to make ends meet, including millinery (Agatha and Mary Wood), midwifery (Phoebe), schoolteaching (Eleanor, Keziah, and Belinda), farming (Hannahette), and odd jobs such as "gleaning, washing" (Sarah).[144] His $26,000 estate, settled in 1867, was divided between ten widows (including Mary Ann Frost) and his children. Between 1884 and 1889, the remaining Pratt widows and children split an additional $13,500 from the proceeds of *Voice of Warning* and *Key to the Science of Theology*.[145] When Eleanor died in 1874, the first widow to join Pratt in death, she was buried in the pauper's section of the Salt Lake City Cemetery; the next wife to die, Keziah, was buried in what was likely a borrowed grave. Eventually, Pratt's wives who did not remarry purchased a family plot in the Salt Lake City Cemetery.[146] Even today, these wives have no individual headstones (only small footstones), mute testament to the poverty that dogged the Pratt name in death as it did in life.

FIGURE 15.1 Parley P. Pratt, daguerreotype by Marsena Cannon, about 1853. Courtesy of Church History Library, The Church of Jesus Christ of Latter-day Saints.

Epilogue

[Sometimes] a man has got to break off in the middle.
—PARLEY PRATT, *the improvised end of a sermon preached
on October 2, 1852, after he sensed (or was told) that he
was running on too long*

PRATT WAS A missionary, hymnist, explorer, politician, theologian, satirist, editor, and historian—but his acute sense of history left him convinced that his definitive role was that of apostle in "the most interesting [dispensation] that ever was." And that same sense shaped his mission as a chronicler. The Acts of the Apostles compiled by Luke, he wrote, "is the kind of history that we desire should be prepared concerning the servants and the works of God, at the present time."[1] Pratt never said which of the original apostles he most closely identified with, but his affinity with Paul was clear. Pratt was called at the dawn of a new dispensation, where the fertile core of a revolutionary gospel awaited the hand of a master missionary, who could expand its doctrine, expound its meaning, and extend its reach. Pratt the theologian and polemicist did more than any other man to turn Joseph Smith's prophetic declarations into a fully formed new religious system. Like the apostle Paul, Pratt traveled thousands of miles, braved imprisonment and hardship for the gospel's sake, and gladly suffered the contempt of his contemporaries for his part in "turning the world upside down" and overthrowing the idols of what he saw as a benighted religious culture. Perhaps even the fate of his predecessor influenced the martyrlike fatalism with which Pratt approached his own death. But if Pratt wanted to leave for posterity a record of his apostolic role in providential history, he also wanted to leave for futurity the story of the flesh and blood Parley P. Pratt.

There may be no such thing as a medium for transparent self-revelation. Journals, in the Early Republic as now, were written with an eye to posterity and public alike. Private letters were often preserved or routinely copied to assure their inclusion into a durable record. Pratt's autobiographical writings and historical texts were no more explicitly self-aware than were his other productions; everything he said and wrote was a self-conscious contribution

to the construction of a persona. The fact that he was Mormon only exacerbated that self-consciousness: "We present a spectacle to the world," he
observed, "that attracts the eyes and the attention of religionists first, philos-
ophers next, and of statesmen and political institutions and courts."
Consequently, he lamented, "we cannot publish an epistle, make a law, publish a speech, drop a word, write out a proclamation or deliver a message...or
preach a discourse or drop a private opinion...that it has not got to be published and republished." Thinking surely of himself rather than a generic institution, he judged with slight exaggeration that what emanated from the
church "is more looked upon...than the sentiment of any one people,
government, or individual."[2]

Pratt delivered his Salt Lake City sermons in the 1850s in the presence of
stenographers and in full awareness of their possible publication. Many of his
sermons, though, were not published and remained virtually unknown until
recently translated from the scribes' cramped nineteenth-century shorthand.
His spontaneous remarks, given to throngs of loyal Saints who knew and
loved him, exude an openness and vulnerability that even his letters often
lack. Delivered in middle age yet in the twilight of his life, they shed clarifying, if not definitive, light on his own self-understanding. Pratt was a product of vigorously competing worldviews, many of which never fully resolved
themselves in his tempestuous character.

He was a self-made individualist, fervent about republican ideals, convinced of America's providential role in Christian history (God favored "those
that best loved liberty," he said of the nation's founding).[3] But he came of age
in an era when widespread intolerance, frontier violence, and the tyranny of
the majority made most of the ideas he associated with his country into a
hollow promise. Steeped in a rhetoric of Mormon Zionism, lieutenant in a
militia, and zealous to defend the rights of his people, he also aspired to the
meekness and gentleness of a disciple and apostle of Jesus Christ. And passionate about the literal fulfillment of prophecy, he both imbibed and exuded
a millennial fervor that seamlessly superimposed the words of biblical
prophecy onto the world events and local developments of the mid-
nineteenth century. The predictions and prophecies of the Book of Mormon,
he proclaimed, led him to contemplate future events "with all of the assurances as if I had seen it myself....I could rely on those predictions,...there
was not a sentence predicted in that book pertaining to our time that I hadn't
gloried over perhaps one hundred times."[4] At the same time, he lived through
the wrenching failure to expel the usurpers who had dispossessed the
Mormons of their New Jerusalem, and he adjusted by learning to at least partially

spiritualize the meaning of Zion. Like so many of his people, he looked across the River Jordan but found the Promised Land a more elusive destination than he expected.

Even his sufferings and death were fraught with competing interpretations. No compatriot, Pratt believed, ever suffered longer imprisonment for his faith—but the charge under which he was held in a Missouri jail resulted from a killing arising out of an armed encounter that left several dead. Proclaimed a martyr by the Saints after his own cold-blooded murder, detractors and many historians today see the episode as a messy outcome of troublesome marriage practices and a frontier code of honor, not religious persecution.

Pratt had lived to see the remarkable stream of prophecies Heber C. Kimball pronounced upon him fulfilled—with the exception of "gold beyond counting." Near the end of his life, he had learned to interpret that prophecy in a spiritual way. Yet his insistent assertions suggest inner irresolution: "I concluded the prayer of faith would reach the banking house of Almighty that is never emptied of its treasures nor fails to pay," he told an audience, reporting on his South American mission. Then he added several reassurances: "we have never accomplished a work by counting up as other men do counting dimes, dollars." Rather, the church leadership accomplished their missions because they did not "reckon the cost" in "dollars and dimes." If he had more missions to fulfill, he would not even take an extra shirt. He gloried in his poverty and apostolic compliance with the injunction to be without purse or script, "valise or money." With undoubtedly painful recognition he acknowledged a responsibility "to feed and clothe those [who] depend on us," but in almost abject self-assurance concluded that "we may think we need money [but] he knows best whether we need or not."[5]

Less ambiguous than the meaning of Pratt's life and death is the influence he exerted in early Mormonism and his enduring legacy as the principal expounder and shaper of the doctrines Joseph Smith proclaimed. The Articles of Faith, Mormonism's official platform of beliefs propounded by Joseph Smith, then later canonized and now memorized by Mormon children in scores of languages, have their genesis in Pratt's earliest systematizing of Mormon doctrine.[6] His pithy exposition underlies the closest thing Mormons have to a creed. But Pratt elaborated, rather than simply organized, Mormon thought. He was first to grasp and expand a Mormon cosmology based on the eternalism of matter, only hinted at in Smith's earliest revelations. He was the first to defend and fully imagine the implications of a human destiny among the gods, before Smith himself explored the literal implications of being "equal with" Christ. And he was the first to give concrete expression to a detailed life and activity in the spirit world, reasoning by analogy and fired by Smith's teachings on vicarious salvation.

With other key doctrines as well Pratt went beyond his prophet prede-cessor, giving new or additional form to founding principles. The sense in which Smith thought of God as the father of human spirits, for example, prob-ably tended more toward an adoptive than a biological model. Intelligence and spirit were to him synonymous, referring to an eternal, uncreated human iden-tity.[7] Pratt (along with brother Orson) developed a two-stage anthropology, explicitly detailing a creation process that Brigham Young and subsequent Mormon leaders have adopted. Imagine, he said in an 1853 sermon, a "spirit liquid invisible" with "a capacity and enjoyment and intellectual power inherent in it." Let it be organized "into an individual being that will see, sense with eye and in the likeness and power that you now see me stand before you with eyes, head, members, mouth, and the gift of hearing, seeing, speaking, thinking with hands, feet, and in short,…you have organized it an individual agent a living, moving, thinking being."[8] Only rarely were his views curbed or constrained; some of his metaphysical speculations dropped out of circulation when reprints of his *Key to the Science of Theology* excised his theories of the Holy Ghost as an omnipresent ether or "spiritual fluid." (His theories of its physiological interactions with corporeal bodies also disappeared.) More often, his ideas simply merged into the stream of unfolding and expanding Mormon doctrine.

At the summit of his influence and intellectual powers, Pratt, though only in his forties, confessed himself the recipient of "many hard knocks"; he was by then wearied by his extensive missions and absences from the home he so loved.[9] His many letters reveal a man whose highest happiness was to be sur-rounded by a teeming domestic world of multiple wives and offspring—yet he refused to acknowledge publicly any hint of exhaustion. "Traveling abroad to preach the gospel is one of the pleasantest and easiest of all the labors of [the] kingdom," he said after the difficult South American mission.[10] Months later, he would boast that upon his return, Young directed him to rest. "Resting," he told his audience, was "the hardest work that a man thus called ever did." Better to dig down a mountain or traverse the sands of Arabia.[11] The pose was not facile façade. Pratt had received "the holy anointing" and was undoubtedly fueled by a preternatural passion to advance the millennial time-table. But he was also moved upon by a fierce sense of duty. Pratt's language was full of "rejoicing" and "gladness," but his contemporaries, as in the Richmond jail, often found him often dour and humorless. Intensity, rather than joviality, dominated his public and private persona. It was not for lack of trying, he explained in a revealing sermon. "A spirit of solemnity rests upon m[e]. I cannot bring my mind down to the trifling joys or amusements of life. It is not that I consider them particularly sinful.... It is not that I am opposed to the enjoyments of the young.... But the feeling [is] like this: I cannot bring my mind to stoop, [I cannot] center my mind to waste my time in much amusement that way....I tremble considerably under the weight of responsibility that is rolling upon us."[12] To Pratt's dutifulness was added the touch of a martyr. He took quite literally his apostolic vocation, finding in the apostlic church a pattern for his own life of trial and sacrifice. God "wants us to get into" taxing circumstances, he said, that we may learn "how we will hold out, how long" we will endure, what "obstacles" we will overcome and "how much faith" we will exercise.[13]

If Pratt was moved by duty, he was also drawn by love. "The individual thinking being," he preached, "never ceases to live and think and act." It "never ceases those sympathies and affections which are...the inherent principles of their eternal existence."[14] Pratt loved deeply and profoundly, and he lived in the hope of the continuation of his associations. Who could look out upon the filled tabernacle, he said in a late sermon, "and not be filled full of...joy...for the privilege of living and communing together with brethren and sisters of one heart and one mind." And to this he added the "hope of eternal joy...dwell[ing] in each other's society in worlds without end."[15] Mormonism offered him a compelling way to enlarge and eternalize that love—with family and his fellow Saints. His passion to extend the community he inhabited and served reaches across the decades since his passing:

Then here is my heart, and here is my hand to every good Saint in this world, in the world of spirits, in the resurrected world, and in all the worlds connected with this warfare and this work—here is my heart and hand! Depend upon it, if I am counted worthy, I will be somewhere about whether I stay here or go there, whether I stay in the flesh or go into the spirit world, or whether in the resurrected world, depend upon it, while my name is Parley P. Pratt, I will be somewhere about.[16]

Pamphlets and Books by Parley P. Pratt

(This list is based on Peter Crawley's article "Parley P. Pratt: Father of Mormon Pamphleteering," *Dialogue: A Journal of Mormon Thought* 15 [Autumn 1982]: 23–26.) Note: Other editions include only those published in Pratt's lifetime.

1. *A short account of a shameful outrage, committed by a part of the inhabitants of the town of Mentor, upon the person of Elder Parley P. Pratt, while delivering a public discourse upon the subject of the gospel; April 7th 1835.* [Kirtland? 1835?] 11 pp.

2. *The Millennium, a poem. To which is added hymns and songs on various subjects, new and interesting, adapted to the dispensation of the fullness of times.* Boston: Printed for Elder Parley P. Pratt, author and proprietor, 1835. 52 pp.

3. *A voice of warning and instruction to all people, containing a declaration of the faith and doctrine of the Church of the Latter Day Saints, commonly called Mormons.* New York: W. Sandford, 1837. 216 pp.

    Other editions: New York, 1839; Manchester, England, 1841; New York, 1842; Nauvoo, 1844; Edinburgh, 1847; Liverpool, 1852; Jersey, 1853 (French); Hamburg, 1853 (German); Liverpool, 1854; Copenhagen, 1855 (Danish); Copenhagen, 1856 (Danish).

4. *Mormonism unveiled; Zion's Watchman unmasked, and its editor, Mr. L. R. Sunderland, exposed: truth vindicated: the Devil mad, and priestcraft in danger!* New York: printed for the publisher, 1838. 47 pp.

    Other editions: New York, 1838 (two editions); Painesville, Ohio, 1838; New York, 1842.

5. *History of the late persecution inflicted by the state of Missouri upon the Mormons, in which ten thousand American citizens were robbed, plundered, and driven from the state, and many others imprisoned, martyred, &c. for their religion, and all this by military force, by order of the executive.* Detroit: Dawson & Bates, 1839. 84 pp.

    Other editions: Mexico, N.Y., 1840; New York, 1840.

6. *The millennium and other poems: to which is annexed, a treatise on the regeneration and eternal duration of matter.* New York: W. Molineux, 1840. 148 pp.

7. *Late persecution of the Church of Jesus Christ, of Latter Day Saints. Ten thousand American citizens robbed, plundered and banished; others imprisoned, and others martyred for their religion. With a sketech of their rise, progress and doctrine.* New York: J. W. Harrison, 1840. 215 pp.

8. *An address by Judge Higbee and Parley P. Pratt, Ministers of the gospel, of the Church of Jesus Christ of "Latter-day Saints," to the citizens of Washington and to the public in general.* Washington, D.C., February 9, 1840. 4 pp.

9. *An address by a minister of the Church of Jesus Christ of Latter-day Saints, to the people of England.* Manchester: W. R. Thomas, 1840. 4 pp.

    Other editions: Manchester, 1840; Bristol, 1841?; New York? 1841? (two editions); Philadelphia? 1843?

10. *Farewell song. Sung at the general conference of the Latter Day Saints, in the city of New York, as six of their elders, viz: B. Young, H. C. Kimball, O. Pratt, G. A. Smith, R. Hadlock [sic], and P. P. Pratt, were about to sail for Europe.* N.p., 1840? Broadside.

11. *Plain facts, showing the falsehood and folly of the Rev. C. S. Bush, (a Church Minister of the Parish of Peover,) being a reply to his tract against the Latter-day Saints.* Manchester: W. R. Thomas, 1840. 16 pp.

12. *A reply to Mr. Thomas Taylor's "Complete Failure," &c., and Mr. Richard Livesey's "Mormonism Exposed."* Manchester: W. R. Thomas, 1840. 12 pp.

13. *An answer to Mr. William Hewitt's tract against the Latter-day Saints.* Manchester: W. R. Thomas, 1840. 12 pp.

14. *An epistle of Demetrius, Junior, the silversmith, to the workmen of like occupation, and all others whom it may concern,—greeting: showing the best way to preserve our craft, & to put down the Latter Day Saints.* Manchester: Wm. Shackleton and Sons, 1840? Broadside.

    Other editions: Birmingham, 1841?; Norwich, 1842?; Peterboro, N.H.? 1842?; Philadelphia? 1842?

15. *A letter to the Queen, touching the signs of the times, and the political destiny of the world.* Manchester: P. P. Pratt, 1841. 12 pp.

    Other editions: Manchester, 1841; New York? 1841?

16. *Truth defended, or a reply to the "Preston Chronicle," and to Mr. J. B. Rollo's "Mormonism Exposed."* Manchester: P. P. Pratt, 1841. 8 pp.

17. *"Dialogue between a Latter-day Saint and an enquirer after truth.* Manchester: P. P. Pratt, 1842. 4 pp.

18. *The true God and His worship contrasted with idolatry.* [Liverpool? 1842?] 8 pp.

19. *The world turned upside down, or heaven on earth.* Liverpool: P. P. Pratt, 1842. 25 pp.

20. *An appeal to the inhabitants of the state of New York, letter to Queen Victoria, (reprinted from the tenth European edition,) the fountain of knowledge; immortality of the body, and intelligence and affection.* Nauvoo, Ill.: John Taylor, 1844. 40 pp. Other editions: Milwaukee, 1844?

21. *Proclamation of the Twelve Apostles of the Church of Jesus Christ, of Latter-day Saints. To all the kings of the world; to the President of the United States of America; to the governors of the several states; and to the rulers and people of all nations.* New York, 1845. 16 pp.

    Other editions: Liverpool, 1845.

22. *A dialogue between Joe. Smith and the devil!* New York? 1845. 12 pp.

    Other editions: Liverpool? 1846? (two editions).

23. *An apostle of the Church of Jesus Christ of Latter-day Saints, was in the Island of great Britain, for the gospel's sake; and being in the spirit on the 21st of November, A.D. 1846, addressed the following words of comfort to his dearly-beloved wife and family, dwelling in tents, in the camp of Israel, at Council Bluffs, Missouri Territory, North America.* London: J. B. Franklin, 1846? Broadside.

    Other editions: London? 1851?

24. *What do the Latter-day Saints believe; or what is "Mormonism?"* Liverpool: J. Sadler, 1851? Broadside.

25. *Proclamation! To the people of the coasts and islands of the Pacific; of every nation, kindred and tongue. By an apostle of Jesus Christ.* Sydney, Australia: William Baker, 1851. 16 pp.

    Other editions: Madras, 1853.

26. *Proclamacion! extraordinaria, para los Americanos Espanoles. Por Parley P. Pratt, apostol de la Iglesia de Jesu Christo, de los Postiros Dias Santos. Proclamation extraordinary! To the Spanish Americans by Parley P. Pratt, apostle of the Church of Jesus Christ of Later [sic] Day Saints.* San Francisco: Monson, Haswell & Co., 1852. 18 pp.

27. *"Mormonism!" "Plurality of wives!" An especial chapter, for the especial edification of certain inquisitive news editors, etc.* San Francisco, 1852. Broadside.

28. *Spiritual communication. A sermon delivered by Elder P. P. Pratt, Senr. before the conference at Salt Lake City, April 7, 1853.* [San Francisco? 1853?] 8 pp.

29. *Repent! Ye people of California! For, know assuredly, the Kingdom of God, has come nigh unto you.* San Francisco, 1854. Broadside.

30. *Key to the science of theology: designed as an introduction to the first principles of spiritual philosophy; religion; law and government; as delivered by the ancients, and as restored in this age, for the final development of universal peace, truth and knowledge.*

    Liverpool: F. D. Richards, 1855. 173 pp.

31. *Marriage and morals in Utah, an address by P. P. Pratt.* Liverpool: F. D. Richards, 1856. 8 pp.

    Other editions: Copenhagen, 1856 (Danish); Abertawy, Wales, 1856 (Welsh); San Francisco, 1856; Geneva, 1857 (French).

APPENDIX 2

Pratt Family Chart

Jared Pratt (b. November 25, 1769; d. November 5, 1839) married (July 7, 1799) Charity Dickinson (b. February 24, 1776; d. May 20, 1849)

THEIR CHILDREN:

Anson Pratt (b. January 9, 1801; d. May 26, 1849)
William Dickinson Pratt (b. September 3, 1802; d. September 15, 1870)
Parley Parker Pratt (b. April 12, 1807; d. May 13, 1857)
Orson Pratt (b. September 19, 1811; d. October 3, 1881)
Nelson Pratt (b. May 26, 1815; d. May 8, 1889)

Parley P. Pratt married (September 9, 1827) Thankful Halsey (b. March 18, 1797; d. March 25, 1837)

THEIR CHILD:

Parley Parker Pratt Jr. (b. March 25, 1837; d. August 26, 1897)

Parley P. Pratt married (May 14, 1837) Mary Ann Frost (b. January 14, 1808; d. August 24, 1891) (divorced)

THEIR CHILDREN:

Nathan Pratt (b. August 31, 1838; d. December 12, 1843)
Olivia Pratt (b. June 2, 1841; d. June 12, 1906)
Susan Pratt (b. April 7, 1843; d. August 1844)
Moroni Llewellyn Pratt (b. December 7, 1844; d. April 18, 1913)

Parley P. Pratt married (July 24, 1843) Elizabeth Brotherton (b. March 27, 1817; d. May 9, 1897)

THEIR CHILD:

Abish Pratt (adopted) (b. 1851; d. 1866)

Parley P. Pratt married (September 9, 1844) Mary Wood (b. June 18, 1818; d. March 5, 1898)

THEIR CHILDREN:

Cornelia Pratt (b. September 5, 1848; d. October 9, 1899)
Helaman Pratt (b. May 31, 1846; d. November 26, 1909)
Mary Wood Pratt (b. September 14, 1853; d. October 25, 1911)
Mathoni Wood Pratt (b. July 6, 1856; d. May 1, 1937)

Parley P. Pratt married (November 2, 1844) Hannahette Snively (b. October 22, 1812; d. February 21, 1898)

THEIR CHILDREN:

Alma Pratt (b. July 31, 1845; d. November 13, 1902)
Lucy Pratt (b. March 9, 1848; d. February 26, 1916)
Henrietta Pratt (b. October 26, 1851; d. May 18, 1918)

Parley P. Pratt married (November 20, 1844) Belinda Marden (b. December 24, 1820; d. February 19, 1894)

THEIR CHILDREN:

Nephi Pratt (b. January 1, 1846; d. April 29, 1910)
Belinda Marden Pratt (b. May 8, 1848; d. December 10, 1893)
Abinadi Pratt (b. May 8, 1848; d. November 1914)
Lehi Pratt (b. June 9, 1851; d. August 15, 1905)
Isabella Eleanor Marden Pratt (b. September 1, 1854; d. April 23, 1912)

Parley P. Pratt married (October 15, 1845) Sarah Houston (b. August 3, 1822; d. May 22, 1886)

THEIR CHILDREN:

Julia Houston Pratt (b. April 1, 1847; d. April 17, 1903)
Mormon Pratt (b. January 8, 1850; d. November 19, 1850)
Teancum Pratt (b. November 15, 1851; d. September 8, 1900)
Sarah Elizabeth Pratt (b. May 31, 1856; d. November 23, 1891)

Parley P. Pratt married (February 8, 1846) Phoebe Elizabeth Soper (b. July 8, 1823; d. September 17 1887)

THEIR CHILDREN:

Mosiah Pratt (b. February 26, 1850; d. March 26, 1850)
Omner Pratt (b. November 30, 1851; d. January 7, 1852)
Phoebe Soper Pratt (b. May 19, 1853; d. October 13, 1922)

Parley P. Pratt married (April 28, 1847) Martha Monks (b. April 28, 1825; d. ?)

THEIR CHILD:

Ether Pratt (b. January 30, 1849; d. February 27, 1849)

Parley P. Pratt married (April 28, 1847) Ann Agatha Walker (b. June 11, 1829; d. June 25, 1908)

THEIR CHILDREN:

Agatha Pratt (b. July 7, 1848; d. August 12, 1914)
Malona Pratt (b. April 15, 1850; d. October 14, 1913)
Marion Pratt (b. November 28, 1851; d. October 6, 1852)
Moroni Walker Pratt (b. October 10, 1853; d. June 28, 1911)
Evelyn Pratt (b. August 8, 1856; d. August 16, 1917)

Parley P. Pratt married (December 27, 1853) Keziah Downes (b. May 10, 1812; d. January 19, 1876)

Parley P. Pratt married (November 14, 1855) Eleanor Jane McComb (b. December 29, 1817; d. October 24, 1874)

Parley P. Pratt had 12 wives, 30 children, and 266 grandchildren.

Notes

INTRODUCTION

1. Parley P. Pratt (hereafter PPP) to William Patterson, 9 May 1853, Parley P. Pratt Collection (hereafter PPP Collection), Church History Library, The Church of Jesus Christ of Latter-day Saints (hereafter CHL).

2. On Paul, see Bart D. Ehrman, *Peter, Paul, and Mary Magdalene: The Followers of Jesus in History and Legend* (New York: Oxford University Press, 2006); Jerome Murphy-O'Connor, *Paul: A Critical Life* (New York: Oxford University Press, 1996); Calvin J. Roetzel, *Paul: The Man and the Myth* (Minneapolis: Fortress Press, 1999); A. N. Wilson, *Paul: The Mind of the Apostle* (New York: W. W. Norton, 1997).

3. *New York World*, 25 September 1870, cited in Stanley P. Hirshson, *The Lion of the Lord: A Biography of Brigham Young* (New York: Knopf, 1969), 323.

4. "Mormonism," *Edinburgh Review* 202 (April 1854): 375.

5. PPP, "Biography of Nathan Pratt," *Times and Seasons*, 15 January 1844, 414–415.

6. PPP to Mary Ann Frost Pratt, 30 May 1839, PPP Collection.

7. PPP to Family, 16 May–13 June 1851, PPP Collection.

8. Dean C. Jessee, ed., *The Papers of Joseph Smith*. Vol. 2: *Journal, 1832–1842* (Salt Lake City, Utah: Deseret Book, 1992), 456. Portions of the letter, including this statement, were later canonized as Doctrine and Covenants 127:2. When citing Joseph Smith's revelations, we generally cite the version that Pratt would have used, particularly the manuscript revelation book recently published by the Joseph Smith Papers Project; the 1833 Book of Commandments (hereafter BC); or the 1835 Doctrine and Covenants (hereafter DC [1835]). The Book of Commandments and the 1835 Doctrine and Covenants have been recently republished in Robin Scott Jensen, Richard E. Turley Jr., and Riley M. Lorimer, *Published Revelations*, Vol. 2 of the Revelations and Translations series of *The Joseph Smith Papers*, edited by Dean C. Jessee, Ronald K. Esplin, and Richard Lyman Bushman (Salt Lake City, Utah: Church Historian's Press, 2011).

9. PPP, *The Autobiography of Parley Parker Pratt, one of the Twelve Apostles of the Church of Jesus Christ of Latter-day Saints, Embracing his Life, Ministry, and Travels*, edited by Parley P. Pratt Jr. (New York: Russell Brothers, 1874). For the sake of accessibility for readers, we use a more recent edition, with the same text but added footnotes and photographs, edited by Scot Facer Proctor and Maurine Jensen Proctor (Salt Lake City, Utah: Deseret Book, 2000).

10. PPP to Patterson, 9 May 1853.

CHAPTER I

1. Orson Pratt to PPP, 11 October 1853, PPP Collection.

2. Val D. Rust, *Radical Origins: Early Mormon Converts and Their Colonial Ancestors* (Urbana: University of Illinois Press, 2004), 67–68.

3. Eve LaPlante, *American Jezebel: The Uncommon Life of Anne Hutchinson, the Woman Who Defied the Puritans* (New York: HarperCollins, 2004), 118, 208.

4. Orson Pratt to PPP, 11 October 1853, PPP Collection.

5. Rust, *Radical Origins*, 45–47; *John Lathrop: Reformer, Sufferer, Pilgrim, Man of God* (Salt Lake City, Utah: Institute of Family Research, 1979).

6. Rust, *Radical Origins*, 5.

7. Frederick W. Chapman, *The Pratt Family: or the Descendants of Lieut. William Pratt* (Hartford, Conn.: Case, Lockwood, 1864), 137–144.

8. James A. Roberts, comp., *New York in the Revolution as Colony and State* (Albany, N.Y.: Brandow, 1898), 238.

9. Chapman, *Pratt Family*, 144.

10. Pratt reflected on his grandfather's Revolutionary War service in *An Appeal to the Inhabitants of the State of New York* (Nauvoo, Ill.: John Taylor, 1844), 1.

11. Obadiah made Jared "early in life a weaver for the family," son Orson Pratt remembered. Elden J Watson, comp., *The Orson Pratt Journals* (Salt Lake City, Utah: Elden J. Watson, 1975), 6.

12. Orson Pratt, "History of Orson Pratt," *Latter-day Saints' Millennial Star* 27, 3 (21 January 1865): 39.

13. Little is known of Parley's half sister, Mary or Polly Pratt. She married twice, had one son, and was described by Parley in a letter to Orson in 1853 as "insane." PPP to Orson Pratt, 25 May 1853, PPP Collection.

14. D. Hamilton Hurd, *History of Otsego County, New York* (Philadelphia: Everts & Fariss, 1878), 101.

15. PPP, *Appeal to the Inhabitants*, 1.

16. David G. Fitz-Enz, *The Final Invasion: Plattsburgh, the War of 1812's Most Decisive Battle* (New York: Cooper Square, 2001).

17. Oliver Goldsmith, *The Deserted Village* (London: W. Griffin, 1770).

18. William Wordsworth, "The Prelude," bk. 12.2: 208–209, in *Poetical Works*, edited by Thomas Hutchinson and Ernest de Selincourt (Oxford: Oxford University Press, 1989).

19. PPP, *Autobiography*, 4.

20. Orson Pratt, "Biographical Sketch of Parley P. Pratt," *Latter-day Saints' Millennial Star* 19, 27 (4 July 1857): 417.

21. Joyce Oldham Appleby, *Inheriting the Revolution: The First Generation of Americans* (Cambridge: Harvard University Press, 2001), 124.

22. PPP, *Autobiography*, 4.

23. For the "four great branches," see Pratt, *Autobiography*, 4; "Oxford Examinations," *Quarterly Journal of Education* 5 (January–April 1833): 330.

24. Watson, *Orson Pratt Journals*, 7.

25. Census records for 1820 indicate that the parents and six other males resided in the household, two in the eighteen-to-twenty-six category, when there was only one son of that age. New Lebanon, Columbia, N.Y., census, 1820.

26. Orson Pratt, "Biographical Sketch," 417.

27. PPP to William Patterson, 9 May 1853, PPP Collection.

28. PPP, *Autobiography*, 209.

29. Ibid., 6.

30. Robert Morgan, *Boone: A Biography* (Chapel Hill, N.C.: Algonquin, 2007), 30–31.

31. PPP, *Autobiography*, 6.

32. Ibid., 7–8.

33. *Oswego Yesterday and Today* (Oswego, N.Y.: Chamber of Commerce, 1906), 42.

34. On Scranton, see Charles Wesley Brooks, *A Century of Missions in the Empire State* (Philadelphia: American Baptist Publication Society, 1900); on Hamilton Seminary, see *Triennial Baptist Register* 2, 2 (1836): 68–71.

35. PPP, *Autobiography*, 11. Italics in original.

36. Ibid., 14.

37. Ibid.

38. PPP, sermon, 9 October 1853, papers of George D. Watt, transcribed by LaJean Purcell Carruth, CHL.

39. Elizabeth Camp, journals, William L. Clements Library, University of Michigan.

40. PPP, *Autobiography*, 16.

41. Pratt mentioned being sixteen years old when he left Thankful four years previous. But Thankful referred to a three years' absence, suggesting that Pratt had seen her again in 1824, between his two farming seasons in Oswego.

42. PPP, *Autobiography*, 19.

43. Ibid., 583, 585n.

44. Watson, *Orson Pratt Journals*, 8.

45. George Frederick Wright, *A Standard History of Lorain County, Ohio: An Authentic Narrative of the Past....* (Chicago: Lewis, 1916), 1:62.

46. Ibid., 41.

47. PPP, *Autobiography*, 22.

48. Thomas Campbell, *Declaration and Address of the Christian Association of Washington* (Washington, Pa.: Brown & Sample, 1809), 4.

49. William E. Tucker and Lester G. McAllister, *Journey in Faith: A History of the Christian Church (Disciples of Christ)* (St. Louis, Mo.: Bethany, 1975), 140.

50. Bill J. Leonard, *Baptists in America* (New York: Columbia University Press, 2005), 146.

51. Richard S. Van Wagoner, *Sidney Rigdon: A Portrait of Religious Excess* (Salt Lake City, Utah: Signature, 1994), 10.

52. Most numerous of these, the Methodists went from less than 3 percent of American church members in 1776 to 34 percent by 1850. Nathan Hatch, "Mormon and Methodist: Popular Religion in the Crucible of the Free Market," edited by Dean L. May and Reid L. Nielson, *The Mormon History Association Tanner Lectures: The First Twenty Years* (Urbana: University of Illinois Press, 2006), 65.

53. Tucker and McAllister, *Journey in Faith*, 133–134.

54. Van Wagoner, *Rigdon*, 44–46.

55. Alexander Campbell and Robert Owen, *Evidences of Christianity: A Debate* (Nashville, Tenn.: McQuiddy, 1957), 504.

56. Frances Trollope, *Domestic Manners of the Americans* (New York: Alfred A. Knopf, 1949), 153.

57. Alexander Campbell, *Memoirs of Alexander Campbell Embracing A View of the Origin, Progress and Principles of the Religious Reformation Which He Advocated,* edited by Robert Richardson, 2 vols. (Philadelphia, 1868), 2:346, in Dan Vogel, *Religious Seekers and the Advent of Mormonism* (Salt Lake City, Utah: Signature, 1988), 37. Early Mormon writers, perhaps stung by Campbell's attacks on the Book of Mormon, became equally vociferous in attacking what they saw as Campbell's diluted restorationism. See *Evening and Morning Star* 2, 17 (February 1834): 131. Other times they attacked restorationists (whom they called "reformers") in general. See *Evening and Morning Star* 2, 20 (May 1834): 153.

58. Campbell and Owen, *Evidences of Christianity*, 104.

59. "Prospectus," *Millennial Harbinger* 1, 1 (4 January 1830).

60. PPP, *Mormonism Unveiled: Zion's Watchman Unmasked* (New York: Pratt & Fordham, 1838), 40; Robert Richardson, ed., *Memoirs of Alexander Campbell,* 2 vols. (Cincinnati: Standard, 1913), 2:345–346, in Grant Underwood, *The Millenarian World of Early Mormonism* (Urbana: University of Illinois Press, 1999), 25.

61. Van Wagoner, *Rigdon*, 50–51.

62. William Sims Bainbridge, "Shaker Demographics, 1840–1900: An Example of the Use of U.S. Census Enumeration Studies," *Journal for the Scientific Study of Religion* 21 (1982): 352–365.

63. Mario de Pillis, "The Development of Mormon Communitarianism, 1826–1846," Ph.D. diss., Yale University, 1960, 66.

64. Larry C. Porter, "The Brigham Young Family: Transition between Reformed Methodism and Mormonism," in *A Witness for the Restoration: Essays in Honor of Robert J. Matthews*, edited by Kent P. Jackson and Andrew C. Skinner (Provo, Utah: Religious Studies Center, Brigham Young University), 253–256.

65. PPP, *Autobiography*, 22.

66. Campbell, *Declaration and Address*, 9.

67. Nathan Hatch, *The Democratization of American Christianity* (New Haven, Conn.: Yale University Press, 1989).

68. David Brion Davis, "Some Themes of Counter-Subversion: An Analysis of Anti-Masonic, Anti-Catholic, and Anti-Mormon Literature," *Mississippi Valley Historical Review* 47, 2 (September 1960): 205–224.

69. For the Mormon case, see Mario De Pillis, "The Quest for Religious Authority and the Rise of Mormonism," *Dialogue: A Journal of Mormon Thought* 1 (Spring 1966): 66–88; Marvin Hill, *Quest for Refuge: The Mormon Flight from American Pluralism* (Salt Lake City, Utah: Signature Books, 1989).

70. One newspaper account dated Pratt's joining with Rigdon, and his commission to preach for them, to August 1829. *Painesville Telegraph* 2, 26 (14 December 1830).

71. PPP, *Autobiography*, 24.

72. *Prophet* 1, 51 (10 May 1845).

73. PPP, *Autobiography*, 27.

74. Andrew Reed and James Matheson, *A Narrative of the Visit to the American Churches,....* (New York: Harper & Brothers, 1835), 1:66, cited in E. Brooks Holifield, *God's Ambassadors: A History of the Christian Clergy in America* (Grand Rapids, Mich.: Eerdmans, 2007), 114.

75. Van Wagoner, *Rigdon*, 9.

76. Eliza Roxie Taylor, "The Life of Elvira Annie Cowles," 2, CHL.

77. John G. Turner, *Mind Your Business: Bringham Young*, chap. 1 (Cambridge: Harvard University Press, forthcoming).

78. Philip Schaff, *The Principle of Protestantism* (Philadelphia: United Church Press, 1964), 150, cited in Holifield, *God's Ambassadors*, 104.

79. PPP, *Autobiography*, 30.

80. Jerald C. Brauer, "Conversion: From Puritanism to Revivalism," *Journal of Religion* 58, 3 (July 1978): 230.

81. Tucker and McAllister, *Journey in Faith*, 140.

82. His early biographer wrote that Pratt fabricated his conversion experience but based her account on undocumented "later claims" by Pratt. Reva Stanley, *The Archer of Paradise: A Biography of Parley P. Pratt* (Caldwell, Idaho: Caxton, 1937), 33.

83. Tucker and McAllister, *Journey in Faith*, 141.

84. PPP, *Autobiography*, 31–32.

85. PPP, 7 September 1856, *Journal of Discourses*, 26 vols., reported by G. D. Watt et al. (Liverpool: F. D. & S. W. Richards et al., 1851–1886; reprint, Salt Lake City: n.p., 1974), 5:194.

86. An excellent treatment of the synthesis of spiritual witness and rational evidence sought by Mormon converts is Steven C. Harper's "Infallible Proofs, Both Human and Divine: The Persuasiveness of Mormonism for Early Converts," *Religion and American Culture* 10, 1 (Winter 2000): 99–118.

87. A. S. Hayden, *Early History of the Disciples of the Western Reserve, Ohio* (Cincinnati: Chase & Hall, 1875), 183.

88. Ibid., 209.

89. PPP, sermon, 31 October 1852, Papers of George D. Watt, transcribed by LaJean Carruth, CHL.

90. PPP, *Voice of Warning and Instruction to all People* (New York: Sandford, 1837), 133–135.

91. PPP, sermon, 31 October 1852.

92. See Roger G. Kennedy, *Hidden Cities: The Discovery and Loss of Ancient North American Civilization* (New York: Free Press, 1994), esp. 225–228; Lee E. Huddleston, *Origins of the American Indians: European Concepts 1492–1729*, Latin American Monographs 11 (Austin: University of Texas Press, 1967); Dan Vogel, *Indian Origins and the Book of Mormon* (Salt Lake City, Utah: Signature, 1986).

93. PPP, *Autobiography*, 32.

94. PPP, sermon, 7 September 1856, *Journal of Discourses* 5:194.

95. PPP, *Autobiography*, 32.

96. Gregory A. Prince, *Power from on High: The Development of Mormon Priesthood* (Salt Lake City, Utah: Signature, 1995), 1–45.

97. BC 24:9.

98. BC 22:1, 8.

99. Pratt, *Autobiography*, 37–38; Reuben Miller, journal, 21 October 1848, in Dan Vogel, *Early Mormon Documents* (Salt Lake City, Utah: Signature, 1998), 2:494.

100. George Q. Cannon, sermon, 16 September 1877, *Journal of Discourses* 19:105.

101. PPP to Edward Hunter, 15 July 1856, CHL.

102. Watson, *Orson Pratt Journals*, 9.

103. PPP, *Autobiography*, 43.

104. Ibid., 45.

105. Robin Scott Jensen, Robert J. Woodford, and Steven C. Harper, *Manuscript Revelation Books*, Vol. 1 of the Revelations and Translations series of *The Joseph Smith Papers*, edited by Dean C. Jessee, Ronald K. Esplin, and Richard Lyman Bushman (Salt Lake City, Utah: Church Historian's Press, 2009), 36–41.

106. BC 30:8.

107. PPP, sermon, 9 October 1853, papers of George D. Watt, transcribed by LaJean Purcell Carruth, CHL.

108. "Testimony of Brother E. Thayre," *Saints Herald* (3 October 1862): 79–80.

109. "History of Parley P. Pratt," *Latter-day Saints' Millennial Star* 26 (24 December 1864): 822.

110. This revelation did not appear in the Book of Commandments, but is in the Kirtland Revelation Book, 83–84 (Jensen, Woodford, and Harper, *Revelations and Translations*, 583–584).

CHAPTER 2

1. Ezra Booth, Letter 8, *Ohio Star* 2, 49 (8 December 1831).
2. The Buffalo Creek Indian Reservation became the town of West Seneca upon the Native Americans' removal to other reservations after a treaty of 1838. See *History of West Seneca, New York*, edited by Truman C. White (Boston: Boston History Co., 1898).
3. John Corrill, *A Brief History of the Church of Jesus Christ of Latter-day Saints* (St. Louis, Mo.: "Printed For the Author," 1839), 7–9.
4. Oliver Cowdery to Joseph Smith and Beloved Brethren, 12 November 1830, Newel Knight, Autobiography and Journal [ca. 1846–1847], CHL.
5. PPP, *Mormonism Unveiled*, 41.
6. Robert Owen and Alexander Campbell, *Debate on the Evidences of Christianity* (Bethany, Va.: Campbell, 1829), 1:91.
7. Hayden, *Disciples of the Western Reserve*, 121.
8. *Times and Seasons* 4, 19 (15 August 1843).
9. Anson Call statement, *Deseret Evening News*, 21 April 1879, in Van Wagoner, *Rigdon*, 59.
10. Hayden, *Disciples of the Western Reserve*, 210. For Rigdon's reaction, see also John Wickliffe Rigdon, 'I Never Knew A Time When I Did Not Know Joseph Smith': A Son's Record of the Life and Testimony of Sidney Rigdon," ed. Karl Keller, *Dialogue* 1, 4 (Winter 1966): 23–24.
11. "Mormonism," *Painesville Telegraph*, 15 February 1831.
12. Lucy Diantha Morley Allen, autobiographical sketch, undated, CHL.
13. Oliver Cowdery to Joseph Smith and Beloved Brethren, 12 November 1830.
14. Lyman Wight, journals, as quoted in Joseph Smith III and Heman C. Smith, *History of the [Reorganized] Church of Jesus Christ of Latter Day Saints* (Independence, Mo.: Herald House, 1897–1903), 1:154.
15. Frederic G. Mather, "The Early Days of Mormonism," *Lippincott's Magazine*, August 1880, 206–207.
16. Levi Ward Hancock, autobiography, ca. 1854, CHL.
17. Philo Dibble, "Philo Dibble's Narrative," *Early Scenes in Church History* (Salt Lake City, Utah: Juvenile Instructor Office, 1882), 76.
18. Hancock, autobiography.
19. Mather, "Early Days," 206–207. Levi Hancock confirmed Card's presence at the morning preaching. See Hancock, autobiography.
20. John Murdock, autobiography and journal, CHL.
21. PPP, *Mormonism Unveiled*, 41.
22. According to the church's *Evening and Morning Star* (1, 11 [April 1833]), there were seventy to eighty members when the missionaries departed. With its converts, the church would have numbered more than two hundred.
23. "The Book of Mormon," *Painesville Telegraph*, 30 November 1830.

24. See, for example, John Riggs, autobiographical sketch, 1880, CHL.

25. "The Golden Bible," *Painesville Telegraph*, 16 November 1830; see also "Golden Bible," *Painesville Telegraph*, 22 September 1829.

26. E. D. Howe, *Mormonism Unvailed* (Painesville, Ohio: Telegraph Press, 1834), 102–103.

27. *Painesville Telegraph*, 30 November 1830, 7 December 1830. On the missionaries' experience in Kirtland, see also Mark Lyman Staker, *Hearken, O Ye People: The Historical Setting of Joseph Smith's Ohio Revelations* (Salt Lake City, Utah: Greg Kofford Books, 2010), 49–69.

28. PPP, *Autobiography*, 53–55.

29. "Beware of Imposters," *Painesville Telegraph*, 14 December 1830.

30. PPP, *Autobiography*, 55.

31. John P. Bowes, *Exiles and Pioneers: Eastern Indians in the Trans-Mississippi West* (Cambridge: Cambridge University Press, 2007), 161.

32. Perl Wilbur Morgan, *History of Wyandotte County, Kansas and its People* (Kansas City: Lewis, 1911), 66.

33. Eleanor Atkinson, "The Winter of the Deep Snow," *Transactions of the Illinois State Historical Society for the Year 1909* (Springfield: State Journal, 1910), 47–62.

34. Ronald E. Romig, "The Lamanite Mission," *John Whitmer Historical Association Journal* 14 (1994): 28.

35. Oliver Cowdery to Joseph Smith, 8 April 1831, Joseph Smith Collection, CHL.

36. Ibid.

37. Richard W. Cummins to William Clark, 15 February 1831, Records of the United States Superintendency of Indian Affairs, St. Louis, Volume 6, Kansas State Historical Society.

38. Peter Whitmer, Jr., journal, 30 December 1831, CHL.

39. William G. McLoughlin, "Cherokees and Methodists, 1824–1834," *Church History* 50, 1 (March 1981): 44.

40. PPP, *Autobiography*, 67–69.

41. BC 30.

42. Ibid., 29:9.

43. Ibid., 39:4.

44. Lavina Fielding Anderson, ed., *Lucy's Book: A Critical Edition of Lucy Mack Smith's Family Memoir* (Salt Lake City, Utah: Signature, 2001), 530–533.

45. BC 42. The current edition of the Doctrine and Covenants inaccurately dates the revelation March 1831. See Jensen, Woodford, and Harper, *Revelations and Translations*, 133.

46. Ashbel Kitchell, who recorded the Mormon mission to the Shakers, remembered only Cowdery by name (and remembered that very imperfectly—as Lowdree). Though Pratt would almost certainly have been one of the "number" of men Kitchell referred to, since he was one of Cowdery's three companions on that journey, Kitchell did not appear to recognize him on his return visit. This is not surprising,

since Cowdery was the spokesperson on the first encounter. Ashbel Kitchell, "A Mormon Interview," in Lawrence R. Flake, ed., "A Shaker View of a Mormon Mission," *BYU Studies* 20, 1 (Fall 1979): 95–99; Robert F. W. Meader, "The Shakers and the Mormons," *Shaker Quarterly* 2 (Fall 1962): 83–96.

47. Richard McNemar, commentary on the Book of Mormon, 28–29 January 1831, Library of Congress, Manuscript Division, Shaker Collection, Item 253, p. 45. Thanks to Christian Goodwillie for this reference.

48. Caroline B. Piercy, *Valley of God's Pleasure* (New York: Stratford House, 1951), 9, 124–27.

49. Kitchell, "Mormon Interview."

50. Many Shakers at this time were experimenting with Grahamism, named after the reformer who linked vegetarianism with sexual continence. See Stephen J. Stein, *The Shaker in America: A History of the United Society of Believers* (New Haven, Conn.: Yale University Press, 1992), 156ff.

51. Jensen, Woodford, and Harper, *Revelations and Translations*, 133–135.

52. Kitchell, "Mormon Interview."

53. Ibid.

54. Reynolds Cahoon, journal, May 1831, p. 1, CHL.

55. Nathan Bangs, *A History of the Methodist Episcopal Church*, 2 vols. (New York: Mason & G. Lane, 1839), 160–161.

56. John Whitmer, "The Book of John Whitmer," 25, Community of Christ Library-Archives, Independence, Missouri.

57. *Painesville Telegraph*, 14 December 1830.

58. PPP, *Autobiography*, 72.

59. Jensen, Woodford, and Harper, *Revelations and Translations*, 137–143.

60. Ibid., 147–151.

61. PPP, *Autobiography*, 83–84; Watson, *Orson Pratt Journals*, 11.

62. 3 Nephi 21.

63. BC 56:9.

64. Dean C. Jessee, ed., *The Papers of Joseph Smith*. Vol. 1: *Autobiographical and Historical Writings* (Salt Lake City, Utah: Deseret, 1989), 357.

65. DC 27:1 (1835).

66. *Elders' Journal* 1, 4 (August 1838): 54.

67. Peter Whitmer Jr., journal, CHL; Oliver Cowdery to Joseph Smith, 8 April 1831.

68. BC 57.

69. Stephen C. Ragan, "Notes on the Pioneer School of Kansas City," *Annals of Kansas City* 1 (December 1922): 173, cited in R. Steven Pratt, "Introduction to 1833 Handbill," unpublished ms., R. Steven Pratt, research files (hereafter SPF).

70. *Evening and the Morning Star* 1, 1 (June 1832): 6.

71. PPP, *Autobiography*, 96.

72. Pratt, *Autobiography*, 96–100; BC 59:62.

73. BC 64:30–32.

74. "Philo Dibble's Narrative," *Early Scenes in Church History* (Salt Lake City, Utah: Juvenile Instructor, 1882), 81.

75. PPP, *Autobiography*, 99–100.

76. Ibid., 100.

77. Ibid., 101.

78. Jan Shipps and John W. Welch, eds., *The Journals of William McLellin* (Provo, Utah: Brigham Young University Studies, 1994; and Urbana: University of Illinois Press, 1994), 89.

79. Ibid., 90.

80. Ibid., 91–92.

81. *Evening and Morning Star* 1, 2 (July 1832): 14; 2, 13 (June 1833): 101.

82. Shipps and Welch, *McLellin*, 93.

83. PPP, sermon, 7 April 1853, papers of George D. Watt, transcribed by LaJean Purcell Carruth, CHL.

84. Shipps and Welch, *McLellin*, 102.

85. PPP, *Autobiography*, 103.

86. John Russell to Laura Ann Spencer Russell, 27 April 1833, Illinois State Historical Library.

87. S. G. Russell, "Prof. John Russell," in *Transactions of the Illinois State Historical Society for the Year 1901* (Springfield: Phillips Bros., 1901), 103. Pratt's subsequent visit to the Russell home must have occurred long after the Missouri problems, since Pratt was imprisoned soon after the Haun's Mill Massacre until July of the next year. Given also the location of Greene County, which is southeast of Nauvoo and not along the route of the flight from Missouri, it is likely that the visit remembered by Russell's son occurred at a time when Pratt was traveling between Nauvoo and St. Louis. He could also be conflating a later visit of Pratt with that of other Saints, such as Newell and Elizabeth Whitney, who did take refuge in Greene County in fall 1838.

88. John Russell, *The Mormoness, or, The Trials of Mary Maverick* (Alton, Ill.: Courier Steam Press, 1853), 55.

89. John Mason Peck, *"Father Clark," or the Pioneer Preacher, Sketches and Incidents of Rev. John Clark, by an Old Pioneer* (New York: Sheldon, Lamport & Blakeman, 1855), 277–278; Edward Miner, *Past and Present of Greene County, Illinois* (Chicago: S. J. Clark, 1905), 121. Pratt remembered his antagonist as Reverend Dotson.

90. See "Mormonism," *Painesville Telegraph*, 21 June 1832, reprinted from *The Pioneer* (Rock Springs, Ill., ca. June 1832).

91. "Abraham Lincoln to Rev. J. M. Peck," 21 May 1848, in John G. Nicolay and John Jay, eds., *Complete Works of Abraham Lincoln* (New York: Francis Tandy, 1894), 2:23–26.

92. J. M. Peck, *A Gazeteer of Illinois* (Jacksonville: Goudy, 1834), 92.

93. Laura Ann Spencer Russell to John Russell, 9 May 1833, Illinois State Historical Library.

94. PPP, *Autobiography*, 109.

95. [John Mason Peck], *Mormonism, one of the delusions of Satan, exposed. By a friend of truth.* [Galena, Ill.? 1835?], copy at the John Mason Peck Collection, St. Louis Mercantile Library Association. Peck's newspaper also continued to attack Mormonism. The *Latter-day Saints' Messenger and Advocate* responded to an article from the *Pioneer* in April 1835 that had advocated the Spaulding theory of the Book of Mormon's origins (1.7, 104–107). Peck later published "Nauvoo, Illinois—The Mormons," *Arthur's Home Magazine* 3, 1 (January 1854): 38–44.

96. DC 7:21 (1835).

97. DC 84:5 (1835).

98. PPP, *Autobiography*, 112.

99. DC 81:2 (1835).

100. Joseph Smith to William W. Phelps, 11 January 1833, in Dean C. Jessee, ed. *The Personal Writings of Joseph Smith* (Salt Lake City, Utah: Deseret, 2002), 292–293.

101. Orson Hyde and Hyrum Smith to "the Bishop his councel and the inhabitents of Zion," 14 January 1833, Joseph Smith Letterbook, Joseph Smith Collection, CHL.

102. Kenneth H. Winn, "The Missouri Context of Antebellum Mormonism and Its Legacy of Violence," in Thomas M. Spencer, ed., *The Missouri Mormon Experience* (Columbia: University of Missouri Press, 2010), 19–26.

103. *Evening and Morning Star* 14 (June 1833): 109, 111.

104. PPP, *Autobiography*, 116–117.

105. "To His Excellency, Daniel Dunklin," *Evening and the Morning Star* 2, 15 (December 1833): 114.

106. Joseph Smith, Sidney Rigdon, Frederick G. Williams, and Martin Harris to Brethren in Zion, 25 June 1833, Joseph Smith Collection, CHL. In spite of Smith's directive, Morley and Corrill were still being referred to as Partridge's counselors in 1835.

107. Minute Book 2 (Far West Record), 11, September 1833, 36–37, CHL.

108. Daniel Dunklin to Edward Partridge et al., 19 October 1833, in Joseph Smith Jr., "History of Joseph Smith," *Times and Seasons* 6, 7 (15 April 1845): 880.

109. PPP, *History of the Late Persecution* (Detroit: Dawson & Bates, 1839), 13–14.

110. Ibid., 15. Oliver Cowdery wrote that Pratt had been "considerably hurt" by the mob. See Oliver Cowdery to Thankful Halsey, 4 March 1834, Oliver Cowdery Letter Book, Huntington Library.

111. "The Outrage in Jackson County, Missouri," *Evening and the Morning Star* 2, 15 (December 1833): 120.

112. PPP, *Late Persecution*, 20–21.

113. PPP, *Autobiography*, 121.

114. PPP, *Late Persecution*, 20–23; PPP, *Autobiography*, 120.

115. PPP, *Autobiography*, 121

116. PPP, *Mormonism Unveiled*, 29–30.

117. Edward Partridge to Joseph Smith, November 1833, Joseph Smith Collection, CHL.

CHAPTER 3

1. The handbill was reprinted in Kirtland, Ohio: Parley P. Pratt, Newel Knight, John Carrill [Corrill], "'The Mormons' So Called," *Evening and the Morning Star. Extra* (February 1834).

2. W. W. Phelps, "The Answer," *Times and Seasons* 5, 24 (1 January 1844): 760.

3. Peter Crawley, *A Descriptive Bibliography of the Mormon Church.* Vol. 1: *1830–1847* (Provo, Utah: Religious Studies Center, Brigham Young University, 1997), 42.

4. "History of Lyman Wight," *Latter-day Saints' Millennial Star* 27 (Liverpool, U.K.: Brigham Young, 1865): 455.

5. Oliver Cowdery to Thankful Halsey, 4 March 1834.

6. Minute Book 1 (Kirtland Council Minute Book), 24 February 1834, 41, CHL.

7. Jensen, Woodford, and Harper, *Revelations and Translations*, 355–361 (first published in the 1844 DC as section 101).

8. Anderson, *Lucy's Book*, 569–570.

9. PPP, *Autobiography*, 133–134.

10. Nauvoo Relief Society Minute Book, 28 April 1842, CHL. Smith singled out Parley, along with Orson Pratt, Orson Hyde, and John Page.

11. Reuben McBride, Reminiscence, undated, CHL.

12. Dean C. Jessee, Mark Ashurst-McGee, and Richard L. Jensen, eds., *Journals, 1832–1839*, Vol. 1 of the Journals Series of *The Joseph Smith Papers*, edited by Dean C. Jessee, Ronald K. Esplin, and Richard Lyman Bushman (Salt Lake City, Utah: Church Historian's Press, 2008), 32, entry for 6 March 1834.

13. Ibid., 34, entry for 10 March 1834.

14. William Hyde, journal, CHL.

15. DC 91 (1835).

16. Watson, *Orson Pratt Journals*, 31 January 1833 and 13 March 1834. Warren Foote recorded that "Landon and others had been cut off for rejecting the vision concerning the three glories." "Autobiography," 5, CHL.

17. *Times and Seasons* 6, 16 (1 November 1845): 1027.

18. PPP, *Autobiography*, 138.

19. Watson, *Orson Pratt Journals*, 12, 44; Orson Pratt recorded in his family history that "a few years previous to their death," his parents were baptized. Orson Pratt, Genealogical Record [ca. 1880], CHL.

20. Scott G. Kenney, *Wilford Woodruff's Journal, 1833–1898* (Salt Lake City, Utah: Signature Books, 1984), 1–25 April 1834, 1:7–8.

21. Roger D. Launius, *Zion's Camp: Expedition to Missouri* (Independence, Mo.: Herald House, 1984), 93.

22. PPP, *Autobiography*, 141–142.

23. George A. Smith, memoirs, 13 May 1834, George A. Smith Papers, CHL.

24. Bushman, *Rough Stone Rolling*, 247–248.

25. Smith, "History of Joseph Smith," *Times and Seasons* 6, 9 (15 May 1845): 912.

26. Governor Daniel Dunklin to Colonel J. Thornton, 6 June 1834, in the *Evening and the Morning Star* 2, 22 (July 1834): 175.

27. PPP, *Autobiography*, 142.

28. Charles C. Rich, diary, 14 June 1834, CHL.

29. See Launius, *Zion's Camp*.

30. The revelation was not published until the 1844 edition of the DC. See Jensen, Woodford, and Harper, *Revelations and Translations*, 375–379.

31. Launius, *Zion's Camp*, 115.

32. George A. Smith, memoirs, 22 June 1834, 38, George A. Smith Papers, CHL.

33. Minute Book 2, 23 June 1834, CHL; Benjamin E. Park, "'Thou Wast Willing to Lay Down Thy Life for they Brethren': Zion's Blessings in the Early Church," *John Whitmer Historical Association Journal* 29 (2009): 28. On Zion's Camp, see also Bushman, *Rough Stone Rolling*, 235–248.

34. PPP, *Autobiography*, 144.

35. Minute Book 2, 3 July 1834, CHL.

36. PPP, *Autobiography*, 144–145.

37. Ibid., 145.

38. Interview of David Whitmer by Zenas H. Gurley, 14 January 1885, in *David Whitmer Interviews*, edited by Lyndon W. Cook (Orem, Utah: Grandin, 1991), 157.

39. Minute Book 1, 14 February 1835, 147, CHL.

40. Ibid., 21 February 1835, 154–155.

41. Ibid., 155–156b.

42. "Apostle," Charles Buck, *A Theological Dictionary* (Philadelphia: Woodward, 1830), 28.

43. Pratt mentioned the addition of his mother to his household but noted of his father, by then 66, only that he was "unable to do for himself or family" (*Autobiography*, 159). When Pratt visited Anson in Detroit four years later, his father—as well as Charity—were in that city, where Jared died shortly thereafter.

44. PPP, *Autobiography*, 161.

45. The record of Oliver Cowdery is not extant, but was described as beginning thus by John Whitmer; Whitmer, "Book of John Whitmer," 25.

46. "I have been laboring in this cause for eight years," he wrote in a letter published in *Messenger and Advocate* 1, 12 (September 1835): 179.

47. Because the press was destroyed while the Book of Commandments was in production, no complete versions were printed, but several partial versions were gathered from the wreckage, bound, and circulated.

48. J. Wickliffe Rigdon, "Life Story of Sidney Rigdon," 24.

49. Winfred Ernest Garrison and Alfred T. DeGroot, *The Disciples of Christ: A History* (St. Louis, Mo.: Bethany, 1958), 188.

50. Alexander Campbell, "Delusions," *Millennial Harbinger* 2 (Bethany, Va.: Campbell, 1831), 93.

51. PPP, *A Short Account of a Shameful Outrage* (Kirtland?: 1835).

52. See Grant Underwood, "Book of Mormon Usage in Early LDS Theology," *Dialogue* 17, 3 (Autumn 1984): 35–72.

53. "The Millennium," *Latter-day Saints' Millennial Star* 1 (August 1840): 75.

54. Brigham Young, sermon, 6 April 1857, *Journal of Discourses* 4:305.

55. PPP, *Shameful Outrage*, 9–10.

56. *Chardon Spectator*, 30 October 1835, in Edwin Brown Firmage and Richard Collin Mangrum, *Zion in the Courts: A Legal History of the Church of Jesus Christ of Latter-day Saints 1830–1900* (Urbana: University of Illinois Press, 2001), 53.

57. Watson, *Orson Pratt Journals*, 61.

58. Quorum of the Twelve Apostles, Record, 22 May 1835, CHL.

59. Shipps and Welch, *McLellin*, 180, 315, 366n.

60. Quorum of the Twelve Apostles, Record, 29 June 1835, 17–18 July 1835.

61. PPP to Asael Smith, 21 July 1835, George A. Smith Collection, University of Utah.

62. Brigham Young, sermon, 6 April 1857, *Journal of Discourses* 4:305.

63. "An Autobiographical Sketch of the Life of the Late Mary Ann Stearns Winters," *Relief Society* 3, 8 (August 1916), 423, 427.

64. Watson, *Orson Pratt Journals*, 70.

65. Ibid., 71.

66. James B. Allen and Glen M. Leonard, *The Story of the Latter-day Saints*, 2nd ed. (Salt Lake City, Utah: Deseret, 1992), 107.

67. See Steven C. Harper, "'A Pentecost and Endowment Indeed': Six Eyewitness Accounts of the Kirtland Temple Experience," in John W. Welch, ed., *Opening the Heavens: Accounts of Divine Manifestations 1820–1844* (Provo: Brigham Young University Press, 2005; and Salt Lake City, Utah: Deseret, 2005), 327–371.

68. Jessee, McGee, and Jensen, *Journals*, 171–172, entry for 22 January 1836.

69. PPP, Family Record of Parley Parker Pratt, CHL.

70. Jessee, McGee, and Jensen, *Journals*, 171–172, entry for 22 January 1836.

71. Ibid., 174–175, entry for 28 January 1836.

72. Jessee, McGee, and Jensen, *Journals*, 181, entry for 6 February 1836.

73. DC 87: 4–5 (1835).

74. PPP, *Autobiography*, 164.

75. Ibid., 164–165.

76. Curiously, Pratt omitted all mention of his brother Orson on this journey.

77. Carl Benn, "Colonial Transformations," in *Toronto: A Short Illustrated History of its First 12,000 Years*, edited by Ronald F. Williamson (Toronto: James Lorimer, 2008), 65–67.

78. John Taylor, *Three Nights' Public Discussion between the Revds. C. W. Cleeve*, James Robertson, and Philip Cater and Elder John Taylor (Liverpool: J. Taylor, 1850), 17.

79. PPP, *Autobiography*, 175.

80. Ibid., 178.

81. PPP to John Whitmer, 9 May 1836, in *Messenger and Advocate* 2, 20 (May 1836): 318.

82. John Taylor, "History of John Taylor by Himself," 10, CHL.

83. PPP to John Whitmer, 318.

84. The letter Pratt sent was most likely his undated "An Epistle Written by an Elder of the Church of Latter Day Saints," CHL.

85. Watson, *Orson Pratt Journals*, 79.

86. Joseph Fielding, journals, 1837–1859, 5–7, CHL.

87. Crawley, *Descriptive Bibliography*, 1:23–24.

88. John Taylor, "History of John Taylor by Himself," 11–12, Histories of the Twelve, 1856–1868, CHL.

89. *Messenger and Advocate* 2, 22 (July 1836): 352.

90. "History of Orson Hyde," *Latter-day Saints' Millennial Star* 26 (1864): 791.

91. PPP, *Autobiography*, 199–205.

92. Ibid., 205.

93. Taylor, "History," 12.

94. David Whitmer, *Address to All Believers in Christ* (Richmond, Mo.: 1887), 32.

95. Kenney, *Woodruff's Journal*, 30 November 1836, 1:110.

96. *Messenger and Advocate* 3, 4 (January 1837): 444.

97. PPP to John Taylor, 27 November 1836, in John Taylor Collection, CHL.

98. BC 24:6.

99. [PPP], "An Epistle Written by an Elder of the Church of Latter Day Saints," CHL. In similar fashion, Oliver Cowdery combined elements from Joseph Smith's 1820 theophany (as he later related them) with the story of Moroni's 1823 visitation. See *Messenger and Advocate* 1, 3 (December 1834): 42–43; and 1, 5 (February 1835): 78–79.

100. PPP, *Autobiography*, 45.

101. PPP to John Taylor, 27 November 1836.

CHAPTER 4

1. Geauga County Tax Records, 1837; Staker, *Hearken*, 442.

2. Joseph Smith Jr., trans., The Book of Mormon (Kirtland, Ohio: Pratt & Goodson, 1837), preface.

3. Edward Leo Lyman, Susan Ward Payne, and S. George Ellsworth, *No Place to Call Home: The 1807–1857 Life Writings of Caroline Barnes Crosby, Chronicler of Outlying Mormon Communities* (Logan: Utah State University Press, 2005), 43.

4. *Messenger and Advocate* 3, 31 (3 April 1837): 496.

5. PPP, *Autobiography*, 209.

6. *Messenger and Advocate* 3, 31 (3 April 1837): 496.

7. PPP, *Autobiography*, 207–208.

8. Parley P. Pratt Jr. to Orson Pratt Jr., 21 July 1897, in Arthur D. Coleman, *Pratt Pioneers of Utah* (Provo, Utah: J. Grant Stevenson, 1967), xxvi.

9. DC 100:2 (1835), received 3 November 1831, in Hiram, Ohio.

10. Jessee, McGee, and Jensen, *Journals*, 168, entry for 21 January 1836.

11. Kimball, Autobiography, cited in James B. Allen, Ronald K. Esplin, and David J. Whittaker, *Men with a Mission 1837–1841: The Quorum of the Twelve Apostles in the British Isles* (Salt Lake City, Utah: Deseret, 1992), 24.

12. PPP, *Autobiography*, 209.

13. John Taylor, discourse, 5 March 1882, *Journal of Discourses* 23:31.

14. John Taylor claimed he was "the first person that wrote a letter to England on the subject of the gospel," but in the letter where he made that claim he referred to his correspondent as already having a copy of the letter "which Elder P. P. Pratt wrote to England" (Taylor, letter, 3 May 1837, reprinted in *Messenger and Advocate* 3, 9 [June 1837]: 513–516). Pratt's letter had been written even before Taylor's baptism, as he mentioned in a letter to John Whitmer dated 9 March 1836 that he had "addressed a letter of eleven pages to that land" (*Messenger and Advocate* 2, 20 (May 1836): 318. If Pratt did indeed send a letter in that year, it most likely was the undated "Epistle Written by an Elder," which internal evidence suggests was written in 1836. The only discrepancy in dating is that the holograph is seven pages, and Pratt mentions eleven. Most likely, the extant holograph is a shorter draft version (it bears insertions and corrections) of the final, but non-extant, letter.

15. [PPP], "An Epistle Written by an Elder," CHL.

16. Thomas Marsh and David Patten to PPP, 10 May 1837, Joseph Smith Letterbook, CHL.

17. See Vilate Kimball to Heber C. Kimball, 6 September 1837, cited in Ronald K. Esplin, *The Emergence of Brigham Young and the Twelve to Mormon Leadership* (Provo, Utah: Joseph Fielding Institute for Latter-day Saint History and BYU Studies, 2006), 109.

18. Jayne Fife, "Story of Mary Ann Frost Stearns Pratt," unpublished manuscript; Lyman, Payne, and Ellsworth, *No Place to Call Home*, 45–46. Mary Ann Winters recorded the marriage date as May 9 ("Autobiographical Sketch of M. A. S. Winters," *Relief Society* 3, 9 [September 1916], 485).

19. "Autobiographical Sketch," 485.

20. *Elders' Journal* 1, 3 (July 1838): 43.

21. DC 101 (1835).

22. Benjamin F. Johnson to George F. Gibbs, 1903, CHL.

23. Whitmer, "Book of John Whitmer," 86.

24. *Elders' Journal* 1, 2 (November 1837): 29.

25. Richard Bushman writes that "Joseph, it appears, married no one else until he wed Louisa Beaman on April 5, 1841, in Nauvoo," while acknowledging that "historians debate the possibility of one other wife in the interim." *Rough Stone Rolling*, 437.

26. *Messenger and Advocate* 3, 32 (May 1837): 510.

27. Ibid., 3, 33 (June 1837): 521.

28. Staker, *Hearken*, 463–465.

29. Kirtland Bank Stock Ledger, Chicago Historical Society, microfilm copy at Utah State Historical Society.

30. Staker, *Hearken*, 503n13.

31. "Minutes of a Conference," 22 December 1836, in *Messenger and Advocate* 3, 4 (January 1837): 443–444.

32. Staker, *Hearken*, 482–487.

33. Daniel Walker Howe, *What Hath God Wrought: The Transformation of America 1815–1848* (New York: Oxford University Press, 2007), 503.

34. PPP to Joseph Smith, 23 May 1837, published in Arthur B. Deming, *Naked Truths about Mormonism* 1, 2 (April 1888): 4. Deming stated that he transcribed the letter from an original held by the Lake County Historical Society in Painesville, Ohio, but this institution no longer has the letter. The letter was sent by Warren Parrish, who had been secretary of the Kirtland Safety Society and had since left Mormonism, to LaRoy Sunderland, editor of *Zion's Watchman*, who published it on 28 March 1838. Sunderland corrected Pratt's spelling and punctuation and omitted the postscript. Pratt claimed, without entering into specifics, that the letter as published was "altered, so as to convey a different idea from the original," though he acknowledged its essential purport and expressed regret and contrition for writing it (*Elders' Journal* 1, 4 [July 1838]: 85–86). Smith justified his profits from land sales as necessary to fund church enterprises, as when he explicitly told Nauvoo immigrants that the higher price they paid for lots was "their sacrifice" to the work of the kingdom. Andrew H. Hedges, Alex D. Smith, and Richard Lloyd Anderson, *Journals, 1841–1843*, Vol. 2 of the Journals Series of *The Joseph Smith Papers*, edited by Dean C. Jessee, Ronald K. Esplin, and Richard Lyman Bushman (Salt Lake City, Utah: Church Historian's Press, forthcoming 2011), entry for 13 April 1843.

35. John Johnson to Parley P. Pratt, 22 May 1837, Geauga County, Deed Records; Staker, *Hearken*, 525–556.

36. PPP to Joseph Smith, 23 May 1837.

37. Ibid.

38. William E. McLellin to James T. Cobb, 14 August 1880, in Larry C. Porter, "William E. McLellan's Testimony of the Book of Mormon," *BYU Studies* 10, 4 (Summer 1970): 486.

39. Sally Parker to Mr. John Kempton, 26 August 1838, in Janiece L. Johnson, "'The Scriptures Is a Fulfilling': Sally Parker's Weave," *BYU Studies* 44, 2 (2005): 116.

40. Lyman Johnson and Orson Pratt, "To the Bishop & his council in Kirtland," 29 May 1837, L. Tom Perry Special Collections, Harold B. Lee Library, Brigham Young University (hereafter BYU), cited in Chad J. Flake, "The Newell K. Whitney Collection," *BYU Studies* 11, 4 (Summer 1971): 327.

41. Minute Book 1, 29 May 1837, 226–227, CHL.

42. Ibid., 229.

43. Heber C. Kimball, "Autobiography," Heber C. Kimball, Papers 1837–1866, CHL.

44. Mary Fielding to Mercy Fielding Thompson, ca. 15 June 1837, Mary Fielding Papers, CHL.

45. Ibid.

46. John Taylor, "History of John Taylor By Himself," 15.

47. Kirtland Bank, Stock Ledger.

48. Stephen Burnett, purchase from PPP, 23 June 1837, Geauga County Land Deeds, vol. 24, 398; Orimel Barney, purchase from PPP, 24 June 1837, Lake County Land Deeds, vol. A, 129. Thanks to Mark Staker for these references.

49. Mary Fielding to Mercy Fielding Thompson, 8 July 1837, Mary Fielding Papers, CHL.

50. "History of Thomas Baldwin Marsh," *Latter-day Saints' Millennial Star* 26 (1864): 391.

51. PPP, *Autobiography*, 210–222.

52. Fielding to Thompson, 8 July 1837. The letter is now too damaged to recapture these original portions, but Esplin reports their essence in *Brigham Young*, 108.

53. *Elders' Journal* 1, 4 (August 1838): 51.

54. Minute Book 1, 3 September 1837, 235, CHL.

55. Mary Ann Stearns Winter recalled that at the time of Pratt's pre-marriage visits to their home (which would have been early May 1837), her mother "told me we were going to New York, and then we could go from there and visit my grandparents and relations in Maine—and all this seemed very natural and right" ("Autobiographical Sketch," 485).

56. Crawley, *Descriptive Bibliography*, 1:70.

57. Pratt, *Autobiography*, 211–213; Mary Ann Stearns Winters, "Mothers in Israel," *Relief Society* (September 1916): 486.

58. C. Leonard Allen, "Baconianism and the Bible in the Disciples of Christ: James S. Lamar and *The Organon of Scripture*," *Church History* 55 (March 1986): 66, cited in Craig James Hazen, *The Village Enlightenment in America: Popular Religion and Science in the Nineteenth Century* (Urbana: University of Illinois Press, 2000), 8–9.

59. Mark A. Noll, *America's God: From Jonathan Edwards to Abraham Lincoln* (New York: Oxford University Press, 2002), 233. The Dwight quotation, cited by Noll, is from *Theology: Explained and Defended* (New Haven, Conn., 1843), 4:260–261.

60. Theodore Dwight Bozeman, *Protestants in an Age of Science: The Baconian Ideal and Antebellum American Religious Thought* (Chapel Hill: University of North Carolina Press, 1977), xiii.

61. PPP, *Voice of Warning and Instruction to all People* (New York: Sandford, 1837), 12.

62. William Godwin, *Enquiry Concerning Political Justice and Its Influence on Modern Morals and Happiness*, bk. 2, chap. 6 (Baltimore: Penguin, 1976), 206.

63. PPP, *Voice*, 20.

64. Orson Pratt, *Prophetic Almanac, for 1845* (New York: *Prophet* office, 1844); Pratt, *Prophetic Almanac for 1846* (New York: *New York Messenger* office, 1846). Orson's almanacs quoted from or reprinted several of Parley's essays. Crawley, *Descriptive Bibliography*, 1:308.

65. PPP, *Voice*, iii–x.

66. PPP, *Autobiography*, 24.

67. For an introduction to the history and scholarship of millennialism, see John J. Collins, Bernard McGinn, and Stephen J. Stein, *Encyclopedia of Apocalypticism* (New York: Continuum, 1998), 3 vols.

68. "Prospectus," *Millennial Harbinger* 1, 1 (4 January 1830).

69. PPP, *The Millennium* (Boston: Pratt, 1835), 5.

70. "The Second Coming of the Savior," *Evening and Morning Star* 2, 13 (June 1833): 99.

71. PPP, *Millennium*, 25.

72. Dean C. Jessee, ed., *The Papers of Joseph Smith*. Vol. 1: *Autobiographical and Historical Writings* (Salt Lake City, Utah: Deseret, 1989), 7, 278–279.

73. Smith eventually named three signs that the latter days were arrived. The other two signs were "the covenants given to the Latter-day Saints, also the translation of the Bible." *Messenger and Advocate* 2, 3 (December 1835): 229.

74. Underwood, *Millenarian World of Early Mormonism*, 28.

75. PPP, *Voice* (1837), 89, 88.

76. Noll, *America's God*, 381.

77. *Evening and Morning Star* 1, 2 (July 1832): 11, 14; 2, 19 (April 1834): 145; 2, 20 (May 1834): 153.

78. "Spiritualizing the Scriptures" (from the *Gospel Reflector*), *Times and Seasons* 3, 5 (1 January 1842): 644–646.

79. Amos 5:15; Ezekiel 37.

80. Alma 46:24.

81. BC 30:9.

82. See Anthony F. C. Wallace, *The Long, Bitter Trail: Andrew Jackson and the Indians* (New York: Hill & Wang, 1993).

83. *Evening and Morning Star*, 1, 7 (December 1832): 54.

84. Ibid., 1, 8 (January 1833): 62; 1 Nephi 22:12.

85. PPP, *Millennium*, 22.

86. PPP, *Autobiography*, 328–329.

87. Kenneth Cmiel, *Democratic Eloquence: The Fight over Popular Speech in Nineteenth-Century America* (New York: William Morrow, 1990).

88. William Wordsworth, "Preface," *Lyrical Ballads*, 1800.

89. John Milton, *The Poetical Works of John Milton*, edited by Edward Philips (New York: D. Appleton & Company, 1872), 4.

90. On antebellum print culture, see Dan Schiller, *Objectivity and the News: The Public and the Rise of Commercial Journalism* (Philadelphia, 1981); David M.

Henkin, *The Postal Age: The Emergence of Modern Communications in Nineteenth-Century America* (Chicago, 2006); Trish Loughran, *The Republic in Print: Print Culture in the Age of U.S. Nation Building, 1770–1870* (New York, 1870).

91. Cmiel, *Democratic Eloquence*, 57, 66, 95.

92. *Evening and Morning Star* 1, 2 (July 1832): 12.

93. PPP, "Preface," *Voice of Warning and Instruction to all People* (Manchester: Sheckleton & Son, 1841 [first European edition]), iv.

94. PPP, *Voice* (1837), ix, 57, 75, 87, 155, 173; (1839), 132.

95. PPP, *Voice* (1837), 107.

96. Richard T. Hughes, ed., *The American Quest for the Primitive Church* (Urbana: University of Illinois Press, 1988).

97. Jessee, *Papers*, 1:5.

98. De Pillis, "Quest for Religious Authority."

99. Alexander Campbell, "Importance of a Pure Version of the Christian Scriptures," *Millennial Harbinger*, 4th ser., 2, 1 (January 1952): 32.

100. PPP, *Voice*, 103.

101. Ibid., 110.

102. Smith once said in reference to "the angel flying through the midst of heaven," simply "Moroni delivered the Book of Mormon." See Andrew F. Ehat and Lyndon W. Cook, *The Words of Joseph Smith: The Contemporary Accounts of the Nauvoo Discourses of the Prophet Joseph* (Orem, Utah: Grandin, 1991), 13. But he remarked in an 1844 sermon that the being referred to was "an angel having the holy Priesthood,.... a special messenger, ordained & prepared for that purpose" (Ehat and Cook, *Words*, 366–367). Similarly, David Patten said the angel of the scripture "must be clothed with the power of all the other dispensations" (To the Saints scattered abroad," *Elders' Journal* 1, 3 [July 1838]: 42).

103. PPP, *Voice*, 122, 125, 133, 171.

104. Zvi Ben-dor Benite, *The Ten Lost Tribes: A World History* (New York: Oxford University Press, 2009), 213.

105. Joseph Wolff, *Researches and Missionary Labours Among the Jews* (London: Nisbet, 1835), 13, quoted in Benite, 213.

106. PPP to Don Carlos Smith, 3 October 1837, *Elders' Journal* 1 (October 1837): 8–9.

107. John Dunmore Lang, *Origin and Migrations of the Polynesian Nation* (Sydney, Australia: George Robertson, 1877), 210–211.

108. PPP, "Preface to the European Edition," *Times and Seasons*, 1 January 1842, 647–648.

109. Parley P. Pratt Jr. et al., to John Taylor, 24 July 1884, CHL.

110. Crawley, *Descriptive Bibliography*, 1:71.

111. John Hyde, *Mormonism: Its Leaders and Designs* (New York: Fetridge, 1857), 134.

112. History of Sara Studevant Leavitt, 1798–1878, ed. Juanita L. Pulsipher, 6, 8, typescript, BYU Library.

113. Annie Clark Tanner, *A Mormon Mother: An Autobiography* (Salt Lake City, Utah: Tanner Trust Fund, 1991), 12, 14.

114. PPP, *Voice of Warning* (Edinburgh, Scotland: H. Armour, 1847), v.

115. Brigham Young to a "Gentleman in New York," 31 October 1864, CHL.

116. *Deseret News*, 22 April 1875; 26 May 1875.

117. "Mormonism," *Baptist Advocate* 31 December 1841; "Memoir of the Mormons," *Southern Literary Messenger* (November 1848).

118. John W. Gunnison, *The Mormons, or Latter-day Saints: A History of Their Rise and Progress* (Philadelphia: Lippincott, 1852), 40.

119. PPP, *Autobiography*, 211–212.

120. Origen Bachelor and Robert Dale Owen, *Discussion on the existence of God and the authenticity of the Bible* (London: James Watson, 1853).

121. Charles Knowlton, *Speech of Dr. Charles Knowlton, in support of Materialism, Against the Argument of Origen Bacheler, the Great Goliath, and Champion of the Cross* (Philadelphia: Society of Free Inquirers, 1838).

122. Origen Bachelor, *Mormonism Exposed, Internally and Externally* (New York, 1838).

123. "The Mormon Church," *Detroit Tribune*, 1 February 1872, republished in *Chicago Tribune*, 4 February 1872. See "Uncle Dale's Readings in Early Mormon History," http://www.sidneyrigdon.com/dbroadhu/IL/mischig.htm

124. Bachelor, *Mormonism Exposed*, 6–7.

125. Ibid., 6–10.

126. PPP to Mary Ann Frost Pratt, 25 November 1837, PPP Collection.

127. PPP, *Autobiography*, 213.

128. Ibid., 214.

129. Wandle Mace, Autobiography, ca. 1890, 11–12, CHL.

130. Mormon 8:26.

131. In 1856, Pratt told Mace that "this was the only time he ever asked a man not a member of the church to lay hands on the sick." Mace, Autobiography, 14–15.

132. Mace, Autobiography, 15–16.

133. PPP, *Autobiography*, 214.

134. Bachelor, *Mormonism Exposed*, 6.

135. Jonathan Baldwin Turner compared the Mormons to Austin. See *Mormonism in All Ages* (New York: Platt & Peters, 1842), 294. Thomas Greenwood and William Goode could only identify Ann Lee as a practitioner of faith healing in America; see Greenwood, *The Latest Heresy: or, Modern Pretensions to the Miraculous Gifts of Healing and of Tongues, Condemned by Reason and Scripture* (London: William Harding, 1832), 15; and Goode, *The Modern Claims to the Possession of the Extraordinary Gifts of the Spirit* (London: Hatchard, 1833), 9.

136. A study of American Baptists could find a parallel to Mormon faith healing only in Scotland and England. See Francis Augustus Cox, James Hoby, *The Baptists in America: A Narrative* (London: T. Ward, 1836), 306.

137. J. R. Jacob, "La Roy Sunderland: Alienation of an Abolitionist," *Journal of American Studies* 6, 1 (April 1972): 1–17.

138. "Mormonism," *Zion's Watchman*, 13 January 1838.

139. PPP, *Mormonism Unveiled*, 3–4.

140. DC 90:2 (1835).

141. The first anti-Mormon pamphlet, Alexander Campbell's *"Delusions: An Analysis of the Book of Mormon"* (Boston: Greene, 1832), and the first anti-Mormon book, Eber D. Howe's *Mormonism Unvailed: A Faithful Account of that Singular Imposition and Delusion* (Painesville, Ohio: E. D. Howe, 1834), employed the fraud theme. Virtually all anti-Mormons writers followed suit until the scandal of polygamy became their new focus in the 1850s.

142. PPP, *Mormonism Unveiled*, 9.

143. Ibid., 27.

144. DC 91:5 (1835).

145. Jensen, Woodford, and Harper, *Revelations and Translations*, 265.

146. Ibid., 509. A post-1838 broadside of a poetic reworking of the revelation ascribes the text—probably referring to the original—to David Patten as singer and Sidney Rigdon as translator. "Mysteries of God," undated broadside, BYU Special Collections.

147. PPP, *Mormonism Unveiled*, 27.

148. PPP, *Key to the Science of Theology* (Liverpool: F. D. Richards, 1855), 33.

149. PPP, *Mormonism Unveiled*, 31.

150. PPP, *An Answer to Mr. William Hewitt's Tract Against the Latter-day Saints* (Manchester: Thomas, 1840), 9.

151. *Messenger and Advocate* 2, 17 (February 1836): 265.

152. Truman Coe, "Mormonism," *Ohio Observer*, 11 August 1836, cited in Milton V. Backman Jr., "Truman Coe's 1836 Description of Mormonism," *BYU Studies* 17, 3 (Spring 1977): 354.

153. PPP, sermons, 9 January 1853, 10 July 1853, papers of George D. Watt, transcribed by LaJean Purcell Carruth, CHL.

CHAPTER 5

1. Jensen, Woodford, and Harper, *Revelations and Translations*, 159. The manuscript has the notation, "Not to be printed at present" and did not appear until the 1835 DC.

2. Manuscript History of the Church, B-1, 26 April 1838, 791, CHL.

3. *Elders' Journal* 1, 3 (July 1838): 47.

4. PPP, *Autobiography*, 217.

5. Thomas Marsh to Wilford Woodruff, 30 April 1838, CHL.

6. Wilford Woodruff said Daniel 2 was quoted by Moroni to Joseph Smith in 1823 (*Journal of Discourses* 24:241). See David Whittaker, "The Book of Daniel in

Early Mormon Thought," in *By Study and Also by Faith: Essays in Honor of Hugh W. Nibley*, edited by John M. Lundquist and Stephen D. Richs (Salt Lake City and Provo, Utah: Deseret and Foundation for Ancient Research and Mormon Studies, 1990), 1:159. Whittaker provides an excellent overview of the pervasiveness of Daniel's "Kingdom of God" rhetoric in the Missouri period and elsewhere.

7. Daniel 2:35.

8. PPP, *Voice of Warning*, 29–31, 96, 107.

9. Whittaker, "Book of Daniel," 174.

10. The July speech was printed and distributed with Smith's blessing as a pamphlet, and it is reproduced in Peter Crawley, "Two Rare Missouri Documents," *BYU Studies* 14, 4 (Summer 1974): 504.

11. Whittaker, "Book of Daniel," 155–201.

12. *Elders' Journal* 1, 4 (August 1838): 61.

13. Alexander L. Baugh, "A Call to Arms: The 1838 Defense of Northern Missouri," PhD. diss., Brigham Young University, 1996, 89.

14. Linda Thatcher, "Women Alone: The Economic and Emotional Plight of Early LDS Women," *Dialogue* 25, 4 (Winter 1992): 46.

15. Mary Ann Stearns Winters, memoirs, diary, 1880–1881, Bennion Family Papers cited in Fife, "Story of Mary Ann Frost Stearns Pratt."

16. *Autobiography of Warren Foote* (Mesa, Ariz.: Dale Foote, 1997), 29.

17. Pratt's successive moves were described in his obituary of Nathan Pratt, *Time and Seasons* 5, 15 January 1844, 414–415.

18. Ebenezer Robinson, "Items of Personal History," *Return* 1, 12 (December 1889): 189.

19. Testimony of Joseph H. McGee, *Document Concerning the Correspondence, Orders, &C. in Relation to the Disturbances with the Mormons; And the Evidence Given Before the Hon. Austin A. King, Judge of the Fifth Judicial Circuit of the State of Missouri, at the Court-House in Richmond, in a Criminal Court of Inquiry, Begun November 12, 1838, on the Trial of Joseph Smith, Jr., and Others, for High Treason and Other Crimes Against the State* (Fayette, Mo.: Boon's Lick *Democrat*, 1841), 110.

20. PPP, *Autobiography*, 223.

21. Ibid., 224.

22. For a detailed account of the battle, see Stephen C. LeSueur, *The 1838 Mormon War in Missouri* (Columbia: University of Missouri Press, 1987); Baugh, "A Call to Arms," 99–113.

23. D. Michael Quinn asserted that Tarwater later pressed charges of attempted murder against Pratt. However, no sources (including the ones that Quinn cites as evidence) indicate Pratt's involvement in Tarwater's mutilation. D. Michael Quinn, *The Mormon Hierarchy: Origins of Power* (Salt Lake City, Utah: Signature Books, 1994), 99.

24. For Cravens's testimony, see *Document Containing the Correspondence*, 109. Lee confused Tarwater with Cravens and alleged that "when [the victim] was some

forty yards from the Mormons, Parley P. Pratt, then one of the Twelve Apostles, stepped up to a tree, laid his gun up by the side of the tree, took deliberate aim, and shot Tarwater [Cravens]. "John D. Lee, *Mormonism Unveiled: or, The Life and Confessions of the Late Mormon Bishop, John D. Lee* (St. Louis, Mo.: Bryan, Brand & Company, 1877), 73–74. Reed Peck, a Mormon who soon became a dissident, later stated that the killer was a "cold hearted villain (I know him well)," but left him unnamed. Quinn accepts Lee's statement and states that Reed pointed to Pratt, but no evidence indicates that Reed had Pratt in mind. Quinn, *Origins of Power*, 99. For an analysis of the episode, see also Baugh, *Call to Arms*, 106–107. LeSueur writes that "the shooting was probably accidental" (*Mormon War*, 141).

25. PPP, *Autobiography*, 218.

26. Jeffrey N. Walker, "Mormon Land Rights in Caldwell and Daviess Counties and the Mormon Conflict of 1838," *BYU Studies* 47, 1 (2008): 5.

27. Contemporary but anonymous letter published in the *Boston Atlas* and reprinted in the *Journal of History* [The Reorganized Church of Jesus Christ of Latter Day Saints] 2 (1909): 434.

28. Walker, "Mormon Land Rights," 41.

29. Daniel Walker Howe, *What Hath God Wrought* (New York: Oxford University Press, 2007), 491.

30. See Baugh, *Call to Arms*, 19–29. See also James B. Whisker, *The Rise and Decline of the American Militia System* (Selinsgrove, Pa.: Susquehanna University Press, 1999).

31. Howe, *What Hath God Wrought*, 430–432, 509.

32. David Grimsted, *American Mobbing, 1828–1861* (New York: Oxford University Press, 1998), 4.

33. Leonard Richards, *"Gentlemen of Property and Standing": Anti-Abolition Mobs in Jacksonian America* (New York: Oxford University Press, 1971).

34. PPP, *Autobiography*, 247.

35. LeSueur, *Mormon War*, 147.

36. Ibid., 150.

37. Lilburn W. Boggs to John B. Clark, 27 October 1838, in *Document Concerning the Correspondence*, 61.

38. Lorenzo D. Young, "Lorenzo Dow Young's Narrative," *Fragments of Experience: Sixth Book of the Faith-Promoting Series* (Salt Lake City, Utah: *Juvenile Instructor* Office, 1882), 52.

39. Baugh notes that thirty-three left on October 31, and six or seven more on November 1. See "The Final Episode of Mormonism in Missouri in the 1830s: The Incarceration of the Mormon Prisoners at Richmond and Columbia Jails, 1838–1839," *John Whitmer Historical Association Journal* 28 (1998): 7.

40. General Samuel Lucas to Governor Lilburn Boggs, 2 November 1838, cited in LeSueur, *Mormon* War, 169.

41. PPP, Testimony before the Municipal Court of the City of Nauvoo, 1 July 1843, CHL.

42. In Pratt's autobiography (235), he conflated the two nights they spent as prisoners in the enemy camp into one. They surrendered late on October 31, and the court-martial was apparently held in the evening of November 1.

43. Peter H. Burnett, *An Old California Pioneer by Peter H. Burnett, First Governor of the State* (Oakland, Calif.: Biobooks, 1946), 37–38, cited in Alexander L. Baugh, "'Tis not for Crimes that I have Done:' Parley P. Pratt's Missouri Imprisonment Letters, 1838–1839," in Gregory Armstrong, Matthew J. Grow, and Dennis Siler, *Parley P. Pratt and the Making of Mormonism* (Norman, Okla.: Arthur Clark Co., forthcoming 2011).

44. Baugh, "Final Episode," 3–4.

45. Affidavit of Lyman Wight, in Clark V. Johnson, ed., *The Mormon Redress Petitions: Documents of the 1833–1838 Missouri Conflict* (Provo, Utah: Religious Studies Center, Brigham Young University, 1992), 661.

46. PPP, *Autobiography*, 237.

47. Ibid., 238–239.

48. PPP, Testimony before the Municipal Court of the City of Nauvoo, 1 July 1843, CHL.

49. PPP to Mary Ann Frost Pratt, 4 November 1838, PPP Collection.

50. "A Card to the Citizens of Jackson County," 5 November 1838, published in the *Ohio Statesman* 28 November 1838, in Baugh, "Imprisonment Letters," 9.

51. PPP, *Autobiography*, 245–46.

52. PPP to Mary Ann Frost Pratt, 4 November 1838.

53. PPP, *Autobiography*, 247–248.

54. Ibid., 262.

55. Pratt initially published this account in a letter written on 7 November 1853 to the *Deseret News*, which was published in the *Deseret News* on 12 November 1853, 3. Pratt also included the portrayal in an 1854 play, "The Mormon Prisoners," PPP Collection.

56. Language in a discourse Smith later gave lends credence to Pratt's account: "I have been chained—I have rattled chains before—in a dungeon for the truth's sake" (26 May 1844, Nauvoo, Illinois, Thomas Bullock Report of 26 May 1844 Nauvoo discourse, CHL, in Ehat and Cook, *Words*, 376).

57. PPP, Testimony before the Municipal Court of the City of Nauvoo, 1 July 1843, CHL; Baugh, "Imprisonment Letters," 12.

58. Ebenezer Robinson, "Personal History," *Return* 2, 3 (March 1890): 236.

59. PPP to Mary Ann Frost Pratt, 1 December 1838, PPP Collection.

60. PPP, *Autobiography*, 293.

61. Robinson, "Personal History," 236.

62. PPP to Mary Ann Frost Pratt, 1 December 1838.

63. PPP to Ruth Haven Rockwood, 9 December 1838, A. P. Rockwood Collection, CHL.

64. PPP and Mary Ann Frost Pratt to Aaron Frost, 9 December 1838, PPP Collection.

65. PPP to Aaron Frost, 20 March 1839, PPP Collection.

66. On anti-Catholicism, see Ray Allen Billington, *The Protestant Crusade, 1800–1860* (New York: Macmillan, 1938); John T. McGreevy, *Catholicism and American Freedom: A History* (New York: W. W. Norton, 2003).

67. Brad Gregory, *Salvation at Stake: Christian Martyrdom in Early Modern Europe* (Cambridge: Harvard University Press, 2001).

68. Robert Paul, "Joseph Smith and the Manchester Library," *BYU Studies* 22, 3 (Summer 1982). Smith himself made reference to having read Fox.

69. John Foxe, *Book of Martyrs*, with alterations and additions by Charles A. Goodrich (Middletown, N.Y.: Edwin Hunt, 1833), iv, 592.

70. Susan Juster, *Doomsayers: Anglo-American Prophecy in the Age of Revolution* (Philadelphia: University of Pennsylvania Press, 2003), 83.

71. PPP, *History of the Late Persecution Inflicted by the State of Missouri Upon the Mormons* (Detroit: Dawson & Bates, 1839), iii.

72. PPP, *The World Turned Upside Down, or Heaven on Earth* (Liverpool, U.K.: Millennial Star, 1842). This was a reworking of his 1840 *Regeneration and Eternal Duration of Matter*.

73. Joseph Smith et al., to the Church members and Edward Partridge, 20 March 1839, in Jessee, *Personal Writings*, 443.

74. Francis G. Bishop to President of High Priests Quorum, 4 February 1840, in *Times and Seasons* 1, 5 (March 1840): 78.

75. Crawley, *Descriptive Bibliography*, 1:88. The committee consisted of three men: Almon Babbitt, Erastus Snow, and Robert Thompson.

76. PPP, *Late Persecution*, 66–67.

77. Ibid., 4.

78. Ibid., 7–8.

79. See Terryl L. Givens, *The Viper on the Hearth: Mormons, Myths, and the Construction of Heresy* (New York: Oxford University Press, 1997), 13–24.

80. PPP, *Autobiography*, 342–345.

81. PPP, *Late Persecution*.

82. See also David W. Grua, "'We Glory in Tribulation': Parley P. Pratt, Martyrology, and the Memory of Persecution," in Armstrong, Grow, and Siler, *Making of Mormonism*; Kenneth Winn, *Exiles in a Land of Liberty: Mormons in America, 1830–1846* (Chapel Hill: University of North Carolina Press, 1990), 147–151.

83. Pratt mentioned her absence of "more than two months" in PPP to Mary Ann Frost Pratt, PPP Collection, 12 May 1839. But in his *Late Persecution*, he wrote that she left on 17 March (58).

84. Dean C. Jessee, "'Walls, Grates and Screeking Iron Doors': The Prison Experience of Mormon Leaders in Missouri, 1838–1839," 30, in Davis Bitton and Maureen Ursenbach Beecher, *New Views of Mormon History: Essays in Honor of Leonard J. Arrington* (Salt Lake City: University of Utah Press, 1987).

85. PPP to Aaron Frost, 20 March 1839, PPP Collection.

86. Orson Hyde to Brigham Young, 30 March 1839, CHL, typescript in SPF.

87. Wandle Mace, Autobiography, 24.

88. B. H. Roberts, *Comprehensive History of the Church of Jesus Christ of Latter-day Saints* (Provo, Utah: Brigham Young University Press, 1965), 2:51.

89. David White Rogers, statement, 1 February 1839, CHL.

90. PPP to Mary Ann Frost Pratt, 12 April–21 April 1839. PPP Collection.

91. Orson F. Whitney, *Life of Heber C. Kimball* (Salt Lake City, Utah: Stevens & Wallis, 1945), 251.

92. PPP, *Autobiography*, 295–296.

93. PPP to Mary Ann Frost Pratt, 12 May 1839. PPP Collection.

94. Ibid.

95. PPP, *Late Persecution*, 80–83.

96. Petition of PPP, Morris Phelps, and Luman Gibbs to Austin A. King, 17 May 1839, in Boone County, Missouri, Circuit Court Records, copy in Lyndon Cook, research collection, Lee Library, BYU. King Follett prepared a separate petition.

97. Austin A. King, Statement, 17 May 1839, in Boone County, Missouri, Circuit Court Records, Miscellaneous, copy in Lyndon Cook, Research Collection, BYU.

98. Edward Leo Lyman, *Amasa Mason Lyman, Mormon Apostle and Apostate: A Study in Dedication* (Salt Lake City: University of Utah Press, 2009), 51–52.

99. Jean A. Pry and Dale A. Whitman, "But for the Kindness of Strangers: The Columbia, Missouri, Response to the Mormon Prisoners and the Jail Break of July 4, 1839," in Spencer, *Missouri Mormon Experience*, 119–138.

100. PPP to Mary Ann Frost Pratt, 30 May 1839. PPP Collection.

101. Ibid.

102. Ibid., 12 May 1839.

103. Ibid., 30 May 1839.

104. Ibid., 8 June 1839. PPP Collection.

105. PPP to Aaron Frost, 17–19 June 1839 (19 June addendum), PPP Collection.

106. Ibid.

107. Heber C. Kimball, journal, July 1839, Heber C. Kimball Papers, CHL.

108. PPP, *Autobiography*, 307–310.

109. PPP to Aaron Frost, 21 July 1839, PPP Collection.

110. PPP, *Autobiography*, 317–318.

111. Ibid, 340–341.

CHAPTER 6

1. Jessee, *Papers of Joseph Smith*, 2:256–257.

2. Theodore Turley's Memorandum, Joseph Smith History Documents, CHL.

3. Wilford Woodruff, sermon, 12 December 1869, *Journal of Discourses* 13:159.

4. Kenney, *Woodruff's Journal*, 26 April 1839, 1:325–327.

5. Ibid., 7 July 1839, 1:344–345.

6. Ibid., 12 July 1839, 1:347.

7. PPP, *Autobiography*, 355.

8. [Helen Mar Whitney, comp.,] *Heber C. Kimball Journal* (Salt Lake City, Utah: Juvenile Instructor, 1882), 81.

9. PPP, *Autobiography*, 355.

10. Mace, Autobiography, 30–31.

11. Jessee, *Papers of Joseph Smith*, 2:329.

12. History of Wilford Woodruff, *Latter-day Saints' Millennial Star* 27, 21 (27 May 1865): 327.

13. PPP, *Autobiography*, 355–356.

14. Ibid., 357–357.

15. Bushman, *Rough Stone Rolling*, 398.

16. PPP to the Editors, 12 October 1833, *Times and Seasons* 1, 3 (January 1840): 43–44.

17. *Latter-day Saints' Millennial Star* 1, 3 (July 1840): 50.

18. PPP, *Autobiography*, 360.

19. PPP to Joseph Smith, 22 November 2009, Joseph Smith Collection, CHL.

20. Kenney, *Woodruff's Journal*, 11 December 1839, 1:372.

21. PPP to Joseph Smith, 22 November 1839, Joseph Smith Collection, CHL.

22. Jessee, Ashurst-McGee, and Jensen, *Journals*, 351.

23. Not published until the 1850s, Smith's vision of Moses referred to the return of the ten tribes "from the land of the north." DC 110:11 (1981).

24. Crawley, *Descriptive Bibliography*, 1:97.

25. Terryl L. Givens, *By the Hand of Mormon: The American Scripture That Launched a New World Religion* (New York: Oxford University Press, 2002), 96–97.

26. Lester E. Bush, "The Spaulding Theory Then and Now," *Dialogue: A Journal of Mormon Thought* 10, 4 (1977): 40–69; Bushman, *Rough Stone Rolling*, 90–91.

27. PPP, *Mormonism Unveiled*, 42.

28. PPP to editor of the *New Era* (New York City), 27 November 1839, reprinted as "The Mormonites," *Times and Seasons* 1:45–46.

29. "The Book of Mormon," *Western Messenger* (Cincinnati) 8 (August 1840): 189–190.

30. T. W. Young, *Mormonism: Its Origins, Doctrine, and Dangers* (Ann Arbor, Mich.: G. Wahr, 1900), 21, suggests Pratt was a mutual friend of Smith and Rigdon, providing a crucial connection for their conspiracy.

31. Peter Crawley, "Parley P. Pratt: Father of Mormon Pamphleteering," *Dialogue* 15, 3 (Autumn 1982): 16.

32. J. P. Landis, "Matter—Eternal or Created?" *Old Testament Student* 4, 4 (December 1884): 146.

33. PPP, *The Millennium, and other Poems: to which is annexed, a Treatise on the Regeneration and Eternal Duration of Matter* (New York: Molineux, 1840), 105.

34. Smith taught the eternal duration of spirit as early as 1833 (DC 93:29), with only a brief nod to the eternal nature of "the elements" (v. 33). An earthly creation ex materia was more comprehensively treated when he published the Book of Abraham in 1842.

35. John Smith, Diary, 30 August 1840, in Ehat and Cook, *Words*, 37.

36. Gerhard May, *Creation ex Nihilo: The Doctrine of "Creation Out of Nothing" in Early Christian Thought*, trans. A. S. Worrall (Edinburgh: T&T Clark, 1994), 57.

37. PPP, *Eternal Duration*, 110.

38. 2 Peter 1:4.

39. PPP, *Eternal Duration*, 137.

40. Thomas Dick, *The Philosophy of a Future State* (Philadelphia: Biddle, 1845), 166.

41. James Ferguson, *Astronomy Explained* (1756), cited in Richard Holmes, *The Age of Wonder* (New York: Harper, 2008), 91–92.

42. Dick, *Philosophy*, 136, 145.

43. PPP, *Eternal Duration*, 112.

44. "Original Sin," *Oxford Dictionary of the Christian Church*, 1195.

45. 2 Nephi 2:26; Moroni 8.

46. DC 73 (1835).

47. PPP, *Eternal Duration*, 126–127.

48. *Times and Seasons* 3, 9 (1 March 1842): 706–710.

49. Kenney, *Woodruff's Journal*, 21 January 1844, 2:342.

50. PPP, *Late Persecution of the Church of Jesus Christ of Latter Day Saints* (New York: J. W. Harrison, 1840), iv–ix. David Whittaker treats the evolution of this Mormon quasi-creed in "The 'Articles of Faith' in Mormon Literature and Thought," in *New Views of Mormon History*, edited by Davis Bitton and Maureen Ursenbach Beecher (Salt Lake City: University of Utah Press, 1987), 63–92.

51. Crawley, *Descriptive Bibliography*, 1:102. Crawley also notes an almost simultaneous reprinting of the Detroit version as a thirty-nine-page pamphlet, in Mexico, New York.

52. PPP to Joseph Smith, 22 November 1839, Joseph Smith Collection, CHL.

53. Jessee, *Papers*. 2:329.

54. PPP, *Autobiography*, 362.

55. PPP, "Sketch of Travels in America, and Voyage to England," *Latter-day Saints' Millennial Star* 3, 1 (July 1840): 51.

56. Several contemporary accounts from this year refer to his private teachings on the subject. The link between eternal marriage and salvation was canonized as DC 131 (1981), but not published as scripture until 1876. Section 132 addressing both plural and eternal marriage also was recorded at this time, though Smith said he had received the revelation years earlier.

57. *Latter-day Saints' Millennial Star* 5, 12 (May 1845): 190.

58. W. W. Phelps, "Letter no. 8," *Messenger and Advocate* 1, 9 (June 1835): 130.

59. PPP, *Autobiography*, 361.

60. Ibid., 361–362.

61. PPP to Joseph Smith, 22 November 1839.

62. Hyrum Smith to PPP, 22 December 1839, Joseph Smith Letterbook, Joseph Smith Collection, CHL.

63. Philadelphia Branch Minutes, 13 January 1840, CHL.

64. PPP to Brigham Young, 4 May 1840, Brigham Young Collection, CHL.

65. High Council Meeting Minutes, 6 March 1840, in Manuscript History of the Church, C-1, 1025–1026, CHL.

66. Matthew L. Davis (a reporter for the *New York Enquirer*) to Mrs. Matthew L. Davis, 6 February 1840, in Ehat and Cook, *Words*, 32–33.

67. Elias Higbee and PPP, *An Address by Judge Higbee and Parley P. Pratt, ... to the citizens of Washington* (Washington, D.C.: Pratt, 1840).

68. Ehat and Cook, *Words*, 34.

69. Higbee and PPP, *An Address*.

70. PPP, "Farewell Song," *Times and Seasons*, May 1840, 111.

71. PPP, *Autobiography*, 366.

72. Foster soon became the major publisher and seller of Mormon books in the eastern United States. Pratt's books, though relatively successful with Mormon readers, never achieved sales numbers sufficient to relieve his debts. Crawley records how vast numbers of his publications were unsold and steeply discounted, years after publication (*Descriptive Bibliography*, 1:24–25).

73. PPP to Mary Ann Frost Pratt, 6 April 1840, PPP Collection.

74. Brigham Young, sermon, 31 August 1856, *Journal of Discourses* 4:35.

75. PPP, *Autobiography*, 371; Brigham Young to the Saints in the United States of America, 17 April 1840, in *Times and Seasons*, June 1840, 119–120.

76. George D. Smith, ed., *An Intimate Chronicle: The Journals of William Clayton* (Salt Lake City, Utah: Signature, 1995), 45.

77. The name was formally suggested by Willard Richards, but Pratt's influence was doubtless a major factor. See Kenney, *Woodruff's Journal* 1:438.

78. *Latter-day Saints' Millennial Star* 1, 1 (May 1840): 1.

79. Ibid., preface to collected edition, 17 April 1841; 1, 1 (May 1840): 17.

80. Allen, Esplin, and Whittaker, *Men with a Mission*, 254.

81. Young to the Saints in the United States of America, 17 April 1840.

82. PPP to Brigham Young, 4 May 1840, Brigham Young Collection, CHL.

83. *A Collection of Sacred Hymns for the Church of Jesus Christ of Latter-day Saints in Europe*, selected by Brigham Young, Parley P. Pratt, and John Taylor (Manchester: W. R. Thomas, 1840), 5–6, 218–219, 103–104.

84. Michael Hicks, *Mormonism and Music* (Urbana: University of Illinois Press, 1989), 28.

85. Karen Lynn Davidson, "Hymns and Hymnody," *Encyclopedia of Mormonism*, ed. Daniel H. Ludlow (New York: Macmillan, 1992), 2:667.

86. Joseph Smith to the Council of Twelve, 15 December 1840, excerpted in *Times and Seasons* 2 (1 January 1841): 258–261.

87. Brigham Young to Willard Richards and Wilford Woodruff, 10 June 1840, CHL, typescript in SPF.

88. PPP to *Times and Seasons*, 19 March 1843, in *Times and Seasons*, 15 April 1843, 162–165.

89. PPP to Mary Ann Frost Pratt, 6 July 1840. PPP Collection.

90. Grant Underwood, "The Religious Milieu of English Mormonism," in *Mormons in Early Victorian Britain*, edited by Richard L. Jensen and Malcolm R. Thorp (Salt Lake City: University of Utah Press, 1989), 31–48; *Latter-day Saints' Millennial Star*, 2, 2 (June 1841): 23.

91. Heber C. Kimball, *President Heber C. Kimball's Journal*, 16, cited in Allen, Esplin, and Whittaker, *Men with a Mission*, 28.

92. Allen, Esplin, and Whittaker, *Men with a Mission*, 47.

93. Ibid., 66.

94. Wilford Woodruff to Willard Richards, 31 March 1840, Willard Richards Collection, CHL, in Allen, Esplin, and Whittaker, *Men with a Mission*, 128.

95. Willard Richards to Editor, 15 May 1840, *Latter-day Saints' Millennial Star* 1, 1 (May 1840): 23.

96. "News from the Elders," *Latter-day Saints' Millennial Star* 2, 1 (June 1840): 44–45.

97. George M. Stephenson, *The Puritan Heritage* (New York: Macmillan, 1952), 157, cited in David J. Whittaker, *Early Mormon Pamphleteering* (Provo, Utah: Joseph Fielding Smith Institute for Latter-day Saint History and BYU Studies, 2003), 2.

98. PPP, *Plain Facts Showing the Falsehood and Folly of The Rev. C. S. Bush* (Manchester, U.K.: W. R. Thomas, 1840), 2–3.

99. PPP to Mary Ann Frost Pratt, 6 July 1840, PPP Collection.

100. PPP, *Autobiography*, 381. Pratt's brother-in-law Samuel Bean subsequently started for Nauvoo with his family, but being "darkened in mind" by "lying tales" en route, changed his mind and died soon afterward (381–382).

101. PPP to Orson Pratt, excerpts in Orson Pratt to George A. Smith, 21 January 1841, George A. Smith Papers, CHL.

102. PPP to Mary Ann Frost Pratt, 6 July 1840, PPP Collection, CHL.

103. PPP to Sidney Rigdon, 8 January 1841, *Times and Seasons* 2, 11 (1 April 1841): 364–366.

104. Elder Reuben Hedlock to PPP, 5 February 1841. *Latter-day Saints' Millennial Star* 1, 11 (March 1841): 284–285.

105. Kenney, *Woodruff's Journal*, 22 August 1841, 2:118–120; George A. Smith to Don Carlos Smith, 18 November 1840, in *Times and Seasons*, 1 February 1841, 307–308.

106. Joseph Fielding, Diary, 1 June 1838, CHL.

107. William E. A. Axon, *The Annals of Manchester: A Chronological Record from the Earliest Times to the End of 1885* (Manchester, U.K.: Heywood, 1886), 211.

108. PPP, *A Reply to Mr. Thomas Taylor's 'Complete Failure,' &c., and Mr. Richard Livesey's 'Mormonism Exposed'* (Manchester, U.K.: W. R. Thomas, 1840), 9.

109. PPP, *Reply*, 10.

110. PPP, *Regeneration*, 105.

111. PPP, *Answer to Mr. William Hewitt's Tract*, 9.

112. Extracts from William Clayton's Private Book, 5 January 1841, in Ehat and Cook, *Words*, 60. On March 9, he repeated the idea that "the Son Had a Tabernicle & so hd the father" (64). The wording of the canonized teaching, now in DC 130:22 ("The Father has a body of flesh and bones as tangible as man's") did not acquire its current formulation until the 1850s.

113. PPP, *An Epistle of Demetrius, Junior, the Silversmith....* (Manchester, U.K.: Shackleton & Sons, 1840[?]).

114. PPP, *Autobiography*, 385–89.

115. Joseph Smith to the Council of Twelve, 15 December 1840, excerpted in *Times and Seasons* 2 (1 January 1841): 258–261.

116. Orson Pratt and G. D. Watt to George A. Smith, 4 December 1840, George A. Smith Collection, CHL. Orson quoted this passage in this letter, from one he had received from Parley.

117. PPP to Rigdon, 8 January 1841.

118. Joseph Fielding, Diary, 18 April 1840; Allen, Esplin, and Whittaker, *Men with a Mission*, 136.

119. "To the Saints Scattered Abroad," September 1840, *Times and Seasons* 1, 12 (October 1840): 177–179.

120. Joseph Fielding, Diary, 3 January 1841, CHL.

121. PPP to Brigham Young, 4 February [1841], Brigham Young Collection, CHL.

122. PPP to George A. Smith, 18 February 1841, George A. Smith Papers, CHL.

123. George Simpson to George A. Smith, 9 February 1841, CHL, typescript in SPF.

124. *Evening and Morning Star* 1, 2 (July 1832): 13.

125. Brigham Young to "Beloved Brother," 1 March 1841, CHL, typescript in SPF.

126. Brigham Young to Willard Richards, 3 March 1841, CHL, typescript in SPF.

127. Kenney, *Woodruff's Journal*, 3 April 1841, 2:80.

128. Ibid., 15 April 1841, 2:88.

129. J. Tompkins & Co to Brigham Young, Heber Kimball, and PPP, 18 April 1841, CHL, typescript in SPF.

130. PPP to *Times and Seasons*, 19 March 1843.

131. Kenney, *Woodruff's Journal*, 7 April 1841, 2:86.

132. Joseph Smith to the Twelve, 15 December 1840, Joseph Smith Collection, CHL.

133. Kenney, *Woodruff's Journal*, 9 April 1841, 2:86–87; Theodore Turley Journal, 4 July 1841, CHL.

134. PPP to Aaron Frost, 19 April 1841, PPP Collection.

135. PPP to *Times and Seasons*, 19 March 1843.

136. PPP, *Letter to the Queen*.

137. The riot is mentioned in Axon, *Annals of Manchester*, 213; Kenney, *Woodruff's Journal*, 21 August 1841, 2:118.

138. William Miller to Brigham Young and Heber C. Kimball, 25 August 1841, in *Times and Seasons*, 15 November 1841, 596–598.

139. Levi Richards to Willard Richards, 10 May 1842, in *Times and Seasons*, 1 July 1842, 843.

140. Lorenzo Dow Barnes to Elijah Malin and Edward Hunter, 8 June 1842, CHL.

141. PPP to Joseph Smith, 24 October 1841, *Times and Seasons* 3 (1 February 1842): 682–683.

142. Steven Marcus, *Engels, Manchester, and the Working Class* (New York: W. W. Norton, 1974), 30, 66.

143. Friedrich Engels, *The Condition of the Working Class in England*, edited by David McLellan (New York: Oxford, 1993), 57–86.

144. PPP to Joseph Smith, 4 December 1841, Joseph Smith Collection, CHL.

145. PPP to Joseph Smith 4 December 1841.

146. "This is the day of the Lamanite, and they are receiving the gospel with great eagerness. Percentagewise, they are increasing more rapidly than the non-Lamanites—Mexico, Central America, South America, the islands of the sea." Spencer W. Kimball, "Church Growth and Lamanite Involvement," address given at Brigham Young University, 7 November 1972.

147. In America, "provisions cost about one sixth part what they cost here," PPP to Joseph Smith, 4 December 1841.

148. "Looker On" to Editor, 26 April 1842, "The Latter-day Saints' Agitation at Birmingham," *The Anti-Socialist Gazette and Christian Advocate* [Chester], 1 May 1842, CHL.

149. Lorenzo Dow Barnes to Elijah Malin and Edward Hunter, 8 June 1842; PPP to *Times and Seasons*, 19 March 1843.

150. Joseph Smith to PPP, 12 June 1842, Joseph Smith Collection, CHL.

151. PPP to First Presidency and Quorum of the Twelve, September 1842, Joseph Smith Collection, CHL.

152. Wilford Woodruff to PPP, 18 June 1842, PPP Collection.

153. PPP to the Authorities and Members of the Church of the Saints in Nauvoo, 12 August–12 September 1841, in *Times and Seasons*, 15 December 1841, 623–625.

154. *Latter-day Saints' Millennial Star* 6, 3 (October 1842): 109.

155. *Times and Seasons* 1, 11 (September 1840): 169–170. Missouri lawmen continued to threaten Pratt even after his arrival in Nauvoo; in June 1843, rumors swirled that officials had arrived in Nauvoo with "state writs" for Pratt and two other former Missouri prisoners, Lyman Wight and Alexander McRae. Anxious reports of "many strangers in the city" led to a doubling of the watch, but the crisis passed without attempted arrests. Joseph Smith, journal, entries for 26–28 June 1843, Joseph Smith Collection, CHL.

156. PPP, *Autobiography*, 403.

157. Hedges, Smith, and Anderson, *Journals*, entry for 8 February 1843.

158. Dan Jones to PPP, ca. 1845, PPP Collection.

159. Hedges, Smith, and Anderson, *Journals*, entry for 12 April 1843.

160. Mary Ann Winters, "Joseph Smith, the Prophet," *Young Woman's Journal* 16 (1905): 557.

CHAPTER 7

1. PPP to *Times and Seasons*, 19 March 1843.

2. Hedges, Smith, and Anderson, *Journals*, entry for 19 April 1843.

3. Melvin B. Banner, *Come After Us: The Lord Has Beheld Our Sacrifice* (North Salt Lake, Utah: DMT Publishing, 2004), 54–65.

4. On the Pratts' Nauvoo home, see Paul DeBry, "The House that Parley Built: Parley P. Pratt's Home in Nauvoo," CHL.

5. PPP to John Van Cott, 7 May 1843, Orson Pratt Collection, CHL.

6. "Dry Goods, Provisions &c.," *Nauvoo Neighbor*, 14 June 1843, 4.

7. Mary Ann Stearns Winters, "Mothers in Israel," 578.

8. Erastus Snow, journal, 1843–1844, 45–46, CHL. The Nauvoo Registry of Licenses, 25 December 1843, CHL, listed $1,800 in goods for Pratt & Snow, with $600 credited to Pratt and $1,200 to Snow.

9. "New Goods, Very Cheap," *Nauvoo Neighbor*, 8 November 1843; Karl Andrew Larson, *Erastus Snow: The Life of a Missionary and Pioneer for the Early Mormon Church* (Salt Lake City: University of Utah Press, 1971), 86–89.

10. Historian's Office, journal, 2 January 1860, CHL. Kimball stated that Pratt "brought about $7,000 worth of merchandise" from England.

11. Erastus Snow, journal, 1843–44, 45–46.

12. Mary Ann Stearns Winters, "Mothers in Israel," 579. On the Frosts, see also Olive Frost to Joshua Grey, 3 March 1844, typescript in author's (Grow) possession.

13. Banner, *Come After Us*, 63.

14. Joseph Smith, journal, 17 August 1843.

15. PPP to Elizabeth Brotherton Pratt, 7 October 1843, PPP Collection.

16. Brigham Young to PPP, 17 July 1842, Young Collection.

17. Breck England, *The Life and Thought of Orson Pratt* (Salt Lake City: University of Utah Press, 1985), 77–80; Bushman, *Rough Stone Rolling*, 458–468.

18. Bushman, *Rough Stone Rolling*, 458–468; Andrew F. Smith, *The Saintly Scoundrel: The Life and Times of Dr. John Cook Bennett* (Urbana: University of Illinois Press, 1997).

19. Breck England, *The Life and Thought of Orson Pratt*, 77–80; Bushman, *Rough Stone Rolling*, 466–468. In 1850, Sarah Marinda Bates Pratt wrote to Bathsheba W. Smith, wife of apostle George A. Smith, about Orson, "I have long since made up my mind that it is no use to fret about those who do not fret about *me*." Pratt to Smith, 4 April 1850, George A. Smith Papers, CHL.

20. PPP and Orson Pratt to John Van Cott, 7 May 1843, Orson Pratt Collection, CHL.

21. Orson Pratt to Brigham Young and Council, 12 January 1846, Young Collection.

22. Glen M. Leonard, Nauvoo: *A Place of Peace, a People of Promise* (Salt Lake City: Deseret Book, 2002), 346.

23. PPP, *Autobiography*, 361.

24. Levi Richards, diary, 9 May 1843, 90, typescript, CHL.

25. Winters, "Mothers in Israel," 580–581. Winters mistakenly dated the steamboat excursion as July 4; see Andrew F. Ehat, "Joseph Smith's Introduction of Temple Ordinances and the 1844 Mormon Succession Question," M.A. thesis, Brigham Young University, 1982, 67; and Fife, "Mary Ann Frost Pratt."

26. Levi Richards, diary, 14 May 1843, 92.

27. Ehat, "Temple Ordinances," 67.

28. Willard Richards to Brigham Young, 19 July 1843, in Ehat and Cook, *Words*, 231; Todd Compton, *In Sacred Loneliness: The Plural Wives of Joseph Smith* (Salt Lake City, Utah: Signature Books, 1997), 549.

29. Stanley, *Archer of Paradise*, 163–164.

30. Vilate Kimball to Heber Kimball, 27 June 1843, CHL. See also Stanley Kimball, *Heber C. Kimball: Mormon Patriarch and Pioneer* (Urbana: University of Illinois Press, 1986), 96–97. This letter was first published in *Woman's Exponent* 11, 8 (15 September 1882), 57–58.

31. Vilate Kimball to Heber Kimball, 27 June 1843.

32. Myrtle Stevens Hyde, *Orson Hyde: The Olive Branch of Israel* (Salt Lake City, Utah: Agreka Books, 2000), 153–159.

33. See Gary J. Bergera, "The Earliest Eternal Sealings for Civilly Married Couples Living and Dead," *Dialogue: A Journal of Mormon Thought* 35, 3 (Fall 2002): 48.

34. PPP, Family Record.

35. Vilate Kimball to Heber Kimball, 27 June 1843.

36. PPP to Mary Wood, 27 June 1843, quoted in Mathoni Wood Pratt, "Mary Wood Pratt," PPP Collection, BYU.

37. Young to William Smith, 10 August 1845, Young Papers, CHL, in Bergera, "Earliest Eternal Sealings," 56.

38. Ehat, "Temple Ordinances," 70.

39. Mary Ann Frost Pratt, affidavit, 3 September 1869, and Elizabeth Brotherton Pratt, affidavit, 2 August 1869, in Affidavits on Celestial Marriage, Joseph F. Smith Collection, CHL. See also Gary J. Bergera, "Identifying the Earliest Mormon Polygamists, 1841–1844," *Dialogue: A Journal of Mormon Thought* 38, 3 (Fall 2005): 19–20; PPP, Family Record; Mary Ann Stearns Winter, "Mothers in Israel," 643. Hyrum may have officiated because of Joseph's illness. See Elizabeth B. Pratt, "Autobiography of Elizabeth Brotherton Pratt," *Woman's Exponent* 19, 12 (1 December 1890): 94–95; 19, 13 (15 December 1890): 102; and 19, 14 (1 January 1891): 110–111.

40. Marriages by proxy between a living spouse and a deceased one had begun the previous year. Bergera, "Earliest Eternal Sealings," 55, 59.

41. Elizabeth B. Pratt, "Autobiography," 94–95.

42. Martha Brotherton, affidavit, 13 July 1842, in *New York Herald*, 25 July 1842; "Conference Minutes," *Times and Seasons* 3, 12 (15 April 1842): 763.

43. "Apostacy," *Latter-day Saints' Millennial Star* 3 (August 1842): 73–74.

44. Elizabeth B. Pratt, "Autobiography," 94–95.

45. PPP to Elizabeth Brotherton Pratt, 7 October 1843, PPP Collection.

46. George Smith, ed., *An Intimate Chronicle: The Journals of William Clayton* (Salt Lake City, Utah: Signature Books, 1995), 20 August 1843, 118.

47. Bushman, *Rough Stone Rolling*, 449.

48. Manuscript History of the Church, C-1, 4 May 1842, 1328–1329, CHL.

49. Kimball to PPP, Mary Ann Frost Pratt, and Olive Frost, 17 June 1842, PPP Collection.

50. Steven C. Bullock, *Revolutionary Brotherhood: Freemasonry and the Transformation of the American Social Order, 1730–1840* (Chapel Hill: University of North Carolina Press, 1996).

51. Kimball to PPP, 17 June 1842.

52. Michael W. Homer, " 'Similarity of Priesthood in Masonry': The Relationship between Freemasonry and Mormonism," *Dialogue: A Journal of Mormon Thought* 27, 3 (Fall 1994): 1–113.

53. Kimball to PPP, 17 June 1842.

54. Joseph Smith, journal, 2 December 1843.

55. Kenney, *Woodruff's Journal*, 21 January 1844, 2:340.

56. Compton, *In Sacred Loneliness*, 586–592.

57. For the DNA study, see Ugo A. Perego, Natalie M. Myers, and Scott R. Woodward, "Reconstructing the Y-Chromosome of Joseph Smith Jr.: Genealogical Applications," *Journal of Mormon History* 32, 2 (Summer 2005): 70–88. Fawn Brodie listed Mary Ann as a wife and Moroni as a possible son of Joseph Smith in *No Man Knows My History: The Life of Joseph Smith* (New York: Alfred A. Knopf, 1963), 336, 484. George D. Smith also mistakenly argues that Smith married Mary Ann on 24 July 1843 (Smith, *Nauvoo Polygamy: "...but we called it celestial marriage"* [Salt Lake City, Utah: Signature Books, 2008]). Bergera suggests that Joseph Smith may have had Hyrum seal Parley and Mary Ann only for time, after which Joseph was sealed to Mary Ann for eternity. Bergera, "Earliest Mormon Polygamists," 23. However, in her 1869 affidavit, Mary Ann stated that Hyrum Smith "married or Sealed" her to Parley "for time and eternity." In the most comprehensive study of Joseph Smith's wives, Todd Compton correctly categorizes Mary Ann as an "Early Posthumous Proxy Marriage" with Smith, rather than a wife during his lifetime. Compton, *Sacred Loneliness*, 2.

58. PPP, Family Record.

59. PPP, "Biography of Nathan Pratt," *Times and Seasons*, 15 January 1844, 414–415.

60. Joseph Smith, journal, 31 December 1843; Jill Mulvay Derr and Karen Lynn Davidson, eds., *Eliza R. Snow: The Complete Poetry* (Provo, Utah: BYU Studies and Brigham Young University Press, 2009), 282–284.

61. PPP, *An Appeal to the Inhabitants of the State of New York; Letter to Queen Victoria; The Fountain of Knowledge; Immortality of the Body; and Intelligence and Affection* (Nauvoo, Ill.: John Taylor, [1844]).

62. PPP, *Autobiography*, 408.

63. PPP, *Angel of the Prairies; A Dream of the Future, by Elder Parley Parker Pratt, One of the Twelve Apostles of the Church of Jesus Christ of Latter-day Saints*, edited by Abinadi Pratt (Salt Lake City, Utah: Deseret News Printing, 1880). See also Jordan Watkins, "'Virtue Fled into the Wilderness': Parley P. Pratt's Mormon Vision of the American Frontier," presentation to Mormon History Association, 2010.

64. PPP, *An Appeal*, 17.

65. Smith, *Journals of William Clayton*, 103–104, entry for 17 May 1843.

66. PPP, *An Appeal*, 21, 25, 29, 31.

67. One classic formulation of this idea was given by Augustine, who argued that time entails change; being changeless, God dwells not in time but in eternity. (Confessions XI, chap. 6).

68. PPP, *An Appeal*, 35.

69. *Elders' Journal* 1, 4 (August 1838): 54.

70. Westminster Confession from John H. Leith, ed., *Creeds of the Churches: A Reader in Christian Doctrine from the Bible to the Present*, 3rd ed. (Atlanta: John Knox, 1982); PPP, *An Appeal*, 37.

71. PPP, *An Appeal*, 37–39.

72. D&C 132:63.

73. PPP, *An Appeal*, 4–6. Pratt read his "Appeal" to Smith and other leaders on 4 December 1843. See Joseph Smith, journal, 4 December 1843.

74. Bushman, *Rough Stone Rolling*, 512–514.

75. Joseph Smith, *General Smith's Views of the Powers and Policy of the Government of the United States* (Nauvoo, Ill.: John Taylor, 1844); Bushman, *Rough Stone Rolling*, 515–517.

76. Joseph Smith, journal, 29 January 1844.

77. Bushman, *Rough Stone Rolling*, 517–519.

78. D. Michael Quinn, "The Council of Fifty and Its Members, 1844–1945," *BYU Studies* 20 (Winter 1980): 166–170.

79. PPP to Joseph Smith, 19 April 1844, Joseph Smith Collection, CHL.

80. Bushman, *Rough Stone Rolling*, 519–525.

81. On the campaign activities, see Margaret C. Robertson, "The Campaign and the Kingdom: The Activities of the Electioneers in Joseph Smith's Presidential Campaign," *BYU Studies* 39, 3 (2000): 147–180.

82. General Church Minutes, 9 April 1844, CHL.

83. Larson, *Erastus Snow*, 89.

84. Walter Nugent, "Demography: Chicago as a Modern World City," *Encyclopedia of Chicago*, http://encyclopedia.chicagohistory.org/pages/962.html.

85. PPP to Joseph Smith and the Twelve Apostles, 19 April 1844, Joseph Smith Collection, CHL.

86. PPP to Mary Ann Frost Pratt, 26 April 1844, PPP Collection.

87. *New York Herald*, 25 August 1844.

88. Ibid.

89. "Jeffersonian Meeting," *Prophet*, 15 June 1844. See also Robert S. Wicks and Fred R. Foister, *Junius and Joseph: Presidential Politics and the Assassination of the First Mormon Prophet* (Logan: Utah State University Press, 127, 140).

90. PPP to Joseph Smith and Orson Spencer, 3 May 1844, appended to PPP to Mary Ann Frost Pratt, 26 April 1844, PPP Collection and Joseph Smith Collection, CHL.

91. Bushman, *Rough Stone Rolling*, 528–32.

92. Ibid., 526–50.

93. Compton, *Sacred Loneliness*, 591.

94. S. George Ellsworth, ed., *The History of Louisa Barnes Pratt, Being the Autobiography of a Mormon Missionary Widow and Pioneer* (Logan: Utah State University Press, 1998), 70.

95. Banner, *Come After Us*, 152–163; Fife, "Mary Ann Frost Pratt."

96. Warren Foote, journal, 28 June 1844, CHL.

CHAPTER 8

1. PPP, *Autobiography*, 409–411.

2. Ibid., 414–415.

3. Gordon S. Wood, "Evangelical America and Early Mormonism," *New York History* 61 (October 1980): 380.

4. D. Michael Quinn, "The Mormon Succession Crisis of 1844," *BYU Studies* 16, 2 (1976), 187.

5. Willard Richards, journal, 10 July 1844, CHL.

6. Smith, *Journals of William Clayton*, 139; Leonard, *Nauvoo*, 430–431.

7. Willard Richards, journal, 11 July–27 July 1844, CHL.

8. James Blakesley to Jacob Scott, 16 August 1844, in Leonard, *Nauvoo*, 430–431.

9. Willard Richards, journal, 4 August 1844; Leonard, *Nauvoo*, 431.

10. Lewis Barney, Reminiscences [ca. 1888], 15, CHL. See also William Adams, autobiography, ca. 1894, BYU.

11. Grant, *Sidney Rigdon*, 25–27.

12. Jedediah M. Grant, *A Collection of Facts, Relative to the Course Taken by Elder Sidney Rigdon in the States of Ohio, Missouri, Illinois, and Pennsylvania* (Philadelphia: Brown, Bicking & Guilbert, 1844), 16–18, 25–26.

13. Kenney, *Woodruff's Journal*, 7 August 1844, 2:434; Leonard, *Nauvoo*, 433–434.

14. Leonard, *Nauvoo*, 435–436.

15. Lynne Watkins Jorgenson, "The Mantle of the Prophet Joseph Passes to Brigham Young: A Collective Spiritual Witness," *Brigham Young University Studies* 36, 4 (1996–1997), 125–204.

16. Kenney, *Woodruff's Journal*, 8 August 1844, 2:436–438.
17. George A. Smith, journal, 3 September 1844, George A. Smith Collection, CHL.
18. Smith, *Journals of William Clayton*, 4 September 1844, 147.
19. Grant, *Sidney Rigdon*.
20. Vickie Cleverley Speek, *"God Has Made Us a Kingdom": James Strang and the Midwest Mormons* (Salt Lake City, Utah: Signature Books, 2006).
21. *Voree Herald* 1 (September 1846), 1, in Robin Scott Jensen, "Gleaning the Harvest: Strangite Missionary Work, 1846–1850," M.A. thesis, Brigham Young University, 2005, 27–28.
22. Kenney, *Woodruff's Journal*, 25 August 1844, 2:454.
23. PPP, Family Record.
24. Nauvoo School Schedule, August–September 1844, kept by Howard Coray, CHL.
25. Lyndon W. Cook, *A Tentative Inquiry into the Office of Seventy, 1835–1845* (Provo, Utah: Grandin Book, 2010), 103–121.
26. Leonard, *Nauvoo*, 349.
27. PPP to Mary Wood, 27 June 1843.
28. Mathoni W. Pratt, "Brief Sketch of the Life of Mary Wood Pratt," 6 July 1934, available at www.pratt-family.org.
29. "Parley P. Pratt, His Twelve Wives," in Kate B. Carter, ed., *Our Pioneer Heritage* (Salt Lake City: Daughters of Utah Pioneers, 1974), 17:215; Colleen Whitley, ed., *Brigham Young's Homes* (Logan: Utah State University Press, 2002), 220.
30. PPP to Hannahette Snively, 5 June 1845, PPP Collection.
31. PPP, Family Record.
32. Belinda Marden Pratt, autobiography, 1884, CHL.
33. Belinda Marden Pratt, autobiography.
34. Mary Cable, "She Who Shall Be Nameless," *American Heritage* 16 (February 1965): 50–55; Leonard J. Arrington, *Brigham Young: American Moses* (Urbana and Chicago: University of Illinois Press, 1986), 364–365.
35. Belinda Marden Pratt, autobiography.
36. Beverly Schwartzberg, "'Lots of Them Did That': Desertion, Bigamy, and Marital Fluidity in Late-Nineteenth-Century America," *Journal of Social History* 37, 3 (Spring 2004): 573–600; Hendrik Hartog, *Man and Wife in America: A History* (Cambridge: Harvard University Press, 2000), 63.
37. PPP to Jesse Little and the Saints in Peterborough, 28 March 1845, *Prophet*, 5 April 1845.
38. Irene M. Bates, "William Smith, 1811–93: Problematic Patriarch," *Dialogue* 16, 2 (1983): 11–23; Peter Amann, "Prophet in Zion: The Saga of George J. Adams," *New England Quarterly* 37, 4 (1964): 477–500; Will Bagley, *Scoundrel's Tale: The Samuel Brannan Papers* (Spokane, Wash.: Arthur H. Clark, 1999).
39. Woodruff to Young, 9–14 October 1844, 3 December 1844, Young Collection.
40. Ibid., 9–14 October 1844.

41. Bagley, *Scoundrel's Tale*, 67.
42. *History of the Trials of Elder John Hardy before the Church of the Latter-day Saints in Boston, for slander, in saying that G. J. Adams, S. Brannan and Wm. Smith were licentious characters* (Boston: Conway & Company, 1844).
43. Woodruff to Young, 3 December 1844; PPP, *Autobiography*, 421. On Winchester, see David J. Whittaker, "East of Nauvoo: Benjamin Winchester and the Early Mormon Church," *Journal of Mormon History* 21, 2 (April 1995): 30–83.
44. *Times and Seasons*, 1 December 1844, 727.
45. PPP to Mary Ann Frost Pratt, 18 December 1844, CHL.
46. Ibid.
47. Belinda Marden Pratt, autobiography.
48. PPP to the Church of Jesus Christ of Latter-day Saints, 1 January 1845, in the *Prophet*, 4 January 1845. For a similar declaration from the apostles, see Alexander L. Baugh and Richard Neitzel Holzapfel, "'I Roll the Burthen and Responsibility of Leading Thus Church Off from My Shoulders on to Yours': The 1844/1845 Declaration of the Quorum of the Twelve Regarding Apostolic Succession" *BYU Studies* 49, 3 (2010): 5–19.
49. PPP to the Church of Jesus Christ of Latter-day Saints, 1 January 1845.
50. Henry Rowe to editor, 20 January 1845, "Mormonism—PPP, &c.," *Boston Investigator*, 29 January 1845, BYU; Rowe to editor, 3 February 1845, "Mormonism—The 'Spiritual Wife' Doctrine, &c." *Boston Investigator*, 12 February 1845, BYU; Henry Rowe to editor, 17 March 1845, "Mormonism—Miracles—Gift of Tongues, &c., &c." *Boston Investigator*, 26 March 1845, BYU.
51. William Smith, letter, 25 January 1845, *Times and Seasons*, 15 February 1845, 814.
52. Manuscript History of the Church, D-1, 1 January 1843, 1433.
53. Pratt, "Regulations for the Publishing Department of the Latter-day Saints in the East" (*Prophet*, in *Times and Seasons*, 15 January 1845, 778). On Pratt's "regulations," see David J. Whittaker, "Early Mormon Pamphleteering," *Journal of Mormon History* 4 (1977): 35–49.
54. PPP to Samuel Brannan, 11 January 1844, in the *Prophet*, 18 January 1844; PPP to John VanCott, 14 January 1845, PPP Collection.
55. PPP to Young, 13 January 1845, Young Collection.
56. PPP to Young and the Twelve Apostles, 7 May 1845, Young Collection.
57. PPP to Young, 7 May 1845, Young Collection, CHL.
58. PPP and Brannan to Wilford Woodruff, 18 January 1845, Wilford Woodruff Collection, CHL; Benjamin Winchester to PPP, 14 January 1845, PPP Collection.
59. PPP to Young, 13 January 1845, Young Collection. On John Hardy's 1843 hymnal, see Crawley, *Descriptive Bibliography*, 1:231.
60. PPP to Young, 9 April 1845, Young Collection.
61. Young to PPP, 22 January 1845, Young Collection.
62. PPP, "Rigdonism!" *Prophet*, 18 January 1845.

63. PPP, "The Bible and the Book of Mormon contrasted," *Prophet*, 12 April 1845. For further remarks about evidences for the ancient origin of the Book of Mormon, see PPP, "Reply to the Athenaeum," *Prophet*, 22 January 1845.

64. PPP, "The remnants of Lehi," *Prophet*, 12 April 1845.

65. PPP, "Materiality," *Prophet*, 24 May 1845. See also "A Sermon delivered by PPP, at New Haven, Ct., March 1845," *Prophet*, 3 May 1845.

66. PPP, "The Great Secret Revealed," *Prophet*, 15 February 1845.

67. PPP, "Celestial Family Organization," *Prophet*, 1 March 1845.

68. PPP, "A word to the Saints on dancing and other amusements," *Prophet*, 22 February 1845.

69. Orson Hyde, sermon, 3 January 1858, *Journal of Discourses* 6:150.

70. PPP, "The Science of Anti-Mormon Suckerology," *Prophet*, May 1845.

71. PPP to Elias Smith, 16 February 1845, Young Collection.

72. *Proclamation of the Twelve Apostles of the Church of Jesus Christ, of Latter-day Saints* (New York, 1845).

73. Ibid., 16.

74. Young to PPP, 26 May 1845, Young Collection.

75. Crawley, *Descriptive Bibliography*, 1:295–296.

76. PPP to Young, 13 January 1845, Young Collection.

77. PPP to Mary Ann Frost Pratt, 13 March 1845, PPP Collection.

78. PPP to Hannahette Snively Pratt, 5 June 1845.

79. PPP, "Presidential Jurisdiction," *Prophet*, 10 May 1845.

80. PPP to Woodruff, 19 June 1845, Woodruff Collection, CHL.

81. PPP to Young, 5 June 1845, Young Collection.

82. PPP, "Remarkable Prophecy by Jesus Christ," *Prophet*, 10 May 1845.

83. PPP, "To the Saints in the Eastern States," *New York Messenger*, 26 July 1845.

84. Minutes of a conference held at Philadelphia, 7 July 1845, Philadelphia Branch Records, CHL.

85. PPP to Young, 3 June 1845, Young Collection.

86. PPP, "This number closes the first volume of the 'Prophet,'" *Prophet*, 24 May 1845.

87. Smith, *Journals of William Clayton*, 23 May 1845, 166.

88. "Conference Minutes," *Times and Seasons*, 1 November 1845.

89. Bagley, *Scoundrel's Tale*, 71.

CHAPTER 9

1. Leonard, *Nauvoo*, 568.

2. PPP to Isaac Rogers and Wife, 6 September 1845, PPP Collection.

3. Leonard, *Nauvoo*, 525–550.

4. Ibid., 518–519, 557.

5. Devery S. Anderson and Gary James Bergera, eds., *The Nauvoo Endowment Companies, 1845–1846: A Documentary History* (Salt Lake City, Utah: Signature Books, 205), 230.

6. Smith, *Journals of William Clayton*, 236.

7. Anderson and Bergera, *Nauvoo Endowment Companies*, 220.

8. "Conference Minutes," *Times and Seasons*, 1 November 1845.

9. Anderson and Bergera, *Nauvoo Endowment Companies*, 377.

10. PPP, Family Record; "Correspondence," obituary of Sarah Houston Pratt, *Deseret News*, 30 June 1886, 3.

11. PPP, Family Record; Anderson and Bergera, *Nauvoo Endowment Companies*, 155, 396.

12. Anderson and Bergera, *Nauvoo Endowment Companies*, 221, 408–409, 451, 515.

13. Orson Pratt to Brigham Young and Council, 12 January 1846, Young Collection.

14. Ibid.

15. Ibid.

16. England, *Orson Pratt*, 109.

17. Stanley B. Kimball, *On the Potter's Wheel: The Diaries of Heber C. Kimball* (Salt Lake City, Utah: Signature Books, 1987), 152, 27 November 1845.

18. PPP, Family Record, 11 March 1850.

19. Moroni L. Pratt to John Taylor, 28 October 1886, CHL.

20. PPP, Family Record, 11 March 1850.

21. Moroni L. Pratt to John Taylor, 28 October 1886; Taylor to Moroni Pratt, 29 October 1886, CHL.

22. Fife, "Mary Ann Frost Pratt"; Compton, *In Sacred Loneliness*, 409, 451, 551, 609.

23. PPP, Family Record.

24. PPP to Isaac Rogers, 6 September 1845; Phoebe Soper, letter, in Carter, "Twelve Wives," 17:222.

25. Endowment House Record, 26 February 1851, cited in R. Steven Pratt, "Family Life of Parley P. Pratt," in Armstrong, Grow, and Siler, *Making of Mormonism*. Several other sealings were performed that same day, February 8, including at least one performed by Brigham Young. Anderson and Bergera, *Nauvoo Endowment Companies*, 620–621.

26. Richard Bennett, *Mormons at the Missouri: Winter Quarters, 1846–1852* (Norman: University of Oklahoma Press, 1987), 25.

27. PPP, *Autobiography*, 426–427. George Whitaker dated the departure as February 9. See Whitaker, autobiography, undated, CHL.

28. Whitaker, autobiography.

29. Ibid.; Fife, "Mary Ann Frost Pratt."

30. Whitaker, autobiography.

31. Bennett, *Mormons at the Missouri*, 37.

32. Whitaker, autobiography.

33. PPP to Orson Pratt, Brigham Young, and Council, 20 March 1846, Young Collection.

34. PPP to Brigham Young, 22 March 1846, Young Collection.

35. Brigham Young to PPP, Orson Pratt, and George Miller, 23 March 1846, Young Collection.

36. PPP, *Autobiography*, 427.

37. Young to PPP, Orson Pratt, and George Miller, 26 March 1846, Young Collection.

38. PPP, *Autobiography*, 427; Smith, *Journals of William Clayton*, 265.

39. PPP, *Autobiography*, 428.

40. Whitaker, autobiography; Young to William Huntington and Council, 14 June 1846, Young Collection.

41. Bennett, *Mormons at the Missouri*, 50–51.

42. Smith, *Journals of William Clayton*, 285; Kenney, *Woodruff's Journal*, 1 July 1846, 3:56; Maurine Carr Ward ed., *Winter Quarters: The 1846–1848 Life Writings of Mary Haskin Parker Richards* (Logan: Utah State University Press, 1996) 68.

43. PPP to "All the Saints," 9 July 1846, PPP Collection. See also Ward, *Winter Quarters*, 69, entry of 12 July 1846.

44. Young to President Samuel Bent and Council, 7 July 1846, in David L. Bigler and Will Bagley, *Army of Israel: Mormon Battalion Narratives* (Logan: Utah State University Press, 2000), 48.

45. Brooks, *Mormon Frontier*, 1:179; Ronald W. Walker, "Sheaves, Bucklers, and the State: Mormon Leaders Respond to the Dilemmas of War," in *New Mormon History: Revisionist Essays on the Past*, edited by D. Michael Quinn (Salt Lake City, Utah: Signature Books, 1992), 273.

46. On the Battalion, see Norma Baldwin Ricketts, *The Mormon Battalion: U.S. Army of the West, 1846–1848* (Logan: Utah State University Press, 1996); Sherman L. Fleek, *History May Be Searched in Vain: A Military History of the Mormon Battalion* (Spokane, Wash.: Arthur H. Clark, 2006).

47. Kenney, *Woodruff's Journal*, 9 July 1846, 3:58.

48. Woodruff to Young, 1 April 1845, Young Collection, CHL.

49. "The Joint Stock Company," *Latter-day Saints' Millennial Star* 8, 7 (1 November 1846): 102–103.

50. Reuben Hedlock, "To the Saints in Great Britain," *Latter-day Saints' Millennial Star* 7, 1 (1 January 1846), 12.

51. Reuben Hedlock, speech, April 1845, *Latter-day Saints' Millennial Star* 5, 11 (April 1845): 171.

52. "General Conference," *Latter-day Saints' Millennial Star* 7, 12 (15 June 1846): 190.

53. Orson Hyde and John Taylor to Young, 22 October 1846, Young Collection.

54. Oliver B. Huntington, journal, 12 January 1847, BYU.

55. PPP, *Autobiography*, 431.

56. Woodruff to Young, 1 October 1845, Young Papers, CHL, in Bennett, *We'll Find the Place*, 50.

57. "The Joint Stock Company," *Latter-day Saints' Millennial Star* 8, 7 (1 November 1846), 102–103.

58. Thomas Ward and Lucius N. Scovil to Brigham Young and the Twelve Apostles, 17 September 1846, Young Collection.

59. Kenney, *Woodruff's Journal*, 15 July 1846, 3:59; Brigham Young to the Church of Jesus Christ of Latter-day Saints in the British Empire, and throughout the

continent of Europe, 16 July 1846, Young Collection, CHL; Willard Richards, journal, 16 July 1846.

60. "English Churches," *Voree Herald* 1 (September 1846): [3], in Jensen, "Gleaning the Harvest," 106–107.

61. Bennett, *We'll Find the Place*, 49.

62. Willard Richards, journal, 24 July 1846.

63. Steven Pratt, "Family Life." According to Willard Richards, Hyde asked Young where the three departing apostles should leave their families during their mission to England. Young responded, "Just where you please." The Twelve Apostles also appointed Orson Spencer and Elias Smith to follow the three Apostles to England to assist "in the printing & publishing departments." Willard Richards, journal, 24 July 1846.

64. PPP, *Autobiography*, 431–433.

65. PPP to Belinda Marden Pratt, 4 September 1846, PPP Collection.

66. "The Archer of Paradise," *Voree Herald*, September 1846.

67. "P. P. Pratt," ibid.

68. PPP to Family, 22 September 1846, PPP Collection.

69. "P. P. Pratt," *Voree Herald*, September 1846.

70. PPP to Belinda Marden Pratt, 14 October 1846, PPP Collection.

71. Cyrus Wheelock, journal, 28 September 1846, CHL.

72. Huntington, journal, 19 October 1846.

73. Ibid., 16 October 1846.

74. Bennett, *We'll Find the Place*, 51, 63–64; Huntington, journal, 19 January 1847.

75. PPP to Family, 21 November 1846, 29 November 1846, PPP Collection. For the broadside, see PPP, *An Apostle of the Church of Jesus Christ of Latter-day Saints. . . . addressed the following words of comfort to his dearly-beloved wife and family* (England?, 1846). Samuel W. Richards sold copies of the poem, and Mary Haskin Parker Richards obtained a copy of Parley's "love letter to his Wife" at Winter Quarters. See Samuel W. Richards, journal, 12 December 1846, CHL; Ward, *Winter Quarters*, 145; Crawley, *Descriptive Bibliography*, 2:270–271.

76. James Ure, journal, 20–25 November 1846, typescript, CHL. Ure estimated that 2000 people attended a meeting at the Music Hall.

77. PPP to Family, 21 November 1846, 29 November 1846, PPP Collection.

78. Melissa Lambert Milewski, ed., *Before the Manifesto: The Life Writings of Mary Lois Walker Morris* (Logan: Utah State University Press, 2007), 73.

79. PPP to Family, 26 December 1846, PPP Collection.

80. PPP to Belinda Marden Pratt, 1 October 1846, PPP Collection. Pratt did not expect to mail his letters to his family, but to deliver them in person the following spring.

81. PPP to Belinda Marden Pratt, 1 October 1846.

82. Ibid., 14 October 1846.

83. PPP to Family, 29 November 1846, PPP Collection.

84. Ibid., 26 December 1846, PPP Collection.

85. Charles Miller, Reminiscences, CHL.

86. Orson Hyde to PPP, 2 November 1846, PPP Collection.

87. PPP to Hyde, 9 November 1846, PPP Collection.

88. Kenney, *Woodruff's Journal*, 24 July 1846, 3:62; Steven Pratt, "Family Life."

89. PPP, "To the Saints in Great Britain," 29 January 1847, *Latter-day Saints' Millennial Star* 9, no. 4 (15 February 1847): 61–62. Pratt wrote this after he and Taylor had returned "after nine days of seafaring life" due to contrary winds.

90. Huntington, journal, 19 January 1847.

91. Andrew Sprowl, journal, 27 December 1846, CHL.

92. Cyrus Wheelock, journal, 25 October 1846, CHL.

93. On the Strangite mission to England, see Jensen, "Gleaning the Harvest," 105–127.

CHAPTER 10

1. Brooks, *Mormon Frontier*, 246, 8 April 1847; Mary Haskin Parker Richards to Samuel W. Richards, 15 April 1847, in Maurine Carr Ward, *Winter Quarters* 135.

2. Bennett, *Mormons at the Missouri*, 162; Bennett, *We'll Find the Place*, 50–51.

3. Elizabeth Brotherton Pratt, "Autobiography," *Woman's Exponent*, 15 December 1890.

4. John Taylor to PPP, 1 January [1847], damaged letter, PPP Collection.

5. Mary Walker to Ann Agatha Walker, 15 February 1847, Ann Agatha Walker Pratt Papers, CHL.

6. Milewski, *Before the Manifesto*, 4–5.

7. Franklin D. Richards, journal, 14 January 1847, CHL; Oliver Huntington, journal, 19 January 1847.

8. Ward, *Winter Quarters*, 142, 21 May 1847.

9. Stephen F. Pratt, "Parley P. Pratt in Winter Quarters and the Trail West," *BYU Studies* 24, 3 (1984), 1.

10. John Miller to Brigham Young, 4 April 1847, Office of Indian Affairs, Council Bluffs Agency, in Pratt, "Winter Quarters," 2.

11. Meeting, 19 April 1847, Miscellaneous Minutes, CHL, in Pratt, " Pratt is Winter Quarters," 3.

12. Pratt, "Pratt in Winter Quarters," 4.

13. Meeting, 25 April 1847, Miscellaneous Minutes, in Pratt, "Pratt is Winter Quarters," 5.

14. Charles Kelly, ed., *Journals of John D. Lee, 1846–47 and 1859* (Salt Lake City: University of Utah Press, 1984).

15. Meeting, 25 April 1847, Miscellaneous Minutes, in Pratt, "Winter Quarters," 5.

16. Pratt, "Pratt in Winter Quarters," 5–7; Brooks, *Mormon Frontier*, 256–257, 25 May 1857.

17. Jonathan Stapley, "Mormon Adoption Ritual: Theology and Practice," *Journal of Mormon History*, forthcoming; Gordon Irving, "The Law of Adoption: One Phase of the Development of the Mormon Concept of Salvation, 1830–1900," *BYU Studies* 14 (Spring 1974): 291–314.

18. Campbell, journal, 15 June 1847, in Pratt, "Winter Quarters," 11.

19. Andrew Siler to PPP, 30 December 1850, PPP to Siler, 6 January 1851, *Deseret News*, 11 January 1851, 2.

20. PPP, *Autobiography*, 452.

21. "Journal History," 15 June 1847, 1.

22. Doctrine and Covenants 136.

23. Bennett, *We'll Find the Place*, 254.

24. John Taylor to Brigham Young and the Council of the Twelve, 18 August 1847, Young Collection.

25. Gatha [Ann Agatha Walker Pratt], "Personal Reminiscences," *Woman's Exponent*, 15 March 1893, 139.

26. Maureen Ursenbach Beecher, *The Personal Writings of Eliza Roxcy Snow* (Logan: Utah State University Press, 2000), 178–179, 16–18 June 1847. Two years later, Parley gave a blessing in which he also spoke in tongues. George Q. Cannon, journal, 7 October 1849.

27. Bennett, *We'll Find the Place*, 254–255.

28. Beecher, *Eliza Roxcy Snow*, 181, 24 June 1847; Daniel Spencer, journal, 24 June 1847, CHL; Isaac Haight, journal, 25 June 1847, CHL.

29. Bennett, *We'll Find the Place*, 256.

30. Donna Toland Smart, ed., *Exemplary Elder: The Life and Missionary Diaries of Perrigrine Sessions, 1814–1893* (Provo, Utah: BYU Studies and Joseph Fielding Smith Institute for Latter-day Saint History, 2002), 116.

31. Gatha [Ann Agatha Walker Pratt], "Personal Reminiscences."

32. Ann Agatha Walker Pratt, Reminiscences, 1907, CHL.

33. Donna Toland Smart, *Mormon Midwife: The 1846–1888 Diaries of Patty Bartlett Sessions* (Logan: Utah State University Press, 1997), 90, entry for 8 July 1847.

34. PPP, *Autobiography*, 454; Smart, *Diaries of Perrigrine Sessions*, 116; Smart, *Diaries of Patty Bartlett Sessions*, 8 July 1847, 90.

35. Smart, *Diaries of Perrigrine Sessions*, 117.

36. Smart, *Diaries of Patty Bartlett Sessions*, 92, entry for 23 July 1847.

37. John Smith, journal, 4 July 1847, CHL.

38. Susanna Musser Sheets, journal, in Elijah Funk Sheets, journals, 1843–1904, Vol. 1, 21 August 1847, CHL; Smart, *Diaries of Patty Bartlett Sessions*, 22 August 1847, 96.

39. PPP Jr., Reminsicences, in Arthur D. Coleman, *Pratt Pioneers of Utah*, xxviii–xxix.

40. Gatha [Ann Agatha Walker Pratt], "Personal Reminiscences"; John Smith, journal, 6 August 1847, CHL; Smart, *Diaries of Perrigrine Sessions*, 117.

41. Smart, *Diaries of Patty Bartlett Sessions*, 16 August 1847, 21 September 1847, 95, 99; John Smith, journal, 11 July 1847, 2 August 1847, 3 September 1847, 21 September 1847.

42. Gatha [Ann Agatha Walker Pratt], "Personal Reminiscences."

43. Taylor to PPP, 28 August 1847, and Pratt and Daniel Spencer to Brethren of the Twelve, 1 September 1847, PPP Collection.

44. Kenney, *Woodruff's Journal*, 4 September 1847, 3:265.

45. General Church Minutes, 3–4 September 1847. For this meeting, see also Bennett, *We'll Find the Place*, 269–272.

46. Kenney, *Woodruff's Journal*, 4 September 1847, 3:265.

47. Ibid.

48. General Church Minutes, 3–4 September 1847.

49. PPP, discourse, 23 May 1847, General Church Minutes, CHL.

50. General Church Minutes, 3–4 September 1847.

51. Bennett, *We'll Find the Place*, 273.

52. General Church Minutes, 3–4 September 1847.

53. Kenney, *Woodruff's Journal*, 4 September 1847, 3:265–266.

54. General Church Minutes, 3–4 September 1847; Bennett, *We'll Find the Place*, 272.

55. Kenney, *Woodruff's Journal*, 8 September 1847, 3:268–269.

56. Brooks, *Mormon Frontier*, 289, entry for 26 November 1847.

57. Gary James Bergera, *Conflict in the Quorum: Orson Pratt, Brigham Young, Joseph Smith* (Salt Lake City, Utah: Signature Books, 2002), 58.

58. Ibid., 57–58.

59. D. Michael Quinn, *The Mormon Hierarchy: Origins of Power*, 660; Brooks, *Mormon Frontier*, 289, entry for 30 November 1847; Minutes of Meetings, 30 November 1847, ser. 9, box 12, 128–135, Leonard Arrington Papers Collection, Utah State University.

60. Kenney, *Woodruff's Journal*, 15 July 1851, 4:38.

61. Gatha [Ann Agatha Walker Pratt], "Personal Reminiscences."

62. PPP, Autobiography, 455.

63. Minutes, High Council of Great Salt Lake City, High Council Minutes, 6 March 1848.

64. PPP, Family Record. On rebaptism, see D. Michael Quinn, "The Practice of Rebaptism at Nauvoo," *BYU Studies* 18, 2 (1978): 1–7.

65. Eugene E. Campbell, *Establishing Zion: The Mormon Church in the American West, 1847–1869* (Salt Lake City, Utah: Signature Books, 1988), 18–19.

66. Willard Snow to Erastus Snow, 6 October 1847, CHL.

67. John Nebeker, "Early Justice in Utah," *Utah Historical Quarterly* 3, 3 (July 1930): 88.

68. Dale Morgan, *The State of Deseret* (Logan: Utah State University Press, 1987), 13.

69. Minutes, High Council of Great Salt Lake City, 24 October 1847, CHL.

70. Morgan, *State of Deseret*, 17–19.

71. "Epistle of the High Council of the City to President Brigham Young and Council," 6 March 1848, in Morgan, *State of Deseret*, 17.

72. Morgan, *State of Deseret*, 17; Campbell, *Establishing Zion*, 20–21. See also Beecher, *Eliza Roxcy Snow*, 215, entry for 26 December 1847.

73. Minutes, High Council of Great Salt Lake City, 24 October 1847, 4 March 1848, CHL.

74. Smart, *Diaries of Patty Bartlett Sessions*, 122, 6 February 1848.

75. "Diary of Lorenzo Dow Young," *Utah Historical Quarterly* (17 January 1848): 165.

76. Nebeker, "Justice in Utah," 88.

77. Minutes, High Council of Great Salt Lake City, 6 May 1848, George A. Smith Papers, CHL, reproduced as appendix in James F. D. Alexander, "Were the Apostles Pratt and Taylor without Authority during the First Year in Salt Lake Valley?" (BYU History 490 Papers, Eugene Campbell, 1976); Campbell, *Establishing Zion*, 22–23.

78. Minutes, High Council, 6 May 1848; Daniel Spencer, journal, 7 May 1848, CHL.

79. Beecher, *Eliza Roxcy Snow*, 223, entry for 10 May 1848.

80. Campbell, *Establishing Zion*, 150–151.

81. Gatha [Ann Agatha Walker Pratt], "Personal Reminiscences."

82. PPP, *Autobiography*, 459–461. See also *A Mormon Chronicle: The Diaries of John D. Lee, 1848–1876*, edited by Robert Glass Cleland and Juanita Brooks (San Marino, Calif.: Huntington Library, 1955), 1:88, entry for 3 February 1849.

83. Gatha [Ann Agatha Walker Pratt], "Personal Reminiscences." See also William G. Hartley, "Mormons, Crickets, and Gulls: A New Look at an Old Story," *Utah Historical Quarterly* 38 (Summer 1970): 224–239.

84. PPP to Brigham Young and Council, 8 August 1848, PPP Collection.

85. George A. Smith and Ezra Taft Benson to Wilford Woodruff, 20 December 1848, CHL; Kenney, *Woodruff's Journal*, 24 January 1849, 3:409.

86. PPP to Brigham Young and Council, 8 August 1848, PPP Collection.

87. PPP, "An Epistle of the Twelve to President Orson Pratt, and the Church of Jesus Christ of Latter-day Saints in the British Isles," 9 March–12 April 1849, *Latter-day Saints' Millennial Star* 11, 16 (15 August 1859): 244–248.

88. Crawley, "The Constitution of the State of Deseret," *BYU Studies* 29 (Fall 1989): 9.

89. Ibid., 9–10.

90. PPP, *Autobiography*, 462. For example, Pratt's contemporary letter to his brother Orson and the British Saints explains the territorial petition, but not the statehood convention: PPP, "An Epistle of the Twelve to President Orson Pratt," 9 March–12 April 1849.

91. Ronald W. Walker, "Thomas L. Kane and Utah's Quest for Self-Government, 1846–51," *Utah Historical Quarterly* 69 (Spring 2001): 100–119.

92. Matthew J. Grow, *Thomas L. Kane, Romantic Reformer* (New Haven, Conn.: Yale University Press, 2009), chap. 5.

93. Crawley, "State of Deseret," 20; PPP, *Autobiography*, 468.

94. PPP, "An Epistle of the Twelve to President Orson Pratt," 9 March–12 April 1849.

95. Gatha [Ann Agatha Walker Pratt], "Personal Reminiscences." Midwife Patty Sessions assisted at the births. See Smart, *Diaries of Patty Bartlett Sessions*, 52, 109.

96. Ann Agatha Walker and PPP to William and Mary Walker, 3 May 1849, Ann Agatha Walker Pratt papers, CHL.

97. PPP, Family Record.

98. Smart, *Mormon Midwife*, 116–117, entry for 28 July 1848.

99. PPP, Family Record.

100. See, for example, William P. MacKinnon, "Sex, Subalterns, and Steptoe: Army Behavior, Mormon Rage, and Utah War Anxieties," *Utah Historical Quarterly* 76, 3 (Summer 2008): 227–246.

101. Turpin was ordained a priest by Wilford Woodruff in May 1836 in Tennessee. He originally came to Utah with a wife, Jane Smith. He later reentered the good graces of church leaders and served as a missionary in the West Indies, the Midwest, and Washington, D.C., before his death in 1854. See "Journal History," 25 November 1836, 26 October 1836, 11 February 1853, 4 March 1853, and 12 September 1854.

102. Mrs. B. G. [Elizabeth Cordelia Ferris, The Mosmons at Home: with Some incidents of Travel from Missouri to California, 1852–3 (New York: Harper & Brothers, 1854) 165–167.

103. Austin N. Ward, *Husband in Utah; or, Sights and Scenes among the Mormons: with Remarks on their Moral and Social Economy*, ed. Maria Ward (New York: Derby & Jackson, 1859), 281

104. Stanley Kimball, "The Mormon Trail in Utah," in Allan Kent Powell, ed., *Utah History Encyclopedia* (Salt Lake City: University of Utah Press, 1994), 380–381.

105. Brigham D. Madsen, *Gold Rush Sojourners in Great Salt Lake City, 1849 and 1850* (Salt Lake City: University of Utah Press, 1983), 27–30.

106. PPP to John Smith and High Council, 30 June 1848, PPP Collection.

107. PPP, John VanCott, and Daniel Spencer to John Smith, 8 July 1848, PPP Collection.

108. PPP, *Autobiography*, 463.

109. Arrington, *Great Basin Kingdom*, 69.

110. PPP, document about toll road, 19 December 1850, PPP Collection.

111. PPP, *Autobiography*, 462.

112. Ann Agatha Pratt, reminiscences.

113. John Pulsipher, autobiography, typescript, 32, CHL.

114. PPP, "The Golden Pass! Or, New Road Through the Mountains," *Deseret News*, 29 June 1850, 1.

115. Kimball, "Mormon Trail."

116. Hal Schindler, "Early Utah Toll Project Was No Road to Riches," *Salt Lake Tribune*, 18 July 1996, A4.

117. PPP, "The Golden Pass!"

118. Ibid.

119. Mary Ann Weston Maughan, journal, 17 August 1850, CHL.

120. Juanita Brooks, ed., *Not by Bread Alone: The Journal of Martha Spence Heywood, 1850–56* (Salt Lake City: Utah State Historical Society, 1978), 56–57, 13 April 1851.

121. Regarding the "Golden Pass," see also J. Roderic Korns and Dale L. Morgan, eds., *West from Fort Bridger: The Pioneering of the Immigrant Trails across Utah, 1846–1850*, rev. Will Bagley and Harold Schindler (Logan: Utah State University Press, 1994), 251–275. For the names, see Journal History, 13 September 1852, 3; 1 July 1860, 7.

122. William B. Smart and Donna T. Smart, eds., *Over the Rim: The PPP Exploring Expedition to Southern Utah, 1849–1850* (Logan: Utah State University Press, 1999), 9. This volume reproduces the journals of Robert Campbell, John Armstrong, John Brown, and Isaac Haight. See also Rick J. Fish, "The Southern Utah Expedition of Parley P. Pratt, 1849–1850," M.A. thesis, Brigham Young University, 1992.

123. Haight, journal, 23 November 1849, in Smart and Smart, *Over the Rim*, 20.

124. Biographical sketches of all of the expedition members are in Smart and Smart, *Over the Rim*, 200–248.

125. Brown, journal, 23 November 1849, in Smart and Smart, *Over the Rim*, 19–20.

126. Smart and Smart, *Over the Rim*, 23–24. After his return from the expedition, Pratt supported a military excursion against the Native Americans as part of a broader colonizing strategy, during which Mormons killed between 40 and 102. Jared Farmer, *On Zion's Mount: Mormons, Indians, and the American Landscape* (Cambridge: Harvard University Press, 2008), 70; Campbell, *Establishing Zion*, 99–100.

127. Campbell, journal, 3 December 1849, in Smart and Smart, *Over the Rim*, 32; PPP to Family, 8 December 1849, PPP Collection.

128. PPP to Family, 25 December 1849, PPP Collection.

129. Campbell, journal, 4 December 1849, in Smart and Smart, *Over the Rim*, 33. See also PPP to Young, Kimball, and Richards, 5 December 1849, in Smart and Smart, *Over the Rim*, 35.

130. PPP to Family, 8 December 1849, PPP Collection.

131. Campbell, journal, 7–8 December 1849, in Smart and Smart, *Over the Rim*, 42.

132. Haight, journal, 8 December 1849, in Smart and Smart, *Over the Rim*, 45–46.

133. Campbell, journal, 8 December 1849, in Smart and Smart, *Over the Rim*, 45.

134. Armstrong, journal, 11 December 1849, Smart and Smart, *Over the Rim*, 49.

135. PPP to Family, 25 December 1849.

136. Ibid.

137. Armstrong, journal, 2 December 1849, in Smart and Smart, *Over the Rim*, 31.

138. Campbell, journal, 10 January 1849, in Smart and Smart, *Over the Rim*, 127.

139. PPP to Family, 25 December 1849.

140. Armstrong, journal, 13 December 1849, in Smart and Smart, *Over the Rim*, 53.

141. Brown, journal, 15 December 1849, in Smart and Smart, *Over the Rim,* 55.

142. Campbell, journal, 16 December 1849, in Smart and Smart, *Over the Rim,* 57.

143. Brown, journal, 16 December 1849, in Smart and Smart, *Over the Rim,* 57.

144. Smart and Smart, *Over the Rim,* 58–59.

145. Brown, journal, 17 December 1849; Campbell, journal, 17 December 1849, in Smart and Smart, *Over the Rim,* 59.

146. Robert Campbell to Brigham Young, Heber C. Kimball, and Willard Richards, 25 December 1849, in Smart and Smart, *Over the Rim,* 77.

147. Brown, journal, 18 December 1849; Campbell, journal, 18 December 1849, in Smart and Smart, *Over the Rim,* 62.

148. Haight, journal, 19 December 1849; Campbell, journal, 19 December 1849, in Smart and Smart, *Over the Rim,* 64.

149. Haight, journal, 20 December 1849; Brown, journal, 20 December 1849, in Smart and Smart, *Over the Rim,* 66.

150. Smart and Smart, *Over the Rim,* 66–70.

151. Haight, journal, 24 December 1849, in Smart and Smart, *Over the Rim,* 75.

152. Campbell, journal, 25 December 1849, in Smart and Smart, *Over the Rim,* 76.

153. PPP to First Presidency, 25 December 1849, Young Collection.

154. PPP to Family, 25 December 1849.

155. Campbell, journal, 30 December 1849–1 January 1850; Brown, journal, 31 December 1849–2 January 1850, in Smart and Smart, *Over the Rim,* 89–97.

156. Brown, journal, 5 January 1849, in Smart and Smart, *Over the Rim,* 101.

157. Armstrong, journal, 7 January 1849, in Smart and Smart, *Over the Rim,* 118–119.

158. Campbell, journal, 8 January 1849, in Smart and Smart, *Over the Rim,* 121–123.

159. Haight, journal, 15 January 1849, in Smart and Smart, *Over the Rim,* 132.

160. Smart and Smart, *Over the Rim,* 134–137.

161. Campbell, journal, 21 January 1850, in Smart and Smart, *Over the Rim,* 136.

162. Ibid., 22 January 1849, 145.

163. Ibid., 145–46.

164. PPP, journal, 21–23 January 1850, in Smart and Smart, *Over the Rim,* 137–139.

165. Brown, journal, 23 January 1850, in Smart and Smart, *Over the Rim,* 139.

166. PPP, journal, 25–26 January 1850; Brown, journal, 26–27 January 1850, in Smart and Smart, *Over the Rim,* 140–142.

167. PPP, journal, 27 January 1850; Haight, 28 January 1850, in Smart and Smart, *Over the Rim,* 141–142.

168. PPP, journal, 28 January 1850, in Smart and Smart, *Over the Rim,* 142.

169. Haight, journal, 30 January 1850, in Smart and Smart, *Over the Rim,* 143.

170. "Journal History," 31 January 1850, 1–6.

171. Smart and Smart, *Over the Rim,* 84; Morris A. Shirts and Kathryn H. Shirts, *A Trial Furnace: Southern Utah's Iron Mission* (Provo, Utah: Brigham Young University Press, 2001).

172. Smart and Smart, *Over the Rim,* 14.

CHAPTER 11

1. Brigham Young to Amasa Lyman and Charles C. Rich, 17 March 1851, Young Collection.

2. PPP, Discourse, 31 October 1852, George D. Watt Papers, CHL, transcription from shorthand by LaJean Purcell Carruth, 2009; PPP, *Proclamation! To the People of the Coasts and Islands, of the Pacific; of Every Nation, Kindred and Tongue. By an Apostle of Jesus Christ* (Sydney, Australia: William Baker, 1851), 1.

3. Laurie F. Maffly-Kipp, "Eastward Ho! American Religion from the Perspective of the Pacific Rim," in *Proclamation to the People: Nineteenth-century Mormonism and the Pacific Basin Frontier*, edited by Maffly-Kipp and Reid L. Neilson (Salt Lake City: University of Utah Press, 2008), 33–34.

4. Manuscript History of the Church, C-1, 1223, 31 August 1841, CHL.

5. Reid L. Neilson and Laurie F. Maffly-Kipp, "Nineteenth-century Mormonism and the Pacific Basin Frontier," in *Proclamation to the People*, 12–13.

6. Richard O. Cowan and William E. Homer, *California Saints: A 150-Year Legacy in the Golden State* (Provo, Utah: Religious Studies Center, Brigham Young University, 1996), 23–39, 94–95.

7. PPP, "An Epistle of the Twelve to President Orson Pratt," 9 March 1849.

8. On the Chilean mission, see A. Delbert Palmer and Mark L. Grover, "Hoping to Establish a Presence: Parley P. Pratt's 1851 Mission to Chile," *BYU Studies* 38 (1999): 115–138; F. Lamond Tullis, "California and Chile in 1851 as Experienced by the Mormon Apostle Parley P. Pratt," *Southern California Quarterly* (Fall 1985): 291–307; and Rodolfo Acevedo, *Los Mormones en Chile* (Santiago, Chile: Impresos y Publicaciones Cumora, 1990), 9–17.

9. Edward Leo Lyman, *San Bernardino: The Rise and Fall of a California Community* (Salt Lake City, Utah: Signature Books, 1996), 35–41.

10. Brigham Young, Heber C. Kimball, and Willard Richards to PPP, 23 October 1851, Young Collection.

11. The missionaries were John Murdock, Rufus Allen, William Perkins, John Stillman Woodbury, Francis A. Hammond, Philo B. Wood, Richard R. Hopkins, and Morris Miner.

12. Phoebe Soper, letter, quoted in Carter, "Twelve Wives," 17: 221–222.

13. PPP, Family Record.

14. PPP to Family, 21 November 1851, PPP Collection.

15. PPP to Belinda Marden Pratt, 25 February 1852, PPP Collection.

16. PPP to Family, 28 March 1851, PPP Collection.

17. PPP to Family, 28 March 1851; PPP, journal, 2 April 1851, BYU.

18. PPP, journal, 25 March 1851.

19. PPP to Brigham Young, 13 April 1851, Young Collection.

20. Ibid.

21. PPP, journal, 12 April 1851.

22. PPP, journal, 20 April 1851; Shirts and Shirts, *A Trial Furnace*, 101–103, 449.

23. Lyman, *San Bernardino*, 39.

24. PPP, journal, 20 April 1851.

25. Lyman, *San Bernardino*, 42; Lyman, *Amasa Lyman*, 191–192.

26. Lyman, *San Bernardino*, 43–45.

27. PPP to Family, 16 May–13 June 1851, Collection, PPP.

28. Probably exaggerated reports sent to Brigham Young indicated that Pratt and Rich had been driven away when they tried to preach. Lyman, *San Bernardino*, 41.

29. PPP, journal, 20–21 May 1851.

30. Ibid., 13 May 1851.

31. PPP to Family, 16 May–13 June 1851.

32. PPP, journal, 23 May 1851.

33. PPP to Family, 16 May–13 June 1851.

34. PPP, journal, 10 June 1851, 20 June 1851.

35. Ibid., 1 June 1851.

36. PPP to Family, 16 May–13 June 1851.

37. PPP, journal, 16 June 1851.

38. PPP to Family, 16 May–13 June 1851.

39. PPP, journal, 19 June 1851.

40. PPP, journal, 19 June 1851.

41. Ibid., 22–29 June 1851.

42. Ibid., 7–11 July 1851.

43. Doris Muscatine, *Old San Francisco: The Biography of a City from Early Days to the Earthquake* (New York: G. P. Putnam's Son, 1975), 49.

44. PPP, Discourse, 31 October 1852.

45. John Boessenecker, *Gold Dust and Gunsmoke: Tales of Gold Rush Outlaws, Gunfighters, Lawmen, and Vigilantes* (New York: John Wiley & Sons, 1999), 5.

46. Roger W. Lotchin, *San Francisco, 1846–1856: From Hamlet to City* (Urbana: University of Illinois Press, 1997), 30, 102.

47. PPP to Brigham Young, 25 July 1851, Young Collection.

48. Jay Monaghan, *Chile, Peru, and the California Gold Rush of 1849* (Berkeley: University of California Press, 1973); Malcolm J. Rohrbough, *Days of Gold: The California Gold Rush and the American Nation* (Berkeley: University of California Press, 1997), 224–226.

49. Tullis, "California and Chile."

50. John Murdock, journal, 13 July 1851, CHL.

51. Thomas Williams to Brigham Young, 30 July 1852, in "Journal History," 30 July 1852, 1.

52. Laurie F. Maffly-Kipp, *Religion and Society in Frontier California* (New Haven, Conn.: Yale University Press, 1994).

53. Sandra Sizer Frankiel, *California's Spiritual Frontiers: Religious Alternatives in Anglo-Protestantism, 1850–1910* (Berkeley: University of California Press, 1988), xi, 4, 14; see also Lotchin, *San Francisco*, 322–328. Historians have argued that during the nineteenth century, the "only major area" where San Francisco deserves its celebrated "reputation for tolerance is that of religion." See Robert W. Cherny,

"Patterns of Toleration and Discrimination in San Francisco: The Civil War to World War I," *California History* 73 (1994): 140; Bradford Luckingham, "Religion in Early San Francisco," *Pacific Historian* 17 (1973): 56–73.

54. PPP to Young, 25 July 1851; for example, see *Daily Alta California*, 15 July 1851.

55. PPP, journal, 21 July 1851; 3 August 1851; 19 August 1851.

56. PPP to Brigham Young, 28 August 1851, Young Collection.

57. PPP to Ann Agatha Walker Pratt, 27 August 1851, PPP Collection.

58. Augusta Joyce Crocheron, *Representative Women of Deseret: A Book of Biographical Sketches* (Salt Lake City, Utah: J. C. Graham, 1884), 106–107.

59. PPP, journal, 1 September 1851; Bagley, *Scoundrel's Tale*, 297.

60. PPP to Ann Agatha Walker Pratt, 27 August 1851.

61. PPP, journal, 19 August 1851.

62. "Minutes of the General Conference of the Church of Jesus Christ of Latter Day Saints, for the State of California," *Deseret News*, 6 November 1852.

63. PPP, journal, 25 August 1851.

64. PPP to Brigham Young, 25 July 1851; PPP to Brigham Young, 28 August 1851, both in Young Collection.

65. PPP, journal, 1 September 1841; John M. Horner to Brigham Young, 28 April 1853, Young Collection; PPP to Ann Agatha Walker Pratt, 27 August 1851.

66. Lyman, *San Bernardino*, 35–83.

67. On Addison Pratt, see S. George Ellsworth, *The Journals of Addison Pratt: Being a Narrative of Yankee Whaling in the Eighteen Twenties, a Mormon Missionary to the Society Islands, and of Early California and Utah in the Eighteen Forties and Fifties* (Salt Lake City: University of Utah Press, 1990); PPP to Addison Pratt, 26 July 1851, PPP, journal.

68. Ellsworth, *Journals of Addison Pratt*, 485.

69. PPP to Young, 28 August 1851.

70. R. Lanier Britsch, *Unto the Islands of the Sea: A History of the Latter-day Saints in the Pacific* (Salt Lake City, Utah: Deseret Book, 1986), 7–20.

71. Brigham Young, Heber C. Kimball, and Willard Richards to PPP, 23 October 1851, Young Collection; Brigham Young, Heber C. Kimball, and Willard Richards to Amasa Lyman and Charles C. Rich, 23 October 1851, Young Collection.

72. PPP, *Autobiography*, 487; R. Lanier Britsch, *Moramona: The Mormons in Hawaii* (Laie, Hawaii: Institute for Polynesian Studies, 1989), 13–22; Davis Bitton, *George Q. Cannon: A Biography* (Salt Lake City, Utah: Deseret Book, 1999), 2–10.

73. George Q. Cannon to PPP, 25 August 1851, PPP Collection.

74. Francis Hammond to PPP, 28 August 1851, PPP Collection.

75. PPP to Family, 31 January 1852, PPP Collection.

76. Neilson and Maffly-Kipp, "Mormonism and the Pacific Basin Frontier," 8.

77. PPP to Young, 28 August 1851.

78. PPP, *Proclamation! To the People of the Coasts and Islands of the Pacific*.

79. PPP, *Proclamation!*

80. Crawley, *Descriptive Bibliography*, 2:262–264.

81. Peter Crawley, "The First Australian Mormon Imprints," *Gradalis Review* 2 (Fall 1973): 38–51; David J. Whittaker, "Parley P. Pratt and the Pacific Mission: Mormon Publishing in 'That Very Questionable Part of the Civilized World,'" in *Mormons, Scripture, and the Ancient World: Studies in Honor of John L. Sorenson,* ed. Davis Bitton (Provo, Utah: Foundation for Ancient Research and Mormon Studies, 1998), 55; Marjorie Newton, *Southern Cross Saints: The Mormons in Australia* (Laie, Hawaii: Institute for Polynesian Studies, 1991), 26–30; S. Reed Murdock, *John Murdock: His Life and Legacy* (Layton, Utah: Summerwood, 2000), 223–252. Murdock slightly altered Pratt's pamphlet, omitting references to San Francisco because of the "very bitter feeling here against California." Murdock and Wandell to PPP, 15 November 1851, PPP Collection. Wandell later became disillusioned with Utah Mormonism and returned to Australia as a missionary for the Reorganized Church of Jesus Christ of Latter Day Saints in 1874.

82. PPP to Ann Agatha Walker Pratt, 27 August 1851; PPP to Brigham Young, 28 August 1851.

83. PPP to Young, 28 August 1851.

84. PPP, *Proclamation! To the People of the Coasts and Islands of the Pacific*; and PPP, *Key to the Science of Theology,* 22–23. While other early Saints also believed Lehi had landed in Chile, the issue was disputed. An editorial in the *Times and Seasons* in 1842 stated that Lehi had arrived a "little south of the Isthmus of Darien," or modern Panama. See Frederick G. Williams III, "Did Lehi Land in Chile? An Assessment of the Frederick G. Williams Statement" (Provo, Utah: FARMS, 1988).

85. Palmer and Grover, "Pratt's 1851 Mission to Chile," 76–77.

86. David Clark Knowlton, "Parley P. Pratt, Mormonism, and Latin America: A Mission's Contribution to LDS Growth," in Armstrong, Grow, and Siler, *Making of Mormonism.*

87. Brigham Young, Heber C. Kimball, and Willard Richards to PPP, 23 October 1851.

88. PPP, Discourse, 31 October 1852.

89. PPP to Franklin D. Richards, 24 November 1851, "The Gospel in South America: Letter from Elder P. P. Pratt," *Latter-day Saints' Millennial Star* 14 (15 February 1852): 54–55.

90. Palmer and Grover, "Pratt's 1851 Mission to Chile," 120.

91. "Sketch of the Life of Rufus Chester Allen," 1905, CHL.

92. PPP to Family, 15 September–21 November 1851, PPP Collection.

93. Ibid.

94. Ibid.

95. PPP to Belinda Marden Pratt, 25 February 1852.

96. Tullis, "California and Chile," 296.

97. PPP to Family, 15 September–21 November 1851.

98. Amasa Lyman to Brigham Young, 14 February 1852, Young Collection. Pratt had earlier mentioned that "Several Young men are with me who will go to Chili & Peru in due time." PPP, journal, 26 July 1851.

99. Palmer and Grover, "Pratt's 1851 Mission to Chile," 120–121; Tullis, "California and Chile," 299.

100. PPP to Belinda Marden Pratt, 25 February 1852.

101. Simon Collier and William F. Sater, *A History of Chile, 1808–1994* (Cambridge, U.K.: Cambridge University Press, 1996), 107–109.

102. PPP to Brigham Young, 13 March 1852, Young Collection.

103. Tullis, "California and Chile," 295.

104. Anthony James Gill, *Rendering unto Caesar: The Catholic Church and the State in Latin America* (Chicago: University of Chicago Press, 1998), 124.

105. Tullis, "California and Chile," 299.

106. Acevedo, *Los Mormones en Chile*, 11.

107. Palmer and Grover, "Pratt's 1851 Mission to Chile," 81–82.

108. PPP, Discourse, 31 October 1852.

109. For comparisons of anti-Catholicism and anti-Mormonism, see David Brion Davis, "Some Themes of Counter-Subversion: An Analysis of Anti-Masonic, Anti-Catholic, and Anti-Mormon Literature," *Mississippi Valley Historical Review* 47 (September 1960): 205–224; Matthew J. Grow, "The Whore of Babylon and the Abomination of Abominations: Nineteenth-Century Catholic and Mormon Mutual Perceptions and Religious Identity," *Church History* 73 (March 2004): 139–167.

110. Revelation 17:5.

111. 1 Nephi 13 and 14.

112. Eric Dursteler, "Inheriting the 'Great Apostasy': The Evolution of Mormon Views on the Middle Ages and the Renaissance," *Journal of Mormon History* 28 (Fall 2002): 23–59.

113. PPP, *Proclamacion! Extraordinaria, para los Americanos Espanoles, or Proclamation Extraordinary! To the Spanish Americans* (San Francisco: Monson, Haswell, 1852).

114. PPP, *Proclamacion!*, 15, 17.

115. Palmer and Grover, "Pratt's 1851 Mission to Chile," 85.

116. Brian E. Loveman, *Chile: The Legacy of Hispanic Capitalism* (New York: Oxford University Press, 1989), 53–71; Collier and Sater, *A History of Chile*, 95–97.

117. PPP to Family, 31 January 1852, PPP Collection.

118. PPP to Ann Agatha Walker Pratt, 9 February 1852.

119. Stanley, *Archer of Paradise*, 257.

120. PPP, Family Record.

121. PPP to Family, 31 January 1852.

122. PPP to Ann Agatha Walker, 9 February 1852.

123. PPP to Family, 31 January 1852.

124. Jeffrey Klaiber, *Religion and Revolution in Peru, 1824–1876* (Notre Dame, Ind.: University of Notre Dame Press, 1977), 13–22.

125. PPP to Brigham Young, 13 March–29 April 1852, Young Collection.

126. PPP to Family, 31 January 1852.

127. PPP, Discourse, 31 October 1852.

128. PPP to Family, 31 January 1852.

129. Palmer and Grover, "Pratt's 1851 Mission to Chile," 88.

130. PPP to Brigham Young, 13 March–29 April 1852.

131. Palmer and Grover, "Pratt's 1851 Mission to Chile," 131.

132. PPP to Brigham Young, 13 March–29 April 1852.

133. Stanley, *Archer of Paradise*, 267–269.

134. PPP to Brigham Young, 13 March–29 April 1852.

135. David J. Whittaker, "The Bone in the Throat: Orson Pratt and the Public Announcement of Plural Marriage," *Western Historical Quarterly* 18 (July 1987): 293–314.

136. PPP, "'Mormonism!' 'Plurality of wives!' An Especial chapter, for the especial edification of certain inquisitive news editors, etc." [San Francisco? 1852?].

137. Ibid. Six months earlier, Orson Hyde had likewise implicitly acknowledged Mormon polygamy in the *Frontier Guardian*. See Crawley, *Descriptive Bibliography*, 2:335.

138. PPP to Ann Agatha Walker Pratt, 24 June 1852, PPP Collection.

139. PPP, *Autobiography*, 508; George Q. Cannon, journal, 21 July 1852.

140. "Minutes of the General Conference of the Church of Jesus Christ of Latter Day Saints, for the State of California," *Deseret News*, 6 November 1852; Ellsworth, *Louisa Barnes Pratt*, 198–199.

141. PPP, *Autobiography*, 509; Knowlton, "Pratt, Mormonism, and Latin America."

142. PPP, Discourse, 31 October 1852.

CHAPTER 12

1. PPP to Family, 28 March 1852, PPP Collection.

2. PPP to Orson Pratt, 25 May 1853, Orson Pratt Collection, CHL.

3. PPP, Family Record, 11 March 1850.

4. PPP to Mary Ann Frost Pratt, 22 October 1852, PPP, journal, BYU.

5. Brigham Young to Mary Ann Frost Pratt, 7 October 1846, Young Collection.

6. Mary Haskin Parker Richards to Samuel W. Richards, 8 June 1847, in Ward, *Winter Quarters*, 175.

7. Fife, "The Story of Mary Ann Frost Stearns Pratt." For her communication with Wilford Woodruff in Maine, see Kenney, *Woodruff's Journal*, 13 August 1849, 3:477; 7 September 1849, 3:480; 14 March 1850, 3:538. For her arrival in Salt Lake, see Smart, *Mormon Midwife*, 180–181, entries for 10 September and 16 September 1852.

8. PPP to Mary Ann Frost Pratt, 22 October 1852, PPP, journal.

9. Divorce Certificate, 5 March 1853, Mary Ann Pratt Smith from PPP, Brigham Young Papers, CHL. On divorce in polygamous Utah, see Eugene E. Campbell

and Bruce L. Campbell, "Divorce Among Mormon Polygamists: Extent and Explanations," *Utah Historical Quarterly* 46 (Winter 1978): 4–23; Kathryn M. Daynes, *More Wives Than One: Transformation of the Mormon Marriage System, 1840–1910* (Urbana: University of Illinois Press, 2001), 141–159.

10. PPP, journal, 6 May 1854.

11. Fife, "The Story of Mary Ann Frost Stearns Pratt."

12. England, *Orson Pratt*, 180–183.

13. Orson Pratt to PPP, 10 March 1853, PPP Collection.

14. James B. Allen, Jessie L. Embry, and Kahlile B. Mehr, *Hearts Turned to the Fathers: A History of the Genealogical Society of Utah, 1894–1994* (Provo, Utah: Brigham Young University Press, 1995), 33–34.

15. Orson Pratt to PPP, 10 March 1853.

16. PPP to Orson Pratt, 25 May 1853.

17. For example, see Alfred A. Pratt to Orson Pratt, 27 March 1853, 25 September 1853; Seth Pratt to Orson Pratt, 8 April 1853; L. C. Pratt to Orson Pratt, 24 October 1853, and Asenath Gorsline to Orson Pratt, 28 May 1853, all in Orson Pratt Collection, CHL.

18. A Kirtland Temple revelation, dated 21 January 1836, described the salvation of Smith's brother Alvin, who had died before the church organization (canonized as D&C 137).

19. PPP, sermon, 7 April 1853, papers of George D. Watt, transcribed by LaJean Purcell Carruth, CHL.

20. Orson Pratt to PPP, ca. late 1856, PPP Collection.

21. England, *Orson Pratt*, 247–248; Chapman, *Pratt Family*.

22. PPP, Family Record.

23. R. Steven Pratt, "Family Life."

24. PPP to Brigham Young, 21 December 1853, PPP Letters, Mormon File, Huntington Library.

25. PPP to Keziah Downes ("Sister Hill"), December 1853, PPP Letters, Mormon File, Huntington Library.

26. PPP, Family Record. Parley and Keziah were sealed again on 13 October 1855, possibly because at the time of their initial marriage, Keziah had not received the temple ritual of the endowment, which occurred on 14 February 1854. Maxine Driggs Belnap, "Notes on the Life of Keziah Downes Pratt," 2007, available at www.pratt-family.org.

27. Belnap, "Keziah Downes Pratt."

28. Charles Miller, to PPP, 15 April 1845, PPP Collection.

29. Keziah Downes Pratt to PPP, 18 October 1854, PPP Collection. Keziah also served as secretary of the Relief Society in the Salt Lake City 14th Ward.

30. PPP to Keziah Downes Pratt, 19 January 1855, PPP Collection.

31. R. Steven Pratt, "Family Life."

32. Church Historian's Office, journal, 29 April 1849, CHL.

33. Ann Agatha Walker Pratt to PPP, 18 July 1854, PPP Collection.

34. PPP to Orson Pratt, 25 May 1853, Orson Pratt Collection, CHL.

35. PPP to Orson Pratt, 30 October 1853, Orson Pratt Collection, CHL.

36. Ann Agatha Walker Pratt to PPP, 18 July 1854, PPP Collection.

37. Francis A. Hammond, "In Early Days: My Introduction to Mormonism," *Juvenile Instructor*, 29, 16 (15 August 1894): 519–520.

38. Brigham Young, Heber C. Kimball, and Willard Richards to PPP, 23 October 1851, Young Collection.

39. PPP to Orson Pratt, 25 May 1853.

40. Ibid., 30 October 1853.

41. Ibid., 25 May 1853.

42. Ibid., 30 October 1853.

43. England, *Orson Pratt*, 137–138.

44. Arrington, *Great Basin Kingdom*, 51.

45. Land records, PPP Collection.

46. PPP to Orson Pratt, 23 August 1853, Orson Pratt Collection, CHL.

47. Ibid.

48. PPP to Orson Pratt, 2 November 1853, PPP Collection.

49. Milewski, *Before the Manifesto*, 107.

50. PPP to Family, 19 May 1854.

51. Ann Agatha Walker Pratt, Reminiscences.

52. PPP to Family, 28 March 1852, BYU.

53. Ferris, *Mormons at Home* 159.

54. Benjamin G. Ferris, *Utah and the Mormons. The History, Government, Doctrines, Customs, and Prospects of the Latter-day Saints* (New York: Harper & Brothers, 1854), 289.

55. The sections on the Pratts were reprinted in several other publications, including Charles Mackay, *The Mormons, or Latter-day Saints: A Contemporary History* (London: Houlston & Wright, 1856, 299–300); *Putnam's Monthly* 9 (October 1855: 380); and in reviews in *Littell's Living Age* 13 (April–June 1856: 606), the *United States Democratic Review* (1856: 343); and *Sharpe's London Magazine* (8, 320).

56. Ferris, *Mormons at Home*, 168–170.

57. Brooks, *Mormon Frontier*, 393, entry for 18 February 1851. Ann Agatha Walker's brother-in-law, John T. Morris, completed the second painting, as well as a "life size bust" painting of Parley. See Milewski, *Before the Manifesto*, 111.

58. Ferris, *Mormons at Home*, 168–170.

59. For anti-polygamy fiction, see Givens, *Viper on the Hearth*, and Gordon, *Mormon Question*, 19–54.

60. Lola Van Wagenen, "Sister-Wives and Suffragists: Polygamy and the Politics of Woman Suffrage, 1870–1896," Ph.D. diss., New York University, 1992; reprint, Provo, Utah: BYU Studies and the Joseph Fielding Smith Institute for LDS History, 2003.

61. Belinda Marden Pratt, *Defence of Polygamy, by a Lady in Utah, in a Letter to her Sister in New Hampshire* [Salt Lake City, 1854].

62. Ibid.

63. William Hepworth Dixon, *The White Conquest* (London: Chatto & Windus, Piccadilly, 1876), Vol. 1, 208.

64. Whittaker, "Mormon Pamphleteering," 350–359.

65. PPP to Mary Wood Pratt, 21 September 1854, PPP Collection.

66. William McBride, journal, 13–14 November 1854, CHL; Francis A. Hammond, journal, 3 June 1854, CHL. It has traditionally been assumed that Belinda's pamphlet was not published until 1854, though Hammond indicated that Pratt sent him a copy in December 1853.

67. PPP to William Patterson, 9 May 1853, PPP Collection.

68. Ann Agatha Walker Pratt, "Reminiscence".

69. Elizabeth B. Pratt, "Autobiography of Elizabeth Brotherton Pratt," *Woman's Exponent* 19, 14 (1 January 1891): 110–111.

70. Phoebe Soper Pratt to Esther, 1851, in Carter, "Twelve Wives," 17:222.

71. Nine of Pratt's sons married, and six had plural wives. Thirteen of Pratt's daughters married, ten to polygamous men.

72. Orson Pratt to PPP, 2 November 1853, PPP Collection.

73. Ibid., 12 September 1853.

74. Ferris, *Utah and the Mormons*, 288.

75. Parley P. Pratt Jr. et al., to John Taylor, 24 July 1884, CHL.

76. PPP to Orson Pratt, 25 May 1853, Orson Pratt Collection, CHL.

77. "Man's Physical and Intellectual Progress," *Latter-day Saints' Millennial Star* 15 (30 July 1853): 500–503.

78. PPP, *Key to the Science of Theology* (Liverpool, U.K.: F. D. Richards, 1855), 37.

79. Samuel T. Coleridge, "Notebooks," *Samuel Taylor Coleridge*, ed. H. J. Jackson (Oxford: Oxford University Press, 1985), 555.

80. PPP, *Key to the Science of Theology*, 33.

81. PPP, "Materiality," *Prophet* 1, 52 (24 May 1845), reprinted in *Latter-day Saints' Millennial Star* 6, 2 (1 July 1845): 19–22.

82. PPP, *Millennium and other Poems*, (1840), 105, iv.

83. PPP, *The World Turned Upside Down, or Heaven on Earth* (Liverpool, U.K.: James & Woodburn, 1842), 14.

84. PPP, *Key to the Science of Theology*, 43–44.

85. Ibid., 46.

86. Ibid., 46–47.

87. Ibid., 33–34.

88. Ibid., 33.

89. PPP, "Eternal Duration of Matter" in *Millennium*, 135–136.

90. This "Old Tabernacle" was later demolished and is distinct from the current tabernacle on Temple Square, which opened in 1867.

91. Ferris, *Mormons at Home*, 147–149; the sermon was on 13 January 1853.

92. Ibid.

93. Ibid., 287–288.

94. John Hyde, Jr., *Mormonism: Its Leaders and Designs* (New York: W. P. Fetridge, 1857), 40.

95. Michael W. Homer, ed., *On the Way to Somewhere Else: European Sojourners in the Mormon West, 1834–1930* (Spokane, Wash.: Arthur H. Clark, 2006), 82.

96. Dr. Greenman, Letter to the Editor, *Princeton Post* [Princeton, Ill.], 23 February 1854.

97. PPP to Orson Pratt, 30 January 1854, Orson Pratt Collection, CHL. In August 1853, Pratt was reelected as a councilor to the Legislative Assembly from Great Salt Lake County. *Deseret News*, 25 August 1853, in "Journal History," 1 August 1853, 1; Legislative Certificate, 23 August 1853, CHL.

98. *Journal of the Council of Utah* (1852–1853 session); *Journal of the House of Representatives, Council, and Joint Sessions, Third Annual Session, 1853–54*, copies at Utah State Historical Society.

99. PPP to Orson Pratt, 30 October 1853, Orsen Pratt Collection, CHL.

100. Ibid., 25 May 1853.

101. Church Historian's Office Journal, 14 November–25 November 1853, CHL; PPP, *Autobiography*, 511; Kenney, *Woodruff's Journal*, 15 November 1853, 4:225; PPP to Willard Richards, 21 November 1853, as "Communication from Elder P. P. Pratt," *Deseret News*, 1 December 1853, 4; Juanita Brooks, *Journal of the Southern Indian Mission: Diary of Thomas D. Brown* (Logan: Utah State University Press, 1972), 17.

102. Ronald G. Watt, *The Mormon Passage of George D. Watt: First British Convert, Scribe for Zion* (Logan: Utah State University Press, 2009), 141–143. On the Deseret Alphabet, see also Douglas D. Alder, Paula J. Goodfellow, and Ronald G. Watt, "Creating a New Alphabet for Zion: The Origin of the Deseret Alphabet," *Utah Historical Quarterly* 52 (1984): 275–286.

103. PPP to Orson Pratt, 30 October 1853.

104. "The New Alphabet," *Deseret News*, 19 January 1854.

105. Ibid.

106. PPP to Orson Pratt, 30 January 1854, Orson Pratt Collection.

107. Watt, *Mormon Passage*, 145.

108. Larry Ray Wintersteen, "A History of the Deseret Alphabet," M.A. thesis, Brigham Young University , 1970, 30; Brooks, *Mormon Frontier*, 581, entry for 2 January 1856.

CHAPTER 13

1. PPP to Brigham Young, 25 October 1854, Young Collection.

2. PPP to Brigham Young, 18 December 1854, Young Collection.

3. Kenney, *Woodruff's Journal*, 6 April 1854, 4:258; Mission Certificate, signed by Brigham Young, Heber C. Kimball, and Jedediah M. Grant, 3 May 1854, PPP Collection.

4. PPP, journal, 21 May 1854.

5. Mission Certificate, 3 May 1854.

6. Edward Partridge Jr., journal, 6 April 1854, CHL; Kenney, *Woodruff's Journal*, 7 April 1854, 4:259; "Journal History," 6 April 1854, 4, 8 April 1854, 1.

7. PPP, journal, 6 April 1854. Before leaving for California, Pratt helped organize a party of twenty-four members of the Southern Indian Mission headed to Harmony, Utah, to build a new fort and preach to Native Americans. Brooks, *Journal of the Southern Indian Mission*, 4–6. Pratt visited the missionaries in Harmony in May while traveling south with Brigham Young's group.

8. PPP, journal, 5 May 1854.

9. Simon N. Carvalho, *Incidents of Travel and Adventure in the Far West; with Col. Fremont's Last Expedition Across the Rocky Mountains* (New York: Derby & Jackson, 1859), 189.

10. Farmer, *On Zion's Mount*, 86; Arrington, *Brigham Young*, 210–222.

11. Kenney, *Woodruff's Journal*, 11 May 1854, 4:272; PPP, journal, 11 May 1854.

12. PPP to Family, 19 May 1854, PPP Collection.

13. Ibid.

14. PPP to Belinda Marden Pratt, 23 August 1854, PPP Collection.

15. PPP to Family, 29 May 1854, PPP Collection.

16. PPP, journal, 21 May 1854; PPP, *Autobiography*, 164–165.

17. Jared Pratt Family Association records.

18. "Journal History," 15 June 1855, 1; Arrington, *Great Basin Kingdom*, 148–156.

19. PPP to Family, 21 May 1854, PPP Collection.

20. Brooks, *Journal of the Southern Indian Mission*, 34–35.

21. Henry, D. Richards, journal, 21 May 1854, CHL.

22. PPP to Family, 21 May 1854.

23. Carvalho, *Travel and Adventure in the Far West*, 194.

24. PPP, Family Record.

25. PPP, journal, 21 May 1854; PPP, *Autobiography*, 512.

26. PPP, journal, 31 May 1854; Partridge, journal, 1 June 1854.

27. PPP, journal, 3 June 1854.

28. Silas Smith, Journal, 3 June 1854.

29. Partridge, journal, 9 June 1854; Henry D. Richards, Journal, 9 June 1854.

30. Partridge, journal, 11 June 1854.

31. PPP, journal, 9 June–24 June 1854; Partridge, journal, 9 June–10 July 1854; PPP to Family, 6 May 1854, PPP Collection.

32. PPP to Ann Agatha Walker Pratt, 17 November 1854, PPP Collection.

33. PPP, journal, 15 August 1854.

34. PPP to Mary Wood Pratt, 21 September 1854, PPP Collection.

35. PPP to Ann Agatha Walker Pratt, 17 November 1854, PPP Collection.

36. PPP to Ann Agatha Walker Pratt, 13 January 1855, PPP Collection.

37. PPP, journal, 1 June 1855.

38. For a discussion of the business and banking crisis in 1854–1855, see Theodore H. Hittell, *History of California* (San Francisco: N. J. Stone & Co., 1898), 3:442–443. For the number of local members, see PPP to Ann Agatha Walker Pratt, Salt Lake City, 13 January 1855, PPP Collection. The five branches were in San Francisco, Santa Clara, Union City, St. John, and Sacramento.

39. PPP to Family, 22 August 1854, PPP Collection. For information on Horner, see Horner, "Adventures of a Pioneer," *Improvement Era* 7 (May–September 1904): 5-part series; and Horner, "Voyage of the Ship 'Brooklyn,'" *Improvement Era* 9 (August–September 1906): 2-part series; and Annaleone Davis Patton, *California Mormons by Sail and Trail* (Salt Lake City, Utah: Deseret Book, 1961).

40. Some Saints did donate significant amounts. For example, Hamilton M. Wallace and Reuben Gates gave a total of $700 to the missionaries. William McBride, journal, 3 October 1854.

41. PPP to Family, 22 August 1854.

42. PPP to Brigham Young, 23 August 1854, Young Collection.

43. Brigham Young to PPP, 29 October 1854, PPP Collection.

44. PPP to Brigham Young, 21 September 1854, Young Collection, CHL; PPP to Mary Wood Pratt, 21 September 1854, PPP Collection.

45. PPP to Ann Agatha Walker Pratt, 17 November 1854, PPP Collection.

46. PPP to Ann Agatha Walker Pratt, 13 January 1854.

47. PPP to Belinda Marden Pratt, 16 May 1855, PPP Collection.

48. PPP to Brigham Young, 18 May 1855, Young Collection, CHL; PPP to Ann Agatha Walker Pratt, 24 February 1855, PPP Collection.

49. Nathan Tanner, journal, 25–26 May 1854, CHL.

50. Amasa Lyman and Charles C. Rich to Brigham Young, June 1854, Young Collection. See also John M. Horner to Brigham Young, 21 July 1854, Young Collection.

51. Silas S. Smith, journal, 11 July–14 August 1854, CHL.

52. Henry Richards, journal, 29 August 1854, CHL.

53. Young to PPP, 19 September 1854, Young Collection, CHL; Newton, *Saints*, 153.

54. PPP to Young, 21 September 1854.

55. PPP to Young, 25 October 1854, Young Collection. Young's last instructions to Pratt in Utah involved San Diego, but Pratt reported to him in November, "I have not seen time and means yet, to take a look that way, but will when it is expedient." PPP to Young, 23 November 1854, Young Collection.

56. PPP to Young, 29 January 1855, Young Collection.

57. Young to PPP, 29 December 1854.

58. Bitton, *George Q. Cannon*, 28–31.

59. PPP to Young, 18 December 1854.

60. PPP, journal, 10 July 1854, CHL; PPP to Young, 21 September 1854.

61. PPP to Family, 22 August 1854, PPP Collection. See also Edward Partridge, journal, 30 July 1854, CHL.

62. George Q. Cannon, journal, 12 August 1854.

63. Henry Richards, journal, 10 September 1854, 17 September 1854, 28 September 1854, CHL.

64. PPP to Young, 23 November 1854.

65. Young to PPP, 19 August 1854, PPP Collection. Lyman and Rich in San Bernardino had earlier suggested this approach to Young. Amasa Lyman and Charles C. Rich, to Brigham Young, June 1854, Young Collection.

66. PPP to Family, 22 August 1854, PPP Collection.

67. Orson Pratt to PPP, 4 April 1854, PPP Collection, CHL; Orson Pratt to PPP, ca. late 1856, PPP Collection.

68. PPP to Family, 22 August 1854, PPP Collection.

69. PPP to George A. Smith, 23 August 1854, PPP Collection.

70. George Q. Cannon, journal, September 1854.

71. PPP to Mary Wood Pratt, 21 September 1854, PPP Collection.

72. Benjamin E. Park, "Parley Pratt's *Autobiography* as Personal Restoration and Redemption," *Journal of Mormon History*, 37, 1 (Winter 2011): 158–163.

73. Davis Bitton listed nearly three thousand diaries and autobiographies in his *Guide to Mormon Diaries and Autobiographies* (Provo, Utah: Brigham Young University Press, 1977). For Mormon autobiographies, see also Neal Lambert, "The Representation of Reality in Nineteenth-Century Mormon Autobiography," *Dialogue* 11 (Summer 1978): 63–74.

74. Orson Pratt to PPP, 12 September 1853, PPP Collection.

75. Scott E. Casper, *Constructing American Lives: Biography and Culture in Nineteenth-Century America* (Chapel Hill: University of North Carolina Press, 1999), 2.

76. R. Steven Pratt, "Autobiography of Parley P. Pratt," unpublished paper. Pratt's writing on the Missouri persecution was partially autobiographical; while in prison, he told Mary Ann, "I am now finishing the Journal of my Life and Sufferings." PPP to Mary Ann Frost Pratt, 8 June 1839, PPP Collection.

77. R. Steven Pratt, "Autobiography of Parley P. Pratt."

78. Kenney, *Woodruff's Journal*, 6 September 1856, 4:444.

79. Isaiah Coombs, journal, 11 October 1856, CHL.

80. PPP to Family, 3 January 1857.

81. R. Steven Pratt, "Autobiography of Parley P. Pratt."

82. John Taylor, "To the Public," *Autobiography of Parley P. Pratt* (New York: Russell Brothers, 1874).

83. R. Steven Pratt, "Autobiography of Parley P. Pratt." The "After Manuscript" is at the CHL.

84. Parley Pratt Jr., "Prospectus to the Life and Writings of the Late Elder Parley Parker Pratt," *Deseret News*, 5 February 1873, 15.

85. *Autobiography of Parley P. Pratt* (New York: Russell Brothers, 1874).

86. Steven P. Sondrup, "Literary Dimensions of Mormon Autobiography," *Dialogue* 11 (Summer 1978): 81.

87. Jonathan Edwards, "Personal Narrative," in George S. Claghorn, ed., *Jonathan Edwards: Letters and Personal Writings*, Vol. 16 of *The Works of Jonathan Edwards* (New Haven, Conn.: Yale University Press, 1998), 790–791.

88. Ronald W. Walker, David J. Whittaker, and James B. Allen, *Mormon History* (Urbana: University of Illinois Press, 2001), 117.

89. David Hall, *Worlds of Wonder, Days of Judgment: Popular Religious Belief in Early New England* (New York: Knopf, 1989).

90. PPP, *Autobiography*, 42.

91. Walker, Whittaker, Allen, *Mormon History*, 119. See also R. A. Christmas, "The Autobiography of Parley P. Pratt: Some Literary, Historical, and Critical Reflections," *Dialogue: A Journal of Mormon Thought* 1 (Spring 1966): 33–43.

92. Wesley Norton, "'Like a Thousand Preachers Flying': Religious Newspapers on the Pacific Coast to 1865," *California Historical Quarterly* 56 (Fall 1977): 194–209.

93. David Dary, *Red Blood and Black Ink: Journalism in the Old West* (New York: Alfred A. Knopf, 1998), 107–111.

94. Gary L. Bunker and Davis Bitton, "Illustrated Periodical Images of Mormons, 1850–1860," *Dialogue: A Journal of Mormon Thought* 10 (Spring 1977), 82–83.

95. "Journal History," 2 February 1855, 7.

96. "Journal History," 4 May 1855, 3. For Mormon attitudes on newspapers, see also David J. Whittaker, "The Web of Print: Towards a History of the Book in Early Mormon Culture," *Journal of Mormon History* 23 (Spring 1997): 15–19.

97. Hittell came to California in 1849, worked as a reporter for the *California Chronicle* from 1852 to 1854, and then moved to the *Alta California*. His lectures led to a book, *The Evidences against Christianity*, which went through two editions (San Francisco, 1856; New York, 1857). Claude Petty, "John S. Hittell and the Gospel of California," *Pacific Historical Review* 24 (February 1955): 3.

98. Henry Richards, journal, 17 September 1854, CHL; PPP to Family, 22 August 1854, PPP Collection.

99. PPP to Young, 21 September 1854.

100. The dailies that dominated the press included the *Alta*, the *California Chronicle*, the *Evening Bulletin*, and the *Herald*. These papers usually had a daily circulation each between three thousand and six thousand. See Lotchin, *San Francisco*, 334–336.

101. Richard H. Dillon, introduction to *The Annals of San Francisco* (Palo Alto, Calif.: Lewis Osborne, 1966), xvii.

102. PPP to John Hittell, 1 September 1854, printed in "A Prophet is Among Us," *Daily California Chronicle*, 2 September 1854.

103. Benjamin G. Ferris, *Utah and the Mormons* (New York: Harper & Brothers, 1854); PPP to Family, 22 August 1854, PPP Collection.

104. PPP to Editors of *Christian Advocate*, September 1854, printed in "Peter Parley Pratt on San Francisco Editors," *Daily California Chronicle*, 23 September 1854.

105. PPP, *Autobiography*, 515–516.

106. Brigham Young to PPP, 19 October 1854, PPP Collection.

107. PPP, Letter to the Editor titled "What is 'Mormonism,'" 2 November 1854, printed in "Another 'Ism' Finding its 'Truth' and Making the Most of it," *Daily California Chronicle*, 8 November 1854.

108. PPP to the Editor, 14 November 1854, printed in "Spiritual Philosophy," *Daily California Chronicle*, 23 November 1854.

109. PPP, Letter to the Editor titled "The Bible!" printed in "Rattles and Bubbles," *Daily California Chronicle*, 26 January 1855.

110. PPP to Young, 16 January 1855, Young Collection.

111. PPP to "People of California," titled "The Future—A Prophecy," 5 February 1855, printed in "The Prophet Pee Pee Pratt on the Oracular Tripod: The Sad Fate of the Old World," *Daily California Chronicle*, 10 February 1855; and "The Prophet 'Parley Parker Pratt' Once More—The American Future—A Prophecy," *Daily California Chronicle*, 27 February 1855.

112. "Another 'Ism' Finding its 'Truth.'"

113. "The Prophet Pee Pee Pratt on the Oracular Tripod."

114. "The Prophet 'Parley Parker Pratt' Once More." In response, Pratt explained that he had used biblical phrases without attribution because of widespread disregard of the Bible among the populace. PPP, Letter to the Editor, 1 March 1855, printed as "Apology and Explanations from Mr. Pratt in regard to his Prophecies," *Daily California Chronicle*, 2 March 1855.

115. "Rattles and Bubbles."

116. "Pee Pee Pratt on things in California," *Daily California Chronicle*, 6 April 1855.

117. "Rattles and Bubbles."

118. "Spiritual Philosophy."

119. PPP to Young, 25 October 1854.

120. Ibid., 15 February 1855. For example, the *Pacific*, a Congregationalist paper, "objected to publication of Mormon communications." See Lotchin, *San Francisco*, 338, citing *Pacific*, 2 February 1855.

121. George A. Smith to PPP, 31 January 1855, PPP Collection, CHL; PPP to Young, 15 February 1855.

122. *St. Louis Luminary*, 24 February 1855, in "Journal History," 27 February 1855, 3.

123. PPP to Young, 25 October 1854. Published in *Deseret News*, 4 January 1855.

124. PPP to Brigham Young, 18 December 1854, Young Collection. Published in *Deseret News*, 8 February 1854.

125. For a discussion of the ways in which the gender imbalance complicated the work of evangelical Protestant missionaries, see Maffly-Kipp, *Religion and Society in Frontier California*, 148–180.

126. PPP to the Editor, 22 November 1854, printed as "A Challenge!" *Daily California Chronicle*, 25 November 1854.

127. "The 'Challenge' Accepted," *Daily California Chronicle*, 13 December 1854.

128. PPP to Young, 18 December 1854; PPP, *Autobiography*, 517–518; see also PPP Scrapbook, CHL, for responses from the Oakland Lyceum to Pratt's challenge

printed in other local newspapers; Nathan Tanner, journal, 10 January 1855, CHL.

129. "Elder P. P. Pratt's Alleged Victory at Oakland!!!" newspaper clipping, Pratt Family Scrapbook, CHL.

130. PPP, *Autobiography*, 523–528.

131. Nathan Tanner, journal, 10 January 1855, CHL.

132. *Daily Alta California*, 11 December 1854. See also "Parley Parker in the Mercantile Library," *Daily California Chronicle*, 9 December 1854.

133. PPP to Brigham Young, 18 December 1854.

134. PPP to Brigham Young, 21 September 1854, 25 October 1854.

135. William McBride, journal, 19–22 October 1854, CHL.

136. PPP, journal, 8 October 1854.

137. PPP to Family, 22 August 1854, PPP Collection.

138. PPP, journal, 29–30 October 1854, 1 November 1854.

139. PPP to Brigham Young, 25 October 1854.

140. Ibid., 18 December 1854.

141. Ibid., 16 January 1855.

142. PPP to Young, 15 February 1855, Young Collection; Whittaker, "Pratt and the Pacific Mission," 64; Britsch, *Moramona*, 26–28.

143. The prospectus described the sixteen-page monthly newspaper as "Historical, Prophetic, Doctrinal and Philosophical." "Prospectus for the Mormon Herald," *Deseret News*, 6 June 1855, 103.

144. PPP to Ann Agatha Walker Pratt, 24 February 1855, 22 March 1855, PPP Collection. The books included five hundred copies each of the Book of Mormon, the Doctrine and Covenants, hymnals, and Lucy Mack Smith's *Biographical Sketches of Joseph Smith*, and an assortment of other pamphlets, including three hundred copies of *Voice of Warning*. See Richards to PPP, 31 August 1854, PPP Collection, CHL; and PPP to Richards, *Latter-day Saints' Millennial Star* 17 (26 May 1855): 331–332.

145. PPP, journal, 12 April 1855; PPP to Family, 16 April 1855, PPP Collection.

146. PPP to Belinda Marden Pratt, 16 May 1855, PPP Collection.

147. "San Francisco Given Over," *Daily California Chronicle*, 22 May 1855.

148. PPP to Brigham Young, 18 May 1855, Young Collection.

149. PPP to Franklin D. Richards, 24 March 1855, in *Latter-day Saints' Millennial Star* 17 (26 May 1855): 331–332.

150. Franklin D. Richards to PPP, 25 May 1855, PPP Collection.

151. D. E. [Dwight Eveleth?] to George Q. Cannon, 4 July 1857, *Western Standard*, 10 July 1857. On the relationship between Pratt, Eleanor McComb, and Hector McLean, see Steven Pratt, "Eleanor McLean and the Murder of Parley P. Pratt," *BYU Studies* 15 (Winter 1975): 225–256; and Patrick Mason, "Honor, the Unwritten Law, and Extralegal Violence: Contextualizing the Murder of Parley P. Pratt," in Armstrong, Grow, and Siler, *Making of Mormonism*.

152. Eleanor J. McComb Pratt, Account of the death of Parley P. Pratt, ca. 1857, 60, CHL.

153. "A Friend of the Oppressed," [PPP] letter to the *Mormon*, written 20 February 1857, published as "Sad Story of Presbyterianism: The Mother and Children," *Mormon*, 14 March 1857.

154. D. E. [Dwight Eveleth?] to George Q. Cannon, 4 July 1857, *Western Standard*, 10 July 1857.

155. Lyman, Payne, and Ellsworth, *No Place to Call Home*, entry for 19 April 1854, 256.

156. Nathan Tanner, journal, 24 May 1854, CHL.

157. Henry W. Bigler, journal, 12 August 1854, CHL.

158. Lyman, Payne, and Ellsworth, *No Place to Call Home*, entry for 24 May 1854, 28 May 1854, 18 June 1854, 264–267; Nathan Tanner, journal, 25–26 May 1854, CHL.

159. Lyman, Payne, and Ellsworth, *No Place to Call Home*, 274, entry for 27 July 1854.

160. PPP, journal, 27 August 1854. In July, missionary Henry Richards stated that Eleanor's sons were "confirmed," likely referring to a blessing rather than the ordinance of confirmation that follows baptism. Henry Richards, journal, 16 July 1854, CHL.

161. "Dreadful Persecution of Mrs. McLean–Her Defence–Murder of P. P. Pratt," *Latter-day Saints' Millennial Star* 19 (4 July 1857): 430–431.

162. Eleanor Pratt, Account, 35.

163. D. E. [Dwight Eveleth?] to George Q. Cannon, 4 July 1857, *Western Standard*, 10 July 1857.

164. PPP to Belinda Marden Pratt, 17 January 1855, PPP Collection. See also PPP to Ann Agatha Walker Pratt, 13 January 1855, PPP Collection.

165. J. Spencer Fluhman, "Anti-Mormonism and the Making of Religion in Antebellum America," Ph.D. diss., University of Wisconsin-Madison, 2006, chap. 2.

166. John R. Young to William G. Black, March 1930, CHL.

167. Lyman, Payne, and Ellsworth, *No Place to Call Home*, 302, entry for 25 January 1855.

168. PPP to Amasa Lyman, 2 March 1855, Amasa Lyman Collection, CHL.

169. PPP to Belinda Marden Pratt, 23 August 1854, PPP Collection.

170. PPP to Belinda Marden Pratt, 16 May 1855, PPP Collection.

171. PPP, journal, 14 June 1855.

172. PPP to George A. Smith, 30 April 1855, George A. Smith Collection, CHL.

173. Minutes of Special Conference, San Francisco Branch, 16 June 1855, CHL.

174. PPP, journal, 3 June 1855, CHL.

175. Minutes of Special Conference, San Francisco Branch, 16 June 1855, CHL.

176. Young to PPP, 28 March 1855, Young Collection.

177. Lyman, Payne, and Ellsworth, *No Place to Call Home*, 333–334, entry for 24 June 1855; George Q. Cannon to Brigham Young, 27 July 1855, Young Collection.

178. Cannon to Young, 27 July 1855; George Q. Cannon, *Writings from the "Western Standard," Published in San Francisco, California* (Liverpool: George Q. Cannon, 1864), vii.

179. For discussion on Cannon's mission and the *Western Standard*, see Whittaker, "PPP and the Pacific Mission," 64–70; Bitton, *George Q. Cannon*, 69–87. The period of Mormon involvement in the San Francisco press ended when the *Western Standard* ceased publication in 1857. The Utah War effectively eliminated an official Mormon presence in California, as the Saints were commanded to return to the Salt Lake Valley.

180. PPP, journal, 30 July 1855; PPP to *Deseret News*, 21 August 1855, in *Deseret News*, 22 August 1855.

CHAPTER 14

1. Ann Agatha Walker Pratt, Reminiscences.

2. On the broader context, see Laurel Thatcher Ulrich, "An American Album, 1857," *American Historical Review* 115 (February 2010): 1–25.

3. "Minutes of the Quarterly Conference Held in Ogden City," *Deseret News*, 4 November 1855, in "Journal History," 4 November 1855, 1.

4. On the legislative session, see PPP to Belinda Marden Pratt, 6 January 1856, PPP Collection.

5. PPP, *Autobiography*, 536–541.

6. Brigham Young, Heber C. Kimball, Jedediah M. Grant, to PPP, 10 September 1856, in PPP, *Autobiography*, 544–545.

7. PPP, discourse, 7 September 1856, *Journal of Discourses* 5:196–197.

8. Blessing of PPP, 4 September 1856, PPP Collection.

9. Kenney, *Woodruff's Journal*, 7 September 1856, 4:445.

10. PPP to Young, 2 September 1856, Young Collection.

11. PPP to Young, 1 September 1856, Young Collection.

12. Kenney, *Woodruff's Journal*, 7 September 1856, 4:446.

13. PPP to Parley P. Pratt Jr., 7 October–9 November 1856, PPP Collection.

14. Thomas Bullock to Orson Pratt, 28 October 1856, in *Latter-day Saints' Millennial Star*, 18, no. 51 (20 December 1856): 811.

15. PPP, *Autobiography*, 546.

16. David Roberts, *Devil's Gate: Brigham Young and the Great Mormon Handcart Tragedy* (New York: Simon & Schuster, 2008).

17. PPP to Parley P. Pratt Jr., 7 October–9 November 1856.

18. "From the Journal and Diary of Isaiah Moses Coombs," in Carter, *Our Pioneer Heritage*, 1:347–348.

19. Simpson Huffaker, diary, 14 October 1857, CHL.

20. Coombs, journal, 6 October 1857, 24 October 1857.

21. PPP to Parley P. Pratt Jr., 7 October–9 November 1856.

22. PPP, *Autobiography*, 546.

23. PPP to John Taylor, 10 November 1856, in "Correspondence of President P. P. Pratt," *Mormon*, 22 November 1856.

24. Taylor to PPP, 27 November 1856, PPP Collection.

25. PPP, *Autobiography*, 546.

26. Coombs, journal, 22 November 1856.

27. E. J. McComb to *Arkansas Intelligencer*, 18 May 1857, in *Mormon*, 13 June 1857.

28. PPP to Orson Pratt, 2 January 1857, Orson Pratt Collection, CHL; PPP, *Autobiography*, 546–557; PPP to Family, 3 January 1857, PPP Collection.

29. PPP, *Autobiography*, 547–548.

30. PPP to Orson Pratt, 2 January 1857, Orson Pratt Collection, CHL; *New York Morning Express*, in "Journal History," 1 January 1857, 1–4.

31. PPP to John Taylor, 1 January 1857, in "Communicated," *Mormon*, 10 January 1857; republished in "Discovery of Gold Plates," *Latter-day Saints' Millennial Star* 19, 7 (14 February 1857): 103–104.

32. "Discovery of Gold Plates"; "More Gold Plates Discovered," *Latter-day Saints' Millennial Star* 19, 40 (3 October 1857): 631–634.

33. PPP to John Taylor, 10 January 1857, published as "Modern Spiritual Manifestations," *Mormon*, 24 January 1857. Pratt denounced Spiritualism in two 1853 discourses; see *Journal of Discourses* 1:43–47; 2:6–15. On Mormonism and Spiritualism, see Michael W. Homer, "Spiritualism and Mormonism: Some Thoughts on the Similarities and Differences," *Dialogue: A Journal of Mormon Thought* 27 (1994): 171–191.

34. PPP to Orson Pratt, 2 January 1857, Orson Pratt Collection, CHL.

35. PPP to Family, 3 January 1857, PPP Collection.

36. PPP to John Taylor, 19 January 1857, published as "A Looking Glass, in which to Examine Ourselves, to see Whether We Be in the Faith," *Mormon*, 31 January 1857.

37. PPP to Orson Pratt, 2 January 1857.

38. PPP to Family, 3 January 1857, PPP Collection.

39. PPP to Family, 3 January 1857.

40. Nelson Pratt to PPP, 22 March 1857, PPP Collection.

41. PPP, *Autobiography*, 551; George A. Smith to Brigham Young, 15 March 1857, Young Collection.

42. PPP, *Autobiography*, 552.

43. PPP to Family, 3 January 1857.

44. PPP to Belinda Marden Pratt, 27 January 1857, PPP Collection.

45. Bertram Wyatt-Brown, *Southern Honor: Ethics and Behavior in the Old South* (New York: Oxford University Press, 1982); Wyatt-Brown, *The Shaping of Southern Culture: Honor, Grace, and War, 1760s–1890s* (Chapel Hill: University of North Carolina Press, 2001); Kenneth Greenberg, *Honor and Slavery: Lies, Duels, Noses, Masks, Dressing as a Woman, Gifts, Strangers, Humanitarianism, Death, Slave*

Rebellions, the Proslavery Argument, Baseball, Hunting, and Gambling in the Old South (Princeton, N.J.: Princeton University Press, 1996).

46. Wyatt-Brown, *Southern Honor.*

47. Hendrik Hartog, "Lawyering, Husbands' Rights, and 'the Unwritten Law' in Nineteenth-Century America," *Journal of American History* 84, 1 (1997): 67–96; Robert M. Ireland, "Insanity and the Unwritten Law," *American Journal of Legal History* 23, 2 (1988): 157–172; Ireland, "The Libertine Must Die: Sexual Dishonor and the Unwritten Law in the Nineteenth-Century United States," *Journal of Social History* 23, 1 (1989): 27–44; Ireland, "Frenzied and Fallen Females: Women and Sexual Dishonor in the Nineteenth-Century United States," *Journal of Women's History* 3, 3 (1992): 95–117; Gordon Morris Bakken, "The Limits of Patriarchy: Women's Rights and 'Unwritten Law' in the West," *Historian* 60, 4 (1998): 702–716.

48. On extralegal violence in the South, see David Grimsted, *American Mobbing, 1828–1861: Toward Civil War* (New York: Oxford University Press, 1998); Bertram Wyatt-Brown, *Honor and Violence in the Old South* (New York: Oxford University Press, 1986).

49. Patrick Q. Mason, *The Mormon Menace: Violence and Anti-Mormonism in the Postbellum South* (New York: Oxford University Press, 2011).

50. Kenneth L. Cannon II, "'Mountain Common Law': The Extralegal Punishment of Seducers in Early Utah," *Utah Historical Quarterly* 51, 4 (1983): 308–327.

51. Hartog, "Unwritten Law."

52. The *St. Louis Evening News*, for instance, stated that it had published the account. See "Recapture of Children Stolen by Mormons—Elder Pratt in Custody," *St. Louis Evening News*, 19 May 1857.

53. "Sad Story of Mormonism: The Mother and Children," *New Orleans Bulletin,* republished in *Mormon*, 14 March 1857.

54. Ibid.

55. On the image of Mormonism, see Givens, *Viper on the Hearth;* Jan Shipps, "From Satyr to Saint: American Perceptions of the Mormons, 1860–1960," in *Sojourner in the Promised Land: Forty Years among the Mormons* (Urbana: University of Illinois Press, 2000); and Sarah Barringer Gordon, *Mormon Question.*

56. "Sad Story of Mormonism: The Mother and Children."

57. "A Friend of the Oppressed" [PPP] to *The Mormon*, 20 February 1857, published as "Sad Story of Presbyterianism: The Mother and Children," *The Mormon*, 14 March 1857.

58. Bushman, *Rough Stone Rolling*, 402; Grow, *"Liberty to the Downtrodden,"* chap. 5.

59. "Sad Story of Presbyterianism: The Mother and Children."

60. Nelson Pratt to PPP, 22 March 1857, PPP Collection.

61. Thomas Sirls Terry to Zera P. Terry, 1 December 1914, CHL; Thomas Sirls Terry, autobiographical sketch, CHL.

62. George A. Smith to Young, 15 March 1857. Former Mormon Isaac Sheen, for instance, boasted that he had assisted McLean by contacting Eleanor's father (Isaac

Sheen to *Cincinnati Commercial*, reprinted in "Mormonism: The Affairs of Parley Pratt and Mrs. McLain," *New York Times*, 12 April 1858); Samuel E. Allen, affidavit, 25 November 1893, CHL.

63. PPP Jr., "Prospectus to the Life and Writings of the Late Elder Parley Parker Pratt," *Deseret News*, 5 February 1873, 15.

64. Erastus Snow to Brigham Young, 14 March 1857, Young Collection.

65. George A. Smith to Young, 15 March 1857, Young Collection.

66. Snow to Young, 25 April 1857, Young Collection.

67. Erastus Snow, journal, March 1857, CHL. See also Thomas Sirls Terry to Zera P. Terry, 1 December 1914.

68. Smith to Young, 15 March 1857.

69. Snow to Young, 25 April 1857.

70. George B. Higginson to Andrew Kimball, March 1892, CHL.

71. PPP to Eleanor Pratt, 11 April 1857, in *Daily Missouri Democrat*, 25 May 1857.

72. Higginson to Kimball, March 1892.

73. H. Wilson to Adjutant General, U.S. Army Department of the West, 11 May 1857.

74. Hector McLean, statement, in "The Killing of Pratt—Letter from Mr. McLean," *Daily Alta California* (San Francisco), 9 July 1857.

75. Wilson to Adjutant General, 11 May 1857.

76. McLean, statement, in "The Killing of Pratt."

77. Wilson to Adjutant General, 11 May 1857.

78. Eleanor Pratt, account, 5–6.

79. Hector H. McLean to Friends, 7 May 1857, published as "Recapture of Children Stolen by the Mormons—Elder Pratt in Custody," *Council Bluffs Nonpareil*, 16 May 1857.

80. McLean, statement, in "The Killing of Pratt."

81. Eleanor Pratt, account, 2–4.

82. Ibid., 5–9.

83. Ibid., 6–8.

84. Ibid., 10.

85. Ibid., 11–14.

86. Ibid., 15–16.

87. William Bennion to Samuel Russell, 22 August 1902, Samuel Russell Collection, CHL.

88. Eleanor Pratt, account, 20–21.

89. Ibid., 21–22; McLean, statement, in "The Killing of Pratt."

90. Eleanor Pratt, account, 40.

91. Ibid.

92. McLean, statement, in "The Killing of Pratt."

93. Bennion to Russell, 22 August 1902; Eleanor Pratt, account, 29–30.

94. Eleanor Pratt, account, 30–31.

95. Bennion to Russell, 22 August 1902.

96. Eleanor Pratt, account, 30.

97. Statement of Frank T. Pomeroy, 11 April 1898, "Journal History," 11 April 1898, 4–6. Pomeroy's information came from John A. Peel, who had lived in western Arkansas and was among the large company that followed McLean and the other two assailants to the scene of murder.

98. Eleanor Pratt, account, 29–31.

99. Bennion to Russell, 22 August 1902.

100. Eleanor Pratt, account, 31–32.

101. Bennion to Russell, 22 August 1902.

102. Eleanor Pratt, account, 24–25.

103. Ibid., 26–27.

104. Ibid., 27–28.

105. Bennion to Russell, 22 August 1902; Eleanor Pratt, account, 32–33.

106. Higginson to Kimball, March 1892.

107. Eleanor Pratt to Erastus Snow, 14 May 1857, Erastus Snow Papers, CHL. For Eleanor's account of Parley's death, see also Eleanor Pratt to "Ye loved ones in Utah," 14 May 1857, CHL.

108. Eleanor Pratt, account, 49; Hector McLean, petition to the Honorable P. H. Morgan, Judge of the Second District Court of New Orleans; order from Second District Court, 1 June 1857, signed by P. H. Morgan.

109. Elias Smith, journal, 23 July 1857, CHL.

110. "Another Startling Tragedy," *New York Times*, 28 May 1857, which reprinted an article from the *St. Louis Democrat* (25 May 1857), itself a reprint of an article from the *Arkansas Intelligencer*.

111. Reprinted in "Terrible Tragedy. The Second Head of the Mormon Church Killed by an Injured Husband," *Texas State Gazette* [Austin], 6 June 1857.

112. Eleanor McComb Pratt to *Arkansas Intelligencer*, published in the *Intelligencer* as "Another Article by Mrs. McLean," in Stanley, *Archer of Paradise*, 317–324.

113. See also "More About the Murder of Parley Pratt, the Mormon Elder by McLean," *New York Herald*, 9 June 1857; "The McLean and Pratt Mormon Tragedy," *North American and United States Gazette* (Philadelphia), 1 June 1857; "The Murder of Parley Pratt," *Daily Chronicle and Sentinel* (Augusta, Georgia), 13 June 1857; "The Death of the Mormon Elder Pratt," *Weekly Raleigh Register* (Raleigh, North Carolina), 17 June 1857. While some of these papers published Eleanor's article without comment, most used the occasion to further celebrate Pratt's death. A sympathetic paper, the *Chicago Weekly Ledger*, noted that Eleanor's statement had "been quite generally published, by the leading papers of the country, but everywhere with a sneer, a cold voice of insult and bitter insinuation." "The Woman's Story—Mrs. McLean," *Chicago Weekly Ledger*, 13 June 1857, in "Journal History," 13 May 1857, 20.

114. Eleanor McComb Pratt, "The Orphans' Lamentation, on Hearing of the Martyrdom of their Father," *Latter-day Saints' Millennial Star* 19, 27 (4 July 1857): 427.

115. *Alta California*, 9 July 1857, in Stanley, *Archer of Paradise*, 330–331.

116. Grow, *Liberty to the Downtrodden*, 256.

117. William Appleby to Young, 1 April 1857, Young Collection.

118. On the Utah War, see William P. MacKinnon, *At Sword's Point: A Documentary History of the Utah War to 1858* (Norman, Okla.: Arthur Clark, 2008); Grow, *Liberty to the Downtrodden*, chaps. 9–10.

119. "Hector H. McLean, the Man Who Killed the Seducer of his Wife," *Jeffersonian Democrat* (Chardon, Ohio), 8 July 1857 (article copied from the *New Orleans Bulletin*).

120. "The Beginning of the End," *Alta California*, 15 July 1857, in Roger Robin Ekins, ed., *Defending Zion: George Q. Cannon and the California Mormon Newspaper Wars of 1856–1857* (Spokane, Wash.: Arthur H. Clark, 2002), 319–24.

121. The *New Orleans Bulletin* presented her as the "victim of this extraordinary imposture." *New Orleans Bulletin*, reprinted in "Terrible Tragedy. The Second Head of the Mormon Church Killed by an Injured Husband," *Texas State Gazette* [Austin], 6 June 1857. Some articles charged Eleanor with insanity; among these are "The Mormon Pratt's Last Victim," *Galveston News*, reprinted in the *New York Times*, 11 June 1857, 3; and "Frightful Effects of Mormonism," *Daily Evening Bulletin*, 18 July 1857.

122. "The Woman's Story—Mrs. McLean," *Chicago Weekly Ledger*, 13 June 1857, in "Journal History," 13 May 1857, 20.

123. "Journal of Philip Margetts," in Kate B. Carter, ed., *Heart Throbs of the West* (Salt Lake City: Daughters of Utah Pioneers, 1945), 6:400; Bagley, *Blood of the Prophets*, 71; Juanita Brooks, *The Mountain Meadows Massacre* (Norman: University of Oklahoma Press 1979), 57–58. See also Horace S. Eldredge to Young, 25 May 1857, Young Collection.

124. Kenney, *Woodruff's Journal*, 23 June 1857, 5:61; "Journal History," 23 June 1857, 1.

125. Kenney, *Woodruff's Journal*, 25 June 1857, 5:62.

126. Brigham Young to Henry G. Boyle, 4 July 1857, Young Collection, CHL; see also Young to George Q. Cannon, 4 July 1857, Young Collection.

127. Thomas D. Brown to Brigham Young, 27 June 1857, Young Collection.

128. Orson Pratt to Brigham Young, 27 June 1857, Young Collection.

129. "Correspondence. Letter from Elder E. T. Benson to His Family," dated 23 June 1857 from London, *Deseret News*, 28 October 1857, 7.

130. "Murder of Parley P. Pratt, One of the Twelve Apostles of the Church of Jesus Christ of Latter-day Saints," *Latter-day Saints' Millennial Star* 19, 27 (4 July 1857): 417, "Biographical Sketch of Parley P. Pratt," *Latter-day Saints' Millennial Star* 19, 27 (4 July 1857): 423–434.

131. Kenney, *Woodruff's Journal*, 3 January 1858, 5:153.

132. Higginson to Kimball, March 1892.

133. Kenney, *Woodruff's Journal*, 1 May 1865, 6:222; "Meeting of Missionaries," typescript minutes, 1 May 1865, CHL.

134. "Mass Meetings," *Deseret News*, 10 March 1858, 5. See also "Mass Meeting. Harmony," *Deseret News*, 24 March 1858, 4.

135. Kenney, *Woodruff's Journal*, 4 September 1869, 6:489; "Martyrs to the Truth," *Deseret News*, 29 December 1888, 16. See also "A Roll of Honor," *Deseret News*, 19 November 1892, 20.

136. Gordon B. Hinckley, "The Miracle of Faith," *Ensign* (May 2001): 67.

137. Ronald W. Walker, Richard E. Turley, and Glen M. Leonard, *Massacre at Mountain Meadows* (New York: Oxford University Press, 2008); Brooks, *Mountain Meadows Massacre*; Bagley, *Blood of the Prophets*.

138. "The Killing of Pratt—Letter from McLean," *Alta California*, 9 July 1857; "The Beginning of the End," *Alta California*, 15 July 1857; John Nugent, "Topics of the Day," *San Francisco Herald*, 12 October 1857, all reproduced in Ekins, *Defending Zion*, 319–24, 368.

139. "The Death of PPP," *Daily Evening Bulletin* (San Francisco), 26 March 1877; "McLean and Mountain Meadows: Reminiscences of the McComb Family in Port Gibson," *Hinds County Gazette* (Raymond, Miss.), 16 May 1877; "Elder Pratt: The Tragedy that Led to the Mountain Meadow Massacre, Described by an Eye-Witness—A Mother's Life Ended in Lunacy," *St. Louis Globe-Democrat* (reprinted from the *New York Sun*), 20 September 1875.

140. Brooks, *Mountain Meadows Massacre*, 57–58. For historical accounts that have linked Pratt's murder with the Mountain Meadows Massacre, see William Alexander Linn, *The Story of the Mormons* (New York: Macmillan, 1923), 519–520; Bagley, *Blood of the Prophets*, 8, 80–81, 98, 380; and Sally Denton, *American Massacre: The Tragedy at Mountain Meadows, September 1857* (New York: Alfred A. Knopf, 2003), 109–112. For a persuasive rebuttal of these arguments, see Richard E. Turley Jr., "The Murder of Parley P. Pratt and the Mountain Meadows Massacre," in Armstrong, Grow, and Siler, *Making of Mormonism*.

141. Kenney, *Woodruff's Journal*, 23 June 1857, 5:62.

142. Teancum Pratt, autobiography, CHL.

143. Sarah married William Taussig as a plural wife, but his first wife persuaded him to abandon Sarah and her children, including two by Taussig, and leave Utah for California. Belinda married Thomas Box as a plural wife, though by 1870 she had stopped living with him. On Brigham Young's advice, Parley's youngest widow, Ann Agatha, married Joseph Ridges, the builder of the Salt Lake Tabernacle organ, in 1860; she bore two children with Ridges. In 1866, Ridges also married her daughter Agatha, leading Ann Agatha to discontinue living with him. See Teancum Pratt, autobiography; Belinda Marden Pratt, journal, 1870, 1887; Ann Agatha Pratt, journals and accounts, CHL.

144. Teancum Pratt, autobiography; Orson Pratt to Nelson Pratt, 15 June 1861, CHL.

145. Settlement of the Estate of Parley Pratt, 11 February 1867; Parley P. Pratt Jr. et al. to John Taylor, 24 July 1884; Parley P. Pratt Jr. et al. to George Q Cannon, 4 October 1889, CHL.

146. Cemetery records, Salt Lake City Cemetery.

EPILOGUE

1. PPP, "Do You Keep a Journal," *Latter-day Saints' Millennial Star* 1, 6 (October 1840): 159–60.
2. PPP, sermon, 9 January 1853, papers of George D. Watt, transcribed by LaJean Purcell Carruth, CHL.
3. Ibid., 29 May 1853.
4. Ibid., 31 October 1852.
5. Ibid., 24 October 1852.
6. In his *Interesting Account of Several Remarkable Visions* (Edinburgh: Ballantyne & Hughes, 1840), Orson Pratt presented sixteen statements beginning "We Believe," some of which survived virtually verbatim in the Smith version. Orson's version was itself much influenced by Parley's introduction to his *Late Persecution*.
7. Ehat and Cook, *Words of Joseph Smith*, 68; Stan Larson, "The King Follett Discourse: A Newly Amalgamated Text," *BYU Studies* 18, 2 (Winter 1978): 196, 204.
8. PPP, sermon, 7 April 1853, papers of George D. Watt, transcribed by LaJean Purcell Carruth, CHL.
9. Ibid., 9 January 1853.
10. Ibid., 31 October 1852.
11. Ibid., 7 April 1853.
12. Ibid., 9 January 1853.
13. Ibid., 24 October 1852.
14. Ibid., 7 April 1853.
15. Ibid., 9 January 1853.
16. PPP, sermon, 7 April 1856, *Journal of Discourses*, 3:316

Index